Videodisc Segment	Video segment from Houghton Mifflin's *The Psychology Show* videodisc. This disc features 19 short, provocative clips. Also available in standard videotape format.
Videodisc Still	Still image or overhead from *The Psychology Show* videodisc.

Student Resource

Sattler/Shabatay reader, 2/e	Reading from Sattler/Shabatay, *Psychology in Context: Voices and Perspectives,* Second Edition. This engaging collection contains literary essays and narratives that exemplify key concepts in introductory psychology.
Freberg, *Perspectives*	Reading from Freberg, *Perspectives.* This collection brings together recent articles relating to key topics in introductory psychology courses.
Freberg, *Stand!*	Reading from Freberg, *Stand!* This collection contains articles that explore contending ideas and opinions relating to fundamental issues in introductory psychology courses.
Personal Learning Activity	*Study Guide* Personal Learning Activity. Each *Study Guide* chapter includes activities designed to help students actively practice using information they are learning.
Critical Thinking Exercise	*Study Guide* Critical Thinking Exercise. Each *Study Guide* chapter provides the opportunity to apply the textbook's five "Thinking Critically" questions to a new scenario.

Additional Materials Available with *Psychology,* Sixth Edition

For the Instructor

- *Online quizzes,* powered by eduSpace: Instructors can assign these quizzes, with multiple-choice, true/false, and fill-in questions, and track student's results in the gradebook.

- *HM ClassPrep with HM Computerized Testing V6.0 CD-ROM*: This instructor CD-ROM collects in one place materials that instructors might want to have available electronically. It contains PowerPoint lecture outlines and art from the textbook, as well as electronic versions of much of the IRM and SG materials to make it easy to incorporate into a web site or lecture/activity. It also has the *Test Bank* questions available in the HM Testing 6.0 package, a new version of our testing software that offers complete delivery over the Internet; a new, easy-to-use interface; complete cross-platform flexibility; as well as other new features to make the product flexible and easy to use.

- *Instructor's web site:* Much of the material from the HM ClassPrep CD-ROM is also available on the web at **psychology.college.hmco.com/instructors.** This web site also has information on how to integrate the students' technology package into the course.

- *Course Cartridges for WebCT and Blackboard:* Ask your Houghton Mifflin representative for details about these course management cartridges. You can utilize many of the instructor resources available with this edition including chapter outlines, PowerPoint slides, and handouts. Additionally, you can access a wealth of testing material specifically developed for this edition including multiple-choice quizzes, NetLabs, Critical Thinking exercises, and Evaluating Research web exercises.

For the Student

- *PsychStart CD-ROM:* This brand-new CD-ROM, which comes packaged with the textbook, contains study guide content to help students study for exams. This consists of The Big Picture (chapter summary); Chapter Walkthrough (students answer different types of questions to build their own detailed chapter summary); What's That? (labeling exercises); Critical Thinking Questions; Practice Tests; and a glossary with pronunciation. The CD is intended especially for students whose reading skills and study habits are poor. It should also help ESL students, not only because of the pronunciations with the glossary but also through the different activities to rehearse content.

- *Student web site*: The student web site contains additional study aids, such as self-tests and flashcards, as well as activities that ask the student to evaluate materials that they find on the web. Additionally, multimedia tutorials are included on topics instructors have identified as the most difficult to teach and the most appropriate for multimedia treatment. These help students learn difficult concepts by experiencing activities in different media and by being asked to respond interactively. All web resources are keyed to the textbook and can be found at **psychology.college.hmco.com/students.**

- *Succeed in College!,* a skills-building booklet and career guide containing selected chapters from Walter Pauk's best-selling study skills text, *How to Study in College,* is packaged automatically with the student text.

PSYCHOLOGY

SIXTH EDITION

Douglas A. Bernstein
University of South Florida
University of Surrey

Louis A. Penner
University of South Florida

Alison Clarke-Stewart
University of California, Irvine

Edward J. Roy
University of Illinois at Urbana–Champaign

Houghton Mifflin Company   Boston New York

To the researchers, past and present, whose work embodies psychology today, and to the students who will follow in their footsteps to shape the psychology of tomorrow.

Senior Sponsoring Editor: Kerry T. Baruth
Development Editors: Marianne Stepanian/Rita Lombard
Editorial Assistant: Nirmal Trivedi
Senior Project Editor: Aileen Mason
Editorial Assistant: Lindsay Frost
Senior Production/Design Coordinator: Sarah Ambrose
Senior Manufacturing Coordinator: Marie Barnes
Senior Marketing Manager: Katherine Greig

Anatomical illustrations by Pat Rossi

CREDITS
Credits begin after the References, on page C-1.

Printed in the U.S.A.

Library of Congress Control Number: 2001133226

ISBN (Student Edition): 0-618-21374-0

ISBN (Instructor's Annotated Edition): 0-618-21990-0

1 2 3 4 5 6 7 8 9-QWV-06 05 04 03 02

BRIEF CONTENTS

CONTENTS

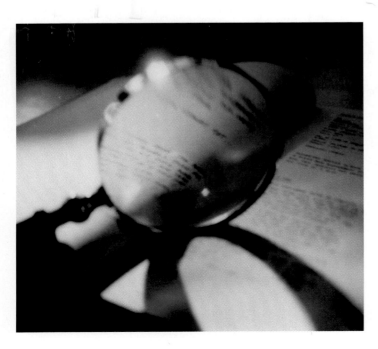

8 Cognition and Language 264

9 Consciousness 308

10 Cognitive Abilities 344

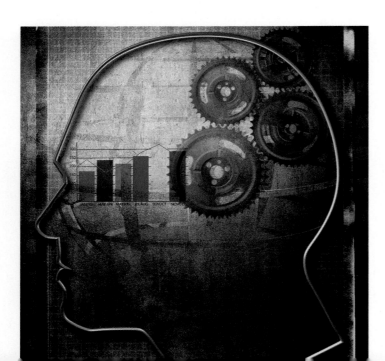

11 Motivation and Emotion 380

12 Human Development 431

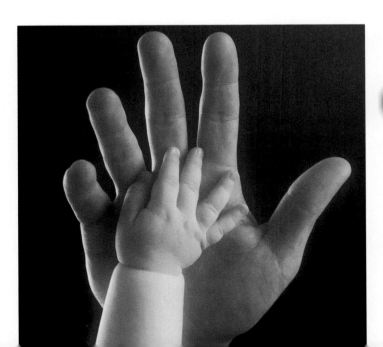

**13 Health, Stress, and
Coping 485**

FEATURES

LINKAGES

FOCUS ON RESEARCH METHODS

THINKING CRITICALLY

PREFACE

In revising *Psychology* we have rededicated ourselves to the goals we pursued in the first five editions:

- To explore the full range of psychology, from cell to society, in an eclectic manner as free as possible of theoretical bias.

- To balance our need to explain the content of psychology with an emphasis on the doing of psychology, through a blend of conceptual discussion and description of research studies.

- To foster scientific attitudes and to help students learn to think critically by examining the ways that psychologists have solved, or failed to solve, fascinating puzzles of behavior and mental processes.

- To produce a text that, without oversimplifying psychology, is clear, accessible, and enjoyable to read.

- To demonstrate that, in spite of its breadth and diversity, psychology is an integrated discipline in which each subfield is linked to other subfields by common interests and overarching research questions. The productive cross-fertilization among social, clinical, and biological psychologists in researching health and illness is just one example of how different types of psychologists benefit from and build on one another's work.

Preparing the Sixth Edition provided us with new ways to do justice to our goals. We sought to respond to the needs of instructors who wanted us to reduce or expand coverage of various topics. For example, many instructors asked us to increase the amount of material on applied psychology without losing the book's emphasis on basic research in psychology. As a result, we have added material relating to applied areas such as industrial/organizational and forensic psychology throughout the book, wherever appropriate.

As always, we sought to strike an ideal balance between classic and current research. The important historic findings of psychological research are here, but so is coverage of much recent work. Approximately one third of the research citations are new to the Sixth Edition, and we have added the latest information on such topics as

- Methods for evaluating claims for the effectiveness of eye movement desensitization ("Research in Psychology")

- Techniques for studying the brain ("Biological Aspects of Psychology")

- The interaction of senses in synesthesia ("Sensation")

- Perceptual grouping principles such as synchrony and connectedness ("Perception")

- Applying learning principles to help diagnose Alzheimer's disease ("Learning")

- Biological bases of memory ("Memory")

- Locating brain areas involved in analogical thinking ("Cognition and Language")

- The controversy over using marijuana for medical purposes ("Consciousness")

- How anxiety over ethnic stereotypes can affect cognitive test performance ("Cognitive Abilities")

- Achievement and happiness ("Motivation and Emotion")

- The challenges facing adults in twenty-first-century families ("Human Development")

- Psychological reactions to stress ("Health, Stress, and Coping")

- Gray's Approach-Inhibition Theory ("Personality")

- The biopsychosocial model of psychological disorder ("Psychological Disorders")

- Empirically validated psychotherapies ("Treatment of Psychological Disorders")

- Terror management theory and social cognitive neuroscience ("Social Cognition")

- Obedience and social power ("Social Influence")

The Sixth Edition also contains substantial material on culture and human diversity. Throughout the text students will encounter recent research on multicultural phenomena occurring in North America and around the world. We introduce this multicultural emphasis in the chapter on introducing psychology, and we follow up on it in other chapters through such topics as

- Selecting human participants for research ("Research in Psychology")

- Culture, experience, and perception ("Perception")

- Classrooms across cultures ("Learning")

- Culture, language, and thought ("Cognition and Language")

- Ethnic differences in IQ ("Cognitive Abilities")

- Flavor, cultural learning, and food selection ("Motivation and Emotion")

- Social and cultural factors in sexuality ("Motivation and Emotion")

- Cultural and gender differences in achievement motivation ("Motivation and Emotion")

- Cultural aspects of emotional expression ("Motivation and Emotion")

- Culture and cognitive development ("Human Development")

- Sociocultural factors in adult development ("Human Development")

- Cultural background and heart disease ("Health, Stress, and Coping")

- Personality, culture, and human development ("Personality")

- Ethnic bias in psychodiagnosis ("Psychological Disorders")

- Sociocultural factors in psychological disorders ("Psychological Disorders")

- Gender and cultural differences in depression and suicide ("Psychological Disorders")

- Cultural factors in psychotherapy ("Treatment of Psychological Disorders")

- Ethnic differences in responses to drug treatment ("Treatment of Psychological Disorders")

- Cultural differences in attribution ("Social Cognition")

- The roots of ethnic stereotyping and prejudice ("Social Cognition")

- Cultural factors and love ("Social Cognition")

- Cultural factors in social norms ("Social Influence")

- Culture and conformity ("Social Influence")

- Culture and social loafing ("Social Influence")

- Cultural factors in aggression ("Social Influence")

We also have updated our coverage of behavioral genetics and evolutionary psychology beginning in the chapters on introducing psychology and research in psychology and in a revised behavioral genetics appendix. They are also explored wherever appropriate—for example, when we discuss

- Gene manipulation research on the causes of Alzheimer's disease ("Biological Aspects of Psychology")

- Biopreparedness for learning ("Learning")

- Genetic components of intelligence ("Cognitive Abilities")

- Genetic components of sexual orientation ("Motivation and Emotion")

- Evolutionary explanations of mate selection ("Motivation and Emotion")

- Innate expressions of emotion ("Motivation and Emotion")

- The genetics of prenatal development ("Human Development")

- The heritability of personality ("Personality")

- Genetic factors in psychological disorders ("Psychological Disorders")

- Evolutionary/genetic explanations for aggression, helping, and altruism ("Social Influence")

Chapter Organization

As always, we have refrained from grouping the book's eighteen chapters into more general sections. We designed each chapter to be a freestanding unit so that you may assign chapters in any order you wish. For example, many instructors prefer to teach the material on human development relatively late in the course, which is why it appears as Chapter 12 in the Sixth Edition. But that chapter can be comfortably assigned earlier in the course as well.

Special Features

Psychology contains a number of special features designed to promote efficient learning and students' mastery of the material. Most of the features from previous editions have been revised and enhanced in the Sixth; two features are entirely new to the Sixth Edition.

Linkages

In our experience, most students enter the introductory course thinking that psychology concerns itself mainly with personality, psychological testing, mental disorders, psychotherapy, and other aspects of clinical psychology. They have little or no idea of how broad and multifaceted psychology is. Many students are surprised, therefore, when we ask them to read about neuroanatomy, neural communication, the endocrine system, sensory and perceptual processes and principles, prenatal risk factors, and many other topics that they tend to associate with disciplines other than psychology.

We have found that students are better able to appreciate the scope of psychology when they see it not as a laundry list of separate topics but as an interrelated set of subfields, each of which contributes to and benefits from the work going on in all of the others. To help students see these relationships, we have built into the book an integrating tool called "Linkages." There are four elements in the Linkages program:

1. Beginning with the chapter on research in psychology, a Linkages diagram presents a set of questions that illustrate three of the ways in which material in the chapter is related to other chapters in the book. For example, the Linkages diagram in the chapter on biological aspects of psychology contains questions that show how biological psychology is related to human development ("How do our brains change over a lifetime?"), consciousness ("Does the brain shut down when we sleep?"), and treatment of psychological disorders ("How do drugs help people who suffer from schizophrenia?").

2. The Linkages diagrams are placed at the end of each chapter so that students will be more familiar with the material to which each linkage refers when they encounter this feature. To help students notice the Linkages diagrams and appreciate their purpose, we provide an explanatory caption with each.

3. The page numbers following each question in the Linkages diagram direct the student to pages that carry further discussion of that question. The relevant material is marked by a Linkages logo in the margin next to the discussion.

4. One of the questions in each chapter's Linkages diagram is treated more fully in a special section in the chapter titled, appropriately enough, Linkages.

The Linkages elements combine with the text narrative to highlight the network of relationships among psychology's subfields. This Linkages program is designed to help students see the "big picture" that is psychology—no matter how many chapters their instructor assigns or in what sequence.

Thinking Critically

We try throughout the book to describe research on psychological phenomena in a way that reveals the logic of the scientific enterprise, that identifies possible flaws in design or interpretation, and that leaves room for more questions and further research. In other words, we try to display critical thinking processes. The Thinking Critically sections in each chapter are designed to make these processes more explicit and accessible by providing a framework for analyzing evidence before drawing conclusions. The framework is built around five questions that the reader should find useful in analyzing not only studies in psychology but other forms of communication as well. These questions, first introduced when we discuss the importance of critical thinking in the chapter on research in psychology, are

1. What am I being asked to believe or accept?

2. What evidence is available to support the assertion?

3. Are there alternative ways of interpreting the evidence?

4. What additional evidence would help to evaluate the alternatives?

5. What conclusions are most reasonable?

All the Thinking Critically sections retained from the Fifth Edition have been extensively revised and updated.

Focus on Research Methods

This feature, appearing in the chapter on biological aspects of psychology through the chapter on social influence, examines the ways in which the research methods described in the chapter on research in psychology have been applied to help advance our understanding of some aspect of behavior and mental processes. To make this feature more accessible, it is organized around the following questions:

1. What was the researcher's question?

2. How did the researcher answer the question?

3. What did the researcher find?

4. What do the results mean?

5. What do we still need to know?

Examples of these Focus on Research Methods sections include the use of neuroimaging technology to locate areas of the brain involved in analogical thinking ("Cognition and Language"), the use of experiments to study attention ("Perception"), learned helplessness ("Learning"), the development of physical knowledge ("Human Development"), and self-esteem ("Social Cognition"). Other sections illustrate the use of quasi-experimental, survey, longitudinal, and laboratory analogue designs. All the Focus on Research Methods sections retained from the Fifth Edition were revised and updated and some new ones were added. A full list of topics appears on p. xiii.

An Emphasis on Active Learning

To help students become active learners, not just passive readers of the material in the Sixth Edition, we have added two features to each chapter that encourage students to become more deeply involved with that material. These "Try This" features include

● Dozens of new figure and photo captions that help students understand and remember a psychological principle or phenomenon by suggesting ways in which they can demonstrate it for themselves. In the chapter on memory, for example, a photo caption suggests that students show the photo to a friend and then ask the friend questions about it to illustrate the operation of constructive memory. These captions are all identified with a "Try This" symbol.

● Placement of "Try This" symbols in page margins at the many places throughout the book where active learning opportunities are encouraged in the narrative. At these points, we ask students to stop reading and try doing something to illustrate or highlight the psychological principle or phenomenon under discussion. For example, in the chapter on perception, we ask the student to focus attention on various targets as a way of appreciating the difference between overt and covert shifts in attention.

Behavioral Genetics Appendix

This feature is designed to amplify the coverage of behavioral genetics methodology that is introduced in the chapter on research in psychology. The revised appendix includes a discussion of the impact of the Human Genome Project. It also includes a section on the basic principles of genetics and heredity, a brief history of genetic research in psychology, a discussion of what it means to say that genes influence behavior, and an analysis of what behavioral genetics research can—and cannot—tell us about the origins of such human attributes as intelligence, personality, and mental disorders.

In Review Charts

In Review charts summarize information in a convenient tabular format. We have placed two or three In Review charts strategically in each chapter to help students synthesize and assimilate large chunks of information—for example, on drug effects, key elements of personality theories, and stress responses and mediators.

Key Terms

New to the Sixth Edition is the listing of key terms and their definitions in the margin where the terms are first used. As always, key terms and their definitions also appear in the glossary at the end of the book.

Teaching and Learning Support Package

Many useful materials have been developed to support *Psychology.* Designed to enhance the teaching and learning experience, they are well integrated with the text and include some of the latest technologies. Several components are new to this edition.

Instructor's Annotated Edition

To help instructors coordinate the many print, software, and video supplements available with the text, an Instructor's Annotated Edition shows which materials correlate to and support the content on every page of the student text. These materials include learning objectives, test questions, discussion and lecture ideas, handouts, active learning and critical thinking activities from the *Study Guide,* videodisc segments and stills, lecture starter videos, overhead transparencies and PowerPoint images, as well as three psychology readers.

Print Ancillaries

Accompanying this book are, among other ancillaries, a *Test Bank,* an *Instructor's Resource Manual,* and a *Study Guide.* Because the lead author and a number of colleagues who have worked with him over the years at the University of Illinois psychology department prepared these items, you will find an especially high level of coordination between the textbook and these supplements. All three are unified by a shared set of learning objectives, and all three have been revised and enhanced for the Sixth Edition.

Test Bank The *Test Bank,* by Ted Powers, David Spurlock, and Douglas A. Bernstein, contains more than 3,000 multiple-choice items plus three essay questions for each chapter of the text. Half the multiple-choice questions are new; in all others, the response alternatives have been scrambled. All multiple-choice items are keyed to pages in the textbook and to the learning objectives listed in the *Instructor's Resource Manual* and *Study Guide.* In addition, questions that ask students to apply their knowledge of the concepts are distinguished from those that require factual recall. More than 2,100 questions have already been class-tested with between 500 and 2,500 students and are accompanied by data indicating the question's discriminative power and level of difficulty, the percentage of students who chose each response, and the relationship between students' performance on a given item and their overall performance on the test in which the item appeared.

Instructor's Resource Manual The *Instructor's Resource Manual,* by Amanda Allman, Sandra Goss Lucas, and Douglas A. Bernstein, contains for each chapter a complete set of learning objectives, detailed chapter outlines, suggested readings, and numerous specific teaching aids—many of them new to the Sixth Edition—including ideas for discussion, class activities, focus on research sections, and the accompanying handouts. It also contains sections on pedagogical strategies such as how to implement active learning and critical thinking techniques and how to make full use of the Linkages and Focus on Research supplements. In addition, it contains material geared toward teachers of large introductory courses, including a section on classroom management and another on the administration of multisection courses.

Study Guide The *Study Guide,* by Kelly Bouas Henry, Linda Lebie, and Douglas A. Bernstein, employs numerous techniques that help students to learn. Each chapter contains a detailed outline, a key terms section that presents fresh examples and aids to remembering, plus a fill-in-the-blank test, learning objectives, a concepts and exercises section that shows students how to apply their knowledge of psychology to everyday issues and concerns, a critical thinking exercise, and personal learning activities. In addition, each chapter concludes with a two-part self-quiz consisting of forty multiple-choice questions. An answer key tells the student not only which response is correct but also why each of the other choices is wrong, and quiz analysis tables enable students to track patterns to their wrong answers, either by topic or by type of question—definition, comprehension, or application.

Succeed in College! *Succeed in College!* is a skills-building booklet containing selected chapters from Walter Pauk's best-selling study skills text *How to Study in College.* This booklet, which offers time-tested advice on notetaking, test-taking, and other topics, as well as a section on careers in psychology by John P. Fiore, can be shrink-wrapped free of charge with new copies of the student text.

Introductory Psychology Readers *Psychology in Context: Voices and Perspectives*, Second Edition, by David N. Sattler and Virginia Shabatay, contains engaging first-person narratives and essays keyed to major psychological concepts. Coursewise Publishing offers two readers by Laura Freberg. *Perspectives: Introductory Psychology* comprises articles relating to key topics in introductory psychology courses, and *Stand! Introductory Psychology* contains articles that explore contending ideas and opinions relating to fundamental issues in introductory psychology courses.

Electronic and Video Ancillaries

In keeping with the technological needs of today's campus, we provide the following electronic and video supplements to *Psychology*:

For the Student

PsychStart CD-ROM This brand-new CD-ROM, which comes packaged with the textbook, contains study guide content to help students study for exams. This consists of The Big Picture (chapter summary), Chapter Walkthough (students answer different types of questions to build their own detailed chapter summary), What's That? (labeling exercises), Critical Thinking Questions, Practice Tests, and a glossary with pronunciation guide. The CD is intended especially for students whose reading skills and study habits are poor. It should also help ESL students, not only because of the pronunciation guide with the glossary but also because of the different activities that help students rehearse the content.

Student Web Site The student web site contains additional study aids, such as self-tests and flashcards, as well as activities that ask the student to evaluate materials that they find on the web. Additionally, multimedia tutorials are included on topics instructors have identified as the most difficult to teach and the most appropriate for multimedia treatment. These help students learn difficult concepts by experiencing activities in different media and by being asked to respond interactively. All web resources are keyed to the textbook and can be found at **psychology.college.hmco. com/students**.

For the Instructor

Online Quizzes Powered by eduSpace Instructors can assign these quizzes, with multiple-choice, true/false, and fill-in questions, and track student's results in the gradebook.

HMClassPrep CD-ROM with Computerized Test Bank This instructor CD-ROM collects in one place materials that instructors might want to have available electronically. It contains PowerPoint lecture outlines and art from the textbook, as well as electronic versions of much of the IRM and SG materials to make it easy to incorporate into a web site or lecture/activity. It also makes the Test Bank questions available in the HMTesting 6.0 package, a new version of our testing software that offers complete delivery over the Internet; a new, easy-to-use interface; complete cross-platform flexibility; and well as other new features to make the product flexible and easy to use.

Instructor's Web Site Much of the material from the HMClassPrep CD-ROM is also available on the web at **psychology.college.hmco.com/instructors**, as well as information on how to integrate the students' technology package into the course.

Course Cartridges for WebCT and Blackboard Ask your Houghton Mifflin representative for details about these course management cartridges. You can utilize many of the instructor resources available with this edition including chapter outlines, PowerPoint slides, and handouts. Additionally, you can access a wealth of testing material specifically developed for this edition including multiple-choice quizzes, NetLabs, Critical Thinking exercises, and Evaluating Research web exercises.

Lecture Starter Video and Guide The Lecture Starter Video contains a series of high-interest, concise segments that instructors can use to begin a class meeting or change to a new topic. The accompanying guide briefly describes each segment, indicates concepts that can be addressed using each segment, and offers suggestions on how to use each segment.

Lecture Starter CD-ROM An additional set of video clips is available on CD-ROM.

The Psychology Show Houghton Mifflin's video supplement for introductory psychology is available in both videodisc and videotape formats to qualified adopters. Containing nineteen motion segments plus nearly 100 still images, The Psychology Show is designed to expand on text coverage and to stimulate class discussion through the length of the course. An accompanying instructor's guide offers information on each motion segment and still image and provides bar codes for videodisc use.

Transparencies The accompanying transparency set contains more than 150 full-color images from both the text and sources outside the text.

Online Teaching Tools Useful and practical information on online teaching tools can be found on the Bernstein 6/e web site, including a link to *Research Online: A Practical*

Guide. Houghton Mifflin also offers a useful print resource *Teaching Online: A Practical Guide* (0-618-00042-9).

Other Multimedia Offerings A range of videos, CD-ROMs, and other multimedia materials relevant to psychology are available free to qualified adopters. Houghton Mifflin sales representatives have further details.

Acknowledgments

Many people provided us with the help, criticism, and encouragement we needed to create the Sixth Edition.

Once again we must thank Katie Steele, who got the project off the ground in 1983 by encouraging us to stop talking about this book and start writing it.

We are indebted to a number of our colleagues for their expert help and advice on the revisions of a number of chapters for the Sixth Edition. These colleagues include, for Chapter 5, Melody Carswell, University of Kentucky; for Chapter 6, J. Bruce Overmier, University of Minnesota; for Chapter 7, Kathleen McDermott, Washington University; for Chapter 8, Paul Whitney, Washington State University; for Chapter 10, Deborah Beidel, University of Maryland; for Chapter 11, Steve Brown, Rockhurst University; for Chapter 13, Catherine Stoney, The Ohio State University; for Chapter 15, Ronald Kleinknecht, Western Washington University; for Chapter 16, Robert DeRubeis, University of Pennsylvania; and for the behavioral genetics appendix, Robert Plomin, University of London.

We also owe an enormous debt to the colleagues who provided prerevision evaluations of, or reviewed the manuscript for, the Sixth Edition as it was being developed: David R. Barkmeier, Northeastern University; Mitchell Berman, University of Southern Mississippi; Evelyn W. Chisholm, Spelman College; Douglas L. Chute, Drexel University; Lawrence D. Cohn, University of Texas at El Paso; Teresa K. Elliott, American University; Keegan D. Greenier, Mercer University; Barry Haimson, University of Massachusetts, Dartmouth; Rona McCall, Regis University; Ann Merriwether, University of Michigan; Michelle Merwin, University of Tennessee at Martin; and Kathleen A. Flannery, Saint Anselm College. Their advice and suggestions for improvement were responsible for many of the good qualities you will find in the book. If you have any criticisms, they probably involve areas these people warned us about. We especially want to thank these friends and colleagues for their help: Sandra Goss Lucas, University of Illinois at Urbana-Champaign; Elizabeth Loftus, University of Washington, and Scott Tindale, Loyola University, Chicago.

The process of creating the Sixth Edition was greatly facilitated by the work of many dedicated people in the College Division at Houghton Mifflin Company. From the sales representatives and sales managers who told us of faculty members' suggestions for improvement, to the marketing staff who developed innovative ways of telling our colleagues about the changes we have made, it seems that everyone in the division had a hand in shaping and improving the Sixth Edition. Several people deserve special thanks, however. Former senior associate editor Jane Knetzger, senior sponsoring editor Kerry Baruth, and former editor-in-chief Kathi Prancan gave us invaluable advice about structural, pedagogical, and content changes for the new edition. Jennifer Wall, our developmental editor, applied her editorial expertise and disciplined approach to helping us create this manuscript. Aileen Mason, senior project editor, contributed her considerable organizational skills and a dedication to excellence that was matched by a wonderfully helpful and cooperative demeanor. We also wish to thank Jessyca Broekman for her stellar work in the creation and updating of the art program for the Sixth Edition, and Naomi Kornhauser for her creativity in developing new photo ideas and for her diligence in selecting and locating them. A big thank-you goes to Mary Berry for her outstanding job of copyediting the manuscript. Thanks also to Debbie Prato, who checked page proof to ensure its typographical accuracy. Without these people, and those who worked with them, this revision simply could not have happened. Finally, we want to express our deepest appreciation to our families and friends. Once again, their love saw us through an exhilarating but demanding period of our lives. They endured our hours at the computer, missed meals, postponed vacations, and occasional irritability during the creation of the First Edition of this book, and they had to suffer all over again during the lengthy process of revising it once more. Their faith in us is more important than they realize, and we will cherish it forever.

D.A.B.

L.A.P.

A.C.-S.

E.J.R.

The authors of this comprehensive, research-oriented text have rededicated themselves to exploring "the full range of psychology from cell to society, as free as possible from theoretical bias." The Sixth Edition emphasizes updates and improvements in applied psychology—such as new findings in organizational and forensic psychology; culture and human diversity; and behavioral genetics and evolutionary psychology.

Written in a lively, contemporary style, *Psychology* offers a skillful balance of classic and contemporary topics. The extensive supplement package has been improved, to provide complete learning and teaching solutions for instructors, students, and teaching assistants.

▶ New! An improved technology package includes a student CD free with all new books; psychology quizzes powered by eduSpace; all-new, extensive PowerPoint slides available on an instructor CD or on the web; plus more depth and variety of student and instructor materials on the web site.

▶ New! The art program has undergone a thorough revision, making illustrations clearer, more effective teaching tools and creating a contemporary, stimulating learning environment.

▶ New! *Try This* icons appear in the margin to encourage active learning in the following ways: figure and photo captions which enable students to demonstrate psychological principles for themselves, and marginal symbols alert students to stop reading and engage in an activity that illustrates the principle or phenomenon under discussion.

▶ New! A Margin Glossary defines key terms in the margin of the page to reinforce key concepts without interrupting the flow of reading or the text.

▶ New! The subject index and glossary have been combined to make information easier to locate.

"Bernstein et al. is a comprehensive overview of the field of psychology. The research discussed is current, and the text is far more accurate than many other books on the market. A strong emphasis on the critical evaluation of research is a central theme, and is presented so the subtleties of psychological research are accessible to the average student."

—Mitchell Berman, University of Southern Mississippi

Thinking Critically

Do your students understand the need for and process of critical thinking?

These dedicated sections in every chapter model the critical-thinking process and encourage students to analyze research studies before drawing conclusions.

The same five questions are repeated in every feature, reinforcing the process:

1. What am I being asked to believe or accept?
2. Is there evidence available to support the claim?
3. Can that evidence be interpreted another way?
4. What evidence would help to evaluate the alternatives?
5. What conclusions are most reasonable?

---

figure 7.17

Retrieval Failures and Forgetting

In Tulving and Psotka's experiment, people's ability to recall a list of items was strongly affected by the number of other lists they learned before being tested on the first one. When item-category (retrieval) cues were provided on a second test, however, retroactive interference from the intervening lists almost disappeared.

Source: Tulving & Psotka (1971).

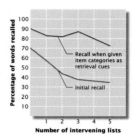

was due to a failure in retrieval. So putting more and more information in long-term memory may be like putting more and more CDs into a storage case. None of the CDs disappears, but it becomes increasingly difficult to find the specific one you are looking for.

Some theorists have concluded that all forgetting from long-term memory is due to some form of retrieval failure (Ratcliff & McKoon, 1989). Does this mean that everything in long-term memory remains there until death, even if you cannot always, or ever, recall it? No one knows for sure, but as described in the next section, this question lies at the heart of some highly controversial court cases.

THINKING CRITICALLY

Can Traumatic Memories Be Repressed, Then Recovered?

In 1989, Eileen Franklin-Lipsker told police in California that when she looked into her young daughter's eyes one day, she suddenly remembered seeing her father kill her childhood friend more than twenty years earlier. Her father, George Franklin, Sr., was sent to prison for murder on the basis of her testimony about that memory (Loftus & Ketcham, 1994). This case sparked a debate that has continued to grow in intensity and involves not only psychologists but the North American legal system as well. The controversy concerns the validity of claims of recovered memory. Some psychologists accept the idea that it is possible for people to *repress*, or push into unconsciousness, memories of traumatic incidents and then recover these memories many years later. Other psychologists are skeptical about recovered memory claims.

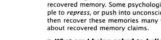 LINKAGES (a link to Consciousness)

● **What am I being asked to believe or accept?**

The prosecution in the Franklin case successfully argued that Eileen had repressed, and then recovered, her memory of a murder. Similar arguments in a number of other cases tried in the early 1990s resulted in the imprisonment of other parents whose now-adult children claimed to have recovered childhood memories of being physically or sexually abused by them. The juries in these trials accepted the assertion that all memory of shocking events can be repressed, or pushed into an inaccessible corner of the mind where for decades, subconscious processes keep it out of awareness, yet potentially subject to accurate recollection (Hyman, 2000). Jurors are not the only believers in this phenomenon. A few years ago a large American news organization reported that the United States had illegally used nerve gas during the war in Vietnam. The story was based, in part, on a Vietnam

---

Focus on Research Methods

How can you help students analyze evidence before drawing conclusions?

In these sections, focused attention on a particular study helps students understand the value of empirical research, the creativity with which it is conducted, and how it furthers understanding of behavior and mental processes.

Five focus questions consistently ask students to make connections between research questions and results:

1. What was the researcher's question?
2. How did the researcher answer the question?
3. What did the researcher find?
4. What do the results mean?
5. What do we still need to know?

---

in review   Body Senses

Sense	Energy	Conversion of Physical Energy to Nerve Activity	Pathways and Characteristics
Touch	Mechanical deformation of skin	Skin receptors (may be stimulated by hair on the skin)	Nerve endings respond to changes in weight (intensity) and location of touch.
Temperature	Heat	Sensory neurons in the skin	Changes in temperature are detected by warm-sensing and cool-sensing fibers. Temperature interacts with touch.
Pain	Increases with intensity of touch or temperature	Free nerve endings in or near the skin surface	Changes in intensity cause the release of chemicals detected by receptors in pain neurons. Some fibers convey sharp pain; others convey dull aches and burning sensations.
Kinesthesia	Mechanical energy of joint and muscle movement	Receptors in muscle fibers	Information from muscle fibers is sent to the spinal cord, thalamus, cerebellum, and cortex.

changes, receptors in the joints transduce this mechanical energy into neural activity, providing information about both the rate of change and the angle of the bones. This coded information goes to the spinal cord and is sent from there to the thalamus, along with sensory information from the skin. Eventually the information goes to the cerebellum and to the somatosensory cortex (see Figures 3.13 and 3.16), both of which are involved in the smooth coordination of movements

Proprioception is a critical sense for success in physical therapy and rehabilitative medicine, especially for people who have to relearn how to move their muscles after strokes or other problems. Research in a branch of physics called *nonlinear dynamics* has been applied to problems in proprioception. Utilizing the discovery that the right amount of random, background noise can actually improve the detection of signals, rehabilitation neurologists have found that adding a small amount of vibration (or "noise") to muscle and joint sensations dramatically increases patients' ability to detect joint movements and position (Glanz, 1997). (See "In Review: Body Senses" for a summary of our discussion of touch, temperature, pain, and kinesthesia.)

FOCUS ON RESEARCH METHODS

The Case of the Disembodied Woman

Early in this chapter we discussed the problem of coding sensation—of translating the physical properties of some stimulus into neural signals that make sense to the brain. In later sections we described how this problem is "solved" for the different senses. But what happens when the brain does not receive the sensory information it needs? The most common examples of this situation are deafness and blindness, but in the case study described next, a person suffered the loss of a proprioceptive sense.

● What was the researcher's question?

Oliver Sacks, a well-known clinical neurologist, has spent years treating people with "neurological deficits"—that is, impairments or incapacities of neurological functions. One of his most memorable cases was that of "Christina," who had apparently lost the sense of kinesthesia and, thus, was unable to feel the position of her own body.

In 1977, Christina was a healthy young woman who entered a hospital in preparation for some minor surgery. The night before her operation, she dreamt that she was unsteady on her feet, "could hardly feel anything in her hands . . . and kept dropping whatever she picked up" (Sacks, 1985, p. 43). Her dream soon became a horrible reality. The next day, Christina tried to get out of bed but flopped onto the floor like a rag doll. She was unable to hold onto objects and had trouble moving. She felt "weird—disembodied." A psychiatrist diagnosed Christina's problem as *conversion disorder*, a psychological condition described in the chapter on psychological disorders as involving apparent, but not actual, damage to sensory or motor systems. Sacks, however, wondered if there might be another reason for Christina's strange symptoms.

● How did the researcher answer the question?

Sacks tested Christina's nerve and muscle functions, performed a spinal tap to examine the fibers that carry sensory information to the brain, and studied the portion of her brain that receives proprioceptive information. His approach exemplifies the *case study* method of research. As noted in the chapter on research in psychology, case studies focus intensively on a particular individual, group, or situation. Sometimes they lead to important insights about clinical problems or other phenomena that occur so rarely that they cannot be studied through surveys or controlled experiments.

● What did the researcher find?

Sacks's examination of Christina ruled out a psychological disorder. His tests of her nerves and muscles disclosed that the signals they normally sent to tell her brain about the location of her body parts were simply not being transmitted. The spinal tap revealed why: The sensory neurons that carry proprioceptive information had, for unknown reasons, degenerated. As a result, Christina seemed to have become disconnected from her body. On one occasion, for example, she became annoyed at a visitor who she thought was tapping her fingers on a table top. But it was Christina, not the visitor, who was doing it. Her hands were acting on their own; her body was doing things she did not know about.

● What do the results mean?

In his analysis of this case, Sacks noted that the sense we have of our bodies is provided partly through our experience of seeing it, but also partly through proprioception. Christina put it this way: "Proprioception is like the eyes of the body, the way the body sees itself. And if it goes, it's like the body's blind." With great effort and determination, Christina was ultimately able to regain some of her ability to move about. If she looked intently at her arms and legs, she could coordinate their movement to some degree. Eventually, she left the hospital and resumed many of her normal activities. But Christina never recovered her sense of self. She still feels like a stranger in her own body.

● What do we still need to know?

The story of Christina and the other fascinating case studies in Sacks's popular

---

Linkages

How well do your students grasp the scope of psychology and the network of relationships among the subfields?

▸ Linkages features help students understand psychology as a whole, linking the content in each chapter and showing how the subfields contribute to and benefit from one another.

▸ Wherever a linkage is discussed in the text, a marginal callout directs students to further discussion.

▸ Every chapter explores one linkage in depth.

▸ Within the active review, a diagram plots out the relationship among the linkages in that chapter.

many short-term experiments and correlational studies in this area and why there is still some uncertainty about the effects of television violence.

● **What conclusions are most reasonable?**
The preponderance of evidence collected so far, including statistical analyses of correlational findings (e.g., Huesmann et al., 1997), makes it reasonable to conclude that watching TV violence may be one cause of violent behavior (Bushman & Anderson, 2001; Robinson et al., 2001; Smith & Donnerstein, 1998). Playing violent video games may be another (Anderson & Bushman, 2001). However, a causal relationship between watching TV violence and acting violently is not inevitable, and there are many circumstances in which the effect does not occur (Charleton, Gunter, & Coles, 1998; Freedman, 1992). Parents, peers, and other environmental influences, along with personality factors, may dampen or amplify the effect of watching televised violence. The viewers most likely to be affected by TV violence may be those who are most aggressive or violence-prone in the first place, a trait that could well have been acquired by observing the behavior of parents or peers (Huesmann et al., 1997). Still, the fact that violence on television *can* have a causal impact on violent behavior is reason for serious concern and continues to influence public debate about what should and should not be aired on television (Glod, 1998).

LINKAGES

 LINKAGES (a link to Perception)

Neural Networks and Learning

Taking a cognitive approach to learning does not mean that associations are unimportant in the learning process. Associations between conditioned stimuli and reflexes or between responses and their consequences play an important role even in the mental processes that allow us to understand which events predict which other events. As a result of experience, some things remind us of other things, which remind us of still others, and so on.

How are associations actually stored in the brain? No one yet knows for sure, but the neural network models discussed in the chapter on perception provide a good way of thinking about this process. Networks of neural connections are believed to play a critical role not only in the rapid and accurate recognition of objects (Hintzman, 1991), but also in the learning process itself (Hergenhahn & Olson, 1997). These associative networks can be very complex. Consider the word *dog.* As shown in Figure 6.15, each person's experience builds many associations to this word, and the strength of each association will reflect the frequency with

figure 6.15
An Associative Network
Here is an example of a network of associations to the word *dog.* Network theorists suggest that the connections shown here represent patterns of neural connections in the brain.

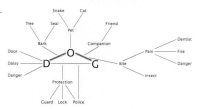

learning effortless (Druckman & Bjork, 1994; Phelps & Exum, 1992). In short, "no pain, no gain."

LINKAGES

As noted in the chapter on introducing psychology, all of psychology's many subfields are related to one another. Our discussion of neural networks as possible models of learning illustrates just one way in which the topic of this chapter, learning, is linked to the subfield of perception, which is covered in the chapter on that topic. The Linkages diagram shows ties to two other subfields as well, and there are many more ties throughout the book. Looking for linkages among subfields will help you see how they all fit together and better appreciate the big picture that is psychology.

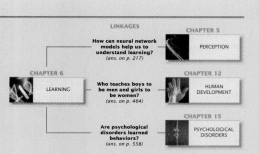

LINKAGES

CHAPTER 5 — PERCEPTION
How can neural network models help us to understand learning? (ans. on p. 217)

CHAPTER 6 — LEARNING

CHAPTER 12 — HUMAN DEVELOPMENT
Who teaches boys to be men and girls to be women? (ans. on p. 464)

CHAPTER 15 — PSYCHOLOGICAL DISORDERS
Are psychological disorders learned behaviors? (ans. on p. 558)

"These linkages increase and reinforce the content presented in a different format. [Because] we emphasize interdisciplinarity and attempt to illustrate the interconnectedness of psychology, these sections provide me an opportunity to have students look beyond the topics immediately being considered."

—Evelyn W. Chisolm, Spelman College

Introducing Psychology

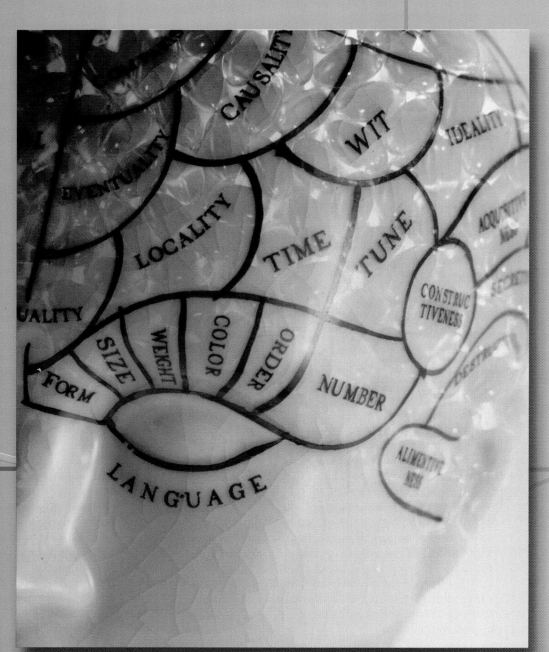

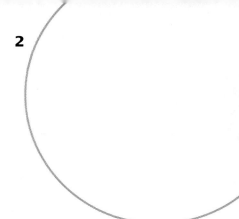

2

See if you can figure out what the following people have in common:

- Kristen Beyer works for the Federal Bureau of Investigation, where she develops questionnaires and conducts interviews aimed at identifying common features in the backgrounds of serial killers.

- David Buss, a professor at the University of Texas, conducts research and teaches courses on how evolution influences aggression, the choice of sexual partners, and other aspects of people's social behavior.

- Anne Marie Apanovitch is employed by a major drug company to study which of the company's marketing strategies are most effective in promoting sales.

- Michael Moon's job at a software company is to find new ways to make Internet web sites more informative and easier for consumers to use.

- Marissa Reddy, co-director of the U.S. Secret Service's Safe Schools initiative, tries to prevent school shootings by identifying risk factors for violent behavior in high school students.

- Sharon Lundgren, founder of Lundgren Trial Consulting, Inc., helps prepare witnesses to testify in court, conducts mock trials in which attorneys rehearse their questioning strategies, and teaches attorneys how to present themselves and their evidence in the most convincing way.

- Evan Byrne works at the National Transportation Safety Board, where he investigates the role of memory lapses, disorientation, errors in using equipment, and other human factors in causing airplane crashes.

- Karen Orts, a captain in the U.S. Air Force, is chief of mental health services at an air base, where among other things, she provides psychotherapy to military personnel suffering combat-related stress disorders and teaches leadership courses to commissioned and noncommissioned officers.

Because Captain Orts offers psychotherapy, you probably guessed that she is a psychologist, but the fact is that *all* these people are psychologists! They may not all fit your image of what psychologists do, but as you will see in this chapter, and throughout this book, psychology is much broader and more diverse than you might have expected.

There are many different kinds of psychologists, doing all sorts of interesting work in one or more of psychology's many *subfields*. Most of these people took their first psychology course without realizing how many of these subfields there are or how many different kinds of jobs are open to psychologists. But like the people we described here, they found something in psychology—perhaps something unexpected—that captured their interest, and they were hooked. And who knows? By the time you have finished this book and this course, you may have found some aspect of psychology so fascinating that you will want to make it your life's work, too. Or not. At the very least, we hope you enjoy learning about psychology, about the work of psychologists, and about how that work benefits people everywhere.

In this chapter, we offer an overview of psychology and its subfields, and how these subfields are linked to one another and to other disciplines. We then tell the story of how psychology came to be and the various ways in which psychologists approach their work.

LSV: Greetings from Doug Bernstein

Videodisc Segment: A Psychologist at Work

ClassPrep PPT 1: Introducing Psychology

IRM Activity 3.12: Question Formation

IRM Handout 7.13: Study Dos and Don'ts

ClassPrep PPT 2: What Do These People Have in Common?

Freburg *Perspectives:* Wiseman et al., "Testing the ESP Claims of SORRAT"

IRM In Your Own Words 1.1: Writing About Psychological Research

ClassPrep PPT 3: The World of Psychology

The World of Psychology: An Overview

Psychology is the science that seeks to understand behavior and mental processes, and to apply that understanding in the service of human welfare. It is a science that covers a lot of territory, as illustrated by the vastly different jobs that occupy the

eight psychologists we described. They are all psychologists, because they are all involved in studying, predicting, improving, or explaining some aspect of behavior and mental processes (Conner, 2001a).

To begin to appreciate all that can fall within the realm of *behavior and mental processes,* take a moment to jot down an answer to this question: Who are you?

Now review your answer. Perhaps you described your personality or your 20/20 vision, your interests or your aspirations, your skills or your accomplishments, your IQ or your cultural background. You could have listed these and dozens of other things about yourself, and every one of them would reflect some aspect of what psychologists mean by behavior and mental processes. It is no wonder, then, that this book's table of contents includes so many different topics, including some—such as vision and hearing—that you might not have expected to see in a book about psychology. The topics have to be diverse in order to capture the full range of behaviors and mental processes that make you who you are and that come together in other ways in people of every culture around the world.

Subfields of Psychology

Let's see what psychologists working in different subfields would emphasize about you.

Biological Psychology   From a biological point of view, you are a collection of cells that form your bones and muscles, your skin and hair, your liver and brain. Your heart beats and your lungs breathe because of activity in these cells, and because the cells are able to communicate with one another. **Biological psychologists,** also called *physiological psychologists,* use high-tech scanning devices and other methods to study how biological processes in the brain and other organs affect, and are affected by, behavior and mental processes (see Figure 1.1). Biological psychologists have found, for example, that when mental patients "hear voices" or "see things" that are not really there, activity appears in regions of the brain that help process information about real sounds and sights (Silbersweig et al., 1995). In the chapter on biological aspects of psychology, you can read more about biological psychologists' research on the processes that allow you to maintain blood pressure, move, speak, cope with stress, fight disease, and perform many other vital functions.

figure 1.1

Visualizing Brain Activity

Magnetic resonance imaging (MRI) techniques allow biological psychologists to study the brain activity accompanying various mental processes. This study found that males (left) and females (right) show different patterns of brain activity (indicated by the brightly colored areas) while reading (Shaywitz et al., 1995).

psychology The science of behavior and mental processes.

biological psychologists Psychologists who analyze the biological factors influencing behavior and mental processes.

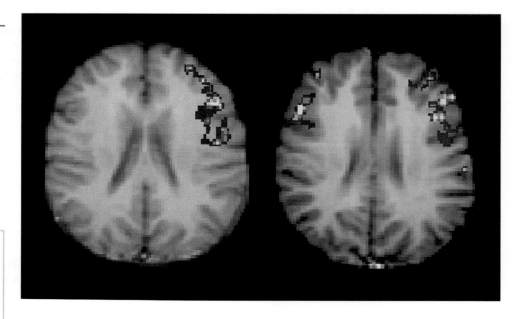

figure 1.2

Where Would You Put a Third Eye?

In a study of how thinking processes develop, children were asked to show where they would place a third eye, if they could have one. Nine-year-old children, who were still in an early stage of mental development, drew the extra eye between their existing eyes, "as a spare." Having developed more advanced thinking abilities, eleven-year-olds drew the third eye in more creative places, such as the palm of their hand "so I can see around corners" (Shaffer, 1973).

Source: Shaffer (1973). Box 4-2.

ClassPrep PPT 7: *Figure 1.2:* Where Would You Put a Third Eye?

Drawing by a nine-year-old　　　　　　Drawing by an eleven-year-old

IRM Activity 7.3: Depth of Processing

 TRY THIS

developmental psychologists Psychologists who seek to understand, describe, and explore how behavior and mental processes change over the course of a lifetime.

cognitive psychologists Psychologists who study the mental processes underlying judgment, decision making, problem solving, imagining, and other aspects of human thought or cognition.

engineering psychology A field in which psychologists study human factors in the use of equipment and help designers create better versions of that equipment.

personality psychologists Psychologists who study the characteristics that make individuals similar to, or different from, one another.

clinical and counseling psychologists Psychologists who seek to assess, understand, and change abnormal behavior.

community psychologists Psychologists who work to obtain psychological services for people in need of help and to prevent psychological disorders by changing in social systems.

Developmental Psychology　　Your cells' ability to divide and take on specific functions allowed you to blossom from the single fertilized cell you once were into the complex human being you are now. **Developmental psychologists** describe these changes, from birth through old age, and try to understand their causes and effects (see Figure 1.2). Their research on the development of memory and other mental abilities, for example, is used by judges and attorneys in deciding how old a child has to be in order to serve as a reliable witness in court, or to responsibly choose which divorcing parent to live with. The chapter on human development describes more research by developmental psychologists and how it is applied in areas such as parenting, evaluating day care, and preserving mental capacity in elderly people.

Cognitive Psychology　　Stop reading for a moment, and look left and right. Your ability to follow this suggestion, to recognize whatever you saw, and to understand the words you are reading right now are the result of mental, or *cognitive,* abilities that allow you to receive information from the outside world, understand it, and act on it. **Cognitive psychologists** (some of whom prefer to be called **experimental psychologists**) focus on these and other mental abilities, including sensation and perception, learning and memory, thinking, consciousness, intelligence, and creativity. Cognitive psychologists have found, for example, that we don't just passively receive incoming information—we mentally manipulate it. Thus, although the drawing in Figure 1.3 does not physically change, two different versions emerge, depending on which of its features *you* emphasize.

Applications of cognitive psychologists' research are all around you. For instance, research by those whose special interest is **engineering psychology**—also known as *human factors*—has helped designers create computer keyboards, Internet web sites, aircraft instrument panels, nuclear power plant controls, and even on-screen VCR programming systems that are logical, easy to use, and less likely to cause errors (Mumford, 2000; Segal & Suri, 1999). The need for human factors consultants on the design of medical equipment was underscored in September 1999, in the neonatal intensive care unit of a hospital in Bournemouth, England. A nurse intended to shut off the alarm on a pump delivering a painkiller to a three-day-old baby, but accidentally pressed a nearby button that increased the drug flow. The infant died twelve hours later (Rayner, 2000). Many chapters of this book deal with human factors and many other interesting aspects of cognitive psychology.

figure 1.3

⭐ *TRY THIS* **Husband and Father-in-Law**
This figure is labeled "husband and father-in-law" (Botwinick, 1961) because you can see an old man or a young man, depending upon how you mentally organize its features. The elderly father-in-law faces to your right, and he is turned slightly toward you. He has a large nose, and the dark areas represent his coat pulled up to his protruding chin. However, the tip of his nose can also be seen as the tip of a younger man's chin; the younger man is in profile, also looking to your right, but away from you. The old man's mouth is the young man's neck band. Both men are wearing a broad-brimmed hat.

ClassPrep PPT 8: *Figure 1.3:* Husband and Father-in-Law

A Bad Design Consultation by human factors psychologists would probably have resulted in changes in the design of the "butterfly" ballot used in Palm Beach County, Florida, and elsewhere, during the U.S. presidential election in November 2000. The candidates' names appeared in two columns to allow for a more readable type size, but many voters said this layout was so confusing that they may have accidentally voted for the wrong candidate (Baron, Roediger, & Anderson, 2000).

Personality Psychology Although you may be like other people in some ways, you are in other ways different from everyone else on earth. **Personality psychologists** study these similarities and differences, often using tests and interviews to create profiles that describe how one individual compares with others in terms of characteristics such as openness to experience, emotionality, reliability, agreeableness, and sociability Some personality psychologists apply their research by examining these profiles for what they might teach us about identifying people who are most likely to develop mental or physical health problems in the face of stress, or who are at greatest risk for becoming violent or abusing drugs. Others use personality assessment tools to better understand the characteristics of people who are prejudiced against others, who tend to be pessimistic or depressed, or even who claim to have been abducted by space aliens. And as part of a recent focus on *positive psychology* (Seligman & Csikszentmihalyi, 2000), personality psychologists have also become involved in identifying the characteristics of people who maintain optimism, even in the face of stress or tragedy, and have achieved happiness in life (Lykken, 1999). You can read more about personality psychology and its applications in the chapter on personality.

Clinical, Counseling, Community, and Health Psychology
Part of your uniqueness as an individual includes the stresses you face and the problems that you might have, whether they be insomnia, academic difficulties, trouble with overeating or smoking, a lack of confidence, or maybe a tendency toward depression or anxiety. **Clinical psychologists** and **counseling psychologists** conduct research on the causes of various kinds of behavior disorders and offer services to help troubled people overcome those disorders. They have found, for example, that many irrational fears, called *phobias,* are learned through the bad experiences people have with dogs, public speaking, or whatever, and that fearful people can literally be taught to overcome their fears (Robbins, 2000). Other clinicians have worked at summarizing research on treatment methods to help therapists choose those methods that have been shown most effective with particular kinds of disorders (DeRubeis & Crits-Christoph, 1998).

Community psychologists work to ensure that psychological services reach the homeless and others who need help but tend not to seek it. They also try to *prevent* psychological disorders by working for changes in schools and other social systems

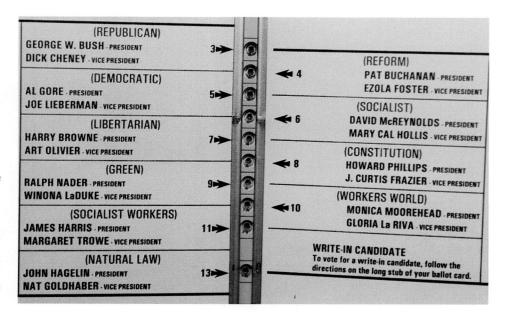

Getting Ready for Surgery Health psychologists have learned that when patients are mentally prepared for a surgical procedure, they are less stressed by it and recover more rapidly. Their research is now routinely applied in hospitals through programs in which children and adults are given more information about what to expect before, during, and after their operations.

Essay Q 1.1

Got a Match? Some commercial dating services apply social psychologists' research on interpersonal attraction in an effort to pair up people whose characteristics are most likely to be compatible.

in hopes of reducing the poverty and other stresses of life that so often lead to disorders. **Health psychologists** study the effects of behavior on health, as well as the effects that illness has on people's behavior and emotions. Their research is applied, for example, in programs that help people reduce the risk of heart disease and stroke by giving up smoking, eating a low-fat diet, and exercising more. You can read more about the work of clinical, counseling, community, and health psychologists in the chapters on health, stress, and coping; psychological disorders; and treatment of psychological disorders.

Social Psychology   Although you are an individual, you live in a social world. **Social psychologists** study several aspects of this world, focusing especially on how we think about, relate to, influence, and are influenced by other people. They have found, for example, that though we may pride ourselves on not being prejudiced, we may actually hold unconscious beliefs about certain ethnic groups that negatively affect the way we relate to people from those groups (Abreu, 1999; Chen & Bargh, 1997). Social psychologists also study persuasion; their research has been applied by advertisers, not only to make television commercials more effective (Kardes, 1999) but also to increase the impact of campaigns to keep young people away from smoking, drugs, and unsafe sex. The chapters on social cognition and social influence describe these and many other examples of research in social psychology.

Other Subfields   Psychologists in still other subfields might think of you in the many social roles you play-perhaps as an employee, a student, an athlete, the occupant of a residence hall or apartment building, or even as a defendant in a lawsuit. In the workplace, for example, **industrial/organizational psychologists** blend research on cooperation, competition, and other aspects of social psychology with studies of motivation, job stress, leadership, and other topics of interest to employers and employees. They explore the ways in which businesses and industrial organizations work—or fail to work—and they make recommendations for improving the efficiency, productivity, and satisfaction of workers, teams, and the organizations that employ them (Krumm, 2001). If you have ever taken a test of skill in order to get a new job, it may have been because an industrial/organizational psychologist recommended it to the company as a way of choosing employees who are most likely to succeed at that job.

In school systems, **educational psychologists** conduct research and develop theories about teaching and learning. The results of their work are applied to improving

Working Underground Before putting its new data-processing center in the basement of a new office building, one large corporation asked an environmental psychologist how employees' performance and morale would be affected by working in a windowless space like this. The psychologist described the possible negative effects and, to combat those effects, recommended the creation of shafts that let in natural light, as well as the installation of plants and artwork depicting nature's beauty (Sommer, 1999).

health psychologists Psychologists who study the effects of behavior and mental processes on health and illness, and vice versa.

social psychologists Psychologists who study how people influence one another's behavior and attitudes, individually and in groups.

industrial/organizational psychologists Psychologists who study ways to improve efficiency, productivity, and satisfaction among workers and the organizations that employ them.

educational psychologists Psychologists who study methods by which instructors teach and students learn, and who apply their results to improving such methods.

school psychologists Psychologists who test IQs, diagnose students' academic problems, and set up programs to improve students' achievement.

sport psychologists Psychologists who explore the relationships between athletic performance and such psychological variables as motivation and emotion.

forensic psychologists Psychologists who create criminal profiles, assist in jury selection, evaluate defendants' mental competence to stand trial, and deal with other issues involving psychology and the law.

environmental psychologists Psychologists who study the effects of the physical environment on behavior and mental processes.

teacher training and to helping students learn more efficiently (Hoy, 1999). For example, they have supported the use of the "jigsaw" technique, a type of classroom activity in which children from various ethnic groups must work cooperatively to complete a task or solve a problem. Research indicates that these cooperative experiences not only promote learning but also generate mutual respect and minimize prejudicial attitudes (Aronson, Wilson, & Akert, 2002). **School psychologists** traditionally specialized in IQ testing, diagnosing learning disabilities and other academic problems, and setting up programs to improve students' achievement and satisfaction in school. Today, however, they are also involved in early detection of students' mental health problems, in crisis intervention following school violence, and the like (DeAngelis, 2000).

In the competitive arena, **sport psychologists** use visualization and relaxation training programs, for example, to help athletes reduce excessive anxiety, focus attention, and make other changes that let them perform at their best (Roberts & Treasure, 1999). In the legal system, **forensic psychologists** create criminal profiles, assist in jury selection, evaluate defendants' mental competence to stand trial, and deal with other issues involving psychology and the law (Otto & Heilbrun, 2002). Finally, **environmental psychologists** study the effects of environmental characteristics on people's behavior and mental processes. The results of their research help architects and interior designers plan or remodel residence halls, shopping malls, auditoriums, hospitals, prisons, offices, and other spaces to make them more comfortable and functional for the people who will occupy them (Sommer, 1999). Our list of psychology's subfields is long, but it is not complete. You can read about more of them in books such as *Psychology: Fields of Application* (Stec & Bernstein, 1999).

Where do the psychologists in all these subfields work? Table 1.1 contains the latest figures on where the approximately 160,000 psychologists in the United States find employment, as well as the kinds of things they typically do in each setting.

Linkages Within Psychology and Beyond

We have listed psychology's subfields as though they were separate, but they often overlap, as do the activities of the psychologists working in them. When developmental psychologists study the growth of children's thinking skills or friendships,

table 1.1
Typical Activities and Work Settings for Psychologists

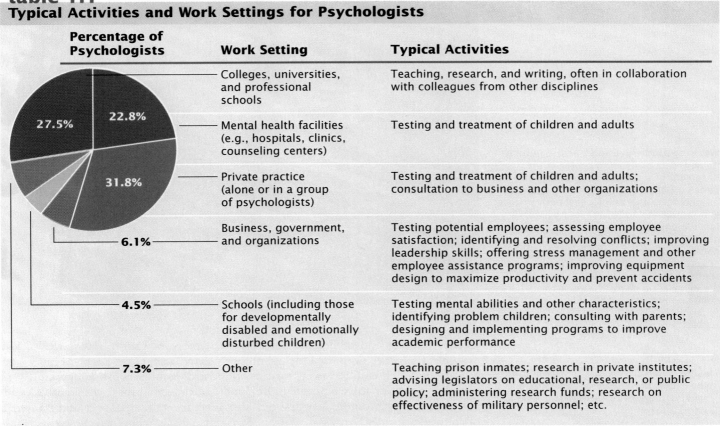

Percentage of Psychologists	Work Setting	Typical Activities
22.8%	Colleges, universities, and professional schools	Teaching, research, and writing, often in collaboration with colleagues from other disciplines
27.5%	Mental health facilities (e.g., hospitals, clinics, counseling centers)	Testing and treatment of children and adults
31.8%	Private practice (alone or in a group of psychologists)	Testing and treatment of children and adults; consultation to business and other organizations
6.1%	Business, government, and organizations	Testing potential employees; assessing employee satisfaction; identifying and resolving conflicts; improving leadership skills; offering stress management and other employee assistance programs; improving equipment design to maximize productivity and prevent accidents
4.5%	Schools (including those for developmentally disabled and emotionally disturbed children)	Testing mental abilities and other characteristics; identifying problem children; consulting with parents; designing and implementing programs to improve academic performance
7.3%	Other	Teaching prison inmates; research in private institutes; advising legislators on educational, research, or public policy; administering research funds; research on effectiveness of military personnel; etc.

The fact that psychologists can work in such a wide variety of settings and do so many interesting—and often well-paying—jobs helps account for the popularity of psychology as an undergraduate major (APA, 2000; National Center for Education Statistics, 1998; Williams, 2000). Psychology courses also provide excellent background for students planning to enter medicine, law, business, and many other fields (Kohout, 2000).

Source: Data from 1999 APA Directory Survey.

ClassPrep PPT 9, OHT: *Table 1.1:* Typical Activities and Work Settings for Psychologists

for example, their research is linked to that of cognitive or social psychologists. Similarly, biological psychologists are working partly in clinical psychology when they look to problems in brain chemistry as a cause of mental disorder. And when social psychologists apply research on persuasion or cooperation to improve anti-smoking campaigns or group activities in the classroom, they are linking up with health psychology or educational psychology.

Even when psychologists do not themselves conduct research that crosses sub-fields, they often draw on, and contribute to, the knowledge developed in other subfields (Conner, 2001b). Recognizing the linkages among subfields is an important part of understanding psychology as a whole. We illustrate three of these link-ages at the end of each chapter in a diagram similar to the one shown here. Each question in these Linkages diagrams illustrates a way in which the topics of two chapters are connected to each other; the number in parentheses tells you the page on which you can find a discussion of each question (look for the linked rings in the margin of that page). One linkage is given special attention in the Linkages section of each chapter. By examining the Linkages diagram in each chapter, you can more easily see how the topic of that chapter is related to other subfields of psychology. We hope that the diagrams will lead you to look for still other linkages that we did not mention. This kind of detective work can be enjoyable, and you may find it easier to remember material in one chapter by relating it to linked material in other chapters.

Much as psychology's subfields are linked to one another, psychology is linked to many other academic disciplines. Sometimes these linkages occur because psychologists and researchers from other disciplines have common interests. For example, *neuroscience* is a multidisciplinary research enterprise that examines

OBJ 1.3: Explain why the field of psychology is unified, despite its many areas of specialization. Describe the linkages between psychology and other fields.

Test Items 1.49–1.53

LINKAGES

By staying alert to the many linkages among psychology's subfields as you read this book, you will come away with not only threads of knowledge about each subfield but also an appreciation of the fabric of psychology as a whole. We discuss one linkage in detail in each chapter in a special Linkages section.

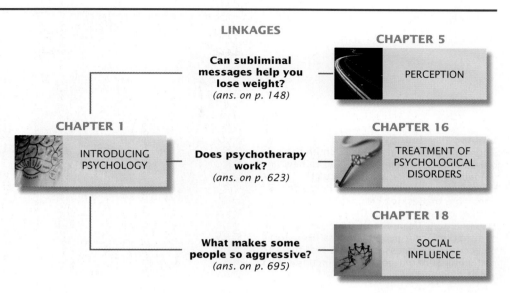

LINKAGES

CHAPTER 1
INTRODUCING PSYCHOLOGY

Can subliminal messages help you lose weight?
(ans. on p. 148)

CHAPTER 5
PERCEPTION

Does psychotherapy work?
(ans. on p. 623)

CHAPTER 16
TREATMENT OF PSYCHOLOGICAL DISORDERS

What makes some people so aggressive?
(ans. on p. 695)

CHAPTER 18
SOCIAL INFLUENCE

the structure and function of the nervous system in animals and humans, at levels ranging from the individual cell to overt behavior. This integrated field includes biological psychologists as well as specialists in neuroanatomy, neurophysiology, neurochemistry, genetics, and computer science. Someday, biological psychologists, like the colleagues with whom they work, may be known simply as "neuroscientists."

Psychology is also linked to other disciplines because research and theory from one discipline are applicable to another. For example, psychologists have applied chaos theory—which was developed in physics and mathematics to understand natural systems such as weather—to detect underlying order in apparently random patterns of brain activity, violence, drug abuse, depression, or family conflict (e.g., Dafilis, Liley, & Cadusch, 2001). Economists and political scientists apply social psychologists' research on cooperation, conflict, and negotiation to help them understand economic trends and explain international tensions. And genetic counselors use psychological knowledge about decision making and stress management to help clients decide whether, given a risky gene profile, they should have children.

This book is filled with examples of other ways in which psychological theories and research have been applied to fields as diverse as medicine, dentistry, law, business, engineering, architecture, aviation, public health, and sports. Cognitive psychologists' research on memory has influenced how lineups are displayed to eyewitnesses attempting to identify criminals, how attorneys question eyewitnesses in court, and how judges instruct juries (e.g., Casell & Bernstein, 2001; Kassin, 1997). Developmental psychologists' work on understanding the social and emotional aspects of aging is reshaping nursing-home policies on sexual behavior, and research by industrial/organizational psychologists is helping Web-based companies and other businesses adjust and survive in an economy under the threat of terrorism in the new millennium.

Research: The Foundation of Psychology

To help face the challenge of dealing with so many aspects of behavior and mental processes, most psychologists rely on a philosophical view known as *empiricism*. Empiricists see knowledge as coming through experience and observation, not through speculation. Accordingly, psychologists use the methods of science to conduct *empirical research*, meaning that they perform experiments and other scientific procedures to systematically gather and analyze information about psychological phenomena.

Linking Psychology and Law
Cognitive psychologists' research on the quirks of human memory has led to new guidelines for police and prosecutors (U.S. Department of Justice, 1999). The guidelines note that asking crime witnesses leading questions (e.g., "Do you remember seeing a gun?") can distort their memory, and that innocent people are less likely to be accused if witnesses are told that the real criminal might not be in a lineup or a set of mug shots (Foxhall, 2000).

IRM In Your Own Words 1.1: Writing About Psychological Research

Personal Learning Activity 1.5

IRM Activity 1.10: Proving the Obvious

For example, Michael Morris and Kaiping Peng (1994) were interested in learning more about how people explain other people's actions. Previous research in North America and other Western cultures had shown that people in those cultures tend to see other people's behavior as caused mainly by their personality traits and other individual characteristics. Morris and Peng wondered if this tendency occurred in all cultures. They had reason to believe it did not. North American cultures tend to place great emphasis on self-esteem, personal achievement, and other individual traits and goals. In other cultures, such as those in China and Japan, individuals tend to be seen as less important than the groups to which they belong. These cultural differences affect the way people think about what is important in life, but could they also affect the way people explain other people's behavior? Morris and Peng predicted that whereas North Americans would tend to see behavior as caused by *personal* characteristics such as laziness or bravery, people from China would tend to see behavior as caused by social pressure, lack of money, or other *situational* factors.

To test this idea, Morris and Peng gave North American students and Chinese students (who were studying in the United States) newspaper stories about two real murders. In one, the murderer was Chinese; in the other, he was North American. After reading the articles, both groups of students were asked to rate the extent to which each murder was due to the personal attributes of the murderer (e.g., personality problems) and the extent to which it was due to the situation in which the murderer found himself (e.g., being provoked by the victim).

The results of this study are presented in Figure 1.4. As Morris and Peng had predicted, North American students were more inclined to attribute the murders to the murderer's personality than to the situation he was in. In contrast, the Chinese students gave more weight to the situation as the cause of the murderer's actions. This study, along with many others described in later chapters, provides part of the empirical basis for psychologists' assertion that cultural factors can have a strong influence on people's thoughts, feelings, and actions.

In other words, psychologists do more than speculate about behavior and mental processes; they also use scientific methods to test the validity of their theories and to reach informed conclusions. Even psychologists who do not personally engage in research are constantly applying the results of their colleagues' studies to enhance the quality, currency, and effectiveness of their own teaching, writing, or service to clients and organizations.

The rules and methods of science that guide psychologists in their research are summarized in the chapter on research in psychology. We have placed our discussion of research methods early in the book to underscore the fact that without scientific methods and the foundation of empirical data they provide, psychologists' statements and recommendations would be no more credible than those of astrologers, tabloid newspapers, or talk-show guests who offer empirically unsupported opinions. Indeed, throughout this book, the results of scientific research in psychology shape our presentation of what psychologists have discovered so far about behavior and mental processes, as well as our evaluation of their efforts to apply that knowledge to improve the quality of human life.

ClassPrep PPT 12: A Brief History of Psychology

A Brief History of Psychology

Psychologists have been studying behavior and mental processes for almost 125 years. The birth date of modern psychology is usually given as 1879, the year that Wilhelm Wundt (pronounced "voont") established the first formal psychology research laboratory at the University of Leipzig, Germany (Benjamin, 2000). However, the roots of psychology can be traced back through centuries of history in philosophy and science. Since at least the time of Socrates, Plato, and Aristotle, there has been debate about such topics as the source of human knowledge, the nature of mind and soul, the relationship of mind to body, and the possibility of scientifically studying these matters (Wertheimer, 1987).

The philosophy of empiricism was particularly important to the development of scientific psychology. Beginning in the seventeenth century, proponents of empiricism—especially the British philosophers John Locke, George Berkeley, and David Hume—challenged the view, held by philosophers from Plato to Descartes, that some knowledge is innate. As mentioned earlier, empiricists see everything we know as coming through the experience of our senses. At birth, they said, our minds are like a blank slate (*tabula rasa*, in Latin) upon which experience writes a lifelong story. ClassPrep PPT 13: Development of Psychology

ClassPrep PPT 14: Structuralism

Wundt and the Structuralism of Titchener
By the nineteenth century, a number of German physiologists, including Hermann von Helmholtz and Gustav Fechner (pronounced "FECK-ner"), were conducting scientific studies of the structure and function of vision, hearing, and the other sensory systems and perceptual processes that empiricism identified as the basis of human knowledge. Fechner's work was especially valuable because he realized that one could study these mental processes by observing people's reactions to changes in sensory stimuli. By exploring, for example, how much brighter a light must become before we see it as twice as bright, Fechner discovered complex, but predictable, relationships between changes in the *physical* characteristics of stimuli and changes in our *psychological experience* of them. Fechner's approach, which he called *psychophysics*, paved the way for much of the research described in the chapter on perception.

As a physiologist, Wundt, too, analyzed sensory-perceptual systems using the methods of laboratory science, but his goal was to study *consciousness*, the immediate experience arising from these systems. Wundt wanted to describe the basic elements of consciousness, how they are organized, and how they relate to one another (Schultz & Schultz, 2000). He developed ingenious laboratory methods to study these elements, including the speed at which decisions and other mental events take place. In an attempt to observe conscious experience, Wundt used the technique of *introspection*, which means "inward looking." He trained research participants in this method, then repeatedly exposed them to a light or sound and asked them to describe the sensations and feelings the stimuli created. Wundt concluded that "quality" (e.g., cold or blue) and "intensity" (e.g., brightness or loudness) are the two essential elements of any sensation and that feelings can be described in terms of pleasure-displeasure, tension-relaxation, and excitement-depression (Schultz &

IRM Activity 1.8: Popular Press Coverage of Psychological Research

OBJ 1.5: Compare the goals and beliefs of structuralism, Gestalt psychologists, psychoanalysis, functionalism, and behaviorism. Describe introspection and the functional analysis of behavior.

Test Items 1.59–1.84

ClassPrep PPT 11: *Figure 1.4:* Morris and Peng (1994)

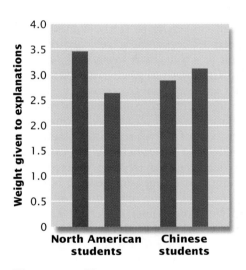

figure 1.4

North American and Chinese Students' Explanations of a Murder

When North American students were asked to explain why someone committed a murder, they tended to attribute the act to the murderer's personal characteristics. Chinese students tended to attribute it to the circumstances in which the murderer found himself. The experiment illustrates how psychologists can design empirical research to objectively study virtually any kind of behavior or mental process. It also illustrates how cultural background can affect people's mental processes.

Source: Morris & Peng (1994); adapted from Figure 8.

Wilhelm Wundt (1832–1920) In a classic experiment on the speed of mental processes, Wundt (third from left) first measured how quickly people could respond to a light by releasing a button they had been holding down. He then measured how much longer the response took when they held down one button with each hand and had to decide—based on the color of the light—which one to release. Wundt reasoned that the additional time taken reflected how long it took to perceive the color and decide which hand to move. As noted in the chapter on cognition and language, the logic behind this experiment remains a part of research on cognitive processes today.

Source: Psychology Archives—The University of Akron

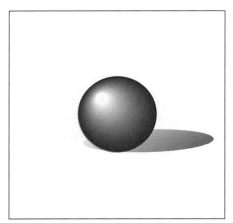

figure 1.5

A Stimulus for Introspection

⭐ **TRY THIS** Look at this object, and try to describe not what it is but only the intensity and clarity of the sensations and images (such as redness, brightness, and roundness) that you experience. If you can do this, you would have been an excellent research participant in Titchener's laboratory.

Schultz, 2000). In short, with Wundt's work, psychology had evolved from the *philosophy* of mental processes to the *science* of mental processes.

Edward Titchener, an Englishman who had been a student of Wundt's, used introspection in his own laboratory at Cornell University to study Wundt's basic elements, as well as images and other aspects of conscious experience that are harder to quantify (see Figure 1.5). One result was that Titchener added "clarity" as an element of sensation (Watson, 1963). Titchener's approach was known as *structuralism* because he tried to define the structure of consciousness.

Wundt was not alone in the scientific study of mental processes, nor was his work universally accepted. In psychology laboratories established by German contemporaries such as Hermann Ebbinghaus, the use of introspection to dissect consciousness was seen as less important than conducting experiments on the capacities and limitations of mental processes such as learning and memory. Ebbinghaus's experiments—in which he himself was the only participant—formed the basis for some of what we know about memory today. Another group of German colleagues, including Max Wertheimer, Kurt Koffka, and Wolfgang Köhler, criticized Wundt on the grounds that introspection can be misleading. Pointing to visual illusions of the type shown in Figure 1.3, they argued that our experience of a whole stimulus pattern is not the same as the sum of its parts. These Gestalt psychologists (*Gestalt* means, roughly, "unified whole" in German) claimed that consciousness can be best understood by observing it as a total experience, not by breaking it down into its component elements. Take movies, for example. Imagine how boring it would be to browse slowly through the thousands of still images that are printed on a reel of film. Yet when those same images are projected onto a screen at just the right speed, they combine to create a rich, emotional experience.

Freud and Psychoanalysis While Wundt and his colleagues in Leipzig were conducting scientific research on consciousness, Sigmund Freud (1856–1939) was in Vienna, beginning to explore the unconscious. As a physician, Freud had presumed that all behavior and mental processes have *physical* causes somewhere in the nervous system. He began to question that assumption in the late 1800s, however, after encountering a series of patients who displayed a variety of physical ailments that had no apparent physical cause. Using hypnosis and other methods, Freud found evidence that convinced him that the roots of these people's "neuroses" lay in shocking experiences from the distant past that the patients had pushed out of

ClassPrep PPT 18: Psychoanalysis

Personal Learning Activity 1.2

ClassPrep PPT 19: Functionalism

consciousness (Breuer & Freud, 1896). He eventually came to believe that all behavior—from everyday slips of the tongue to severe forms of mental disorder—is motivated by *psychological* processes, especially conflicts within ourselves that occur without our awareness, at an unconscious level. For the next forty years, Freud developed his ideas into a body of work known as *psychoanalysis*, which included a theory of personality and mental disorder, as well as a set of treatment methods. Freud's ideas were (and still are) controversial, but they have had an undeniable influence on the thinking of many psychologists around the world.

James and Functionalism

It was also during the late 1800s that scientific research in psychology took root outside Europe, especially in the United States and Canada. The first U.S. psychology laboratory was founded by William James at Harvard University, at around the same time Wundt established his laboratory in Leipzig. Most historians believe that James used his laboratory mainly for conducting demonstrations for his students; it was not until 1883 that G. Stanley Hall, at Johns Hopkins University, established the first psychology research laboratory in the United States. Six years later, in 1889, the first Canadian laboratory was established at the University of Toronto by James Mark Baldwin, Canada's first modern psychologist and a pioneer in research on child development.

Like the Gestalt psychologists, William James rejected both Wundt's approach and Titchener's structuralism. Influenced by Charles Darwin's theory of evolution, James was more interested in understanding how consciousness *functions* to help people adapt to their environments (James, 1890, 1892). This idea came to be called *functionalism*, and it focused on the ongoing "stream" of consciousness—the ever-changing pattern of images, sensations, memories, and other mental events. James wanted to know how the whole process works for the individual. Why, for example, do we usually remember recent events better than things that happened in the remote past?

James's focus on the *functions* of mental processes encouraged North American psychologists to look not only at how those processes work to our advantage but also at how they vary from person to person. Accordingly, some psychologists began to measure individual differences in learning, memory, and other mental processes associated with intelligence, made recommendations for improving educational practices in the schools, and even worked with teachers on programs tailored to children in need of special help (Nietzel et al., 2003).

William James's Lab William James (1842–1910) established this psychology demonstration laboratory at Harvard University in the late 1870s. Like the Gestalt psychologists, James saw the approach used by Wundt and Titchener as a scientific dead end; he noted that trying to understand consciousness by studying its components is like trying to understand a house by looking at individual bricks (James, 1884). He preferred to study instead the functions served by consciousness.

Watson and Behaviorism   Besides fueling James's functionalism, Darwin's theory of evolution led psychologists—especially those in North America after 1900—to study animals as well as humans. If all species evolved in similar ways, perhaps their behavior and mental processes followed similar laws. If so, we could learn something about people by studying animals. Psychologists could not expect cats or rats or chickens to introspect, so they observed animal behavior in mazes and other experimental situations. From these observations, they made *inferences* about conscious experience and about what they hoped would become general laws of learning, memory, and other mental processes.

John B. Watson, a psychology professor at Johns Hopkins University, agreed that overt behavior in animals and humans was the most important source of scientific information for psychology. However, Watson believed it was utterly unscientific to use behavior as the basis for making inferences about consciousness, as structuralists and functionalists did—let alone about the unconscious, as Freudians did. In 1913, Watson published an article called "Psychology As the Behaviorist Views It." In it, he argued that psychologists should ignore mental events and base psychology only on what they can actually observe about overt behavior and its response to various stimuli (Watson, 1913, 1919). Watson's *behaviorism* recognized the existence of consciousness but considered it useless as a target of research, because it would always be private and unobservable by scientific methods. Preoccupation with consciousness, said Watson, would prevent psychology from ever being a true science. Influenced by Ivan Pavlov's research on classical conditioning in dogs (described in the chapter on learning), Watson believed that *learning* is the most important determinant of behavior, and that it is through learning that organisms are able to adapt to their environments. He was famous for claiming that with enough control over the environment, he could create learning experiences that would turn any infant into a doctor, a lawyer, or even a criminal.

American psychologist B. F. Skinner was another early champion of behaviorism. From the 1930s until his death in 1990, Skinner worked on mapping out the details of how rewards and punishments shape, maintain, and change behavior through what he termed "operant conditioning." His *functional analysis of behavior* helped explain, for example, how children's tantrums are sometimes inadvertently encouraged by the attention they attract from parents and teachers, and how a virtual addiction to gambling can result from the occasional and unpredictable rewards it brings.

Many psychologists were drawn to Watson's and Skinner's vision of psychology as the learning-based science of observable behavior. Behaviorism dominated psychological research from the 1920s through the 1960s, whereas the study of consciousness received less attention, especially in the United States. ("In Review: The Development of Psychology" summarizes behaviorism and the other schools of thought that have influenced psychologists in the last century.)

Psychology Today   Psychologists continue to study all kinds of overt behavior in humans and in animals. By the 1960s, however, many had become dissatisfied with the limitations imposed by behaviorism (some, especially in Europe, had never accepted it in the first place). They grew uncomfortable ignoring mental processes that might be important in more fully understanding behavior (e.g., Ericsson & Simon, 1994). With the dawn of the computer age, these psychologists began to think about mental activity in a new way—as information processing. Computers also enabled psychologists to measure mental activity far more accurately than ever before. At the same time, progress in computer-supported biotechnology began to offer psychologists exciting new ways to study the biological bases of mental processes—to literally see what is going on in the brain when, for example, a person thinks or makes decisions (see Figure 1.1).

Armed with ever more sophisticated research tools, psychologists today are striving to do what Watson thought was impossible: to study mental processes with

in review The Development of Psychology			
School of Thought	**Founders**	**Goals**	**Methods**
Structuralism	Edward Titchener, trained by Wilhelm Wundt	To study conscious experience and its structure	Experiments; introspection
Gestalt psychology	Max Wertheimer	To describe organization of mental processes: "The whole is greater than the sum of its parts."	Observation of sensory/ perceptual phenomena
Psychoanalysis	Sigmund Freud	To explain personality and behavior; to develop techniques for treating mental illness	Study of individual cases
Functionalism	William James	To study how the mind works in allowing an organism to adapt to the environment	Naturalistic observation of animal and human behavior
Behaviorism	John B. Watson, B. F. Skinner	To study only observable behavior and explain behavior via learning principles	Observation of the relation-ship between environmental stimuli and behavioral responses

precision and scientific objectivity. In fact, there are probably as many contemporary psychologists studying cognitive and biological processes as there are those studying observable behaviors. So mainstream psychology has come full circle, once again accepting consciousness—in the form of cognitive processes—as a legitimate topic for scientific research and justifying the definition of psychology as the science of behavior and mental processes (Kimble, 2000; Robins, Gosling, & Craik, 1999).

 Unity and Diversity in Psychology

Psychologists today are unified by their commitment to empiricism and scientific research, by their linked interests in behavior and mental processes, and by the debt they owe to predecessors whose work has shaped psychology over its 125-year history (Kimble, 1999). In other ways, however, psychologists are an amazingly diverse group. This diversity is reflected not only in the many subfields they choose but also in who they are and how they approach their work.

Our photographs of psychology's founders might suggest that all psychologists are Caucasian men, but this is certainly not the case. White males did dominate in psychology—much as they did in other academic disciplines—through the early part of the twentieth century. However, almost from the beginning, women and people of color made important contributions to psychology (Schultz & Schultz, 2000). Throughout this book you will find the work of their modern counterparts. Psychology research, service, and teaching by women and members of ethnic minority groups have all increased in tandem with their growing representation in the field.

In the United States, women now constitute about 46.1 percent of all psychologists holding doctoral degrees (National Science Foundation, 2001), and they are earning 66 percent of the new psychology doctorates awarded each year (National Science Foundation, 2000). Moreover, 16 percent of new doctoral degrees in psychology are being earned by members of ethnic minority groups (National Science Foundation, 2000). These numbers reflect continuing efforts by psychological organizations and governmental bodies, especially in the United States and Canada, to promote the recruitment, graduation, and employment of women and ethnic minorities in psychology (O'Conner, 2001; Rabasca, 2000).

IRM Activity 1.7: Sociocultural Diversity

ClassPrep PPT 21: Unity and Diversity in Psychology

Mary Whiton Calkins (1863–1930)
Mary Whiton Calkins studied psychology at Harvard University, where William James described her as "brilliant." Because she was a woman, though, Harvard refused to grant her a doctoral degree. They offered her the degree through Radcliffe, an affiliated school, but she refused it and went on to do research on memory. In 1905, she became the first woman president of the American Psychological Association (APA). Margaret Washburn (1871–1939) encountered similar sex discrimination at Columbia University, so she transferred to Cornell University, became the first woman to earn a doctorate in psychology, and in 1921 became the second woman president of the APA.

The Biology of Emotion Robert Levenson, a biological psychologist at the University of California at Berkeley, measures heart rate, muscle tension, and other physical reactions in couples as they discuss problems in their relationships.

Approaches to Psychology

Diversity among psychologists can also be seen in the different ways in which they think about, study, and try to change behavior and mental processes. Suppose, for example, that you are a psychologist, and you want to know why some people stop to help a sick or injured stranger and others just keep walking. Where would you start? You could look for answers in people's brain cells and hormones, in their genetic background, in their personality traits, and in what they have learned from family, friends, and cultural traditions, to name just a few possibilities. With so many research directions available, you'd have to decide which sources of information were most likely to explain helping behavior.

Psychologists have to make the same kinds of decisions, not only about where to focus their research but also about what kind of treatment methods to use, or what other services to provide to schools, businesses, government agencies, or other clients. Their decisions are guided mainly by their overall *approach* to psychology—that is, by the assumptions, questions, and methods they believe will be most helpful in their work. The approaches we described earlier as structuralism and functionalism are gone now, but the psychodynamic and behavioral approaches remain, along with others known as biological, evolutionary, cognitive, and humanistic approaches. Some psychologists adopt just one of these approaches, but most psychologists are *eclectic*. This means that they blend assumptions and methods from two or more approaches in an effort to more fully understand behavior and mental processes (e.g., Cacioppo et al., 2000). Some approaches to psychology are more influential than others these days, but we should review the main features of all of them so you understand the differences among them, and how they have affected psychologists' work over the years.

The Biological Approach
As its name implies, the **biological approach** to psychology assumes that behavior and mental processes are largely shaped by biological processes. Psychologists who take this approach study the psychological effects of hormones, genes, and the activity of the nervous system, especially the brain. So if they are studying memory, they might try to identify the changes taking

Gilbert Haven Jones (1883–1966)
When Gilbert Haven Jones graduated from the University of Jena in Germany in 1909, he became one of the first African Americans to earn a doctorate in psychology. Many others were to follow, including J. Henry Alston, who was the first African American to publish research in a major U.S. psychology journal (Alston, 1920).

place in the brain as information is stored there (Figure 7.18, in the chapter on memory, shows an example of these changes). Or if they are studying thinking, they might look for patterns of brain activity associated with, say, making quick decisions or reading a foreign language.

Research discussed in nearly every chapter of this book reflects the enormous influence of the biological approach on psychology today. To help you better understand the terms and concepts used in that research, we have included an appendix on the principles of genetics and a chapter on biological aspects of psychology.

The Evolutionary Approach   Biological processes also figure prominently in the **evolutionary approach** to psychology. The foundation for this approach was Charles Darwin's book *The Origin of Species*. Darwin argued that the forms of life we see today are the result of *evolution*—of changes in life forms that occur over many generations—and more specifically, that evolution occurs through *natural selection*. Darwin believed that natural selection operates at the level of individuals, but most evolutionists now see it operating at the level of genes. At either level, the process is the same. Genes that result in characteristics and behaviors that are adaptive and useful in a certain environment will enable the creatures that inherited them to survive and reproduce, thereby passing those genes on to subsequent generations. Genes that result in characteristics that are not adaptive in that environment are not passed on to subsequent generations, because the creatures possessing them don't survive to reproduce. Thus, evolutionary theory says that many (but not all) of the genes we possess today are the result of natural selection.

In psychology, the evolutionary approach assumes that the *behavior* of animals and humans today is also the result of evolution through natural selection. Psychologists who take this approach see aggression, for example, as a form of territory protection, and gender differences in mate-selection preferences as reflecting different ways of helping one's genes to survive in future generations. The evolutionary approach has generated a growing body of research (Buss, 1999; Kurzban & Leary, 2001). You will encounter it again in later chapters in relation to topics such as helping and altruism, mental disorders, temperament, and interpersonal attraction.

A Father's Love   Mothers are solely responsible for the care and protection of their offspring in 95 percent of mammalian species. If all these species survive without male involvement in parenting, why are some human fathers so active in child rearing? Do evolutionary forces make fathering more adaptive for humans? Is it a matter of learning to care? Is it a combination of both? Psychologists who take an evolutionary approach study these questions and others relating to the origins of human social behavior (Buss, 1999; Geary, 2000).

biological approach An approach to psychology in which behavior and behavior disorders are seen as the result of physical processes, especially those relating to the brain and to hormones and other chemicals.

evolutionary approach An approach to psychology that emphasizes the inherited, adaptive aspects of behavior and mental processes.

figure 1.6

What Do You See?

TRY THIS   Take a moment to jot down what you see in these clouds. According to the psychodynamic approach to psychology, what we see in cloud formations and other vague patterns reflects wishes, impulses, and other mental processes of which we may be unaware. The chapter on personality discusses the value of personality tests based on this assumption.

ClassPrep PPT 24: *Figure 1.6:* What Do You See?

ClassPrep PPT 23: Approaches (cont.)

ClassPrep PPT 23: Approaches (cont.)

The Psychodynamic Approach   The **psychodynamic approach** to psychology offers a different slant on the role of inherited instincts and other biological forces in human behavior. Rooted in Freud's psychoanalysis, this approach asserts that all behavior and mental processes reflect constant, and mostly unconscious, psychological struggles raging within each person (see Figure 1.6). Usually, these struggles involve conflict between the impulse to satisfy instincts (such as for food, sex, or aggression) and the need to abide by the restrictions imposed by society. Psychologists taking the psychodynamic approach would see aggression, for example, as a case of primitive urges overcoming a person's defenses against expressing those urges. They would see anxiety, depression, or other disorders as overt signs of inner turmoil.

Freud's original theories are not as influential today as they once were (Robins, Gosling, & Craik, 1999), but as you will see in later chapters, modern versions of the psychodynamic approach still appear in various theories of personality, psychological disorders, and psychotherapy.

The Behavioral Approach   The assumptions of the **behavioral approach** to psychology contrast sharply with those of the psychodynamic, biological, and evolutionary approaches. As founded by John Watson, behaviorism characterizes behavior as primarily the result of *learning*. From a strict behaviorist point of view, biological, genetic, and evolutionary factors simply provide "raw material," which is then shaped by learning experiences into what we see in each individual's actions. So behaviorists would seek to understand all behavior—whether it is aggression or drug abuse, shyness or sociability, confidence or anxiety—by looking at the individual's learning history, especially the patterns of reward and punishment the person has experienced. They also believe that people can change problematic behaviors, from overeating to criminality, by unlearning old habits and developing new ones.

Many of today's behaviorists have broadened their approach to include thoughts, or cognitions, as well as overt behavior. Those who take this *cognitive-behavioral, or social-cognitive,* approach explore how learning affects the development of thoughts and beliefs and, in turn, how these learned cognitive patterns affect overt behavior.

The Cognitive Approach   The growth of the cognitive-behavioral perspective reflects the influence of a broader **cognitive approach** to psychology. The

psychodynamic approach A view developed by Freud that emphasizes the interplay of unconscious mental processes in determining human thought, feelings, and behavior.

behavioral approach An approach to psychology emphasizing that human behavior is determined mainly by what a person has learned, especially from rewards and punishments.

cognitive approach A way of looking at human behavior that emphasizes research on how the brain takes in information, creates perceptions, forms and retrieves memories, processes information, and generates integrated patterns of action.

Why Is He So Aggressive?
Psychologists taking the cognitive-behavioral approach suggest that children *learn* to be aggressive. They say it happens partly through seeing family and friends acting aggressively, but also through hearing people talking about others as being threatening and about aggression as the only way to deal with disagreements (Shahinfar, Kupersmidt, & Matza, 2001).

cognitive approach focuses on how people take in, mentally represent, and store information; how they perceive and process that information; and how cognitive processes are related to the behavior we see. In other words, the cognitive approach leads psychologists to study the rapid series of mental events—including those taking place outside of awareness—that accompany overt behavior. Here is how a psychologist would use the cognitive approach to describe the information processing that occurs during an aggressive incident outside a movie theater: The aggressor (1) *perceives* that someone has cut into the theater line, (2) uses information stored in memory to *decide* that this act is inappropriate, (3) *attributes* the act to the culprit's obnoxious personality, (4) *considers* possible responses and their likely consequences, (5) *decides* that shoving the person is the best response, and (6) *executes* that response.

Psychologists who adopt the cognitive approach explore how people process information in domains ranging from decision making and interpersonal attraction to intelligence testing and group problem solving, to name but a few. Some of them work with researchers from computer science, the biological sciences, engineering, linguistics, philosophy, and other disciplines in a multidisciplinary field called *cognitive science*. Cognitive scientists attempt to discover the building blocks of cognition and to determine how these components produce complex behaviors such as remembering a fact, naming an object, or writing a word (Reisberg, 1997).

The Humanistic Approach   Mental events play a different role in the **humanistic approach** to psychology (also known as the *phenomenological approach*). Psychologists who favor the humanistic perspective see behavior as determined primarily by each person's capacity to choose how to think and act. They see these choices as dictated not by instincts, biological processes, or rewards and punishments, but by each individual's unique perceptions of the world. So if, to you, the world is a friendly place, you are likely to be optimistic and secure. If you perceive it as full of hostile people, you will probably be defensive and anxious.

Like their cognitively oriented colleagues, psychologists who choose the humanistic approach would see aggression in a theater line as stemming from a perception that aggression is justified. But where those favoring the cognitive approach search for general laws governing *all* people's thoughts and actions, humanistic psychologists try to understand how each individual's immediate and unique experiences guide *that* person's thoughts and actions. In fact, many proponents of the humanistic approach say that behavior and mental processes can be fully understood *only*

ClassPrep PPT 23: Approaches (cont.)

Personal Learning Activity 1.4

humanistic approach An approach to psychology that views behavior as controlled by the decisions that people make about their lives based on their perceptions of the world.

Cognitive Science at Work
Psychologists and other cognitive scientists are working on a "computational theory of the mind," in which they create computer programs that simulate how humans process information. In the chapter on cognition and language, we discuss their progress in creating artificial intelligence in computers that can help make medical diagnoses and perform other complex cognitive tasks.

by appreciating the perceptions and feelings experienced by each individual. Humanistic psychologists also believe that people are essentially good, that they are in control of themselves, and that their main innate tendency is to grow toward their highest potential.

The humanistic approach began to attract attention in North America in the 1940s through the writings of Carl Rogers (1902–1987), a psychologist who had been trained in, but later rejected, the psychodynamic approach. We describe his views on personality and his psychotherapy methods in the chapters on personality and the treatment of psychological disorders. The humanistic approach also shaped the famous hierarchy-of-needs theory of motivation proposed by Abraham Maslow (1908–1970) and discussed in the chapters on motivation and emotion and

Personal Learning Activity 1.3

in review	Approaches to Psychology
Approach	**Characteristics**
Biological	Emphasizes activity of the nervous system, especially of the brain; the action of hormones and other chemicals; and genetics.
Evolutionary	Emphasizes the ways in which behavior and mental processes are adaptive for survival.
Psychodynamic	Emphasizes internal conflicts, mostly unconscious, which usually pit sexual or aggressive instincts against environmental obstacles to their expression.
Behavioral	Emphasizes learning, especially each person's experience with rewards and punishments.
Cognitive	Emphasizes mechanisms through which people receive, store, retrieve, and otherwise process information.
Humanistic	Emphasizes individual potential for growth and the role of unique perceptions in guiding behavior and mental processes.

personality. Today, however, the impact of the humanistic approach to psychology is limited, mainly because many psychologists find humanistic concepts and predictions too vague to be expressed and tested scientifically. (For a summary of the approaches we have discussed, see "In Review: Approaches to Psychology.")

Human Diversity and Psychology

A final aspect of the diversity in psychology can be seen in the range of people whom psychologists study and serve. This was not always the case. Many psychologists once presumed that all people are essentially the same, and that whatever principles emerged from research with local volunteer research participants would apply to everyone, everywhere. Since about 90 percent of researchers in psychology work at universities in North America and Europe, they tended to study local college students, mostly white and middle-class, and more often men than women (Graham, 1992). Most of the psychologists, too, tended to be white, middle-class, and male (Walker, 1991).

From one perspective, studying a narrow sample of people need not limit the usefulness of psychological research, because in many ways, people *are* very much alike. They tend to live in groups; have religious beliefs; and create social rules, music, dances, and games. And reactions to heat or a sour taste are the same in men and women the world over, as is their recognition of a smile.

But are people's moral values, motivation to achieve, or patterns of interpersonal communication universal as well? Do the principles derived from research on European American males living in the midwestern United States apply to African American women or to people in Greece, Korea, Argentina, or Egypt? Not always. What people experience and what they learn from that experience are shaped by *sociocultural factors,* including differences in gender, ethnicity, social class, and culture. As in the study about how people from different countries explained a murderer's actions, these variables create many significant differences in behavior and mental processes, especially from one culture to another (Cross & Markus, 1999; Sue et al., 1999).

Culture has been defined as the accumulation of values, rules of behavior, forms of expression, religious beliefs, occupational choices, and the like for a group of people who share a common language and environment (Fiske et al., 1998). Culture is an organizing and stabilizing influence. It encourages or discourages particular behaviors and mental processes; it also allows people to understand and anticipate the behavior of others in that culture. It is a kind of group adaptation, passed along by tradition and example rather than by genes from one generation to the next. Culture determines, for example, whether children's education will focus on skill at hunting or reading, how close people stand when they converse, and whether or not they form lines in public places (Munroe & Munroe, 1994).

Psychologists and anthropologists have isolated many respects in which cultures differ (Triandis, 1998). Table 1.2 outlines one way of analyzing these differences; it shows that many cultures can be described as either individualist or collectivist. Many people in *individualist* cultures, such as those typical of North America and Western Europe, tend to value personal rather than group goals and achievement. Competitiveness to distinguish oneself from others is common in these cultures, as is a sense of isolation. By contrast, many people in *collectivist* cultures, such as Japan, tend to think of themselves mainly as part of family or work groups. Cooperative effort aimed at advancing the welfare of such groups is highly valued, and whereas loneliness is seldom a problem, fear of rejection by the group is common. Many aspects of U.S. culture—from self-reliant cowboy heroes and bonuses for "top" employees to the invitation to "help yourself" at a buffet table—reflect its tendency toward an individualist orientation (see Table 1.3).

Culture is often associated with a particular country, but in fact most countries are *multicultural*; in other words, they host many *subcultures* within their borders.

OBJ 1.7: Explain why psychologists have become increasingly interested in the influence of culture on behavior and mental processes. Define and give examples of sociocultural variables. Compare and contrast individualist and collectivist cultures.

Test Items 1.144–1.165

IRM Activity 1.9: Who Are You?

ClassPrep PPT 27: Human Diversity and Psychology

Personal Learning Activity 1.5

IRM Activity 1.7: Sociocultural Diversity

culture The accumulation of values, rules of behavior, forms of expression, religious beliefs, occupational choices, and the like for a group of people who share a common language and environment.

The Impact of Culture   Culture helps shape virtually every aspect of our behavior and mental processes, from how we dress to how we think to what we think is important. Because we grow up immersed in our culture, we may be unaware of its influence on our own thoughts and actions until—like these participants at a United Nations World Conference on Women—we encounter people whose culture has shaped them in different ways.

ClassPrep PPT 28, 29, OHT: Some Characteristics of Individualist vs. Collectivist Cultures

Often, these subcultures are formed by people of various ethnic origins. The population of the United States, for instance, encompasses African Americans, Hispanic Americans, Asian Americans, and American Indians, as well as European Americans whose families came from Italy, Germany, Britain, Poland, Ireland, and many other places (see Figure 1.7). In each of these groups, the individuals who identify with their cultural heritage tend to share behaviors, values, and beliefs based on their culture of origin and, thus, form a subculture (Phinney, 1996).

Like fish unaware of the water in which they are immersed, people often fail to notice how their culture or subculture has shaped their patterns of thinking and behavior until they come in contact with people whose culture or subculture has shaped different patterns. For example, an American teaching in Korea discovered

Cultures don't make everyone in them exactly the same, but they do create certain tendencies in behavior and mental processes (Fiske et al., 1998; Oyserman, Coon, & Kemmelmeier, 2002). For example, individualist cultures support the idea of placing one's personal goals before the goals of the extended family or work group, whereas collectivist cultures tend to encourage putting the goals of those groups ahead of personal goals (Smith & Bond, 1999). Cultures also vary in the degree to which they impose tight or loose rules for social behavior, value achievement or self-awareness, seek dominance over nature or integration with it, and emphasize the importance of time (Abi-Hashem, 2000; Triandis, 1996).

table 1.2
Some Characteristics of Behavior and Mental Processes Typical of Individualist Versus Collectivist Cultures

Variable	Individualist	Collectivist
Personal identity	Separate from others	Connected to others
Major goals	Self-defined; be unique; realize your personal potential; compete with others	Defined by others; belong; occupy your proper place; meet your obligations to others; be like others
Criteria for self-esteem	Ability to express unique aspects of the self; ability to be self-assured	Ability to restrain the self and be part of a social unit; ability to be self-effacing
Sources of success and failure	Success comes from personal effort; failure, from external factors	Success is due to help from others; failure is due to personal faults
Major frame of reference	Personal attitudes, traits, and goals	Family, work group

TRY THIS The statements listed here appeared in advertisements in Korea and the United States. Those from Korea reflect collectivist values, whereas those from the United States emphasize a more individualist orientation (Han & Shavitt, 1994). See if you can tell which are which; then check the bottom of the next page for the answers. You can follow up on this exercise by identifying cultural values in ads you see in newspapers and magazines, as well as on billboards and television. By surfing the Web or scanning international newspapers, you can compare the values conveyed by ads in your culture with those in ads from other cultures.

ClassPrep PPT 31: Korean or U.S. Advertisements?

table 1.3
Cultural Values in Advertising

1. "She's got a style all her own."

2. "You, only better."

3. "A more exhilarating way to provide for your family."

4. "We have a way of bringing people closer together."

5. "Celebrating a half-century of partnership."

6. "How to protect the most personal part of the environment: Your skin."

7. "Our family agrees with this selection of home furnishings."

8. "A leader among leaders."

9. "Make your way through the crowd."

10. "Your business success: Harmonizing with (company name)."

Source: Brehm, Kassin, & Fein (2002).

that some people there believe it is in poor taste to write a student's name in red ink (Stevens, 1999). He was told that doing so conveys a prediction or wish that the person will die, because red ink was traditionally used to record new names in official death registers. Even some of the misunderstandings that occur between men and women in the same culture are traceable to subtle, culturally influenced differences in their communication patterns (Tannen, 1994). In the United States, for example, women's efforts to connect with others by talking may be perceived by many men as "pointless" unless the discussion is aimed at solving a specific problem; thus women often feel frustrated and misunderstood by men, who tend to offer, instead of conversation, well-intentioned but unwanted advice.

For decades, psychologists interested in cross-cultural research have studied cultural differences (Triandis, 1964), but now the influence of sociocultural variables is of growing interest to psychologists in general (Miller, 1999; Sampson, 2000). As psychology strives to be the science of *all* behavior and mental processes, researchers are increasingly taking into account gender, nationality, and other sociocultural variables (Miller, 1999). You will see this trend in much of the research described in the chapters to come.

IRM Activity 1.8: Popular Press Coverage of Psychological Research

ClassPrep PPT 32: Cultural Diversity in the United States

figure 1.7

Cultural Diversity in the United States

The people of the United States represent a wide array of cultural backgrounds. Notice that these figures total more than 100 percent because many people see themselves belonging to two or more groups.

Source: U.S. Bureau of the Census (2001).

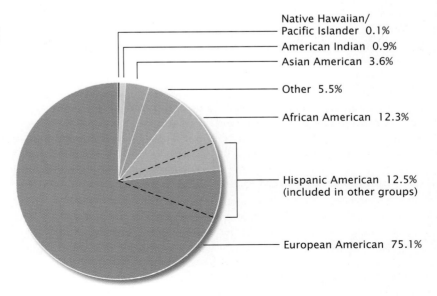

Native Hawaiian/ Pacific Islander 0.1%

American Indian 0.9%

Asian American 3.6%

Other 5.5%

African American 12.3%

Hispanic American 12.5% (included in other groups)

European American 75.1%

SUMMARY

Psychology is the science that seeks to understand behavior and mental processes, and to apply that understanding in the service of human welfare.

The World of Psychology: An Overview

The concept of "behavior and mental processes" is a broad one, encompassing virtually all aspects of what it means to be a human being.

Subfields of Psychology

Because the subject matter of psychology is so diverse, most psychologists work in particular subfields within the discipline. For example, *biological psychologists,* also called *physiological psychologists,* study topics such as the role played by the brain in regulating normal and disordered behavior. *Developmental psychologists* specialize in trying to understand the development of behavior and mental processes over a lifetime. *Cognitive psychologists,* some of whom prefer to be called *experimental psychologists,* focus on basic psychological processes such as learning, memory, and perception; they also study judgment, decision making, and problem solving. *Engineering psychology,* the study of human factors in the use of equipment, helps designers create better versions of that equipment. *Personality psychologists* focus on characteristics that set people apart from one another. *Clinical psychologists* and *counseling psychologists* provide direct service to troubled people and conduct research on abnormal behavior. *Community psychologists* work to prevent mental disorders and to extend mental health services to those who need them. *Health psychologists* study the relationship between behavior and health and help promote healthy lifestyles. *Social psychologists* examine questions regarding how people influence one another. *Industrial/organizational psychologists* study ways to increase efficiency and productivity in the workplace. *Educational psychologists* conduct and apply research on teaching and learning, whereas *school psychologists* specialize in assessing and alleviating children's academic problems. *Sport psychologists, forensic psychologists,* and *environmental psychologists* exemplify some of psychology's many other subfields.

Linkages Within Psychology and Beyond

Psychologists often work in more than one subfield and usually share knowledge with colleagues in many subfields. Psychologists also draw on, and contribute to, knowledge in other disciplines, such as physics, economics, and political science.

Research: The Foundation of Psychology

Psychologists use the methods of science to conduct empirical research. This means that they perform experiments and use other scientific procedures to systematically gather and analyze information about psychological phenomena.

A Brief History of Psychology

The founding of modern psychology is usually marked as 1879, when Wilhelm Wundt established the first psychology research laboratory. Wundt used laboratory methods to study consciousness in a manner that, as expanded by Edward Titchener, became known as *structuralism.* It was in the late 1800s, too, that Freud, in Vienna, began his study of the unconscious, while in the United States, William James's perspective, known as functionalism, suggested that psychologists should study how consciousness functions to help us adapt to our environments. In 1913, John B. Watson founded behaviorism, arguing that to be scientific, psychologists should study only the behavior they can see, not private mental events. Behaviorism dominated psychology for decades, but psychologists are once again studying consciousness in the form of cognitive processes.

Unity and Diversity in Psychology

Psychologists are unified by their commitment to empirical research and scientific methods, by their linked interests, and by the legacy of psychology's founders, but they are diverse in their backgrounds, in their activities, and in the approaches they take to their work. Most of the prominent figures in psychology's early history were white males, but women and members of minority groups made important contributions from the start, and continue to do so.

Approaches to Psychology

Psychologists differ in their approaches to psychology—that is, in the assumptions, questions, and methods they believe will be most helpful in their work. Some adopt one particular approach; many combine features of two or more approaches. Those adopting a *biological approach* focus on how physiological processes shape behavior and mental processes. Psychologists who prefer the *evolutionary approach* emphasize the inherited, adaptive aspects of behavior and mental processes. In the *psychodynamic approach,* behavior and mental processes are seen as reflecting struggles to resolve conflicts between impulses and the demands made by society to control those impulses. Psychologists who take the *behavioral approach* view behavior as determined primarily by learning based on experiences with rewards and punishments. The *cognitive approach* assumes that behavior can be understood through analysis of the basic mental processes that underlie it. To those adopting the *humanistic approach,* behavior is controlled by the decisions that people make about their lives based on their perceptions of the world.

Human Diversity and Psychology

Psychologists are increasingly taking into account the influence of culture and other sociocultural variables such as gender and ethnicity in shaping human behavior and mental processes.

Answer key for Table 1.3: U.S. ads are numbers 1, 2, 6, 8, and 9.

Research in Psychology

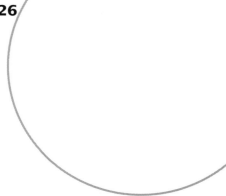

Freburg *Stand!:* Marano, "When Planets Collide," and Grottman & DeClaire, "Calling It Splits"

Francine Shapiro, a clinical psychologist in northern California, had an odd experience one day in 1987 while taking a walk. She had been thinking about some distressing events when she noticed that her emotional reaction to them was fading away (Shapiro, 1989a). In trying to figure out why this should be, she realized that she had been moving her eyes from side to side. Could these eye movements have caused the change in her emotions? To test this possibility, she made more deliberate eye movements and found that the emotion-reducing effect was even stronger. Was this a fluke, or would the same thing happen to others? Curious, she first tested the effects of side-to-side eye movements with friends and colleagues, and then with clients who had suffered traumatic experiences such as sexual abuse, military combat, or rape. She asked these people to think about unpleasant experiences in their lives while keeping their eyes on her finger as she moved it rapidly back and forth in front of them. Like her, they found that during and after these eye movement sessions, their reactions to unpleasant thoughts faded away. Most notably, her clients reported that their emotional flashbacks, nightmares, fears, and other trauma-related problems had decreased dramatically (Shapiro, 1989a).

Based on the success of these cases, Shapiro developed a treatment method she calls *eye movement desensitization and reprocessing,* or *EMDR* (Shapiro, 1991). Since 1990, she and her associates at EMDR Institute, Inc., have trained more than 30,000 therapists in 52 countries to use EMDR in the treatment of adults and children with problems ranging from simple phobias to severe emotional disorders (EMDR Institute, 2001; Greenwald, 1999; Smith & Yule, 1999).

Suppose you had an anxiety-related problem. Would the growth of EMDR be enough to convince you to spend your own money on it? If not, what would you want to know about EMDR before deciding? As a cautious person, you would probably ask some of the same questions that have occurred to many scientists in psychology: Are the effects of EMDR caused by the treatment itself, or by the faith that clients might have in *any* new and impressive treatment? And are EMDR's effects faster, stronger, and longer lasting than those of other treatments?

Asking questions about cause and effect, quality, and value are part of a *critical thinking* process that can help us make informed decisions, not only about psychotherapy options but also about all sorts of other things—such as which pain reliever or Internet service to choose, which college to attend, what apartment to rent, which candidate to vote for, and whether we believe that cell phones can cause cancer or that shark cartilage can cure it. Finding answers to these kinds of questions requires us to translate critical thinking into research. For most people, this means reading *Consumer Reports,* surfing the Web, listening to speeches, or tapping other sources for information about the products, services, institutions, people, and issues we are considering. For psychologists, research means using scientific methods to gather information about behavior and mental processes.

In the pages that follow, we summarize some basic questions that emerge from thinking critically about psychology, describe the scientific research methods psychologists use, and show how some of those methods have been applied in evaluating EMDR. We end the chapter by considering the importance of research ethics in psychology.

Freburg *Perspectives:* Wiseman et al., "Testing the ESP Claims of SORRAT"

Thinking Critically About Psychology (or Anything Else)

Ask several friends and relatives if humans and animals are more aggressive during the full moon, if psychics help the police solve crimes, and if people sometimes suddenly burst into flames for no reason. Most people you ask will probably agree with at least one of these statements, even though not one of them is true (see Table 2.1). Perhaps you already knew that, but don't feel too smug. At one time or another, we all accept something we are told simply because the information seems to come

ClassPrep PPT 1: Ch 2: Research in Psychology

IRM Activity 2.7: Applying Research Methods to "Psychic" Demonstrations

ClassPrep PPT 5: Thinking Critically About Psychology (or anything else)

IRM Thinking Critically 2.1: A Free Trip

IRM Activity 2.6: Critical Thinking About Advertising Claims

table 2.1
Some Popular Myths

Myth	Fact
Many children are injured each year in the United States when razor blades, needles, or poison is put in Halloween candy.	Reported cases are rare, most turn out to be hoaxes, and in the only documented case of a child dying from poisoned candy, the culprit was the child's own parent (Brunvald, 1989).
If your roommate commits suicide during the school term, you automatically get A's in all your classes for that term.	No college or university anywhere has ever had such a rule.
People have been known to burst into flames and die from fire erupting within their own bodies.	In rare cases, humans have been consumed by fires that caused little or no damage to the surrounding area. However, this phenomenon has been duplicated in a laboratory, and each alleged case of "spontaneous human combustion" has been traced to an external source of ignition (Benecke, 1999; Nienhuys, 2001).
Most big-city police departments rely on the advice of psychics to help them solve murders, kidnappings, and missing persons cases.	Only about 35% of urban police departments ever seek psychics' advice, and that advice is virtually never more helpful than other means of investigation (Nickell, 1997; Wiseman, West, & Stemman, 1996).
Murders, suicides, animal bites, and episodes of mental disorder are more likely to occur when the moon is full.	Records of crimes, dog bites, and mental hospital admissions do not support this common belief (Bickis, Kelly, & Byrnes, 1995; Chapman & Morrell, 2000; Rotton & Kelly, 1985).
You can't fool a lie detector.	Lie detectors can be helpful in solving crimes, but they are not perfect; their results can free a guilty person or send an innocent person to jail (see the chapter on motivation and emotion).
Viewers never see David Letterman walking to his desk after the opening monologue because his contract prohibits him from showing his backside on TV.	When questioned about this story on the air, Letterman denied it and, to prove his point, lifted his jacket and turned a full circle in front of the cameras and studio audience (Brunvald, 1989).
Psychics have special abilities to see into the future.	Even the most famous psychics are almost always wrong, as in these predictions for the year 2000: "Prince Charles will fly in the space shuttle," "An earthquake will destroy Los Angeles and San Francisco," and "O. J. Simpson will admit his guilt." None predicted the September 11, 2001, terrorist attacks on New York and Washington. The few correct predictions are usually vague ("Dolly Parton *may* write a book") or obvious ("Brad Pitt and Jennifer Aniston will marry") (Emery, 2001).

ClassPrep PPT 2, 3, 4: Fact or Fiction?

ClassPrep PPT 2, 3, 4: Fact or Fiction? (cont.)

Many people believe in the statements listed here, but critical thinkers who take the time to investigate them will discover that they are not true.

from a reliable source or because "everyone knows" it is true. If this were not the case, advertisers, politicians, salespeople, social activists, and others who seek our money, our votes, or our loyalty would not be as successful as they are. These people want you to believe their promises or claims without careful thought; they don't want you to think critically.

Often, they get their wish. Millions of people waste billions of dollars every year on worthless predictions by telephone "psychics"; on bogus cures for cancer, heart

Uncritically accepting claims for the value of "psychic" readings, "get-rich-quick" schemes, new therapies, or proposed government policies can be embarrassing, expensive, and dangerous. Critical thinkers carefully evaluate evidence for *and* against such claims before reaching a conclusion about them.

disease, and arthritis; on phony degrees offered by nonexistent Internet "universities"; and on "miracle" defrosting trays, eat-all-you-want weight-loss programs, "effortless" exercise gadgets, and other consumer products that simply don't work—not to mention the millions more lost in investment scams and fraudulent charity appeals (Cassel & Bernstein, 2001).

Critical thinking is the process of assessing claims and making judgments on the basis of well-supported evidence (Wade, 1988). We can apply critical thinking to EMDR—or to any other topic—by asking the following five questions:

1. *What am I being asked to believe or accept?* In this case, the assertion to be examined is that EMDR causes the reduction or elimination of anxiety-related problems.

2. *What evidence is available to support the assertion?* Shapiro experienced a reduction in her own emotional distress following certain kinds of eye movements. Later, she found the same effect in others.

3. *Are there alternative ways of interpreting the evidence?* The dramatic effects experienced by Shapiro and others might be due not to EMDR itself but instead to the motivation of these individuals to change or their desire to prove her right. And who knows? They might have eventually improved on their own, without any treatment. Even the most remarkable evidence cannot be accepted as confirming an assertion until equally plausible alternative assertions like these have been ruled out. Doing that leads to the next step in critical thinking: conducting scientific research.

4. *What additional evidence would help to evaluate the alternatives?* The ideal method for collecting further evidence about the value of EMDR would be to identify three groups of emotionally troubled people who were alike in every way except for the anxiety treatment they received. Now suppose the people in the EMDR group improved much more than those getting an equally motivating, but useless, treatment or no treatment at all. Such results would make it less likely that the improvements seen following EMDR can be explained by client motivation or the mere passage of time.

5. *What conclusions are most reasonable?* So far, additional research evidence has not ruled out alternative explanations for the effects of EMDR. People's belief in EMDR, rather than the treatment itself, may be largely responsible for its positive effects. So the only reasonable conclusions to be drawn at this point are that (a) EMDR seems to have a positive impact on some clients and (b) further research is needed in order to understand the nature and origins of those effects (Herbert et al., 2000).

Does that sound wishy-washy? Critical thinking sometimes does seem indecisive, because even though scientists would prefer to find quick, clear, and final answers, their conclusions must be tempered by the evidence available. In the long run, though, critical thinking opens the way to understanding. To help you hone your

critical thinking   The process of assessing claims and making judgments on the basis of well-supported evidence.

Taking Your Life in Your Hands?
Does exposure to microwave radiation from cell phone antennas cause brain tumors (Carlo & Schram, 2001)? And what about the possible dangers and benefits of herbal remedies, dietary supplements, and other controversial treatments for cancer, AIDS, and depression? These questions have generated intense speculation, strong opinions, and a lot of wishful thinking, but the best answers will depend on scientific research based on critical thinking. For example, although there is no evidence that cell phones cause tumors, scientists continue to study the effects of long-term or heavy exposure (e.g., Carlo & Thibodeau, 2001; Inskip et al., 2001).

own critical thinking skills, we include in each subsequent chapter of this book a section called "Thinking Critically," in which we examine an issue by asking the same five questions we raised here about EMDR.

Critical Thinking and Scientific Research

Scientific research often begins with curious questions, such as "Can eye movements reduce anxiety?" Like many seemingly simple questions, however, this one is actually rather complex. Are we talking about horizontal, vertical, or diagonal eye movements? How long do they continue in each session, and how many sessions should there be? What kind of anxiety will we address, and how will we measure improvement? In other words, a scientist must ask *specific* questions in order to get meaningful answers.

Psychologists and other scientists clarify their questions about behavior and mental processes by phrasing them in terms of a **hypothesis**—a specific, testable proposition about something they want to study. Researchers state hypotheses in order to establish in clear, precise terms what they think may be true, and how they will know if it is not. In the case of EMDR, the hypothesis might be as follows: *EMDR treatment causes significant reduction in anxiety.* To make it easier to understand and objectively evaluate hypotheses, scientists employ **operational definitions**, which are statements describing the exact operations or methods they will use in their research. In the hypothesis just presented, "EMDR treatment" might be operationally defined as inducing a certain number of back-and-forth eye movements per second for a particular period of time, whereas "significant reduction in anxiety" might be operationally defined as a decline of ten points or more on a scale that measures clients' self-reported anxiety. The kind of treatment a client is given (say, EMDR versus no treatment) and the results of that treatment (how much anxiety

IRM Activity 2.8: Design a Study

ClassPrep: Critical Thinking and Objective Research

OBJ 2.2: Define hypothesis, operational definition, and variable.

Test Items 2.4–2.12

IRM In Your Own Words 2.2: A Check on Research Terminology

IRM Discussion 2.3: Steps in Scientific Research

IRM Activity 2.7: Applying Research Methods to "Psychic" Demonstrations

hypothesis In scientific research, a prediction stated as a specific, testable proposition about a phenomenon.
operational definitions Statements that define the exact operations or methods used in research.

reduction occurred) are examples of research **variables**, the specific factors or characteristics that are manipulated and measured in research.

To evaluate whether the results of a study support a hypothesis, the researcher usually looks at objective, quantifiable evidence—numbers or scores that represent the variables of interest and provide the basis for conclusions. This kind of evidence is usually called **data** (which is the plural of *datum*), or a *data set*. Even though data themselves are objective, it is all too easy for scientists to look only for those numbers or scores that confirm a hypothesis, especially if they expect the hypothesis to be true or hope that it is. This common human failing, called *confirmation bias,* is described in the chapter on cognition and language. Scientists have a special responsibility to combat confirmation bias by looking for evidence that contradicts their hypotheses, not just evidence that supports those hypotheses.

Scientists must also assess the *quality* of the evidence they collect. Usually, the quality of evidence is evaluated in terms of two characteristics: reliability and validity. *Reliability* is the degree to which the data are stable and consistent; the *validity* of data is the degree to which they accurately represent the topic being studied. For example, the initial claims for EMDR stemmed from Shapiro's use of this treatment with colleagues and clients. If she had not been able to repeat, or *replicate,* the initial effects—if clients sometimes showed improvement and sometimes did not—she would have had to question the reliability of her data. Alternatively, if the clients' reports of improvement were not supported by, say, the reports of their close relatives, she would have had to doubt the validity of her data.

The Role of Theories

After examining the evidence from research on particular phenomena, scientists often begin to favor certain explanations. Sometimes, they organize these explanations into a **theory**, which is a set of statements designed to account for, predict, and even suggest ways of controlling certain phenomena. For example, Shapiro's theory about the effects of EMDR suggests that eye movements activate parts of the brain

I Love It! When we want something—or someone—to be perfect, we may ignore all evidence to the contrary. This is one reason why people end up in faulty used cars—or in bad relationships. Psychologists and other scientists must be especially careful to keep this confirmation bias from distorting the conclusions they draw from their research.

variables Factors or characteristics that are manipulated or measured in research.

data Numbers that represent research findings and provide the basis for research conclusions.

theory An integrated set of propositions that can be used to account for, predict, and even control certain phenomena.

Where Does Prejudice Come From?
In September 2001, local Protestants shouted insults, threw rocks, and even exploded a bomb as terrified Catholic children were escorted by their parents to classes at Holy Cross Primary school in Belfast, Northern Ireland. Researchers have proposed several theories about the causes of such prejudice—and how to prevent it (see the chapter on social cognition). The testing of these theories by other researchers is an example of how theory and research go hand in hand. Without research results, there would be nothing to explain; without explanatory theories, the results might never be organized in a useful way. The knowledge generated by psychologists over the past 125 years has been based on this constant interaction of theory and research.

where information about trauma or other unpleasant experiences has been stored but never fully processed. EMDR, she says, promotes the "accelerated information processing" required for the resolution of emotional and behavioral problems (Shapiro, 1995, 1999). In the chapter on introducing psychology, we reviewed broader and more famous examples of explanatory theories, including Charles Darwin's theory of evolution and Sigmund Freud's theory of psychoanalysis.

Theories are tentative explanations that must be subjected to scientific evaluation based on critical thinking. For example, Shapiro's theory about EMDR has been criticized as being vague; lacking empirical support; and being less plausible than other, simpler explanations (e.g., Herbert et al., 2000; Keane, 1998). In other words, theories are based on research results, but they also generate hypotheses for further research. The predictions of one psychologist's theory will be tested by many other psychologists. If research does not support a theory, the theory will be revised or abandoned.

The constant formulation, evaluation, reformulation, and abandonment of psychological theories have resulted in several competing explanations for color vision, memory, sleep, aggression, and many other behaviors and mental processes. A sometimes frustrating consequence of this continuing search for answers in psychology is that we cannot offer as many definite conclusions as you might want. The conclusions we *do* draw about many of the phenomena described in this book are always based on what is known so far, and we always cite the need for additional research. This is because research often raises at least as many questions as it answers. The results of one study might not apply in every situation, or to all people. For example, herbal remedies containing St.-John's-Wort appear to reduce mild depression but have little or no impact on severe depression (Shelton et al., 2001). Keep this point in mind the next time you hear a talk-show guest confidently offering simple solutions to complex problems such as depression or anxiety, or presenting easy formulas for a happy marriage and perfect children. These self-proclaimed experts—called "pop" (for *popular*) psychologists by the scientific community—tend to oversimplify issues, cite evidence for their views without concern for its reliability or validity, and ignore good evidence that contradicts the pet theories that they live on.

Psychological scientists must be far more cautious. It is often necessary that they suspend final judgments about complex aspects of behavior and mental processes until they have enough high-quality data to make responsible statements and recommendations. Still, psychological research has led to an enormous body of knowledge that is being put to good use in many ways. And psychologists in all subfields are using today's knowledge as the foundation for the research that will increase tomorrow's understanding of behavior and mental processes. In the rest of this chapter, we describe their research methods and some of the pitfalls that lie in the path of progress toward their goals.

Research Methods in Psychology

OBJ 2.4: Name the four scientific goals of psychology.

Test Items 2.16–2.23

Essay Q 2.1

Like other scientists, psychologists strive to achieve four main goals in their research: to *describe* a phenomenon, to make *predictions* about it, and to introduce enough *control* over the variables in their research to allow them to *explain* the phenomenon with some degree of confidence. Certain methods are especially useful for gathering the evidence needed to attain each of these goals. Specifically, psychologists tend to use *naturalistic observation, case studies,* and *surveys* to describe and predict behavior and mental processes. They use *experiments* to control variables and thus establish *cause-effect relationships,* in which one variable can be shown to have actually caused a change in another. Thus, Shapiro initially *described* the effects of EMDR on the basis of observations of her own reactions; then she tested her *prediction* that similar results might occur in other people. Later we discuss an experiment designed to introduce enough *control* over the variables of interest to begin evaluating alternative explanations for EMDR effects, and thus to explore whether the treatment is actually the cause of clients' improvement. Let's look at how these goals and methods are blended in psychologists' work, beginning with how researchers select the participants in their studies.

ClassPrep PPT 10: Selecting Human Participants for Research

Selecting Human Participants for Research

Just as visitors from another galaxy would be wildly mistaken if they tried to describe the typical earthling after meeting only Jackie Chan, Michael Jackson, Madonna, and Sparky the Wonder Dog, psychologists can go astray in their research if the participants they choose to study are not typical of the larger population of people or animals about which they want to draw conclusions.

OBJ 2.5: Define sampling, random sample, and biased sample. Discuss the importance of sampling in data collection.

Test Items 2.24–2.32

Essay Q 2.2

The process of selecting participants for research is called **sampling.** Sampling is an extremely important component of the research enterprise because it can affect not only what results a psychologist gets but also what those results mean. If all the participants in a study come from a particular subgroup (say, male Asian American musicians), the research results might apply, or *generalize,* only to people like them. This outcome would be especially likely if the researcher is studying a behavior or mental process that is affected by age, gender, ethnicity, cultural background, socioeconomic status, sexual orientation, disability, or other characteristics specific to the participants. When, as is often the case, these variables are likely to have an impact on research results, the sample of participants studied must be representative of people in general if the researcher wants results that are applicable to people in general.

If every member of a population to be studied has the same chance of being chosen as a research participant, the individuals selected constitute a **random sample.** If not everyone has a chance of participating, those selected constitute a **biased sample.** Because it is so difficult and expensive to select a truly random sample from, say, "all college students," "all Canadians," or any other large group, most researchers draw their participants, as randomly as possible, from the population available to them. Depending on their research budget, this population might include, for example, all college students on a local campus or on several campuses around the country, all citizens in the Toronto phone book, or the like. Participants chosen in this way provide a *representative sample* of the population from which they were selected. These samples might represent an even larger population as well, but researchers cannot merely assume that. Before drawing broad conclusions from their research, they must conduct additional studies to show that those conclusions apply to people who differ on sociocultural characteristics such as age, gender, and ethnicity (APA Office of Ethnic Minority Affairs, 2000; Case & Smith, 2000; Gray-Little & Hafdahl, 2000).

Sometimes, however, representative samples of the general population are not necessary, or even desirable. If you are studying unusual mental abilities, it might be more valuable to focus on those rare individuals who can do complex math problems in their heads than to test a representative sample of adults. Further, if you *want* to learn about male Asian American musicians, or pregnant teenagers, or Hispanic American women executives, all your participants should be randomly selected from those groups, not from among people in general.

sampling   The process of selecting participants who are members of the population that the researcher wishes to study.

random sample   A group of research participants selected from a population, each of whose members had an equal chance of being chosen.

biased sample   A group of research participants selected from a population each of whose members did not have an equal chance of being chosen.

No matter how they select their samples, psychologists must guard against allowing their preconceptions about people to influence the questions they ask; the research designs they create; and the way they analyze, interpret, and report their data (Denmark et al., 1988; Hall, 1997). When designing a study on gender and job commitment, for example, the researcher must be sure to sample men and women in jobs of equal status. Comparing male executives with female secretaries might create a false impression of greater male commitment, because people in lower-status positions tend to change jobs more often, regardless of gender. Similarly, researchers who use an all-male sample should give this fact the same prominence

Selecting Research Participants Imagine that as a social psychologist, you want to study people's willingness to help each other. You have developed a method for testing helpfulness, but now you want a random sample of people to test. Take a minute to think about the steps necessary to select a truly random sample; then ask yourself how you might obtain a representative sample, instead.

in their research report as is customarily the case when only females are studied (Ader & Johnson, 1994). To do otherwise would imply that males provide a standard against which females' behavior and mental processes are to be compared. Finally, researchers must report whatever results appear. After all, it is just as valuable to know that men and women, or African Americans and European Americans, did *not* differ on a test of leadership ability as to know that they did. Stephanie Riger (1992) suggests that one of psychologists' greatest challenges is to "disengage themselves sufficiently from commonly shared beliefs so that those beliefs do not predetermine research findings" (p. 732).

Let's now consider some specific research methods that psychologists use to describe, predict, control, and explain the behavior and mental processes of the participants they select for study.

Naturalistic Observation: Watching Behavior

Sometimes, the best way to describe behavior is through **naturalistic observation**, the process of watching without interfering as behavior occurs in the natural environment. This method is especially valuable in cases where other methods are likely to be disruptive or misleading. For example, if you studied animals only by observing them in the laboratory, you might conclude that learning determines most of what they do. If you saw them in the wild, however, you might realize that they also display unlearned actions that are automatically triggered by signals in their natural habitat.

Naturalistic observation of people can be just as important. For example, much of what we know about gender differences in how children play and communicate has come from psychologists' observations in classrooms and playgrounds. Observations of adults have helped psychologists see that the gender differences evident in childhood might underlie some of the conflict and miscommunication that occurs later in intimate relationships (Bradbury, Campbell, & Fincham, 1995). And understanding gender differences that first came to light through observational research helps therapists who work with couples in conflict.

naturalistic observation The process of watching without interfering as a phenomenon occurs in the natural environment.

An Ethologist at Work   Konrad Lorenz helped to found *ethology*, the scientific study of animal behavior in the natural environment. Using naturalistic observation, Lorenz described many examples of inborn, but environmentally triggered, behaviors. For example, baby geese follow their mother because her movement and honking provide signals that are naturally attractive. After Lorenz squatted and made mother-goose noises in front of orphaned newborn geese, the goslings began following him wherever he went.

Although naturalistic observation can provide large amounts of information, it is not problem-free (Nietzel et al., 2003). For one thing, when people know they are being observed (and ethics usually requires that they do know), they tend to act differently than they otherwise would. Researchers typically combat this problem by observing long enough for participants to get used to the situation and begin behaving more naturally. Observational data can also be distorted if observers *expect* to see certain behaviors. If, in a study of EMDR's effects on anxiety, observers know which participants received EMDR and which did not, they might tend to rate the treated participants as less anxious, no matter how they actually behave. To get the most out of naturalistic observation, psychologists must counteract problems such as these. In the treatment study just mentioned, for example, the researchers might ask observers to rate participants' anxiety as seen in videotaped interviews, and without telling them which participants had been given treatment.

LSV: "An Example of a Brain Structure: The Cerebellum," "Phantom Limb," "Narcolepsy"

Case Studies: Taking a Closer Look

Observations are often an important part of a **case study**, which is an intensive examination of behavior or mental processes in a particular individual, group, or situation. Case study examinations may also include tests; interviews; and analysis of letters, school transcripts, or other written records. Case studies are especially useful when studying something that is new, complex, or relatively rare. Shapiro's EMDR treatment, for example, first attracted psychologists' attention through case studies of its remarkable effects on her clients (Shapiro, 1989a).

Case studies have a long tradition in clinical work. Freud's theory of psychoanalysis, for example, was largely developed from case studies of people whose paralysis or other physical symptoms disappeared when they were hypnotized or asleep. Case studies have also played a special role in *neuropsychology*, the study of the relationships among brain activity, thinking, and behavior. Consider the case of Dr. P., a patient described by Oliver Sacks (1985). A distinguished musician with superior intelligence, Dr. P. began to display odd symptoms, such as the inability to recognize familiar people or to distinguish between people and objects. During a visit to a neurologist, Dr. P. mistook his foot for his shoe. When he rose to leave, he tried to lift off his wife's head—like a hat—and put it on his own. He could not

IRM Discussion 2.3: Steps in Scientific Research

ClassPrep PPT 12: Case Studies

TRY THIS **Naturalistic Observation** Observing people in natural settings can provide important clues to understanding social interaction, but it is not easy. Imagine you are studying these children at play. Make a list of the *exact* behaviors you would count as "aggressive," "cooperative," and "competitive."

Learning from Rare Cases Dustin Hoffman's character in *Rain Man* was based on the case of "Joseph," an autistic man who can, for example, mentally multiply or divide six-digit numbers. Other case studies have described *autistic savants* who can correctly identify the day of the week for any date in the past or the future, or tell at a glance that, say, exactly 125 paper clips are scattered on the floor. By carefully studying such rare cases, cognitive psychologists are learning more about human mental capacities and how they might be maximized in everyone (L. K. Miller, 1999; Snyder & Mitchell, 1999).

name common objects when he looked at them, although he could describe them. When handed a glove, for example, he said, "A continuous surface, infolded on itself. It appears to have . . . five outpouchings, if this is the word. . . . A container of some sort." Only later, when he put it on his hand, did he exclaim, "My God, it's a glove!" (Sacks, 1985, p. 13).

Using case studies like this one, pioneers in neuropsychology noted the difficulties suffered by people with particular kinds of brain damage or disease (Banich, 2003). Eventually, neuropsychologists were able to tie specific disorders to certain types of injuries, tumors, poisons, and other causes. (Dr. P.'s symptoms may have been caused by a large brain tumor.) Case studies do have their limitations, however. They may contain only the evidence that a particular researcher considered important, and of course, they are unlikely to be representative of people in general. Nonetheless, case studies can provide valuable raw material for further research. They can also be vital sources of information about particular people, and they serve as the testing ground for new treatments, training programs, and other applications of research.

Surveys: Looking at the Big Picture

Whereas case studies provide close-up views of individuals, surveys provide wide-angle portraits of large groups. In a **survey**, researchers use interviews or questionnaires to ask people about their behavior, attitudes, beliefs, opinions, or intentions. Just as politicians and advertisers rely on opinion polls to gauge the popularity of policies or products, psychologists use surveys to gather descriptive data on just about anything related to behavior and mental processes, from parenting practices to sexual behavior. However, the validity of survey data depends partly on how questions are worded (Schwarz, 1999). This point was illustrated in the results of a 1998 Gallup poll conducted just after then-president Bill Clinton admitted to an adulterous affair with White House intern Monica Lewinsky. This survey suggested that only 40 percent of a national sample had a favorable opinion of Clinton—a 20-point drop from previous polls assessing his popularity. However, the wording of the question differed from the previous surveys. The 1998 poll asked, "Thinking

case study A research method involving the intensive examination of some phenomenon in a particular individual, group, or situation.

survey A research method that involves giving people questionnaires or special interviews designed to obtain descriptions of their attitudes, beliefs, opinions, and intentions.

of Bill Clinton *as a person,* do you have a favorable or unfavorable opinion of him?" The earlier polls had presented respondents with the names of several well-known people, including Clinton. As each name was read, respondents were asked, "Do you have a favorable or unfavorable opinion *of this person*?" When this original wording was used again in a survey conducted one day later, 55 percent of respondents said they had a favorable opinion of Clinton. This figure represented a drop of only 5 percentage points from earlier polls (New York Times, August 20, 1998).

A survey's validity also depends on the sample of people surveyed. As mentioned earlier in relation to all research methods, if you want to draw conclusions about a large population, the sample of people surveyed must be representative of that population. If only people who had voted for Bill Clinton had been sampled in the post-Lewinsky survey, his favorability rating would probably have been even higher than it was. But that result would have reflected the views of Clinton supporters, not U.S. citizens in general.

Other limitations of the survey method are more difficult to avoid. For example, the American Society for Microbiology found that 95 percent of the 1,021 U.S. adults it surveyed said that they wash their hands after using toilet facilities. However, naturalistic observations of 7,836 people in public restrooms across the United States revealed that the figure is closer to 67 percent (ASM, 2000). In short, people may be reluctant to admit undesirable or embarrassing things about themselves, or they may say what they believe they *should* say about an issue. And sometimes, those who respond to a survey hold views that differ from those who do not respond (Rogelberg & Luong, 1998). Survey results—and the conclusions drawn from them—will be distorted to the extent that such tendencies distort people's responses and researchers' access to responses (Turner, Miller, & Rogers, 1998). Still, surveys provide an efficient way to gather large amounts of data about people's attitudes, beliefs, or other characteristics.

Experiments: Exploring Cause and Effect

Naturalistic observation, case studies, and surveys provide valuable descriptions of behavior and mental processes. The relationships revealed by these research methods help psychologists to evaluate existing explanations—and to form new

OBJ 2.7: Define an experiment and give an example of it.

Test Items 2.63–2.67

OBJ 2.8: Explain why an experiment allows investigation of causation.

Test Items 2.68–2.71

ClassPrep PPT 14, OHT: *Figure 2.1:* What Is Causing What?

ClassPrep PPT 15: Experiments

Designing Survey Research How do people feel about gay men and lesbians serving openly in the U.S. military? To appreciate the difficulties of survey research, try writing a question about this issue that you think is clear enough and neutral enough to generate valid data. Then ask some friends whether or not they agree it would be a good survey question, and why.

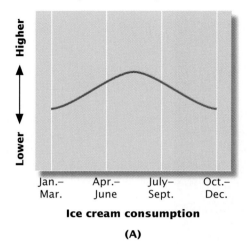

Ice cream consumption

(A)

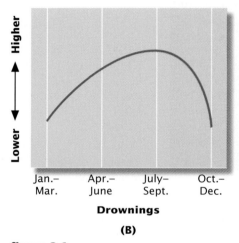

Drownings

(B)

figure 2.1

What Is Causing What?

As these graphs show, ice cream consumption and drownings in the United States tend to rise and fall together. Does this mean that eating ice cream *causes* drowning? No. The relationship between them probably reflects a third variable—time of year—that affects both ice cream sales and the likelihood of swimming and boating (Brenner et al., 2001).

OBJ 2.9: Define and explain the role of independent and dependent variables and of experimental and control groups in an experiment. Define confounding variables.

experiments Situations in which the researcher manipulates one variable and then observes the effect of that manipulation on another variable, while holding all other variables constant.

independent variable The variable manipulated by the researcher in an experiment.

dependent variable In an experiment, the factor affected by the independent variable.

hypotheses—about why people think and act as they do. For example, observations that children who watch a lot of violence on television tend to be more aggressive than other children led to the hypothesis that exposure to media violence can cause aggressiveness (see the chapter on learning.). Surveys showing that sex criminals consume more pornography than other men do suggested that exposure to pornography might cause rape and other sex-related crimes (see the chapter on social influence). And observations that children in day care for more than thirty hours a week are more aggressive than those who stay home with their mothers raised concerns that day care can cause behavior problems (see the chapter on human development).

Establishing Cause and Effect

Do violent television, pornography, and day care actually *cause* the problems with which they are associated? They might, but the most obvious explanations of what is causing what in observational, case study, and survey results may not always be the correct ones (see Figure 2.1). Accordingly, psychologists must consider and test a number of hypotheses to determine which one best explains their research results. Perhaps children who are most aggressive in the first place are the ones who watch the most violent television; maybe sex criminals exaggerate the impact of pornography in hope of escaping punishment; and the aggressiveness seen in day care might have something to do with certain children's pre-existing characteristics, not just their separation from a parent.

One way to evaluate possibilities like these is to analyze observations, case studies, and surveys for trends that support or conflict with certain hypotheses. One trend in the day-care study, for example, was for the most aggressive preschoolers to be the ones who spent the most time in day care each week. This trend supports the hypothesis that separation from the mother can cause aggressiveness. However, it was also the case that 83 percent of the children in day care did *not* show any behavior problems. This second trend suggests that whatever effect separation has, it may be different for different children. It would have been ideal if the children in day care and those at home had been the same in every way except for where they spent their time, but this was not the case. It was the parents, not the researchers, who decided whether to place a particular child in day care, and for how long. The researchers could only describe the results of these decisions and then try to figure out the most reasonable explanation for those results.

The Experimental Method

A better way to evaluate explanatory hypotheses and establish cause-effect relationships is to exert some *control* over research variables ahead of time, not just describe them after the fact. This kind of research usually takes the form of an experiment. **Experiments** are situations in which the researcher manipulates one variable and then observes the effect of that manipulation on another variable, while holding all other variables constant. The variable controlled by the experimenter is called the **independent variable.** The variable to be observed is called the **dependent variable** because it is affected by, or depends on, the independent variable.

Consider the experiment Shapiro conducted in an attempt to better understand the effects of EMDR. As illustrated in Figure 2.2, she first identified twenty-two people suffering the ill effects of traumas such as rape or military combat. These were her research participants. She assigned the participants to two groups. The first group received a single fifty-minute session of EMDR treatment; the second group focused on their unpleasant memories for eight minutes, but without moving their eyes back and forth (Shapiro, 1989b). The experimenter controlled whether EMDR treatment was administered to each participant, so the presence or absence of treatment was the independent variable. The participants' anxiety level while thinking about their traumatic memories was the dependent variable.

Test Items 2.72–2.89

Essay Q 2.2

Unthinkable Experiments   It would be much easier to draw cause-effect conclusions about the impact of day care if researchers assigned similar children to either day care or home care. And keeping one group of pregnant women drug-free while giving others varying amounts of alcohol would allow firmer conclusions about the amount of alcohol it takes to cause birth defects. But these controlled experiments would be utterly unethical, which is why psychologists explore some important research questions only by comparing the outcomes of people's differing decisions about day care, drug use, dropping out of school, and the like.

Personal Learning Activity 2.3

IRM Discussion 2.4: On the Use of Animals in Scientific Research

IRM Research Focus 2.5: Listening to Music While Studying

experimental group   In an experiment, the group that receives the experimental treatment.

control group   In an experiment, the group that receives no treatment or provides some other baseline against which to compare the performance or response of the experimental group.

confounding variable   In an experiment, any factor that affects the dependent variable, along with or instead of the independent variable

random variables   In an experiment, confounding variables in which uncontrolled or uncontrollable factors affect the dependent variable, along with or instead of the independent variable.

random assignment   The procedure by which random variables are evenly distributed in an experiment by putting participants into various groups through random process.

placebo   A physical or psychological treatment that contains no active ingredient but produces an effect because the person receiving it believes it will.

The group that receives the experimental treatment is called, naturally enough, the **experimental group.** The group that receives no treatment or some other treatment is called the **control group.** Control groups provide baselines against which to compare the performance of other groups. In Shapiro's experiment, having a control group allowed her to measure how much change in anxiety could be expected from exposure to bad memories without EMDR treatment. If everything about the two groups was exactly the same *before* the experiment, then any difference in anxiety between the groups *afterward* should have been due to the treatment given. At the same time, hypotheses about alternative causes of improvement, such as the mere passage of time, became less plausible.

The results of the Shapiro (1989b) experiment showed that participants who received EMDR treatment experienced a complete and nearly immediate reduction in anxiety related to their traumatic memories, whereas those in the control group showed no change. This difference suggests that EMDR caused the improvement. But look again at the structure, or design, of the experiment. The EMDR group's session lasted about fifty minutes, but the control group focused on their memories for only eight minutes. Would the people in the control group have improved, too, if they had spent fifty minutes focusing on their memories? We don't know, because the experiment did not compare methods of equal duration.

Anyone who conducts or relies on research must be on guard for such flaws in experimental design and control. Before drawing any conclusions from research, experimenters must consider other factors—especially variables that could confound, or confuse, interpretation of the results. Any factor that might have affected the dependent variable, along with or instead of the independent variable, may be such a **confounding variable.** When confounding variables are present, the experimenter cannot know whether the independent variable or the confounding variable produced the results. Let's examine three sources of confounding: random variables, participants' expectations, and experimenter bias.

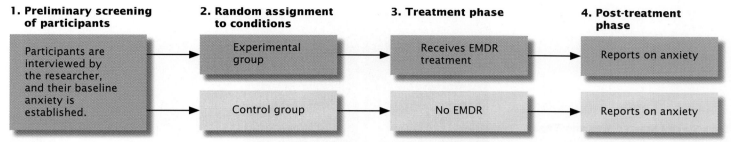

1. Preliminary screening of participants	2. Random assignment to conditions	3. Treatment phase	4. Post-treatment phase
Participants are interviewed by the researcher, and their baseline anxiety is established.	Experimental group	Receives EMDR treatment	Reports on anxiety
	Control group	No EMDR	Reports on anxiety

figure 2.2

A Simple Two-Group Experiment

Ideally, the only difference between the experimental and control groups in experiments like this one is whether the participants receive the treatment the experimenter wishes to evaluate. Under such ideal circumstances, any difference in the two groups' reported levels of anxiety (the dependent variable) at the end of the experiment would be due only to whether or not they received treatment (the independent variable).

ClassPrep PPT 16, OHT: *Figure 2.2:* A Simple Two-Group Experiment

They Are All the Same Scientists in Hawaii succeeded in cloning dozens of mice and then creating a second generation of clones from the original group. Having lots of genetically identical animals is important because they can be assigned to various experimental and control groups without having to worry about the effects of individual differences on the dependent variable. Ethical concerns rule out creating a pool of cloned people, so random assignment will remain a vital component of psychological research with human beings.

ClassPrep PPT 17: Sources for Confounding Variables

OBJ 2.10 Discuss the problems presented by confounding variables in the interpretation of experimental results. Define random variables, random assignment, and placebo.

Test Items 2.90–2.100

Random Variables In an ideal research world, everything about the experimental and control groups would be identical except for their exposure to the independent variable (such as whether or not they received treatment). In reality, however, there are always other differences, especially those introduced by **random variables.** Random variables are uncontrolled, sometimes uncontrollable, factors such as differences among the participants—in terms of their backgrounds, personalities, physical health, or vulnerability to stress, for example—as well as differences in research conditions such as the time of day, temperature, or noise level.

Differences among participants can be so numerous that no experimenter can create groups that are equivalent on all of them. A common solution to this problem is to flip a coin or use some other random process to assign each research participant to experimental or control groups. Such procedures—called **random assignment**—are intended to distribute the impact of these uncontrolled variables randomly (and probably about equally) across groups, thus minimizing the chance that they will distort the results of the experiment (Shadish, Cook, & Campbell, 2002).

Notice that although the names are similar, *random assignment* is not the same as *random sampling*. As mentioned earlier, random sampling is used in many kinds of research to ensure that the people studied are representative of some larger group, whereas random assignment is used in experiments to create equivalence among various groups.

Participants' Expectations After eight minutes of focusing on unpleasant memories, participants in the control group in Shapiro's (1989b) experiment were asked to begin moving their eyes. At that point they, too, started to experience a reduction in anxiety. Was this improvement caused by the eye movements themselves, or could it be that the instructions made the participants feel more confident that they were now getting "real" treatment? This question illustrates a second source of confounding: differences in what people *think* about the experimental situation. If participants who receive an impressive treatment expect that it will help them, they may try harder to improve than those in a control group who receive no treatment or a less impressive one. Improvement created by a participant's knowledge and expectations is called the *placebo effect*. A **placebo** (pronounced "pla-SEE-boe") is a treatment that contains nothing known to be helpful, but that nevertheless produces benefits because a person believes it will be beneficial.

How can researchers determine the extent to which a result is caused by the independent variable or by a placebo effect? Usually, they include a special control group that receives *only* a placebo treatment. Then they compare results for the experimental group, the placebo group, and those receiving no treatment. In one smoking-cessation study, for example, participants in a placebo group took sugar

Ever Since I Started Wearing These Magnets . . .   Placebo-controlled experiments are vital for establishing cause-effect relationships between treatment and outcome with human participants. For example, many people swear that magnets held against their joints relieve the pain of sports injuries and even arthritis. But experiments show that magnets are no more effective than placebo treatment with an identical, but nonmagnetic, metal object (e.g., Carter et al., 2002; Collacott et al., 2000). Something other than magnets—wishful thinking, perhaps—appears to be causing the reported benefits.

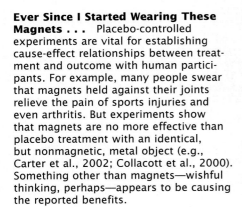

IRM Research Focus 16.8: "Uppers" for "Hyper" Kids

IRM Activity 2.7: Applying Research Methods to "Psychic" Demonstrations

experimenter bias   A confounding variable that occurs when an experimenter unintentionally encourages participants to respond in a way that supports the hypothesis.

double-blind design   A research design in which neither the experimenter nor the participants know who is in the experimental group and who is in the control group.

pills described by the experimenter as "fast-acting tranquilizers" that would help them learn to endure the stress of giving up cigarettes (Bernstein, 1970). These people did far better at quitting than did those in a no-treatment group; in fact, they did as well as participants in the experimental group, who received extensive treatment. This result suggested that the success of the experimental group may have been due largely to the participants' expectations, not to the treatment methods. Placebo effects may not be as strong as experimenters once assumed (Hrobjartsson & Gotzsche, 2001), but some people do improve after receiving medical or psychological treatment, not because of the treatment itself but because they believe that it will help them.

Research on EMDR treatment suggests that the eye movements themselves may not be responsible for improvement, inasmuch as staring, finger tapping, or listening to rapid clicks or tones while focusing on traumatic memories has also produced benefits (e.g., Carrigan & Levis, 1999; Cusack & Spates, 1999; Rosen, 1999). In fact, although EMDR appears to have some positive effects on some clients (e.g., Feske & Goldstein, 1997), its failure to outperform impressive placebo treatments (or other established methods for helping clients deal with unpleasant images) has led many researchers to conclude that EMDR should not be a first-choice treatment for anxiety-related disorders (Davison & Parker, 2001; Goldstein et al., 2000; Herbert et al., 2000). Accordingly, mental health professionals volunteering to work with traumatized people in the days following the September 11, 2001, terrorist attack on the World Trade Center were asked by New York authorities not to use EMDR (P. Fraenkel, personal communication, October 28, 2001).

Experimenter Bias   Another potential confounding variable comes from **experimenter bias**, the unintentional effect that experimenters may exert on their results. Robert Rosenthal (1966) was one of the first to demonstrate the power of one kind of experimenter bias: *experimenter expectancies*. His research participants were laboratory assistants whose job was to place rats in a maze. Rosenthal told some of the assistants that their rats had been bred to be particularly "maze-bright"; he told the others that their rats were "maze-dull." In fact, both groups of rats were randomly drawn from the same population and had equal maze-learning capabilities. But the "maze-bright" animals learned the maze significantly faster than the "maze-dull" rats. Why? Rosenthal concluded that the result had nothing to do with

Keeping Experimenters "Blind" Suppose you are a sport psychologist conducting an experiment in which the independent variable is coaching style (standard methods versus a new relaxation-based technique) for reducing athletic performance anxiety (the dependent variable). How would you create a double-blind design to prevent experimenter bias? Would it be possible to keep coaches in the dark about which method is expected to produce the best results?

OBJ 2.11: Describe the relationship between a double-blind design and experimenter bias.

Test Items 2.101–2.109

Personal Learning Activity 2.4

the rats and everything to do with the experimenters. He suggested that the assistants' expectations about their rats' supposedly superior (or inferior) capabilities caused them to slightly alter their training and handling techniques, which in turn speeded (or slowed) the animals' learning. Similarly, when administering different kinds of anxiety treatments to different groups, experimenters who believe one treatment will be the best may do a slightly better job with that treatment and thus unintentionally improve its effects.

To prevent experimenter bias from confounding results, experimenters often use a **double-blind design.** In this arrangement, both the research participants and those giving the treatments are unaware of, or "blind" to, who is receiving a placebo, and they do not know what results are expected from various treatments. Only the director of the study—a person who makes no direct contact with participants—has this information, and he or she does not reveal it until the experiment is over. The fact that double-blind studies of EMDR have not yet been conducted is another reason for caution in drawing conclusions about this treatment.

In short, experiments are vital tools for examining cause-effect relationships between variables, but like the other methods we have described (see "In Review: Methods of Psychological Research"), they are vulnerable to error. To maximize the value of their experiments, psychologists try to eliminate as many confounding variables as possible, replicate their work to ensure consistent results, and then temper their interpretation of the results to take into account the limitations or problems that remain.

To best control for participant expectancies and experimenter bias, neither experimenters nor participants should know who is getting the experimental treatment and who is getting placebo treatment.

By permission of Johnny Hart and Creators Syndicate, Inc.

THE WIZARD OF ID   Brant parker and Johnny hart

in review   Methods of Psychological Research

Method	Features	Strengths	Pitfalls
Naturalistic observation	Observation of human or animal behavior in the environment where it typically occurs	Provides descriptive data about behavior presumably uncontaminated by outside influences	Observer bias and participant self-consciousness can distort results
Case studies	Intensive examination of the behavior and mental processes associated with a specific person or situation	Provide detailed descriptive analyses of new, complex, or rare phenomena	May not provide representative picture of phenomena
Surveys	Standard sets of questions asked of a large number of participants	Gather large amounts of descriptive data relatively quickly and inexpensively	Sampling errors, poorly phrased questions, and response biases can distort results
Experiments	Manipulation of an independent variable and measurement of its effects on a dependent variable	Can establish a cause-effect relationship between independent and dependent variables	Confounding variables may prevent valid conclusions

ClassPrep: Statistical Analysis of Research Results

Statistical Analysis of Research Results

OBJ 2.12: Summarize the use of descriptive and inferential statistics in evaluating research results.

Test Items 2.110–2.112

IRM Discussion S.1: Statistics

IRM Handout S.2: A Handy Statistical Reference

OBJ 2.13: Discuss the role of measures of central tendency in summarizing and describing research results.

Naturalistic observations, case studies, surveys, and experiments generate a large amount of information, or data. *Statistical analyses* are the methods most often used to summarize and analyze those data. These methods include **descriptive statistics**, which are the numbers that psychologists use to describe and present their data, and **inferential statistics**, which are mathematical procedures used to draw conclusions from data and to make inferences about what they mean. Here, we describe a few statistical terms that you will encounter in later chapters; you can find more information about these terms in the statistics appendix.

Descriptive Statistics

The three most important *descriptive statistics* are *measures of central tendency*, which describe the typical score (or value) in a set of data; *measures of variability*, which describe the spread, or dispersion, among the scores in a set of data; and *correlation coefficients*, which describe relationships between variables.

descriptive statistics Numbers that summarize a set of research data.

inferential statistics A set of procedures that provides a measure of how likely it is that research results came about by chance.

mode A measure of central tendency that is the value or score that occurs most frequently in a data set.

median A measure of central tendency that is the halfway point in a set of data: Half the scores fall above the median, and half fall below it.

mean A measure of central tendency that is the arithmetic average of the scores in a set of data.

Measures of Central Tendency   Suppose you wanted to test the effects of EMDR treatment on fear of the dark. Looking for participants, you collect the eleven self-ratings of anxiety listed on the left side of Table 2.2. What is the typical score, the central tendency, that best represents the anxiety level of this group of people? There are three measures designed to capture this typical score: the mode, the median, and the mean.

The **mode** is the value or score that occurs most frequently in a data set. You can find it by arranging the scores from lowest to highest. On the left side of Table 2.2, the mode is 50, because the score of 50 occurs more often than any other. Notice, however, that in this data set the mode is actually an extreme score. Sometimes, the mode acts like a microphone for a small but vocal minority that, though it speaks most frequently, does not represent the views of the majority.

Unlike the mode, the median takes all of the scores into account. The **median** is the halfway point in a set of data: Half the scores fall above the median, and half

Here are scores representing people's self-ratings, on a 1–100 scale, of their fear of the dark.

ClassPrep PPT 19: Descriptive Statistics

ClassPrep PPT 20: *Table 2.2:* A Set of Pretreatment Anxiety Ratings

table 2.2

A Set of Pretreatment Anxiety Ratings

Data from 11 Participants		Data from 12 Participants	
Participant Number	**Anxiety Rating**	**Participant Number**	**Anxiety Rating**
1	20	1	20
2	22	2	22
3	28	3	28
4	35	4	35
5	40	5	40
6	45 (Median)	6	45
7	47	7	47 (Median = 46*)
8	49	8	49
9	50	9	50
10	50	10	50
11	50	11	50
		12	100

Measures of central tendency
Mode = 50
Median = 45
Mean = 436/11 = 39.6

Measures of central tendency
Mode = 50
Median = 46
Mean = 536/12 = 44.7

Measures of variability
Range = 30
Standard deviation = 11.064

Measures of variability
Range = 80
Standard deviation = 19.763

*When there is an even number of scores, the exact middle of the list lies between two numbers. The median is the value halfway between those numbers.

Test Items 2.113–2.127

IRM Activity S.3: Quick and Simple Normal Distributions

IRM Activity S.4: Cognitive Individual Differences and a Normal Distribution

fall below it. For the scores on the left side of Table 2.2, the halfway point—the median—is 45.

The third measure of central tendency is the **mean**, which is the *arithmetic average* of a set of scores. When people talk about the "average" in everyday conversation, they are usually referring to the mean. To find the mean, add the scores and divide by the number of scores. For the data on the left side of Table 2.2, the mean is 436/11 = 39.6.

Like the median (and unlike the mode), the mean reflects all the data to some degree, not just the most frequent data. Notice, however, that the mean reflects the actual values of all the scores, whereas the median gives each score equal weight, whatever its value. This distinction can have a big effect on how well the mean and median represent the scores in a particular set of data. Suppose, for example, that

Descriptive statistics are valuable for summarizing research results, but we must evaluate them carefully before drawing conclusions about what they mean. Given this executive's reputation for uncritical thinking, you can bet that Dogbert's impressive-sounding restatement of the definition of *median* will win him an extension of his pricey consulting contract.

DILBERT reprinted by permission of United Feature Syndicate, Inc.

you add to your sample a twelfth participant, whose anxiety rating is 100. When you re-analyze the anxiety data (see the right side of Table 2.2), the median hardly changes, because the new participant counts as just one more score. However, when you compute the new mean, the actual *amount* of the new participant's rating is added to everyone else's ratings; as a result, the mean jumps five points. Sometimes, as in this example, the median is a better measure of central tendency than the mean because the median is less sensitive to extreme scores. But because the mean is more representative of the values of all the data, it is often the preferred measure of central tendency.

Measures of Variability   The variability (also known as *spread* or *dispersion*) in a set of data is described by statistics known as the *range* and the *standard deviation*. The **range** is simply the difference between the highest and the lowest scores in a data set (it would be 30 for the data on the left side of Table 2.2 and 80 for the data on the right side). In contrast, the **standard deviation**, or **SD**, measures the average difference between each score and the mean of the data set. It provides information on the extent to which scores in a data set vary, or differ, from one another. The more variable the data are, the higher the standard deviation will be. For example, the SD for the eleven participants on the left side of Table 2.2 is 11.064, but it rises to 19.763 once the very divergent twelfth score is added on the right side. In the statistics appendix, we show how to calculate the standard deviation.

Correlation and Correlation Coefficients   Does the number of fears people have tend to decrease with age? In general, yes (Kleinknecht, 1991);

OBJ 2.14: Discuss the role of measures of variability in summarizing and describing research results.

Test Items 2.128–2.134

IRM Activity S.5: Why Measures of Variability Matter

Personal Learning Activity 2.5

IRM Activity 2.9: Exercises in Correlations and Experiments

★ TRY THIS   **The Impact of Variability**
Suppose that on your first day as a substitute teacher at a new school, you are offered either of two classes. The mean IQ score in both classes is 100, but the standard deviation (SD) of scores is 16 in one class and 32 in the other. Before you read the next sentence, ask yourself which class you would choose if you wanted an easy day's work, or a tough challenge. (Higher standard deviation means more variability, so students in the class with the SD of 32 will vary more in ability, thus creating a greater challenge.)

range   A measure of variability that is the difference between the highest and the lowest values in a data set.

standard deviation (SD)   A measure of variability that is the average difference between each score and the mean of the data set.

correlation   In research, the degree to which one variable is related to another.

correlation coefficient   A statistic, *r*, that summarizes the strength and direction of a relationship between two variables.

ClassPrep PPT 21, OHT: Correlation

OBJ 2.15: Define correlation. Describe how the absolute value and sign of a correlation coefficient are interpreted.

Test Items 2.135–2.144

ClassPrep PPT 22: Correlation Coefficient

IRM Activity 2.11: Statistics Worksheet: Correlations

but to test hypotheses about questions such as this, psychologists must have a way to measure how, and to what extent, variables such as age and fearfulness are correlated.

Correlation means just what it says: "co-relation." In statistics, correlation refers both to how strongly one variable is related to another and to the direction of the relationship. A *positive correlation* means that two variables increase together or decrease together. A *negative correlation* means that the variables move in opposite directions: When one increases, the other decreases. For example, James Schaefer observed 4,500 customers in 65 bars and found that the tempo of jukebox music was negatively correlated with the rate at which the customers drank alcohol; the slower the tempo, the faster the drinking (Schaefer et al., 1988).

Does this mean Schaefer could wear a blindfold and predict exactly how fast people are drinking by timing the music? Or could he plug his ears and determine the musical tempo by watching how fast people drink? No and no, because the accuracy of predictions about one variable from knowledge of another depends on the strength of the correlation. Only a perfect correlation between two variables would allow you to predict the exact value of one from a knowledge of the other. The weaker the correlation, the less one variable can tell you about the other.

To describe the strength of a correlation, psychologists use a statistic called the **correlation coefficient** (the statistics appendix shows how to calculate it). The correlation coefficient is given the symbol r, and it can vary from $+1.00$ to -1.00. Thus, the coefficient includes (1) an absolute value, such as .20 or .50, and (2) either a plus sign or a minus sign.

The actual value of r indicates the strength of the relationship. An r of $+.01$ between people's shoe size and the age of their cars, for example, indicates that there is virtually no relationship between the variables, whereas an r of $+1.00$ indicates a perfectly predictable relationship between two variables (see Figure 2.3).

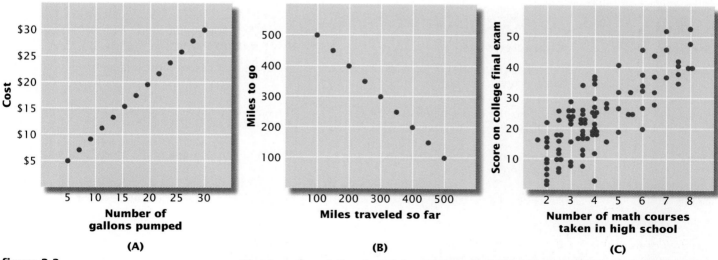

(A)   (B)   (C)

figure 2.3

Three Correlations

The strength and direction of the correlation between variables can be seen in a graph called a *scatterplot*. Here are three examples. In Part A, we have plotted the cost of a gasoline purchase against the number of gallons pumped. The number of gallons is *positively* and perfectly correlated with their cost, so the scatterplot appears as a straight line, and you can predict the value of either variable from a knowledge of the other. Part B shows a perfect *negative* correlation between the number of miles you have traveled toward a destination and the distance remaining. Again, one variable can be exactly predicted from the other. Part C illustrates a correlation of +.81 between the number of math courses students had in high school and their scores on a college math exam; each dot represents one student (Hays, 1981). As correlations decrease, they are represented by ever-greater dispersion in the pattern of dots. A correlation of 0.00 would appear as a shapeless cloud.

ClassPrep PPT 23: Uses of Correlation
Coefficients

OBJ 2.16: Explain why correlations do not imply
causation. Describe the role of alternative
hypotheses in the interpretation of a correlation.

Test Items 2.145–2.151

IRM Activity 2.9: Exercises in Correlations and
Experiments

IRM Activity 2.10: Correlation and Causation

ClassPrep PPT 24: Inferential Statistics

Unfortunately, the variables of interest in psychology are seldom perfectly correlated. Throughout this book, you will find many correlation coefficients whose absolute values range from .20 to .90, reflecting relationships of intermediate strength in which knowing about one variable tells us something, but not everything, about the other.

The *sign* of a correlation coefficient indicates its direction. A plus sign signifies a *positive* correlation between variables; a minus sign indicates a *negative* correlation.

Psychologists use correlation coefficients to help them describe the results of their research, to evaluate existing hypotheses, and often, to generate new hypotheses. As mentioned earlier, however, they must be very careful when drawing conclusions about what correlations mean. Think back to that positive correlation between watching violent television programs and behaving violently. Does seeing violence on TV cause viewers to be violent, or does being violent to begin with cause a preference for violent shows? Perhaps neither causes the other; violent behavior and TV choices could both be due to some third factor, such as examples set by friends. Finding that two variables are *correlated* doesn't guarantee that one is *causing* an effect on the other. And even if one *does* affect the other, a correlation coefficient can't tell us which variable is influencing which. In short, correlations can reveal and describe relationships, but correlations alone cannot explain them.

Inferential Statistics

The task of understanding the meaning of research results summarized in correlations or other descriptive statistics is not an easy one. For example, how did researchers conclude that compared with other anxiety treatments or a placebo, the benefits of EMDR were not great enough to justify recommending it as a treatment of choice (Goldstein et al., 2000)? Such conclusions are based largely on the results of analyses that use *inferential statistics*.

---

in review   Descriptive and Inferential Statistics

Statistic	Characteristics	Information Provided
Mode	Describes the central tendencies of a set of scores	The score that occurs most frequently in a data set
Median	Describes the central tendencies of a set of scores	The halfway point in a data set; half the scores fall above this score, half below
Mean	Describes the central tendencies of a set of scores	The arithmetic average of the scores in a data set
Range	Describes the variability of a set of scores	The difference between the highest and lowest scores in a data set
Standard deviation	Describes the variability of a set of scores	The average difference between each score and the mean of a data set
Correlation coefficient	Describes the relationship between two variables	How strongly the two variables are related and whether the relationship is positive (variables move in same direction) or negative (variables move in opposite directions)
Tests of significance	Help make inferences about the relationships between descriptive statistics	How likely it is that the difference between measures of central tendencies or the size of a correlation coefficient is due to chance alone

Inferential statistics employ certain rules to evaluate the possibility that a correlation or a difference between groups represents a real and reliable phenomenon rather than the operation of chance factors of some kind. Suppose, for example, that participants who received EMDR showed a mean decrease of 10 points on an anxiety test, whereas the scores of a no-treatment control group decreased by a mean of 7 points. Does this difference reflect the greater impact of EMDR or some random fluctuation in people's scores that made EMDR appear more powerful than it actually is? Traditionally, psychologists have answered questions like this by using tests of statistical significance to estimate how likely it is that an observed difference was due to chance alone (Krueger, 2001). When such tests show that a correlation coefficient or the difference between two means is larger than would be expected by chance alone, that correlation or difference is said to be **statistically significant.** In the statistics appendix we describe some of these tests and discuss the factors that affect their results.

Keep in mind, however, that statistical significance tests alone do not necessarily constitute proof that a particular treatment is effective or ineffective. In fact, some psychologists have begun to suggest that other methods of analysis be used in addition to, or instead of, such tests to evaluate research findings (e.g., Cohen, 1994; Hunter, 1997; Krueger, 2001; Loftus, 1996). But whatever quantitative methods are used, psychological scientists are more confident in, and pay the most attention to, correlations or other research findings that statistical analyses suggest are robust and not flukes. (For a review of the statistical measures discussed in this section, see "In Review: Descriptive and Inferential Statistics.")

Statistics and Research Methods as Tools in Critical Thinking

As you think critically about evidence for or against any hypothesis, remember that part of the process is to ask whether a researcher's results have withstood careful statistical analysis—and whether they can be replicated. Using your critical thinking skills to evaluate the statistical and methodological aspects of research becomes especially important when you encounter results that are dramatic or unexpected. This point was well illustrated when Douglas Biklen (1990) began promoting a procedure called "facilitated communication (FC)" to help people with severe autistic disorder use language for the first time (autistic disorder is described in the chapter on psychological disorders). Biklen claimed that these people have language skills and coherent thoughts, but no way to express them. He reported case studies in which autistic people were apparently able to answer questions and speak intelligently using a special keyboard, but only when assisted by a "facilitator" who physically supported their unsteady hands. Controlled experiments showed this claim to be groundless, however (Jacobson, Mulick, & Schwartz, 1995). The alleged communication abilities of these autistic people disappeared under conditions in which the facilitator (1) did not know the question being asked of the participant or (2) could not see the keyboard (Delmolino & Romanczyk, 1995). The discovery that facilitators were—perhaps inadvertently (Spitz, 1997)—guiding participants' hand movements has allowed those who work with autistic people to see FC in a different light.

The role of experiments and other scientific research methods in understanding behavior and mental processes is so important that in each chapter to come, we include a special feature called "Focus on Research Methods." These features describe in detail the specific procedures employed in a particularly interesting research project. Our hope is that by reading these sections, you will see how the research methods discussed in this chapter are applied in every subfield of psychology.

OBJ 2.17: Define statistically significant. Describe the role of statistical significance in thinking critically about scientific research.

Test Items 2.152–2.155

statistically significant A term used to describe the results of an experiment when the outcome of a statistical test indicates that the probability of those results occurring by chance is small.

The Social Impact of Research   The impact of research in psychology depends partly on the quality of the results and partly on how people feel about those results. Despite negative results of controlled experiments on facilitated communication, the Facilitated Communication Institute's web site continues to announce training for the many professionals and relatives of autistic people who still believe in its value (Gorman, 1999). The fact that some people ignore, or even attack, research results that challenge cherished beliefs reminds us that scientific research has always affected, and been affected by, the social and political values of the society in which it takes place (Bjork, 2000; Hagen, 2001; Hunt, 1999; Oellerich, 2000; Tavris, 1998).

ClassPrep PPT 24: Ethical Guidelines for Psychologists

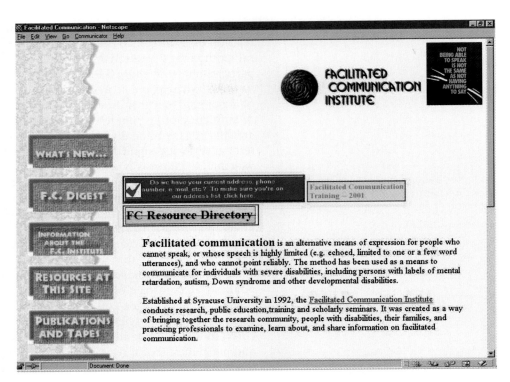

Ethical Guidelines for Psychologists

OBJ 2.18: Describe the ethical guidelines that psychologists must follow.

Test Items 2.156–2.160

The obligation to analyze and report research fairly and accurately is one of the many ethical requirements that guide psychologists in their work. Preserving the welfare and dignity of research participants, both animal and human, is another. So although researchers *could* measure severe anxiety by putting a loaded gun to people's heads, or study marital conflicts by telling one partner that the other has been unfaithful, such methods are potentially harmful and therefore unethical. Whatever their research topic, psychologists' first priority is to investigate it in accordance with the highest ethical standards. They must find ways to protect their participants from harm while still gathering data that will have potential benefits for everyone. To measure anxiety, for example, a researcher might ask people to enter a situation that is anxiety provoking, but not traumatic (e.g., approaching a feared animal, riding in an elevator, or sitting in a dark room). And research on marital conflict usually involves observing couples as they discuss controversial issues in their relationship.

Psychologists take very seriously their obligation to minimize any discomfort or risk involved in their research projects, as well as the need to protect participants from long-term negative consequences. Accordingly, they take care to inform potential participants about every aspect of the study that might influence their decision to participate and ensure that each person's involvement is voluntary. But what if the purpose of the study is to, say, measure emotional reactions to being insulted? Participants might not react as they otherwise would if they know ahead of time that an "insult" will be part of the experiment. When some deception is necessary to create certain experimental conditions, ethical standards require the researcher to "debrief" participants as soon as the study is over by revealing all relevant information about the research and correcting any misconceptions it created.

Local review committees—and standards issued by organizations such as the Association for the Accreditation of Human Research Protection Programs—help psychologists think through these and other ethical implications of any research that might have the slightest risk of harm to human participants. Their review

Caring for Animals in Research
Psychologists are careful to protect the welfare of animal participants in research. They do not wish to see animals suffer, and besides, undue stress on animals can create reactions that can act as confounding variables. For example, in a study of how learning is affected by food rewards, the researcher could starve animals to make them hungry enough to want the rewards. But this would introduce discomfort that would make it impossible to separate the effects of the reward from the effects of starvation.

IRM Discussion 2.4: On the Use of Animals in Scientific Research

ClassPrep: Linkages to Research in Psychology

ClassPrep: Linkages: Psychological Research and Behavioral Genetics

determines whether the planned project's potential benefits, in terms of new knowledge and human welfare, outweigh any potential harm.

The obligation to protect participants' welfare also extends to animals, which are used in a small percentage of psychological research studies (Plous, 1996). Psychologists study animals partly because their behavior is interesting in and of itself and partly because research with animals can yield information that would be impossible or unethical to collect from humans (Mason, 1997). For example, researchers can randomly assign animals to live alone or with others, and then look at how these conditions affect later social interactions. The same thing could not ethically be done with people, but studies like this can provide clues about how social isolation might affect humans (see the chapter on motivation and emotion).

Contrary to the claims of some animal-rights activists, animals used in psychological research are not routinely subjected to extreme pain, starvation, or other inhumane conditions (Novak, 1991). Even in the small proportion of studies that require the use of electric shock, the discomfort created is mild, brief, and not harmful. The *Animal Welfare Act,* the National Institutes of Health's *Guide for the Care and Use of Laboratory Animals*, the American Psychological Association's *Principles on Animal Use*, and other laws and regulations set high standards for the care and treatment of animal participants. In those relatively rare studies that require animals to undergo short-lived pain or other forms of moderate stress, legal and ethical standards require that funding agencies—as well as local committees charged with monitoring animal research—first determine that the discomfort is justified by the expected benefits to human welfare.

The responsibility for conducting research in the most humane fashion is just one aspect of the *Ethical Principles of Psychologists and Code of Conduct* developed by the American Psychological Association (1992b). This document not only emphasizes the importance of ethical behavior but also describes specific ways in which psychologists can protect and promote the welfare of society and the particular people with whom they work in any capacity. Here are some examples: As teachers, psychologists should give students complete, accurate, and up-to-date coverage of each topic rather than a narrow, biased point of view. Psychologists should perform only those services and use only those techniques for which they are adequately trained; a psychologist untrained in clinical methods, for example, should not try to offer psychotherapy. Except in the most unusual circumstances (discussed in the chapter on treatment of psychological disorders), psychologists should not reveal information obtained from clients or students, and they should avoid situations in which a conflict of interest might impair their judgment or harm someone else. They should not, for example, have sexual relations with their clients, their students, or their employees.

Despite these guidelines, doubt and controversy arise in some cases about whether a proposed experiment or a particular practice, such as deceiving participants, is ethical (e.g., D. N. Bersoff, 1999). The American Psychological Association has published a casebook to help psychologists resolve such issues (Nagy, 1999). The ethical principles themselves must continually be updated to deal with complex new questions—such as how to protect the confidentiality of e-mail communications—that psychologists face in their ever-expanding range of work (Jones, 2001).

 LINKAGES (a link to Biological Aspects of Psychology)

Psychological Research and Behavioral Genetics

One of the most fascinating and difficult challenges in psychology is to find research methods that can help us understand the ways in which people's genetic inheritance (their biological *nature*) intertwines with environmental events and conditions before and after birth (often called *nurture*) to shape their

OBJ 2.19: Define behavioral genetics.

Test Items 2.161–2.163

LSV: "Origins of Nature" and "Origins of Nurture"

Videodisc Segment: The Widow's Peak

ClassPrep: Linkages: Psychological Research and Behavioral Genetics (cont.)

OBJ 2.20: Explain how family, twin, and adoption studies help to establish the relative roles of genetic and environmental variables.

Test Items 2.164–2.165

Videodisc Segment & Still: Monozygotic and Dizygotic Twins

behavior and mental processes. In the chapters to come, you will encounter questions about nature and nurture in relation to perception, personality, mental ability, mental disorder, and many other topics. Psychologists' efforts to explore the influences of nature and nurture in relation to these phenomena have taken them into the field of **behavioral genetics**, the study of how genes and heredity affect behavior. In this section, we describe the logic—and some results—of research methods in behavioral genetics. The basic principles of genetics and heredity that underlie these methods are described as part of a more detailed discussion in the behavioral genetics appendix.

Researchers in behavioral genetics realize that most behavioral tendencies can be influenced by many different genes, but also by the environment. Accordingly, research in behavioral genetics is designed to explore the relative roles of genetic and environmental factors in creating differences in behavioral tendencies and, most recently, to identify specific genes that contribute to hereditary influences.

Early research in behavioral genetics relied on the selective breeding of animals. For example, Robert Tryon (1940) mated rats who were fast maze learners with other fast learners and mated slower learners with other slow learners. After repeating this procedure for several generations, he found that the offspring of the fast learners were significantly better at maze learning than those of the slow learners.

Selective-breeding studies must be interpreted with caution, however, because it is not specific behaviors that are inherited but rather differing sets of physical structures, capacities, and the like, which in turn make certain behaviors more or less likely. These behavioral tendencies are often narrow, and they can be altered by the environment (Gottlieb, 2000). For example, "maze-dull" rats performed just as well as "maze-bright" rats on many tasks other than maze learning (Searle, 1949). And when raised in an environment containing tunnels and other stimulating features, "dull" animals did as well at maze learning as "bright" ones; both groups did equally poorly in the maze after being raised in an environment that lacked stimulating features (Cooper & Zubek, 1958).

Research on behavioral genetics in humans must be interpreted with even more caution, because environmental influences have an enormous impact on human behavior and because legal, moral, and ethical considerations prohibit manipulations such as selective breeding. Instead, research in human behavioral genetics depends on studies where control is imperfect. Some of the most important designs in behavioral genetics research are family studies, twin studies, and adoption studies (Plomin et al., 2001; Rutter et al., 2001).

In *family studies*, researchers examine whether similarities in behavior and mental processes are greater among people who are closely related than among more distant relatives or unrelated individuals. If increasing similarity is associated with closer family ties, the similarities might be inherited. For example, data from family studies suggest a genetic basis for schizophrenia because this severe mental disorder appears much more often in the closest relatives of schizophrenics than in other people (see Figure 2.4). But family studies alone cannot establish the role of genetic factors in mental disorders or other characteristics, because close relatives tend to share environments, as well as genes. So similarities among close relatives might stem from environmental factors instead of, or in addition to, genetic ones.

Twin studies explore the heredity-environment mix by comparing the similarities seen in identical twins with those of nonidentical pairs. Twins usually share the same environment and may also be treated very much the same by parents and others. Therefore, if identical twins (whose genes are exactly the same) are more alike on some characteristic than nonidentical twins (whose genes are no more similar than those of other siblings), that characteristic may have a significant genetic component. As we will see in later chapters, this pattern of results holds for a number of characteristics, including some measures of intelligence and some mental disorders. For example, Figure 2.4 shows that if one member of an identical twin pair is schizophrenic, the chances are about 45 percent that the other

behavioral genetics The study of the effect of genes on behavior.

figure 2.4

Family and Twin Studies of Schizophrenia

The risk of developing schizophrenia, a severe mental disorder described in the chapter on psychological disorders, is highest for the siblings and children of schizophrenics and lowest for those genetically unrelated to a schizophrenic. Does this mean that schizophrenia is inherited? These results are consistent with that interpretation, but the question cannot be answered through family studies alone. Environmental factors, such as stressors that close relatives share, could also play an important role. Studies comparing identical and nonidentical twins also suggest a genetic influence on schizophrenia, but even twin studies do not eliminate the role of environmental influences.

ClassPrep: Linkages (cont.) *Figure 2.4:* Family and Twin Studies of Schizophrenia

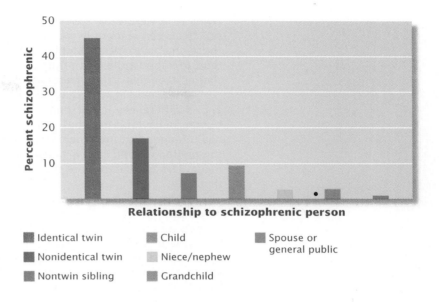

Relationship to schizophrenic person

- Identical twin
- Nonidentical twin
- Nontwin sibling
- Child
- Niece/nephew
- Grandchild
- Spouse or general public

twin will be schizophrenic, too. Those chances drop to about 17 percent if the twins are nonidentical.

Adoption studies take scientific advantage of cases in which babies are adopted very early in life. The logic underlying these studies is that if adopted children's characteristics are more like those of their biological parents than those of their adoptive parents, genetically inherited ingredients in the nature-nurture mix play a clear role in those characteristics. For example, as described in the chapter on personality, the personalities of young adults who were adopted at birth tend to be more like those of their biological parents than those of their adoptive parents. Adoption studies can be especially valuable when they focus on identical

Research in Behavioral Genetics Like other identical twins, each member of this pair has identical genes. Twin studies and adoption studies help to reveal the interaction of genetic and environmental influences on human behavior and mental processes. Cases in which identical twins who had been separated at birth are found to have similar interests, personality traits, and mental abilities suggest that these characteristics have a significant genetic component.

twins who were separated at or near birth. If identical twins show similar characteristics after years of living in very different environments, the role of heredity in those characteristics is highlighted. Adoption studies of intelligence, for example, tend to support the role of genetics in variations in mental ability, but they show that environmental influences are important as well.

As you read in later chapters about the role of genetics in human development and in differences in personality and mental abilities, remember that research on human behavioral genetics can help illuminate the relative roles of heredity and environment that underlie differences *among* individuals, but it cannot determine the degree to which a *particular* person's behavior is due to heredity or environment. The two factors are too closely entwined in an individual to be separated that way.

Family, twin, and adoption studies will continue to be an important part of behavioral genetics research, but the future of behavioral genetics will also be shaped by the results of the Human Genome Project, which has now deciphered the genetic code contained in the DNA that makes each human being unique (International Human Genome Sequencing Consortium, 2001; Venter et al., 2001; see the behavioral genetics appendix). This achievement has allowed behavioral geneticists and other scientists to begin pinpointing some of the many genes that contribute to individual differences in disorders such as autism, learning disabilities, hyperactivity, and Alzheimer's disease, as well as to the normal variations in personality and mental abilities that we see all around us. Finding the DNA differences responsible for the role of heredity in psychology will eventually make it possible to understand exactly how heredity interacts with the environment as development unfolds. Analysis of DNA—collected by rubbing a cotton swab inside an individual's cheek—may someday be used not only in behavioral genetics research but also in clinics where it will help psychologists more precisely diagnose clients' problems and choose the most appropriate treatments (Plomin & Crabbe, 2000).

ClassPrep: Linkages to Research in Psychology

LINKAGES

As noted in the chapter on introducing psychology, all of psychology's subfields are related to one another. Our discussion of behavioral genetics illustrates just one way in which the topic of this chapter, research in psychology, is linked to the subfield of biological psychology (see the chapter on biological aspects of psychology). The Linkages diagram shows ties to two other subfields as well, and there are many more ties throughout the book. Looking for linkages among subfields will help you see how they all fit together and help you better appreciate the big picture that is psychology.

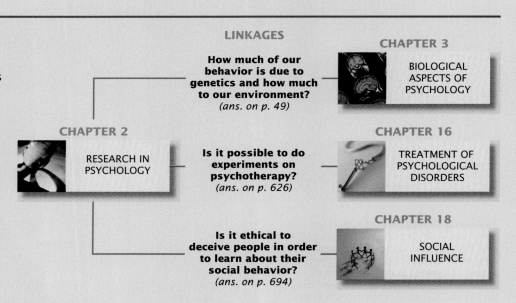

LINKAGES

How much of our behavior is due to genetics and how much to our environment?
(ans. on p. 49)

CHAPTER 3
BIOLOGICAL ASPECTS OF PSYCHOLOGY

CHAPTER 2
RESEARCH IN PSYCHOLOGY

Is it possible to do experiments on psychotherapy?
(ans. on p. 626)

CHAPTER 16
TREATMENT OF PSYCHOLOGICAL DISORDERS

Is it ethical to deceive people in order to learn about their social behavior?
(ans. on p. 694)

CHAPTER 18
SOCIAL INFLUENCE

SUMMARY

Thinking Critically About Psychology (or Anything Else)

Critical thinking is the process of assessing claims and making judgments on the basis of well-supported evidence.

Critical Thinking and Scientific Research

Often, questions about behavior and mental processes are phrased in terms of *hypotheses* about *variables* that have been specified by *operational definitions*. Tests of hypotheses are based on objective, quantifiable evidence, or *data,* representing the variables of interest. If data are to be useful, they must be evaluated for reliability and validity.

The Role of Theories

Explanations of phenomena often take the form of a *theory,* which is a set of statements that can be used to account for, predict, and even suggest ways of controlling certain phenomena. Theories must be subjected to rigorous evaluation.

Research Methods in Psychology

Research in psychology, as in other sciences, focuses on four main goals: description, prediction, control, and explanation.

Selecting Human Participants for Research

Psychologists' research can be limited if their *sampling* procedures do not give them a fair cross-section of the population they want to study and about which they want to draw conclusions. Anything other than a *random sample* is said to be a *biased sample* of participants. In most cases, samples consist of people who are representative of specified target populations rather than of the general population.

Naturalistic Observation: Watching Behavior

Naturalistic observation entails watching without interfering as behavior occurs in the natural environment. This method can be revealing, but care must be taken to ensure that observers are unbiased and do not alter the behavior being observed.

Case Studies: Taking a Closer Look

Case studies are intensive examinations of a particular individual, group, or situation. They are useful for studying new or rare phenomena and for evaluating new treatments or training programs.

Surveys: Looking at the Big Picture

Surveys ask questions, through interviews or questionnaires, about behavior, attitudes, beliefs, opinions, and intentions. They provide an efficient way to gather large amounts of data from many people at a relatively low cost, but their results can be distorted if questions are poorly phrased, if answers are not given honestly, or if respondents do not constitute a representative sample.

Experiments: Exploring Cause and Effect

In *experiments*, researchers manipulate an *independent variable* and observe the effect of that manipulation on a *dependent variable*. Participants receiving experimental treatment are called the *experimental group*; those in comparison conditions are called *control groups*. Experiments can reveal cause-effect relationships between variables, but only if researchers use *random assignment*, *placebo* conditions, *double-blind designs*, and other strategies to avoid being misled by *random variables*, participants' expectations, *experimenter bias*, and other *confounding variables*.

Statistical Analysis of Research Results

Psychologists use *descriptive statistics* and *inferential statistics* to summarize and analyze data.

Descriptive Statistics

Descriptive statistics include measures of central tendency (such as the *mode, median,* and *mean*), measures of variability (such as the *range* and *standard deviation,* or *SD*), and *correlation coefficients*. Although valuable for describing relationships, *correlations* alone cannot establish that two variables are causally related, nor can they determine which variable might affect which, or why.

Inferential Statistics

Psychologists employ inferential statistics to guide conclusions about data and, especially, to determine if correlations or differences between means are *statistically significant*—that is, larger than would be expected by chance alone.

Statistics and Research Methods as Tools in Critical Thinking

Scientific evaluation of research requires the use of critical thinking to carefully assess the statistical and methodological aspects of even the most dramatic or desirable results.

Ethical Guidelines for Psychologists

Ethical guidelines promote the protection of humans and animals in psychological research. They also set the highest standards for behavior in all other aspects of psychologists' scientific and professional lives.

3

Biological Aspects of Psychology

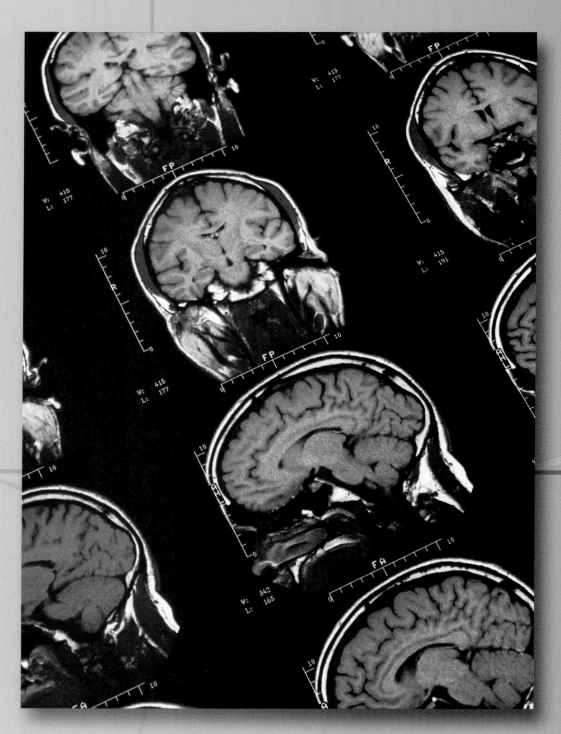

D o you drink coffee? Do you like beer or wine? Are you still unable to quit smoking? If so, you know that caffeine, alcohol, and nicotine can change the way you feel. The effects of these substances are based largely on their ability to change the chemistry of your brain. There are many other examples of how our mental experiences, and our identity as individuals, are rooted in biological processes. Each year, millions of people who suffer anxiety, depression, and other psychological disorders take prescription drugs that alter brain chemistry in ways that relieve their distress. And severe brain disorders such as Alzheimer's disease cause their victims to "lose themselves" as they become progressively less able to think clearly, to express themselves, to remember events, or even to recognize members of their families.

These examples of biological influences on behavior and mental processes reflect the biological approach to psychology discussed in the chapter on introducing psychology. The popularity and impact of that approach stems from the fact that brain cells, hormones, genes, and other biological factors are intimately related to everything you think and feel and do, from the fleeting memory you had a minute ago, to the anxiety or excitement or fatigue you felt last night, to the movements of your eyes as you read right now. In this chapter, we describe these biological factors in more detail. Reading it will take you into the realm of **biological psychology**, which is the study of the cells and organs of the body and the physical and chemical changes involved in behavior and mental processes. It is here that we begin to consider the relationship between your body and your mind, your brain and your behavior.

It is a complex relationship. Scientific psychologists are no doubt correct when they say that every thought, every feeling, and every action are represented somehow in the nervous system and that none of these events could occur without it. However, we must be careful not to oversimplify or overemphasize biological explanations in psychology. Many people assume, for example, that if a behavior or mental process has a strong biological *basis,* it is beyond our control—that "biology is destiny." Accordingly, many smokers do not even try to quit, simply because they assume that their biological addiction to nicotine will doom them to failure. This is not necessarily true, as millions of ex-smokers can attest. The fact that all behavior and mental processes are *based* on biological processes does not mean that they can be fully understood through the study of biological processes alone.

Reducing all of psychology to the analysis of brain chemicals would vastly underestimate the complexity of the interactions between our biological selves and our psychological experiences, between our genes and our environments. Just as all behaviors and mental processes are influenced by biology, all biological processes are influenced by the environment. We will see later, for example, that the experiences we have in the environment can change our brain chemistry and even our brain anatomy. Similarly, your height is a biological characteristic, but how tall you actually become depends heavily on nutrition and other environmental factors (Tanner, 1992). As described in the chapter on research in psychology and the behavioral genetics appendix, hereditary and environmental influences also combine to determine intelligence, personality, mental disorders, and all our other characteristics.

In short, understanding behavior and mental processes requires that we combine information mined at many levels of analysis, ranging from the activity of cells and organ systems to the activity of individuals and groups in social contexts. This chapter focuses on the biological level, not because it reveals the whole story of psychology but because it tells an important part of that story.

We begin by considering your **nervous system**, a complex combination of cells that tells you what is going on inside and outside your body and allows you to make appropriate responses. For example, if you are jabbed with a pin, your nervous system gets the message and immediately causes you to flinch. But your nervous system can do far more than detect information and execute responses. When information

biological psychology The psychological specialty that researches the physical and chemical changes that cause, and occur in response to, behavior and mental processes.

nervous system A complex combination of cells whose primary function is to allow an organism to gain information about what is going on inside and outside the body and to respond appropriately.

figure 3.1

Three Functions of the Nervous System

The nervous system's three main functions are to receive information (input), integrate that information with past experiences (processing), and guide actions (output). When the alarm clock goes off, this person's nervous system, like yours, gets the message, recognizes what it means, decides what to do, and then takes action, by getting out of bed or perhaps hitting the snooze button.

ClassPrep PPT 4, OHT: *Figure 3.1:* Three Functions of the Nervous System

Essay Q 3.1

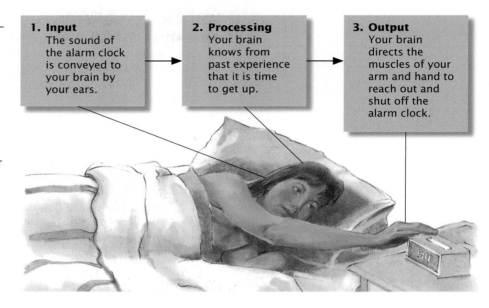

1. Input The sound of the alarm clock is conveyed to your brain by your ears.

2. Processing Your brain knows from past experience that it is time to get up.

3. Output Your brain directs the muscles of your arm and hand to reach out and shut off the alarm clock.

about the world reaches the brain, that information is *processed*—meaning that it is combined with information about past experiences and current wants and needs to make a decision about how to respond. The chosen action is then taken (see Figure 3.1). In other words, your nervous system displays the characteristics of an information-processing system: it has input, processing, and output capabilities.

The processing capabilities of this system are especially important, not only because the brain interprets information, makes decisions, and guides action but also because the brain can actually adjust the impact of incoming information. This phenomenon helps explain why you can't tickle yourself. In one study, simply telling ticklish people that they were about to be touched on the bottom of their feet caused marked activation in the brain region that receives sensory input from the foot (Carlsson et al., 2000). The *anticipation* of being touched made these people all the more sensitive to that touch. However, when they were asked to touch the bottom of their *own* feet, there was far less advance activation of this brain region, and they did not overreact to their touch. Why? The explanation is that when the brain plans a movement, it also predicts which of its own touch-detecting regions will be affected by that movement. So predictable, self-controlled touches, even in a normally "ticklish" spot, reduce activation of the sensory regions associated with that spot (Blakemore et al., 2000).

The nervous system is able to do what it does partly because it is made up of cells that *communicate with each other*. Like all cells in the body—indeed, like all living cells—those in the nervous system can respond to outside influences. Many of the signals that cells respond to come in the form of *chemicals* released by other cells. So even as various cells specialize during prenatal development to become skin, bone, hair, and other tissues, they still "stay in touch" through chemical signals. Bone cells, for example, add or drop calcium in response to hormones secreted in another part of the body. Cells in the bloodstream respond to viruses and other invaders by destroying them. We focus first on the cells of the nervous system, because their ability to communicate is the most efficient and complex.

The Nervous System

Scientists have studied many aspects of the nervous system, from the workings of molecules and cells to the wonders of how vast networks of brain cells accomplish such tasks as recognizing visual patterns and learning a language. We begin our

exploration of the nervous system at the "bottom," with a description of the individual cells and molecules that compose it. Then we consider how these cells are organized to form the structures of the human nervous system.

Cells of the Nervous System

One of the most striking findings of research on the cells of the nervous system is how similar they are to other cells in the body, and how similar all cells are in all living organisms, from bacteria to plants to humans. For example, bacteria, plant cells, and brain cells all synthesize similar proteins when they are subjected to reduced oxygen or elevated temperatures. Because of this similarity, we can learn much about humans by studying animals, and much about brain cells by studying cells in simple organisms. For example, recent studies of cells in simple worms have provided clues to the causes of Alzheimer's disease (Okochi et al., 2000).

Figure 3.2 illustrates three of the characteristics that cells of the nervous system share with every other kind of cell in the body. First, they have an *outer membrane* that, like a fine screen, lets some substances pass in and out while blocking others. Second, nervous system cells have a *cell body*, which contains a *nucleus*. The nucleus carries the genetic information that determines how a cell will function. Third, nervous system cells contain *mitochondria*, which are structures that turn oxygen and glucose into energy. This process is especially vital to brain cells. Although the brain accounts for only 2 percent of the body's weight, it consumes more than 20 percent of the body's oxygen (Sokoloff, 1981). All of this energy is required because brain cells transmit signals among themselves to an even greater extent than do cells in the rest of the body.

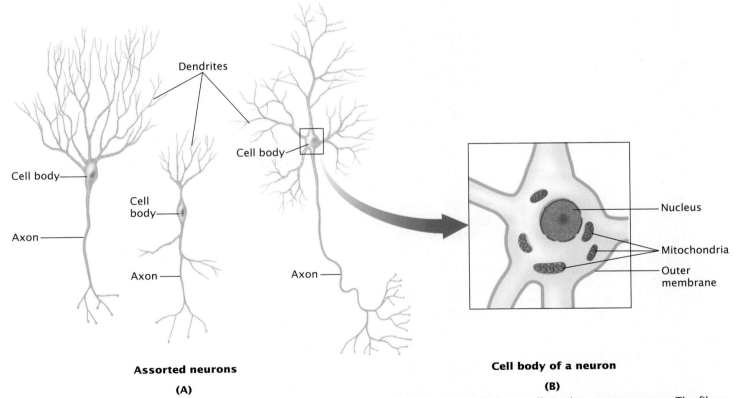

Assorted neurons

(A)

Cell body of a neuron

(B)

figure 3.2

The Neuron

Part A shows three examples of neurons, which are cells in the nervous system. The fibers extending outward from the cell body—the axons and dendrites—are among the features that make neurons unique. Part B is an enlarged drawing of the cell body of a neuron. The cell body of every neuron has typical cell elements, including an outer membrane, a nucleus, and mitochondria.

ClassPrep PPT 5: Cells of the Nervous System

OBJ 3.3: Compare and contrast neurons and glial cells with other body cells.

Test Items 3.7–3.9

Two major types of cells—neurons and glial cells—allow the nervous system to carry out its complex signaling tasks so efficiently. **Neurons** are cells that are specialized to rapidly respond to signals and quickly send signals of their own. Most of Zour discussion of brain cells will be about neurons, but glial cells are important as well. *Glial* means "glue," and scientists had long believed that glial cells did no more than hold neurons together. Recent research shows, however, that **glial cells** also help neurons communicate by directing their growth, keeping their chemical environment stable, providing energy, secreting chemicals to help restore damage, and even responding to signals from neurons (Laming et al., 2000; Smit et al., 2001). Without glial cells, neurons could not function.

Neurons have three special features that enable them to communicate signals efficiently. The first is their structure. Although neurons come in many shapes and sizes, they all have long, thin fibers that extend outward from the cell body (see Figure 3.2). When these fibers get close to other neurons, communication between the cells can occur. The intertwining of all these fibers with fibers from other neurons allows each neuron to be in close proximity to thousands or even hundreds of thousands of other neurons.

OBJ 3.4: Name and describe the functions of the neuronal parts that allow them to communicate with one another.

Test Items 3.10–3.15

The fibers extending from a neuron's cell body are called axons and dendrites. **Axons** are the fibers that carry signals away from the cell body, out to where communication occurs with other neurons. Each neuron generally has only one axon leaving the cell body, but that one axon may have many branches. Axons can be very short or several feet long, like the axon that sends signals from your spinal cord all the way down to your big toe. **Dendrites** are the fibers that receive signals from the axons of other neurons and carry those signals to the cell body. A neuron can have many dendrites. Dendrites, too, usually have many branches. Remember that *axons* carry signals *away* from the cell body, whereas *dendrites* *detect* signals from other cells.

The neuron's ability to communicate efficiently also depends on two other features: the "excitable" surface membrane of some of its fibers and the tiny gap between neurons, called a **synapse**. In the following sections we examine how these features allow a signal to be sent rapidly from one end of a neuron to the other and from one neuron to another.

IRM Activity 3.3: "Acting Out" the Structure and Function of Neurons

IRM Activity 3.5: Mental Chronometry and Speed of Neural Transmission

Action Potentials   **Videodisc Segment & Still:** The Action Potential

To understand how signals are sent in the nervous system, you first need to know something about nerve cell membranes and the chemicals within and outside these cells. As we mentioned earlier, the cell membrane lets some chemical molecules pass through, but excludes others. Many of these molecules carry a positive or negative electrical charge. Normally, the cell pumps positively charged molecules out through its membrane, making the inside of the cell slightly more negative than the outside. When this happens, the cell membrane is said to be *polarized*. Molecules with a positive charge are attracted to those with a negative charge, creating a force called an *electrochemical potential*, which drives positively charged molecules toward the inside of the cell.

Many of these positively charged molecules are kept out by the cell membrane, but some enter by passing through special openings, or *channels*, in the membrane. These channels are distributed along the axon and dendrites and act as gates that can be opened or closed. Normally the channels along the axon are closed, but changes in the environment around the cell can *depolarize* part of its membrane, causing the gates in that area to swing open and allowing positively charged molecules to rush in (see Figure 3.3). When this happens, the next area of the axon becomes depolarized, causing the neighboring gate to open. This sequence continues, creating a wave of changes in electrochemical potential that spreads rapidly all the way down the axon.

neurons Fundamental units of the nervous system; nerve cells.

glial cells Cells in the nervous system that hold neurons together and help them communicate with one another.

axons Fibers that carry signals from the body of a neuron out to where communication occurs with other neurons.

dendrites Neuron fibers that receive signals from the axons of other neurons and carry those signals to the cell body.

synapse The tiny gap between neurons across which they communicate.

ClassPrep PPT 7, OHT: *Figure 3.3:* The Beginning of an Action Potential

OBJ 3.5: Describe the electrical and chemical changes that lead to an action potential. Define myelin and discuss its effects.

Test Items 3.16–3.23

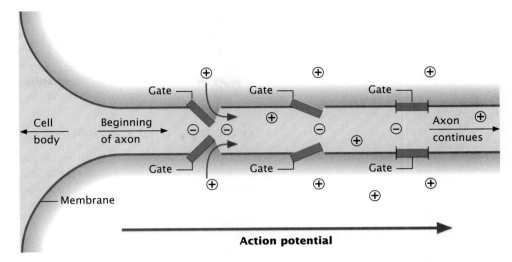

Action potential

figure 3.3

The Beginning of an Action Potential

This highly simplified view of a polarized nerve cell shows the normally closed gates in the cell membrane. The electrochemical potential across the membrane is generated by an uneven distribution of positively and negatively charged molecules. For example, there are more positively charged molecules on the outside than on the inside. There are also more negatively charged molecules on the inside than on the outside. If stimulation causes depolarization near a particular gate, that gate may swing open, allowing positively charged molecules to rush through the membrane; this, in turn, depolarizes the neighboring region of the membrane and stimulates the next gate to open, and so on down the axon. This wave of depolarization is called an *action potential*. Membrane gates allow action potentials to spread along dendrites in a similar fashion.

Personal Learning Activity 3.1

Sattler/Shabatay reader, 2/e: Mairs, "Carnal Acts: Living with Multiple Sclerosis"

Videodisc Segment & Still: A Myelinated Neuron

This abrupt wave of electrochemical changes in the axon is called an **action potential.** When an action potential shoots down an axon, the neuron is said to have "fired." This term is appropriate because action potentials in axons are like gunshots: the cell either fires at full strength or it does not fire at all. For many years, scientists believed that only axons were capable of generating action potentials. However, more recent research has revealed that action potentials also occur in dendrites (Magee & Johnston, 1997). In many neurons, action potentials beginning in the axon go in both directions—down the axon and also "backward" through the cell body and into the dendrites. Action potentials that spread into the dendrites from the cell body appear to reach some dendritic branches and not others, leading scientists to conclude that these messages may be important in strengthening particular connections between neurons that are important to learning and memory (Stuart & Hausser, 2001).

The speed of the action potential as it moves down an axon is constant for a particular cell, but in different cells the speed ranges from 0.2 meters per second to 120 meters per second (about 260 miles per hour). The speed depends on the diameter of the axon—larger ones are faster—and on whether myelin is present. **Myelin** (pronounced "MY-a-lin") is a fatty substance that wraps around some axons and speeds action potentials. Larger, myelinated cells are usually found in parts of the nervous system that carry the most urgently needed information. For example, the sensory neurons that receive information from the environment about oncoming cars, hot irons, and other dangers are fast-acting, myelinated cells. Multiple sclerosis (MS), a severe brain disorder that destroys myelin, probably occurs because some viruses are very similar to components of myelin (Martin et al., 2001). When the MS victim's immune system attacks such viruses, it attacks and destroys vital myelin as well, resulting in disruption of vision, speech, balance, and other important functions.

Although each neuron fires or does not fire in an "all-or-none" fashion, its *rate* of firing can vary. It can fire over and over, because the membrane gates open only

action potential An abrupt wave of electrochemical changes traveling down an axon when a neuron becomes depolarized.

myelin A fatty substance that wraps around some axons and increases the speed of action potentials.

OBJ 3.6: Explain how polarization and refractory periods affect signal transduction in the nervous system.

Test Items 3.24–3.31

LSV: "Neurons and the Nervous System"

briefly and then close. Between firings there is a very short rest, called a **refractory period**, during which the membrane becomes repolarized. At that point the neuron can fire again. Because the refractory period is so short, a neuron can send action potentials down its axon at rates of up to 1,000 per second. The *pattern* of repeated action potentials amounts to a coded message. We describe some of the codes used by the nervous system in the chapter on sensation

Synapses and Communication Between Neurons

How does an action potential occurring in one neuron affect other neurons? For communication to occur *between* cells, a signal must be transmitted across the synapse, or gap, between neurons. Usually, the axon of one cell delivers its signals across a synapse to the dendrites of a second cell; those dendrites, in turn, transmit the signal to their cell body, which may relay the signal down its axon to a third cell, and so on. But other communication patterns also occur. Axons can signal to other axons or even directly to the cell body of another neuron; dendrites of one cell can send signals to the dendrites of other cells (Didier et al., 2001). These varied communication patterns allow the brain to conduct extremely complex information-processing tasks.

OBJ 3.7: Define neurotransmitters and synapse, and describe their roles in nervous-system activity.

Test Items 3.32–3.36

Videodisc Segments: Neurotransmitters, Animation, Neurotransmitters and Receptors, Lock and Key

OBJ 3.8: Describe the role of receptors in the communication process between neurons.

Test Items 3.37–3.38

Neurotransmitters   Communication between neurons across the synapse relies first on chemical messengers called **neurotransmitters.** These chemicals are stored in numerous little "bags," called *vesicles*, at the tips of axons (see Figure 3.4). When an action potential reaches the end of an axon, a neurotransmitter is released into the synapse, where it spreads to reach the next, or *postsynaptic*, cell (see Figure 3.5).

When they reach the membrane of the postsynaptic cell, neurotransmitters attach to proteins called **receptors.** Like a puzzle piece fitting into its proper place, a neurotransmitter snugly fits, or "binds" to, its own receptors but not to receptors for other neurotransmitters (see Figure 3.6). Although each receptor "recognizes" only one type of neurotransmitter, each neurotransmitter type can bind to several different receptor types. As a result, the same neurotransmitter can have different effects depending on the type of receptor to which it binds.

When a neurotransmitter binds to a receptor, it stimulates channels in the membrane of the postsynaptic cell to open, allowing charged molecules to flow in or out. The flow of these charged molecules into and out of the postsynaptic cell produces a change in its membrane potential; thus, the *chemical* signal that crosses the synapse creates an *electrochemical* signal in the postsynaptic cell.

ClassPrep PPT 8: *Figure 3.4:* A Synapse

figure 3.4

A Synapse

This photograph taken through an electron microscope shows part of a neural synapse magnified 50,000 times. It shows the mitochondria; the neurotransmitter-containing vesicles in the ending of the presynaptic cell's axon; the synapse itself, which is the narrow gap between cells; and the dendrite of the postsynaptic cell.

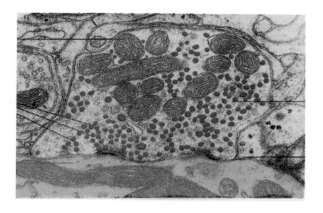

figure 3.5

Communication Between Neurons

When a neuron fires, an action potential shoots to the end of its axon, triggering the release of a neurotransmitter into the synapse. This process stimulates neighboring neurons and may cause them to fire their own action potentials.

ClassPrep PPT 9, OHT: Figure 3.5: Communication Between Neurons

Personal Learning Activity 3.1

IRM Activity 3.3: "Acting Out" the Structure and Function of Neurons

OBJ 3.9: Compare and contrast action potentials and postsynaptic potentials.

Test Items 3.39–3.45

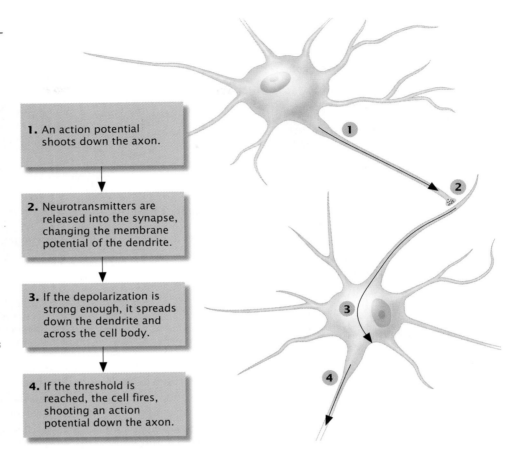

1. An action potential shoots down the axon.

2. Neurotransmitters are released into the synapse, changing the membrane potential of the dendrite.

3. If the depolarization is strong enough, it spreads down the dendrite and across the cell body.

4. If the threshold is reached, the cell fires, shooting an action potential down the axon.

OBJ 3.10: Define excitatory and inhibitory postsynaptic potentials. Describe their role in the creation of an action potential in the postsynaptic cell.

Test Items 3.46–3.47

---

refractory period A short rest period between action potentials.

neurotransmitters Chemicals that assist in the transfer of signals from one neuron to another.

receptors Sites on the surface of cells that allow only one type of neurotransmitter to fit into them, triggering a chemical response that may lead to an action potential.

postsynaptic potential The change in the membrane potential of a neuron that has received stimulation from another neuron.

excitatory postsynaptic potential A postsynaptic potential that depolarizes the neuronal membrane, bringing the cell closer to the threshold for firing an action potential.

inhibitory postsynaptic potential A postsynaptic potential that hyperpolarizes the neuronal membrane, making a cell less likely to fire an action potential.

Excitatory and Inhibitory Signals The change taking place in the membrane potential of the dendrite or cell body of the postsynaptic cell is called the **postsynaptic potential.** The change can make the cell either more likely or less likely to fire. For example, if positively charged molecules of chemicals such as sodium or calcium flow *into* the neuron, it becomes slightly *less* polarized. Because this *depolarization* of the membrane can lead the neuron to fire an action potential, a depolarizing postsynaptic potential is called an **excitatory postsynaptic potential,** or **EPSP.** However, if positively charged molecules (such as potassium) flow *out* of the neuron, or if negatively charged molecules flow in, the neuron becomes slightly *more* polarized. This *hyperpolarization* makes it less likely that the neuron will fire an action potential. For this reason, a hyperpolarizing postsynaptic potential is called an **inhibitory postsynaptic potential,** or **IPSP.**

The postsynaptic potential spreads along the membrane of the postsynaptic cell. But unlike the action potential in an axon, which remains at a constant strength, the postsynaptic potential fades as it goes along. Usually, it is not strong enough to pass all the way along the dendrite and through the cell body to the axon, so a single EPSP will not cause a neuron to fire. However, each neuron is constantly receiving EPSPs and IPSPs. The combined effect of rapidly repeated potentials or potentials from many locations can create a signal strong enough to reach the junction of the axon and cell body, a specialized region where new action potentials are generated.

Whether or not the postsynaptic cell fires and how rapidly it fires depend on whether, at a given moment, there are more excitatory ("fire") or more inhibitory ("don't fire") signals from other neurons at this junction (see Figure 3.7). So as neurotransmitters transfer information across many neurons, each neuron constantly integrates or processes this information.

figure 3.6

The Relationship Between Neurotransmitters and Receptors

Neurotransmitters influence postsynaptic cells by stimulating special receptors on the surface of those cells' membranes. Each type of receptor receives only one type of neurotransmitter; the two fit together like puzzle pieces or like a lock and its key. Stimulation of a cell's receptors by their neurotransmitter causes them to either help or hinder the generation of a wave of depolarization in that cell's dendrites.

ClassPrep PPT 10, OHT: *Figure 3.6:* The Relationship Between Neurotransmitters and Receptors

ClassPrep PPT 12: Neuronal Transmission: A Review

ClassPrep PPT 13: Axon

ClassPrep PPT 14: Dendrite

ClassPrep PPT 15: Synapse

ClassPrep PPT 16: Neurotransmitter

ClassPrep PPT 17: Receptors

Videodisc Stills: Neurotransmitters and Receptors, Lock and Key

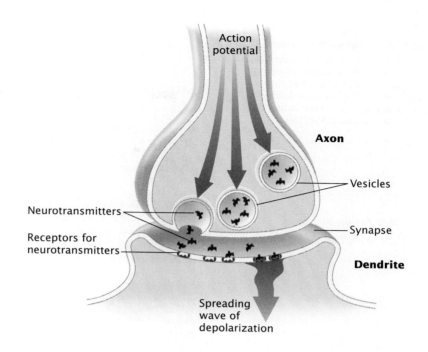

ClassPrep PPT 11: *Figure 3.7:* Integration of Neural Signals

figure 3.7

Integration of Neural Signals

Most of the signals that a neuron receives arrive at its dendrites or at its cell body. These signals, which typically come from many neighboring cells, can contain conflicting messages. Some are excitatory, telling the cell to fire; others are inhibitory, telling the cell not to fire. Whether or not the cell actually fires at any given moment depends on whether excitatory or inhibitory messages predominate at the junction of the cell body and the axon.

Neurotransmitters are involved in every aspect of behavior and mental processes, as you will see later in this chapter and in other chapters, too. In the chapter on sensation, for example, we describe some of the neurotransmitters used in pathways that convey pain messages throughout the brain and spinal cord. In the chapter on psychological disorders, we discuss the role that neurotransmitters play in schizophrenia and depression. And in the chapter on the treatment of psychological disorders, we consider how prescription drugs act on neurotransmitters and the cells they affect.

Organization and Functions of the Nervous System

Impressive as individual neurons are (see "In Review: Neurons, Neurotransmitters, and Receptors"), we can best understand their functions by looking at how they operate in groups. In the brain and spinal cord, neurons are organized into groups called **neural networks.** Many neurons in a network are closely connected, sending axons to the dendrites of many other neurons in the network. Signals from one network also go to other networks, and small networks are organized into bigger

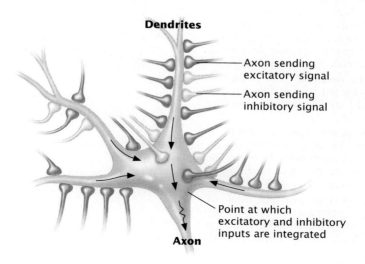

in review — Neurons, Neurotransmitters, and Receptors

Part	Function	Type of Signal Carried
Axon	Carries signals away from the cell body	The action potential, an all-or-nothing electrochemical signal that shoots down the axon to vesicles at the tip of the axon, releasing neurotransmitters
Dendrite	Detects and carries signals to the cell body	The postsynaptic potential, an electrochemical signal moving toward the cell body
Synapse	Provides an area for the transfer of signals between neurons, usually between axon and dendrite	Chemicals that cross the synapse and reach receptors on another cell
Neurotransmitter	A chemical released by one cell that binds to the receptors on another cell	A chemical message telling the next cell to fire or not to fire its own action potential
Receptor	Protein on the cell membrane that receives chemical signals	Recognizes certain neurotransmitters, thus allowing it to begin a postsynaptic potential in the dendrite

OBJ 3.11: Define sensory system and motor system. Describe their role in two components of information processing.

Test Items 3.48–3.49

collections. By studying these networks, neuroscientists have begun to see that the nervous system conveys information not so much by the activity of single neurons sending single messages with a particular meaning, but by the activity of *groups* of neurons firing together in varying combinations. So the same neurons may be involved in producing different patterns of behavior, depending on which combinations of them are active.

The groups of neurons in the nervous system that provide input about the environment are known as the senses, or **sensory systems**. These systems—including hearing, vision, taste, smell, and touch—are described in the chapter on sensation. Integration and processing of information occur mainly in the brain. Output flows through **motor systems**, which are the parts of the nervous system that influence muscles and other organs to respond to the environment.

Still a Super Man If axons, dendrites, or other components of the nervous system are damaged or disordered, serious problems can result. For example, the spinal cord injury that actor Christopher Reeve suffered in a riding accident cut the neural communication lines that had allowed him to feel most of his body and to move most of his muscles.

neural networks Neurons that operate together to perform complex functions.

sensory systems The parts of the nervous system that provide information about the environment.

motor systems The parts of the nervous system that influence muscles and other organs to respond to the environment in some way.

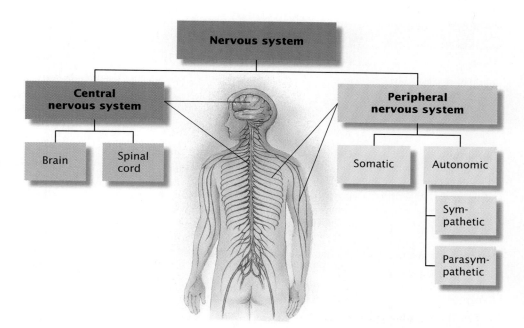

figure 3.8

Organization of the Nervous System

The brain and spinal cord make up the bone-encased central nervous system (CNS), the body's central information processor, decision maker, and director of actions. The peripheral nervous system, which is not housed in bone, functions mainly to carry messages. The somatic subsystem of the peripheral nervous system transmits information to the CNS from the outside world and conveys instructions from the CNS to the muscles. The autonomic subsystem conveys messages from the CNS that alter the activity of organs and glands, and it sends information about that activity back to the brain.

The nervous system has two major divisions, which work together: the peripheral nervous system and the central nervous system (see Figure 3.8). The **peripheral nervous system (PNS)**, which includes all of the nervous system that is not housed in bone, carries out sensory and motor functions. The **central nervous system (CNS)** is the part encased in bone. It includes the brain, which is inside the skull, and the spinal cord, which is inside the spinal column (backbone). The CNS is often called the "central executive" of the body because information is usually sent to the CNS to be processed and acted on. Let's take a closer look at these divisions of the nervous system.

The Peripheral Nervous System: Keeping in Touch with the World

As shown in Figure 3.8, the peripheral nervous system has two components, each of which performs both sensory and motor functions.

The Somatic Nervous System

The first of these components is the **somatic nervous system**; it transmits information from the senses to the CNS and carries signals from the CNS to the muscles that move the skeleton. For example, when you lie in the sun at the beach, the somatic nervous system sends signals from the skin to the brain that become sensations of warmth. The somatic nervous system is also involved in every move you make. Neurons extend from the spinal cord to the muscles, where the release of a neurotransmitter onto them causes the muscles to contract. In fact, much of what we

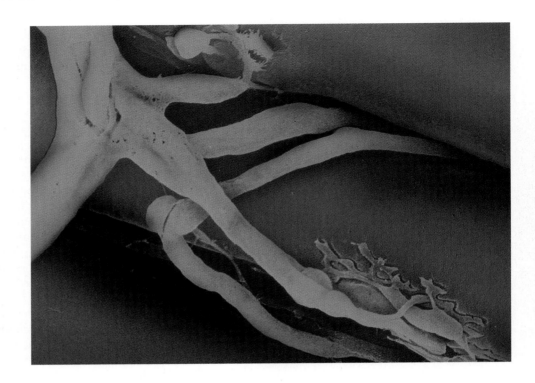

The Neuromuscular Junction When nerve cells (shown here as green fibers) release neurotransmitters onto muscle tissue, the muscle contracts.

know about neurotransmitters was discovered in laboratory studies of this "neuro-muscular junction," especially in the frog's hind leg. At the neuromuscular junction, the action of a neurotransmitter allows a quick response that can mean the difference between life and death, for a frog or any other animal, including humans.

The Autonomic Nervous System

The second component of the peripheral nervous system, the **autonomic nervous system,** carries messages back and forth between the CNS and the heart, lungs, and other organs and glands (Berthoud & Neuhuber, 2000). These messages increase or decrease the activity of the organs and glands to meet varying demands placed on the body. As you lie on the beach, it is your autonomic nervous system that makes your heart beat a little faster when an attractive person walks by and smiles.

The name *autonomic* means "autonomous" and suggests independent operation. This term is appropriate because, although the autonomic nervous system is influenced by the brain, it controls activities that are normally outside of conscious control, such as digestion and perspiration (sweating). The autonomic nervous system exercises this control through its two divisions: the sympathetic and parasympathetic branches. Generally, the *sympathetic system* mobilizes the body for action in the face of stress; the responses that result are sometimes collectively referred to as the *fight-or-flight response.* The *parasympathetic system* regulates the body's functions to conserve energy. These two branches often create opposite effects. For example, the sympathetic nervous system can make your heart beat faster, whereas the parasympathetic nervous system can slow it down.

The functions of the autonomic nervous system may not get star billing, but you would miss them if they were gone. Just as a race-car driver is nothing without a good pit crew, the somatic nervous system depends on the autonomic nervous system to get its job done. For example, when you want to move your muscles, you create a demand for energy; the autonomic nervous system fills the bill by increasing sugar fuels in the bloodstream. If you decide to stand up, you need increased blood pressure so that your blood does not flow out of your brain and settle in your legs. Again, the autonomic nervous system makes the adjustment. Disorders of the

peripheral nervous system The parts of the nervous system not housed in bone.

central nervous system The parts of the nervous system encased in bone, including the brain and the spinal cord.

somatic nervous system The subsystem of the peripheral nervous system that transmits information from the senses to the central nervous system and carries signals from the central nervous system to the muscles.

autonomic nervous system A subsystem of the peripheral nervous system that carries messages between the central nervous system and the heart, lungs, and other organs and glands.

autonomic nervous system can make people sweat uncontrollably or faint whenever they stand up; they can also lead to other problems, such as an inability to have sex. We examine the autonomic nervous system in more detail in the chapter on motivation and emotion.

The Central Nervous System: Making Sense of the World

The amazing speed and efficiency of the neural networks that make up the central nervous system—the brain and spinal cord—have prompted many people to compare it to the central processor in a computer. In fact, to better understand how human and other brains work and how they relate to sensory and motor systems, *computational neuroscientists* have created neural network models on computers (Koch & Davis, 1994). Figure 3.9 shows an example of how the three components of the nervous system (input, processing, and output) might be represented in a neural network model. Notice that input simultaneously activates several paths in the network, so information is processed in various places at the same time. Accordingly, the activity of these models is described as *parallel distributed processing*. In the chapters on sensation, perception, learning, and memory, we describe how parallel distributed processing often characterizes the activity of the brain.

Although neural network models were initially intended to help scientists better understand the nervous system, the principles of neural networks have been applied to a variety of problems that are not directly related to neurons or the brain. Specifically, neural network models can be programmed into computers, allowing them to perform functions that previously only humans could do. For example, computers using neural networks are able to determine the quality of pork from scans of pig carcasses (Berg, Engel, & Forrest, 1998) and to predict which cancer patients will relapse after chemotherapy (Burke et al., 1998).

Neural network models are neatly laid out like computer circuits or the carefully planned streets of a new suburb, but the flesh-and-blood central nervous system is more difficult to follow. In fact, the CNS looks more like Boston or Paris, with distinct neighborhoods, winding back streets, and multilaned expressways. Its "neighborhoods" are collections of neuronal cell bodies called **nuclei.** The "highways" of the central nervous system are made up of axons that travel together in bundles called **fiber tracts** or **pathways.** Like a freeway ramp, the axon from a given cell may merge with and leave fiber tracts, and it may send branches into other tracts. The pathways travel from one nucleus to other nuclei, and scientists have learned much about how the brain works by tracing the connections among nuclei. To begin our description of some of these nuclei and anatomical connections, let's consider a practical example of nervous system functioning.

At 6 A.M., your alarm goes off. The day begins innocently enough with what appears to be a simple case of information processing. Input in the form of sound

OBJ 3.15: Define nuclei and fiber tracts.

Test Items 3.71–3.72

Essay Q 3.1

ClassPrep PPT 21: *Figure 3.9:* A Neural Network Model

figure 3.9

A Neural Network Model

This simple computer-based neural network model includes three basic components: an input layer, a processing layer, and an output layer. Notice that each element in each layer is connected to every other element in each of the other layers. As in the brain itself, these connections can be either excitatory or inhibitory, and the strength of the connections between elements can be modified depending on the results of the output; in other words, a computerized neural network model has the capacity to learn.

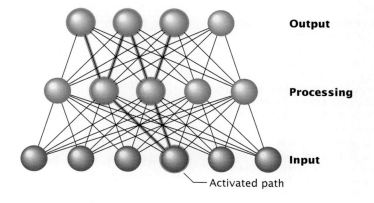

Output

Processing

Input

└─ Activated path

figure 3.10

A Reflex Pathway

 Sit on a chair, cross one leg over the other, and then use the handle of a butter knife or some other solid object to gently tap your top knee, just below the joint, until you get a "knee jerk" reaction. Tapping your knee at just the right spot sets off an almost instantaneous sequence of events that begins with stimulation of sensory neurons that respond to stretch. When those neurons fire, their axons, which end within the spinal cord, cause spinal neurons to fire. This, in turn, stimulates the firing of motor neurons with axons ending in your thigh muscles. The result is a contraction of those muscles and a kicking of the lower leg and foot. Information about the knee tap and about what the leg has done also goes to your cerebral cortex, but the reflex is completed without waiting for guidance from the brain.

ClassPrep PPT 22, OHT: *Figure 3.10:* A Reflex Pathway

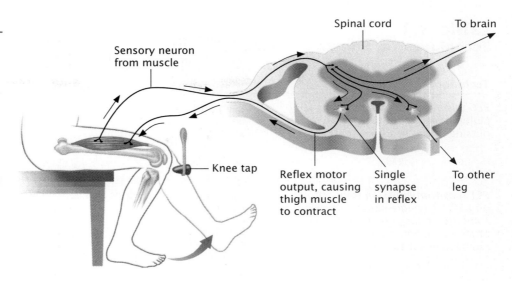

Spinal cord

To brain

Sensory neuron
from muscle

Knee tap

Reflex motor output, causing thigh muscle to contract

Single synapse in reflex

To other leg

OBJ 3.16: Name the type of neurons found in the spinal cord and describe their function. Define reflex.

Test Items 3.73–3.81

IRM Activity 3.4: Reinforcing Reflexes

IRM Activity 3.5: Mental Chronometry and Speed of Neural Transmission

nuclei Collections of nerve cell bodies in the central nervous system.

fiber tracts Axons in the central nervous system that travel together in bundles.

spinal cord The part of the central nervous system within the spinal column that relays signals from peripheral senses to the brain and conveys messages from the brain to the rest of the body.

reflexes Involuntary, unlearned reactions in the form of swift, automatic, and finely coordinated movements in response to external stimuli.

from the alarm clock is received by your ears, which convert the sound into neural signals that reach your brain. Your brain compares these signals with previous experiences stored in memory and correctly associates the sound with "alarm clock." However, your output is somewhat impaired because your brain's activity has not yet reached the waking state. It directs your muscles poorly: You get out of bed and shuffle into the kitchen, where, in your drowsy condition, you touch a hot burner as you reach for the coffeepot. Now things get more lively. Heat energy activates sensory neurons in your fingers, and action potentials flash along fiber tracts going into the spinal cord.

The Spinal Cord

The **spinal cord** receives signals from peripheral senses, including pain and touch from the fingertips, and relays those signals to the brain through fibers within the cord. Neurons in the spinal cord also carry signals downward, from the brain to the muscles. In addition, cells of the spinal cord can direct some simple behaviors without instructions from the brain. These behaviors are called **reflexes** because the response to an incoming signal is directly "reflected" back out (see Figure 3.10).

For example, when you touched that hot burner, impulses from sensory neurons in your fingers reflexively activated motor neurons, which caused muscles in your arm to contract and quickly withdraw your hand. Because spinal reflexes like this one include few time-consuming synaptic links, they are very fast. And because spinal reflexes occur without instructions from the brain, they are considered involuntary; but they also send action potentials along fiber tracts going to the brain. Thus, you officially "know" you have been burned a fraction of a second after your reflex got you out of further trouble.

The story does not end there, however. When a simple reflex set off by touching something hot causes one set of arm muscles to contract, an opposing set of muscles relaxes. If this did not happen, the arm would go rigid. Furthermore, muscles have receptors that send impulses to the spinal cord to let it know how extended they are, so that a reflex pathway can adjust the muscle contraction to allow smooth movement. This is an example of a *feedback system*, a series of processes in which information about the consequences of an action goes back to the source of the action so that adjustments can be made.

In the spinal cord, sensory neurons are often called *afferent* neurons and motor neurons are termed *efferent* neurons, because *afferent* means "coming toward" and *efferent* means "going away." To remember these terms, notice that *afferent* and *approach* both begin with *a*; *efferent* and *exit* both begin with *e*.

table 3.1
Techniques for Studying Human Brain Function and Structure

Technique	What It Shows	Advantages (+) and Disadvantages (−)
EEG (electroencephalography) Multiple electrodes are pasted to the outside of the head **ClassPrep PPT 24 & 25:** EEG (Electroencephalography)	Lines that chart the summated electrical fields resulting from the activity of billions of neurons	+ Detects very rapid changes in electrical activity, allowing analysis of stages of cognitive processing − Provides poor spatial resolution of the source of electrical activity
PET (positron emission tomography) and SPECT (single photon emission computed tomography): Positrons and photons are emissions from radioactive substances **ClassPrep PPT 26:** PET (Positron Emission Tomography)	An image of the amount and localization of any molecule that can be injected in radioactive form, such as neurotransmitters, drugs, or tracers for blood flow or glucose use (which indicates specific changes in neuronal activity)	+ Allows functional and biochemical studies + Provides visual image corresponding to anatomy − Requires exposure to low levels of radioactivity − Provides spatial resolution better than that of EEG but poorer than that of MRI − Cannot follow rapid changes (faster than 30 seconds)
MRI (magnetic resonance imaging): Exposes the brain to a magnetic field and measures radiofrequency waves **ClassPrep PPT 28:** MRI (Magnetic Resonance Imaging)	The traditional MRI provides a high-resolution image of brain anatomy, and the newer functional MRI (fMRI) provides images of changes in blood flow (which indicate specific changes in neuronal activity)	+ Requires no exposure to radioactivity + Provides high spatial resolution of anatomical details (<1 mm) + Provides high temporal resolution ($<\frac{1}{10}$ second)
MEG (magnetoencephalography) **ClassPrep PPT 30 & 31:** MEG (Magnetoencephalography)	Detects the magnetic fields produced by electrical currents in neurons; detects and localizes brain activity, usually combined with a structural image from MRI	+ Like EEG, detects very rapid changes in electrical activity, allowing analysis of cognitive processing + Allows millimeter resolution of source of electrical activity for surface sources such as cerebral cortex − Has poor spatial resolution of brain activity in structures below the cortex − Requires very expensive equipment

LSV: "The Brain"

OBJ 3.17: Name and define the three major subdivisions of the brain and describe their functions.

The Brain
Videodisc Segments & Stills: The Brain from Below, from Inside (a), from Inside (b)

The brain has three major subdivisions: the hindbrain, the midbrain, and the forebrain. Table 3.1 and Figures 3.11 and 3.12 describe and illustrate some of the techniques scientists use to learn about these structures and how they function.

The Hindbrain
Incoming signals first reach the **hindbrain,** which is actually a continuation of the spinal cord. As you can see in Figure 3.13, the hindbrain lies just inside the skull. Blood pressure, heart rate, breathing, and many other vital autonomic functions are controlled by nuclei in the hindbrain, particularly in an area called the **medulla.** Threading throughout the hindbrain and into the midbrain

hindbrain An extension of the spinal cord contained inside the skull where nuclei control blood pressure, heart rate, breathing, and other vital functions.

medulla An area in the hindbrain that controls blood pressure, heart rate, breathing, and other vital functions.

figure 3.11

Combining a PET Scan and an MRI

Researchers have superimposed images from PET scans and MRI to construct a three-dimensional view of the living brain. Here you can see the brain of a young epileptic girl. The picture of the outer surface of the brain is from the MRI; the pink area is from the PET scan and shows the source of epileptic activity. The images at the right are the MRI and PET images at one plane, or "slice," through the brain (indicated by the line on the brain at the left).

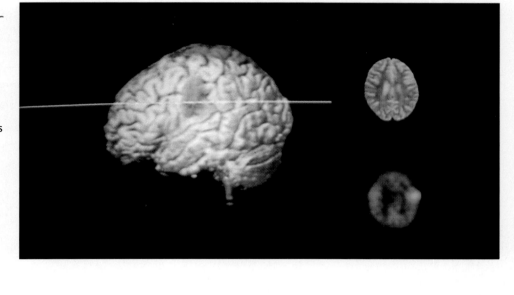

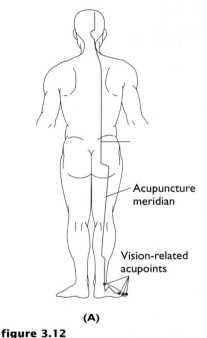

(A)

figure 3.12

Linking Eastern Medicine and Western Neuroscience Through Functional MRI

Videodisc Segment: MRI

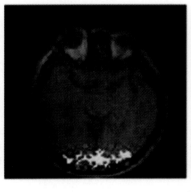 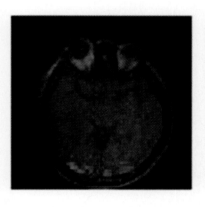

(B)

Acupuncture is an ancient Asian medical practice in which physical disorders are treated by stimulating specific locations in the skin with needles. Most acupuncture points are distant from the organ being treated. For example, vision and hearing problems are treated by inserting needles at different "acupoints" in the foot (Part A). Scientists have begun to investigate the role of the brain in the effects of acupuncture (Cho et al., 1998). In Part B, similar areas of the brain are activated by direct sensory stimulation and stimulation of the related acupoints on the foot. The MRI images on the left are produced by visual stimuli. On the right is the MRI image showing activation of the same brain areas in response to acupuncture at a vision-related spot in the foot. These acupoints are located near nerves, but the pathways to the specific parts of the brain have not been charted.

reticular formation A network of cells and fibers threaded throughout the hindbrain and midbrain that alters the activity of the rest of the brain.

locus coeruleus A small nucleus in the reticular formation that contains about half of the cell bodies of neurons in the brain that use norepinephrine.

is a collection of cells that are not arranged in any well-defined nucleus. Because the collection resembles a net, it is called the **reticular formation** (*reticular* means "net-like"). This network is very important in altering the activity of the rest of the brain. It is involved, for example, in arousal and attention; if the fibers from the reticular system are disconnected from the rest of the brain, a permanent coma results. Some of the fibers carrying pain signals from the spinal cord make connections in the reticular formation, which immediately arouses the rest of the brain from sleep. Within seconds, the hindbrain causes your heart rate and blood pressure to increase.

Activity of the reticular formation also leads to activity in a small nucleus within it called the **locus coeruleus** (pronounced "LO-kus seh-ROO-lee-us"), which means

figure 3.13

Major Structures of the Brain (with Hindbrain Highlighted)

This side view of a section cut down the middle of the human brain reveals the forebrain, midbrain, hindbrain, and spinal cord. Many of these subdivisions do not have clear-cut borders, because they are all interconnected by fiber tracts. The anatomy of the mammalian brain reflects its evolution over millions of years. Newer structures (such as the cerebral cortex, which is the outer surface of the forebrain) that handle higher mental functions were built on older ones (such as the medulla) that coordinate heart rate, breathing, and other more basic functions.

ClassPrep PPT 34, OHT: *Figure 3.13:* Major Structures of the Brain

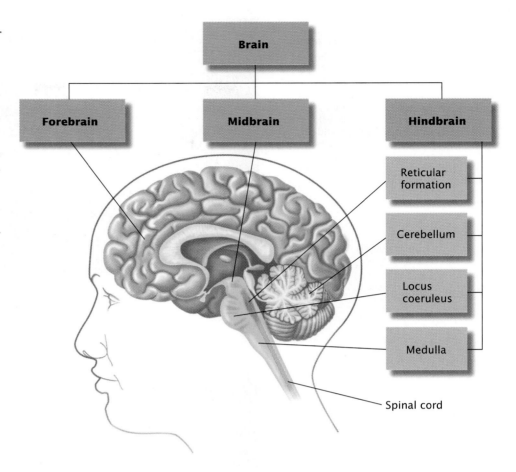

OBJ 3.18: Name and define the structures in the hindbrain. Describe their functions.

Test Items 3.84–3.93

Personal Learning Activity 3.3

Freburg *Perspectives:* Richardson, "Tarzan's Little Brain"

LSV: An Example of a Brain Structure: The Cerebellum

IRM Research Focus 3.6: Mapping the Mind's Eye

cerebellum　The part of the hindbrain whose function is to control finely coordinated movements and to store learned associations that involve movement.

"blue spot" (see Figure 3.13). There are relatively few cells in the locus coeruleus—only about 30,000 of the 100 billion or so in the human brain (Foote, Bloom, & Aston-Jones, 1983)—but each sends out an axon that branches extensively, making contact with as many as 100,000 other cells. Studies of rats, monkeys, and humans suggest that the locus coeruleus is involved in directing attention (Aston-Jones, Chiang, & Alexinsky, 1991; Smythies, 1997). In humans, abnormalities in the locus coeruleus have been linked to depression (Leonard, 1997).

The **cerebellum** is also part of the hindbrain. It allows the eyes to track a moving target accurately (Krauzlis & Lisberger, 1991), and it may be the storehouse for well-rehearsed movements, such as those associated with ballet, piano playing, and athletics (McCormick & Thompson, 1984). For a long time its primary function was thought to be control of finely coordinated movements, such as threading a needle. But compared with other species, the human cerebellum has grown more in size than any other brain structure, so researchers have begun to rethink and reinvestigate the cerebellum's role in more uniquely human tasks such as language and symbolic thought.

Recent work on the function of the cerebellum highlights the fact that there are different ways to think about what various parts of the brain do. For instance, you can think of coordinated movements simply as "motor functioning" or as an example of the more general activity of "sequencing and timing" (Gibbon et al., 1997). The importance of sequencing has become increasingly apparent in the study of nonmovement activities, particularly language. To speak fluently, you must put together a sequence of words rapidly and in the correct order and temporal rhythm. It appears that the cerebellum plays a vital role in normal speech by integrating moment-to-moment feedback about vocal sounds with a sequence of precise movements of the lips and tongue (Leiner, Leiner, & Dow, 1993). When this process of

A Field Sobriety Test The cerebellum is involved in the balance and coordination required for walking. When the cerebellum's activity is impaired by alcohol, these skills are disrupted, which is why the police ask people suspected of driving under the influence of alcohol to walk a straight line.

IRM Activity 3.12: Question Formation

OBJ 3.19: Name and define the structures in the midbrain. Describe their functions.

Test Items 3.94–3.95

ClassPrep: The Midbrain

IRM Discussion 9.11: A "Designer" Drug Gone Bad

midbrain A small structure, between the hindbrain and forebrain, that relays information from the eyes, ears, and skin and that controls certain types of automatic behaviors.

substantia nigra An area of the midbrain involved in the smooth initiation of movement.

striatum A structure within the forebrain that is involved in the smooth initiation of movement.

forebrain The most highly developed part of the brain; it is responsible for the most complex aspects of behavior and mental life.

integration and sequencing is disrupted, stuttering can result. Even nonstutterers who hear their own speech with a slight delay begin to stutter. (This is why radio talk-show hosts ask callers to turn off their radios. A momentary gap occurs before the shows are actually broadcast, and listening to the delayed sound of their own voice on the radio can cause callers to stutter.) Recent magnetic resonance imaging (MRI) studies indicate that the cerebellum is one of a number of brain regions that are concurrently involved in stuttering (Fox et al., 2000).

Reflexes and feedback systems are important to the functioning of the hindbrain, just as they are in the spinal cord. For example, if blood pressure drops, heart action increases reflexively to compensate for that drop. If you stand up very quickly, your blood pressure can drop so suddenly that it produces lightheadedness until the hindbrain reflex "catches up." If the hindbrain does not activate autonomic nervous system mechanisms to increase blood pressure, you will faint.

The Midbrain Above the hindbrain is the **midbrain.** In humans it is a small structure, but it serves some very important functions. Certain types of automatic behaviors that integrate simple movements with sensory input are controlled there. For example, when you move your head, midbrain circuits allow you to move your eyes smoothly in the opposite direction, so that you can keep your eyes focused on an object despite the movement of your head. And when a loud noise causes you to turn your head reflexively and look in the direction of the sound, your midbrain circuits are at work.

One vital nucleus in the midbrain is the **substantia nigra,** meaning "black substance." This small area and its connections to the **striatum** (named for its "striped" appearance) in the forebrain are necessary in order to smoothly begin movements. Without them, you would find it difficult, if not impossible, to get up out of a chair, lift your hand to swat a fly, move your mouth to form words, or reach for that coffeepot at 6:00 A.M.   Sattler/Shabatay reader, 2/e: Dorros, "Parkinson's: A Patient's View"

The Forebrain Like the cerebellum, the human **forebrain** is another region that has grown out of proportion to the rest of the brain, so much so that it folds back over and completely covers the other parts. It is responsible for the most complex aspects of behavior and mental life. As Figure 3.14 shows, the forebrain includes a variety of structures.

figure 3.14

Major Structures of the Forebrain

The structures of the forebrain are covered by an outer "bark" known as the *cerebral cortex*. This diagram shows some of the structures that lie within the fore-brain. The amygdala, the hippocampus, the septum, and portions of the cerebral cortex are part of the limbic system.

ClassPrep PPT 35, OHT: *Figure 3.14:* Major Structures of the Forebrain

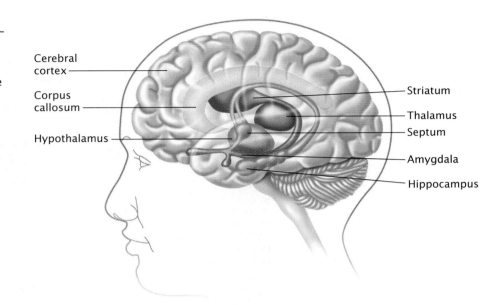

Cerebral cortex — Corpus callosum — Hypothalamus — Striatum — Thalamus — Septum — Amygdala — Hippocampus

OBJ 3.20: Name and define the structures in the forebrain. Describe their function.

Test Items 3.96–3.102

Freburg *Perspectives:* Nimmens, "Sex and the Brain"

Freburg *Stand!:* Billings & Beckwith, "Born Gay?"

thalamus   A forebrain structure that relays signals from most sense organs to higher levels in the brain and plays an important role in processing and making sense out of this information.

hypothalamus   A structure in the forebrain that regulates hunger, thirst, and sex drives.

suprachiasmatic nuclei   Nuclei in the hypothalamus that generate biological rhythms.

amygdala   A structure in the forebrain that, among other things, associates features of stimuli from two sensory modalities.

hippocampus   A structure in the forebrain associated with the formation of new memories.

limbic system   A set of brain structures that play important roles in regulating emotion and memory.

Two of these structures lie deep within the brain. The first is the **thalamus**, which relays pain signals from the spinal cord, as well as signals from the eyes and most other sense organs, to upper levels in the brain. It also plays an important role in processing and making sense out of this information. The other is the **hypothalamus**, which lies under the thalamus (*hypo* means "under") and is involved in regulating hunger, thirst, and sex drives. It has many connections to and from the autonomic nervous system, as well as to other parts of the brain. Destruction of one section of the hypothalamus results in an overwhelming urge to eat (see the chapter on motivation and emotion). Damage to another area of a male's hypothalamus causes his sex organs to degenerate and his sex drive to decrease drastically. There is also a fascinating part of the hypothalamus that contains the brain's own time-piece: the **suprachiasmatic nuclei**. The suprachiasmatic (pronounced "soo-pra-kye-as-MAT-ik") nuclei keep an approximately twenty-four-hour clock that determines your biological rhythms. We discuss these rhythms in the chapter on consciousness

Two other forebrain structures, the **amygdala** (pronounced "ah-MIG-duh-luh") and the **hippocampus**, are important in memory and emotion. For example, the amygdala associates features of stimuli from two different senses, as when we link the shape and feel of objects in memory (Murray & Mishkin, 1985). It is also involved in fear and other emotions (LeDoux, 1995; Whalen, 1998); its activity has been found to be altered in people suffering from posttraumatic stress disorder (Shin et al., 1997; see the chapter on health, stress, and coping). Damage to the hippocampus results in an inability to form new memories of events. In one case, a patient known as R.B. suffered a stroke (an interruption of blood flow in the brain) that damaged only his hippocampus. Although tests indicated that his intelligence was above average and he could recall old memories, he was almost totally unable to build new memories (Squire, 1986). Research using MRI scans and tests of the decline of memory function in normal elderly people suggests that memory ability is correlated with the size of the hippocampus (Golomb et al., 1994); a small hippocampus predicts severe memory problems even before they are evident (Kaye et al., 1997). Animal studies have also shown that damage to the hippocampus within a day of a mildly painful experience erases memories of the experience, but that removal of the hippocampus several days after the experience has no effect on the memory. So memories are not permanently stored in the hippocampus but are transferred elsewhere. As described in the chapter on memory, your storehouse of memories depends on the activities of many parts of the brain.

figure 3.15

Alzheimer's Disease and Brain Atrophy

These human brains, photographed after death, show that compared with a normal brain (bottom), the brain of a person with Alzheimer's disease (top) shows considerable degeneration, especially in limbic regions and the cerebral cortex (Callan et al., 2001). For example, the hippocampus of a person with Alzheimer's disease is about 40 percent smaller than normal. In fact, a smaller-than-average hippocampus in the elderly predicts the onset of the disease (Jack et al., 1999).

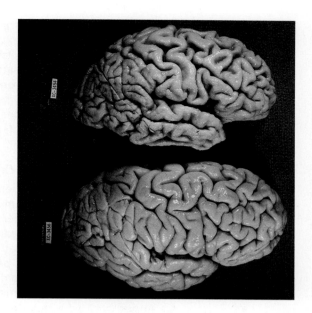

ClassPrep PPT 37, OHT: The Limbic System

ClassPrep PPT 38: *Figure 3.15:* Alzheimer's Disease and Brain Atrophy

LSV: Alzheimer's Disease

Videodisc Segment & Still: The Limbic System

The hippocampus and amygdala, and other interconnected structures such as the hypothalamus and the septum, are part of the **limbic system.** The limbic system plays an important role in regulating emotion and memory. Studies of the brains of people who died from Alzheimer's disease have found severe degeneration of neurons in the hippocampus and other limbic structures (see Figure 3.15). This may explain why Alzheimer's disease is a major cause of *dementia*, the deterioration of cognitive capabilities often associated with aging. About 10 percent of people over the age of sixty-five, and more than 47 percent of people over eighty-five, suffer from this disorder (Small et al., 1997; U.S. Surgeon General, 1999). The financial cost of Alzheimer's disease in the United States alone is more than $100 billion a year (Small et al., 1997); the cost in human suffering is incalculable. It is no wonder, then, that the search for its causes and cures has a high priority among researchers who study the brain.

FOCUS ON RESEARCH METHODS

Manipulating Genes in Animal Models of Human Disease

Alzheimer's disease is named for Alois Alzheimer, a German neurologist. Almost a century ago, Alzheimer examined the brain of a woman who had died after years of progressive mental deterioration and dementia. He was looking for the cause of her disorder, and he found that cells in her cerebral cortex were bunched up like a rope tied in knots and that cellular debris had collected around the affected nerves. These features came to be known as tangles and plaques. *Tangles* are twisted fibers within neurons; their main protein component is called *tau*. *Plaques* are deposits of protein and parts of dead cells found between neurons. The major component of plaques was found to be a small protein called *beta-amyloid*, which is produced from a larger protein called *beta-amyloid precursor protein*. Ever since Alzheimer described plaques and tangles, researchers have been trying to learn about the role they play in Alzheimer's disease.

ClassPrep PPT 51: Focus on Research Methods: Manipulating Genes in Animal Models of Human Disease

OBJ 3.21: Describe the experimental methods used by scientists in their study of Alzheimer's disease.

Test Items 3.103–3.104

Personal Learning Activity 3.2

● **What was the researchers' question?**

One specific question that researchers have addressed is whether the biochemicals found in plaques and tangles actually *cause* Alzheimer's disease.

As noted in the chapter on research in psychology, a causal relationship cannot be inferred from a correlation. Therefore, to discover if beta-amyloid and tau might cause the death of neurons seen in Alzheimer's disease, researchers needed to conduct controlled experiments, which means manipulating an independent variable and measuring its effect on a dependent variable. In this case, the experiment would involve creating plaques and tangles (the independent variable) and looking for their effects on memory (the dependent variable). Because such experiments cannot ethically be conducted on humans, scientists began looking for Alzheimer's-like conditions in some other species of animal. Progress in finding the causes of Alzheimer's disease depended on their finding an "animal model" of the disease.

● How did the researchers answer the question?

Previous studies of the genes of people with Alzheimer's disease had revealed that a mutation in the beta-amyloid precursor protein was associated with the disease. However, many Alzheimer's patients exhibited mutations not in this protein but in another one, which researchers called *presenilin* because it was associated with senility. (It turns out that presenilin is related to Alzheimer's disease because it affects the way in which beta-amyloid precursor protein is modified.) At this point, the researchers hoped to determine whether these mutated proteins actually cause the brain damage and memory impairment associated with Alzheimer's disease. Armed with new genetic engineering tools, they began to create, literally, an animal model of Alzheimer's disease with mutated human genes.

The first attempts to create this animal model involved the insertion of a mutant form of beta-amyloid precursor protein into the cells of mice. If Alzheimer's disease is caused by faulty beta-amyloid precursor protein, so the logic went, inserting the gene for this faulty protein into mouse cells should cause deposits of beta-amyloid and the loss of neurons in the same parts of the brain as those seen in human Alzheimer's victims. No such changes should be observed in a control group of untreated animals.

● What did the researchers find?

Of course, finding this result just once is not enough; an experiment's results must be replicable in order to be reliable. This principle was reinforced in 1992, when a group of scientists reported success in creating a model of Alzheimer's disease in mice, only to retract their statements when they could not repeat their results. Three years later, researchers at a biotechnology company encountered a different problem. Although they succeeded in implanting the faulty protein into mice and found damage characteristic of Alzheimer's disease (Games et al, 1995), they did not observe any memory impairment in the mice.

Since then, however, other scientists have found that a variety of different mutations of beta-amyloid precursor protein inserted into mice produce both brain damage and memory impairment (Hsiao et al., 1996; Nalbantoglu et al., 1997). One group subsequently claimed that the best animal model of Alzheimer's disease appears to involve mice with mutations in both beta-amyloid precursor protein and presenilin. These mice exhibit both severe brain pathology and memory impairment at a younger age than that seen in other experiments (Arendash et al., 2001; Holcomb et al., 1998). Another group has claimed that its model better mimics the tau-containing tangles of Alzheimer's disease in humans (Sturchler-Pierrat et al., 1997).

Unfortunately, none of these "transgenic" mouse models yet fully reproduces the brain pathology seen in Alzheimer's disease (Chapman et al., 2001). Nevertheless, these mice have paved the way for an exciting new possibility for the treatment for Alzheimer's disease: a vaccine against beta-amyloid. Transgenic mice given this vaccine have shown not only improvements in memory but also a reversal of beta-amyloid deposits in their brains (Morgan et al., 2000; Younkin 2001). Researchers have begun clinical trials of beta-amyloid vaccines in humans, but it is too soon to tell how beneficial they might be. At first they appeared safe (Ingram, 2001), but serious side effects have halted some trials.

IRM Discussion 2.4: On the Use of Animals in Scientific Research

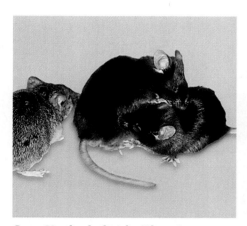

Gene Manipulation in Mice In one study, the gene for a particular type of neurotransmitter receptor was "knocked out" in these black mice. As shown here, these animals were much more aggressive than a control group of brown mice (Nelson et al., 1995).

● What do the results mean?

Regardless of whether this particular vaccine works, scientists will continue to use transgenic mice to evaluate the roles of mutations in beta-amyloid precursor protein, presenilin, *tau,* and other proteins in causing Alzheimer's disease. This research is important not only because it might eventually solve the mystery of this terrible disorder but also because it illustrates the power of experimental modification of animal genes for testing all kinds of hypotheses about biological factors influencing behavior. Besides inserting new or modified genes into brain cells, scientists also can manipulate an independent variable by "knocking out" specific genes, then looking at the effect on dependent variables. One research team has shown, for example, that knocking out a gene for a particular type of neurotransmitter receptor causes mice to become obese and to overeat even when given appetite-suppressant drugs (Tecott et al., 1995). And genetic elimination of proteins that modify neurotransmitter activity in mice canceled out the stimulating effects of cocaine (Sora et al., 2001).

Of course, researchers must be careful not to inadvertently affect other genes while modifying the particular gene they are interested in. And they must be sure that the modified gene has not influenced the mice's behavior in unexpected and important ways. For example, if the gene significantly affects sensory or motor functions, a behavioral change could mistakenly be attributed to a change in brain function. (After all, a mouse with defective legs cannot run through a memory-testing maze.) Careful behavioral analyses of the mouse model of Alzheimer's disease will also be needed to determine what components of memory processes are impaired.

● What do we still need to know?

The scarcity of animal models of obesity, drug addiction, and other problems has impeded progress in finding biological treatments for them. As animal models for these conditions become more available through gene modification techniques, they will pave the way for new types of animal studies that are directly relevant to human problems. The next challenge will be to use these animal models to develop and test treatments that might effectively be applied to humans.

The Cerebral Cortex

So far, we have described some key structures *within* the forebrain; now we turn to a discussion of other structures on its surface. The outermost part of the brain appears rather round and has right and left halves that are similar in appearance. These halves are called the **cerebral hemispheres.** The outer part of the cerebral hemispheres, the **cerebral cortex,** has a surface area of one to two square feet—an area that is larger than it looks because of the folds that allow the cortex to fit compactly inside the skull. The cerebral cortex is much larger in humans than in most other animals (dolphins are an exception). It is associated with the analysis of information from all the senses, control of voluntary movements, higher-order thought, and other complex aspects of human behavior and mental processes.

The left side of Figure 3.16 shows the *anatomical* or physical features of the cerebral cortex. The folds of the cortex give the surface of the human brain its wrinkled appearance—its ridges and valleys. The ridges are called *gyri* (pronounced "ji-rye"), and the valleys are called *sulci* (pronounced "sulk-eye") or *fissures.* As you can see in the figure, several deep sulci divide the cortex into four areas: the *frontal, parietal, occipital,* and *temporal* lobes. Thus, the gyri and sulci provide landmarks for describing the appearance of the cortex. The right side of Figure 3.16 depicts the areas of the cerebral cortex in which various *functions* or activities occur. The functional areas do not exactly match the anatomical areas, inasmuch as some functions

cerebral hemispheres The left and right halves of the rounded, outermost part of the brain.

cerebral cortex The outer surface of the brain.

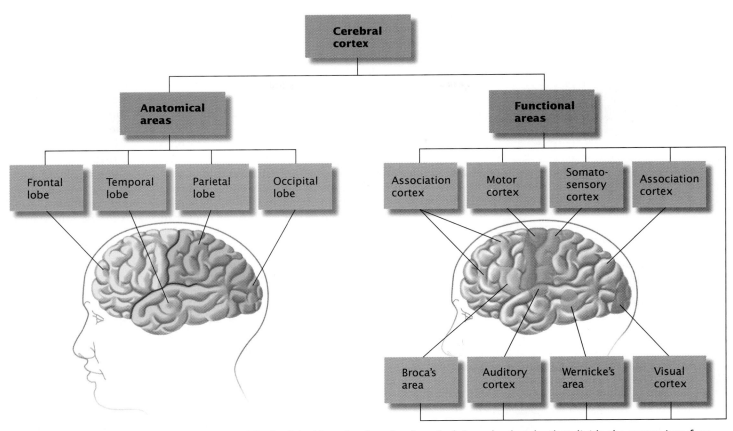

figure 3.16

The Cerebral Cortex (Viewed from the Left Side)

The brain's ridges (gyri) and valleys (sulci) are landmarks that divide the cortex into four lobes: the frontal, parietal, occipital, and temporal. These terms describe where the regions are (the lobes are named for the skull bones that cover them), but the cortex is also divided in terms of function. These functional areas are the motor cortex (which controls movement), sensory cortex (including somatosensory, auditory, and visual areas that receive information from the senses), and association cortex (which integrates information). Also labeled are Wernicke's area and Broca's area, two regions that are found only on the left side of the cortex and that are vital to the interpretation and production of speech.

OBJ 3.23: Name the three functional divisions of the cortex and describe their functions.

Test Items 3.110–3.113

IRM Research Focus 3.6: Mapping the Mind's Eye

IRM Activity 3.7: Brain Structure and Function

Videodisc Segment & Still: The Sensory Cortex

sensory cortex The parts of the cerebral cortex that receive stimulus information from the senses.

motor cortex The part of the cerebral cortex whose neurons control voluntary movements in specific parts of the body.

occur in more than one area. Three of these functional areas—the sensory cortex, the motor cortex, and the association cortex—are discussed below, along with related areas.

Sensory Cortex   The **sensory cortex** lies in the parietal, occipital, and temporal lobes and is the part of the cerebral cortex that receives information from our senses. Different regions of the sensory cortex receive information from different senses. Visual information is received by the *visual cortex*, made up of cells in the occipital lobe; auditory information is received by the *auditory cortex*, made up of cells in the temporal lobe; and information from the skin about touch, pain, and temperature is received in the *somatosensory cortex*, made up of cells in the parietal lobe.

Information about skin sensations from neighboring parts of the body comes to neighboring parts of the somatosensory cortex, as Figure 3.17 illustrates. It is as if the outline of a tiny person, dangling upside down, determined the location of the information. This pattern is called the *homunculus*, which is Latin for "little man." The organization of the homunculus has long been assumed to be unchanging, but recent work has shown that the amount of sensory cortex that responds to particular sensory inputs can be modified by experience. The experience may be as traumatic as the loss of a limb (whereby sensory areas of the brain formerly stimulated

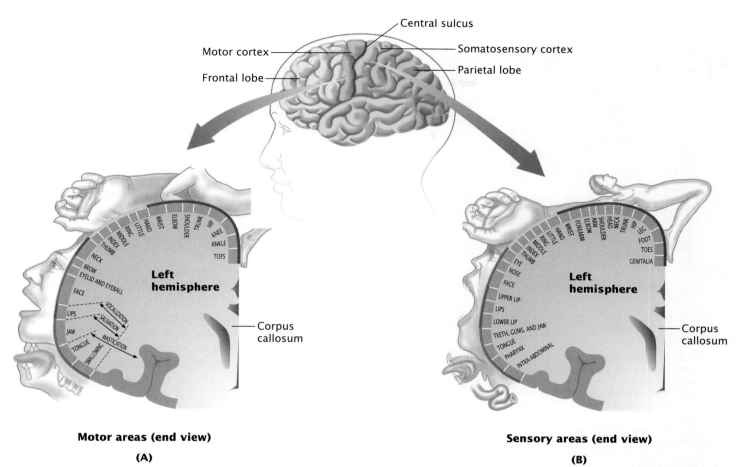

Motor areas (end view)

(A)

Sensory areas (end view)

(B)

figure 3.17

Motor and Somatosensory Cortex

ClassPrep PPT 40, OHT: *Figure 3.17:* Motor and Somatosensory Cortex

The areas of cortex that move parts of the body (motor cortex) and receive sensory input from body parts (somatosensory cortex) appear in both hemispheres of the brain. Here we show cross-sections of only those on the left side, looking from the back of the brain toward the front. Areas controlling movement of neighboring parts of the body, such as the foot and leg, occupy neighboring parts of the motor cortex. Areas receiving input from neighboring body parts, such as the lips and tongue, are near one another in the somatosensory cortex. Notice that the size of these areas is uneven; the larger the area devoted to each body part, the larger that body part appears on the "homunculus."

Note: Did you notice the error in this class drawing? (The figure shows the right side of the body, but the left hand and left side of the face.)

Source: Penfield & Rasmussen (1968).

THE FAR SIDE　　By GARY LARSON

"Whoa! *That* was a good one! Try it, Hobbs — just poke his brain right where my finger is."

by that limb are now stimulated by other regions of skin) or something as mundane as practicing the violin (which can increase the number of neurons responding to touch). These changes appear to be coordinated partly by brain areas outside the cerebral cortex, which reassign more neurons to process particular sensory inputs. For example, activity in the basal nucleus of the forebrain can generate a massive reorganization of the sensory cortex involved in sound processing (Kilgard & Merzenich, 1998).

Videodisc Segment: The Motor Cortex

Motor Cortex　　Neurons in specific areas of the **motor cortex**, which is in the frontal lobe, create voluntary movements in specific parts of the body. Some control movement of the hand; others stimulate movement of the foot, the knee, the head, and so on. The specific muscles activated by these regions are linked not to specific neurons but, as mentioned earlier, to the patterned activity of many neurons. For example, some of the same neurons are active in moving more than one finger. In other words, different parts of the motor cortex homunculus overlap somewhat

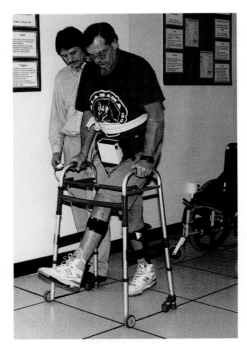

Movement and the Brain Smooth movements require the coordination of neural activity in both the brain and the spinal cord. This presents a challenge to researchers developing devices to restore movement in paralyzed individuals. Delivering computer-controlled electrical stimulation to the leg muscles allows walking movements to occur, but they are jerkier than movements that the brain normally produces.

 LINKAGES (a link to Cognition and Language)

OBJ 3.24: Name and describe the role of the areas in the association cortex involved in understanding and producing language.

Test Items 3.114–3.117

IRM Research Focus 8.13: Male and Female Brains and Language

association cortex Those parts of the cerebral cortex that receive information from more than one sense or that combine sensory and motor information to perform complex cognitive tasks.

corpus callosum A massive bundle of fibers that connects the right and left cerebral hemispheres and allows them to communicate with each other.

(Indovina & Sanes, 2001). As you can see in Figure 3.17, the motor homunculus mirrors the somatosensory homunculus; the parts of the motor cortex that control the hands, for instance, are near parts of the somatosensory cortex that receive sensory information from the hands.

Controlling the movement of the body may seem simple: You have a map of body parts in the motor cortex, and you activate cells in the hand region if you want to move your hand. But the actual process is much more complex. Recall again your sleepy reach for the coffeepot. The motor cortex must first translate the coffeepot's location in space into a location relative to your body; for example, your hand might have to be moved forward and a certain number of degrees to the right or to the left of your body. Next, the motor cortex must determine which muscles must be contracted to produce those movements. Populations of neurons work together to produce just the right combinations of direction and force in the particular muscle groups necessary to create the desired effects. Many interconnected areas of the motor cortex are involved in making these determinations.

Association Cortex   The parts of the cerebral cortex not directly involved with either receiving specific sensory information or initiating movement are referred to as **association cortex**. These are the areas that perform complex cognitive tasks, such as associating words with images. The term *association* is appropriate because these areas either receive information from more than one sense or combine sensory and motor information. Association cortex occurs in all of the lobes and forms a large part of the cerebral cortex in human beings. For this reason, damage to association areas can create severe losses, or deficits, in all kinds of mental abilities.

One of the most devastating deficits, called *aphasia*, creates difficulty in understanding or producing speech and can involve all the functions of the cerebral cortex. Language information comes from the auditory cortex (for spoken language) or from the visual cortex (for written language); areas of the motor cortex produce speech (Geschwind, 1979). But the complex function known as language also involves activity in association cortex.

In the 1800s, two areas of association cortex involved in different aspects of language were delineated. Paul Broca described the difficulties that result from damage to the association cortex in the frontal lobe near motor areas that control facial muscles, an area now called *Broca's area* (see Figure 3.16). When Broca's area is damaged, the mental organization of speech suffers. Victims have great difficulty speaking, and what they say is often grammatically incorrect. Each word comes slowly. Other language problems result from damage to a portion of the association cortex first described by Carl Wernicke (pronounced "VER-nick-ee") and thus called *Wernicke's area*. As Figure 3.16 shows, it is located in the temporal lobe, near an area of the cortex that receives information from the ears and eyes. Wernicke's area is involved in the interpretation of both speech and written words. Damage to this area can leave a person able to speak, but it disrupts the ability to understand the meaning of words or to speak comprehensibly.

One study illustrates the different effects of damage to each area (Lapointe, 1990). In response to the request "Tell me what you do with a cigarette," a person with chronic Broca's aphasia replied, "Uh . . . uh . . . cigarette (pause) smoke it." Though halting and ungrammatical, this speech was meaningful. In response to the same request, a person with chronic Wernicke's aphasia replied, "This is a segment of a pegment. Soap a cigarette." This speech, by contrast, was fluent but without meaning. A fascinating aspect of Broca's aphasia is that when a person with the disorder sings, the words come fluently and correctly. Presumably, words set to music are handled by a different part of the brain than spoken words (Besson et al., 1998). Capitalizing on this observation, "melodic intonation" therapy helps Broca's aphasia patients gain fluency in speaking by teaching them to speak in a "singsong" manner (Lapointe, 1990).

It appears that differing areas of association cortex are activated, depending on whether language is spoken or written and whether particular grammatical and conceptual categories are involved. For example, consider the cases of two women who had strokes that damaged different language-related parts of their association cortex (Caramazza & Hillis, 1991). Neither woman had difficulty speaking or writing nouns, but both had difficulty with verbs. One woman could write verbs but could not speak them: She had difficulty pronouncing *watch* when it was used as a verb in the sentence "I watch TV," but she spoke the same word easily when it appeared as a noun in "My watch is slow." The other woman could speak verbs but had difficulty writing them. Another odd language abnormality following brain damage, known as "foreign accent syndrome," was illustrated by a thirty-two-year-old stroke victim whose native language was English. His speech was slurred immediately after the stroke, but as it improved, he began to speak with a Scandinavian accent, adding syllables to some words ("How are you today-ah?") and pronouncing *hill* as "heel." His normal accent did not fully return for four months (Takayama et al., 1993). Case studies of "foreign accent syndrome" suggest that specific regions of the brain are involved in the sound of language, whereas others are involved in various aspects of its meaning.

Regions of association cortex long assumed to be involved mainly with spoken or written language also appear to be involved in processing the "language" of music. For example, recent studies using magnetoencephalography have found that Broca's area is activated when people hear a chord in a progression that disobeys musical "rules of grammar" (Maess et al., 2001).

The Divided Brain in a Unified Self

A striking idea emerged from observations of people with damage to the language areas of the brain. Researchers noticed that damage to limited areas of the *left hemisphere* impaired the ability to use or comprehend language, whereas damage to corresponding parts of the *right hemisphere* usually did not. Perhaps, they reasoned, the right and left halves of the brain serve different functions.

This concept was not entirely new. It had long been understood, for example, that most sensory and motor pathways cross over as they enter or leave the brain. As a result, the *left hemisphere* receives information from, and controls movements of, the *right* side of the body, whereas the *right hemisphere* receives input from and controls the *left* side of the body. However, both sides of the brain perform these functions. In contrast, the fact that language centers, such as Broca's area and Wernicke's area, are almost exclusively on the left side of the brain suggested that each hemisphere might be specialized to perform some functions almost independently of the other hemisphere.

Videodisc Segment: Gazzaniga: The Split Brain

Split-Brain Studies   As far back as the late 1800s, scientists had wanted to test the hypothesis that the cerebral hemispheres might be specialized, but they had no techniques for doing so. Then, during the 1960s, Roger Sperry, Michael Gazzaniga, and their colleagues began to study *split-brain* patients—people who had undergone a surgical procedure in an attempt to control severe epilepsy. Before the surgery, their seizures began in one hemisphere and then spread to engulf the whole brain. As a last resort, surgeons isolated the two hemispheres from each other by severing the **corpus callosum**, a massive bundle of more than a million fibers that connects the two hemispheres (see Figure 3.18).

After the surgery, researchers used a special apparatus to present visual images to only one side of these patients' split brains (see Figure 3.19). They found that severing the tie between the hemispheres had dramatically affected the way these people thought about and dealt with the world. For example, when the image of a spoon was presented to the left, language-oriented side of one patient's split brain, she could say what the spoon was; but when the spoon was presented to the right

OBJ 3.25: Describe split brain studies and explain the function of the corpus callosum.

Test Items 3.118–3.123

ClassPrep PPT 41, OHT: *Figure 3.18:* The Brain's Left and Right Hemispheres

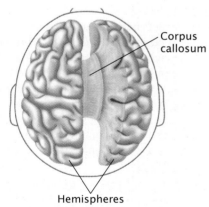

Corpus callosum

Hemispheres

figure 3.18

The Brain's Left and Right Hemispheres

The brain's two hemispheres are joined by a core bundle of nerve fibers known as the *corpus callosum*; in this figure the corpus callosum has been cut, and the hemispheres are separated. The two cerebral hemispheres look nearly the same but perform somewhat different tasks. For one thing, the left hemisphere receives sensory input from, and controls movement on, the right side of the body. The right hemisphere senses and controls the left side of the body.

figure 3.19

**Apparatus for Studying
Split-Brain Patients**

When the person stares at the dot on the screen, images briefly presented on one side of the dot go to only one side of the brain. For example, a picture of a spoon presented on the left side of the screen goes to the right side of the brain. The right side of the brain can find the spoon and direct the left hand to touch it; but because the language areas on the left side of the brain did not see it, the person is not able to say what it is.

ClassPrep PPT 42: *Figure 3.19:* Apparatus for Studying Split-Brain Patients

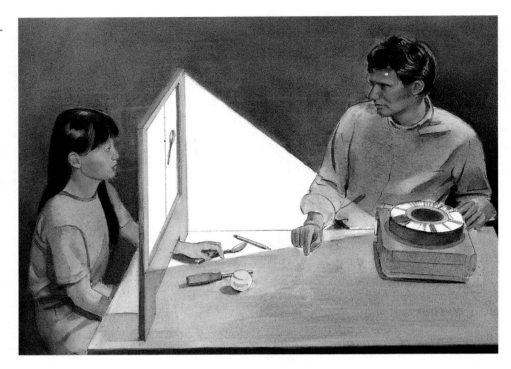

Freburg _Perspectives:_ Shreeve, "Music of the Hemispheres"

OBJ 3.26: Describe the lateralization of the cerebral hemispheres.

Test Items 3.124–3.126

IRM Discussion 3.8: Two Brains in One?

Personal Learning Activity 3.4

lateralized   Referring to the tendency for one cerebral hemisphere to excel at a particular function or skill compared with the other hemisphere.

side of her brain, she could not describe the spoon in words. She still knew what the object was, however. Using her left hand (controlled by the right hemisphere), she could pick out the spoon from a group of other objects by its shape. But when asked what she had just grasped, she replied, "A pencil." The right hemisphere recognized the object, but the patient could not describe it because the left (language) half of her brain did not see or feel it (Sperry, 1968).

Although the right hemisphere has no control over spoken language in split-brain patients, it does have important capabilities, including some related to nonspoken language. For example, a split-brain patient's right hemisphere can guide the left hand in spelling out words with Scrabble tiles (Gazzaniga & LeDoux, 1978). Thanks to this ability, researchers discovered that the right hemisphere of split-brain patients has self-awareness and normal learning abilities. In addition, it is superior to the left hemisphere on tasks dealing with spatial relations (especially drawing three-dimensional shapes) and at recognizing human faces.

Lateralization of Normal Brains   Sperry (1974) concluded from his studies that each hemisphere in the split-brain patient has its own "private sensations, perceptions, thoughts, and ideas all of which are cut off from the corresponding experiences in the opposite hemisphere. . . . In many respects each disconnected hemisphere appears to have a separate mind of its own." But when the hemispheres are connected normally, are certain functions, such as mathematical reasoning or language skills, lateralized? A **lateralized** task is one that is performed more efficiently by one hemisphere than by the other.

To find out, researchers presented images to just one hemisphere of people with normal brains and then measured how fast they could analyze information. If information is presented to one side of the brain and that side is specialized to analyze that type of information, a person's responses will be faster than if the information must first be transferred to the other hemisphere for analysis. These studies have confirmed that the left hemisphere has better logical and language abilities than the right, whereas the right hemisphere has better spatial, artistic, and musical abilities (Springer & Deutsch, 1989). Positron emission tomography (PET) scans of normal people receiving varying kinds of auditory stimulation also demonstrate these asymmetries of function (see Figure 3.20). We know that the language abilities of the left

figure 3.20

Lateralization of the Cerebral Hemispheres: Evidence from PET Scans

These PET scans show overhead views of a section of a person's brain that was receiving different kinds of stimulation. At the upper left, the person was resting, with eyes open and ears plugged. Note that the greatest brain activity (as indicated by the red color) was in the visual cortex, which was receiving input from the eyes. As shown at the lower left, when the person listened to spoken language, the auditory cortex in the left temporal lobe became more active, but the right temporal lobe did not. When the person listened to music (lower right), there was intense activity in the right temporal lobe but little in the left. When the person heard both words and music, the temporal cortex on both sides of the brain became activated. Here is visual evidence of the involvement of each side of the brain in processing different kinds of information (Phelps & Mazziotta, 1985).

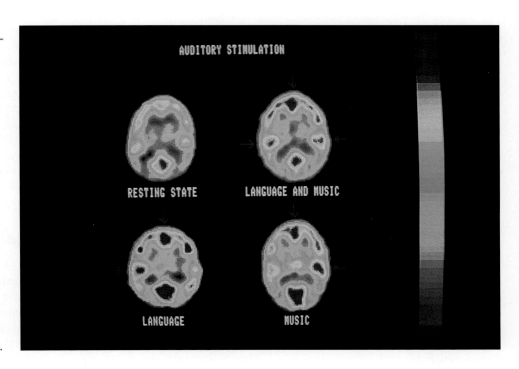

hemisphere are not specifically related to auditory information, though, because people who are deaf also use the left hemisphere more than the right for sign language (Hickok, Bellugi, & Klima, 1996).

The precise nature and degree of lateralization vary quite a bit among individuals. For example, in about a third of left-handed people, either the right hemisphere or both hemispheres control language functions (Springer & Deutsch, 1989). In contrast, only about 5 percent of right-handed people have language controlled by the right hemisphere. Evidence about sex differences in brain laterality comes from studies on the cognitive abilities of normal men and women, the effects of brain damage on cognitive function, and anatomical differences between the sexes. Among normal individuals there are sex differences in the ability to perform tasks that are known to be lateralized in the brain. For example, women tend to do better than men at perceptual fluency tasks, such as rapidly identifying matching items, and at arithmetic calculations. Men tend to be better at imagining the rotation of an object in space and tasks involving target-directed motor skills, such as guiding projectiles or intercepting them, in real or virtual-reality situations (Halperin, 1992; Waller, 2000).

Damage to just one side of the brain is more debilitating to men than to women. In particular, men show larger deficits in language ability than women when the left side is damaged (McGlone, 1980). This difference may reflect a wider distribution of language abilities in the brains of women compared with those of men. When participants in one study performed language tasks, such as thinking about whether particular words rhyme, MRI scans showed increased activity on the left side of the brain for men but on both sides for women (Shaywitz et al., 1995; see also Figure 1.1 in the chapter on introducing psychology). Women appear to have proportionately more of their association cortex devoted to language tasks (Harasty et al., 1997). Note, however, that although humans and animals show definite sex differences in brain anatomy and metabolism (Allen et al., 1989; Gur et al., 1995), no particular anatomical feature has been identified as underlying sex differences in lateralization. One highly publicized report claimed that the corpus callosum is larger in women than men (de Lacoste-Utamsing & Holloway, 1982), but numerous subsequent investigations have all failed to replicate this finding (Olivares et al., 2000). (The original report of a sex difference in the corpus callosum continues to be cited, however, despite overwhelming evidence against it, suggesting that scientists are sometimes not entirely unbiased.)

Having two somewhat specialized hemispheres allows the brain to more efficiently perform some tasks, particularly difficult ones (Hoptman & Davidson, 1994), but the differences between the hemispheres should not be exaggerated. The corpus callosum usually integrates the functions of the "two brains"; this role is particularly important in tasks that require sustained attention (Rueckert et al., 1999). As a result, the hemispheres work so closely together, and each makes up so well for whatever lack of ability the other may have, that people are normally unaware that their brains are made up of two partially independent, somewhat specialized halves (Banich & Heller, 1998; Staudt et al., 2001).

Plasticity: Repairing Damage in the Central Nervous System

The central nervous system has a remarkable property called **synaptic plasticity**, which is the ability to strengthen neural connections at synapses, as well as to establish new synapses. This ability, which depends partly on neurons and partly on glial cells (Ullian et al., 2001), provides the basis for the learning and memory processes described in other chapters. Plasticity occurs continuously throughout the nervous system; even the simplest reflex in the spinal cord can be modified by experience (Feng-Chen & Wolpaw, 1996).

Unfortunately, plasticity is limited when it comes to repairing damage to the brain and spinal cord. Although there are cases of heroic recovery from brain damage following a stroke, for example, most victims are permanently disabled in some way. In fact, until recently, scientists had good reason to be skeptical that a damaged central nervous system could ever heal its own wounds. For one thing, available evidence suggested that neurons divide and multiply during prenatal development, but that they virtually stop dividing by adulthood. They can still grow new axons, but except in the case of canaries and certain other songbirds (Nottebohm, 1985; Scharff et al., 2000), adult neurons appeared incapable of dividing into new ones, even in response to injury (Eriksson et al., 1998). Second, even if adults *could* generate new neurons, their axons and dendrites would have to reestablish all their former communication links. In the peripheral nervous system, glial cells form "tunnels" that guide the regrowth of axons. But in the central nervous system, reestablishing communication links is almost impossible, because glial cells actively suppress new connections (Olson, 1997).

Still, the brain does try to heal itself. Healthy neurons attempt to take over for damaged ones, partly by changing their own function and partly by sprouting axons whose connections help neighboring regions take on new functions (Cao et al., 1994). Although these changes rarely result in total restoration of lost functions, recent research is creating hope for better outcomes and optimism about finding ways to help the process along.

For example, special mental and physical exercise programs appear helpful in "re-wiring" the brains of stroke victims so as to reverse some forms of paralysis and improve some cognitive abilities (Blakeslee, 2001; Liepert et al., 2000; Robertson & Murre, 1999). Scientists have also discovered a protein called Nogo that prevents newly sprouted axons from making connections with other neurons in the central nervous system. Blocking the action of Nogo in rats allowed surviving neurons to make new axonal connections and actually repair spinal cord damage (Chen et al., 2000). The regeneration process can be greatly accelerated by inserting genes for growth proteins into adult neurons (Bomze et al., 2001; Condic, 2001). And in a preliminary study from the newly developing field *of tissue engineering*, immature cells from an adult rat's spinal cord were stimulated to grow and then implanted into the gap in other rats' severed spinal cords. Within a few months, some of these

ClassPrep PPT 44: Repairing Damage in the Central Nervous System

OBJ 3.27: Define synaptic plasticity. Explain why it is impossible for the brain to heal damaged neurons. Describe the methods used to help people recover from brain damage today.

Test Items 3.127–3.130

Freburg *Perspectives:* Nash, "Fertile Minds"

synaptic plasticity   The ability to create new synapses and to change the strength of synapses.

A Patient with Parkinson's Disease
Cells from a person's own adrenal gland have been used as an alternative to brain tissue in a transplant treatment for Parkinson's disease. Adrenal gland cells act like neurons when placed in the brain, and the benefits appear to be enhanced when the adrenal tissue is mixed with peripheral nerve tissue (Watts et al., 1997). Considered radical just ten years ago, the treatment is now well established, but only partly effective (Lopez-Lozano, Mata, & Bravo, 2000). Scientists hope that stem cells will work even better (Sawamoto et al., 2001).

previously paralyzed rats were able to stand and walk (Noble, 2000). Much more research is needed on methods such as these, of course, but if they are successful and found to apply to the human central nervous system, they might someday help people like Christopher Reeve to walk again (Schwab, 2002).

Another approach to repairing brain damage involves replacing lost tissue with tissue from another brain. Scientists have transplanted, or grafted, tissue from a still-developing fetal brain into the brain of an adult animal of the same species. If the receiving animal does not reject it, the graft sends axons out into the brain and makes some functional connections. This treatment has reversed animals' learning difficulties, movement disorders, and other results of brain damage. The technique has also been used to treat a small number of people with *Parkinson's disease*—a disorder characterized by tremors, rigidity of the arms and legs, difficulty in initiating movements, and poor balance (Lindvall & Hagell, 2001). The initial results were encouraging, but improvement faded after a year, and some patients suffered side effects involving uncontrollable movements (Freed et al., 2001).

Exciting new work with animals has shown that the effectiveness of brain-tissue grafts can be greatly enhanced by adding naturally occurring proteins called *growth factors,* or *neurotrophic factors,* which promote the survival of neurons (Hoglinger et al., 2001). One of the most effective of these proteins is glial cell line-derived neurotrophic factor, or GDNF, which actually causes neurons to produce the neurotransmitter needed to reverse the effects of Parkinson's disease (Kordower et al., 2000; Theofilopoulos et al., 2001).

The brain-tissue transplant procedure is promising, but because its use with humans requires tissue from aborted fetuses, it has generated considerable controversy. Two newer transplant treatments are designed to get around this problem. In one, Russian physicians transplanted neural tissue from fruit flies into the brains of Parkinson's patients, with therapeutic benefits and no reported side effects (Saveliev et al., 1997). In the other, U.S. researchers found that immune-resistant cells taken from testes have growth-promoting effects on some neurotransmitters, and that cells from the testes transplanted into the brains of rats with Parkinson's disease reduced their symptoms (Willing et al., 1999).

In yet another approach to treating brain diseases and damage, researchers have "engineered" cells from rats to produce *nerve growth factor*, a substance that helps stimulate and guide the growth of newly sprouted axons in the central nervous system. When the engineered cells were implanted into the brains of rats with brain damage or disease, the cells secreted nerve growth factor. In many cases, brain damage was reversed, with surviving neurons sprouting axons that grew toward the graft (Rosenberg et al., 1988). Based on these animal studies, nerve growth factor has been infused directly into the brain of a person with Alzheimer's disease (Seiger et al., 1993). The results were encouraging, and trials with other patients are in progress.

Most promising of all is recent research showing that new neurons can appear not only in adult songbirds but also in the brains of adult mammals, including mice, rabbits, primates, and humans (Blakeslee, 2000; Eriksson et al., 1998; Gould et al., 1999). These new cells have been found in areas such as the hippocampus, which is critical to the formation of new memories and is vulnerable to degeneration through Alzheimer's disease. The rate at which new neurons form in these areas appears to be affected by chemicals naturally secreted during stress, and possibly by those contained in certain drugs (Gould et al., 2000). For example, running in an activity wheel caused new neurons to form in mice, and these additional neurons apparently improved the animals' ability to learn (van Praag et al., 1999). Drugs normally prescribed to fight depression have also been shown to increase the formation of new hippocampal neurons (Malberg et al., 2000).

New neurons in mammals' central nervous system arise from a special type of glial cell called a *neural stem cell* (Alvarez-Buylla et al., 2001), which many scientists now believe may hold the key to reversing the consequences of brain damage and neurodegenerative diseases. They hope that someday, patients suffering from Parkinson's disease and Alzheimer's disease might be cured by treatments that replace damaged or dying neurons with new ones grown from stem cells (Kondo & Raff, 2000; Lennard & Jackson, 2000; Phillips et al., 2000; Sanchez-Ramos et al., 2000; Woodbury et al., 2000).

Human Development and the Changing Brain

Fortunately, most of the changes that take place in the brain throughout life are not the kind that produce degenerative diseases. What are these changes, and what are their effects? How are they related to the developments in sensory and motor capabilities, mental abilities, and other characteristics described in the chapter on human development?

Classical anatomical studies—and more recently, PET scans and functional MRI scans—are beginning to answer these questions. They have uncovered some interesting correlations between changes in neural activity and the behavior of human newborns and young infants. Among newborns, activity is relatively high in the thalamus but low in the striatum. This pattern may be related to the way newborns move: They make nonpurposeful, sweeping movements of the arms and legs, much like adults who have a hyperactive thalamus and a degenerated striatum (Chugani & Phelps, 1986). During the second and third months after birth, activity increases in many regions of the cortex, a change that is correlated with the loss of subcortically controlled reflexes such as the grasping reflex. When infants are around eight or nine months old, activity in the frontal cortex increases, a development that correlates well with the apparent beginnings of cognitive activity in infants (Chugani & Phelps, 1986). The brain continues to mature even through adolescence, showing evidence of ever more efficient neural communication in its major fiber tracts (Paus et al., 1999; Thompson et al., 2000).

These changes mainly reflect brain plasticity, not the appearance of new cells. After birth, the number of dendrites and synapses increases. In one area of the cortex, the number of synapses increases tenfold from birth to twelve months of age

figure 3.21

Changes in Neurons of the Cerebral Cortex During Development

During childhood, the brain overproduces neural connections, establishes the usefulness of certain connections, and then "prunes" the extra connections. Overproduction of synapses, especially in the frontal cortex, may be essential for infants to develop certain intellectual abilities. Some scientists believe that connections that are used survive, whereas others die.

Source: Reprinted by permission of the publisher from *The Postnatal Development of the Human Cerebral Cortex*, Vol. I–VIII by Jesse LeRoy Conel, Cambridge, Mass.: Harvard University Press, Copyright © 1939–1975 by the President and Fellows of Harvard College.

Freburg *Perspectives:* Nash, "Fertile Minds"

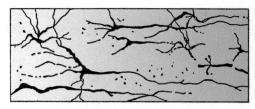

At birth

(A)

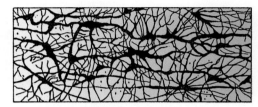

Six years old

(B)

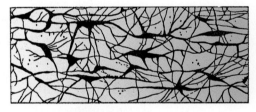

Fourteen years old

(C)

IRM Discussion 3.10: Do We Only Use Ten Percent of Our Brain?

(Huttenlocher, 1990). By the time children are six or seven years old, their brains have more dendrites and use twice as much metabolic fuel as those of adults (Chugani & Phelps, 1986). Then, in early adolescence, the number of dendrites and neural connections begins to drop, so that the adult level is reached by about the age of fourteen (see Figure 3.21). MRI scans show an actual loss of gray-matter volume in the cortex throughout the adolescent years as adult cognitive abilities develop (Sowell et al., 2001). In other words, as we reach adulthood, we develop more brainpower with less brain.

Even as dendrites are reduced, the brain retains its plasticity and "rewires" itself to form new connections throughout life. Our genes apparently determine the basic pattern of growth and the major lines of connections—the "highways" of the brain and its general architecture. (For a summary of this architecture, see "In Review: Organization of the Brain.") But the details of the connections depend on experience, including such factors as how complex and interesting the environment is. For example, researchers have compared the brains of rats raised alone with only a boring view of the side of their cages to the brains of rats raised with interesting toys and stimulating playmates. The cerebral cortex of those from the enriched environment had more and longer dendrites, as well as more synapses and neurotrophic factors, than the cortex of animals from barren, individual housing (Klintsova & Greenough, 1999; Torasdotter et al., 1998). Furthermore, the number of cortical synapses increased when isolated animals were moved to an enriched environment. To the extent that these ideas and research findings apply

in review	Organization of the Brain	
Major Division	**Some Important Structures**	**Some Major Functions**
Hindbrain	Medulla	Regulation of breathing, heart rate, and blood pressure
	Reticular formation (also extends into midbrain)	Regulation of arousal and attention
	Cerebellum	Control of finely coordinated movements and sequences
Midbrain	Various nuclei	Relay of sensory signals to forebrain; creation of automatic responses to certain stimuli
	Substantia nigra	Smooth initiation of movement
Forebrain	Hypothalamus	Regulation of hunger, thirst, and sex drives
	Thalamus	Interpretation and relaying of sensory information
	Hippocampus	Formation of new memories
	Amygdala	Connection of sensations and emotions
	Cerebral cortex	Analysis of sensory information; control over voluntary movements, abstract thinking, and other complex cognitive activity
	Corpus callosum	Transfer of information between the two cerebral hemispheres

to humans, they hold obvious implications for how people raise children and treat the elderly.

In any event, this line of research highlights the interaction of environmental and genetic factors. Some overproduced synapses may reflect genetically directed preparation for certain types of experiences. Generation of these synapses is an "experience-expectant" process, and it accounts for sensitive periods during development when certain things can be most easily learned. But overproduction of synapses also occurs in response to totally new experiences; this process is "experience dependent" (Greenough, Black, & Wallace, 1987). Within constraints set by genetics, interactions with the world mold the brain itself.

The Chemistry of Psychology

So far, we have described how the cells of the nervous system communicate by releasing neurotransmitters at their synapses, and we have outlined some of the basic structures of the nervous system and their functions. Let's now pull these topics together by considering two questions about neurotransmitters and the nervous system. First, which neurotransmitters occur in which structures? As noted earlier, different sets of neurons use different neurotransmitters; a group of neurons that communicates using the same neurotransmitter is called a **neurotransmitter system.** Second, how do neurotransmitter systems affect behavior? It appears that certain

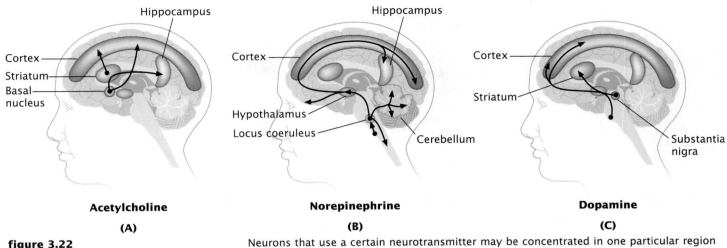

Acetylcholine

(A)

Norepinephrine

(B)

Dopamine

(C)

figure 3.22

Examples of Neurotransmitter Pathways

Neurons that use a certain neurotransmitter may be concentrated in one particular region (indicated by dots) and send fibers into other regions with which they communicate (see arrows). Here are examples for three major neurotransmitters.

neurotransmitter systems play a dominant role in particular functions, such as emotion or memory, and in particular problems, such as Alzheimer's disease. Our discussion will also reveal that certain drugs affect behavior and mental processes by altering these systems. Details about how these *psychoactive drugs* work are presented in other chapters, where we discuss drugs of abuse—such as cocaine and heroin (see the chapter on consciousness)—and drugs used in treating mental disorders (see the chapter on the treatment of psychological disorders).

Chemical neurotransmission was first demonstrated, in frogs, by Otto Loewi in 1921. Since then, more than a hundred different neurotransmitters have been identified. Some of the chemicals that act on receptors at synapses have been called *neuromodulators,* because they act slowly and often modify or "modulate" a cell's response to other neurotransmitters. The distinction between neurotransmitter and neuromodulator is not always clear, however. Depending on the type of receptor it acts on at a given synapse, the same substance can function as either a neuromodulator or a neurotransmitter.

Three Classes of Neurotransmitters

The neurotransmitters used in the nervous system fall into three main categories, based on their chemical structure: *small molecules, peptides,* and *gases.* In the following sections we discuss some examples found in each category.

Small Molecules　　The *small-molecule* neurotransmitters were discovered first, partly because they occur in both the central nervous system and the peripheral nervous system. For example, **acetylcholine** (pronounced "a-see-tull- KO-leen") is used by neurons of the parasympathetic nervous system to slow the heartbeat and activate the gastrointestinal system, and by neurons that make muscles contract. In the brain, neurons that use acetylcholine (called *cholinergic* neurons) are especially plentiful in the midbrain and striatum, where they occur in circuits that are important for movement (see Figure 3.22). Axons of cholinergic neurons also make up major pathways in the limbic system, including the hippocampus, and in other areas of the forebrain that are involved in memory. Drugs that interfere with acetylcholine prevent the formation of new memories. In Alzheimer's disease, there is a nearly complete loss of cholinergic neurons in a nucleus in the forebrain that sends fibers to the cerebral cortex and hippocampus—a nucleus that normally enhances plasticity in these regions (Kilgard & Merzenich, 1998).

---

neurotransmitter system　A group of neurons that communicates by using the same neurotransmitter.

acetylcholine　A neurotransmitter used by neurons in the peripheral and central nervous systems in the control of functions ranging from muscle contraction and heart rate to digestion and memory.

IRM Discussion 16.7: The Controversy over Prozac

Three other small-molecule neurotransmitters are known as *catecholamines* (pronounced "cat-ah-KO-lah-meens"). They include *norepinephrine, serotonin,* and *dopamine.* **Norepinephrine** (pronounced "nor-eppa-NEF-rin"), also called *noradrenaline,* occurs in both the central and peripheral nervous systems; in both places, it contributes to arousal. Norepinephrine (and its close relative, epinephrine, or adrenaline) are the neurotransmitters used by the sympathetic nervous system to activate you and prepare you for action. Approximately half of the norepinephrine in the entire brain is contained in cells of the locus coeruleus, which is near the reticular formation in the hindbrain (see Figure 3.22). Because norepinephrine systems cover a lot of territory, it is logical that norepinephrine would affect several broad categories of behavior. Indeed, norepinephrine is involved in the appearance of wakefulness and sleep, in learning, and in the regulation of mood.

Serotonin is similar to norepinephrine in several ways. First, most of the cells that use it as a neurotransmitter occur in an area along the midline of the hindbrain. Second, axons from neurons that use serotonin send branches throughout the forebrain, including the hypothalamus, the hippocampus, and the cerebral cortex. Third, serotonin affects sleep and mood. Serotonin differs from norepinephrine, however, in that the brain can get one of the substances from which it is made, *tryptophan,* directly from food. As a result, what you eat can affect the amount of serotonin in your brain. Carbohydrates increase the amount of tryptophan getting into the brain and therefore affect how much serotonin is made; so a meal high in carbohydrates produces increased levels of serotonin. Serotonin, in turn, normally causes a reduction in the desire for carbohydrates. Some researchers suspect that malfunctions in the serotonin feedback system are responsible for the disturbances of mood and appetite seen in certain types of obesity, premenstrual tension, and depression (Wurtman & Wurtman, 1995). Serotonin has also been implicated in aggression and impulse control. One of the most consistently observed relationships between a particular neurotransmitter system and a particular behavior is the low level of serotonin metabolites in the brains of suicide victims, who tend to show a combination of depressed mood, self-directed aggression, and impulsivity (Oquendo & Mann, 2000).

IRM In Your Own Words 3.2: Reaction Paper

IRM Discussion 9.11: A "Designer" Drug Gone Bad

Dopamine is the neurotransmitter used in the substantia nigra and striatum, which are important for movement. Malfunctioning of the dopamine-using (or *dopaminergic*) system in these regions contributes to movement disorders, including Parkinson's disease. As dopamine cells in the substantia nigra degenerate, Parkinson's disease victims experience severe shakiness and difficulty in beginning movements. Parkinson's disease is most common in elderly people, and it may result in part from sensitivity to environmental toxins. These toxins have not yet been identified, but there is evidence from animal studies that chemicals in some common garden pesticides damage dopaminergic neurons (Jenner 2001). Parkinson's disease has been treated, with partial success, using drugs that enable neurons to make more dopamine (Chase, 1998). Malfunctioning of dopaminergic neurons whose axons go to the cerebral cortex may be partly responsible for schizophrenia, a severe disorder in which perception, emotional expression, and thought are severely distorted (Marenco & Weinberger, 2000).

Other dopaminergic systems that send axons from the midbrain to the forebrain are important in the experience of reward or pleasure (Wise & Rompre, 1989). Animals will work intensively to receive a direct infusion of dopamine into the forebrain. These dopamine systems play a role in the rewarding properties of many drugs, including cocaine.

Two other small-molecule neurotransmitters—*GABA* and *glutamate*— are amino acids. Neurons in widespread regions of the brain use **GABA**, or gamma-amino butyric acid. GABA reduces the likelihood that postsynaptic neurons will fire an action potential; in fact, it is the major inhibitory neurotransmitter in the central nervous system. When you fall asleep, neurons that use GABA deserve part of the credit.

norepinephrine A neurotransmitter involved in arousal, as well as in learning and mood regulation.

serotonin A neurotransmitter used by cells in parts of the brain involved in the regulation of sleep, mood, and eating.

dopamine A neurotransmitter used in the parts of the brain involved in regulating movement and experiencing pleasure.

GABA A neurotransmitter that inhibits the firing of neurons.

Malfunctioning of GABA systems has been implicated in a variety of disorders, including severe anxiety and *Huntington's disease*, an inherited and incurable disorder in which the victim is plagued by uncontrollable jerky movement of the arms and legs, along with dementia. Huntington's disease results in the loss of many GABA-containing neurons in the striatum. Normally these GABA systems inhibit dopamine systems; so when they are lost through Huntington's disease, the dopamine systems may run wild, impairing many motor and cognitive functions. Because drugs that block GABA receptors produce intense repetitive electrical discharges, known as *seizures,* researchers suspect that malfunctioning GABA systems probably contribute to *epilepsy,* a brain disorder associated with seizures and convulsive movements. Repeated or sustained seizures can result in permanent brain damage; drug treatments can reduce their frequency and severity, but completely effective drugs are not yet available.

Glutamate is the major excitatory neurotransmitter in the central nervous system. Glutamate is used by more neurons than any other neurotransmitter; its synapses are especially plentiful in the cerebral cortex and the hippocampus. Glutamate is particularly important because it plays a major role in the ability of the brain to "strengthen" its synaptic connections—that is, to allow messages to cross the synapse more efficiently. This process is necessary for normal development and may be at the root of learning and memory (Pennartz et al., 2000). At the same time, overactivity of glutamate synapses can cause neurons to die. In fact, this overactivity is the main cause of the brain damage that occurs when oxygen is cut off from neurons during a stroke. Glutamate can "excite neurons to death," so blocking glutamate receptors immediately after a brain trauma can prevent permanent brain damage (Dawson et al., 2001). Glutamate may also contribute to the loss of cells from the hippocampus that occurs in Alzheimer's disease (Cha et al., 2001).

Peptides

Hundreds of chemicals called *peptides* have been found to act as neurotransmitters. The first of these were discovered in the 1970s, when scientists were investigating *opiates,* which are substances derived from poppy flowers. Opiates such as morphine and heroin can relieve pain, produce euphoria, and in high doses, bring on sleep. After marking morphine with a radioactive substance, researchers traced where it became concentrated in the brain. They found that opiates bind to receptors that were not associated with any known neurotransmitter. Because it was unlikely that the brain had developed opiate receptors just in case a person might want to use morphine or heroin, researchers reasoned that the body must contain a substance similar to opiates. This hypothesis led to the search for a naturally occurring, or endogenous, morphine, which was called *endorphin* (short for endogenous morphine). As it turned out, there are many natural opiate-like compounds. So the term **endorphin** refers to any neurotransmitter that can bind to the same receptors stimulated by opiates. Neurons in several parts of the brain use endorphin, including neuronal pathways that modify pain signals to the brain.

Gases

The concept of what neurotransmitters can be was radically altered following the recent discovery that *nitric oxide* and *carbon monoxide*—two toxic gases that contribute to air pollution—can act as neurotransmitters (Baranano et al., 2001). When nitric oxide or carbon monoxide is released by a neuron, it spreads to nearby neurons, sending a signal that affects chemical reactions inside those neurons rather than binding to receptors on their surface. Nitric oxide is not stored in vesicles, as most other neurotransmitters are; it can be released from any part of the neuron. Nitric oxide appears to be one of the neurotransmitters responsible for such diverse functions as penile erection and the formation of memories—not at the same site, obviously. (For a summary of the main neurotransmitters and the consequences of malfunctioning neurotransmitter systems, see "In Review: Classes of Neurotransmitters.")

ClassPrep PPT 47: Other Classes of Neurotransmitters

glutamate An excitatory neurotransmitter that helps strengthen synaptic connections between neurons.

endorphin One of a class of neurotransmitters that bind to opiate receptors and moderate pain.

in review Classes of Neurotransmitters		
Neurotransmitter Class	**Normal Function**	**Disorder Associated with Malfunction**
Small Molecules		
Acetylcholine	Memory, movement	Alzheimer's disease
Norepinephrine	Mood, sleep, learning	Depression
Serotonin	Mood, appetite, impulsivity	Depression
Dopamine	Movement, reward	Parkinson's disease, schizophrenia
GABA	Sleep, movement	Anxiety, Huntington's disease, epilepsy
Glutamate	Memory	Damage after stroke
Peptides		
Endorphins	Pain control	No established disorder
Gases		
Nitric oxide	Memory	No established disorder

THINKING CRITICALLY

ClassPrep PPT 52: Thinking Critically: Are There Drugs That Can Make You Smarter?

Are There Drugs That Can Make You Smarter?

OBJ 3.30: Describe the effects of nootropic drugs and the conclusions that are most reasonable about their use as "smart" drugs.

Test Items 3.142–3.143

Neurotransmitter systems provide humans with all sorts of remarkable capabilities. It is hard not to be impressed by how effectively and efficiently these systems work to affect behavior and mental processes. And it is hard not to be concerned by the severe disorders that occur when major neurotransmitter systems malfunction, as is the case with Alzheimer's disease. Some people believe that drugs designed to correct these malfunctions might also improve the functioning of neurotransmitters in normal individuals. Advertisements and articles in many health magazines and on tens of thousands of web sites describe an incredible array of "smart drugs" and dietary supplements. (The drugs are called *nootropics*—from *noos,* which is Greek for "mind.") It is claimed that these substances will improve mental sharpness and reduce or slow the effects of degenerative brain diseases. Belief in the value of nootropics is not confined to health-food fanatics, however; many respected scientists agree with some of the less extreme claims about some of these substances. The use of "smart drugs" is increasing in the United States, and in some other countries (India, for example), it is even more common (Geary, 1997). Are "smart drugs" really effective, or are they modern-day snake oil, giving no more than the illusion of a sharpened mind?

● **What am I being asked to believe or accept?**

Proponents of "smart drugs" and dietary supplements claim that these substances can enhance memory and reverse the effects of degenerative brain diseases. This notion was popularized in the 1990s by two books by John Morgenthaler and Ward Dean. In an interview, Morgenthaler said he had been taking "smart drugs" for ten years, about eight pills twice a day. He explained, "It's not a scientific study; I may have gotten smarter just from growing up, educating myself and stimulating my brain. But I do stop taking the drugs every now and then, and I know that I have better concentration, attention and memory when I'm on them" (Greenwald, 1991).

● **What evidence is available to support the assertion?**

There is certainly an element of truth to the idea that some of these drugs can improve cognitive performance under some circumstances. Animals given the drugs under controlled conditions show statistically significant improvements in performance on tasks requiring attention and memory. The chemicals used in these drugs include *piracetam,* extracts from the herb *Ginkgo biloba,* and *vasopressin.* The drugs not only affect behavior but also have measurable biochemical effects on the brain. Some have general effects on brain metabolism and also increase blood sugar levels; others affect specific neurotransmitters such as acetylcholine, glutamate, serotonin, and dopamine (Dormehl et al., 1999; Pepeu, 1994).

Do "smart drugs" work with humans? One review of the scientific literature on the effects of nootropics in elderly people describes improvement in cognitive functioning associated with forty-five different medications (van Reekum et al., 1997). One study of elderly people with general brain impairment found improvement after twelve weeks of treatment with "smart drugs." Other studies have shown memory improvement in elderly people whose problems were due to poor blood circulation to the brain (Balestreri, Fontana, & Astengo, 1987). Positive effects have also been reported in younger people. In one study, college students did better on tests of memory after taking some of these drugs (File, Fluck, & Fernandes, 1999). In other words, you can probably find a study supporting the effectiveness of virtually any nootropic drug.

● **Are there alternative ways of interpreting the evidence?**

One alternative explanation of the data on nootropics is that they represent *placebo effects.* As noted in the chapter on research in psychology, placebo effects occur when a person's *beliefs* about a drug, not the drug itself, are responsible for any changes that occur. In their first book on "smart drugs," Morgenthaler and Dean (1990) acknowledge the possibility that placebo effects may be responsible for many of the glowing testimonials about these drugs; but then they themselves present such testimonials to help readers decide which substances to take, and they encourage readers to send in their own accounts of the benefits they have derived from a particular food or dietary supplement. This is hardly the kind of objective, empirical evidence that psychologists seek when evaluating theories and treatments.

Steven Rose (1993) suggests other serious flaws in many of the experiments that apparently show the benefits of nootropic drugs. Specifically, some researchers used only small numbers of participants in their studies, and others failed to test whether positive findings could be reproduced in their own or other researchers' laboratories. Studies that have examined whether the effects of "smart drugs" can be reproduced have yielded mixed results. For example, some experimenters have reported positive effects of *Ginkgo biloba,* while others—using exactly the same dosages and memory tasks—have not (Warot et al., 1991).

One's view of the effects of "smart drugs" must also be tempered by the fact that these effects are not very substantial. For example, the first drug (*tacrine*) approved by the U.S. Food and Drug Administration for the treatment of Alzheimer-related memory problems has repeatedly been shown to "significantly" improve memory, but the actual improvement is always minor. Other nootropic drugs that have positive effects on memory or other cognitive abilities primarily affect attentiveness; they are no more effective than coffee, or even lemonade (Metzger, 2000; Service, 1994). Overall, the evidence from properly designed studies shows nootropic drugs to be a major disappointment (Lobaugh et al., 2001; Riedel & Jolles, 1996).

Finally, the effects of "smart drugs" must be interpreted in light of their possible side effects. For example, tacrine carries the risk of potentially fatal liver damage. Aricept, a similar drug, does not damage the liver, but does cause nausea and diarrhea (Dunn et al., 2000). Even "natural" remedies that people assume are safe can have unwanted effects. For example, ephedrine, a common ingredient in herbal remedies, is a potent stimulant that has lead to cardiac arrest and death in some cases. Ephedrine, *Ginkgo biloba,* and several other herbal substances can also interfere with the action of prescription drugs and raise the risk of bleeding during surgical procedures (Ang-Lee, Moss, & Yuan, 2001).

● **What additional evidence would help to evaluate the alternatives?**

Researchers are evaluating several promising new categories of nootropic drugs in animals (Qizilbash & Emre, 2001). However, it will take years of study to determine which drugs are truly effective for memory enhancement, and under what circumstances. It will also take time to learn whether the results with animals are applicable to humans. Research with humans will require carefully controlled double-blind studies that eliminate the effects of participants' and investigators' expectancies so that the direct effects of the drugs or other treatments can be separated from placebo effects. One critical question to be addressed in such research is whether drugs that can reduce the memory loss associated with Alzheimer's disease will also improve the memories of normal, healthy people and vice versa. And of course, we still need to determine how these drugs work, what their potential side effects are, and whether they affect memory alone or also related processes such as motivation or attention.

● **What conclusions are most reasonable?**

The scientific community is somewhat divided regarding the present benefits and the long-term potential of nootropic drugs. It is much too soon to hail them as the long-sought cure for all sorts of problems in cognitive functioning, but also too soon to write them off as a pseudoscientific fad. Moreover, although the drugs currently available for improving memory are limited in effectiveness, proponents argue that even if such drugs only delay the institutionalization of Alzheimer's patients for several months, the savings to society are substantial. Accordingly, researchers continue to investigate new nootropic drugs, while the scientific jury continues to deliberate about the value of existing ones.

The same wait-and-see attitude is not justified by evidence about the herbs, potions, and drinks that are supposed to make normal people smarter. You can buy them in health-food stores and "smart bars," but their effect on mental powers is minimal. In fact, the strategies described in the chapter on memory are likely to be far more effective in helping you remember information and do well in school. There is also evidence that "exercising your brain" has long-term benefits on memory and brain function. For example, educational achievement and a life of working at a job that engages the mind have been associated with a lowered risk for Alzheimer's disease (Evans et al., 1997), perhaps because education and other factors that increase cerebral blood flow reduce the risk of this disorder (Crawford, 1998).

The Endocrine System: Coordinating the Internal World

Videodisc Segment: The Endocrine Glands

endocrine system Cells that form organs called glands and that communicate with one another by secreting chemicals called hormones.

glands Organs that secrete hormones into the bloodstream.

hormones Chemicals secreted by a gland into the bloodstream, which carries them throughout the body.

As noted earlier, neurons are not the only cells that can use chemicals to communicate with one another in ways that affect behavior and mental processes. Another class of cells with this ability resides in the **endocrine system** (pronounced "EN-doh-krinn"), which regulates functions ranging from stress responses to physical growth. The cells of endocrine organs, or **glands**, communicate by secreting chemicals, much as neurons do. In the case of endocrine organs, the chemicals are called **hormones**. Figure 3.23 shows the location and functions of some of the major endocrine glands.

Hormones secreted from the endocrine organs are similar to neurotransmitters. In fact, many of these chemicals, including norepinephrine and the endorphins, act both as hormones and as neurotransmitters. However, whereas neurons release neurotransmitters into synapses, endocrine organs put their chemicals into the bloodstream, which carries them throughout the body. In this way, endocrine glands can stimulate cells with which they have no direct connection. But not all cells receive the hormonal message. Hormones, like neurotransmitters, can influence only those cells with receptors capable of receiving them (McEwen, 1994). Organs whose cells have receptors for a hormone are called *target organs*.

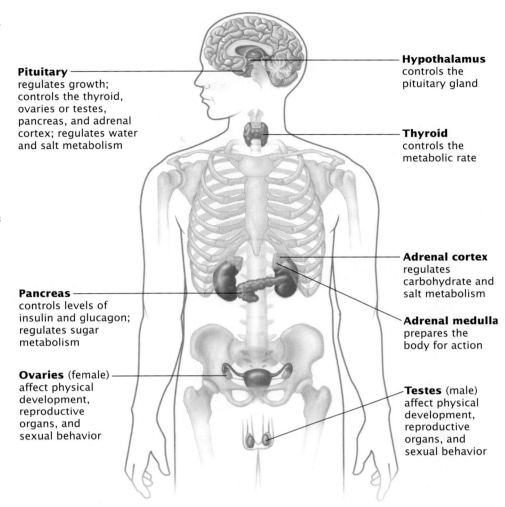

Pituitary regulates growth; controls the thyroid, ovaries or testes, pancreas, and adrenal cortex; regulates water and salt metabolism

Hypothalamus controls the pituitary gland

Thyroid controls the metabolic rate

Adrenal cortex regulates carbohydrate and salt metabolism

Adrenal medulla prepares the body for action

Pancreas controls levels of insulin and glucagon; regulates sugar metabolism

Ovaries (female) affect physical development, reproductive organs, and sexual behavior

Testes (male) affect physical development, reproductive organs, and sexual behavior

Each hormone acts on many target organs, producing coordinated effects throughout the body. For example, when the sex hormone *estrogen* is secreted by a woman's ovaries, it activates her reproductive system. It causes the uterus to grow in preparation for nurturing an embryo; it enlarges the breasts to prepare them for nursing; it stimulates the brain to enhance interest in sexual activity; and it stimulates the pituitary gland to release another hormone that causes a mature egg to be released by the ovary for fertilization. Pituitary hormones cause the male sex organs to secrete *androgens* (which are sex hormones such as testosterone), stimulate the maturation of sperm, increase a male's motivation for sexual activity, and increase his aggressiveness (Rubinow & Schmidt, 1996).

Can differences between hormones in men and women account for some of the differences between the sexes? During development and in adulthood, sex differences in hormones are relative rather than absolute: Both men and women have androgens and estrogens, but men have relatively higher concentrations of androgens, whereas women have relatively higher concentrations of estrogens. There is plenty of evidence from animal studies that the presence of higher concentrations of androgens in males during development creates both structural sex differences in the brain and sex differences in adult behaviors. Humans, too, may be similarly affected by hormones early in development. For example, studies of girls who were exposed to high levels of androgens before birth found that they were later more aggressive than their sisters who had not had such exposure (Berenbaum & Resnick, 1997). And as shown in Figure 1.1, MRI studies have revealed specific brain regions that function differently in men and women. However, such sex differences may not be simple, inevitable, or due to the actions of hormones alone. For example, just the act of practicing finger tapping for ten minutes a day over several weeks can create alterations in the activity of the motor cortex that are detectable with functional MRI (Karni et al., 1998). Most likely, the sex differences we see in behavior depend not only on hormones but also on complex interactions of biological and social forces, as described in the chapter on motivation and emotion.

The brain has ultimate control over the secretion of hormones. Through the hypothalamus, it controls the pituitary gland, which in turn controls endocrine organs in the body. The brain is also one of the target organs for most endocrine secretions. In fact, the brain creates some of the same hormones that are secreted in the endocrine system, and uses them for neural communication (Compagnone & Mellon, 2000). In summary, the endocrine system typically involves four elements: the brain, the pituitary gland, an endocrine organ, and the target organs, which include the brain. Each element in the system uses hormones to signal to the next element, and the secretion of each hormone is stimulated or suppressed by other hormones.

For example, in stress-hormone systems, the brain controls the pituitary gland by signaling the hypothalamus to release hormones that stimulate receptors of the pituitary gland, which secretes another hormone, which stimulates another endocrine gland to secrete its hormones. Specifically, when the brain interprets a situation as threatening, the pituitary releases *adrenocorticotropic hormone (ACTH)*, which causes the adrenal glands to release the hormone *cortisol* into the bloodstream. These hormones, in turn, act on cells throughout the body, including the brain. One effect of cortisol, for example, is to activate the emotion-related limbic system, making it more likely that you will remember stressful or traumatic events (Cahill & McGaugh, 1998). The combined effects of the adrenal hormones and the activation of the sympathetic system result in a set of responses called the **fight-or-flight syndrome**, which, as mentioned earlier, prepares the animal or person for action in response to danger or other stress. The heart beats faster, the liver releases glucose into the bloodstream, fuels are mobilized from fat stores, and the organism usually enters a state of high arousal.

The hormones provide feedback to the brain, as well as to the pituitary gland. Just as a thermostat and furnace regulate heat, this feedback system regulates hor-

OBJ 3.32: Define the fight-or-flight syndrome.

Test Items 3.153–3.155

Hormones at Work   The appearance of a threat activates a pattern of hormonal secretions and other physiological responses that prepare animals and humans to confront, or flee, the danger. This pattern is known as the *fight-or-flight syndrome.*

Freburg *Perspectives:* Furlow, "The Smell of Love"

fight-or-flight syndrome   Physical reactions initiated by the sympathetic nervous system that prepare the body to fight or to run from a threatening situation.

OBJ 3.33: Define negative feedback systems.

Test Items 3.156–3.157

mone secretion so as to keep it within a certain range. If a hormone rises above a certain level, feedback about this situation signals the brain and pituitary to stop stimulating that hormone's secretion. So after the immediate threat is over, feedback about cortisol's action in the brain and in the pituitary terminates the secretion of ACTH and, in turn, cortisol. Because the feedback suppresses further action, this arrangement is called a *negative feedback system.*

The Immune System: Defending the Body

OBJ 3.34: Compare and contrast the functionality of the immune system to the nervous and endocrine systems. Define autoimmune disorder.

Test Items 3.158–3.163

ClassPrep PPT 49, OHT: *Figure 3.24:* Relations Among the Nervous System, Endocrine System, and Immune System

Like the nervous system and endocrine system, the **immune system** serves as both a sensory system and a security system. It monitors the internal state of the body and detects unwanted cells and toxic substances that may have invaded. It recognizes and remembers foreign substances, and it engulfs and destroys foreign cells as well as cancer cells. Individuals whose immune system is impaired—AIDS patients, for example—face death from invading bacteria or malignant tumors. However, if the system becomes overactive, the results can be just as devastating: Many diseases, including arthritis, diabetes, and multiple sclerosis, are now recognized as **autoimmune disorders**, in which cells of the immune system attack normal cells of the body, including brain cells (Marrack, Kappler, & Kotzin, 2001).

The immune system is as complex as the nervous system, and it contains as many cells as the brain. Some of these cells are in organs such as the thymus and

figure 3.24

Relations Among the Nervous System, Endocrine System, and Immune System

All three systems interact and influence one another. The nervous system affects the endocrine system by controlling the secretion of hormones via the pituitary gland. It also affects the immune system through the autonomic nervous system's action on the thymus gland. The thymus, spleen, and bone marrow are sites of generation and development of immune cells. Hormones of the pituitary gland and adrenal gland modulate immune cells. Immune cells secrete cytokines and antibodies to fight foreign invaders; cytokines are blood-borne messengers that regulate the development of immune cells and also influence the central nervous system.

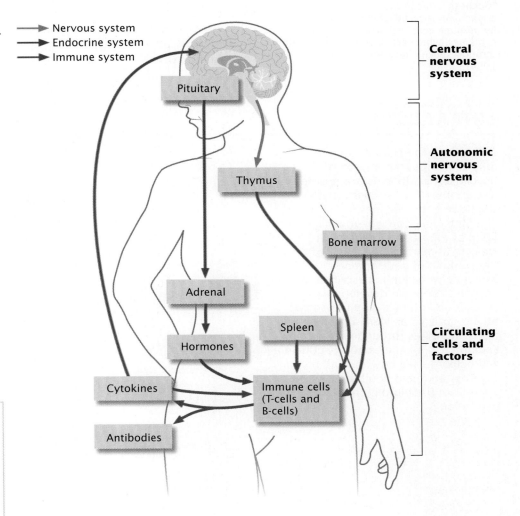

OBJ 3.35: Describe the interaction of the immune, nervous, and endocrine systems.

Test Items 3.164–3.165

LSV: Stress and Disease, Responding to Stress

immune system The body's system of defense against invading substances and microorganisms.

autoimmune disorders Physical problems caused when cells of the body's immune system attack normal body cells as if they were foreign invaders.

The Common Cold   The interaction of the immune system and the nervous system can be seen in some of the symptoms associated with routine "sickness." Sleepiness, nausea, and fever are actually a result of chemicals released by immune cells, collectively called *cytokines,* which act directly on the brain through specific receptors (Pousset, 1994).

spleen, whereas others circulate in the bloodstream and enter tissues throughout the body (see Figure 3.24). In the chapter on health, stress, and coping, we describe a few of the immune system's many cell types and how they work.

The nervous system and the immune system were once thought of as completely separate (Ader, Felten, & Cohen, 1990). However, five lines of evidence suggest important interactions between the two. First, stress can alter the outcome of disease in animals, and as discussed in the chapter on health, stress, and coping, there is growing evidence that psychological stressors also affect disease processes in humans (Sternberg, 2001). Second, immune responses can be "taught" using some of the principles outlined in the chapter on learning. In one study with humans, for example, exposure to the taste of sherbet was repeatedly associated with an injection of epinephrine, which increases immune system activity. Later, an increase in immune system activity could be prompted by the taste of sherbet alone (Exton et al., 2000). Third, animal studies have shown that stimulating or damaging specific parts of the hypothalamus, the cortex, or the brainstem that control the autonomic nervous system can enhance or impair immune functions (Felten et al., 1998). Fourth, activation of the immune system can produce changes in the electrical activity of the brain, in neurotransmitter activity, in hormonal secretion, and in behavior—including symptoms of sickness (Kronfol & Remick, 2000). Finally, some of the same chemical messengers are found in both the brain and the immune system (Maier & Watkins, 1998).

These converging lines of evidence point to important relationships that illustrate the intertwining of biological and psychological functions, the interaction of body and mind. They highlight the ways in which the immune system, nervous system, and endocrine system—all systems of communication between and among cells—are integrated to form the biological basis for a smoothly functioning self that is filled with interacting thoughts, emotions, and memories and is capable of responding to life's challenges and opportunities with purposeful and adaptive behavior.   **Personal Learning Activity 3.5**

LINKAGES

As noted in the chapter on introducing psychology, all of psychology's subfields are related to one another. Our discussion of developmental changes in the brain illustrates just one way in which the topic of this chapter, biological aspects of psychology, is linked to the subfield of developmental psychology, which is described in the chapter on human development. The Linkages diagram shows ties to two other subfields as well, and there are many more ties throughout the book. Looking for linkages among subfields will help you see how they all fit together and help you better appreciate the big picture that is psychology.

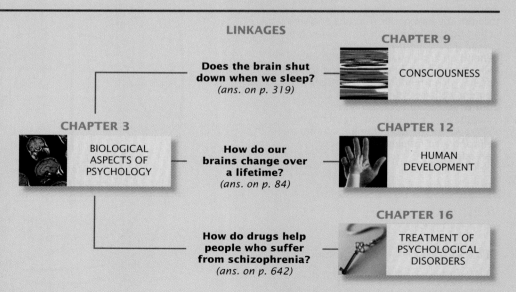

LINKAGES

CHAPTER 3

BIOLOGICAL ASPECTS OF PSYCHOLOGY

Does the brain shut down when we sleep?
(ans. on p. 319)

CHAPTER 9

CONSCIOUSNESS

How do our brains change over a lifetime?
(ans. on p. 84)

CHAPTER 12

HUMAN DEVELOPMENT

How do drugs help people who suffer from schizophrenia?
(ans. on p. 642)

CHAPTER 16

TREATMENT OF PSYCHOLOGICAL DISORDERS

SUMMARY

Biological psychology focuses on the biological aspects of our being, including the nervous system, which provide the physical basis for behavior and mental processes. The *nervous system* is a system of cells that allows an organism to gain information about what is going on inside and outside the body and to respond appropriately.

The Nervous System

Much of our understanding of the biological aspects of psychology has stemmed from research on animal and human nervous systems at levels ranging from single cells to complex organizations of cells.

Cells of the Nervous System

The main units of the nervous system are cells called *neurons* and *glial cells*. Neurons are especially good at receiving signals from, and transmitting signals to, other neurons. Neurons have cell bodies and two types of fibers, called *axons* and *dendrites*. Axons usually carry signals away from the cell body, whereas dendrites usually carry signals to the cell body. Neurons can transmit signals because of the structure of these fibers, the excitable surface of some of the fibers, and the *synapses*, or gaps, between cells.

Action Potentials

The membranes of neurons normally keep the distribution of electrically charged molecules uneven between the inside of cells and the outside, creating an electrochemical force, or potential. The membrane surface of the axon can transmit a disturbance in this potential, called an *action potential*, from one end of the axon to the other. The speed of the action potential is fastest in neurons sheathed in *myelin*. Between firings there is a very brief rest, called a *refractory period*.

Synapses and Communication Between Neurons

When an action potential reaches the end of an axon, the axon releases a chemical called a *neurotransmitter*. This chemical crosses the synapse and interacts with the postsynaptic cell at special sites called *receptors*. This interaction creates *a postsynaptic potential*—either an *excitatory postsynaptic potential (EPSP)* or an *inhibitory postsynaptic potential (IPSP)*—that makes the postsynaptic cell more likely or less likely to fire an action potential. So whereas communication within a neuron is electrochemical, communication between neurons is chemical. Because the fibers of neurons have many branches, each neuron can interact with thousands of other neurons. Each neuron constantly integrates signals received at its many synapses; the result of this integration determines how often the neuron fires an action potential.

Organization and Functions of the Nervous System

Neurons are organized in *neural networks* of closely connected cells. *Sensory systems* receive information from the environ-ment, and *motor systems* influence the actions of muscles and other organs. The two major divisions of the nervous system are the *peripheral nervous system (PNS)* and the *central nervous system (CNS)*, which includes the brain and spinal cord.

The Peripheral Nervous System: Keeping in Touch with the World

The peripheral nervous system has two components.

The Somatic Nervous System

The first component of the peripheral nervous system is the *somatic nervous system*, which transmits information from the senses to the CNS and carries signals from the CNS to the muscles that move the skeleton.

The Autonomic Nervous System

The second component of the peripheral nervous system is the *autonomic nervous system*; it carries messages back and forth between the CNS and the heart, lungs, and other organs and glands.

The Central Nervous System: Making Sense of the World

The CNS is laid out in interconnected groups of neuronal cell bodies, called *nuclei*, whose collections of axons travel together in *fiber tracts*, or *pathways*.

The Spinal Cord

The *spinal cord* receives information from the peripheral senses and sends it to the brain; it also relays messages from the brain to the periphery. In addition, cells of the spinal cord can direct simple behaviors, called *reflexes*, without instructions from the brain.

The Brain

The brain's major subdivisions are the *hindbrain*, *midbrain*, and *forebrain*. The hindbrain includes the *medulla*, the *cerebellum*, and the *locus coeruleus*. The midbrain includes the *substantia nigra*. The *reticular formation* is found in both the hindbrain and the midbrain. The forebrain is the largest and most highly developed part of the brain; it includes many structures, including the *hypothalamus* and *thalamus*. A part of the hypothalamus called the *suprachiasmatic nuclei* maintains a clock that determines biological rhythms. Other forebrain structures include the *striatum*, *hippocampus*, and *amygdala*. Several of these structures form the *limbic system*, which plays an important role in regulating emotion and memory.

The Cerebral Cortex

The outer surface of the *cerebral hemispheres* is called the *cerebral cortex*; it is responsible for many of the higher functions of the brain, including speech and reasoning. The functional areas of the cortex include the *sensory cortex*, *motor cortex*, and *association cortex*.

The Divided Brain in a Unified Self

The right and left hemispheres of the cerebral cortex are specialized to some degree in their functions. In most people, the left hemisphere is more active in language and logical tasks and the right hemisphere, in spatial, musical, and artistic tasks. A task that is performed more efficiently by one hemisphere than the other is said to be *lateralized*. The hemispheres are connected through the *corpus callosum*, allowing them to operate in a coordinated fashion.

Plasticity: Repairing Damage in the Central Nervous System

The brain's *synaptic plasticity*, the ability to strengthen neural connections at its synapses as well as to establish new synapses, forms the basis for learning and memory. Scientists are studying ways to increase plasticity following brain damage.

The Chemistry of Psychology

Neurons that use the same neurotransmitter form a *neurotransmitter system*.

Three Classes of Neurotransmitters

There are three classes of neurotransmitters: small-molecules, peptides, and gases. *Acetylcholine* systems in the brain influence memory processes and movement. *Norepinephrine* is released by neurons whose axons spread widely throughout the brain; it is involved in arousal, mood, and learning. *Serotonin*, another pervasive neurotransmitter, is active in systems regulating mood and appetite. *Dopamine* systems are involved in movement and higher cognitive activities; both Parkinson's disease and schizophrenia involve a disturbance of dopamine systems.

GABA is an inhibitory neurotransmitter involved in anxiety and epilepsy. *Glutamate* is the most common excitatory neurotransmitter; it is involved in learning and memory and, in excess, may cause neuronal death. *Endorphins* are peptide neurotransmitters that affect pain pathways. Nitric oxide and carbon monoxide are gases that function as neurotransmitters.

The Endocrine System: Coordinating the Internal World

Like nervous system cells, those of the *endocrine system* communicate by releasing a chemical that signals to other cells. However, the chemicals released by endocrine organs, or *glands*, are called *hormones* and are carried by the bloodstream to remote target organs. The target organs often produce a coordinated response to hormonal stimulation. One of these responses is the *fight-or-flight syndrome*, which is set off by adrenal hormones that prepare for action in times of stress. Hormones also modulate the development of the brain, contributing to sex differences in the brain and behavior. Negative feedback systems are involved in the control of most endocrine functions. The brain is the main controller: Through the hypothalamus, it controls the pituitary gland, which in turn controls endocrine organs in the body. The brain is also a target organ for most endocrine secretions.

The Immune System: Defending the Body

The *immune system* serves both as a sensory system that monitors the internal state of the body and as a protective system for detecting, and then destroying, unwanted cells and toxic substances that may invade the body. *Autoimmune disorders* result when cells of the immune system attack normal cells of the body. There are important reciprocal relationships among the immune system, nervous system, and endocrine system.

Sensation

4

100

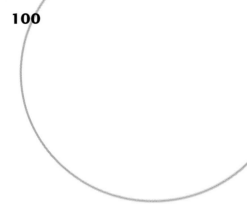

Years ago, Fred Aryee lost his right arm below the elbow in a boating accident, yet he still "feels" his missing arm and hand (Shreeve, 1993). Like Aryee, many people who have lost an arm or a leg continue to experience itching and other sensations from a "phantom limb." When asked to "move" it, they can feel it move, and some people feel intense pain when their missing hand spontaneously tightens into a fist, digging nonexistent fingernails into a phantom palm. Worse, they may be unable to "open" their hand to relieve the pain. In an effort to help these people, scientists have seated them at a table in front of a mirror, then angled the mirror to create the illusion that their amputated arm and hand have been restored. When these patients moved their real hand while looking in the mirror, they not only "felt" movement occurring in their phantom hand but could now "unclench" their phantom fist and stop their excruciating pain (Ramachandran & Rogers-Ramachandran, 2000). This clever strategy arose from research on how vision interacts with the sense of touch. To experience this interaction yourself, sit across a table from someone, and ask that person to stroke the tabletop while stroking your knee under the table in exactly the same way, in exactly the same direction. If you watch the person's hand stroking the table, you will soon experience the touch sensations coming from the table, not your knee! If the person's two hands do not move in synch, however, the illusion will not occur.

This illusion illustrates several points about our senses. It shows, first, that the streams of information coming from different senses can interact. Second, it reveals that experience can change the sensations we receive. Third, and most important, the illusion suggests that "reality" differs from person to person. This last point sounds silly if you assume that there is an "objective reality" that is the same for everyone. After all, the seat you sit on and the book you are reading are solid objects. You can see and feel them with your senses, so they must look and feel the same to you as they would to anyone else. But sensory psychologists tell us that reality is not that simple—that the senses do not reflect an objective reality. Just as people can feel a hand that is not objectively "there," the senses of each individual actively shape information about the outside world to create a *personal reality*. The sensory experiences of different species—and individual humans—vary. You do not see the same world a fly sees, people from California may not hear music quite the same way as do people from Singapore, and different people experience color differently.

In order to understand how sensory systems create reality, consider some basic information about the senses. A **sense** is a system that translates information from outside the nervous system into neural activity. For example, vision is the system through which the eyes convert light into neural activity. This neural activity tells the brain something about the source of the light (e.g., that it is bright) or about objects from which the light is reflected (e.g., that there is a round, red object out there). These messages from the senses are called **sensations**. Because they provide the link between the self and the world outside the brain, sensations help shape many of the behaviors and mental processes studied by psychologists.

Traditionally, psychologists have distinguished between *sensation*—the initial message from the senses—and *perception*, the process through which messages from the senses are given meaning. They point out, for example, that you do not actually sense a cat lying on the sofa; you sense shapes and colors—visual sensations. You use your knowledge of the world to interpret, or perceive, these sensations as a cat. However, it is impossible to draw a clear line between sensation and perception. This is partly because the process of interpreting sensations begins in the sense organs themselves. For example, a frog's eye immediately interprets any small black object as "fly!"—thus enabling the frog to attack the fly with its tongue without waiting for its brain to process the sensory information (Lettvin et al., 1959).

This chapter covers the first steps of the sensation-perception process; the chapter on perception deals with the later phases. Together, these chapters illustrate how we human beings, with our sense organs and brains, create our own realities. In

---

ClassPrep PPT 2: Why Is It Important to Learn About Our Senses?

Personal Learning Activities: 4.1, 4.2, and 4.3

IRM In Your Own Words 4.2: Which Sense Would You Give Up?

IRM Handout 4.3: Review of Sensory Modalities

OBJ 4.1: Define sense and sensation. Be able to explain the differences between sensation and perception.

Test Items 4.1–4.3

ClassPrep PPT 3: Important Terms

sense A system that translates information from outside the nervous system into neural activity.

sensations Messages from the senses that make up the raw information that affects many kinds of behavior and mental processes.

accessory structures Structures, such as the lens of the eye, that modify a stimulus.

transduction The process of converting incoming energy into neural activity through receptors.

sensory receptors Specialized cells that detect certain forms of energy.

adaptation The process through which responsiveness to an unchanging stimulus decreases over time.

this chapter we explore how sensations are produced, received, and acted upon. First, we consider what sensations are and how they inform us about the world. Then we examine the physical and psychological mechanisms involved in the auditory, visual, and chemical senses. And finally, we turn to a discussion of the somatic senses, which enable us to feel things, to experience temperature and pain, and to know where our body parts are in relation to one another. Together, these senses play a critical role in our ability as humans to adapt to and survive in our environment.

Sensory Systems

The senses gather information about the world by detecting various forms of energy, such as sound, light, heat, and physical pressure. Specifically, the eyes detect light energy, the ears detect the energy of sound, and the skin detects the energy of heat and pressure. Humans depend primarily on vision, hearing, and the skin senses to gain information about the world; they depend less than other animals on smell and taste. To your brain, "the world" also includes the rest of your body, and there are sensory systems that provide information about the location and position of your body parts.

All of these senses must detect stimuli, encode them into neural activity, and transfer this coded information to the brain. Figure 4.1 illustrates these basic steps in sensation. At each step, sensory information is "processed" in some way: The information that arrives at one point in the system is not the same as the information that goes to the next step.

In some sensory systems, the first step in sensation involves **accessory structures,** which modify the energy created by something in the environment—such as a person talking or a flashing sign (Step 1 in Figure 4.1). The outer part of the ear is an accessory structure that collects sound; the lens of the eye is an accessory structure that changes incoming light by focusing it.

The second step in sensation is **transduction,** which is the process of converting incoming energy into neural activity (Step 2 in Figure 4.1). Just as a radio receives energy and transduces it into sounds, the ears receive sound energy and transduce it into neural activity that people recognize as voices, music, and other auditory experiences. Transduction takes place at structures called **sensory receptors,** specialized cells that detect certain forms of energy. Sensory receptors are somewhat like the neurons that we describe in the chapter on biological aspects of psychology; they respond to incoming energy by firing an action potential and releasing neurotransmitters that send a signal to neighboring cells. (However, some sensory receptors do not have axons and dendrites, as neurons do.) Sensory receptors respond best to changes in energy. A constant level of stimulation usually produces **adaptation,** a process through which responsiveness to an unchanging stimulus decreases over time. This is why the touch sensations you get from items such as glasses or a wristwatch disappear shortly after you have put them on.

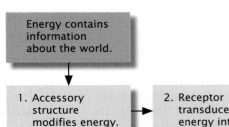

figure 4.1

Elements of a Sensory System

Objects in the world generate energy that is focused by accessory structures and detected by sensory receptors, which convert the energy into neural signals. The signals are then relayed through parts of the brain, which process them into perceptual experiences.

Next, sensory nerves carry the output from receptors to the central nervous system, including the brain (Step 3 in Figure 4.1). For all the senses except smell, the information is taken first to the thalamus (Step 4), which relays it to the sensory portion of the cerebral cortex (Step 5). It is in the sensory cortex that the most complex processing occurs.

The Problem of Coding

When receptors transduce energy, they must somehow code the physical properties of the stimulus into patterns of neural activity that, when analyzed by the brain, allow you to make sense of the stimulus—to determine, for example, whether you are looking at a cat, a dog, or a person. For each psychological dimension of a sensation, such as the brightness or color of light, there must be a corresponding physical dimension coded by sensory receptors.

As a way of thinking about the problem of coding, imagine that for your birthday you receive a Pet Brain. You are told that your Pet Brain is alive, but it does not respond when you open the box and talk to it. You remove it from the box and show it a hot-fudge sundae; no response. You show it pictures of other attractive brains; still no response. You are about to deposit your Pet Brain in the trash when you suddenly realize that the two of you are probably not talking the same language. As described in the chapter on biological aspects of psychology, the brain usually receives information from sensory neurons and responds via motor neurons. So if you want to communicate with your Pet Brain, you will have to stimulate its sensory nerves (so that you can send it messages) and record signals from its motor nerves (so that you can read its responses).

After having this brilliant insight and setting up an electric stimulator and recorder, you are faced with an awesome problem. How do you describe a hot-fudge sundae to sensory nerves so that they will pass on the correct information to the brain? This is the problem of coding. **Coding** is the translation of the physical properties of a stimulus into a pattern of neural activity that specifically identifies those physical properties.

If you want the brain to visualize the sundae, you should stimulate the optic nerve (the nerve from the eye to the brain) rather than the auditory nerve (the nerve from the ear to the brain). This idea is based on the **doctrine of specific nerve energies:** Stimulation of a particular sensory nerve provides codes for that one sense, no matter how the stimulation takes place. For example, if you apply gentle pressure to your eyeball, you will produce activity in the optic nerve and sense little spots of light.

TRY THIS

Having chosen the optic nerve to convey visual information, you must next develop a code for the specific attributes of the sundae: the soft white curves of the vanilla ice cream, the dark richness of the chocolate, the bright red roundness of the cherry on top. These dimensions must be coded in the language of neural activity—that is, in the firing of action potentials.

Some attributes of a stimulus are coded relatively simply. For example, a bright light will cause some neurons in the visual system to fire faster than will a dim light. This is a **temporal code,** because it involves changes in the *timing* of firing. Temporal codes can be more complex as well; for example, a burst of firing followed by a slower firing rate means something different than a steady rate. The other basic type of code is a **spatial code,** in which the *location* of firing neurons relative to their neighbors provides information about the stimulus. For example, neurons that carry sensations from the fingers travel close to those carrying information from the arms, but far from those carrying information from the feet. Information can be re-coded at several relay points as it makes its way through the brain.

> **coding** Translating the physical properties of a stimulus into a pattern of neural activity that specifically identifies those properties.
> **doctrine of specific nerve energies** The discovery that stimulation of a particular sensory nerve provides codes for that sense, no matter how the stimulation takes place.
> **temporal codes** Coding attributes of a stimulus in terms of changes in the timing of neural firing.
> **spatial codes** Coding attributes of a stimulus in terms of the location of firing neurons relative to their neighbors.

If everything goes as planned in your coding system, your Pet Brain will know what a sundae looks like. In short, the problem of coding is solved by means of sensory systems, which allow the brain to receive detailed, accurate, and useful information about stimuli in its environment. Later, we discuss how this remarkable feat is accomplished.

What Is It?   In the split second before you recognized this stimulus as a hot-fudge sundae, sensory neurons in your visual system detected the light reflected off this page and transduced it into a neural code that your brain could interpret. This amazing process of coding occurs so quickly and efficiently in all our senses that we are seldom aware of it.

 LINKAGES (a link to Biological Aspects of Psychology)

OBJ 4.6: Describe the six characteristics of sensory representation for vision, hearing, and the skin senses. Define topographical representation and primary cortex.

Test Items 4.21–4.23

Sensation and Biological Aspects of Psychology

As sensory systems transfer information to the brain, they also organize that information. This organized information is called a *representation.* If you have read the chapter on biological aspects of psychology, you are already familiar with some characteristics of sensory representations. In humans, representations of vision, hearing, and the skin senses in the cerebral cortex share the following features:

1. The information from each of these senses reaches the cortex via the thalamus. (Figure 3.14 shows where these areas of the brain are.)

2. The representation of the sensory world in the cortex is *contralateral,* or opposite, to the part of the world being sensed. For example, the left side of the visual cortex "sees" the right side of the world, whereas the right side of that cortex "sees" the left side of the world. This happens because nerve fibers from each side of the body cross on their way to the thalamus. Why they cross is still a mystery.

3. The cortex contains maps, or *topographical representations,* of each sense. Accordingly, features that are next to each other in the world stimulate neurons that are next to each other in the brain. For example, two notes that are similar in pitch activate neighboring neurons in the auditory cortex, and the neurons that respond to sensations in the elbow and in the forearm are relatively close to one another in the somatosensory cortex. There are multiple maps representing each sense, but the area that receives input directly from the thalamus is called the *primary cortex* for that sense.

4. The density of nerve fibers in any part of a sense organ determines its representation in the cortex. For example, the skin on a fingertip, which has a higher density of receptors for touch than the skin on the back, has a larger area of cortex representing it than does the back.

5. Each region of primary sensory cortex is divided into columns of cells that have similar properties. For example, some columns of cells in the visual cortex respond most to diagonal lines.

6. For each of the senses, regions of cortex other than the primary areas do additional processing of sensory information. As described in the chapter on biological aspects of psychology, these areas of *association cortex* may contain representations of more than one sense, thus setting the stage for the interaction of sensory information described at the beginning of this chapter.

In summary, sensory systems convert some form of energy into neural activity, as described in Figure 4.1. Often the energy is first modified by accessory structures; then a sensory receptor converts the energy to neural activity. The pattern of neural activity encodes physical properties of the energy. The codes are modified as the information is transferred to the brain and processed further. In the remainder of this chapter we describe these processes in specific sensory systems.

LSV: Hearing

Hearing

In 1969, when Neil Armstrong became the first human to step onto the moon, millions of people back on earth heard his radio transmission: "That's one small step for a man, one giant leap for mankind." But if Armstrong had taken off his space helmet and shouted, "Whoo-ee! I can moonwalk!" another astronaut, a foot away, would not have heard him. Why? Because Armstrong would have been speaking into airless, empty space. **Sound** is a repetitive fluctuation in the pressure of a medium, such as air. In a place like the moon, which has almost no atmospheric medium, sound cannot exist.

OBJ 4.7: Define sound. Describe the physical characteristics of sound, including amplitude, wave length, and frequency.

Test Items 4.24–4.28

IRM Handout 4.3: Review of Sensory Modalities

Sound

Sattler/Shabatay reader, 2/e: Wright, "Deafness: An Autobiography"

Vibrations of an object produce the fluctuations in pressure that constitute sound. Each time the object moves outward, it increases the pressure in the medium around it. As the object moves back, the pressure drops. In speech, for example, the vibrating object is the vocal cord, and the medium is air. When you speak, your vocal cords vibrate, producing fluctuations in air pressure that spread as waves. A *wave* is a repetitive variation in pressure that spreads out in three dimensions. The wave can move great distances, but the air itself barely moves. Imagine a jam-packed line of people waiting to get into a rock concert. If someone at the rear of the line shoves the next person, a wave of people jostling against people may spread all the way to the front of the line, but the person who shoved first is still no closer to getting into the theater.

ClassPrep PPT 7: *Figure 4.2:* Sound Waves and Waveforms

ClassPrep PPT 8: Psychological Dimensions of Sound

Physical Characteristics of Sound   Sound is represented graphically by waveforms like those in Figure 4.2. A *waveform* represents a wave in two-dimensions, but remember that waves actually move through the air in all directions.

Three characteristics of the waveform are important in understanding sounds. First, the difference in air pressure from the baseline to the peak of the wave is the **amplitude** of the sound, or its intensity. Second, the distance from one peak to the next is called the **wavelength.** Third, a sound's **frequency** is the number of complete waveforms, or cycles, that pass by a given point in space every second. Frequency is described in a unit called *hertz*, abbreviated *Hz* (for Heinrich Hertz, a nineteenth-century physicist). One cycle per second is 1 hertz. Because the speed of sound is constant in a given medium, wavelength and frequency are related: The longer the wavelength, the lower the frequency; the shorter the wavelength, the higher the frequency. Most sounds are mixtures of many different frequencies and amplitudes. In contrast, a pure tone is made up of only one frequency and can be represented, by what is known as a *sine wave* (Figure 4.2 shows such sine waves).

sound A repetitive fluctuation in the pressure of a medium like air.

amplitude The difference between the peak and the baseline of a waveform.

wavelength The distance from one peak to the next in a waveform.

frequency The number of complete waveforms, or cycles, that pass by a given point in space every second.

loudness A psychological dimension of sound determined by the amplitude of a sound wave.

pitch How high or low a tone sounds.

timbre The mixture of frequencies and amplitudes that make up the quality of sound.

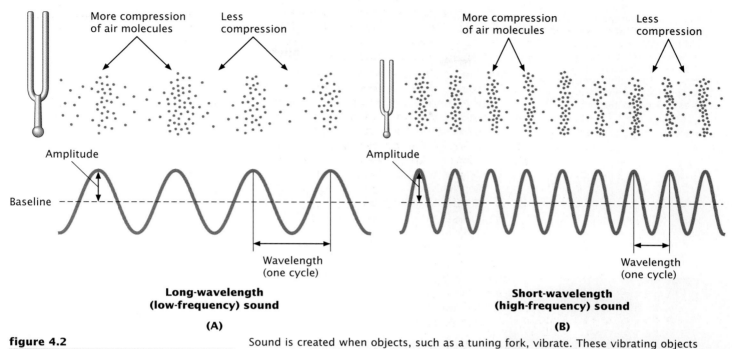

More compression of air molecules   Less compression

Amplitude

Baseline

Wavelength (one cycle)

Long-wavelength (low-frequency) sound

(A)

More compression of air molecules   Less compression

Amplitude

Wavelength (one cycle)

Short-wavelength (high-frequency) sound

(B)

figure 4.2

Sound Waves and Waveforms

Sound is created when objects, such as a tuning fork, vibrate. These vibrating objects create alternating regions of greater and lesser compression of air molecules, which can be represented as a waveform. The point of greatest compression is the peak of the graph. The lowest point, or trough, is where compression is least.

OBJ. 4.8: Describe the psychological characteristics of sound, including loudness, pitch, and timbre. Discuss the relationship among pitch, frequency, and wavelength, as well as that between amplitude and loudness.

Test Items 4.29–4.34

Psychological Dimensions of Sound

The amplitude and frequency of sound waves determine the sounds that you hear. These physical characteristics of the waves produce the psychological dimensions of sound known as *loudness*, *pitch*, and *timbre*.

Loudness is determined by the amplitude of the sound wave; waves with greater amplitude produce sensations of louder sounds. Loudness is described in units called *decibels*, abbreviated *dB*. By definition, 0 decibels is the minimal detectable sound for normal hearing. Table 4.1 gives examples of the loudness of some common sounds.

Pitch, or how high or low a tone sounds, depends on the frequency of sound waves. High-frequency waves are sensed as sounds of high pitch. The highest note on a piano has a frequency of about 4,000 hertz; the lowest note has a frequency of about 50 hertz. Humans can hear sounds ranging from about 20 hertz to about 20,000 hertz. Almost everyone experiences pitch as a relative dimension; that is, they can tell whether one note is higher than, lower than, or equal to another note. However, some people have *perfect pitch,* which means they can identify specific frequencies and the notes they represent. They can say, for example, that a 262-hertz tone is middle C. It was once thought that perfect pitch occurs only in gifted people; but we now know that children who are taught before the age of six can learn that specific frequencies are particular notes (Takeuchi & Hulse, 1993).

Timbre (pronounced "tam-ber") is the quality of sound; it is determined by complex wave patterns that are added onto the lowest, or *fundamental*, frequency of a sound. The extra waves allow you to tell, for example, the difference between a note played on a flute and the same note played on a clarinet.

Noise Eliminators   Complex sound, including noise, can be analyzed into its component, simple sine waves by means of a mathematical process called *Fourier analysis*. This technique can be used to eliminate engine and wind noise in airplanes, trains, and other moving vehicles. After the waveforms are analyzed, a sound synthesizer produces the opposite waveforms. The opposing waves cancel each other out, and the amazing result is silence. Several versions of these noise eliminators are now sold to the public, and related devices are being developed to treat chronic tinnitus, or "ringing in the ear."

Sound intensity varies across an extremely wide range. A barely audible sound is, by definition, 0 decibels. Every increase of 20 decibels reflects a tenfold increase in the amplitude of sound waves. So the 40-decibel sounds of an office are actually 10 times as intense as a 20-decibel whisper, and traffic noise of 100 decibels is 10,000 times as intense as that whisper.

ClassPrep PPT 9: *Table 4.1:* Intensity of Sound Sources

OBJ 4.9: Name and describe the accessory structures of the ear.

Test Items 4.35–4.38

table 4.1
Intensity of Sound Sources

Source	Sound Level (dB)
Spacecraft launch (from 45 m)	180
Loudest rock band on record	160
Pain threshold (approximate)	140
Large jet motor (at 22 m)	120
Loudest human shout on record	111
Heavy auto traffic	100
Conversation (at about 1 m)	60
Quiet office	40
Soft whisper	20
Threshold of hearing	0

IRM Activity 4.4: The Pinna's Role in Hearing

An Accessory Structure Some animals, like Annie here, have a large pinna that can be rotated to help localize the source of a sound.

OBJ 4.10: Describe the role of the cochlea, basilar membrane, hair cells, and auditory nerve in the process of auditory transduction. Name and describe the types of deafness.

---

tympanic membrane A membrane in the middle ear that generates vibrations that match the sound waves striking it.

cochlea A fluid-filled spiral structure in the ear in which auditory transduction occurs.

basilar membrane The floor of the fluid-filled duct that runs through the cochlea.

auditory nerve The bundle of axons that carries stimuli from the hair cells of the cochlea to the brain.

The Ear

The human ear converts sound energy into neural activity through a series of accessory structures and transduction mechanisms.

Auditory Accessory Structures   Sound waves are collected in the outer ear, beginning with the *pinna,* the crumpled part of the ear visible on the side of the head. The pinna funnels sound down through the ear canal (see Figure 4.3). At the end of the ear canal, the sound waves reach the middle ear, where they strike a tightly stretched membrane known as the *eardrum,* or **tympanic membrane.** The sound waves set up matching vibrations in the tympanic membrane.

Next, the vibrations of the tympanic membrane are passed on by a chain of three tiny bones: the *malleus,* or *hammer;* the *incus,* or *anvil;* and the *stapes* (pronounced "STAY-peez"), or *stirrup* (see Figure 4.3). These bones amplify the changes in pressure produced by the original sound waves, by focusing the vibrations of the tympanic membrane onto a smaller membrane, the *oval window.*

IRM Activity 4.5: The Basilar Membrane's Traveling Wave in Audition

Auditory Transduction   When sound vibrations pass through the oval window, they enter the inner ear, reaching the **cochlea** (pronounced "COCK-lee-ah"), the structure in which transduction occurs. The cochlea is wrapped into a coiled spiral. (*Cochlea* is derived from the Greek word for "snail.") If you unwrapped the spiral, you would see that a fluid-filled tube runs down its length. The **basilar membrane** forms the floor of this long tube (see Figure 4.4). Whenever a sound wave passes through the fluid in the tube, it moves the basilar membrane, and this movement deforms *hair cells* of the *organ of Corti,* a group of cells that rests on the membrane. These hair cells connect with fibers from the **auditory nerve,** a bundle of axons that goes into the brain. Mechanical deformation of the hair cells stimulates the auditory nerve, changing the electrical activity of some of its neurons and thus sending a coded signal to the brain about the amplitude and frequency of sound waves, which you sense as loudness and pitch.

Deafness   Problems with the three tiny bones of the middle ear are one cause of deafness. Sometimes the bones fuse together, preventing accurate reproduction of vibrations. This condition is called *conduction deafness.* It may be treated by breaking the bones apart or by replacing the natural bones with plastic ones; a hearing aid that amplifies the input can also be helpful.

If the auditory nerve or, more commonly, the hair cells are damaged, *nerve deafness* results. Hair cell damage occurs gradually with age, but it can also be

figure 4.3

Structures of the Ear

The outer ear (pinna and ear canal) channels sounds into the middle ear, where the vibrations of the tympanic membrane are amplified by the delicate bones that stimulate the cochlea. In the cochlea in the inner ear, the vibrations are transduced into changes in neural activity, which are sent along the auditory nerve to the brain.

ClassPrep PPT 10, OHT: *Figure 4.3:* Structures of the Ear

Video Segments & Stills: The Ear: The Cochlea (coiled); The Ear: The Cochlea (uncoiled)

Test Items 4.39–4.48

IRM Discussion & Activity 4.6: Deafness

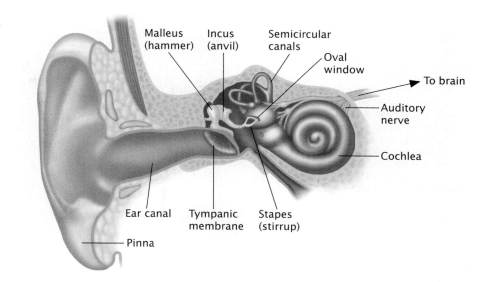

caused by loud noise, such as that created by jet engines, noisy equipment, and intense rock music (Goldstein, 1999; see Figure 4.5). For example, some rock musicians from the 1970s, including Stephen Stills and Pete Townshend, have become partially deaf as a result of their many years of performing extremely loud music (Ackerman, 1995). In the United States and other industrialized countries, people born after World War II are experiencing hearing loss at a younger age than did their forebears, possibly because noise pollution has increased during the past fifty years (Levine, 1999).

Although hair cells can regenerate in chickens (who seldom listen to rock music), such regeneration was long believed to be impossible in mammals (Salvi et al., 1998). However, recent evidence that mammals can regenerate a related kind of inner-ear hair cell has fueled optimism about finding a way to stimulate regeneration of human auditory hair cells (Malgrange et al., 1999). The feat might be accomplished by treating damaged areas with growth factors similar to those used to repair damaged brain cells (see the chapter on biological aspects of psychology). Hair cell regeneration could revolutionize the treatment of nerve deafness, because this form of deafness cannot be overcome by conventional hearing aids. Meanwhile, scientists have developed an artificial cochlea for use as *cochlear implants* that can stimulate the auditory nerve in cases involving congenital nerve deafness (Lee et al., 2001). However, implanting these devices in deaf children is controversial. Some members of the deaf community argue that cochlear implants prevent children from fully entering the deaf culture while at the same time failing to adequately repair the children's hearing deficit (Clay, 1997).

ClassPrep PPT 11, OHT: *Figure 4.4:* The Cochlea

figure 4.4

The Cochlea

This drawing shows how vibrations of the stapes, or stirrup, set up vibrations in the fluid inside the cochlea. The coils of the cochlea are unfolded in this illustration to show the path of the fluid waves along the basilar membrane. Movements of the basilar membrane stimulate the hair cells of the organ of Corti, which transduce the vibrations into changes in neural firing patterns.

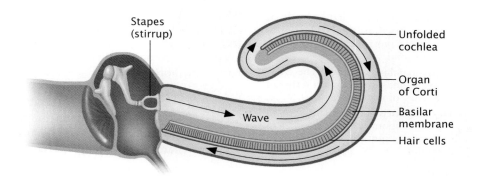

figure 4.5

Effects of Loud Sounds

High-intensity sounds can actually destroy the hair cells of the inner ear. Part A shows the organ of Corti of a normal guinea pig. Part B shows the damage caused by exposure to 24 hours of 2,000-hertz sound at 120 decibels. Generally, any sound loud enough to produce tinnitus (ringing in the ears) causes some damage. In humans, small amounts of damage can accumulate over time to produce a significant hearing loss by middle age—as many middle-aged rock musicians can attest.

ClassPrep PPT 12: *Figure 4.5:* Effects of Loud Sounds

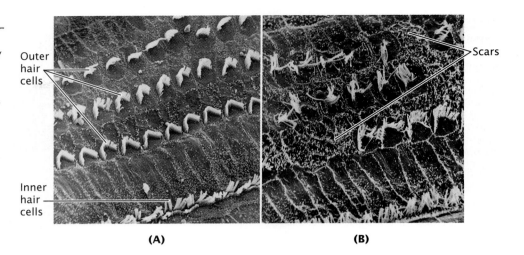

(A)   (B)

Coding Intensity and Frequency

People can hear an incredibly wide range of sound intensities. The faintest sound that can be heard moves the hair cells less than the diameter of a single hydrogen atom (Hudspeth, 1997). Sounds more than a trillion times more intense can also be heard. Between these extremes, the auditory system codes intensity in a straightforward way: The more intense the sound, the more rapid the firing of a given neuron.

Recall that the pitch of a sound depends on its frequency. How do people tell the differences among frequencies? Differences in frequency appear to be coded in two ways, which are described by place theory and frequency-matching theory.

OBJ 4.11: Describe the process of coding auditory information. Discuss the relationship between place theory and the frequency-matching theory, or volley theory, in frequency coding.

Test Items 4.49–4.55

ClassPrep PPT 13: How Do We Code the Pitch of Sound?

Place Theory

Georg von Bekesy performed some pioneering experiments in the 1930s and 1940s to figure out how frequency is coded (von Bekesy, 1960). Studying human cadavers, he made a hole in the cochlear wall and observed the basilar membrane. He then presented sounds of different frequencies by vibrating a rubber membrane that was installed in place of the oval window. With sensitive optical instruments, von Bekesy observed ripples of waves moving down the basilar membrane. He noticed that the outline of the waves, called the *envelope,* grows and reaches a peak; then it quickly tapers off to smaller and smaller fluctuations, much like an ocean wave that crests and then dissolves.

As shown in Figure 4.6, the critical feature of this wave is that the place on the basilar membrane where the envelope peaks depends on the frequency of the sound. High-frequency sounds produce a wave that peaks soon after it starts down the basilar membrane. Lower-frequency sounds produce a wave that peaks farther along the basilar membrane, farther from the oval window.

ClassPrep PPT 14: How Do We Code the Pitch of Sound? (cont.)

How does the location of the peak affect the coding of frequency? According to **place theory,** also called *traveling wave theory,* the greatest response by hair cells occurs at the peak of the wave. Because the location of the peak varies with the frequency of the sound, it follows that hair cells at a particular place on the basilar membrane respond most to a particular frequency of sound, called a *characteristic frequency.* In other words, place theory describes a *spatial,* or place-related, code for frequency. One important result of this arrangement is that if extended exposure to a very loud sound of a particular frequency destroys hair cells at one spot on the basilar membrane, the ability to hear sounds of that frequency is lost as well.

place theory   A theory that hair cells at a particular place on the basilar membrane respond most to a particular frequency of sound.

frequency-matching theory The view that some sounds are coded in terms of the frequency of neural firing.

primary auditory cortex The area in the brain's temporal lobe that is first to receive information about sounds from the thalamus.

Frequency-Matching Theory

Although place theory accounts for a great deal of data on hearing, it cannot explain the coding of very low frequencies, such as that of a deep bass note, because there are no auditory nerve fibers that have very low characteristic frequencies. Because humans can hear frequencies as low as

figure 4.6

Movements of the Basilar Membrane
As vibrations of the cochlear fluid spread along the basilar membrane, the membrane is bent and then recovers. As shown in these three examples, the point at which the bending of the basilar membrane reaches a maximum is different for each sound frequency. According to place theory, these are the locations at which the hair cells receive the greatest stimulation.

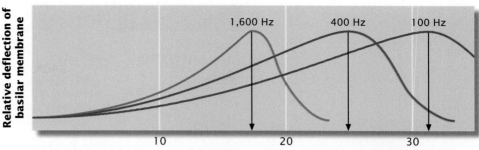

Distance along basilar membrane from oval window in millimeters

20 hertz, however, the frequencies must be coded somehow. The answer is provided by **frequency-matching theory,** which is based on the fact that the firing rate of a neuron in the auditory nerve matches the frequency of a sound wave. Frequency matching provides a *temporal,* or timing-related, code for frequency. For example, one neuron might fire at every peak of a wave. So a sound of 20 hertz could be coded by a neuron that fires 20 times per second.

Frequency matching by individual neurons would apply only up to about 1,000 hertz, however, because no neuron can fire faster than 1,000 times per second. However, frequency matching can code frequencies somewhat above 1,000 hertz because these moderately higher frequencies are matched not by the firing of a single neuron but by the summed activity of a group of neurons. Some neurons in the group might fire, for example, at every other wave peak, others at every fifth peak, and so on, producing a *volley* of firing at a combined frequency higher than any could manage alone. Accordingly, frequency-matching theory is sometimes called the *volley theory* of frequency coding.

In summary, the nervous system uses more than one way to code the range of audible frequencies. The lowest sound frequencies are coded by frequency matching, whereby the frequency is matched by the firing rate of auditory nerve fibers. Low to moderate frequencies are coded by both frequency matching and the place on the basilar membrane where the wave peaks. High frequencies are coded exclusively by the place where the wave peaks.

Auditory Pathways and Representations

OBJ 4.12: Describe how information is relayed to the primary auditory cortex, how the cortex codes the frequency and location of sounds, and why this coding is important for language.

Test Items 4.56–4.58

ClassPrep PPT 15: Auditory Pathways

Before sounds can be heard, the information coded in the activity of auditory nerve fibers must be conveyed to the brain and processed further. (For a review of how changes in air pressure become signals in the brain that are perceived as sounds, see "In Review: Hearing.") The auditory nerve, the bundle of axons that conveys this information, crosses the brain's midline and reaches the thalamus. From the thalamus, the information is relayed to the **primary auditory cortex.** As discussed in the chapter on biological aspects of psychology, this is an area located in the temporal lobe of the cerebral cortex, close to areas of the brain involved in language perception and production (see Figure 3.16).

Various aspects of sound are processed separately as the auditory nerve stimulates the auditory cortex. For example, information about the source of a sound and information about the sound's frequency components are processed in different regions of the cortex (Rauschecker, 1997). Neighboring cells in the cortex have similar preferred frequencies and are arranged so that they create at least three separate maps of sound frequencies (Kaas & Hackett, 2000). In the auditory nerve, too, each neuron has a characteristic frequency to which it best responds, though each also responds to some extent to a range of frequencies. The auditory cortex must examine the pattern of activity of a number of neurons in order to determine the

in review	Hearing	
Aspect of Sensory System	**Elements**	**Key Characteristics**
Energy	Sound—pressure fluctuations of air produced by vibrations	The amplitude, frequency, and complexity of sound waves determine the loudness, pitch, and timbre of sounds.
Accessory structures	Ear—pinna, tympanic membrane, malleus, incus, stapes, oval window, basilar membrane	Changes in pressure produced by the original wave are amplified.
Transduction mechanism	Hair cells of the organ of Corti	Frequencies are coded by the location of the hair cells receiving the greatest stimulation (place theory) and by the firing rate of neurons (frequency-matching theory).
Pathways and representations	Auditory nerve to thalamus to primary auditory cortex	Neighboring cells in the auditory cortex have similar preferred frequencies, thus providing a map of sound frequencies

Shaping the Brain The primary auditory cortex is larger in trained musicians than in people whose jobs are less focused on fine gradations of sound. How much larger this area becomes is correlated with how long the musicians have studied their art. This finding reminds us that, as described in the chapter on biological aspects of psychology, the brain can literally be shaped by experience and other environmental factors (Pantev et al., 1998).

frequency of a sound. Certain parts of the auditory cortex process certain types of sounds. One part, for example, specializes in responding to information coming from human voices (Belin et al., 2000).

Sensing the pitch of sound is not always as simple as you might expect, because most sounds are mixtures of frequencies. The mixtures that make up musical chords and voices, for example, can produce sounds of ambiguous pitch. As a result, different individuals may perceive the "same" sound as different pitches (Patel & Balaban, 2001). In fact, a given sequence of chords can sound like an ascending scale to one person and a descending scale to another. Pitch-recognition abilities are influenced by genetics (Drayna et al., 2001), but cultural factors are partly responsible for the way in which pitch is sensed. For instance, people in the United States tend to hear *ambiguous scales* as progressing in directions that are opposite to the way they are heard by people from Canada and England (Dawe, Platt, & Welsh, 1998). This cross-cultural difference appears to be a reliable one, though researchers do not yet know exactly why it occurs.

Analysis of the location of sound sources is based partly on the very slight difference in when a sound arrives at each of your two ears (it reaches the closer ear slightly earlier) and on the difference in its intensity at each ear (sounds that are closer to one ear are slightly louder in that ear). As a result, you can determine where a voice or other sound is coming from even when you can't see its source. The brain determines the location of the sound source by analyzing the activities of groups of neurons that, individually, signal only a rough approximation of the location (Fitzpatrick, Olsen, & Suga, 1998). The combined firing frequencies of these many neurons in the auditory cortex thus create a *temporal* "Morse code" that describes where a sound is coming from (Middlebrooks et al., 1994; Wright & Fitzgerald, 2001).

Hearing and Language   Language is the auditory stimulation that humans depend upon most, and scientists are learning how the cortex processes

Processing Language As this student and teacher communicate using American Sign Language, the visual information they receive from each other's hand movements is processed by the same areas of their brains that allow hearing people to understand spoken language. Studies show that the primary auditory cortex is also activated when you watch someone speak (but not when the person makes other facial movements). This is the biological basis for the lip reading that helps you to hear what people say (Calvert et al., 1997).

sound signals that we recognize as words. We already know, for example, that temporal processing is particularly important in distinguishing some consonants; in fact, research suggests that children with language learning problems often have deficits in the temporal processing of sounds in general (Merzenich et al., 1996). Fortunately, these children can be trained to more efficiently process the temporal aspects of sounds. Such training dramatically improves their language acquisition (Tallal et al., 1996). It is interesting to note that the brain regions involved in processing language are the same whether the language comes to hearing individuals in the form of sounds or to deaf individuals in the form of sign language (Neville et al., 1998).

Soaring eagles have the incredible ability to see a mouse move in the grass from a mile away. Cats have special "reflectors" at the back of their eyes that help them to see even in very dim light. Through natural selection, over eons of time, each species has developed a visual system uniquely adapted to its way of life. The human visual system is also adapted to do many things well: It combines great sensitivity and great sharpness, enabling people to see objects near and far, during the day and at night. Our night vision is not as acute as that of some animals, but our color vision is excellent. This is not a bad tradeoff; being able to appreciate a sunset's splendor seems worth an occasional stumble in the dark. In this section, we consider the human visual sense and how it responds to light.

OBJ 4.13: Define visible light.

Test Items 4.59–4.61

OBJ 4.14: Define light intensity and wavelength. Describe how both are related to what you sense.

Test Items 4.62–4.64

Light

Light is a form of energy known as *electromagnetic radiation*. Most electromagnetic radiation—including x-rays, radio waves, television signals, and radar—passes through space undetected by the human eye. **Visible light** is electromagnetic radiation that has a wavelength from just under 400 nanometers to about 750 nanometers (a *nanometer* is one-billionth of a meter; see Figure 4.7). Unlike sound, light does not need a medium to pass through. So, even on the airless moon, astronauts can see one another, even if they can't hear one another without radios. Light waves

visible light Electromagnetic radiation that has a wavelength of about 400 nanometers to about 750 nanometers.

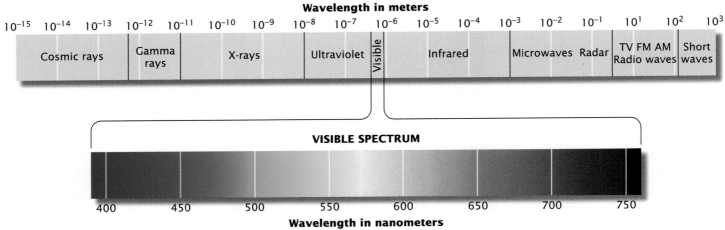

figure 4.7

The Spectrum of Electromagnetic Energy

OBJ 4.15: Define and describe the accessory structures of the eye, including the cornea, iris, pupil, and lens.

OBJ 4.16: Define retina and explain how accommodation affects the image on the retina.

The range of wavelengths that the human eye can see as visible light is very limited—encompassing a band of only about 370 nanometers within the overall spectrum of electromagnetic energy. To detect energy outside this range, people rely on electronic instruments such as radios, TV sets, radar, and infrared night-vision scopes that can "see" this energy, just as the eye sees visible light.

Test Items 4.65–4.69

are like particles that pass through space, but they vibrate with a certain wavelength. Thus, light has some properties of waves and some properties of particles, and it is correct to refer to light as either *light waves* or *light rays*.

Sensations of light depend on two physical dimensions of light waves: intensity and wavelength. **Light intensity** refers to how much energy the light contains; it determines the brightness of light, much as the amplitude of sound waves determines the loudness of sound. What color you sense depends mainly on **light wavelength**. At a given intensity, different wavelengths produce sensations of different colors, much as different sound frequencies produce sensations of different pitch. For instance, 440-nanometer light appears violet blue, and 700-nanometer light appears orangish red.

ClassPrep PPT 17: What Influences Sensations of Light?

IRM Discussion 4.7: Problems in Vision

Focusing Light

light intensity   A physical dimension of light waves that refers to how much energy the light contains; it determines the brightness of light.

light wavelength   The distance between peaks in light waves.

cornea   The curved, transparent, protective layer through which light rays enter the eye.

pupil   An opening in the eye, just behind the cornea, through which light passes.

iris   The colorful part of the eye, which constricts or relaxes to adjust the amount of light entering the eye.

lens   The part of the eye behind the pupil that bends light rays, focusing them on the retina.

retina   The surface at the back of the eye onto which the lens focuses light rays.

accommodation   The ability of the lens to change its shape and bend light rays so that objects are in focus.

photoreceptors   Nerve cells in the retina that code light energy into neural activity.

photopigments   Chemicals in photoreceptors that respond to light and assist in converting light into neural activity.

dark adaptation   The increasing ability to see in the dark as time in the dark increases.

Just as sound energy is converted to neural activity in the ear, light energy is transduced into neural activity in the eye. First, the accessory structures of the human eye focus light rays into a sharp image. The light rays enter the eye by passing through the curved, transparent, protective layer called the **cornea** (see Figure 4.8). Then the light passes through the **pupil,** the opening just behind the cornea. The **iris,** which gives the eye its color, adjusts the amount of light allowed into the eye by constricting to reduce the size of the pupil or relaxing to enlarge it. Directly behind the pupil is the **lens.** The cornea and the lens of the human eye are both curved so that, like the lens of a camera, they bend light rays. The light rays are focused into an image on the surface at the back of the eye; this surface is called the **retina.**

The lens of the human eye bends light rays from a point source so that they meet at a point on the retina (see Figure 4.9). If the rays meet either in front of the retina or behind it, the image will be out of focus. The muscles that hold the lens adjust its shape so that either near or far objects can be focused on the retina. If you peer at something very close, for example, your muscles must tighten the lens, making it more curved, to obtain a focused image. This ability to change the shape of the lens to bend light rays is called **accommodation.** Over time, the lens loses some of its flexibility, and accommodation becomes more difficult. This is why most older people become "farsighted," seeing distant objects clearly but needing glasses for

figure 4.8

Major Structures of the Eye

As shown in this top view of the eye, light rays bent by the combined actions of the cornea and the lens are focused on the retina, where the light energy is transduced into neural activity. Nerve fibers known collectively as the *optic nerve* pass out the back of the eye and continue to the brain.

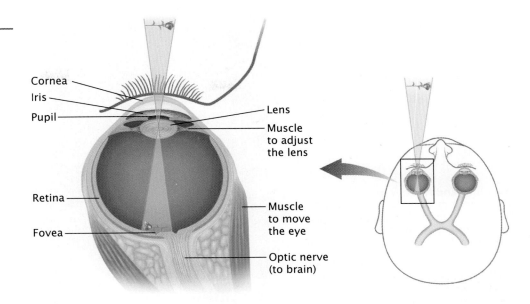

reading or close work. A more common problem in younger people is nearsightedness, in which close objects are in focus but distant ones are blurry. This condition has a genetic component, but it may be influenced by the environment, too (Quinn et al., 1999; Zadnik, 2001).

Converting Light into Images

Visual transduction, the conversion of light energy into neural activity, takes place in the retina. The word *retina* is Latin for "net"; the retina is an intricate network of cells. Before transduction can occur, light rays must actually pass through several layers in this network to reach photoreceptor cells.

Photoreceptors   **Photoreceptors** are specialized cells in the retina that convert light energy into neural activity. They contain **photopigments,** chemicals that respond to light. When light strikes a photopigment, the photopigment breaks apart, changing the membrane potential of the photoreceptor cell. This change in membrane potential provides a signal that can be transferred to the brain.

After a photopigment has broken down in response to light, new photopigment molecules are put together. This takes a little time, however. So when you first come from bright sunshine into, say, a dark theater, you cannot see because your photoreceptors do not yet have enough photopigment. In the dark, your photoreceptors synthesize more photopigments, and your ability to see gradually increases. This increasing ability to see in the dark as time passes is called **dark adaptation.** Overall,

figure 4.9

The Lens and the Retinal Image

Light rays from the top of an object are focused at the bottom of the image on the retinal surface, whereas rays from the right side of the object end up on the left side of the retinal image. The brain rearranges this upside-down and reversed image so that people see the object as it really is.

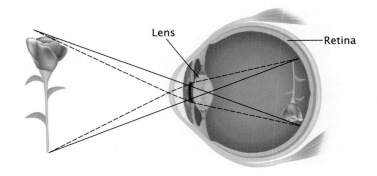

Reading and Nearsightedness   Visual experience can modify the eye. When chicks are raised with goggles that allow only diffused, unpatterned light through, their eyeballs become elongated and they become nearsighted (Wallman et al., 1987). Humans may be vulnerable to the same elongation because reading presents areas around the fovea with a constant, relatively unpatterned image.

OBJ 4.18: Define rods, cones, and fovea. Explain why acuity is greatest in the fovea.

Test Items 4.78–4.86

IRM Activity 4.12: Color Vision-Distribution of Rods and Cones in the Retina

rods   Highly light-sensitive, but color-insensitive, photoreceptors in the retina that allow vision even in dim light.

cones   Photoreceptors in the retina whose color-sensitive photopigment helps us to distinguish colors.

fovea   A region in the center of the retina where cones are highly concentrated.

acuity   Visual clarity, which is greatest in the fovea because of its large concentration of cones.

lateral inhibition   A process in which lateral connections allow one photoreceptor to inhibit the responsiveness of its neighbor, thus enhancing the sensation of visual contrast.

your sensitivity to light increases about 10,000-fold after about half an hour in a darkened room.

The retina has two basic types of photoreceptors: **rods** and **cones.** As their names imply, these cells differ in shape. They also differ in composition and response to light. The photopigment in rods includes a substance called *rhodopsin* (pronounced "row-DOP-sin"), whereas the photopigment in cones includes one of three varieties of *iodopsin.* The multiple forms of iodopsin provide the basis for color vision, which we explain later. Because rods have only one pigment, they are unable to discriminate colors. However, the rods are more sensitive to light than cones. So rods allow you to see even when there is very little light, as on a moonlit night. In dim light, you are seeing with your rods, which cannot discriminate colors; at higher light intensities, the cones, with their ability to detect colors, become most active. As a result, you may put on what you thought was a matched pair of socks in a darkened bedroom, only to go outside and discover that one is dark blue and the other is dark green.

Rods and cones also differ in their distribution in the eye. Cones are concentrated in the center of the retina, a region called the **fovea,** where the eye focuses the light coming from objects you look at. This concentration makes the ability to see details, or **acuity,** greatest in the fovea. Variations in the density of cones in the fovea probably account for individual differences in visual acuity (Curcio et al., 1987). There are no rods in the human fovea. With increasing distance from the fovea, though, the number of cones gradually decreases, and the proportion of rods gradually increases. So, if you are trying to detect a small amount of light, like that from a faint star, it is better to look slightly away from where you expect to see it. This focuses the weak light on the rods outside the fovea, which are very sensitive to light. Because cones do not work well in low light, looking directly at the star will make it seem to disappear.

Interactions in the Retina   If the eye simply transferred to the brain the stimuli that are focused on the retina, the resulting images would resemble a somewhat blurred TV picture. Instead, the eye actually sharpens visual images. How? The key lies in the interactions among the cells of the retina, which are illustrated in Figure 4.10. The most direct connections from the photoreceptor cells to the brain go first to *bipolar cells* and then to *ganglion cells;* the axons of the ganglion cells form the optic nerve, which extends out of the eye and into the brain. However, this direct path to the brain is modified by interactions with other cells.

Rods and Cones This electron microscope view of rods (blue) and cones (aqua) shows what your light receptors look like. Rods are more light sensitive, but they do not detect color. Cones can detect color, but they require more light in order to be activated. To experience the difference in how these cells work, look at an unfamiliar color photograph in a room where there is barely enough light to see. Even this dim light will activate your rods and allow you to make out images in the picture. But because there is not enough light to activate your cones, you will not be able to see colors in the photo.

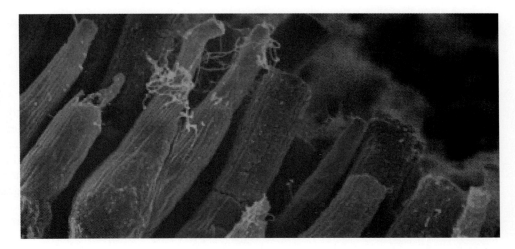

OBJ 4.19: Define lateral inhibition and describe the interactions in the retina that produce it.

Test Items 4.87–4.93

IRM Activity 4.8: The Pathway of Light

IRM Activity 4.10: Brightness Contrast—A Quick Demonstration

These interactions change the information reaching the brain, enhancing the sensation of contrast, for example. How? Most of the time, the amount of light reaching any two photoreceptors will differ slightly. When this happens, the photoreceptor receiving more light inhibits the output to the brain from the photoreceptor receiving less light, making it seem as if there is less light at that cell than there really is. This process, called **lateral inhibition**, is aided by *interneurons*, which are cells that make sideways, or lateral, connections between photoreceptors (see Figure 4.10). In other words, the brain actually receives a *comparison* of the light hitting two neighboring points, and whatever difference that exists between the light

figure 4.10

Cells in the Retina

Light rays actually pass through several layers of cells before striking photo-receptors, the rods and cones. Signals generated by the rods and cones then go back toward the surface of the retina, passing through bipolar cells and ganglion cells, and on to the brain. Interconnections among interneurons, bipolar cells, and ganglion cells allow the eye to begin analyzing visual information even before that information leaves the retina.

ClassPrep PPT 20, OHT: *Figure 4.10:* Cells in the Retina

Videodisc Still: Detail of the Retina

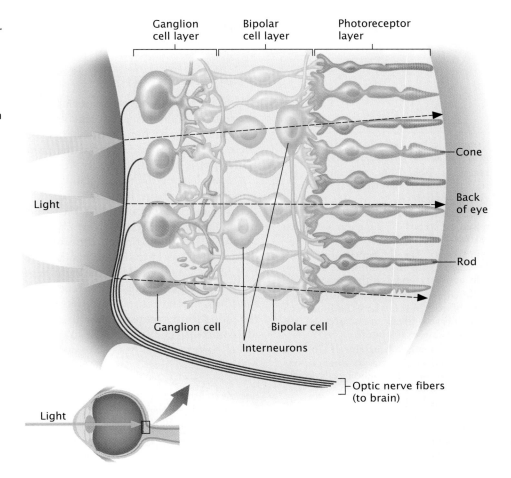

reaching the two photoreceptors is exaggerated. This exaggeration is important, because specific features of objects can create differences in amounts of incoming light. For example, the visual image of the edge of a table contains a transition from a lighter region to a darker region. Lateral inhibition in the retina amplifies this difference, creating contrast that sharpens the edge and makes it more noticeable.

Ganglion Cells and Their Receptive Fields   Photoreceptors and bipolar cells communicate by releasing neurotransmitters. But as discussed in the chapter on biological aspects of psychology, neurotransmitters cause only small, graded changes in the membrane potential of the next cell, which cannot travel the distance from eye to brain. The cells in the retina that generate action potentials capable of traveling that distance are the **ganglion cells,** whose axons extend out of the retina to the brain.

What message do ganglion cells send to the brain? The answer depends on each cell's **receptive field,** which is the part of the retina and the corresponding part of the visual world to which a cell responds (Sekuler & Blake, 1994). Most ganglion cells have *center-surround receptive fields.* That is, most ganglion cells compare the amount of light stimulating the photoreceptors in the center of their receptive fields with the amount of light stimulating the photoreceptors in the area surrounding the center. This comparison results from the interactions in the retina that enhance contrast. Some center-surround ganglion cells *(center-on cells)* are activated by light in the center of their receptive field; light in the regions surrounding the center inhibits their activity (see Figure 4.11). Other center-surround ganglion cells *(center-off cells)* work in just the opposite way. They are inhibited by light in the center and activated by light in the surrounding area.

The center-surround receptive fields of ganglion cells make it easier for you to see edges and, as illustrated in Figure 4.12, also create a sharper contrast between darker and lighter areas than actually exists. By enhancing the sensation of important features, the retina gives your brain an "improved" version of the visual world.

Visual Pathways   IRM Discussion 3.8: Two Brains in One?

The brain performs even more elaborate processing of visual information than does the retina. The information reaches the brain via the axons of ganglion cells, which leave the eye as a bundle of fibers called the **optic nerve** (see Figure 4.8). Because there are no photoreceptors at the point where the optic nerve exits the eyeball, a **blind spot** is created, as Figure 4.13 shows.

After leaving the retina, about half the fibers of the optic nerve cross over to the opposite side of the brain at a structure called the **optic chiasm.** (*Chiasm* means "cross" and is pronounced "KYE-az-um.") Fibers from the inside half of each eye, nearest to the nose, cross over; fibers from the outside half of each eye do not (see Figure 4.14). This arrangement brings all the visual information about the right half of the visual world to the left hemisphere of the brain and information about the left half of the visual world to the right hemisphere of the brain.

The optic chiasm is part of the bottom surface of the brain; beyond the chiasm, the fibers ascend into the brain itself. The axons from most of the ganglion cells in the retina form synapses in the thalamus, in a specific region called the **lateral geniculate nucleus (LGN).** Neurons in the LGN then send the visual input to the **primary visual cortex,** which lies in the occipital lobe at the back of the brain. Visual information is also sent from the primary visual cortex for processing in many other areas of cortex. In studies of monkeys, thirty-two separate visual areas interconnected by more than three hundred pathways have been identified so far (Van Essen, Anderson, & Felleman, 1992).

The retina is organized to create a topographical map of the visual world, such that neighboring points on the retina receive information from neighboring points

---

OBJ 4.20: Describe the center-surround receptive field of ganglion cells.

Test Items 4.94–4.96

OBJ 4.21: Describe the path that visual information follows on its way to the brain, including the roles of the optic nerve, the optic chiasm, the lateral geniculate nucleus, and the primary visual cortex. Know what creates the blind spot.

Test Items 4.97–4.101

Essay Q 4.2

ganglion cells   Cells in the retina that generate action potentials.

receptive field   The portion of the retina, and the world, that affects a given ganglion cell.

optic nerve   A bundle of fibers composed of axons of ganglion cells that carries visual information to the brain.

blind spot   The light-insensitive point at which axons from all of the ganglion cells converge and exit the eyeball.

optic chiasm   Part of the bottom surface of the brain where half of each optic nerve's fibers cross over to the opposite side of the brain.

lateral geniculate nucleus (LGN)   A region of the thalamus in which axons from most of the ganglion cells in the retina end and form synapses.

primary visual cortex   An area at the back of the brain, to which neurons in the lateral geniculate nucleus relay visual input.

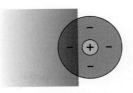

Medium activity (light on center and surround)

Higher activity (light on center; dark on surround)

Low activity (dark on both center and surround)

figure 4.11

Center-Surround Receptive Fields of Ganglion Cells

Center-surround receptive fields allow ganglion cells to act as edge detectors. An edge is a region of light next to a region of relative darkness. If, as shown at the left, an edge is outside the receptive field of a center-on ganglion cell, there will be a uniform amount of light on both the excitatory center and the inhibitory surround, thus creating a moderate amount of activity. If, as shown in the middle drawing, the dark side of an edge covers a large portion of the inhibitory surround but leaves light on the excitatory center, the output of the cell will be high, signaling an edge in its receptive field. When, as shown at right, the dark area covers both the center and the surround of the ganglion cell, its activity will be lower, because neither segment of the cell's receptive field is receiving much stimulation.

in the visual world. This topographical map is also maintained in the brain, in the primary visual cortex, and in each of the many other visual areas of the cortex. So neighboring points in the retina are represented in neighboring cells in the brain. (This is a spatial coding system.) The map is a distorted one, however. A larger area of cortex is devoted to the areas of the retina that have many photoreceptors. For example, the fovea, which is densely packed with photoreceptors, is represented in an especially large segment of cortex.

Visual Representations

So the apparently effortless experience of sight is due to a very complex system, in which visual sensations are transmitted from the retina through various cortical regions. We can appreciate some of these complexities by considering the receptive fields of neurons at each point along the way. Two of the processes that characterize these receptive fields are *parallel processing of visual properties* and *hierarchical processing of visual information.*

figure 4.12

The Hermann Grid

There seem to be dark spots at the intersections of the *Hermann grid,* until you look directly at them. To understand why, look at the black boxes in the smaller grid at right. The circles superimposed on this smaller grid represent the receptive fields of two center-on ganglion cells. At the intersections, a center-on ganglion cell has more whiteness shining on its inhibitory surround. Because its output is reduced compared with that of the cell on the right, the spot on the left appears darker. The spot disappears when you look directly at the intersection because ganglion cells in the fovea have smaller receptive fields than do ganglion cells elsewhere in the retina, so more excitatory centers are being stimulated, creating a greater sensation of whiteness.

figure 4.13

Find Your Blind Spot

TRY THIS There is a blind spot where axons from the ganglion cells leave the eye and become the optic nerve. To "see" your blind spot, cover your left eye, and stare at the cross inside the circle. Move the page closer and then farther away, and at some point the dot to the right should disappear. However, the vertical lines around the dot will probably look continuous, because the brain tends to fill in visual information at the blind spot. We are normally unaware of this "hole" in our vision because the blind spot of one eye is in the visual field of the other eye.

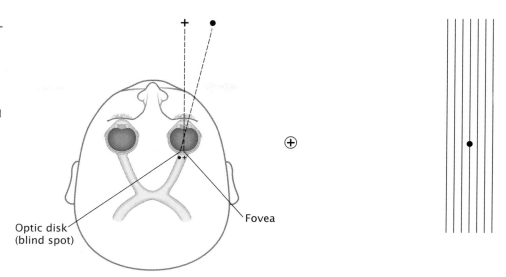

Optic disk
(blind spot)

Fovea

OBJ 4.22: Describe parallel processing of visual properties and hierarchical processing of visual information using feature detectors.

Test Items 4.102–4.108

ClassPrep PPT 24: Parallel Processing of Visual Properties

ClassPrep PPT 23, OHT: *Figure 4.14:* Pathways from the Ganglion Cells into the Brain

Parallel Processing of Visual Properties   Like ganglion cells, neurons of the LGN in the thalamus have center-surround receptive fields. However, the LGN is organized in multiple layers of neurons, and each layer contains a complete map of the retina. Neurons in different layers respond to particular aspects of visual stimuli. In fact, four separate aspects of a visual scene are simultaneously handled by *parallel processing systems* (Livingstone & Hubel, 1987). The *form* of objects and their *color* are handled by one system (the "what" system), whereas their *movement* and *cues to distance* are handled by another (the "where" system).

These sensations are then sent to the cortex, but the question of where in the cortex they are finally assembled into a unified conscious experience is still being debated. Some researchers argue that there is no one region where all the separate streams of processing converge (Engel et al., 1992). Instead, they say, connections among the regions of cortex that process separate aspects of visual sensation appear to integrate their activity, making possible a distributed, but unified, experience (Gilbert, 1992).

figure 4.14

Pathways from the Ganglion Cells into the Brain

Light rays from the right side of the visual field (the right side of what you are looking at) end up on the left half of each retina (shown in red). Light rays from the left visual field end up on the right half of each retina (shown in blue). From the right eye, axons from the nasal side of the retina (the side nearer the nose, which receives information from the right visual field) cross over the midline and travel to the left side of the brain with those fibers from the left eye that also receive input from the right side of the visual world. A similar arrangement unites left visual-field information from both eyes in the right side of the brain.

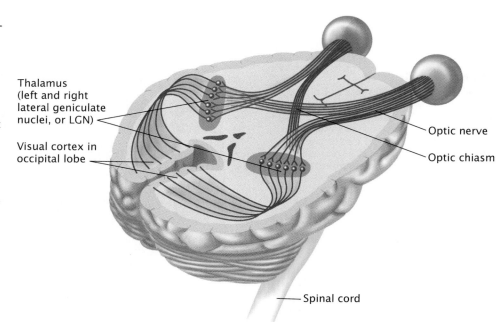

Thalamus
(left and right
lateral geniculate
nuclei, or LGN)

Visual cortex in
occipital lobe

Optic nerve

Optic chiasm

Spinal cord

figure 4.15

Construction of a Feature Detector

The output from several center-on ganglion cells goes to cells in the lateral geniculate nucleus (LGN) and is then fed into one cell in the cortex. This "wiring" makes the cortical cell respond best when all of its LGN cells are excited, and they are most excited when light falls on the center of the receptive fields of their ganglion cells. Because those receptive fields lie in an angled row, it takes a bar-shaped light at that angle to stimulate all their centers. In short, this cortical cell responds best when it detects a bar-shaped feature at a particular angle. Rotating the bar to a different orientation would no longer stimulate this particular cortical cell.

ClassPrep PPT 25: *Figure 4.15:* Construction of a Feature Detector

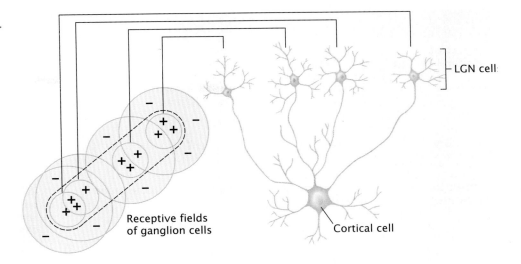

Receptive fields of ganglion cells

LGN cell

Cortical cell

Positron emission tomography (PET) scans, too, have provided evidence of separate processing channels in humans. One area of visual cortex is activated when a person views a colorful painting; a different area is activated by viewing black-and-white moving images (Zeki, 1992). Brain damage may also reveal these separate channels. Damage in one area can leave a person unable to see colors or even remember them, but still able to see and recognize objects. Damage in another area can leave a person able to see only stationary objects; as soon as the object moves, it disappears. People with brain damage in still other regions can see only moving objects, not stationary ones (Zeki, 1992). Even in visual imagination, the same separate processing channels apparently operate. So some patients with brain damage can recall parts of a visual image, but not their correct spatial relationship. For example, they may be able to "see" a mental image of a bull's horns and ears but be unable to assemble them mentally to form a bull's head (Kosslyn, 1988).

Hierarchical Processing of Visual Information   Multiple inputs from the LGN converge on single cells of the cortex, as Figure 4.15 illustrates. Cells of the cortex that receive input from the LGN in the thalamus have more complex receptive fields than the center-surround fields of LGN cells. For example, a specific cell in the cortex might respond only to vertical edges, but it responds to vertical edges anywhere in its receptive field. Another class of cells responds only to moving objects; a third class responds only to objects with corners. Because cortical cells respond to specific characteristics of objects in the visual field, they have been described as **feature detectors** (Hubel & Wiesel, 1979).

Feature detectors illustrate how cortical processing is partly *hierarchical*, or stepwise, in nature. Complex feature detectors may be built up out of more and more complex connections among simpler feature detectors (Hubel & Wiesel, 1979). For example, several center-surround cells might feed into one cortical cell to make a line detector, and several line detectors might feed into another cortical cell to make a cell that responds to a particular spatial orientation, such as vertical. With further connections, a more complex detector, such as a "box detector," might be built from simpler line and corner detectors.

Cells with similar receptive-field properties are organized into columns in the cortex. The columns are arranged at right angles to the surface of the cortex. For example, if you locate a cell that responds to diagonal lines in a particular spot in the visual field, most of the cells in a column above and below that cell will also respond to diagonal lines. Other properties, too, are represented by whole columns of cells; for example, there are columns in which all of the cells are most sensitive

feature detectors Cells in the cortex that respond to a specific feature of an object.

in review   Seeing

Aspect of Sensory System	Elements	Key Characteristics
Energy	Light—electromagnetic radiation from about 400 nm to about 750 nm	The intensity and wavelength of light waves determine the brightness and color of visual sensations.
Accessory structures	Eye—cornea, pupil, iris, lens	Light rays are bent to focus on the retina.
Transduction mechanism	Photoreceptors (rods and cones) in the retina	Rods are more sensitive to light than cones, but cones discriminate among colors. Sensations of color depend first on the cones, which respond differently to different light wavelengths. Interactions among cells of the retina exaggerate differences in the light stimuli reaching the photoreceptors, enhancing the sensation of contrast.
Pathways and representations	Optic nerve to optic chiasm to LGN of thalamus to primary visual cortex	Neighboring points in the visual world are represented at neighboring points in the LGN and primary visual cortex. Neurons there respond to particular aspects of the visual stimulus—such as color, movement, distance, or form.

to a particular color. Research has also revealed that individual neurons in the cortex perform several different tasks, allowing complex visual processing (Schiller, 1996). ("In Review: Seeing" summarizes how the nervous system gathers the information that allows people to see.)

Seeing Color

Like beauty, color is in the eye of the beholder. Many animals see only shades of gray, even when they look at a rainbow, but for humans color is a prominent feature of vision. A marketer might tell you about the impact of color on buying preferences, a poet might tell you about the emotional power of color, but we will tell you about how you see colors—a process that is itself a thing of beauty and elegance.

Wavelengths and Color Sensations   We noted earlier that at a given intensity, each wavelength of light is sensed as a certain color (look again at Figure 4.7). However, the eye is seldom, if ever, presented with pure light of a single wavelength. Sunlight, for example, is a mixture of all wavelengths of light. When sunlight passes through a droplet of water, the different wavelengths of light are bent to different degrees, separating into a colorful rainbow. The spectrum of color found in the rainbow illustrates an important concept: The sensation produced by a mixture of different wavelengths of light is not the same as the sensations produced by separate wavelengths. So just as most sounds are a mixture of sound waves of different frequencies, most colors are a mixture of light of different wavelengths.

Characteristics of the mixture of wavelengths striking the eyes determine the color sensation. There are three separate aspects of this sensation: hue, saturation, and brightness. These are *psychological* dimensions that correspond roughly to the

hue   The essential "color," determined by the dominant wavelength of light.
saturation   The purity of a color.
brightness   The overall intensity of all of the wavelengths that make up light.

OBJ 4.23: Define hue, saturation, and brightness.

Test Items 4.109–4.112

ClassPrep PPT 26: Psychological Dimensions of Light

physical properties of light. **Hue** is the essential "color," determined by the dominant wavelength in the mixture of the light. For example, the wavelength of yellow is about 570 nanometers, and that of red is about 700 nanometers. Black, white, and gray are not considered hues, because no wavelength predominates in them. **Saturation** is related to the purity of a color. A color is more saturated and more pure if just one wavelength is relatively more intense—contains more energy—than other wavelengths. If many wavelengths are added to a pure hue, the color is said to be *desaturated*. For example, pastels are colors that have been desaturated by the addition of whiteness. **Brightness** refers to the overall intensity of all of the wavelengths making up light.

The color circle shown in Figure 4.16 arranges hues according to their perceived similarities. If lights of two different wavelengths but equal intensity are mixed, the color you sense is at the midpoint of a line drawn between the two original colors on the color circle. This process is known as *additive color mixing,* because the effects of the wavelengths from each light are added together. If you keep adding different colored lights, you eventually get white (the combination of all wavelengths). You are probably more familiar with a different form of color mixing, called *subtractive color mixing,* which occurs when paints are combined. Like other physical objects, paints reflect certain wavelengths and absorb all others. For example, grass is green because it absorbs all wavelengths except wavelengths that are sensed as green. White objects are white because they reflect all wavelengths. Light reflected from paints or other colored objects is seldom a pure wavelength, so predicting the color resulting from mixing paint is not as straightforward as combining pure wavelengths of light. But if you keep combining different colored paints, all of the wavelengths will eventually be subtracted, resulting in black. (The discussion that follows refers to *additive color mixing,* the mixing of light.)

By mixing lights of just a few wavelengths, we can produce different color sensations. How many wavelengths are needed to create any possible color? Figure 4.17 illustrates an experiment that addresses this question, using a piece of white paper, which reflects all wavelengths and therefore appears to be the color of the light shined upon it. The answer to the question of how many lights are needed to create all colors helped lead scientists to an important theory of how people sense color.

Videodisc Segment & Still: The Color Wheel

ClassPrep PPT 27: *Figure 4.16:* The Color Circle

figure 4.16

The Color Circle

Ordering colors according to their psychological similarities creates a color circle that predicts the result of additive mixing of two colored lights. The resulting color will be on a line between the two starting colors, the exact location on the line depending on the relative proportions of the two colors. For example, mixing equal amounts of pure green and pure red light will produce yellow, the color that lies at the midpoint of the line connecting red and green. (*Nm* stands for *nanometers,* the unit in which wavelengths are measured.)

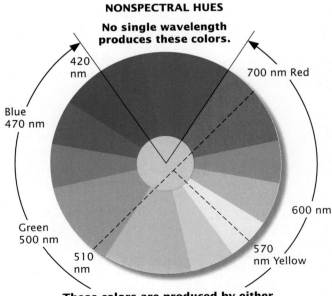

NONSPECTRAL HUES
No single wavelength produces these colors.

420 nm

700 nm Red

Blue 470 nm

600 nm

Green 500 nm

570 nm Yellow

510 nm

These colors are produced by either a single wavelength or a mixture.

SPECTRAL HUES

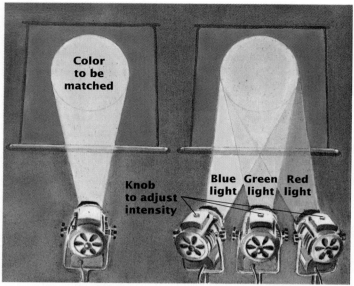

figure 4.17

Matching a Color by Mixing Lights of Pure Wavelengths

A target color is presented on the left side of this display; the participant's task is to adjust the intensity of different pure-wavelength lights until the resulting mixture looks exactly like the target. A large number of colors can be matched with just two mixing lights, but *any* color can be matched by mixing three pure-wavelength lights. Experiments like this generated the information that led to the trichromatic theory of color vision.

OBJ 4.24: Describe the trichromatic and opponent-process theories of color vision. Discuss the phenomena each explains, including complementary colors.

Test Items 4.113–4.119

Essay Q 4.3

ClassPrep PPT 29: Trichromatic Theory of Color Vision

trichromatic theory A theory of color vision identifying three types of visual elements, each of which is most sensitive to different wavelengths of light.

opponent-process theory A theory of color vision stating that color-sensitive visual elements are grouped into red-green, blue-yellow, and black-white elements.

The Trichromatic Theory of Color Vision

Early in the nineteenth century, Thomas Young and, later, Hermann von Helmholtz established that they could match any color by mixing pure lights of only three wavelengths. For example, by mixing blue light (about 440 nanometers), green light (about 510 nanometers), and red light (about 700 nanometers) in different ratios, they could produce *any* other color. Young and Helmholtz interpreted this evidence to mean that there must be three types of visual elements, each of which is most sensitive to different wavelengths, and that information from these three elements combines to produce the sensation of color. This theory of color vision is called the *Young-Helmholtz theory,* or the **trichromatic theory.**

Support for the trichromatic theory has come from recordings of the responses of individual photoreceptors to particular wavelengths of light and from electrical recordings from human cones (Schnapf, Kraft, & Baylor, 1987). This research reveals that there are three types of cones. Although each type responds to a broad range of wavelengths, each type is most sensitive to particular wavelengths. *Short-wavelength* cones respond most to light in the blue range. *Medium-wavelength* cones are most sensitive to light in the green range. Finally, *long-wavelength* cones respond best to light in the reddish yellow range (although these have traditionally been called "red cones").

Note that no single cone, by itself, can signal the color of a light. It is the *ratio* of the activities of the three types of cones that indicates what color will be sensed. In other words, color vision is coded by the *pattern of activity* of the different cones. For example, a light is sensed as yellow if it has a pure wavelength of about 570 nanometers; this light stimulates both medium- and long-wavelength cones, as illustrated by arrow A in Figure 4.18. But yellow is also sensed whenever any mixture of other lights stimulates the same pattern of activity in these two types of cones. The trichromatic theory was applied in the creation of color television screens, which contain microscopic elements of red, green, and blue. A television broadcast excites these elements to varying degrees, mixing their colors to produce many other colors. You see color mixtures—not patterns of red, green, and blue dots—because the dots are too small and close together to be seen individually.

ClassPrep PPT 30: Problem

The Opponent-Process Theory of Color Vision

Brilliant as it is, the trichromatic theory in its simplest form cannot explain some aspects of color

figure 4.18

Relative Responses of Three Cone Types to Different Wavelengths of Light

Each type of cone responds to a range of wavelengths but responds more to some wavelengths than to others. This makes it possible to generate the same pattern of output—and hence the same sensation of color—by more than one combination of wavelengths. For example, a pure light of 570 nanometers (A in the figure) stimulates long-wavelength cones at 1.0 relative units and medium-wavelength cones at about 0.7 relative units. This ratio of cone activity (1/0.7 = 1.4) yields the sensation of yellow. Any combination of wavelengths at the proper intensity that generates the same ratio of activity in these cone types will produce the sensation of yellow.

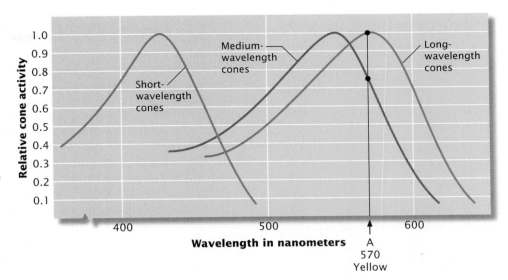

ClassPrep PPT 31, OHT: Flag

ClassPrep PPT 33: Opponent-Process Theory of Color Vision

IRM Activity 4.9: Negative Afterimages, Opponent-Processing, and Sensation

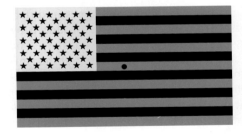

figure 4.19

Afterimages Produced by the Opponent-Process Nature of Color Vision

 Stare at the dot in the center of the flag for at least thirty seconds; then fixate on the dot in the white space below it.

vision. For example, it cannot account for the fact that if you stare at the flag in Figure 4.19 for thirty seconds and then look at the blank white space below it, you will see a color afterimage. What was yellow in the original image will be blue in the afterimage, what was green before will appear red, and what was black will now appear white.

This type of phenomenon led Ewald Hering to offer an alternative to the trichromatic theory of color vision, called the **opponent-process theory.** It holds that the visual elements sensitive to color are grouped into three pairs and that the members of each pair oppose, or inhibit, each other. The three pairs are a *red-green element*, a *blue-yellow element*, and a *black-white element*. Each element signals one color or the other—red or green, for example—but never both. This theory explains color afterimages. When one part of an opponent pair is no longer stimulated, the other is activated. So, as in Figure 4.19, if the original image you look at is green, the afterimage will be red.

The opponent-process theory also explains the phenomenon of complementary colors. Two colors are *complementary* if gray results when lights of the two colors are mixed together. Actually, the neutral color of gray can appear as anything from white to gray to black, depending on the intensity of the light. On the color circle shown in Figure 4.16, complementary colors are roughly opposite each other. Red and green lights are complementary, as are yellow and blue. Notice that complementary colors are *opponent* colors in Hering's theory. According to opponent-process theory, complementary colors stimulate the same visual element (e.g., red-green) in opposite directions, canceling each other out. This theory helps explain why mixing lights of complementary colors produces gray.

A Synthesis and an Update The trichromatic and opponent-process theories seem quite different, but both are correct to some extent, and together they can explain most of what is known about color vision. Electrical recordings made from different types of cells in the retina paved the way for a synthesis of the two theories.

At the level of the photoreceptors, a slightly revised version of the trichromatic theory is correct. As a general rule, there *are* three types of cones that have three different photopigments. However, molecular biologists who isolated the genes for cone pigments have found variations in the genes for the cones sensitive to middle-wavelength and long-wavelength light. These variants have slightly different sensitivities to different wavelengths of light. So a person can have two, three, or even four genes for long-wavelength pigments (Neitz & Neitz, 1995). Individual differences in people's long-wavelength pigments become apparent in color-matching tasks. When asked to mix a red light and a green light to match a yellow light, a person with one kind of long-wavelength pigment will choose a different red-to-green ratio than someone with a different long-wavelength pigment. Women are more likely than men to have four distinct photopigments, and the women who do have the four photopigments have a richer experience of color. They can detect more shades of color than people with the more common three photopigments, but their experience of color pales in comparison to that of certain shrimp. These tropical shrimp live on colorful coral reefs and have twelve different photopigments, which allows them to see colors even in the ultraviolet range, which no human—male or female—can sense (Marshall & Oberwinkler, 1999).

But color vision works a little differently at the level of ganglion cells. Information about light from many photoreceptors feeds into each ganglion cell, and the output from each ganglion cell goes to the brain. Recall that the receptive fields of most ganglion cells are arranged in center-surround patterns. The center and the surround are color coded, as illustrated in Figure 4.20. The center responds best to one color, and the surround responds best to a different color. This color coding arises because varying proportions of the three cone types feed into the center and the surround of the ganglion cell.

When either the center or the surround of a ganglion cell is stimulated, the other area is inhibited. In other words, the colors to which the center and the surround of a given ganglion cell are most responsive are opponent colors. Recordings from many ganglion cells show that three very common pairs of opponent colors are those predicted by Hering's opponent-process theory: red-green, blue-yellow, and black-white. Stimulating both the center and the surround cancels the effects of either light, producing gray. Black-white cells receive input from all types of cones, so it does not matter what color stimulates them. Cells in specific regions of the visual cortex, too, respond in opponent pairs sensitive to the red-green and blue-yellow input coming from ganglion cells in the retina (Engel, Zhang, & Wandell, 1997).

In summary, color vision is possible because the three types of cones have different sensitivities to different wavelengths, as the trichromatic theory suggests. The sensation of different colors results from stimulating the three cone types in different ratios. Because there are three types of cones, any color can be produced by mixing three different wavelengths of light. But the story does not end there. The output from cones is fed into ganglion cells, and the center and surround of the ganglion cells respond to different colors and inhibit each other. This activity provides the basis for afterimages. Therefore, the trichromatic theory describes the properties of the photoreceptors, whereas the opponent-process theory describes the properties of the ganglion cells. Both theories are needed to account for the complexity of visual sensations of color.

figure 4.20

Color Coding and the Ganglion Cells

The center-surround receptive fields of ganglion cells form the anatomical basis for opponent colors. Some ganglion cells, like G$_2$, have a center whose photoreceptors respond best to red wavelengths and a surround whose photoreceptors respond best to green wavelengths. Other ganglion cells pair blue and yellow, whereas still others receive input from all types of photoreceptors.

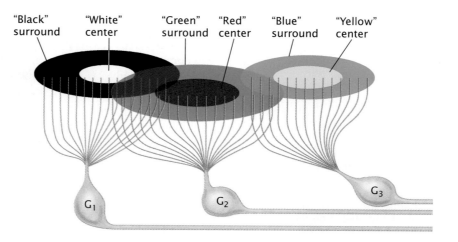

figure 4.21

Are You Colorblind?

TRY THIS At the upper left is a photo as it appears to people who have all three cone photopigments. The other photos simulate how colors appear to people who are missing photopigments for short wavelengths (lower left), long wavelengths (upper right), or medium wavelengths (lower right). If any of these photos look to you just like the one at the upper left, you may have a form of colorblindness.

ClassPrep PPT 35: *Figure 4.21:* Are You Colorblind?

OBJ 4.25: Describe the physical problem that causes colorblindness.

Test Items 4.120–4.123

Colorblindness   People who have cones containing only two of the three possible color-sensitive pigments are described as *colorblind* (see Figure 4.21). They are not actually blind to all color; they simply discriminate fewer colors than other people. Two centuries ago, a colorblind chemist named John Dalton carefully described the colors he sensed—to him, a red ribbon appeared the same color as mud—and hypothesized that the fluid in his eyeball must be tinted blue. He instructed his doctor to examine the fluid after he died, but it turned out to be clear. His preserved retinas were examined recently by molecular biologists. The scientists were not surprised to find that just as most colorblind people today lack the genes that code one or more of the pigments, Dalton had no gene for medium-wavelength pigments (Hunt et al., 1995).

The Interaction of Vision and Hearing: Synesthesia

OBJ 4.26: Define synesthesia.

Test Items 4.124–4.125

At the beginning of this chapter, we gave examples of the interaction of two senses, namely, vision and touch. Vision also interacts with hearing. For example, hearing a brief sound just as lights are flashed can make it appear that there are more lights than there actually are (Shams, Kamitani, & Shimojo, 2000). And hearing a sound as objects collide can affect your perception of their motion (Watanabe & Shimojo, 2001). Sound can also improve your ability to see an object at the sound's source, which could be a vital aid in avoiding or responding to danger (McDonald, Teder-Salejarvi, & Hillyard, 2000). These interactions occur in everyone, but some people also report **synesthesia** (pronounced "sin-ess-THEE-zhah"), a more unusual mixing of sensory modalities or dimensions within modalities. These people may say that they "feel" colors or sounds as touches, or that they "taste" shapes; others claim that they sense certain colors, such as red, when they hear certain sounds, such as a trumpet. Some report experiencing certain tastes, numbers, or letters as vivid patterns or particular colors.

Once dismissed as poetic delusions, some of these claims have recently received scientific support from experiments such as the one illustrated in Figure 4.22 (Mattingly et al., 2001; Ramachandran & Hubbard, 2001). Researchers speculate that synesthesia occurs partly because brain areas that process colors are near areas that process letters and numbers, and partly because the connections between these neighboring areas may be more extensive in people who experience synesthesia.

synesthesia A blending of sensory experience that causes some people to "see" sounds or "taste" colors, for example.

figure 4.22

Synesthesia

In this experiment on synesthesia, a triangular pattern of H's was embedded in a background of other letters, as shown at left. Most people find it difficult to detect the triangle, but "J.C.," a person with synesthesia, easily picked it out because, as depicted at right, he saw the H's as green, the F's as yellow, and the P's as red (Ramachandran & Hubbard, 2001).

Source: Figure 3 from Ramachandran & Hubbard (2001).

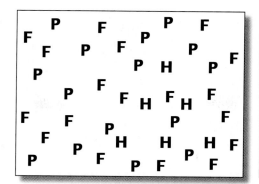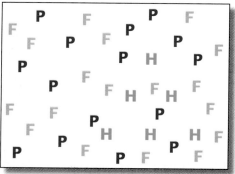

They suggest that similar, but less extensive, connections may underlie widely used metaphors, such as saying that a shirt is "loud," that a cheese is "sharp," or as one wine expert put it, that the taste of a particular wine had "a light straw color with greenish hues" (Martino & Marks, 2001).

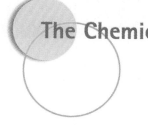

The Chemical Senses: Smell and Taste

There are animals without vision, and there are animals without hearing, but there are no animals without some form of chemical sense—some sense that arises from the interaction of chemicals and receptors. **Olfaction** (our sense of smell) detects chemicals that are airborne, or volatile. **Gustation** (our sense of taste) detects chemicals in solution that come into contact with receptors inside the mouth.

Olfaction

People sense odors in the upper part of the nose (see Figure 4.23). Odor molecules can reach olfactory receptors there either by passing directly through the nostrils or by rising through an opening in the palate at the back of the mouth, allowing us to sample odors from food as we eat it. The olfactory receptors themselves are located on the dendrites of specialized neurons that extend into the moist lining of the nose. Odor molecules bind to these receptors, causing depolarization of the dendrites' membrane, which in turn leads to changes in the firing rates of the neurons. A single molecule of an odorous substance can cause a change in the membrane potential of an olfactory neuron, but detection of the odor by a human normally requires about fifty such molecules (Menini, Picco, & Firestein, 1995); the average hot pizza generates lots more than that.

Olfactory neurons are continuously replaced with new ones, as each lives only about two months. Scientists are very interested in this process because, as noted in the chapter on biological aspects of psychology, most neurons cannot divide to create new ones. An understanding of how new olfactory neurons are generated—and how they make appropriate connections in the brain—may someday be helpful in treating brain damage.

Substances that have similar chemical structures tend to have similar odors. The precise means by which olfactory receptors in the nose discriminate various smells and send coded messages about them to the brain has only recently been determined (Buck, 1996). In contrast to vision, which makes use of only four basic receptor types (rods and three kinds of cones), the olfactory system employs about a thousand different types of receptors. The genes for these olfactory receptors make up about 1 to 2 percent of the human genome. A given odor stimulates these receptors to varying degrees, and the combination of receptors stimulated creates codes for a particular odor (Kajiya et al., 2001). The many combinations possible allow humans to discriminate tens of thousands of different odors.

olfaction   The sense of smell.

gustation   The sense of taste.

olfactory bulb   A brain structure that receives messages regarding olfaction.

pheromones   Chemicals released by one animal and detected by another that shape the second animal's behavior or physiology.

vomeronasal organ   A portion of the mammalian olfactory system that is sensitive to pheromones.

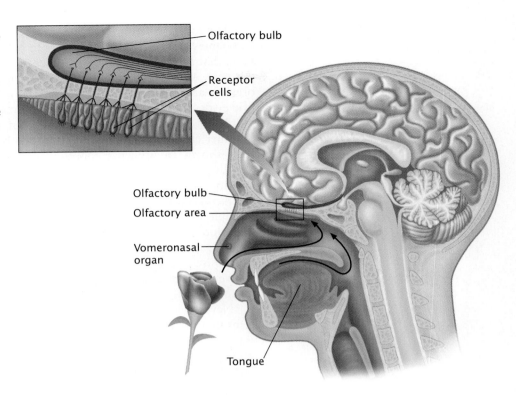

figure 4.23

The Olfactory System: The Nose and the Rose

Airborne chemicals from the rose reach the olfactory area through the nostrils and through the back of the mouth. Fibers pass directly from the olfactory area to the olfactory bulb in the brain, and from there signals pass to areas such as the hypothalamus and amygdala, which are involved in emotion.

ClassPrep PPT 23, OHT: *Figure 4.23:* The Olfactory System

Videodisc Segment & Still: The Nose

ClassPrep PPT 39: Olfaction

Freburg *Perspectives:* Furlow, "The Smell of Love"

Sattler/Shabatay reader, 2/e: Ackerman, "A Natural History of the Sense"

A "Mating Ball" Among snakes there is intense competition for females. Dozens of males will wrap themselves around a single female in a "mating ball." Snakes' forked tongues allow them to sample airborne chemicals at two different points and, hence, to follow an olfactory trail (Schwenk, 1994). Males with the best olfactory tracking abilities are the ones most likely to reach a female first, enabling them to pass on their genes to the next generation.

Olfaction is the only sense that does not send its messages through the thalamus. Instead, axons from neurons in the nose extend through a bony plate and directly into the brain, where they have a synapse in a structure called the **olfactory bulb.** Connections from the olfactory bulb spread diffusely through the brain's olfactory cortex (Zou et al., 2001), and connections are especially plentiful in the amygdala, a part of the brain involved in emotional experience.

These features of the olfactory system may account for the strong relationship between olfaction and emotional memory. For example, associations between a certain experience and a particular odor are not weakened much by time or subsequent experiences (Lawless & Engen, 1977). So catching a whiff of the scent once worn by a lost loved one can reactivate intense feelings of love or sadness associated with that person. Odors can also bring back accurate memories of significant experiences linked with them (Engen, Gilmore, & Mair, 1991).

The mechanisms of olfaction are remarkably similar in species ranging from humans to worms. Different species vary considerably, however, in their sensitivity to smell, and in the degree to which they depend on it for survival. For example, humans have about 9 million olfactory neurons, whereas there are about 225 million such neurons in dogs, which are far more dependent on smell to identify food, territory, and receptive mates. In addition, dogs and many other species have an accessory olfactory system that is able to detect pheromones. **Pheromones** (pronounced "FAIR-o-mones") are chemicals that are released by one animal and, when detected by another, can shape the second animal's behavior or physiology. For example, when male snakes detect a chemical exuded on the skin of female snakes, they are stimulated to "court" the female.

In mammals, pheromones can be nonvolatile chemicals that animals lick and pass into a portion of the olfactory system called the **vomeronasal organ.** In female mice, for example, the vomeronasal organ detects chemicals in the male's urine; by this means a male can cause a female to ovulate and become sexually receptive, and an unfamiliar male can cause a pregnant female to abort her pregnancy (Bruce, 1969).

IRM Thinking Critically 4.1: Do Humans Have Pheromones?

ClassPrep PPT 40: Pheromones

The role of pheromones in humans is much more controversial. Some perfume companies want potential customers to believe that they have created sexual attractants that act as pheromones to subconsciously influence the behavior of desirable partners. At the other extreme are those who argue that in humans, the vomeronasal organ is an utterly nonfunctional vestige, like the appendix. The best current scientific evidence suggests that the human vomeronasal organ is capable of responding to certain hormonal substances and can influence certain hormonal secretions (Berliner et al., 1996). Further, odorants that cannot be consciously detected have been shown to influence mood, suggesting a pheromone-like action (Jacob & McClintock, 2000), and a possible gene for pheromone receptors has been found in humans (Rodriguez et al., 2000). Pheromones themselves are definitely capable of producing physiological changes in humans that are related to reproduction. For example, pheromonal signals secreted in the perspiration of a woman can shorten or prolong the menstrual cycle of other women nearby (Stern & McClintock, 1998). In such cases, pheromones are responsible for *menstrual synchrony*, the tendency of women living together to menstruate at the same time. However, despite some suggestive findings (e.g., Cutler, Friedmann, & McCoy, 1998), there is still no solid evidence for a sexual attractant pheromone in humans, or even in nonhuman primates.

Nevertheless, learned associations between certain odors and emotional experiences may enhance a person's readiness for sex. People also use olfactory information in other social situations. For example, after just a few hours of contact, mothers can usually identify their newborn babies by the infants' smell (Porter, Cernich, & McLaughlin, 1983). And if infants are breastfed, they can discriminate their own mothers' odor from that of other breastfeeding women, and appear to be comforted by it (Porter, 1991). In fact, individual mammals, including humans, have a distinct "odortype," which is determined by their immune cells and other inherited physiological factors (Beauchamp et al., 1995). During pregnancy, a woman's own odortype combines with the odortype of her fetus to form a third odortype. Each of these three odors is distinguishable, suggesting that recognition of odortypes may help establish the mother-infant bonds discussed in the chapter on human development.

OBJ 4.28: Define gustation and papillae. Describe the relationship among taste, smell, and flavor.

Test Items 4.136–4.139

Personal Learning Activity 4.4

ClassPrep PPT 41, OHT: The Tongue and Taste

Gustation

The chemical sense system in the mouth is gustation, or taste. The receptors for taste are in the taste buds, which are grouped together in structures called **papillae** (pronounced "pa-PILL-ee"). Normally, there are about 10,000 taste buds in a person's mouth, mostly on the tongue but also on the roof of the mouth and on the back of the throat.

In contrast to the olfactory system, which can discriminate thousands of different odors, the human taste system detects only a few elementary sensations. The most familiar of these are sweet, sour, bitter, and salty. Each taste bud responds best to one or two of these categories, but it also responds weakly to others. The sensation of a particular substance appears to result from the responses of taste buds that are relatively sensitive to a specific category. Behavioral studies and electrical recordings from taste neurons have also established two additional taste sensations (Rolls, 1997). One, called *umami*, enhances other tastes and is produced by certain proteins, as well as by monosodium glutamate (MSG). The other, called *astringent*, is the taste produced by tannins, which are found in teas, for example.

Different tastes are transduced into neural activity by quite different types of taste receptors, and in different ways (Stewart, DeSimone, & Hill, 1997). For example, sweet and bitter are signaled when chemicals fit into specific receptor sites (Montmayeur et al., 2001), whereas sour and salty act through more direct effects on the ion channels in membranes of taste cells. Knowledge of the chemistry of sweetness is allowing scientists to design new chemicals that fit into sweetness receptors and taste thousands of times sweeter than sugar. Many of these substances are

papillae Structures on the tongue containing groups of taste receptors, or taste buds.

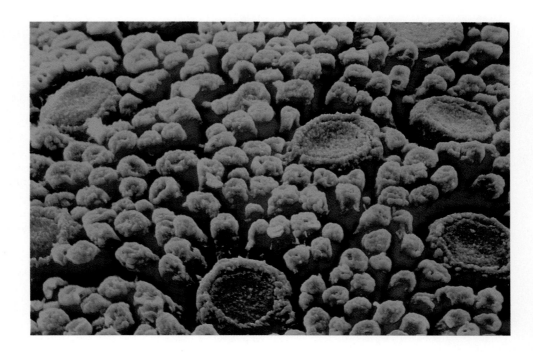

Taste Receptors Taste buds are grouped into structures called *papillae.* Two kinds of papillae are visible in this greatly enlarged photo of the surface of the human tongue.

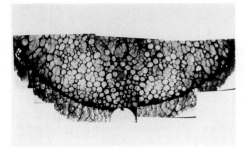

figure 4.24

Are You a Supertaster?

TRY THIS This photo shows the large number of papillae on the tongue of a "supertaster." If you don't mind a temporary stain on your mouth and teeth, you can look at your own papillae by painting the front of your tongue with a cotton swab soaked in blue food coloring. Distribute the dye by moving your tongue around and swallowing; then look into a magnifying mirror as you shine a flashlight on your tongue. The pink circles you see against the blue background are papillae, each of which has about six taste buds buried in its surface. Get several friends to do this test, and you will see that genes create wide individual differences in taste bud density.

now being tested for safety and may soon allow people to enjoy low-calorie hot-fudge sundaes.

A taste component in its own right, saltiness also enhances the taste of food by suppressing bitterness (Breslin & Beauchamp, 1997). In animals, taste responses to salt are determined during early development, before and after birth. Research with animals has shown that if mothers are put on a low-salt diet, their offspring are less likely to prefer salt (Hill & Przekop, 1988). In humans, experiences with salty foods over the first four years of life may alter the sensory systems that detect salt and contribute to enduring preferences for salty foods (Hill & Mistretta, 1990).

There may be genetically determined differences in the ability to taste things. About 25 percent of the population are "supertasters"—individuals who have an especially large number of papillae on their tongues (Bartoshuk, 2000). Supertasters have thousands of taste buds, whereas "nontasters" have only hundreds of buds (see Figure 4.24). Most people fall between these extremes. Supertasters are more sensitive than other people to bitterness, as revealed in their reaction to foods such as broccoli, soy products, and grapefruit. Having different numbers of taste buds may help account for differences in people's food intake, as well as weight problems. For example, Linda Bartoshuk has found that compared with overweight people, thin people have many more taste buds (Duffy et al., 1999). Perhaps they do not have to eat as much to experience the good tastes of food.

Smell, Taste, and Flavor ClassPrep PPT 43: Smell, Taste, and Flavor

If you have a stuffy nose, everything tastes like cardboard. Why? Because smell and taste act as two components of a single system, known as *flavor* (Rozin, 1982). Most of the properties that make food taste good are actually odors detected by the olfactory system, not activities of the taste system. The olfactory and gustatory pathways converge in the *orbitofrontal cortex* (Rolls, 1997), where neurons also respond to the sight and texture of food. The responses of neurons in this "flavor cortex" are also influenced by conditions of hunger and satiety ("fullness").

Both tastes and odors prompt strong emotional responses. For tastes, the reaction to bitter flavors is inborn, but the associations of emotions with odors are all learned (Bartoshuk, 1991). Many animals easily learn taste aversions to particular

in review	Smell and Taste	
Aspect of Sensory System	**Elements**	**Key Characteristics**
Energy	Smell: volatile chemicals Taste: chemicals in solution	The amount, intensity, and location of the chemicals determine taste and smell sensations.
Structures of taste and smell	Smell: chemical receptors in the mucous membrane of the nose Taste: taste buds grouped in papillae in the mouth	Odor and taste molecules stimulate chemical receptors.
Pathways to the brain	Olfactory bulb and taste buds	Axons from the nose bypass the thalamus and extend directly to the olfactory bulb.

ClassPrep PPT 44: Smell, Taste, and Flavor (cont.)

foods when the taste is associated with nausea, but humans learn aversions to odors more readily than to tastes (Bartoshuk & Wolfe, 1990).

Variations in one's nutritional state affect taste and flavor, as well as the motivation to consume particular foods. For example, food deprivation or salt deficiency makes sweet or salty things taste better. Intake of protein and fat are influenced more indirectly. Molecules of protein and fat have no inherent taste or smell; the tastes and smells of foods that contain these nutrients actually come from small amounts of other volatile substances. So adjustments in the intake of these nutrients are based on associations between olfactory cues from the volatile substances and the nutritional consequences of eating the foods (Bartoshuk, 1991). These findings have implications for dieting, which is discussed in the chapter on motivation and emotion.

IRM Discussion 11.8: The Curiosity of Chili Pepper: Anatomy of a Motivation

Flavor includes other characteristics of food as well: its tactile properties (how it feels in your mouth) and, especially, its temperature. Temperature does not alter saltiness, but warm foods are experienced as sweeter; in fact, simply warming a person's taste receptors creates a sensation of sweetness (Cruz & Green, 2000). Aromas released from warm food rise from the mouth into the nose and create more flavor sensations. This is why some people find hot pizza delicious and cold pizza disgusting. Spicy "hot" foods actually stimulate pain fibers in the mouth because they contain a substance called *capsaicin* (pronounced "kap-SAY-uh-sin"), which opens specific ion channels in pain neurons that are also opened by heat. As a result, these foods are experienced as physiologically "hot" (Caterina et al., 1997). Why do people eat spicy foods even though they stimulate pain? The practice may have originated because many "hot" spices have antibacterial properties. In fact, researchers have found a strong correlation between frequent use of antibacterial spices and living in climates that promote bacterial contamination (Billing & Sherman, 1998). ("In Review: Smell and Taste" summarizes our discussion of these senses.)

ClassPrep PPT 45: Somatic Senses and the Vestibular System

Somatic Senses and the Vestibular System

Some senses are not located in a specific organ, such as the eye or the ear. These are the **somatic senses,** also called *somatosensory systems,* which are spread throughout the body. The somatic senses include the skin senses of touch, temperature, and

OBJ 4.29: Define somatic sense or somatosensory system. Describe the transduction process in the skin senses, including touch, temperature, and pain.

Test Items 4.140–4.144

ClassPrep PPT 46: Touch

pain, as well as kinesthesia, the sense that tells the brain where the parts of the body are. Closely related to kinesthesia is the vestibular system, which tells the brain about the position and movements of the head. Although not strictly a somatosensory system, the vestibular system will also be considered in this section.

Touch and Temperature   **LSV:** Phantom Limb

Touch is crucial. People can function and prosper without vision, hearing, or smell, but a person without touch would have difficulty surviving. Without a sense of touch, you could not even swallow food, because you could not tell where it was in your mouth and throat.   **Videodisc Segment & Still:** The Skin

Stimulus and Receptors for Touch
The energy detected by the sense of touch is the mechanical deformation of tissue, usually of the skin. The skin covers nearly two square yards of surface and weighs more than twenty pounds. The hairs distributed virtually everywhere on the skin do not sense anything directly, but when bent, they deform the skin beneath them. The receptors that transduce this deformation into neural activity are in, or just below, the skin.

Many nerve endings in the skin are candidates for the role of touch receptor. Some neurons come from the spinal cord, enter the skin, and simply end; these are called *free nerve endings*. Many other neurons end in a variety of elaborate, specialized structures. However, there is generally little relationship between the type of nerve ending and the type of sensory information carried by the neuron. Many types of nerve endings respond to mechanical stimuli, but the exact process through which they transduce mechanical energy is still unknown. These somatosensory neurons are unusual in that they have no dendrites. Their cell bodies are outside the spinal cord, and their axon splits and extends both to the skin and to the spinal cord. Action potentials travel from the nerve endings in the skin to the spinal cord, where they communicate across a synapse to dendrites of other neurons.

We do more than just passively respond to whatever happens to come in contact with our bodies. For humans, touch is also an active sense that is used to get specific information. In much the same way as you can look as well as just see, you can also touch as well as feel. When people are involved in active sensing, they usually use the part of the sensory apparatus that has the greatest sensitivity. For vision, this is the fovea; for touch, the fingertips. (The area of primary somatosensory cortex devoted to the fingertips is correspondingly large.) Fingertip touch is the principal way people explore the textures of surfaces. It can be extremely sensitive, as evidenced by blind people who can read Braille as rapidly as 200 words per minute (Foulke, 1991).

IRM Activity 5.8: A Somatosensory Illusion

Adaptation of Touch Receptors
Constant input from all your touch neurons would provide an abundance of unnecessary information. Once you get dressed, for example, you do not need to be constantly reminded that you are wearing clothes. Thanks in part to the process of adaptation mentioned earlier, you do not continue to feel your clothes against your skin.

Changes in touch (as when a shoelace breaks, making your shoe feel loose) constitute the most important sensory information. The touch sense emphasizes these changes and filters out the excess information. How? Typically, a touch neuron responds with a burst of firing when a stimulus is applied, then quickly returns to baseline firing rates, even though the stimulus may still be in contact with the skin. If the touch pressure increases, the neuron again responds with an increase in firing rate, but then it again slows down. A few neurons adapt more slowly, continuing to fire at an elevated rate as long as pressure is applied to the skin. By attending to this input, you can sense a constant stimulus (try doing this by focusing on sensations from your glasses or shoes).

somatic senses Senses of touch, temperature, pain, and kinesthesia.

The Complex Nature of Pain If pain were based only on the nature of incoming stimuli, this participant in a purification ceremony in Singapore would be hurting. However, as described in the chapter on consciousness, the experience of pain is a complex phenomenon affected by psychological and biological variables that can make it more, or as in this case less, intense.

Coding and Representation of Touch Information

The sense of touch codes information about two aspects of an object in contact with the skin: its weight and its location. The *intensity* of the stimulus—how heavy it is—is coded by both the firing rate of individual neurons and the number of neurons stimulated. A heavy object produces a higher rate of firing and stimulates more neurons than a light object. The *location* of touch is coded much as it is for vision: by the spatial organization of the information.

Touch information is organized such that signals from neighboring points on the skin stay next to one another other, even as they ascend from the skin through the spinal cord to the thalamus and on to the somatosensory cortex. So just as there is a topographical map of the visual field in the brain, the area of cortex that receives touch information resembles a map of the surface of the body (see Figure 3.17). As with the other senses, these representations are contralateral; that is, input from the left side of the body goes to the right side of the brain, and vice versa. In nonhuman primates, however, touch information from each hand is sent to both sides of the brain. This arrangement appears to amplify information from manual exploration of objects and to improve feedback from hand movements (Iwamura, Iriki, & Tanaka, 1994).

Temperature

When you dig your toes into a sandy summer beach, the pleasant experience you get comes partly from the sensation of warmth. Touch and temperature seem to be separate senses, and to some extent they are; but the difference between the two senses is not always clear.

Some of the skin's sensory neurons respond to a change in temperature, but not to simple contact. There are "warm fibers," which are nerve fibers that increase their firing rates when the temperature changes in the range of about 95 to 115°F (35 to 47°C). Temperatures above this range are painful and stimulate different fibers. Other nerve fibers are "cold fibers"; they respond to a broad range of cool temperatures. However, many of the fibers that respond to temperature also respond to touch, so sensations of touch and temperature sometimes interact. For example, warm and cold objects can feel up to 250 percent heavier than body-temperature objects (Stevens & Hooper, 1982). Also, if you touch an object made up of alternating warm and cool bars, you will have the sensation of intense heat (Thunberg, 1896, cited in Craig & Bushnell, 1994).

Stimulation of the touch sense can have some interesting psychological and physiological effects. For example, premature infants gain weight 47 percent faster when they are given massages; they do not eat more but, rather, process the food more efficiently. In children with asthma, massage therapy increases air flow (Field et al., 1998); in children with arthritis, it reduces pain and lowers stress hormone levels (Field et al., 1997). In adults, massage can reduce anxiety, increase brainwave (EEG) patterns associated with alertness, and improve performance on math tests (Field et al., 1996).

Pain

The skin senses can convey a great deal of pleasure, but a change in the intensity of the same kind of stimulation can create a distinctly different sensation: pain. Pain provides you with information about the impact of the world on your body; it can tell you, "A hammer just crushed your left thumb." Pain also has a distinctly negative emotional component. Researchers have focused on the information-carrying aspects of pain, its emotional components, and the various ways that the brain can adjust the amount of pain that reaches consciousness.

Pain as an Information Sense

The information-carrying aspect of pain is very similar to that of touch and temperature. The receptors for pain are free nerve endings. As mentioned earlier, for example, capsaicin, the active ingredient in

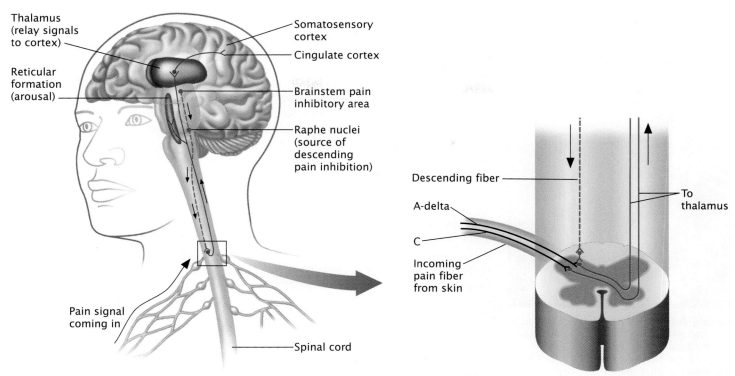

Thalamus (relay signals to cortex)

Reticular formation (arousal)

Somatosensory cortex

Cingulate cortex

Brainstem pain inhibitory area

Raphe nuclei (source of descending pain inhibition)

Pain signal coming in

Spinal cord

Descending fiber

A-delta

C

Incoming pain fiber from skin

To thalamus

figure 4.25

Pain Pathways

Pain messages are carried to the brain by way of the spinal cord. Myelinated *A-delta fibers* carry information about sharp pain. Unmyelinated *C fibers* carry several types of pain, including chronic, dull aches. Pain fibers make synapses in the reticular formation, causing arousal. They also project to the thalamus and from there to the cortex.

ClassPrep PPT 51, OHT: *Figure 4.25:* Pain Pathways

Videodisc Segment & Still: The Pain Gate

OBJ 4.30: Describe the gate-control theory of pain sensation. Define analgesia. Know the names of the body's natural analgesics.

Test Items 4.145–4.152

ClassPrep PPT 52: Modulating Pain

chili peppers, creates pain in the mouth by specifically stimulating these pain nerve endings. Painful stimuli cause the release of chemicals that fit into specialized receptors in pain neurons, causing them to fire. The axons of pain-sensing neurons release neurotransmitters not only near the spinal cord, sending information to the brain, but also near the skin, causing local inflammation.

Two types of nerve fibers carry pain signals from the skin to the spinal cord. *A-delta fibers* carry sharp, pricking pain sensations; they are myelinated to carry the sharp pain message quickly. *C fibers* carry chronic, dull aches and burning sensations. Some of these same C fibers also respond to nonpainful touch, but with a different pattern of firing.

Both A-delta and C fibers carry pain impulses into the spinal cord, where they form synapses with neurons that carry the pain signals to the thalamus and other parts of the brain (see Figure 4.25). Different pain neurons are activated by different degrees of painful stimulation. Numerous types of neurotransmitters are used by different pain neurons, a phenomenon that has allowed the development of a variety of new drugs for pain management.

The role of the cerebral cortex in experiencing pain is still being explored. Earlier studies of humans undergoing brain surgery for epilepsy concluded that pain has little, if any, cortical representation (Penfield & Rasmussen, 1968). More recently, functional magnetic resonance imaging (MRI) studies of healthy volunteers have compared cortical activity during a pain experience with cortical activity during an attention-demanding task (Davis et al., 1997). The scans showed activation of the somatosensory cortex under both conditions, and additional activity during pain in the *anterior cingulate cortex,* an evolutionarily primitive region thought to be important in emotions. When hypnosis has been used to manipulate the unpleasantness of pain, there are corresponding changes in cingulate cortex activity but not in somatosensory cortex activity. This is yet another finding consistent with the hypothesized role of this brain region in pain perception (Rainville et al., 1997).

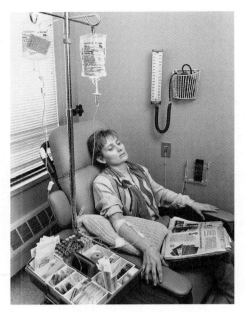

Easing Pain   Candy containing capsaicin is sometimes given for the treatment of painful mouth sores associated with cancer chemotherapy (Berger et al., 1995). Capsaicin is what makes chili peppers "hot," but eating enough of it results in desensitization and a corresponding reduction in pain sensations (Bevan & Geppetti, 1994).

Natural Analgesia   The stress of athletic exertion causes the release of endorphins, natural painkillers that have been associated with pleasant feelings nicknamed "runner's high."

Research also suggests that pain can be experienced without any external stimulation of pain receptors. In such cases, the pain appears to originate in the thalamus and in cortical regions of the brain (Canavero & Bonicalzi, 1998; Gawande, 1998).

Emotional Aspects of Pain   All senses can have emotional components, most of which are learned responses. For example, the smell of baking cookies can make you feel good if it has been associated with happy childhood times. The emotional response to pain is more direct. Specific pathways carry an emotional component of the painful stimulus to areas of the hindbrain and reticular formation (see Figure 4.25), as well as to the cingulate cortex via the thalamus (Craig et al., 1994; Johansen, Fields, & Manning, 2001).

Nevertheless, the overall emotional response to pain depends greatly on cognitive factors (Keefe & France, 1999; Pincus & Morley, 2001). For example, experimenters compared responses to a painful stimulus in people who were informed about the nature of the stimulus, and when to expect it, with responses in people who were not similarly informed. Knowing about pain seemed to make it less objectionable, even though the sensation was reported to be just as noticeable (Mayer & Price, 1982). Another factor affecting emotional responses to pain sensations is the use of pain-reducing strategies, such as focusing on distracting thoughts (Young et al., 1995).

Modulation of Pain: The Gate Control Theory   Pain is extremely useful, because in the long run it protects you from harm. However, there are times when enough is enough. Fortunately, the nervous system has several mechanisms for controlling the experience of pain.

One explanation of how the nervous system controls the amount of pain that reaches the brain is the **gate control theory** (Melzack & Wall, 1965). It holds that there is a "gate" in the spinal cord that either lets pain impulses travel upward to the brain or blocks their progress. The details of the original formulation of this theory turned out to be incorrect, but later work supports the idea that natural mechanisms can block pain sensations (Stanton-Hicks & Salamon, 1997). For example, input from other skin senses can come into the spinal cord at the same time the pain gets there and "take over" the pathways that the pain impulses would have used. This appears to be why rubbing the skin around a wound temporarily reduces the pain that is felt, and why electrical stimulation of the skin around a painful spot relieves the pain. Gate control theory may also partially explain why scratching relieves itching, because itch sensations involve activity in fibers located close to pain fibers (Andrew & Craig, 2001).

The brain can also close the gate to pain impulses by sending signals down the spinal cord. The control of sensation by messages descending from the brain is a common aspect of sensory systems (Willis, 1988). In the case of pain, these messages from the brain block incoming pain signals at spinal cord synapses. The result is **analgesia**, the absence of the sensation of pain in the presence of a normally painful stimulus. For example, if part of a rat's hindbrain is electrically stimulated, pain signals generated in the skin never reach the brain (Reynolds, 1969). Permanently implanting stimulating electrodes in the same region of the human brain has reduced severe pain in some patients, but unfortunately it also produces a profound sense of impending doom (Hoffert, 1992).

Natural Analgesics   At least two substances play a role in the brain's ability to block pain signals: (1) the neurotransmitter *serotonin,* which is released by neurons descending from the brain, and (2) natural opiates called *endorphins.* As described in the chapter on biological aspects of psychology, endorphins are natural painkillers that act as neurotransmitters at many levels of the pain pathway, including the spinal cord, where they block the synapses of the fibers that carry pain signals. Endorphins may also relieve pain when the adrenal and pituitary glands secrete them into the bloodstream as hormones. The more endorphin receptors a person has inherited, the more pain tolerance that person has (Benjamin, Wilson, & Mogil, 1999; Uhl, Sora, & Wang, 1999).

Several conditions are known to cause the body to ease its own pain. For example, endorphins are released by immune cells that arrive at sites of inflammation (Cabot, 2001). And during the late stages of pregnancy, an endorphin system is activated that will reduce the mother's labor pains (Dawson-Basoa & Gintzler, 1997). An endorphin system is also activated when people believe they are receiving a painkiller even when they are not (Benedetti & Amanzio, 1997); this may be one reason for the placebo effect, discussed in the chapter on research in psychology. Remarkably, the resulting pain inhibition is experienced in the part of the body where it was expected to occur, but not elsewhere (Benedetti, Arduino, & Amanzio, 1999). Physical or psychological stress, too, can activate natural analgesic systems. Stress-induced release of endorphins may account for cases in which injured soldiers and athletes continue to perform in the heat of battle or competition with no apparent pain.

There are also mechanisms for reactivating pain sensitivity once a crisis is past. Studies with animals show that they can learn that certain situations signal "safety," and that these safety signals prompt the release of a neurotransmitter that counteracts endorphins' analgesic effects (Wiertelak, Maier, & Watkins, 1992). Blocking these "safety signals" increases the painkilling effects brought on by a placebo (Benedetti & Amanzio, 1997).

THINKING CRITICALLY

OBJ 4.31: Describe the evidence concerning acupuncture and the conclusions that are most reasonable.

Test Items 4.153–4.155

ClassPrep PPT 60: Thinking Critically: Does Acupuncture Relieve Pain?

Does Acupuncture Relieve Pain?

Acupuncture is an ancient and widely used treatment in Asian medicine that is alleged to relieve pain. The method is based on the idea that body energy flows along lines called *channels* (Vincent & Richardson, 1986). There are fourteen main channels, and a person's health supposedly depends on the balance of energy flowing in them. Stimulating the channels by inserting very thin needles into the skin and twirling them is said to restore a balanced flow of energy. The needles produce an aching and tingling sensation called *Teh-ch'i* at the site of stimulation, but they relieve pain at distant, seemingly unrelated parts of the body.

● **What am I being asked to believe or accept?**

Acupuncturists assert that twirling a needle in the skin can relieve pain caused by everything from tooth extraction to cancer.

● **What evidence is available to support the assertion?**

There is no scientific evidence for the existence of energy channels as described in the theory underlying acupuncture. However, as described in the chapter on biological aspects of psychology, some of the sites for stimulation are very near peripheral nerves, and there is evidence from MRI scans that stimulating these sites changes activity in brain regions related to the targets of treatment (Cho et al., 1998).

What about the more specific assertions that acupuncture relieves pain and that it does so through direct physical mechanisms? Numerous studies show positive results in 50 to 80 percent of patients treated by acupuncture for various kinds of pain (Richardson & Vincent, 1986). In one controlled study of headache pain, for example, 33 percent of the patients in a placebo group improved following mock electrical nerve stimulation (which is about the usual proportion of people responding to a placebo), but 53 percent reported reduced pain following real acupuncture (Dowson, Lewith, & Machin, 1985). Another headache study found both acupuncture and drugs to be superior to a placebo. Each reduced the frequency of headaches, but the drugs were more effective than acupuncture at

gate control theory A theory suggesting that a functional "gate" in the spinal cord can either let pain impulses travel upward to the brain or block their progress.

analgesia The absence of pain sensations in the presence of a normally painful stimulus.

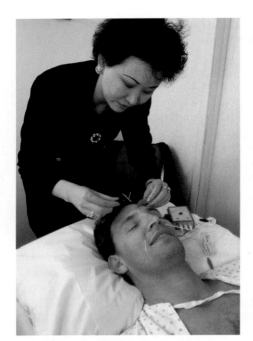

How Does Acupuncture Work? This acupuncturist is inserting fine needles in her patient's face in hopes of treating poor blood circulation in his hands and feet. Acupuncture treatments appear to alleviate a wide range of problems, including many kinds of pain, but the mechanisms through which it works are not yet determined.

reducing the severity of headache pain (Hesse, Mogelvang, & Simonsen, 1994). Such well-controlled studies are rare, however, and their results are often contradictory (Ter Riet, Kleijnen, & Knipschild, 1990). Recent studies of patients with back or neck pain, for example, found acupuncture to be no better than a placebo or massage therapy (Cherkin et al., 2001; Irnich et al., 2001).

There is evidence that acupuncture activates the endorphin system. It is associated with the release of endorphins in the brain, and drugs that slow the breakdown of opiates also prolong the analgesia produced by acupuncture (He, 1987). Furthermore, the pain-reducing effects of acupuncture during electrical stimulation of a tooth can be reversed by *naloxone,* a substance that blocks the painkilling effects of endorphins (and other opiate drugs). This finding suggests that acupuncture somehow activates the body's natural painkilling system. In cases where acupuncture activates endorphins, is this activation brought about only through the placebo effect? Probably not entirely, because acupuncture produces naloxone-reversible analgesia in monkeys and rats, who could not have developed positive expectancies by reading about acupuncture (Ha et al., 1981; Kishioka et al., 1994).

● Are there alternative ways of interpreting the evidence?

Yes. Evidence about acupuncture might be interpreted as simply confirming that the body's painkilling system can be stimulated by external means. Acupuncture may merely provide one activating method; there may be other, even more efficient methods for doing so. We already know, for example, that successful placebo treatments for human pain appear to operate by activating the endorphin system.

● What additional evidence would help to evaluate the alternatives?

More placebo-controlled studies of acupuncture are needed, but it is difficult to control for the placebo effect in acupuncture treatment, especially in double-blind fashion (e.g., Kaptchuk, 2001). (How could a therapist not know whether the treatment being given was acupuncture or not? And from the patient's perspective, what placebo treatment could look and feel like having a needle inserted and twirled in the skin?) Nevertheless, researchers have tried to separate the psychological and physical effects of acupuncture—for example, by using sham needles; mock electrical nerve stimulation, in which electrodes are attached to the skin but no electrical stimulation is given; or stimulation at other sites on the skin (Park, White, & Ernst, 2001).

Researchers also need to go beyond focusing on the effects of acupuncture to consider the general relationship between internal painkilling systems and external methods for stimulating them. Regarding acupuncture itself, scientists do not yet know what factors govern whether it will activate the endorphin system. Other important unknowns include the types of pain for which acupuncture is most effective, the types of patients who respond best, and the precise procedures that are most effective.

● What conclusions are most reasonable?

There seems little doubt that in some circumstances, acupuncture relieves pain. It is not a panacea, however. For example, committees convened in the United States and the United Kingdom have concluded that acupuncture can be effective for the treatment of pain and nausea (British Medical Association, 2000; National Institutes of Health, 1998), but more than $2 million in research has failed to show that acupuncture is better than the best antinausea drugs or conventional painkilling procedures (Taub, 1998). While critics argue that further expenditures for acupuncture research are not warranted, proponents point out that acupuncture's effects can go beyond pain reduction. One study, for example, found that preoperative acupuncture reduced postoperative pain and nausea, decreased the need for pain-relieving drugs, and reduced patients' stress responses (Kotani et al., 2001). Further studies are likely to continue; the quality of their methodology and the nature of their results will determine whether acupuncture finds a prominent place in Western medicine.

Balancing Act   The smooth coordination of all physical movement, from scratching your nose to complex feats of balance, depends on kinesthesia, the sense that provides information about where each part of the body is in relation to all the others.

ClassPrep PPT 53–55: Proprioception; Vestibular Sense; Kinesthesia

Personal Learning Activity 4.5

proprioceptive senses   The sensory systems that allow us to know about where we are and what each part of our body is doing.

vestibular sense   The proprioceptive sense that provides information about the position of the head (and hence the body) in space and about its movements.

vestibular sacs   Organs in the inner ear that connect the semicircular canals and the cochlea, and contribute to the body's sense of balance.

otoliths   Small crystals in the fluid-filled vestibular sacs of the inner ear that, when shifted by gravity, stimulate nerve cells that inform the brain of the position of the head.

semicircular canals   Tubes in the inner ear whose fluid, when shifted by head movements, stimulates nerve cells that tell the brain about those movements.

kinesthesia   The sense that tells you where the parts of your body are with respect to one another.

Proprioception

OBJ 4.32: Name the proprioceptive senses and explain how they differ from other sensory systems.

Most sensory systems receive information from the external world, such as the light reflected from a flower or the feeling of cool water. But as far as the brain is concerned, the rest of the body is "out there," too. You know about the position of your body and what each of its parts is doing only because sensory systems provide this information to the brain. These sensory systems are called **proprioceptive senses** (*proprioceptive* means "received from one's own").

Vestibular Sense

OBJ 4.33: Describe the types of information that the vestibular sense provides. Discuss the role of the vestibular sacs, otoliths, and semicircular canals in the sensation of vestibular information.

The **vestibular sense** tells the brain about the position of the head (and hence the body) in space and about its general movements. It is often thought of as the *sense of balance*. People usually become aware of the vestibular sense only when they overstimulate it and become dizzy.   Test Items 4.156–4.161

The organs for the vestibular sense are two vestibular sacs and three semicircular canals that are part of the inner ear. (You can see the semicircular canals in Figure 4.3; the vestibular sacs connect these canals and the cochlea.) The **vestibular sacs** are filled with fluid and contain small crystals called **otoliths** ("ear stones") that rest on hair endings. The **semicircular canals** are fluid-filled, arc-shaped tubes; tiny hairs extend into the fluid in the canals. When your head moves, the otoliths shift in the vestibular sacs and the fluid moves in the semicircular canals, stimulating hair endings. This process activates neurons that travel with the auditory nerve, signaling to the brain the amount and direction of head movement.

The vestibular system has neural connections to the cerebellum, to the part of the autonomic nervous system (ANS) that affects the digestive system, and to the muscles of the eyes. The connections to the cerebellum help coordinate bodily movements. The connections to the ANS are partly responsible for the nausea that sometimes follows overstimulation of the vestibular system—on amusement park rides, for example. Finally, the connections to the eye muscles create *vestibular-ocular reflexes*. For instance, when your head moves in one direction, your eyes reflexively move in the opposite direction. This reflex allows your eyes to fixate on a point in space even when your head is moving, so you can track a ball in flight as you are running to catch it. You can experience this reflex by having a friend spin you around on a stool for a while; when you stop, try to fix your gaze on one point in the room. You will be temporarily unable to do so, because the excitation of the vestibular system will cause your eyes to move repeatedly in the direction opposite to that in which you were spinning. Because vestibular reflexes adapt to the lack of gravity in outer space, astronauts returning to earth have postural and movement difficulties until their vestibular systems readjust to the effects of gravity (Paloski, 1998).   Videodisc Segment & Still: The Vestibular Organ

Kinesthesia

The sense that tells you where the parts of your body are with respect to one another is **kinesthesia** (pronounced "kin-es-THEE-zha"). You probably do not think much about kinesthetic information, but you definitely use it, and you can demonstrate it for yourself. Close your eyes, hold your arms out in front of you, and try to touch your two index fingertips together. You probably did this well because your kinesthetic sense told you where each finger was with respect to your body. You also depend on kinesthetic information to guide all your movements. Otherwise, it would be impossible to develop or improve any motor skill, from basic walking to complex athletic movements. These movement patterns become simple and fluid because with practice, the brain uses kinesthetic information automatically.

Normally, kinesthetic information comes primarily from the joints but it also comes from muscles. Receptors in muscle fibers send information to the brain about the stretching of muscles (McCloskey, 1978). When the position of the bones

in review Body Senses

Sense	Energy	Conversion of Physical Energy to Nerve Activity	Pathways and Characteristics
Touch	Mechanical deformation of skin	Skin receptors (may be stimulated by hair on the skin)	Nerve endings respond to changes in weight (intensity) and location of touch.
Temperature	Heat	Sensory neurons in the skin	Changes in temperature are detected by warm-sensing and cool-sensing fibers. Temperature interacts with touch.
Pain	Increases with intensity of touch or temperature	Free nerve endings in or near the skin surface	Changes in intensity cause the release of chemicals detected by receptors in pain neurons. Some fibers convey sharp pain; others convey dull aches and burning sensations.
Kinesthesia	Mechanical energy of joint and muscle movement	Receptors in muscle fibers	Information from muscle fibers is sent to the spinal cord, thalamus, cerebellum, and cortex.

OBJ 4.34: Define kinesthesia. Name the source of kinesthetic information and explain what went wrong with Christina, who was the subject of the case study.

Test Items 4.162–4.165

changes, receptors in the joints transduce this mechanical energy into neural activity, providing information about both the rate of change and the angle of the bones. This coded information goes to the spinal cord and is sent from there to the thalamus, along with sensory information from the skin. Eventually the information goes to the cerebellum and to the somatosensory cortex (see Figures 3.13 and 3.16), both of which are involved in the smooth coordination of movements

Proprioception is a critical sense for success in physical therapy and rehabilitative medicine, especially for people who have to relearn how to move their muscles after strokes or other problems. Research in a branch of physics called *nonlinear dynamics* has been applied to problems in proprioception. Utilizing the discovery that the right amount of random, background noise can actually improve the detection of signals, rehabilitation neurologists have found that adding a small amount of vibration (or "noise") to muscle and joint sensations dramatically increases patients' ability to detect joint movements and position (Glanz, 1997). (See "In Review: Body Senses" for a summary of our discussion of touch, temperature, pain, and kinesthesia.)

FOCUS ON RESEARCH METHODS

ClassPrep PPT 60: Focus on Research Methods: The Case of the Disembodied Woman

The Case of the Disembodied Woman

Early in this chapter we discussed the problem of coding sensation—of translating the physical properties of some stimulus into neural signals that make sense to the brain. In later sections we described how this problem is "solved" for the different senses. But what happens when the brain does not receive the sensory information it needs? The most common examples of this situation are deafness and blindness, but in the case study described next, a person suffered the loss of a proprioceptive sense.

● What was the researcher's question?

Oliver Sacks, a well-known clinical neurologist, has spent years treating people with "neurological deficits"—that is, impairments or incapacities of neurological functions. One of his most memorable cases was that of "Christina," who had apparently lost the sense of kinesthesia and, thus, was unable to feel the position of her own body.

In 1977, Christina was a healthy young woman who entered a hospital in preparation for some minor surgery. The night before her operation, she dreamt that she was unsteady on her feet, "could hardly feel anything in her hands . . . and kept dropping whatever she picked up" (Sacks, 1985, p. 43). Her dream soon became a horrible reality. The next day, Christina tried to get out of bed but flopped onto the floor like a rag doll. She was unable to hold onto objects and had trouble moving. She felt "weird—disembodied." A psychiatrist diagnosed Christina's problem as *conversion disorder,* a psychological condition described in the chapter on psychological disorders as involving apparent, but not actual, damage to sensory or motor systems. Sacks, however, wondered if there might be another reason for Christina's strange symptoms.

● How did the researcher answer the question?

Sacks tested Christina's nerve and muscle functions, performed a spinal tap to examine the fibers that carry sensory information to the brain, and studied the portion of her brain that receives proprioceptive information. His approach exemplifies the *case study* method of research. As noted in the chapter on research in psychology, case studies focus intensively on a particular individual, group, or situation. Sometimes they lead to important insights about clinical problems or other phenomena that occur so rarely that they cannot be studied through surveys or controlled experiments.

● What did the researcher find?

Sacks's examination of Christina ruled out a psychological disorder. His tests of her nerves and muscles disclosed that the signals they normally sent to tell her brain about the location of her body parts were simply not being transmitted. The spinal tap revealed why: The sensory neurons that carry proprioceptive information had, for unknown reasons, degenerated. As a result, Christina seemed to have become disconnected from her body. On one occasion, for example, she became annoyed at a visitor who she thought was tapping her fingers on a table top. But it was Christina, not the visitor, who was doing it. Her hands were acting on their own; her body was doing things she did not know about.

● What do the results mean?

In his analysis of this case, Sacks noted that the sense we have of our bodies is provided partly through our experience of seeing it, but also partly through proprioception. Christina put it this way: "Proprioception is like the eyes of the body, the way the body sees itself. And if it goes, it's like the body's blind." With great effort and determination, Christina was ultimately able to regain some of her ability to move about. If she looked intently at her arms and legs, she could coordinate their movement to some degree. Eventually, she left the hospital and resumed many of her normal activities. But Christina never recovered her sense of self. She still feels like a stranger in her own body.

● What do we still need to know?

The story of Christina and the other fascinating case studies in Sacks's popular books, such as *The Man Who Mistook His Wife for a Hat* (1985) and *An Anthropologist on Mars* (1996), not only contribute substantially to our knowledge of sensory and neurological systems but also illustrate the incredible complexity and fragility of sensory processes. However, the case study methodology, by itself, does not provide a full understanding of how sensory processes work and what happens when they go wrong. As noted in the chapter on research in psychology, it is difficult to identify causes using case studies alone. The immediate source of Christina's difficulty was selective degeneration of nerve fibers. But what was the cause of that degeneration? Case studies can rarely answer this kind of question.

Although the case study of Christina did not confirm any hypotheses or identify causal relationships, as an experiment might have, it did focus attention on a rare kinesthetic disorder. This condition was almost unknown when Sacks first reported it, but it has since been diagnosed in several individuals. Specifically, it is found among people taking megadoses of vitamin B6, also known as pyridoxine (Sacks, 1985). These high doses—but also lower doses taken over a long period of time—can damage sensory neurons (Dordain & Deffond, 1994). We still need to learn how vitamin B6 might cause such damage and whether kinesthetic disorders like Christina's can have other causes. So, much research remains to be done. Through this work, psychologists and other scientists will continue to unravel the mysteries of our sensory processes.

LINKAGES

As noted in the chapter on introducing psychology, all of psychology's subfields are related to one another. Our discussion of the representation of the sensory systems in the brain illustrates just one way in which the topic of this chapter, sensation, is linked to the subfield of biological psychology, which is the focus of the chapter on biological aspects of psychology. The Linkages diagram shows ties to two other subfields as well, and there are many more ties throughout the book. Looking for linkages among subfields will help you see how they all fit together and help you appreciate the big picture that is psychology.

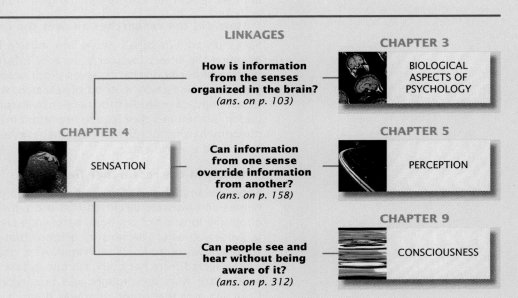

SUMMARY

A *sense* is a system that translates information from outside the nervous system into neural activity. Messages from the senses are called *sensations*.

Sensory Systems

The first step in sensation involves *accessory structures,* which collect and modify sensory stimuli. The second step is *transduction,* the process of converting incoming energy into neural activity; it is accomplished by *sensory receptors,* cells specialized to detect energy of some type. *Adaptation* takes place when receptors receive unchanging stimulation. Neural activity is transferred through the thalamus (except in the case of olfaction) and on to the cortex.

The Problem of Coding

Coding is the translation of physical properties of a stimulus into a pattern of neural activity that specifically identifies those physical properties. It is the language the brain uses to describe sensations. Coding is characterized by the *doctrine of specific nerve energies:* Stimulation of a particular sensory nerve provides codes for that one sense, no matter how the stimulation takes place. There are two basic types of sensory codes: *temporal codes* and *spatial codes.*

Hearing

Sound is a repetitive fluctuation in the pressure of a medium such as air. It travels in waves.

Sound

The *frequency* (which is related to *wavelength*) and *amplitude* of sound waves approximately correspond to the psychological dimensions of *pitch* and *loudness,* respectively. *Timbre,* the quality of sound, depends on complex wave patterns added to the lowest frequency of the sound.

The Ear

The energy from sound waves is collected and transmitted to the *cochlea* through a series of accessory structures, including the *tympanic membrane.* Transduction occurs when sound energy stimulates hair cells of the organ of Corti on the *basilar membrane* of the cochlea, which in turn stimulate the *auditory nerve.*

Coding Intensity and Frequency

The intensity of a sound stimulus is coded by the firing rate of auditory neurons. *Place theory* describes the coding of higher frequencies: They are coded by the place on the basilar membrane where the wave envelope peaks. Each neuron in the auditory nerve is most sensitive to a specific frequency (its characteristic frequency). Very low frequencies are coded by frequency matching, which refers to the fact that the firing rate of a neuron matches the frequency of a sound wave; according to *frequency-matching theory,* or volley theory, some frequencies may be matched by the firing rate of a group of neurons. Low to moderate frequencies are coded through a combination of these methods.

Auditory Pathways and Representations

Auditory information is relayed through the thalamus to the *primary auditory cortex* and to other areas of auditory cortex. Sounds of similar frequency activate neighboring cells in the cortex, but loudness is coded temporally.

Vision

Light

Visible light is electromagnetic radiation with a wavelength of about 400 nanometers to about 750 nanometers. *Light intensity,* or the amount of energy in light, determines its brightness. Differing *light wavelengths* are sensed as different colors.

Focusing Light

Accessory structures of the eye include the *cornea, pupil, iris,* and *lens.* Through *accommodation* and other means, these structures focus light rays on the *retina,* the netlike structure of cells at the back of the eye.

Converting Light into Images

Photoreceptors in the retina—*rods* and *cones*—have *photopigments* and can transduce light into neural activity. Rods and cones differ in their shape, their sensitivity to light, their ability to discriminate colors, and their distribution across the retina. The *fovea,* the area of highest *acuity,* has only cones, which are color sensitive. Rods are more sensitive to light but do not discriminate colors; they are distributed in areas around the fovea. Both types of photoreceptors contribute to *dark adaptation.* From the photoreceptors, energy transduced from light is transferred to bipolar cells and then to *ganglion cells,* aided by lateral connections between photoreceptors, bipolar cells, and ganglion cells. Through *lateral inhibition,* the retina enhances the contrast between dark and light areas. Most ganglion cells, in effect, compare the amount of light falling on the center of their *receptive fields* with that falling on the surrounding area.

Visual Pathways

The ganglion cells send action potentials out of the eye, at a point where a *blind spot* is created. Axons of ganglion cells leave the eye as a bundle of fibers called the *optic nerve;* half of these fibers cross over at the *optic chiasm* and terminate in the *lateral geniculate nucleus (LGN)* of the thalamus. Neurons in the LGN send visual information on to the *primary visual cortex.*

Visual Representations

Visual form, color, movement, and distance are processed by parallel systems. Complex *feature detectors* in the visual cortex are hierarchically built out of simpler units that detect and respond to features such as lines, edges, and orientations.

Seeing Color

The color of an object depends on which of the wavelengths striking it are absorbed and which are reflected. The sensation of color has three psychological dimensions: *hue, saturation,* and *brightness.* According to the *trichromatic* (or Young-Helmholtz) *theory,* color vision results from the fact that the eye includes three types of cones, each of which is most sensitive to short, medium, or long wavelengths; information from the three types combines to produce the sensation of color. Individuals may have variations in the number and sensitivity of their cone pigments. According to the *opponent-process* (or Hering) *theory,* there are red-green, blue-yellow, and black-white visual elements; the members of each pair inhibit each other so that only one member of a pair may produce a signal at a time. This theory explains color afterimages, as well as the fact that lights of complementary colors cancel each other out and produce gray when mixed together.

The Interaction of Vision and Hearing: Synesthesia

Various dimensions of vision interact, and vision can also interact with hearing and other senses in a process known as *synesthesia.* For example, some people experience certain colors when stimulated by certain letters, numbers, or sounds.

The Chemical Senses: Smell and Taste

The chemical senses include olfaction (smell) and gustation (taste).

Olfaction

Olfaction detects volatile chemicals that come into contact with olfactory receptors in the nose. Olfactory signals are sent to the *olfactory bulb* in the brain without passing through the thalamus. *Pheromones* are odors from one animal that change the physiology or behavior of another animal; in mammals, pheromones act through the *vomeronasal organ*.

Gustation

Gustation detects chemicals that come into contact with taste receptors in *papillae* on the tongue. Elementary taste sensations are limited to sweet, sour, bitter, salty, umami, and astringent. The combined responses of many taste buds determine a taste sensation.

Smell, Taste, and Flavor

The senses of smell and taste interact to produce flavor.

Somatic Senses and the Vestibular System

The *somatic senses*, or somatosensory systems, include skin senses and proprioceptive senses. The skin senses include touch, temperature, and pain.

Touch and Temperature

Nerve endings in the skin generate touch sensations when they are mechanically stimulated. Some nerve endings are sensitive to temperature, and some respond to both temperature and touch. Signals from neighboring points on the skin stay next to one another all the way to the cortex.

Pain

Pain provides information about damaging stimuli. Sharp pain and dull, chronic pain are carried by different fibers—A-delta and C fibers, respectively. The emotional response to pain depends on how the painful stimulus is interpreted. According to the *gate control theory*, incoming pain signals can be blocked by a "gate" in the spinal cord; messages sent from the brain down the spinal cord also can block pain signals, producing *analgesia*. Endorphins act at several levels of the pain systems to reduce sensations of pain.

Proprioception

Proprioceptive senses provide information about the body. The *vestibular sense* provides information about the position of the head in space through the *otoliths* in *vestibular sacs* and the *semicircular canals*, and *kinesthesia* provides information about the positions of body parts with respect to one another.

Perception

5

143

144

At a traffic circle in Scotland, fourteen fatal accidents occurred in a single year, partly because drivers failed to slow down as they approached the circle. When warning signs failed to solve the problem, Gordon Denton, a British psychologist, proposed an ingenious solution. White lines were painted across the road leading to the circle, in a pattern that looked something like this:

/   /   /   /   /   / / /

Drivers crossing these progressively more closely spaced lines at a constant speed got the impression that they were speeding up, and their automatic response was to slow down (Denton, 1980). During the fourteen months after Denton's idea was implemented, there were only two fatalities at the traffic circle. The same striping is now being used to slow drivers on roads approaching small towns in the United States (Associated Press, 1999). Denton's solution to this problem relied heavily on his knowledge of the principles of human perception.

Perception is the process through which sensations are interpreted, using knowledge and understanding of the world, so that they become meaningful experiences. Perception is not a passive process of simply absorbing and decoding incoming sensations. If it were, our experience of the environment would be a constantly changing, utterly confusing mosaic of light and color. Instead, our brains take sensations and create a coherent world, often by filling in missing information and using past experience to give meaning to what we see, hear, or touch. For example, the raw sensations coming from the stimuli in Figure 5.1 convey only the information that there is a series of intersecting lines. But your perceptual system automatically interprets this image as a rectangle (or window frame) on its side.

We begin this chapter by considering these perceptual processes and the various approaches that psychologists have taken in trying to understand them. Then we explore how people detect incoming sensory stimuli, organize these sensations into distinct and stable patterns, and recognize those patterns. We also examine the role of attention in guiding the perceptual system to analyze some parts of the world more closely than others. Finally, we provide some examples of how research on perception has been applied to some practical problems.

Sattler/Shabatay reader, 2/e: Sacks, "To See and Not See"

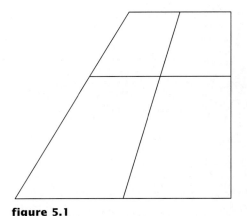

figure 5.1

What Do You See?

ClassPrep PPT 2: *Figure 5.1:* What Do You See?

The Perception Paradox

As discovered by drivers who find themselves slowing because of lines painted on pavement, a lot of our perceptual work is done automatically, without conscious awareness. This quick, often effortless aspect of perceptual processing suggests that perception is a rather simple affair, but it contains a basic contradiction, or paradox: What is so easy for the perceiver to do is not easy for psychologists to understand and explain. The difficulty lies in the fact that to function so effectively and efficiently, our perceptual systems must be exceedingly complex.

To illustrate the workings of these complex systems, psychologists draw attention to *perceptual failures,* cases in which our perceptual experience differs from the actual characteristics of some stimulus. Figure 5.2 provides a good example. Perceptual errors provide clues to the problems that perception must solve, such as estimating length, and to the solutions that it achieves. Ask yourself, for example, why you saw the two lines in Figure 5.2 as differing in length even though they are the same. Part of the answer is that your visual system tries to interpret all stimuli as three-dimensional, even when they are not. A three-dimensional interpretation of this drawing would lead you to see the two lines as defining the edges of two parallel paths, one of which ends closer to you than the other. Because your eyes tell you that the two paths originate from about the same point (the castle entrance), you solve the perceptual problem by assuming that the closer line must be the longer of the two.

OBJ 5.1: Define perception. Compare and contrast perception and sensation.

Test Items 5.1–5.3

perception The process through which people take raw sensations from the environment and interpret them, using knowledge, experience, and understanding of the world, so that the sensations become meaningful experiences.

figure 5.2

Misperceiving Reality

TRY THIS   Which line is longer—line A-C or line A-B? They are exactly the same length, but you probably perceived A-C as longer. Understanding why our perceptual systems make this kind of error has helped psychologists understand the basic principles of perception.

Three Approaches to Perception

Psychologists have taken three main approaches in their efforts to understand human perception. Those who take the **computational approach** try to determine the *computations* that a machine would have to perform to solve perceptual problems. Understanding these computations in machines, they believe, will help explain how complex computations within the nervous systems of humans and animals might turn raw sensory stimulation into a representation of the world (Green, 1991). The computational approach owes much to two earlier, but still influential, views of perception: the constructivist approach and the ecological approach.

Psychologists who take the **constructivist approach** argue that our perceptual systems construct a representation of reality from fragments of sensory information.

Is Anything Missing? Because you know what animals look like, you perceive a whole cat in this picture even though its midsection is hidden from view. The constructivist approach to perception emphasizes our ability to use knowledge and expectations to fill in the gaps in incomplete objects and to perceive them as unified wholes, not disjointed parts.

computational approach An approach to perception that focuses on how computations by the nervous system translate raw sensory stimulation into an experience of reality.

constructivist approach A view of perception taken by those who argue that the perceptual system uses fragments of sensory information to construct an image of reality.

They are particularly interested in situations in which the same stimulus creates different perceptions in different people. Stimuli such as those in Figure 5.2, for example, create optical illusions in some cultures but may not do so in those where people have not had experience with the objects or perspectives shown (Leibowitz et al., 1969). Constructivists emphasize that perception is strongly influenced by past experiences and prior knowledge, and by the expectations and inferences that arise from them (Rock, 1983). So if a desk prevents you from seeing the lower half of a person seated behind it, you still "see" the person as a complete human being. Experience tells you to expect that people remain intact even when parts of them are obscured.

Researchers influenced by the **ecological approach** to perception claim that rather than depending on interpretations, inferences, and expectations, most of our perceptual experience is due directly to the wealth of information contained in the stimuli presented by the environment. For example, J. J. Gibson (1979), founder of the ecological approach, argues that the primary goal of perception is to *support actions,* such as walking, grasping, or driving, by "tuning in" to the part of the environmental stimulus array that is most important for performing those actions. These researchers would be less interested in our *inferences* about the person behind the desk than in how we would *use* visual information from that person, from the desk, and from other objects in the room to guide us as we walk toward a chair and sit down (Nakayama, 1994).

In summary: To explain perception, the computational approach focuses on the nervous system's manipulations of incoming signals, the constructivist approach emphasizes the inferences that people make about the environment, and the ecological approach emphasizes the information provided by the environment. Later, we discuss evidence in support of each of these approaches.

Psychophysics

How can psychologists measure people's perceptions when there is no way to get inside people's heads to experience what they are experiencing? One solution to this problem is to present people with lights, sounds, and other stimuli and ask them to report their perception of the stimuli, using special scales of measurement. This

ecological approach An approach to perception maintaining that humans and other species are so well adapted to their natural environment that many aspects of the world are perceived without requiring higher-level analysis and inferences.

psychophysics An area of research focusing on the relationship between the physical characteristics of environmental stimuli and the psychological experiences those stimuli produce.

subliminal stimuli Stimuli that are too weak or brief to be perceived.

supraliminal stimuli Stimuli that fall above the absolute threshold and thus are consistently perceived.

absolute threshold The minimum amount of stimulus energy that can be detected 50 percent of the time.

table 5.1
Some Absolute Thresholds

Human Sense	Absolute Threshold Is Equivalent to:
Vision	A candle flame seen at 30 miles on a clear night
Hearing	The tick of a watch under quiet conditions at 20 feet
Taste	1 teaspoon of sugar in 2 gallons of water
Smell	1 drop of perfume diffused into the entire volume of air in a 6-room apartment
Touch	The wing of a fly falling on your cheek from a distance of 1 centimeter

TRY THIS Absolute thresholds can be amazingly low. Here are examples of stimulus equivalents at the absolute threshold for the five primary senses in humans. Set up the conditions for testing the absolute threshold for sound, and see if you can detect this minimal amount of auditory stimulation. If you can't hear it, the signal-detection theory we discuss later in this chapter may help explain why.

Source: Galanter (1962).

figure 5.3

The Absolute Threshold

The curve shows the relationship between the physical intensity of a signal and the likelihood that it will be detected. If the absolute threshold were truly absolute, all signals at or above a particular intensity would always be detected, and no signal below that intensity would ever be detected (see green line). But this response pattern almost never occurs, so the "absolute" threshold is defined as the intensity at which the signal is detected with 50 percent accuracy.

ClassPrep PPT 7, OHT: *Figure 5.3:* The Absolute Threshold

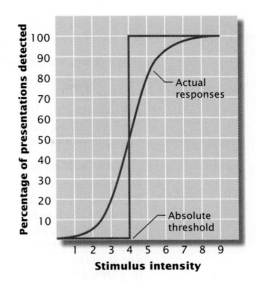

OBJ 5.3: Define psychophysics and absolute threshold. Explain the influence of noise and response criterion on perception.

Test Items 5.12–5.21

Personal Learning Activity 5.1

IRM Research Focus 5.4: A Case of Perception Without Awareness

OBJ 5.4: Define subliminal and supraliminal stimuli. Discuss the debate about the degree to which people's behavior can be influenced by subliminal perception.

Test Items 5.22–5.27

IRM Thinking Critically 5.1: Can People Perceive What Cannot Be Sensed?

method of studying perception, called **psychophysics**, describes the relationship between *physical energy* in the environment and our *psychological experience* of that energy.

Absolute Thresholds: Is Something Out There?

How much stimulus energy is needed to trigger a conscious perceptual experience? The minimum amount of light, sound, pressure, or other physical energy we can detect is called the *absolute threshold* (see Table 5.1). Stimuli below this threshold—stimuli that are too weak or too brief for us to notice—are traditionally referred to as **subliminal stimuli**. Stimuli that fall above the absolute threshold—stimuli that are consistently perceived—are referred to as **supraliminal stimuli.**

If you were participating in a typical experiment to measure the absolute threshold for vision, you would sit in a darkened laboratory. After your eyes adapted to the darkness, you would be presented with many brief flashes of light that varied in brightness. After each one, you would be asked if you saw the stimulus. If your absolute threshold were truly "absolute," your detection accuracy should jump from 0 to 100 percent at the exact level of brightness where your threshold is; this is illustrated by the point at which the green line in Figure 5.3 suddenly rises. But research shows that the average of your responses over many trials would actually form a curve much like the purple line in that figure. In other words, the "absolute" threshold is not really an all-or-nothing phenomenon. Notice in Figure 5.3 that a flash whose brightness (intensity) is 3 is detected 20 percent of the time and missed 80 percent of the time. Is that stimulus *subliminal* or *supraliminal*? Psychologists have dealt with questions of this sort by redefining the **absolute threshold** as the minimum amount of stimulus energy that can be detected 50 percent of the time.

THINKING CRITICALLY

Can Subliminal Stimuli Influence Your Behavior?

In 1957, an adman named James Vicary claimed that a New Jersey theater flashed messages such as "buy popcorn" and "drink Coke" on a movie screen, too briefly to be noticed, while customers watched the movie *Picnic*. He said that these subliminal messages caused a 15 percent rise in sales of Coca-Cola and a 58 percent increase in popcorn sales. Can such "mind control" really work? Many people seem to think so: They spend millions of dollars each year on audiotapes and videos that

LINKAGES (a link to
Introducing Psychology)

IRM Activity 5.10: Subliminal
Messages

promise subliminal help to lose weight, raise self-esteem, quit smoking, make more money, or achieve other goals.

● What am I being asked to believe or accept?

Two types of claims have been made about subliminal stimuli. The more general claim is that subliminal stimuli can influence our behavior. The second, more specific assertion is that subliminal stimuli provide an effective means of changing people's buying habits, political opinions, self-confidence, and other complex attitudes and behaviors, with or without their awareness or consent.

● What evidence is available to support the assertion?

Most evidence for the first claim—that subliminal stimuli can influence behavior in a general way—comes from research on visual perception. For example, using a method called *subliminal priming,* participants are shown clearly visible (supraliminal) stimuli, such as pictures of people, and then asked to make some sort of judgment about them. Unbeknownst to the participants, however, each of the visible pictures is preceded by other pictures or words flashed so briefly that the participants are unaware of them. The critical question is whether the information in the subliminal stimuli influences—or, more specifically, has a "priming effect" on—participants' responses to the supraliminal stimuli that follow them.

In one subliminal priming study, supraliminal pictures of individuals were preceded by subliminal pictures that were either "positive" (e.g., happy children) or "negative" (e.g., a monster). The participants in this study judged the people in the visible pictures as more likable, polite, friendly, successful, and reputable when their pictures had been preceded by a subliminal picture that was positive rather than negative (Krosnick et al., 1992). Another study found that people with eating disorders ate more crackers after being exposed to a subliminal presentation of the phrase "Mama is leaving me" than after either a supraliminal presentation of that phrase or a subliminal presentation of the neutral phrase "Mama is loaning it" (Masling, 1992). More recently, researchers have found that subliminally presented words can influence decisions about the meaning of words. For example, after being exposed to subliminal presentations of a man's name (e.g., *"Tom"*), participants were able to decide more rapidly whether a supraliminal stimulus (e.g., *"John"*) was a man's or woman's name. However, the impact of the subliminally presented name lasted for only about one-tenth of a second (Greenwald, Draine, & Abrams, 1996).

Other research shows that subliminal stimuli can lead to a change in people's physiological responses. In one study, participants were shown words at subliminal speed while researchers recorded their *galvanic skin resistance (GSR),* a measure of physiological arousal. Although the words were flashed too quickly to be perceived consciously, participants had higher GSR measurements following words such as "No one loves me" than after nonemotional messages such as "No one lifts it" (Masling & Bornstein, 1991). In another study, participants were exposed to subliminal photos of snakes, spiders, flowers, and mushrooms. Even though the photos were impossible to perceive at a conscious level, participants who were afraid of snakes or spiders showed increased GSR measurements (and reported fear) in response to snake and spider photos (Öhman & Soares, 1994).

The results of studies like these support the claim that subliminal information can have at least a temporary impact on judgment and emotion, but they say little or nothing about the effects of subliminal advertising or the value of subliminal self-help tapes. We have only the claims of people who believe in subliminal selling and the reports of satisfied customers (e.g., Key, 1973; McGarvey, 1989).

● Are there alternative ways of interpreting the evidence?

Many claims for subliminal advertising—including those reported in the New Jersey theater case we mentioned—have turned out to be publicity stunts using fabricated data (Haberstroh, 1995; Pratkanis, 1992). And testimonials from people who have purchased subliminal tapes may be biased by what these people *want* to believe about the product they bought. This interpretation is supported by experiments that manipulate the beliefs of participants regarding the messages on subliminal tapes. In one study, half the participants were told that they would be hearing tapes whose subliminal messages would improve their memory; the other half were told that the subliminal messages would improve their self-esteem. However, half the participants expecting self-esteem tapes actually received memory-improvement tapes, and half the participants expecting memory-improvement tapes actually received self-esteem tapes. Regardless of which tapes they actually heard, participants who *thought* they had heard memory-enhancement messages reported improved memory; those who *thought* they had heard self-esteem messages said that their self-esteem had improved (Pratkanis, Eskenazi, & Greenwald, 1994). In other words, the effects of the tapes were determined by the listeners' expectations—not by the tapes' subliminal content.

● **What additional evidence would help to evaluate the alternatives?**

To fully evaluate the effectiveness of subliminal products such as self-help tapes, researchers must conduct further experiments—like the one just mentioned—that carefully control for expectations. For example, in a *double-blind, placebo-controlled experiment,* some participants would hear a tape whose subliminal content was consistent with the stated purpose of the tapes (e.g., weight control). Others would hear a tape whose subliminal content was irrelevant to the tapes' stated purpose (e.g., French grammar), or that contained no subliminal messages. Further, neither the participants nor the researchers would know who listened to which tape until after all the results were in. Ultimately, the effects of the three types of tapes would be compared with one another and with the effects of tapes containing supraliminal (audible) self-help messages.

● **What conclusions are most reasonable?**

Available scientific evidence suggests that subliminal perception does occur, but that it has no potential for "mind control" (Greenwald, Klinger, & Schuh, 1995). Subliminal effects are usually small and short-lived, and they mainly affect simple judgments and general measures of overall arousal. Most researchers agree that subliminal messages have no special power to induce major changes in people's needs, goals, skills, or actions (Pratkanis, 1992). In fact, advertisements, political speeches, and other messages that people *can* perceive consciously have far stronger persuasive effects.

Signal-Detection Theory

OBJ 5.5: Define and describe signal-detection theory. Be sure to include sensitivity to stimuli and response criterion in your answer. Describe how information can change the response criterion.

Test Items 5.28–5.34

ClassPrep PPT 8: Why Does an "Absolute" Threshold Vary?

ClassPrep PPT 9: Signal-Detection Theory

Look again at Figure 5.3. It shows that stimuli just above and just below the absolute threshold are sometimes detected and sometimes missed. For example, a stimulus at intensity level 3 appears to be subliminal, even though you will perceive it 20 percent of the time; a stimulus at level 5 is above threshold, but it will be missed 20 percent of the time. Why should the "absolute" threshold vary this way? The two most important reasons have to do with sensitivity and our response criterion.

Sensitivity refers to our ability to pick out a particular stimulus, or *signal.* Sensitivity is influenced by the *intensity of the signal* (stronger ones are easier to detect), the *capacity of sensory systems* (good vision or hearing makes us more sensitive), and the *amount of background stimulation,* or *noise,* arriving at the same time. Some noise comes from outside the person, as when electrical equipment hums or overhead lights flicker. There is also noise coming from the spontaneous, random firing of cells of our own nervous system. Varying amounts of this *internal noise* is always occurring, whether or not we are stimulated by physical energy. You might think of it as a little like "snow" on a television screen or static between radio stations.

sensitivity The ability to detect a stimulus.

Detecting Vital Signals According to signal-detection theory, the likelihood that security personnel will detect the outline of a bomb or other weapon in x-ray images of a passenger's luggage depends partly on the sensitivity of their visual systems and partly on their response criterion. That criterion is affected by their expectations that weapons might appear, as well as by how motivated they are to look carefully for them. To help keep inspectors' response criteria sufficiently low, airport security officials occasionally attempt to smuggle a simulated weapon through a checkpoint. This procedure both evaluates the inspectors and helps keep them focused on their vital task.

The second source of variation in absolute threshold comes from the **response criterion**, which reflects our willingness to respond to a stimulus. Motivation—wants and needs—as well as expectancies affect the response criterion. For example, if you would be punished for reporting that a faint light appeared when it did not, then you might be motivated to raise your response criterion. That is, you would report the light only when you were sure you saw it. Similarly, expecting a faint stimulus to occur lowers the response criterion. Suppose, for example, that you worked at an airport security checkpoint, where you spent hours looking at x-ray images of people's handbags, briefcases, and luggage. The signal to be detected in this situation is a weapon, whereas the "noise" consists of harmless objects in a person's luggage, vague or distorted images on the viewing screen, and anything else that is not a weapon. If there has been a recent terrorist attack, or if the threat of one has just been issued, your airport will be on special alert. Accordingly, your response criterion for saying that some questionable object on the x-ray image might be a weapon will be much lower than if terrorism were not so likely. In other words, expecting a stimulus makes it more likely that you will detect it than if it is unexpected.

When researchers realized that detecting a signal depends on a combination of each person's sensitivity *and* response criterion, they concluded that the measurement of absolute thresholds could never be more precise than the 50 percent rule mentioned earlier. As a result, they abandoned the notion of absolute thresholds and focused instead on **signal-detection theory,** a mathematical model of how our personal sensitivity and response criterion combine to determine decisions about whether or not a near-threshold stimulus has occurred (Green & Swets, 1966).

Once again, imagine that you are participating in a threshold experiment. When presented with faint signals, you may find it impossible to distinguish accurately between trials involving noise alone and those involving a signal plus noise. Sometimes, external or internal noise levels may be so high that you think something must surely be "out there," in which case you report that the stimulus is present when, in fact, it is not. This type of error is called a *false alarm*. At other times, the signal is so faint that it does not produce enough stimulation for you to detect it—causing an error known as a *miss*. But a person with a more sensitive sensory system might correctly detect the stimulus—a situation called a *hit*.

Because it allows precise measurement of people's sensitivity to stimuli of any kind, signal-detection theory provides a way to understand and predict responses in

response criterion The internal rule a person uses to decide whether or not to report a stimulus.

signal-detection theory A mathematical model of what determines a person's report that a near-threshold stimulus has or has not occurred.

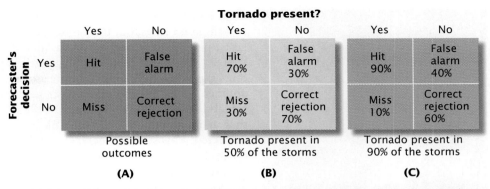

figure 5.4

Signal Detection

Part A shows the possible outcomes of examining a radar display for signs of a tornado: a *hit* (correctly detecting the tornado), a *miss* (failing to detect the tornado), a *correct rejection* (seeing no tornado when there is none), or a *false alarm* (reporting a tornado when none exists). The rest of the figure illustrates the impact of two different response criteria: Part B represents outcomes of a high response criterion, which is set under conditions where tornadoes are seen only 50 percent of the time; Part C represents outcomes of a low response criterion, which operates under conditions where tornadoes are seen 90 percent of the time.

a wide range of situations (Swets, 1992). Consider weather forecasting. Signal-detection theory can be valuable in understanding why weather forecasters, using the latest radar systems, sometimes fail to warn of a tornado that local residents can see with the naked eye (Stevens, 1995). The forecaster's task is not easy, because the high-tech systems they use may respond not only to dangerous shifts in wind direction (wind shear) and a tornado's spinning funnel, but also to such trivial stimuli as swirling dust and swarming insects. So the telltale radar "signature" of a tornado appears against a potentially confusing background of visual "noise." Whether or not that signature will be picked out and reported depends both on the forecaster's sensitivity to the signal and on the response criterion being used. In establishing the criterion for making a report, the forecaster must consider certain consequences. Setting the criterion too high might cause a tornado to go unnoticed. Such a miss could cost many lives if it left a populated area with no warning of danger. If the response criterion were set too low, however, the forecaster might deliver a false alarm that would unnecessarily disrupt people's lives, activate costly emergency plans, and reduce the credibility of future tornado warnings (see Figure 5.4A). In short, there is a tradeoff. To minimize false alarms, the forecaster could set a very high response criterion, but doing so would also make misses more likely.

Let's examine how various kinds of expectations or assumptions can change the response criterion and how those changes might affect the accuracy of a forecaster's decisions. If a forecaster knows it's a time of year when tornadoes exist in only about 50 percent of the storm systems seen on radar, a rather high response criterion is likely to be used; it will take relatively strong evidence to trigger a tornado warning. The hypothetical data in Figure 5.4(B) show that under these conditions, the forecaster correctly detected 70 percent of actual tornadoes but missed 30 percent of them; also, 30 percent of the tornado reports were false alarms. Now suppose the forecaster learns that a different kind of storm system is on the way, and that about 90 percent of such systems spawn tornadoes. This information is likely to increase the forecaster's expectancy for seeing a tornado signature, thus lowering the response criterion. The forecaster will now require less visual evidence of a tornado before reporting one. Under these conditions, the hit rate might rise from 70 percent to, say, 90 percent, but the false-alarm rate might also increase from 30 percent to 40 percent (see Figure 5.4C).

Sensitivity to tornado signals will also affect a forecaster's hit rate and false-alarm rate. Forecasters with greater sensitivity to these signals will have high hit

Perfect! This chef's ability to taste the difference in his culinary creation before and after he has adjusted the spices depends on psychophysical laws that also apply to judging differences in visual, auditory, and other sensory stimuli.

Test Items 5.35–5.44

OBJ 5.6: Describe Weber's law. Define difference threshold and just-noticeable difference (JND). Explain the equation JND = KI.

ClassPrep PPT 12: *Table 5.2:* Weber's Fraction (K) for Different Stimuli

table 5.2

Weber's Fraction *(K)* for Different Stimuli

Stimulus	*K*
Pitch	.003
Brightness	.017
Weight	.02
Odor	.05
Loudness	.10
Pressure on skin	.14
Saltiness of taste	.20

The value of Weber's fraction, *K,* differs from one sense to another. Differences in *K* demonstrate the adaptive nature of perception. Humans, who depend more heavily on vision than on taste for survival, are more sensitive to vision than to taste.

rates and low false-alarm rates. Forecasters with less sensitivity are still likely to have high hit rates, but their false-alarm rates will also be higher. As Figure 5.4 suggests, people do sometimes make mistakes at signal detection, whether it involves spotting tornadoes, inspecting luggage, diagnosing medical conditions, searching for oil, or looking for clues at a crime scene. Research on these and other perceptual abilities has led psychologists to suggest ways of improving people's performance on signal-detection tasks (Wickens, 1992a). For example, psychologists recommend that manufacturers occasionally place flawed items among a batch of objects to be inspected. This strategy increases inspectors' expectations of seeing flaws, thus lowering the response criterion and raising the hit rate.

Personal Learning Activity 5.2

Judging Differences: Has Anything Changed?

Sometimes our perceptual task is not to detect a faint stimulus but rather to notice small differences as a stimulus changes, or to judge whether there are differences between two stimuli. For example, when tuning up, musicians are concerned about whether the notes played by two instruments are the same or different. When repainting part of a wall, you must judge whether the new color matches the old. And you have to decide if your soup tastes any spicier after you have added some pepper.

The smallest difference between stimuli that we can detect is called the **difference threshold** or **just-noticeable difference (JND)**. How small is that difference? The size of a JND is determined by two factors. The first is how much of a stimulus there was to begin with. The weaker the stimuli are, the easier it is to detect small differences between them. For example, if you are comparing the weight of two envelopes, you will be able to detect a difference of as little as a fraction of an ounce. But if you are comparing two boxes weighing around fifty pounds, you may not notice a difference unless it is a pound or more. The second factor affecting people's ability to detect differences is which sense is being stimulated.

The relationship between these two factors is described by one of the oldest laws in psychology. Named after the nineteenth-century German physiologist Ernst Weber (pronounced "VAY-ber"), **Weber's law** states that the smallest detectable difference in stimulus energy is a constant fraction of the intensity of the stimulus. This fraction, often called *Weber's constant* or *Weber's fraction*, is given the symbol *K.* As shown in Table 5.2, *K* is different for each of the senses. The smaller *K* is, the more sensitive a sense is to stimulus differences.

Specifically, Weber's law says that *JND = KI*, where *K* is the Weber's constant for a particular sense, and *I* is the amount, or intensity, of the stimulus. To compute the JND for a particular stimulus, we must know its intensity and what sense it is stimulating. For example, as shown in Table 5.2, the value of *K* for weight is .02. If an object weighs 25 pounds *(I)*, the JND is only half a pound (.02 × 25 pounds). So while carrying a 25-pound bag of groceries, you would have to add or remove a half a pound before you would be able to detect a change in heaviness. But candy snatchers beware: It takes a change of only two-thirds of an ounce to determine that someone has been into a 2-pound box of chocolates!

Weber's constants vary somewhat among individuals, and as we get older we tend to become less sensitive to stimulus differences. There are exceptions to this rule, however. If you like candy, you will be happy to know that Weber's fraction for sweetness stays fairly constant throughout life (Gilmore & Murphy, 1989). Weber's law does not hold when stimuli are very intense or very weak, but it does apply to complex, as well as simple, stimuli. We all tend to have our own personal Weber's fractions that describe how much prices can increase before we notice or worry about the change. For example, if your Weber's fraction for cost is .10, then you would surely notice, and perhaps protest, a fifty-cent increase in a one-dollar bus fare. But the same fifty-cent increase in monthly rent would be less than a JND and thus unlikely to cause notice, let alone concern.

figure 5.5

Length Illusions

People can usually estimate line lengths very accurately, but this ability can be impaired under certain conditions. The pairs of lines marked A and B are the same length in each drawing, but most people report that line A appears longer than line B. These optical illusions, like the one in Figure 5.2, occur partly because of our tendency to see two-dimensional figures as three-dimensional. With the exception of the "top hat," all or part of line A in each drawing can easily be interpreted as being farther away than line B. When two equal-sized objects appear to be at different distances, the visual system tends to infer that the more distant object must be larger.

ClassPrep PPT 14, OHT: *Figure 5.5:* Length Illusions

IRM Activity 5.3: The Size-Weight Illusion

IRM Discussion 5.5: Illusions

IRM Discussion 5.6: The Moon Illusion

IRM Activity 5.7: Analyzing the Moon Illusion

ClassPrep PPT 13: Magnitude Estimation

OBJ 5.7: Describe Fechner's law.

Test Items 5.45–5.48

Videodisc Segments & Stills: Variations on the Müller-Lyer Illusion, Six Perceptual Illusions

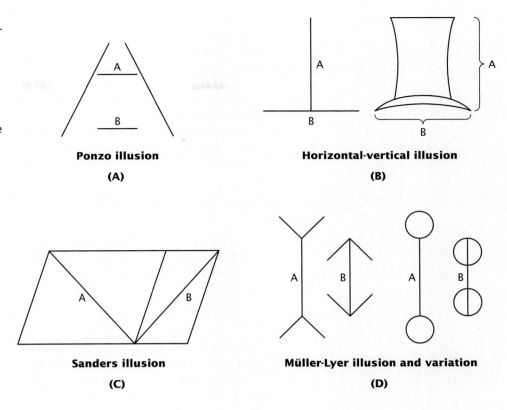

Ponzo illusion
(A)

Horizontal-vertical illusion
(B)

Sanders illusion
(C)

Müller-Lyer illusion and variation
(D)

Magnitude Estimation: How Intense Is That?

How much would you have to increase the volume on your stereo to make it sound twice as loud as your neighbor's? How much would you have to turn it down to make it sound only half as loud as it was before your neighbor complained? These are questions about *magnitude estimation*—about how our perception of stimulus intensity is related to actual stimulus strength. In 1860, Gustav Fechner (pronounced "FECK-ner") used Weber's law to study the relationship between the *physical* magnitude of a stimulus and its *perceived* magnitude. He reasoned that if just-noticeable differences get progressively larger as stimulus magnitude increases, then so, too, must the amount of change in the stimulus required to double or triple the perceived intensity of the stimulus. He was right. For example, it takes only a small increase in volume to make a soft sound seem twice as loud, but imagine how much additional volume it would take to make a rock band seem twice as loud. To put it another way, constant increases in physical energy will produce progressively smaller increases in perceived magnitude. This observation, when expressed as a mathematical equation relating actual stimulus intensity to perceived intensity, became known as *Fechner's law*.

Fechner's law applies to most, but not all, stimuli. Whereas it takes larger and larger increases in light or sound to create the same amount of change in perceived magnitude, the reverse is true for the perceived intensity of electric shock. It takes a relatively large increase in shock intensity to make a weak shock seem twice as intense, but if the shock is already painful, it takes only a small increase in intensity before you would perceive it was twice as strong. S. S. Stevens offered another formula (known as *Stevens's power law*) for magnitude estimation that works for a wider array of stimuli, including electric shock, temperature, and sound and light intensity. Stevens's law is still used today by psychologists who want to determine how much larger, louder, longer, or more intense a stimulus must be for people to perceive a specific difference or amount of change.

just-noticeable difference (JND) The smallest detectable difference in stimulus energy.
Weber's law A law stating that the smallest detectable difference in stimulus energy is a constant fraction of the intensity of the stimulus.

Overall, people do well at estimating differences between stimuli. For example, we are very good at estimating how much longer one line is than another. Yet as shown in Figure 5.2, this perceptual comparison process can be disrupted when the lines are embedded in more complex figures. (See Figure 5.5 for some additional examples of lines that appear to be different lengths but are not.) The perceptual laws that we have discussed, as well as the exceptions to these laws, emphasize a central principle in perception—that perception is not absolute, but relative. Our experience of one stimulus depends on its relationship to others. The way in which the human perceptual system relates one stimulus to another is the focus of research on our next topic, perceptual organization.

Organizing the Perceptual World

Suppose you are driving on a busy road while searching for Barney's Diner, an unfamiliar restaurant where you are to meet a friend. The roadside is crammed with signs of all shapes and colors, some flashing and some rotating. If you are ever to recognize the sign that says "Barney's Diner," you must impose some sort of organization on this overwhelming array of visual information.

Perceptual organization is the task performed by the perceptual system to determine what edges and other stimuli go together to form an object. In this case, the object would be the sign for Barney's Diner. It is perceptual organization, too, that makes it possible for you to separate the sign from its background of lights, colors, letters, and other competing stimuli. Figure 5.6 shows some of the ways in which your perceptual system can organize stimuli. For example, the figure appears as a hollow cube, but notice that you can see it from two angles: either looking down at the top of the cube or looking up toward the bottom of the cube. And notice that the "cube" is not really a cube at all but rather a series of unconnected arrows and Ys. Your perceptual system organized these elements into a cube by creating imaginary connecting lines called *subjective contours*. That system can also change the apparent location of the cube. You probably saw it first as "floating" in front of a background of large black dots, but those dots can also be "holes" through which you see the cube against a solid black background "behind" the page. It may take a little time to see this second perceptual organization, but when you do, notice that the subjective contours you saw earlier are gone. They disappear because your perceptual system adjusts for the fact that when an object is partially obscured, we should not be able to see all of it.

OBJ 5.8: Describe the two basic principles of perceptual organization: figure-ground and grouping. Define and give examples of proximity, similarity, continuity, closure, common fate, synchrony, common region, and connectedness.

Test Items 5.49–5.64

ClassPrep PPT 15: *Figure 5.6:* Organize This!

figure 5.6

Organize This!

Psychologists have employed the principles of figure-ground organization and grouping to help explain how your visual system allows you to perceive these disconnected lines as a cube, as well as to see this cube from above or below, and as being in front of the page or behind it.

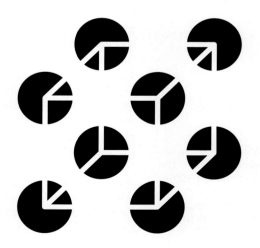

(A)

(B)

figure 5.7

Reversible Figures

TRY THIS   *Reversible figures* can be organized by your perceptual system in two ways. If you perceive Part A as the word *figure*, the space around the letters becomes meaningless background. Now emphasize the word *ground*, and what had stood out a moment ago now becomes background. In Part B, when you emphasize the white vase, the two black profiles become background; if you organize the faces as the figure, what had been a vase now becomes background.

perceptual organization The task of determining what edges and other stimuli go together to form an object.

Basic Processes in Perceptual Organization

To explain phenomena like these and to understand the way our perceptual systems organize more naturalistic scenes, psychologists have focused on two basic processes: *figure-ground organization* and *grouping*.

Figure-Ground Organization

When you look at a complex scene or listen to a noisy environment, your perceptual apparatus automatically picks out certain features, objects, or sounds to be emphasized and relegates others to be *ground*—the less relevant background. For example, as you drive toward an intersection, a stop sign becomes a figure, standing out clearly against the background of trees, houses, and cars. A *figure* is the part of the visual field that has meaning, stands in front of the rest, and always seems to include the contours or edges that separate it from the less relevant background (Rubin, 1915). As described in the chapter on sensation, edges are one of the most basic features detected by our visual system; they combine to form figures.

To fully appreciate the process of figure-ground organization, look at the drawings in Figure 5.7. These drawings are called *reversible figures,* because you can repeatedly reverse your perceptual organization of what is figure and what is ground. Your ability to do this shows that perception is not only an active process but a categorical one as well. People usually organize sensory stimulation into one perceptual category or another, but rarely into both or into something in between. In Figure 5.7, for instance, you cannot easily see both faces *and* a vase, or the words *figure* and *ground*, at the same time.

Grouping

To distinguish figure from ground, our perceptual system must first identify stimulus elements in the environment, such as the edges of a stop sign or billboard, that belong together as figures. We tend to group certain elements together more or less automatically; in the early 1900s, several German psychologists began to study how this happens. They argued first of all that people perceive sights and sounds as organized wholes. These wholes, they said, are different from, and more than, just the sum of the individual sensations, much as water is something more than just an assortment of hydrogen and oxygen atoms. Because the German word meaning (roughly) "whole figure" is *Gestalt* (pronounced "ge-SHTALT"), these researchers became known as *Gestalt psychologists*. They proposed a number of principles, or "Gestalt laws," that describe how perceptual systems group stimuli into a world of shapes and objects. Some of the most enduring of these principles are the following:

1. *Proximity.* The closer objects or events are to one another, the more likely they are to be perceived as belonging together, as Figure 5.8(A) illustrates.

2. *Similarity.* Similar elements are perceived to be part of a group, as in Figure 5.8(B).

3. *Continuity.* Sensations that appear to create a continuous form are perceived as belonging together, as in Figure 5.8(C).

4. *Closure.* We tend to fill in missing contours to form a complete object, as in Figure 5.8(D). The gaps are easy to see, but as illustrated in Figure 5.6, the tendency to fill in missing contours can be so strong that you may see faint connections that are not really there.

5. *Common fate.* Sets of objects that are moving in the same direction at the same speed are perceived together. Choreographers and marching-band directors often use the principle of common fate, arranging for groups of dancers or musicians to move identically, creating the illusion of waves of motion or of large moving objects.

figure 5.8

Gestalt Principles of Perceptual Grouping

We tend to perceive Part A as two groups of two circles plus two single circles, rather than as, say, six single circles. In Part B, we see two columns of Xs and two columns of Os, not four rows of XOXO. We see the X in Part C as being made out of two continuous lines, not a combination of the odd forms shown. We perceive the disconnected segments in Part D as a triangle and a circle. In Part E, we tend to pair up dots in the same oval, even though they are far apart. Part F shows that connected objects are grouped together.

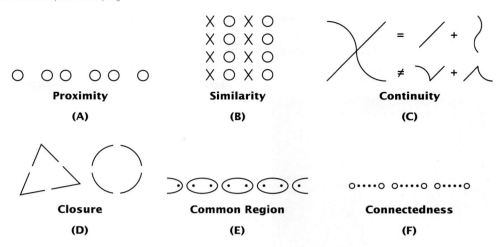

Proximity (A)

Similarity (B)

Continuity (C)

Closure (D)

Common Region (E)

Connectedness (F)

THE FAR SIDE By GARY LARSON

Chronicle Features, 1982

"Wait! Wait! . . . Cancel that, I guess it says 'help.' "

The principle of closure allows us to fill in the blanks in what we see and hear. Without it, the world would appear as fragmented images and sounds that would confuse everyone, including would-be rescuers.

auditory scene analysis The perceptual process through which sounds are mentally represented and interpreted.

Stephen Palmer (1999) has introduced the following three additional grouping principles, which may be more important than many of the traditional laws:

1. *Synchrony.* Stimuli that occur at the same time are likely to be perceived as belonging together. For example, if you see a car ahead stop violently at the same instant you hear a crash, you will probably perceive these visual and auditory stimuli as part of the same event.

2. *Common region.* Elements located within some boundary tend to be grouped together. The boundary can be created by an enclosing perimeter, as in Figure 5.8(E); a region of color; or other factors.

3. *Connectedness.* Elements that are connected by other elements tend to be grouped together. Figure 5.8(F) demonstrates how important this law is. The circles connected by dotted lines seem to go together even though they are farther apart than some pairs of unconnected circles. In this situation, the principle of connectedness appears more important than the principle of proximity.

Why do these grouping principles guide human perceptual organization? One answer is that they reflect the way stimuli are likely to be organized in the natural world. Two nearby elements are, in fact, more likely to be part of an object than are widely separated elements. Likewise, stimulus elements moving in the same direction at the same rate are likely to be part of the same object. Your initial impression of the cube in Figure 5.6 reflects this *likelihood principle* in action. At first glance, you probably saw the cube as being below you rather than above you. This tendency makes adaptive sense, because cubes (such as boxes) are more likely to be on the ground than hanging in midair. The likelihood principle is consistent with both the ecological and constructivist approaches to perception. From the ecological perspective, the likelihood principle evolved because it worked, giving our ancestors reliable information about how the world is most likely to be organized, and thus increasing their chances of survival. Constructivists point out, however, that our personal experiences in the world also help determine the likelihood of interpreting a stimulus array in one way over another. The likelihood principle operates automatically and accurately most of the time. As shown in Figure 5.9, however, when we try using it to organize very *unlikely* stimuli, it can lead to frustrating misperceptions.

Complementing the likelihood principle is the *simplicity principle,* which says that we organize stimulus elements in a way that gives us the simplest possible perception (Pomerantz & Kubovy, 1986). Your visual system, for example, will group stimulus elements so as to reduce the amount of information that you must process.

Common Fate When numerous objects, such as a large flock of birds, move together, we see them as a group or even as a single large object in the sky. Marching-band directors put this perceptual grouping process to good use. By arranging for musicians to move together, they make it appear as though huge letters and other large "objects" are in motion on the field during half-time shows at football games.

Test Items 5.65–5.67

ClassPrep PPT 20: Auditory Scene Analysis

ClassPrep PPT 21: *Figure 5.9:* Impossible Objects

figure 5.9

Impossible Objects

These objects can exist as two-dimensional drawings, but not as the three-dimensional objects that experience tells us to expect them to be. When we try to use the likelihood principle to organize them in three-dimensional space, we eventually discover that they are "impossible."

You can see the simplicity principle in action in Figure 5.6; it was simpler to see a single cube than an assortment of separate, unrelated arrows and Ys.

Auditory Scene Analysis   Grouping principles such as similarity, proximity, closure, and continuity apply to what we hear as well as to what we see (Bartlett, 1993). For example, sounds that are similar in pitch tend to be grouped together, much like sounds that come close together in time. Through closure, we hear a tone as continuous even if it is repeatedly interrupted by bursts of static. **Auditory scene analysis** (Bregman, 1990) is the perceptual process of mentally representing and interpreting sounds. First, the flow of sound energy is organized into a series of segments based on characteristics such as frequency, intensity, location, and the like. Sounds with similar characteristics are then grouped into separate *auditory streams,* which are sounds perceived as coming from the same source. It is through auditory scene analysis that the potentially overwhelming world of sound is organized into separate, coherent patterns of speech, music, or even noise.

Perception of Location and Distance

One of the most important perceptual tasks we face is to determine where objects and sound sources are located. This task involves knowing both their two-dimensional position (left or right, up or down) and their distance from us.

Two-Dimensional Location   Visually determining whether an object is to your right or your left appears to be simple. All the perceptual system has to do, it seems, is determine where the object's image falls on the retina. For example, if the image falls on the center of the retina, then the object must be straight ahead. But when an object is, say, far to your right, and you focus its image on the center of your retina by turning your head and eyes toward it, you do not assume it is straight ahead. A computational approach to this location problem suggests that your brain estimates the object's true location relative to your body using an equation that takes information about where an image strikes the retina and adjusts it based on information about the movement of your eyes and head.

As mentioned in the chapter on sensation, localization of sounds depends on cues about differences in the information received by your two ears. If a sound is

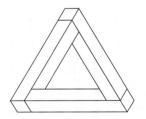

continuous, sound waves coming toward the right side of your head will reach the right ear before reaching the left ear. Similarly, a sound coming toward the right side of your head will seem a little bit louder to the right ear than to the left ear, because the head blocks some of the sound to the latter. The brain uses these slight differences in the timing and the intensity of a sound as cues to locate its source. Visual cues are often integrated with auditory cues to determine the exact identity and location of the sound source. Most often, information from the eyes and the ears converges on the same likely sound source. However, there are times when the two senses produce conflicting impressions; in such cases, we tend to believe our eyes rather than our ears. This bias toward using visual information is known as *visual dominance*. The phenomenon is illustrated by our impression that the sound of a television program is coming from the screen rather than the speaker. Next time you are watching someone talking on TV, close your eyes. If your television has a single speaker below or to the side of the screen, you will notice that the sound no longer seems to be coming from the screen but instead seems to be coming from the speaker itself. As soon as you open your eyes, however, the false impression resumes; words once again seem to come from the obvious visual source of the sound—the person on the screen.

Depth Perception

One of the oldest puzzles in psychology relates to **depth perception,** our ability to perceive distance. How are we able to experience the world in three-dimensional depth even though the visual information we receive from it is projected onto two-dimensional retinas? The answer lies in the many

LINKAGES (a link to Sensation)

IRM Discussion 5.12: Three-D Illusions in Posters and Books

OBJ 5.10: Define and describe depth perception.

Test Items 5.68–5.69

ClassPrep PPT 22, OHT: *Figure 5.10:* Stimulus Cues for Perception of Depth and Distance

figure 5.10

Stimulus Cues for Depth Perception

See if you can identify the cues of relative size, interposition, linear perspective, height in the visual field, textural gradient, and shadows that combine to create a sense of three-dimensional depth in this drawing.

Freburg *Perspectives:* Zimmer, "Wallpaper for the Mind"

LSV: Perception (Unit #8)

depth perception Perception of distance, one of the most important factors underlying size and shape constancy.

interposition A depth cue whereby closer objects block one's view of things farther away.

relative size A depth cue whereby larger objects are perceived as closer than smaller ones.

A Case of Depth Misperception The runner in this photo is actually farther away than the man on the pitcher's mound. But because he is lower, not higher, in the visual field—and because his leg can be seen as being in front of, not behind, the pitcher's leg—the runner appears smaller than normal rather than farther away.

OBJ 5.11: Describe the stimulus cues that influence depth perception. Your answer should include interposition, relative size, height in the visual field, texture gradient, linear perspective, and motion parallax.

Texture Gradient The details of a scene fade gradually as distance increases. This texture gradient helps us to perceive the less detailed birds in this photo as farther away.

Test Items 5.70–5.84

Essay Q 5.1

Personal Learning Activity 5.4

Videodisc Segment: Convergence of Parallel Lines

---

height in the visual field A depth cue whereby objects higher in the visual field are perceived as more distant.

texture gradient A graduated change in the texture, or grain, of the visual field, whereby objects with finer, less detailed textures are perceived as more distant.

linear perspective A depth cue whereby objects closer to the point where two lines appear to converge are perceived as being at a greater distance.

---

depth cues provided by the environment and by some special properties of the visual system.

To some extent, people perceive depth through the same cues that artists use to create the impression of depth and distance on a two-dimensional canvas. These cues are actually characteristics of visual stimuli and therefore illustrate the ecological approach to perception. Figure 5.10 demonstrates several of these cues:

- One of the most important depth cues is **interposition,** or *occlusion:* Closer objects block the view of things farther away. This cue is illustrated in Figure 5.10 by the person walking nearest the car; because his body blocks out part of the car, we perceive him as being closer than the car.

- The two people at the far left side of Figure 5.10 illustrate the cue of **relative size:** When two objects are assumed to be about equal in size, the one that casts the larger image on the retina is perceived to be closer.

- Another cue comes from **height in the visual field:** On the ground, more distant objects are usually higher in the visual field than those nearby. Because the buildings in Figure 5.10 are higher than the people in the foreground, the buildings appear to be farther away.

- A cue known as **texture gradient** involves a graduated change in the "grain" of the visual field. Texture appears less detailed as distance increases, so as the texture of a surface changes across the retinal image, people perceive a change in distance. In Figure 5.10, you can see a texture gradient as the grass, the sidewalk, and the street become less distinct toward the "back" of the drawing.

- The small figure crossing the center line in Figure 5.10 is seen as very far away, partly because she is near the horizon line, which we know is quite distant. She appears far away also because she is near a point where the road's edges, like all parallel lines that recede into the distance, appear to converge toward a single point. This apparent convergence provides a cue called **linear perspective.** Objects that are nearer the point of convergence are seen as farther away.

Still other depth cues depend on *clarity, color,* and *shadows.* Distant objects often appear hazier and tend to take on a bluish tone. (Art students are taught to

figure 5.11

Light, Shadow, and Depth Perception

TRY THIS The shadows cast by these protruding rivets and deep dents make it easy to see them in three dimensions. But if you turn the book upside down, the rivets now look like dents, and the dents look like bumps. This reversal in depth perception occurs partly because people normally assume that illumination comes from above and interpret the pattern of light and shadow accordingly. With the picture upside down, light coming from the top would produce the observed pattern of shadows only if the circles were dents, not rivets.

ClassPrep PPT 23: *Figure 5.11:* Light, Shadow, and Depth Perception

ClassPrep PPT 24: Cues Based on Properties of the Visual System

OBJ 5.12: Describe the cues to depth provided by accommodation, convergence, and binocular disparity.

Test Items 5.85–5.93

IRM Activity 5.9: The Floating Hot Dog

ClassPrep PPT 25: Cues Based on Properties of the Visual System (cont.)

Videodisc Segment: Convergence of Parallel Lines

motion parallax A depth cue whereby a difference in the apparent rate of movement of different objects provides information on the relative distance of those objects.

accommodation The ability of the lens of the eye to change its shape and bend light rays so that objects are in focus.

convergence A depth cue involving the rotation of the eyes to project the image of an object on each retina.

binocular disparity A depth cue based on the difference between two retinal images of the world.

add a little blue when mixing paint for distant background features.) Light and shadow also contribute to the perception of depth (Ramachandran, 1988). The buildings in the background of Figure 5.10 are seen as three-dimensional, not flat, because of the shadows on their right faces. Figure 5.11 offers a more dramatic example of shadows' effect on depth perception.

An important visual depth cue that cannot be demonstrated in Figure 5.10, or in any other still picture, comes from looking at moving objects. You may have noticed, for example, that when you look out the window of a moving car, objects nearer to you seem to speed across your visual field, whereas objects in the distance seem to move slowly, if at all. This difference in the apparent rate of movement is called **motion parallax,** and it provides cues to differences in the distance of various objects.

Several additional depth cues result from the way human eyes are built and positioned. One of these cues is related to facts discussed in the chapter on sensation. To bring an image into focus on the retina, the lens of the eye changes shape, or *accommodates,* so as to bend light rays. To accomplish this feat, muscles surrounding the lens either tighten, to make the lens more curved for focusing on close objects, or relax, to flatten the lens for focusing on more distant objects. Information about that muscle activity is relayed to the brain, and this **accommodation** cue helps create the perception of distance.

The relative location of our two eyes produces two other depth cues. One is **convergence:** Because each eye is located at a slightly different place on the skull, the eyes must converge, or rotate inward, to project an image on each retina. The brain receives and processes information from the eye muscles about this activity. The closer the object, the more the eyes must converge, which sends more intense stimulation to the brain.

Second, because of their differing locations, each eye receives a slightly different view of the world. The difference between the two retinal images of an object is called **binocular disparity.** For any particular object, this difference gets smaller as distance increases. The brain combines the two images, processes information about the amount of disparity, and generates the impression of a single object having depth as well as height and width. View-Master slide viewers and 3-D movies create the appearance of depth by displaying to each eye a separate photograph of a scene, each taken from a slightly different angle.

 Binocular Disparity The difference between each eye's view of an object is smaller for distant objects and greater for closer ones. These binocular disparity cues help to create our perception of distance. To see how distance affects binocular disparity, hold a pencil vertically about six inches in front of your nose; then close one eye and notice where the pencil is in relation to the background. Now open that eye, close the other one, and notice how much the pencil "shifts." These are the two different views your eyes have of the pencil. Repeat the procedure while holding the pencil at arm's length. There is now less disparity, or "shift," because there is less difference in the angles from which your two eyes see the pencil.

looming A motion cue involving a rapid expansion in the size of an image so that it fills the available space on the retina.

The wealth of depth cues available to us is consistent with the ecological approach to perception. However, researchers taking the constructivist and computational approaches argue that even when temporarily deprived of these depth cues, we can still move about and locate objects in an environment. In one study, for example, participants viewed an object from a particular vantage point. Then, with their eyes closed, they were guided to a point well to the side of the object and asked to walk toward it from this new position. The participants were amazingly accurate at this task, leading the researchers to suggest that seeing an object at some point in space creates a spatial model in our minds—a model that remains intact even when immediate depth cues are removed.

Perception of Motion

Sometimes an object's most important property is not its size or shape or distance but its motion—how fast it is going and where it is heading. For example, a car in front of you may change speed or direction, requiring that you change your own speed or direction, often in a split second.

How are you able to perceive such changes in motion? As with the detection of location and depth, the answer seems to be that you can efficiently "tune in" to a host of useful cues. Many of these cues make use of *optical flow*, or the changes in retinal images across the entire visual field. One particularly meaningful pattern of optical flow is known as **looming,** the rapid expansion in the size of an image so that it fills the retina. When an image looms, you tend to interpret it as an approaching stimulus. Your perceptual system quickly assesses whether the expansion on the retina is about equal in all directions or greater to one side than to the other. If it is greater to the right, for example, the approaching stimulus will miss you and pass to your right. However, if the retinal expansion is approximately equal in all directions, then duck!

Two questions, in particular, have interested psychologists who study motion perception. First, how do we know whether the flow of images across the retina is due to the movement of objects in the environment or to our own movements? If changes in retinal images were the only factor contributing to motion perception, then moving your eyes would create the perception that everything in the visual field was moving. This is not the case, though, because as noted earlier, the brain also receives and processes information about the motion of the eyes and head. If you look around the room right now, tables, chairs, and other stationary objects will not appear to move, because your brain determines that all the movement of images on your retinas is due to your eye and head movements. But now close one eye, and wiggle your open eyeball by gently pushing your lower eyelid. Because your brain receives no signals that your eye is being moved by its own muscles, everything in the room will appear to move.

A second question about motion perception involves the time lag of about one-twentieth of a second between the moment when an image is registered on the retina and the moment when messages about that image reach the brain. In theory, each momentary perception of, say, a dog running toward you is actually a perception of where the dog was approximately one-twentieth of a second earlier. How does the perceptual system deal with this time lag so as to accurately interpret information about both motion and location? Psychologists have found that when a stimulus is moving along a relatively constant path, the brain corrects for the image delay by predicting where the stimulus should be one-twentieth of a second in the future (Nijhawan, 1997).

Motion perception is of great interest to sport psychologists. They try to understand, for example, why some individuals are so proficient at perceiving motion. One team of British psychologists discovered a number of cues and computations apparently used by "expert catchers." In catching a ball, these individuals seem to be especially sensitive to the angle between their "straight ahead" gaze (i.e., a

Stroboscopic Motion   If this series of still photographs of an athlete's hand-spring were presented to you, one at a time, in quick succession, an illusion called *stroboscopic motion* would cause you to perceive him to be moving.

Test Items 5.94–5.100

LINKAGES (a link to Sensation)

Personal Learning Activity 5.5

OBJ 5.14: Define perceptual constancy. Give examples of size, shape, and brightness constancy.

Test Items 5.101–5.107

ClassPrep PPT 28: Size Constancy

stroboscopic motion   An illusion in which lights or images flashed in rapid succession are perceived as moving.

perceptual constancy   The perception of objects as constant in size, shape, color, and other properties despite changes in their retinal image.

position with the chin parallel to the ground) and the gaze used when looking up at a moving ball. Their task is to move the body continuously, and often quickly, to make sure that this "gaze angle" never becomes too small (such that the ball falls in front of them) or too large (such that the ball sails overhead). In other words, these catchers appear to unconsciously use a specific mathematical rule: "Keep the tangent of the angle of gaze elevation to zero" (McLeod & Dienes, 1996).

Sometimes, people perceive motion when there is none. Psychologists are interested in these motion illusions because they can tell us something about how the brain processes various kinds of movement-related information. When you accelerate in a car, for example, the experience of motion does not come only from the flow of visual information across your retinas; it also comes from touch information as you are pressed against the seat and vestibular information as your head tilts backward. If a visual flow suggests that you are moving, but you don't receive appropriate sensations from other parts of your body, particularly the vestibular senses, you may experience a nauseating movement illusion. This form of motion sickness often occurs when people watch some 3-D movies; operate motion simulators; or play certain video games, especially those with virtual reality technology.

Other illusions of motion are much less unpleasant. The most important of these, called **stroboscopic motion,** occurs because of our tendency to interpret as continuous motion a series of still images flashed in rapid succession. Stroboscopic motion is the basis for our ability to see movement in the still images on films and videos. Films consist of sequences of snapshots presented at a rate of twenty-four per second. Each snapshot is slightly different from the preceding one, and each is separated by a brief blank-out produced by the shutter of the film projector. Videotapes show thirty snapshots per second. As we watch, the "memory" of each image lasts long enough in the brain to bridge the gap until the next image appears. Thus, we are usually unaware that we are seeing a series of still pictures and that, about half the time, there is actually no image on the screen!

Perceptual Constancy

Suppose that one sunny day you are watching someone walking toward you along a tree-lined sidewalk. The visual sensations produced by this person are actually rather bizarre, if you think about them. For one thing, the size of the image on your retinas keeps getting larger as the person gets closer. To see this for yourself, hold out a hand at arm's length and look at someone far away. The retinal image of that person will be so small that you can cover it with your hand. If you do the same

figure 5.12

A Size Illusion

The monster that is higher in the drawing probably appears larger than the other one, but they are actually the same size. Why does this illusion occur? The converging lines of the tunnel provide strong depth cues telling us that the higher monster is farther away, but because that monster casts an image on our retinas that is just as big as the "nearer" one, we assume that the more distant monster must be bigger. (Look again at Figure 5.5 for other examples of this illusion.)

Shape Constancy Trace the outline of this floating object onto a piece of paper. The tracing will be oval shaped, but shape constancy leads you to perceive it as the circular life ring that it actually is. Sometimes, constancy mechanisms are so good at creating perceptions of a stable world that they can keep us from seeing changes. In one study, for example, participants looking at a computer display of a person's head failed to notice that as the head turned, it morphed gradually into the head of a different person (Wallis & Bülthoff, 2001).

when the person is three feet away, the retinal image will be much larger than your hand, but you will perceive the person as being closer now, not bigger. Similarly, if you watch people pass from bright sunshine through the shadows of trees, your retinas receive images that are darker, then lighter, then darker again. Still, you perceive individuals whose coloring remains the same.

These examples illustrate **perceptual constancy,** the perception of objects as constant in size, shape, color, and other properties despite changes in their retinal image. Without perceptual constancy, the world would be an Alice-in-Wonderland kind of place in which objects continuously changed their properties.

Size Constancy Why does the perceived size of objects remain more or less constant, no matter what changes occur in the size of their retinal image? One explanation emphasizes the computational aspects of perception. It suggests that as objects move closer or farther away, the brain perceives the change in distance and automatically adjusts the perception. More specifically, the *perceived size* of an object is equal to the size of the retinal image multiplied by the perceived distance (Holway & Boring, 1941). As an object moves closer, its retinal image increases, but the perceived distance decreases at the same rate, so the perceived size remains constant. If, instead, a balloon is inflated in front of your eyes, perceived distance remains constant, and the perceived size (correctly) increases as the retinal image size increases.

The computational perspective is reasonably good at explaining most aspects of size constancy, but it cannot fully account for the fact that people are better at judging the true size (and distance) of familiar rather than unfamiliar objects. This phenomenon suggests that there is an additional mechanism for size constancy—one that is consistent with the constructivists' emphasis on the knowledge-based aspects of perception: Your knowledge and experience tell you that most objects (aside from balloons) do not suddenly change size.

The perceptual system usually produces size constancy correctly and automatically, but it can sometimes fail, resulting in size illusions such as the one illustrated in Figure 5.12. Because this figure contains strong linear perspective cues (lines converging in the "distance"), and because objects nearer the point of convergence are interpreted as farther away, we perceive the monster near the top of the figure as the bigger of the two, even though it is exactly the same size as the other one. The consequences of such illusions can be far more serious when the objects involved are, say, moving automobiles. If there are few other depth cues available, we may perceive objects with smaller retinal images to be farther away than those with larger images. This error may explain why in countries where cars vary greatly in size, small cars have higher accident rates than large ones (Eberts & MacMillan, 1985). A small car produces a smaller retinal image than a large one at the same distance, easily causing the driver of a following vehicle to overestimate the distance to the small car (especially in dim light) and therefore fail to brake in time to avoid a collision. Such misjudgments illustrate the *inferential* nature of perception emphasized by constructivists: People make logical inferences or hypotheses about the world based on the available cues. Unfortunately, if the cues are misleading or the inferences are wrong, perceptual errors may occur.

Shape Constancy The principles behind shape constancy are closely related to those of size constancy. To see shape constancy at work, remember what page you are on, close this book, and tilt it toward and away from you several times. The book will continue to look rectangular, even though the shape of its retinal image changes dramatically as you move it. The brain automatically integrates information about retinal images and distance as movement occurs. In this case, the distance information involves the difference in distance between the near and far edges of the book.

figure 5.13

Brightness Contrast

 At first glance, the inner rectangle on the left probably looks lighter than the inner rectangle on the right. But carefully examine the inner rectangles alone (covering their surroundings), and you will see that both are of equal intensity. The brighter surround in the right-hand figure leads you to perceive its inner rectangle as relatively darker.

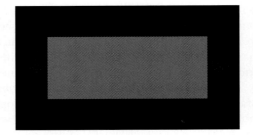

TRY THIS

As with size constancy, much of the ability to judge shape constancy depends on automatic computational mechanisms in the nervous system, but expectations about the shape of objects also play a role. For example, in Western cultures, most corners are at right angles. Knowledge of this fact helps make "rectangle" the most likely interpretation of the retinal image shown in Figure 5.1.

Brightness Constancy   Even with dramatic changes in the amount of light striking an object, the object's perceived brightness remains relatively constant (MacEvoy & Paradiso, 2001). Place a piece of charcoal in sunlight and a piece of white paper in nearby shade. The charcoal will look very dark and the paper very bright, even though a light meter would reveal much more light energy reflected from the sun-bathed coal than from the shaded paper. One reason the charcoal continues to look dark, no matter what the illumination, is that you *know* that charcoal is nearly black, illustrating once again the knowledge-based nature of perception. Another reason is that the charcoal is still the darkest object relative to

in review	Principles of Perceptual Organization and Constancy	
Principle	**Description**	**Example**
Figure-ground processing	Certain objects or sounds are automatically identified as figures, whereas others become meaningless background.	You see a person standing against a building, not a building with a person-shaped hole in it.
Grouping (Gestalt laws)	Properties of stimuli lead us to automatically group them together. These include proximity, similarity, continuity, closure, common fate, synchrony, common region, and connectedness.	People who are sitting together, or who are dressed similarly, are perceived as a group.
Perception of location and depth	Knowing an object's two-dimensional position position (left and right, up and down) and distance enables us to locate it. The image on the retina and the orientation of the head position provide information about the two-dimensional position of visual stimuli; auditory localization relies on differences in the information received by the ears. Depth or distance perception uses stimulus cues such as interposition, relative size, height in the visual field, texture gradients, linear perspective, clarity, color, and shadow.	Large, clear objects appear closer than small, hazy objects.
Perceptual constancy	Objects are perceived as constant in size, shape, brightness, color, and other properties, despite changes in their retinal images.	A train coming toward you is perceived as getting closer, not larger; a restaurant sign is perceived as rotating, not changing shape.

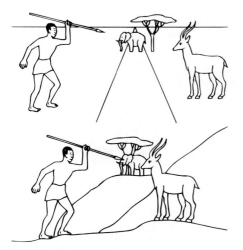

figure 5.14

Culture and Depth Cues

Participants in research on the influence of experience on perception were shown drawings like these and asked to judge which animal is closer to the hunter. People in cultures where pictured depth cues are familiar choose the antelope, which is at the same distance from the viewer as the hunter. People in cultures less familiar with such cues might choose the elephant, which though closer to the hunter on the page, is more distant when depth cues are considered (Hudson, 1960).

Source: Hudson (1960).

ClassPrep PPT 32: *Figure 5.14:* Culture and Depth Cues

OBJ 5.16: Compare and contrast bottom-up processing and top-down processing.

Test Items 5.111–5.121

IRM Activity 5.13: Top-Down Processing

LSV: Perception (Unit #8)

top-down processing   Aspects of recognition that are guided by higher-level cognitive processes and psychological factors such as expectations.

its background in the sunlight, and the paper is the brightest object relative to its background in the shade. As shown in Figure 5.13, the brightness of an object is perceived in relation to its background.

For a summary of this discussion, see "In Review: Principles of Perceptual Organization and Constancy."   **IRM Activity 1.7:** Sociocultural Diversity

Culture, Experience, and Perception

So far, we have talked as if all aspects of perception work or fail in the same way for everyone. Differing experiences, however, do affect people's perceptions. To the extent that people in different cultures are exposed to substantially different visual environments, some of their perceptual experiences may be different as well. For example, researchers have compared responses to depth cues by people from cultures that do and do not use pictures and paintings to represent reality (Derogowski, 1989). This research suggests that people in cultures that provide minimal experience with pictorial representations, such as the Me'n or the Nuba in Africa, have a more difficult time judging distances shown in pictures (see Figure 5.14). These individuals also tend to have a harder time sorting pictures of three-dimensional objects into categories, even though they can easily sort the objects themselves (Derogowski, 1989).

Other research shows that the perception of optical illusions varies from culture to culture and is related to cultural differences in perceptual experiences. In one study, researchers enhanced the Ponzo illusion, shown in Figure 5.5(A), by superimposing its horizontal lines on a picture of railroad tracks. This familiar image added depth cues for participants in the United States, but not for people in Guam, which had no railroad tracks at the time of the research (Leibowitz et al., 1969). In short, although the structure and principles of human perceptual systems tend to create generally similar views of the world for all of us, our perception of reality is also shaped by experience, including the experience of living in a particular culture. Unfortunately, as more and more cultures are "westernized," the visual stimulation they present to their children will become less distinctive; eventually, research on the impact of differential experience on perception may become impossible.

Recognizing the Perceptual World

In discussing how people organize the perceptual world, we have set the stage for addressing one of the most vital questions that perception researchers must answer: How do people recognize what objects are? If you are driving in search of Barney's Diner, exactly what happens when your eyes finally locate the pattern of light that spells out its name?

To know that you have finally found what you have been looking for, your brain must analyze incoming patterns of information and compare them with information stored in memory. If your brain finds a match, recognition takes place, and the stimulus is classified into a *perceptual category*. Once recognition occurs, your perception of a stimulus may never be the same again. Look at Figure 5.15. Do you see anything familiar? If not, turn to Figure 5.20, later in the chapter; then look at Figure 5.15 again. You should now see it in an entirely new light. The difference between your "before" and "after" experiences of Figure 5.15 is the difference between the sensory world before and after a perceptual match occurs and recognition takes place.

Exactly how does such matching occur? Some aspects of recognition are guided by knowledge, expectations, and other psychological factors. This phenomenon is called **top-down processing,** because it involves higher-level, knowledge-based information. Other aspects of recognition rely on specific, detailed information elements

figure 5.15

Categorizing Perceptions

TRY THIS What do you see here? If you can't recognize this pattern of information as falling into any perceptual category, turn to Figure 5.20 for some help in doing so.

ClassPrep PPT 33: Figure 5.15: Perceptual Categorization

IRM In Your Own Words 5.2: Top-Down and Bottom-Up Processing at a Band Concert!

ClassPrep PPT 35: Perceptual Processing

from the sensory receptors that are integrated and assembled into a whole. This latter phenomenon is called **bottom-up processing,** because it begins with basic information units that serve as a foundation for recognition. Let's consider the contributions of bottom-up and top-down processing to recognition, as well as the use of neural network models to understand both.

Bottom-Up Processing

OBJ 5.17: Explain how feature analysis works in bottom-up processing.

Test Items 5.122–5.123

ClassPrep PPT 36, OHT: Figure 5.16: Feature Analysis

Research on the visual system is providing a detailed picture of how bottom-up processing works. As described in the chapter on sensation, all along the path from the eye to the brain, certain cells respond to selected features of a stimulus so that the stimulus is actually analyzed into basic features before these features are recombined to create the perceptual experience.

What features undergo separate analysis? As also noted in the chapter on sensation, certain cells specialize in responding to stimuli having specific orientations in space (Hubel & Wiesel, 1979). For example, one cell in the cerebral cortex might

figure 5.16

Feature Analysis

Feature detectors operating at lower levels of the visual system detect such features of incoming stimuli as the corners and angles shown in the center of this figure. Later in the perceptual sequence, bottom-up processing might recombine these features to aid in pattern recognition, as in the examples on the right.

bottom-up processing Aspects of recognition that depend first on the information about the stimulus that comes up to the brain from the sensory receptors.

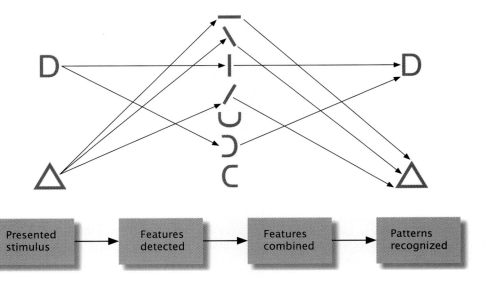

figure 5.17

The Face Looks Familiar

Who are these people? Most people first see Vice President Dick Cheney and President George W. Bush, but look more closely. The image on the left is actually a composite, combining the head shape and glasses of Cheney with the facial features of Bush. The tendency to identify this composite as Cheney suggests that large-scale features, such as overall shape, may be more important than eyes or other small-scale features in the initial recognition of people.

ClassPrep PPT 37: *Figure 5.17:* The Face Looks Familiar

IRM Activity 4.9: Negative Afterimages, Opponent-Processing, and Sensation

IRM Handout 4.3: Review of Sensory Modalities

IRM Activity 5.15: Active Processes in Perception

ClassPrep PPT 38: *Figure 5.18:* Recognizing Objects from Geons

figure 5.18

Recognizing Objects from Geons

TRY THIS Research suggests that we use geons—the forms in the top row—to recognize complex objects. Some examples of objects that can be recognized based on the layout and combination of only two or three geons are shown in the bottom row. The cup, for example, is made up of geons 2 and 4. Other combinations, such as an elongated cylinder (geon 2) on top of a cone (geon 3), might produce a broom. Can you make a kettle out of these geons? The solution is on page 168.

Source: Taken from Belderman, I., Matching Image Edges to Object Memory, from the Proceedings of the IEEE First International Conference on Computer Vision, pp. 364–382, 1987, IEEE © 1997 IEEE.

fire only in response to a diagonal line, so it acts as a *feature detector* for diagonal lines. Figure 5.16 illustrates how the analysis by such feature detectors, early in the information-processing sequence, may contribute to recognition of letters or judgments of shape. Color, motion, and even corners are other sensory features that appear to be analyzed separately in different parts of the brain prior to full perceptual recognition (Beatty, 1995; Cowey, 1994).

Features such as color, motion, overall shape, and fine details can all contribute to our ability to recognize objects, but some carry more weight than others in various situations. In the case of face recognition, for example, not all features are equally weighted when we decide who it is that we are seeing (Sinha & Poggio, 1996). Take just a quick look at Figure 5.17, and see if you recognize the person on the *left*. If you are like most people, it will take a second look to realize that your first glance led you to an erroneous conclusion. Such recognition errors are evidence that at least initially, we tend to rely on large-scale features, such as hair and head shape, to recognize people.

How do psychologists know that feature analysis is actually involved in pattern recognition? Recordings of brain activity indicate that the sensory features we have listed here cause particular sets of neurons to fire. In fact, scientists have recently shown that it is possible to determine what category of object a person is looking at (e.g., a face vs. a house) based on the pattern of activity occurring in visual processing areas of the person's brain (Haxby et al., 2001). Further, as described in the chapter on sensation, people with certain kinds of brain damage show selective impairment in the ability to perceive certain sets of sensory features, such as an object's color or movement (Banks & Krajicek, 1991). Irving Biederman (1987) has

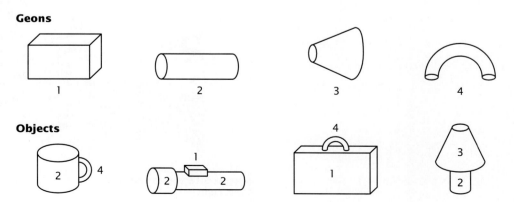

Geons

Objects

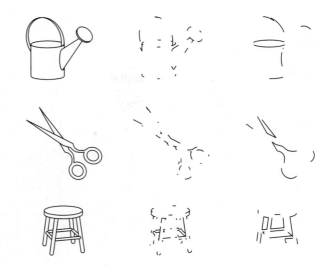

figure 5.19

Recognition of Objects With and Without Their Geons Destroyed

The drawings in columns 2 and 3 have had the same amount of ink removed, but in column 3 the deletions have destroyed many of the geons used in object recognition. The drawings in column 2 are far easier to recognize, because their geons are intact.

ClassPrep PPT 39: *Figure 5.19:* Recognition of Objects With and Without Their Geons Destroyed

IRM Activity 5.10: Subliminal Messages

IRM Activity 5.11: Figure-Ground and Expectancy

IRM Activity 5.13: Top-Down Processing

IRM Activity 5.16: Active Tactile Perception

IRM Activity 7.9: Constructive Memory: The Rumor Chain

proposed that people recognize three-dimensional objects by detecting and then combining simple forms, which he calls *geons;* Figure 5.18 shows some of these geons and how they can be combined to form a variety of recognizable objects. Evidence for Biederman's theory comes from experiments in which people must identify drawings when some of the details have been eliminated. Recognition becomes particularly difficult when the geons are no longer intact, as Figure 5.19 demonstrates.

Top-Down Processing

Bottom-up feature analysis can explain why you recognize the letters in a sign for Barney's Diner. But why is it that you will recognize the sign more easily if it appears where you were told to expect it rather than a block earlier? And why can you recognize it even if a few letters are missing from the sign? Top-down processing seems

figure 5.20

Another Version of Figure 5.15

Now that you can identify a dog in this figure, it should be much easier to recognize when you look back at the original version.

ClassPrep PPT 34: *Figure 5.20:* Now Do You See It?

In figure 5.18 you can create a kettle by adding a cone (geon 3) to a combination of geons 2 and 4 (the cup).

figure 5.21

What Does It Look Like to You?

TRY THIS Many people have reported seeing a demonic face in the smoke pouring from New York's World Trade Center after terrorists attacked it on September 11, 2001. This perceptual categorization results from a combination of bottom-up and top-down recognition processes. Feature detectors automatically register the edges and colors of images, whereas knowledge, beliefs, and expectancies give meaning to these features. A person who does not expect to see a face in the smoke—or whose cultural background does not include the concept of "the devil"—might not see one until that interpretation is suggested. To assess that possibility, show this photo to people from various religious and cultural backgrounds who have not seen it before (don't tell them what to look for) and make a note of which individuals require prompting in order to identify a demonic face.

OBJ 5.18: Discuss the influences on top-down processing. Your answer should include expectancy, motivation, and schemas.

Test Items 5.124–5.136

Essay Q 5.2

IRM Activity 7.10: Remembering an Absent Memory

Personal Learning Activity 5.3

schemas Mental representations of what we know and have come to expect about the world.

to be at work in these cases. Fo- ex-mp-e, y-u c-n r-ad -hi- se-te-ce -it- ev-ry -hi-d l-tt-r m-ss-ng. In top-down processing, people use their knowledge in making inferences or "educated guesses" to recognize objects, words, or melodies, especially when sensory information is vague or ambiguous (DeWitt & Samuel, 1990; Rock, 1983). Once you knew that there was a dog in Figure 5.15, it became much easier for you to perceive it in Figure 5.20. Similarly, police officers find it easy to recognize familiar people on blurry security camera videos, but it is much more difficult for them to recognize strangers (Burton et al., 1999).

Many aspects of perception can best be explained by higher-level cognitive influences, especially by expectancy and context. Consider again the two faces in Figure 5.17. Do you think that you'd have been as likely to mistakenly identify the man on the left as Dick Cheney if the person on the right had been, say, British prime minister Tony Blair or John Travolta? Probably not. Through bottom-up processing you correctly identified the combination of features on the right as President Bush; and given your knowledge of him, you reasonably expected to see certain individuals at his side, such as Cheney. In other words, your perceptual system made a quick "educated guess" that turned out to be wrong.

Top-down processing is also involved in sightings of unusual images or "visions." For example, look at Figure 5.21, which shows the World Trade Center under attack. Some people see an image of the devil in the smoke. This interpretation requires some knowledge of paintings and other representations of the devil. Expectancy plays a role, too. Many people who have not heard about the image through the news media do not see a demonic face in this photo.

These examples illustrate that top-down processing can have a strong influence on pattern recognition. Our experiences create **schemas**, which are mental representations of what we know and have come to expect about the world. Schemas can bias our perception toward one recognition or another by creating a *perceptual set*, a readiness or predisposition to perceive a stimulus in a certain way. This predisposition can also be shaped by the immediate context in which a stimulus occurs. In one case we know of, a woman saw a masked man in the darkened hallway of a house she was visiting. Her first perception was that the man who lived there was playing a joke; in fact, she had confronted a burglar. Context has biasing effects for sounds as well as sights. Gunfire heard in public places is often perceived as firecrackers or a car backfiring; at a rifle range, it would immediately be interpreted as shots. In short, top-down processing saves time. It allows us to identify objects even before examination of features is complete, or even when features are missing, distorted, or ambiguous; but as in Figure 5.17, it can sometimes lead us to jump to false conclusions.

The Eye of the Beholder   Top-down processing can affect our perception of people, as well as objects. As noted in the chapter on social cognition, for example, if you expect everyone in a certain ethnic or social group to behave in a certain way, you may perceive a particular group member's behavior in line with this prejudice. In contrast, have you ever come to perceive someone as physically more attractive or less attractive as you got to know the person better? This change in perception occurs largely because new information alters, in top-down fashion, your interpretation of the raw sensations you get from the person.

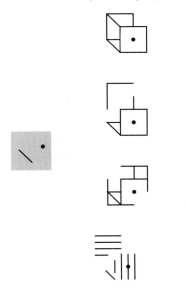

figure 5.22

The Object Superiority Effect

When people are asked to say whether the feature at the left appears in patterns briefly flashed on a computer screen, the feature is more likely to be detected when it appears in patterns like those at the top right, which most resemble three-dimensional objects. This object superiority effect supports the importance of network processing in perception.

Source: Reprinted with permission from figures by Weisstein & Harris, *Science,* 1974, 186, 752–755. Copyright © 1974 by American Association of the Advancement of Science.

ClassPrep PPT 41: *Figure 5.22:* The Object Superiority Effect

Class Prep PPT 42: Parallel Distributed Processing (PDP) Models

ClassPrep PPT 43: *Figure 5.23:* Recognizing a Word

Motivation is another aspect of top-down processing that can affect perception. A hungry person might misperceive a sign for "Burger's Body Shop" as indicating a place to eat. Similarly, if you have ever watched an athletic contest, you probably remember a time when an obviously demented referee incorrectly called a foul on your favorite team. You knew the call was wrong because you clearly saw the other team's player at fault. But suppose you had been cheering for that other team. The chances are good that you would have seen the referee's call as the right one.
Test Items 5.137–5.140

Network Processing

Researchers taking a computational approach to perception have attempted to explain various aspects of object recognition in terms of both top-down *and* bottom-up processing. In one study, participants were asked to say whether a particular feature, like the dot and angle at the left side of Figure 5.22, appeared within a pattern that was briefly flashed on a computer screen. The participants detected this feature faster when it was embedded in a pattern resembling a three-dimensional object than when it appeared within a random pattern of lines (Purcell & Stewart, 1991). This result is called the *object superiority effect*. There is also a *word superiority effect*: When strings of letters are briefly flashed on a screen, people's ability to detect target letters is better if the string forms a word than if it is a nonword (Prinzmetal, 1992).

Neural network models have been used to explain findings such as these. As described in the chapter on biological aspects of psychology, each element in these networks is connected to every other element, and each connection has a specific strength. Applying network processing models to pattern recognition involves focusing on the interactions among the various feature analyzers we have discussed (Rumelhart & Todd, 1992). More specifically, some researchers explain recognition using **parallel distributed processing (PDP) models** (Rumelhart & McClelland, 1986). According to PDP models, the units in a network operate in parallel—simultaneously. Connections between units either excite or inhibit other units. If the connection is excitatory, activating one unit spreads the activation to connected units. Using a connection may strengthen it.

How does this process apply to recognition? According to PDP models, recognition occurs as a result of the simultaneous operation of connected units. Units are

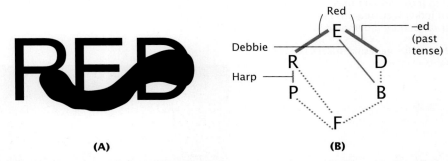

(A)   **(B)**

figure 5.23

Recognizing a Word

You probably recognized the pattern shown in Part A as the word *RED,* even though the first letter of the word shown could be *R* or *P;* the second, *E* or *F;* and the third, *D* or *B.* According to PDP models, your recognition occurred because, together, the letters excite each other's correct interpretation. This mutual excitation process is illustrated in Part B by a set of letter "nodes" (corresponding to activity sites in the brain) and some of the words they might activate. These nodes will be activated if the feature they detect appears in the stimulus array. They will also be activated if nodes to which they are linked become active. All six letter nodes shown in Part B will initially be excited when the stimulus in Part A is presented, but mutual excitement along the strongest links will guarantee that the word *RED* is perceived (Rumelhart & McClelland, 1985).

Source: Rumelhart & McClelland (1986).

in review Mechanisms of Pattern Recognition

Mechanism	Description	Example
Bottom-up processing	Raw sensations from the eye or the ear are analyzed into basic features, such as form, color, or movement; these features are then recombined at higher brain centers, where they are compared with stored information about objects or sounds.	You recognize a dog as a dog because its features—four legs, barking, panting— match your perceptual category for "dog."
Top-down processing	Knowledge of the world and experience in perceiving allow people to make inferences about the identity of stimuli, even when the quality of raw sensory information is low.	On a dark night, what you see as a small, vague blob pulling on the end of a leash is recognized as a dog because the stimulus occurs at a location where you would expect a dog to be.
Network, or PDP, processing	Recognition depends on communication among feature-analysis systems operating simultaneously and enlightened by past experience.	A dog standing behind a picket fence will be recognized as a dog even though each disjointed "slice" of the stimulus may not look like a dog.

activated when matched by features in a stimulus. To the extent that features, such as the letters in a word or the angles in a box, have occurred together in the past, their connective links will be stronger, and detection of any of them will be made more likely by the presence of all the others. This appears to be what happens in the word and object superiority effects, and the same phenomenon is illustrated in Figure 5.23. PDP models, sometimes called *connectionist models,* clearly represent the computational approach to perception. Researchers have achieved many advances in theories of pattern recognition by programming computers to carry out the kinds of complex computations that neural networks are assumed to perform in the human perceptual system (Grossberg, 1988). These computers have "learned" to read and recognize speech, and even faces, in a manner that is strikingly similar to the way humans learn and perform the same perceptual tasks (see "In Review: Mechanisms of Pattern Recognition").

LINKAGES (a link to Human Development)

ClassPrep: Linkages: Perception and Human Development

parallel distributed processing (PDP) models An approach to understanding object recognition in which various elements of the object are thought to be simultaneously analyzed by a number of widely distributed, but connected, neural units in the brain.

Perception and Human Development

We have seen the important role that knowledge and experience play in recognition, but are they also required for more basic aspects of perception? Which perceptual abilities are babies born with, and which do they acquire by seeing, hearing, smelling, touching, and tasting things? How do their perceptions compare with those of adults? To learn about infants' perception, psychologists have studied two inborn patterns, *habituation* and *dishabituation.* For example, infants stop looking when they repeatedly see stimuli that are perceived to be the same. This is habituation. If a stimulus appears that is perceived to be different, infants resume looking. This is dishabituation. Researchers have used the habituation and dishabituation phenomena, along with measurements of electrical responses in the brain, to study color perception in infants. It seems that newborns can perceive differences among stimuli showing different amounts of black-and-white contrast, but they are unable to distinguish among particular hues (Burr, Morrone, & Fiorentini, 1996). Other researchers have used similar methods to show that newborns can perceive differences in the angles of lines (Slater et al., 1991). These

figure 5.24

Infants' Perceptions of Human Faces
Newborns show significantly greater interest in the face-like pattern at the far left than in any of the other patterns. Evidently, some aspects of face perception are innate.

Source: Johnson et al. (1991).

Face   **Configuration**   **Linear**   **Scrambled**

ClassPrep PPT 58: *Figure 5.24:* Infants' Perception of Human Faces

ClassPrep: Linkages (cont.): Perception and Human Development

OBJ 5.20: Describe an infant's perceptual abilities.

Test Items 5.141–5.146

studies and others suggest that we are born with some, but not all, of the basic components of feature detection.

Do we also have an innate ability to combine features into perceptions of whole objects? This question generates lively debate among specialists in infant perception. Some research indicates that at one month of age, infants concentrate their gaze on one part of an object, such as the corner of a triangle (Goldstein, 1999). By two months, though, the eyes systematically scan all the edges of the object, suggesting that only then has the infant begun to perceive the pattern of the object, or its shape, rather than just its component features. However, other researchers have found that once newborns have become habituated to specific combinations of features, they show dishabituation (i.e., they pay attention) when those features are combined in a novel way. The implication is that even newborns notice, and keep track of, the way some features are put together (Slater et al., 1991).

There is evidence that infants may be innately tuned to perceive at least one important complex pattern—the human face. In one study of newborns, some less than an hour old, patterns like those in Figure 5.24 were moved slowly past the infants' faces (Johnson et al., 1991). The infants moved their heads and eyes to follow these patterns, but they tracked the face-like pattern shown on the left side of Figure 5.24 significantly farther than any of the nonfaces. The difference in tracking indicates that the infants could discriminate between faces and nonfaces and were more interested in the faces. Why should this be? The investigators suggest that interest in human faces is adaptive, in evolutionary terms, because it helps newborns focus on their only source of food and care.

ClassPrep: Linkages (cont.): Learning to Judge Depth

Other research on perceptual development suggests that our ability to use certain distance cues develops more slowly than our recognition of object shapes (see Figure 5.25). For example, infants' ability to use binocular disparity and relative

figure 5.25

The Visual Cliff
The *visual cliff* is a glass-topped table that creates the impression of a sudden drop-off. A ten-month-old placed at what looks like the edge will calmly crawl across the shallow side to reach a parent but will hesitate and cry rather than crawl over the "cliff" (Gibson & Walk, 1960). Changes in heart rate show that infants too young to crawl also perceive the depth but are not frightened by it. Here again, nature and nurture interact adaptively: Depth perception appears shortly after birth, but fear and avoidance of dangerous depths do not develop until an infant is old enough to crawl into trouble.

motion cues to judge depth appears to develop some time after about three months of age (Yonas, Arterberry, & Granrud, 1987). Infants do not use texture gradients and linear perspective as cues about depth until they are five to seven months old (Arterberry, Yonas, & Bensen, 1989).

In summary, there is little doubt that many of the basic building blocks of perception are present within the first few days after birth. The basics include organ-based cues to depth, such as accommodation and convergence. Maturation of the visual system adds to these basics as time goes by. For example, over the first few months after birth, the eye's fovea gradually develops the number of cone cells necessary for high visual acuity and perception of small differences in hue (Goldstein, 1999). However, visual experience may also be necessary if the infant is to recognize some unified patterns and objects in frequently encountered stimuli, to interpret depth and distance cues, and to use them in moving safely through the world. In other words, like so many aspects of human psychology, perception is the result of a blending of heredity and environment. From infancy onward, the perceptual system creates a personal reality based in part on the experience that shapes each individual's feature-analysis networks and knowledge-based expectancies.

LSV: Attention

ClassPrep PPT 44 & 45: Attention

Attention

Believe it or not, you still haven't found Barney's Diner! By now, you understand *how* you will recognize the right sign when you perceive it, but how can you be sure you *will* perceive it? As you drive, the diner's sign will appear as but one piece in a sensory puzzle that also includes road signs, traffic lights, sirens, talk radio, and dozens of other stimuli. You can't perceive all of them at once, so to find Barney's you are going to have to be sure that the information you select for perceptual processing includes the stimuli that will help you reach your goal. In short, you are going to have to pay attention.

OBJ 5.21: Define attention. Describe the research on covert shifting of attention.

Attention is the process of directing and focusing certain psychological resources to enhance perception, performance, and mental experience. We use attention to *direct* our sensory and perceptual systems toward certain stimuli, to *select* specific information for further processing, to *ignore* or screen out unwanted stimuli, to *allocate* the mental energy required to process selected stimuli, and to *regulate* the flow of resources necessary for performing a task or coordinating several tasks at once (Wickens & Carswell, 1997).

Test Items 5.147–5.156

Psychologists have discovered three important characteristics of attention. First, it *improves mental processing;* you often need to concentrate attention on a task to do your best at it. If your attentional system temporarily malfunctions, you might drive right past Barney's Diner. Second, attention takes *effort.* Prolonged concentration of attention can be draining (McNay, McCarty, & Gold, 2001), and when you are tired, focusing attention on anything becomes more difficult. Third, attentional resources are *limited.* When your attention is focused on reading this book, for example, you have less attention left over to listen to a conversation in the next room.

ClassPrep PPT 46: Characteristics of Attention

ClassPrep PPT 47: Controlling Attention

Freburg *Stand!:* Hallowell, "What I've Learned from A.D.D.," and Armstrong, "A.D.D.: Does It Really Exist?"

To experience attention as a process, try "moving it around" a bit. When you finish reading this sentence, look at something behind you, then face forward and notice the next sound you hear, then visualize your best friend, and then focus on how your tongue feels. You just used attention to direct your perceptual systems toward different aspects of your external and internal environments. Sometimes, as when you looked behind you, shifting attention involves *overt orienting*—pointing sensory systems at a particular stimulus. But you were able to shift attention to an image of your friend's face without having to move a muscle; this is called *covert orienting*. There is a rumor that students sometimes use covert orienting to shift their attention from their lecturer to thoughts that have nothing to do with the lecture.

Freburg *Perspectives:* Lentwyler, "Paying Attention"

attention The process of directing and focusing certain psychological resources to enhance perception, performance, and mental experience.

FOCUS ON RESEARCH METHODS

An Experiment in "Mind Reading"

Everyone knows what it is like to covertly shift attention, but how can we tell when someone else is doing it? The study of covert attention requires the sort of "mind reading" that has been made possible by innovative experimental research methods. These techniques are helping psychologists to measure where a person's attention is focused.

● What was the researchers' question?

Michael Posner and his colleagues were interested in finding out what changes in perceptual processing occur when people covertly shift their attention to a specific location in space (Posner, Nissen, & Ogden, 1978). Specifically, the researchers addressed the question of whether these attentional shifts lead to more sensitive processing of stimuli in the location attended to.

● How did the researchers answer the question?

Posner and his colleagues took advantage of an important property of mental events: Even though such events do not produce movements that can be observed and recorded, they do take time. Moreover, the time taken by mental events can vary considerably, thus providing important clues about internal processes such as covert attention.

The researchers designed a study in which participants were asked to focus their eyes on a fixation point that appeared at the center of a computer screen. One second later, a tiny square appeared at either the right or left edge of the screen. The participants were then asked to indicate, by pressing a key as quickly as possible, when they detected the square. However, because their vision was focused on the fixation point, they could detect the square only out of the "corners" of their eyes.

On any given trial, a participant could never be sure where the square would be located. However, the researchers provided "hints" on some of the trials. At the start of some trials, participants were given a cue at the fixation point. Sometimes, the cue was an arrow pointing to the right edge of the screen (→). This cue was correct 80 percent of the time. On other trials, participants were presented with an arrow pointing to the left edge of the screen (←); this cue was also correct 80 percent of the time. On still other trials, participants saw a plus sign (+), which indicated that the square was equally likely to appear on the left or the right.

The researchers reasoned that when the plus sign appeared, the best strategy for quickly detecting the square would be to maintain visual attention on the center of the screen and to shift it only after the square appeared. However, when one of the arrow cues was presented, the best strategy would involve covertly shifting attention in the direction indicated by the arrow before the square appeared. If the participants were actually using covert attention shifts, they should have been able to detect the square fastest when the cue provided accurate information about the location of the target square, even though they were not actually moving their eyes.

The dependent variable in this study was the speed of target detection, measured in milliseconds. The independent variable was the type of cue given: valid, invalid, or neutral. Valid cues were arrows that correctly predicted the target location; invalid ones were arrows that pointed the wrong way. Neutral cues gave no guidance.

● What did the researchers find?

As shown in Figure 5.26, the square stimulus was detected significantly faster when the cue gave valid information about where the square would appear. Invalid

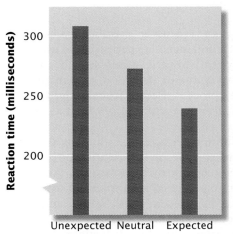

figure 5.26

Measuring Covert Shifts in Attention

It took people less time (measured in thousandths of a second) to detect a square appearing at an expected location than at an unexpected location on a computer screen. This result suggests that even though their eyes did not move, they covertly shifted attention to the expected location before the stimulus was presented.

cues, however, resulted in a distinct cost to performance: When participants were led to shift their attention in the wrong direction, they were much slower in detecting the square.

● What do the results mean?

The data provide evidence that the participants used cues to shift their attention to the expected location, thus readying their perceptual systems to detect information there. When a cue led them to shift their attention to the wrong location, they were less ready to detect information at the correct location, and their detection was slowed. In short, attention can enhance the processing of information at one retinal location, but it does so at the expense of processing information elsewhere.

● What do we still need to know?

More recent research on the costs and benefits associated with perceptual expectancies has been generally consistent with the findings of Posner's pioneering team (e.g., Ball & Sekuler, 1992; Carrasco & McElree, 2001). However, there are still many unanswered questions about how covert attention actually operates. How quickly can we shift attention from one location to another? And how quickly can we shift attention between sensory modalities, say, from watching to listening? These questions are methodologically difficult to address, but they are fundamental to understanding our ability to deal with the potentially overwhelming load of stimuli that reaches our sensory receptors. Experiments designed to answer such questions not only expand our understanding of attention but also illustrate the possibility of measuring hidden mental events through observation of overt behavior (Wolfe, Alvarez, & Horowitz, 2000).

Directing Attention

As shown in Posner's experiment on "mind reading," attending to some stimuli makes us less able to attend to others. In other words, attention is *selective;* it is like a spotlight that can illuminate only a part of the external or internal environment at any particular moment. How do you control, or allocate, your attention?

OBJ 5.22: Describe the influences that determine the ease of directing or dividing our attention.

Test Items 5.157–5.161

Control over attention can be voluntary or involuntary (Yantis, 1993). *Voluntary,* or goal-directed, attention control occurs when you purposely focus your attention in order to perform a task, such as reading a book in a noisy room or watching for a friend in a crowd. Voluntary control reflects top-down processing, because attention is guided by knowledge-based factors such as intentions, beliefs, expectations, and motivation. As people learn certain skills, they voluntarily direct their attention to information they once ignored. For example, when rounding a bend, a newly licensed driver will attend to the outside of the curve; the experienced driver will attend to the inside of the curve, which actually conveys more information about where to steer. If you are watching a sports event, learning where to allocate your attention is important if you are to understand what is going on. And if you are a competitor, the proper allocation of attention is absolutely essential for success on the playing field (Moran, 1996).

When, in spite of these top-down factors, some aspect of the environment—such as a loud noise—diverts your attention, attentional control is said to be *involuntary.* In this case, it is a bottom-up, or stimulus-driven, process. Stimulus characteristics that tend to capture attention include abrupt changes in lighting or color (such as flashing signs), movement, and the appearance of unusual shapes (Folk, Remington, & Wright, 1994). Some psychologists use the results of attention research to help design advertisements, logos, and product packaging that "grab" potential customers' attention.

Ignoring Information

When the spotlight of your attention is voluntarily or involuntarily focused on one part of the environment, you may ignore stimuli occurring in other parts. This ability, called *inattentional blindness* (Mack & Rock, 1998), can be helpful when it allows us to ignore construction noise while we are taking an exam, but it can also endanger us if we ignore information—such as a stop sign—that we should be attending to. Inattentional blindness can result in our missing some rather dramatic changes in our environment (Most et al., 2001). In one study, a researcher asked college students for directions to a campus building (Simons & Levin, 1997). During each conversation, two other researchers dressed as workmen passed between the first researcher and the student, carrying a large door. As the door hid the researcher from the student's view, one of the "workmen" took his place. This new person then resumed the conversation with the student as though nothing had happened.

figure 5.27

Change Blindness

TRY THIS These two photos are almost, but not exactly, alike. If you can't see the difference, or if it took you a while, you may have been focusing your attention on the similarity of main features, resulting in blindness to one small, but obvious, change. (See page 179 for the answer.)

ClassPrep PPT 48: *Figure 5.27:* Change Blindness

Amazing as it seems, only half of the students noticed that they were suddenly talking to a new person! The rest had apparently been paying so much attention to the researcher's question or to the map he was showing that they did not notice his appearance. And half the participants in another study were so focused on their assigned task of counting the passes made during a videotaped basketball game that they did not notice a woman in a gorilla suit who walked in front of the camera, beat her chest, and walked away (Simons & Chabris, 1999). Magicians take advantage of this phenomenon whenever they direct our attention elsewhere while making switches that we would otherwise clearly see. To experience a type of inattentional blindness known as "change blindness," take a look at the photographs in Figure 5.27.

Divided Attention   LSV: Attention

In many situations, people can divide their attention efficiently enough to allow them to perform more than one activity at a time (Damos, 1992). In fact, as Figure 5.28 illustrates, it is sometimes difficult to keep our attention focused rather than divided. We can walk while talking or drive while listening to music, but we find it virtually impossible to read and talk at the same time. Why is it sometimes so easy and at other times so difficult to do two things at once?

When one task is so *automatic* that it requires little or no attention, it is usually easy to do something else at the same time, even if the other task takes some attention (Schneider, 1985). When two tasks both require attention, it may still be possible to perform them simultaneously, as long as each taps into different kinds of attentional resources (Wickens, 1992a). For example, some attentional resources are devoted to perceiving incoming stimuli, whereas others handle making responses. This specialization of attention allows a skilled pianist to read musical notes and press keys simultaneously, even the first time through a piece. Apparently, the human brain has more than one type of attentional resource and more than one spotlight of attention (Wickens, 1989). This notion of different types of attention also helps explain why a driver can listen to the radio while steering safely and why voice control can be an effective way of performing a second task in an aircraft while the pilot's hands are busy manipulating the controls (Wickens, 1992a). If two tasks require the same kind of attention, however, performance on both tasks will suffer (Just et al., 2001)

Attention and Automatic Processing

Your search for Barney's Diner will be aided by your ability to voluntarily allocate attention to a certain part of the environment, but it would be even easier if you knew that Barney's had the only bright red sign on that stretch of road (see "In Review: Attention"). Your search would not take much effort in this case because you could simply "set" your attention to filter out all signs except red ones. The process of actively ignoring certain information will help you find Barney's, but it will also continue to affect your perceptions for some time afterward. Suppose, for example, that while you are ignoring blue signs, you pass one showing a giant blue palm tree. Researchers have found that your efforts to ignore certain stimuli may create *negative priming* (Rock & Gutman, 1981), making you slightly less able than before to identify palm trees of any color for several minutes, hours, or days (Deschepper & Treisman, 1996).

Psychologists describe the ability to search for targets rapidly and automatically as *parallel processing*; it is as if you can examine all nearby locations at once (in parallel) and rapidly detect the target no matter where it appears. So if the sign you are looking for is bright red and twice as large as any other one on the road, you could conduct a parallel search, and it would quickly "pop out." The automatic, parallel processing that allows detection of color or size suggests that these features are

Essay Q 5.3

ClassPrep PPT 49: The Stroop Task

ClassPrep PPT 50: Now Name the Color of the INK in which Each Word Is Printed

OBJ 5.23: Explain parallel processing.

Test Items 5.162–5.163

Videodisc Segment: Stroop Task

BLUE	GREEN
GREEN	ORANGE
PURPLE	ORANGE
GREEN	BLUE
RED	RED
GRAY	GRAY
RED	BLUE
BLUE	PURPLE

figure 5.28

The Stroop Task

TRY THIS Look at these words, and as rapidly as possible, call out the *color of the ink* in which each word is printed. This Stroop task (Stroop, 1935) is not easy, because your brain automatically processes the *meaning* of each word, which then competes for attention with the response you are supposed to give. To do well, you must focus on the ink color and not allow your attention to be divided between color and meaning. Children just learning to read have less trouble with this task, because they do not yet process word meanings as automatically as experienced readers do.

in review   Attention

Characteristics	Functions	Mechanisms
Improves mental functioning	Directs sensory and perceptual systems toward stimuli	Overt orienting (e.g., cupping your ear to hear a whisper)
Requires effort		
Has limits	Selects specific information for further processing	Covert orienting (e.g., thinking about spring break while looking at the notes in front of you)
	Allows us to ignore some information	Voluntary control (e.g., purposefully looking for cars before crossing a street)
	Allocates mental energy to process information	Involuntary control (e.g., losing your train of thought when you're interrupted by a thunderclap)
	Regulates the flow of resources necessary for performing a task or coordinating multiple tasks	Automatic processing (e.g., no longer thinking about grammar rules as you become fluent in a foreign language)
		Divided attention (e.g., looking for an open team-mate while you dribble a soccer ball down the field)

analyzed before the point at which attention is required. However, if the target you seek shares many features with others nearby, you must conduct a slower, serial search, examining each one in turn (Treisman, 1988).

Attention and the Brain

If directing attention to a task causes extra mental work to be done, there should be evidence of that work in brain activity. Such evidence has been provided by positron emission tomography (PET) and magnetic resonance imaging (MRI) scans, which reveal increased blood flow and greater neural activity in regions of the brain associated with the mental processing necessary for the task. In one study, for example, people were asked either to focus attention on reporting only the color of a stimulus or to divide attention in order to report its color, speed of motion, and shape (Corbetta et al., 1991). When attention was focused on color alone, increased blood flow appeared only in the part of the brain where that stimulus feature was analyzed; when attention was divided, the added supply of blood was shared between two locations. Similarly, increased neural activity occurs in two different areas of the brain when participants perform two different tasks, such as deciding whether sentences are true while also deciding whether two three-dimensional objects are the same or different (Just et al., 2001).

Because attention appears to be a linked set of resources that improve information processing at several levels and locations in the brain, it is not surprising that no single brain region has been identified as an "attention center" (Posner & Peterson, 1990; Sasaki et al., 2001). However, scientists have found regions in the base of the brain and in the parietal lobe of the cerebral cortex that are involved in the *switching* of visual attention from one stimulus element or location to another (Posner & Raichle, 1994).

Applications of Research on Perception

Throughout this chapter we have mentioned ways in which perceptual systems shape people's ability to handle a variety of tasks, from recognizing restaurant signs to detecting tornadoes. We have also seen how research on perception explains the

principles behind movies and videos and affects the design of advertisements. In this section we examine three other areas in which perception research has been applied: aviation, human-computer interaction, and traffic safety.

Aviation Psychology

Much of the research on perception in aviation has stemmed from efforts to understand accidents that were caused in part by failures of perception (O'Hare & Roscoe, 1991; Wiener & Nagel, 1988). To land an aircraft safely, for example, pilots must make accurate judgments of how far they are from the ground, as well as how fast and from what angle they are approaching the runway. The ecological approach to perception emphasizes that the perceptual cues providing this information are rich and redundant. Normally, this is the case, and pilots' perceptions are correct (Gibson, 1979). Consistent with the constructivist view, pilots can also use their experience-based expectations about the approaching ground surface, thus adding top-down processing to produce an accurate perception of reality.

But suppose there are few depth cues because the landing occurs at night, and suppose the lay of the land differs from what the pilot normally experiences. With both bottom-up and top-down processing impaired, the pilot's interpretation of reality may be disastrously incorrect. If, for example, the runway is much smaller than a pilot expects, it might be perceived as farther away than it actually is—especially at night—and thus may be approached too fast (O'Hare & Roscoe, 1991). (This illusion is similar to the one mentioned earlier in which drivers overestimate their distance from small cars.) Or if a pilot expects the runway to be perfectly flat but it actually slopes upward, the pilot might falsely perceive that the aircraft is too high. Misguided attempts to "correct" a plane's altitude under these circumstances have caused pilots to fly in too low, resulting in a series of major nighttime crashes in the 1960s (Kraft, 1978). Psychologists have helped to prevent similar tragedies by recommending that airline training programs remind pilots about the dangers of visual illusions and the importance of relying on their flight instruments during landings, especially at night.

Unfortunately, the instruments in a traditional aircraft cockpit present information that bears little resemblance to the perceptual world. A pilot depending on these instruments must do a lot of time-consuming and effortful serial processing to perceive and piece together the information necessary to understand the aircraft's position and movement. To address this problem, engineering psychologists have helped to develop displays that present a realistic three-dimensional image of the flight environment—similar in some ways to a video-game display. This image more accurately captures the many cues for depth perception that the pilot needs (Haskell & Wickens, 1993; Lintern, 1991; Theunisson, 1994).

Research on auditory perception has also contributed to aviation safety, both in the creation of warning signals that are most likely to catch the pilot's attention and in efforts to minimize errors in cockpit communications. Air-traffic control communications use a special vocabulary and standardized phrases to avoid misunderstandings. But as a result, these communications are usually short, with little of the built-in redundancy that in normal conversation allows people to understand a sentence even if some words are missing. For example, if a pilot eager to depart on time perceives an expected message as "clear for takeoff" when the actual message is "hold for takeoff," the results can be catastrophic. Problems like these are being addressed "bottom up," through "noise-canceling" microphones and visual message displays (Kerns, 1991), as well as through the use of slightly longer messages that aid top-down processing by providing more contextual cues.

Avoiding Perceptual Overload The pilot of a modern commercial jetliner is faced with a potentially overwhelming array of visual and auditory signals that must be correctly perceived and interpreted to ensure a safe flight. Engineering psychologists are helping to design instrument displays, warning systems, and communication links that make this task easier and make errors less likely.

ClassPrep PPT 51: Applications of Research on Perception

OBJ 5.24: Describe the influence of perceptual studies on the development of aviation and computer displays.

Test Items 5.164–5.165

The difference between the photos in Figure 5.27 is that in the top photo, there is a clump of trees just to the left of the sphinx.

Freburg *Perspectives:* Kitz, "How Virtual Reality
Can Affect You," and Levy, "Man vs. Machine"

Human-Computer Interaction

The principles of perception are also being applied by engineering psychologists who serve as key members of design teams at various computer manufacturers and software companies. For example, in line with the ecological approach to perception, they are trying to duplicate in the world of computer displays many of the depth cues that help people navigate in the physical world (Preece et al., 1994). The next time you use a word-processing or spreadsheet program, notice how shading cues make the "buttons" on the application toolbar at the top or bottom of the screen seem to protrude from their background, as real buttons would. Similarly, when you open several documents or spreadsheets, notice that interposition cues make them appear to be lying on top of one another.

The results of research on attention have even been applied to your cursor. It blinks to attract your attention, making it possible to do a quick parallel search rather than a slow serial search when you are looking for it amid all the other stimuli on the screen (Schneiderman, 1992). Perceptual principles have also guided creation of the pictorial images, or icons, that are used to represent objects, processes, and commands in your computer programs (Preece et al., 1994). These icons speed your use of the computer if their features are easy to detect, recognize, and interpret (McDougall, de Bruijn, & Curry, 2000; Niemela & Saarinen, 2000). This is why a little trash-can icon is used in some software programs to show you where to click when you want to delete a file; a tiny eraser or paper shredder would also work, but its features might be harder to recognize, making the program confusing. In short, psychologists are applying research on perception to make computers easier to use.

Traffic Safety

Research on perception is being applied in many ways to enhance traffic safety. For example, psychologists are involved in the design of automotive night vision displays that make it easier for drivers to see low-visibility targets, such as pedestrians dressed in dark clothing, or animals (Essock, et al., 1999). Further, research on divided attention is informing the debate over the use of cell phones while driving. The demands of traffic safety groups and the example set by countries such as Britain and Japan have led the state of New York to outlaw drivers' use of cell phones; thirty-four other U.S. states are considering such bans (Clines, 2001). Cell phone manufacturers agree that phone use while driving can be dangerous, but only

Driven to Distraction?   About 85 percent of the more than 110 million cell phone owners in the United States use their phones while driving (Clines, 2001). Some cell phone manufacturers claim that hands-free models can eliminate any dangers associated with using a phone while driving, but perception research indicates that using any kind of phone can create distractions that impair driving performance and may contribute to accidents.

because looking at the handset, pushing its buttons, and holding it in place during the call can distract the driver from steering and watching the road. They claim that hands-free phones that feature headsets and voice-controlled dialing eliminate any dangers associated with cell phone use. That argument is contradicted by recent research showing that driving performance is impaired while talking on *any* cell phone, even if it is a hands-free model (Strayer & Johnston, 2001). The research also suggests that the dangers of driving while using a phone do not stem simply from listening to someone speak, or even from talking. The driving performance of research participants was not impaired by listening to books on tape or by repeating words that they heard. Performance *did* decline, though, when participants were asked to do more elaborate processing of auditory information, such as rephrasing what they heard. (You may have experienced similar effects if you have ever missed a turn or had a near-accident while deeply engaged in conversation with a passenger.) These results suggest that using a cell phone while driving is dangerous not only because it can take your eyes off the road and a hand off the wheel but also because the phone conversation competes for the cognitive/attentional resources you need to drive safely. Perception researchers suggest that this competition and the dangers associated with it are unlikely to be reduced by hands-free car phones (Just et al., 2001).

ClassPrep: Linkages to Perception

LINKAGES

As noted in the chapter on introducing psychology, all of psychology's subfields are related to one another. Our discussion of how perceptual processes develop in infants illustrates just one way in which the topic of this chapter, perception, is linked to the subfield of developmental psychology (which is the topic of the chapter on human development). The Linkages diagram shows ties to two other subfields as well, and there are many more ties throughout the book. Looking for linkages among subfields will help you see how they all fit together and help you better appreciate the big picture that is psychology.

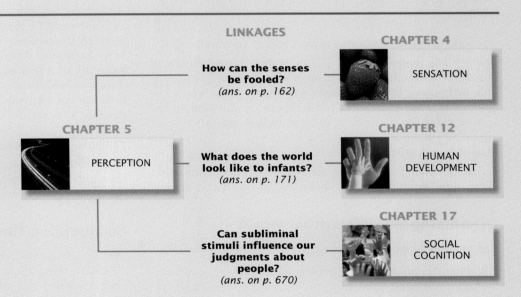

LINKAGES

CHAPTER 5 — PERCEPTION

How can the senses be fooled? *(ans. on p. 162)* — CHAPTER 4 — SENSATION

What does the world look like to infants? *(ans. on p. 171)* — CHAPTER 12 — HUMAN DEVELOPMENT

Can subliminal stimuli influence our judgments about people? *(ans. on p. 670)* — CHAPTER 17 — SOCIAL COGNITION

SUMMARY

Perception is the process through which people actively use knowledge and understanding of the world to interpret sensations as meaningful experiences.

The Perception Paradox

Because perception often seems so rapid and effortless, it appears to be a rather simple operation; however, this is not the case. An enormous amount of processing is required to transform energy received by receptors into perceptual experience.

The complexity of perception is revealed by various perceptual errors (e.g., illusions).

Three Approaches to Perception

The *computational approach* to perception emphasizes the computations performed by the nervous system. The *constructivist approach* suggests that the perceptual system constructs the experience of reality, making inferences and applying knowledge in order to interpret sensations. The *ecological approach* holds that the environment itself provides the cues that people use to form perceptions.

Psychophysics

Psychophysics is the study of the relationship between stimulus energy and the psychological experience of that energy.

Absolute Thresholds: Is Something Out There?

Psychophysics has traditionally been concerned with matters such as determining absolute thresholds for the detection of stimuli. Research shows that this threshold is not, in fact, absolute. Thus, the *absolute threshold* has been redefined as the minimum amount of stimulus energy that can be detected 50 percent of the time. *Supraliminal stimuli* fall above this threshold; *subliminal stimuli* fall below it.

Signal-Detection Theory

Signal-detection theory describes how people respond to faint or ambiguous stimuli. Detection of a signal is affected by external and internal noise, *sensitivity,* and the *response criterion.* Signal-detection theory has been applied to understanding decision making and performance in areas such as the detection of tornadoes on radar.

Judging Differences: Has Anything Changed?

Weber's law states that the minimum detectable amount of change in a stimulus—the *difference threshold,* or *just-noticeable difference (JND)*—increases in proportion to the initial amount of the stimulus. The less the initial stimulation, the smaller the change must be in order to be detected.

Magnitude Estimation: How Intense Is That?

Fechner's law and Stevens's power law describe the relationship between the magnitude of a stimulus and its perceived intensity.

Organizing the Perceptual World

Basic Processes in Perceptual Organization

Perceptual organization is the process whereby order is imposed on the information received by your senses. The perceptual system automatically distinguishes figure from ground, and it groups stimuli into patterns. Gestalt psychologists and others identified laws or principles that guide such grouping: proximity, similarity, continuity, closure, common fate, synchrony, common region, and connectedness. These laws appear to ensure that perceptual organization creates interpretations of incoming information that are simple and most likely to be correct. The process of mentally representing and interpreting sounds is called *auditory scene analysis.*

Perception of Location and Distance

Visual localization requires information about the position of the body and eyes, as well as information about where a stimulus falls on the retinas. Auditory localization depends on detecting differences in the information that reaches the two ears, including differences in timing and intensity. Perception of distance, or *depth perception,* depends partly on stimulus cues and partly on the physical structure of the visual system. Some of the stimulus cues for depth perception are *interposition, relative size, height in the visual field, texture gradient, linear perspective,* and *motion parallax.* Cues based on the structure of the visual system include *accommodation* (the change in the shape of the lenses as objects are brought into focus), *convergence* (the fact that the eyes must move to focus on the same object), and *binocular disparity* (the fact that the eyes are set slightly apart).

Perception of Motion

The perception of motion results, in part, from the movement of stimuli across the retina. Expanding or *looming* stimulation is perceived as an approaching object. Movement of the retinal image is interpreted along with information about movement of the head, eyes, and other parts of the body so that one's own movement can be discriminated from the movement of external objects. *Stroboscopic motion* is an illusion that accounts for our ability to see smooth motion in films and videos.

Perceptual Constancy

Because of *perceptual constancy,* the brightness, size, and shape of objects can be seen as constant even though the sensations received from those objects may change. Size constancy and shape constancy depend on the relationship between the retinal image of an object and the knowledge-based perception of its distance. Brightness constancy depends on the perceived relationship between the brightness of an object and its background.

Culture, Experience, and Perception

To the extent that visual environments of people in different cultures differ, their perceptual experiences—as evidenced by their responses to perceptual illusions—may differ as well.

Recognizing the Perceptual World

Both *bottom-up processing* and *top-down processing* may contribute to recognition of the world. The ability to recognize objects is based on finding a match between the pattern of sensations organized by the perceptual system and a pattern that is stored in memory.

Bottom-Up Processing

Bottom-up processing seems to be accomplished by the analysis of stimulus features or combinations of features, such as form, color, and motion.

Top-Down Processing

Top-down processing is influenced by expectancy and motivation. *Schemas* based on past experience can create a perceptual set, the readiness or predisposition to perceive stimuli in certain ways. Expectancies can also be created by the context in which a stimulus appears.

Network Processing

Research on pattern recognition has focused attention on network models, or *parallel distributed processing (PDP) models,* of perception. These emphasize the simultaneous activation and interaction of feature-analysis systems and the role of experience.

Attention

Attention is the process of focusing psychological resources to enhance perception, performance, and mental experience. We can shift attention overtly—by moving the eyes, for example—or covertly, without any movement of sensory systems.

Directing Attention

Attention is selective; it is like a spotlight that illuminates different parts of the external environment or various mental processes. Control over attention can be voluntary and knowledge based or involuntary and driven by environmental stimuli.

Ignoring Information

Sometimes attention can be so focused that it results in inattentional blindness, a failure to detect or identify normally noticeable stimuli.

Divided Attention

Although there are limits to how well people can divide attention, they can sometimes attend to two tasks at once. For example, tasks that have become automatic can often be performed along with more demanding tasks, and tasks that require very different types of processing, such as gardening and talking, can be performed together because each task depends on a different supply of mental resources.

Attention and Automatic Processing

Some information can be processed automatically, in parallel, whereas other situations demand focused attention and a serial search.

Attention and the Brain

Although the brain plays a critical role in attention, no single brain region has been identified as the main attention center.

Applications of Research on Perception

Research on human perception has numerous practical applications.

Aviation Psychology

Accurate size and distance judgments, top-down processing, and attention are all important to safety in aviation.

Human-Computer Interaction

Perceptual principles relating to recognition, depth cues, and attention are being applied by psychologists who work with designers of computers and computer programs.

Traffic Safety

Research on divided attention is being applied to help understand the potential dangers of driving while using various kinds of cell phones.

6

Learning

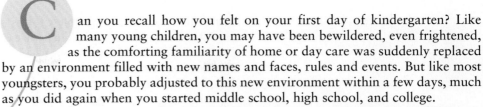

Can you recall how you felt on your first day of kindergarten? Like many young children, you may have been bewildered, even frightened, as the comforting familiarity of home or day care was suddenly replaced by an environment filled with new names and faces, rules and events. But like most youngsters, you probably adjusted to this new environment within a few days, much as you did again when you started middle school, high school, and college.

Your adjustment, or *adaptation,* to these new environments occurred in many ways. Ringing bells, lunch lines, midterm grades, and other once-strange new school events not only became part of your expectations about the world but also began to serve as signals. You soon realized that if a note was delivered to your teacher during class, someone would be called to the main office. If a substitute teacher appeared, it meant an easy lesson, or a chance to act up. And if your teacher arrived with a box of papers, you'd know the tests had been graded. Adapting to school also meant developing new knowledge about what behaviors were appropriate and inappropriate in the new situations you encountered. Although your parents might have encouraged you to talk whenever you wanted to at home, perhaps you found that at school, you had to raise your hand first. And the messy finger painting that got you in trouble at home might have earned you praise in art class. You found, too, that there were things you could do—such as paying attention in class and getting to school on time—to reap rewards and avoid punishment. Finally, of course, you adapted to school by absorbing facts about the world and developing skills ranging from kickball and reading to writing and debating.

The entire process of development, from birth to death, involves adapting to increasingly complex, ever-changing environments, using continuously updated knowledge gained through experience. Although perhaps most highly developed in humans, the ability to adapt to changing environments appears to varying degrees in members of all species. According to the evolutionary approach to psychology, it is individual variability in the capacity to adapt that shapes the evolution of appearance and behavior in animals and humans. As Charles Darwin noted, individuals who don't adapt may not survive to reproduce.

Many forms of animal and human adaptation follow the principles of learning. **Learning** is the process through which experience modifies pre-existing behavior and understanding. The pre-existing behavior and understanding may have been present at birth, acquired through maturation, or learned earlier. Learning plays a central role in the development of most aspects of human behavior, from the motor skills we need to walk or tie a shoe to the language skills we use to communicate to the object categories—such as "food," "vehicle," or "animal"—that help us organize our perceptions and think logically about the world. Sayings such as "Once burned, twice shy" and "Fool me once, shame on you; fool me twice, shame on me" reflect this vital learning process. If you want to know who you are and how you became the person you are today, examining what and how you have learned is a good place to start.

People learn primarily by experiencing events, observing relationships between those events, and noting the regularity in the world around them. When two events repeatedly take place together, people can predict the occurrence of one from knowledge of the other. They learn that a clear blue sky means dry weather, that too little sleep makes them irritable, that they can reach someone via e-mail by typing a certain address, and that screaming orders motivates some people and angers others. Some learning takes place consciously, as when we study for an exam, but as mentioned later, we can also learn things without being aware we are doing so (Watanabe, Náñez, & Sasaki, 2001).

Psychological research on learning has been guided by three main questions: (1) Which events and relationships do people learn about? (2) What circumstances determine whether and how people learn? and (3) Is learning a slow process requiring lots of practice, or does it involve sudden flashes of insight? In this chapter we provide some of the answers to these questions.

learning The modification through experience of pre-existing behavior and understanding.

We first consider the simplest forms of learning—learning about sights, sounds, and other individual stimuli. Then we examine the two major kinds of learning that involve *associations* between events—classical conditioning and operant conditioning. Next we consider some higher forms of learning and cognition, and we conclude by discussing how research on learning might help people learn better. As you read, notice that learning principles operate in education, the workplace, medical treatment, psychotherapy, and many other aspects of people's lives.

Learning About Stimuli

IRM Activity 6.3: Habituation

OBJ 6.2: Define habituation and explain why it is an example of non-associative learning.

Test Items 6.3–6.4

ClassPrep PPT 4: Non-Associative Learning

In a changing world, people are constantly bombarded by stimuli. If we tried to pay attention to every sight and sound, our information-processing systems would be overloaded, and we would be unable to concentrate on anything. People appear to be genetically tuned to attend to certain kinds of events, such as loud sounds, special tastes, or pain. *Novel* stimuli—stimuli we have not experienced before—also tend to attract our attention. By contrast, our response to *unchanging* stimuli decreases over time. This aspect of adaptation is a simple form of learning called **habituation,** which can occur in relation to sights, sounds, smells, tastes, or touches, including ones that originally caused excitement, fear, or even a startle reaction. Through habituation, you eventually fail to notice that you are wearing glasses or a watch. And after having been in a room for a while, you no longer smell that musty or flowery odor or hear that loudly ticking clock. In fact, you may become aware of the clock again only when it stops, because now, something in your environment has changed. Habituation occurs in all animals, from simple sea snails to humans (Pinel, 1993).

Habituation provides organisms with a useful way to adapt to their environments, but notice that this kind of learning results from the impact of one particular stimulus, not because a person or animal learned to associate one stimulus with another (Barker, 1997). For this reason, habituation is an example of *nonassociative learning*. In another form of nonassociative learning called *sensitization,* people and animals show exaggerated responses to unexpected, potentially threatening sights or sounds, especially if they are emotionally aroused at the time. So while breathlessly exploring a dark, spooky house, you might scream, run, or violently throw something in response to the unexpected creaking of a door.

According to Richard Solomon's *opponent-process theory,* habituation may help explain some of the dangers associated with certain drugs. Consider, for example, what happens as someone continues to use a drug such as heroin. The pleasurable reaction (the high) obtained from a particular dose of the drug begins to decrease with repeated doses. This habituation occurs, Solomon says, because the initial, pleasurable reaction to the drug is eventually followed by an unpleasant, opposing reaction that counteracts the drug's primary effects. The opposing reaction becomes quicker and stronger the longer the drug is taken. As drug users become habituated, they must take progressively larger doses to get the same high. According to Solomon, these opponent processes form the basis of drug tolerance and addiction.

Solomon's analysis may also explain some accidental drug overdoses. Suppose the unpleasant reaction that counteracts a drug's initial effects becomes associated with a particular room, person, or other stimulus that is always present when the drug is taken. This stimulus may eventually come to trigger the counteracting process, allowing tolerance of larger doses. Now suppose that a person takes this larger drug dose in an environment where this stimulus is not present. The strength of the drug's primary effect will remain the same, but without the familiar environmental stimulus, the counteracting process may be weaker. The net result may be a stronger-than-usual drug reaction, possibly leading to an overdose (Siegel et al., 1982; Turkkan, 1989).

Learning to Live with It　People who move to a big city may be distracted at first by the din of traffic, low-flying aircraft, and other urban sounds, but after a while the process of habituation makes all this noise far less noticeable.

Sensitization The documentary film makers portrayed in *The Blair Witch Project* demonstrated the nonassociative learning process called *sensitization* as their behavioral reactions to sudden stimuli became more and more extreme.

Notice that this explanation of drug overdoses is based not just on simple habituation and sensitization but also on a *learned association* between certain environmental stimuli and certain responses. Indeed, the nonassociative processes of habituation and sensitization cannot, by themselves, explain many of the behaviors and mental processes that are the focus of psychology. To better understand how learning affects our thoughts and behaviors, we need to consider forms of learning that involve the building of associations between various stimuli, as well as between stimuli and responses. One major type of associative learning is called *classical conditioning*.

Classical Conditioning: Learning Signals and Associations

At the opening bars of the national anthem, a young ballplayer's heart may start pounding; those sounds signal that the game is about to begin. A flashing light on a control panel may make an airplane pilot's adrenaline flow, because it means that something may be wrong. People are not born with these reactions; they learn them by observing relationships or *associations* between events in the world. The experimental study of this kind of learning was begun, almost by accident, by Ivan Petrovich Pavlov.

Pavlov's Discovery

Pavlov is one of the best-known figures in psychology, but he was not a psychologist. A Russian physiologist, Pavlov won a Nobel Prize in 1904 for his research on the digestive processes of dogs. In the course of this work, Pavlov noticed a strange phenomenon: The first stage of the digestive process—salivation—sometimes occurred when no food was present. His dogs salivated, for example, when they saw the assistant who normally brought their food, even if the assistant was empty-handed.

Pavlov devised a simple experiment to determine why salivation occurred in the absence of an obvious physical cause. First he performed a simple operation to

habituation The process of adapting to stimuli that do not change.

figure 6.1

Apparatus for Measuring Conditioned Responses

In this more elaborate version of Pavlov's original apparatus, the amount of saliva flowing from a dog's cheek is measured and then recorded on a slowly revolving drum of paper.

ClassPrep PPT 6: *Figure 6.1:* Apparatus for Measuring Conditioned Responses

Pen recording on cylinder

IRM Activity 6.6: Classical Conditioning: Assorted Demonstrations

OBJ 6.3: Define classical conditioning, unconditioned stimulus, unconditioned response, conditioned stimulus, and conditioned response. Describe how classical conditioning works by using the stimuli and responses in an example.

Test Items 6.5–6.13

Essay Q 6.1

Personal Learning Activity 6.1

---

classical conditioning A procedure in which a neutral stimulus is paired with a stimulus that elicits a reflex or other response until the neutral stimulus alone comes to elicit a similar response.

unconditioned stimulus (UCS) A stimulus that elicits a response without conditioning.

unconditioned response (UCR) The automatic or unlearned reaction to a stimulus.

conditioned stimulus (CS) The originally neutral stimulus that, through pairing with the unconditioned stimulus, comes to elicit a conditioned response.

conditioned response (CR) The response that the conditioned stimulus elicits.

---

divert a dog's saliva into a container so that the amount of salivation could be measured precisely. He then placed the dog in an apparatus similar to the one shown in Figure 6.1. The experiment had three phases.

In the first phase of the experiment, Pavlov and his associates (Anrep, 1920) confirmed that when meat powder was placed on the dog's tongue, the dog salivated, but that it did not salivate in response to a neutral stimulus—a musical tone, for example. Thus, the researchers established the existence of the two basic components for Pavlov's experiment: a natural reflex (the dog's salivation when meat powder was placed on its tongue) and a neutral stimulus (the sound of the tone). A *reflex* is the swift, automatic response to a stimulus, such as shivering in the cold or jumping when you are jabbed with a needle. A *neutral stimulus* is a stimulus that initially does not trigger the reflex being studied, although it may cause other responses. For example, when the tone is first sounded, the dog will prick up its ears, turn toward the sound, and sniff around, but it will not salivate.

It was the second and third phases of the experiment that showed how one type of associative learning can occur. In the second phase, the tone sounded, and then a few seconds later meat powder was placed in the dog's mouth. The dog salivated. This *pairing*—the tone followed immediately by meat powder—was repeated several times. The tone predicted that the meat powder was coming, but the question remained: Would the animal learn this relationship and associate the tone with the meat powder? Yes. In the third phase of the experiment, the tone was sounded, and even though no meat powder was presented, the dog again salivated. In other words, the tone by itself now elicited salivation.

Pavlov's experiment was the first laboratory demonstration of a basic form of associative learning. Today, it is called **classical conditioning**—a procedure in which a neutral stimulus is repeatedly paired with a stimulus that already triggers a reflexive response until the neutral stimulus alone comes to evoke a similar response. Figure 6.2 shows the basic elements of classical conditioning. The stimulus that elicits a response without conditioning, like the meat powder in Pavlov's experiment, is called the **unconditioned stimulus** (UCS). The automatic, unlearned reaction to this stimulus is called the **unconditioned response** (UCR). The new stimulus being paired with the unconditioned stimulus is called the **conditioned stimulus** (CS), and the response it comes to elicit is the **conditioned response** (CR).

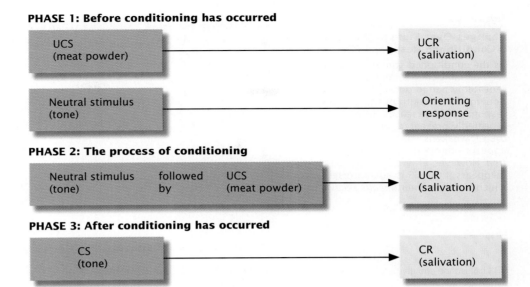

PHASE 1: Before conditioning has occurred

UCS (meat powder) → UCR (salivation)

Neutral stimulus (tone) → Orienting response

PHASE 2: The process of conditioning

Neutral stimulus (tone) followed by UCS (meat powder) → UCR (salivation)

PHASE 3: After conditioning has occurred

CS (tone) → CR (salivation)

figure 6.2
Classical Conditioning

Before classical conditioning has occurred, meat powder on a dog's tongue produces salivation, but the sound of a tone—a neutral stimulus—does not. During the process of conditioning, the tone is repeatedly paired with the meat powder. After classical conditioning has taken place, the sound of the tone alone acts as a conditioned stimulus, producing salivation.

Conditioned Responses over Time: Extinction and Spontaneous Recovery

Continued pairings of a conditioned stimulus with an unconditioned stimulus strengthen conditioned responses. The curve on the left side of Figure 6.3 shows an example: Repeated associations of a tone (CS) with meat powder (UCS) caused Pavlov's dogs to increase their salivation (CR) to the tone alone.

What if the meat powder is no longer given? In general, unless the unconditioned stimulus continues to be paired at least occasionally with the conditioned stimulus, the conditioned response will gradually disappear through a process known as **extinction** (see the center section of Figure 6.3). If the conditioned stimulus and the unconditioned stimulus are again paired after the conditioned response has been extinguished, the conditioned response returns to its original strength very quickly, often after only one or two trials. This quick relearning of a conditioned response after extinction is called **reconditioning**. Because reconditioning takes much less time than the original conditioning, extinction must not have completely erased the learned association.

Additional evidence for this conclusion is illustrated on the right side of Figure 6.3: An extinguished conditioned response will temporarily reappear if, after some time delay, the conditioned stimulus is presented again—even without the unconditioned stimulus. This reappearance of the conditioned response after extinction (and without further CS-UCS pairings) is called **spontaneous recovery**. In general, the longer the time between extinction and the re-presentation of the conditioned stimulus, the stronger the recovered conditioned response. (However, unless the UCS is again paired with the CS, extinction rapidly occurs again.) Spontaneous recovery is at work when a person hears a song or smells a scent associated with a long-lost lover and experiences a ripple of emotion—a conditioned response. Through its association with that person, the song or fragrance, which originally had no particular significance, became a conditioned stimulus that—even years later—can provoke conditioned emotional reactions.

extinction The gradual disappearance of a conditioned response due to elimination of the association between conditioned and unconditioned stimuli.

reconditioning The quick relearning of a conditioned response following extinction.

spontaneous recovery The reappearance of the conditioned response after extinction and without further pairings of the conditioned and unconditioned stimuli.

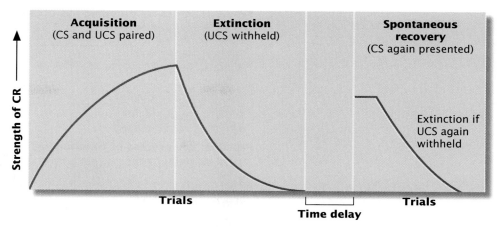

figure 6.3

Changes Over Time in the Strength of a Conditioned Response (CR)

As the conditioned stimulus (CS) and the unconditioned stimulus (UCS) are repeatedly paired during initial conditioning, the strength of the conditioned response (CR) increases. If the CS is repeatedly presented without the UCS, the CR weakens—and eventually disappears—through a process called *extinction*. However, after a brief period the CR reappears if the CS is again presented, which is called *spontaneous recovery.*

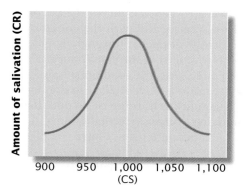

Sound of buzzer (hertz)

figure 6.4

Stimulus Generalization

The strength of a conditioned response (CR) is greatest when the original conditioned stimulus (CS) occurs, but the CR also appears following stimuli that closely resemble the CS. Here, the CS is the sound of a buzzer at 1,000 hertz, and the CR is salivation. Notice that the CR generalizes well to stimuli at 990 or 1,010 hertz, but it gets weaker and weaker following stimuli that are less and less similar to the CS.

Stimulus Generalization and Discrimination

After a conditioned response is learned, stimuli that are similar but not identical to the conditioned stimulus also elicit the response—but to a lesser degree. This phenomenon is called **stimulus generalization.** Usually the greater the similarity between a new stimulus and the conditioned stimulus, the stronger the conditioned response will be. Figure 6.4 shows an example.

Stimulus generalization has obvious adaptive advantages. For example, it is important for survival that a person who becomes sick after drinking sour-smelling milk later avoids dairy products that give off an odor resembling the smell associated with the illness. Generalization, however, would be a problem if it had no limits. Like most people, you would probably be frightened if you found a lion in your home, but imagine the disruption if your fear response generalized so widely that you were panicked by a picture of a lion, or even by reading the word *lion.*

Stimulus generalization does not run wild because it is balanced by a complementary process called **stimulus discrimination.** Through stimulus discrimination, people and animals learn to differentiate among similar stimuli. Many parents find that the sound of their own baby whimpering may become a conditioned stimulus that triggers a conditioned response that wakes them up. That conditioned response might not occur if a visiting friend's baby whimpers.

The Signaling of Significant Events

Is classical conditioning entirely automatic? Pavlov's research suggested that it is—that classical conditioning allows the substitution of one stimulus (the CS) for another (the UCS) in producing an automatic, reflexive response. This kind of learning helps animals and people prepare for events involving food, pain, or other unconditioned stimuli. For years the study of classical conditioning focused mainly on its role in the control of such automatic, involuntary behavior. However, psychologists now recognize the wider implications of classical conditioning (Hollis, 1997). Some argue that organisms acquire conditioned responses when one event reliably predicts, or *signals,* the appearance of another. These psychologists believe that instead of giving rise to simple robot-like reflexes, classical conditioning leads to responses based on the information provided by conditioned stimuli. As a result, animals and people develop *mental representations* of the relationships between important events in their environment and expectancies about when such events will occur (Rescorla, 1988). These representations and expectancies aid adaptation and survival (Williams, Butler, & Overmier, 1990).

What determines whether and how a conditioned response is learned? Important factors include the timing, predictability, and strength of signals; the amount of attention they receive; and how easily the signals can be associated with other stimuli.

ClassPrep PPT 11: Factors Influencing the Learning of Conditioned Responses

OBJ 6.6: Describe the role that timing, predictability, and strength of signals play in the speed and strength of conditioned response development. Indicate which type of conditioning produces the strongest type of conditioned response.

Test Items 6.27–6.33

Timing   If your instructor always dismisses class at 9:59 and a bell rings at 10:00, the bell cannot act as a signal to prepare you for the dismissal. For the same reason, classical conditioning works best when the conditioned stimulus precedes the unconditioned stimulus. In this arrangement, known as *forward conditioning,* the conditioned stimulus signals that the unconditioned stimulus is coming.

There is also an arrangement, called *backward conditioning,* in which the conditioned stimulus *follows* the unconditioned stimulus. When this happens, however, a conditioned response develops very slowly, if at all. (Part of the explanation is that the CS in backward conditioning comes too late to signal the approach of the UCS. In fact, the CS signals the *absence* of the UCS and eventually triggers a response that is opposite to the conditioned response, thus inhibiting its development.)

When the conditioned stimulus and unconditioned stimulus occur at the same time (an arrangement known as *simultaneous conditioning*), conditioning is much less likely to take place than it is in either forward or backward conditioning, and special techniques are required to detect its occurrence.

Research shows that forward conditioning usually works best when there is an interval between the conditioned stimulus and the unconditioned stimulus. This interval can range from a fraction of a second to a few seconds to more than a minute, depending on the particular CS, UCS, and UCR involved (Longo, Klempay, & Bitterman, 1964; Ross & Ross, 1971). Classical conditioning will always be weaker if the interval between the CS and the UCS is longer than what is ideal for the stimuli and responses in a given situation. This makes adaptive sense. Normally, the appearance of food, predators, or other significant events is most reliably predicted by smells, growls, or other stimuli that occur at varying intervals before those events (Einhorn & Hogarth, 1982). So it is logical that organisms are "wired" to form associations most easily between things that occur in a relatively tight time sequence.

Predictability   Is it enough that the conditioned stimulus precedes the unconditioned stimulus—that the two events are close together in time—in order for classical conditioning to occur? Think about it. Suppose two dogs, Moxie and Fang, have very different personalities. When Moxie growls, she sometimes bites, but sometimes she doesn't. Other times, she bites without growling first. Fang, however, growls *only* before biting. Your conditioned fear response to Moxie's growl will probably occur slowly, if at all, because her growl is a stimulus that does not reliably signal the danger of a bite. But you are likely to quickly develop a classically conditioned fear response to Fang's growl, because classical conditioning proceeds most rapidly when the conditioned stimulus *always* signals the unconditioned stimulus, and *only* the unconditioned stimulus. So even if both dogs provide the same number of pairings of the conditioned stimulus (growl) and the unconditioned stimulus (bite), it is only in Fang's case that the conditioned stimulus *reliably* predicts the unconditioned stimulus (Rescorla, 1968).

Signal Strength   A conditioned response will be greater if the unconditioned stimulus is strong than if it is weak. So a predictive signal associated with a strong UCS, such as an intense shock, will come to evoke more fear than one associated with a weak shock. As with timing and predictability, the effect of signal strength on classical conditioning makes adaptive sense: It is more important to be prepared for major events than for events that have little impact.

How quickly a conditioned response is learned also depends on the strength of the conditioned stimulus. As described in the chapter on perception, louder tones, brighter lights, or other, more intense stimuli events tend to get attention, so they are most rapidly associated with an unconditioned stimulus—as long as they remain reliable predictive signals.

Attention   In the laboratory, a single neutral stimulus is presented, followed shortly by an unconditioned stimulus. In the natural environment, however, several

stimulus generalization A phenomenon in which a conditioned response is elicited by stimuli that are similar but not identical to the conditioned stimulus.

stimulus discrimination A process through which individuals learn to differentiate among similar stimuli and respond appropriately to each one.

stimuli might be present just before an unconditioned stimulus occurs. Suppose you are at the beach, sipping lemonade, reading a magazine, listening to a Sting CD, and inhaling the scent of sunscreen, when you are suddenly bitten by a wasp. Where your attention was focused at that moment can influence which potential conditioned stimulus—lemonade, magazine, Sting, or sunscreen—becomes associated with that painful unconditioned stimulus. The stimulus you were attending to most closely—and thus most fully perceiving—is the one likely to be more strongly associated with pain than any of the others (Hall, 1991).

Second-Order Conditioning

When a child suffers the pain of an injection (an unconditioned stimulus) at a doctor's office, noticeable stimuli—such as the doctor's white coat—that precede and predict the unconditioned stimulus can become conditioned stimuli for fear. Once the white coat can trigger a conditioned fear response, it may take on some properties of an unconditioned stimulus. So at future visits, the once-neutral sight of the doctor's waiting room can become a conditioned stimulus for fear because it signals the appearance of the doctor's white coat, which in turn signals pain. When a conditioned stimulus acts like an unconditioned stimulus, creating conditioned stimuli out of events associated with it, the phenomenon is called **second-order conditioning.**

Conditioned fear, along with the second-order conditioning that can be based on it, illustrates one of the most important adaptive characteristics of classical conditioning: the ability to prepare a person or an animal for threatening events—unconditioned stimuli—that are reliably signaled by a conditioned stimulus. Unfortunately, second-order conditioning can also cause problems. For example, medical patients known as *white coat hypertensives* (Myers et al., 1996) appear to have high blood pressure because the presence of a doctor or nurse has become a conditioned stimulus for fear. This conditioned fear response includes a temporary rise in blood pressure.

Biopreparedness

After Pavlov's initial demonstration of classical conditioning, many psychologists believed that associations formed through classical conditioning were like Velcro. Just as Velcro pieces of any size or shape can be attached

The Power of Second-Order Conditioning Cancer patients may feel queasy when they enter a chemotherapy room because they have associated the room with nausea-producing treatment. Through second-order conditioning, almost anything associated with that *room* can also become a conditioned stimulus for nausea. One cancer patient, flying out of town on a business trip, became nauseated just by seeing her hospital from the air.

© Herb Lingl/aerialarchives.com

Taste Aversions Humans can develop classically conditioned taste aversions, even to preferred foods. Ilene Bernstein (1978) gave one group of cancer patients Mapletoff ice cream an hour before they received nausea-provoking chemotherapy. A second group ate the same kind of ice cream on a day they did not receive chemotherapy. A third group got no ice cream. Five months later, the patients were asked to taste several ice cream flavors. Those who had never tasted Mapletoff and those who had not eaten it in association with chemotherapy chose it as their favorite. Those who had eaten Mapletoff before receiving chemotherapy found it very distasteful.

second-order conditioning A phenomenon in which a conditioned stimulus acts like an unconditioned stimulus, creating conditioned stimuli out of events associated with it.

with equal ease, it was believed that any conditioned stimulus—such as the taste of food, the pain of an insect bite, or the sight of a dog—has an equal potential for becoming associated with any unconditioned stimulus, as long as the two stimuli occur in the right time sequence. This view, called *equipotentiality*, was later challenged by experiments showing that certain signals or events are especially suited to form associations with other events (Logue, 1985). This apparent natural tendency for certain events to become linked suggests that humans and animals are "biologically prepared" or "genetically tuned" to develop certain conditioned associations.

The most dramatic example of this *biopreparedness* is seen in conditioned taste aversion. Consider the results of a study in which rats were either shocked or made nauseous in the combined presence of a bright light, a loud buzzer, and saccharin-flavored water. Only certain conditioned associations were formed. Specifically, the animals that had been shocked developed a conditioned fear response to the light and the buzzer, but not to the flavored water. Those animals that had been made nauseous developed a conditioned aversion to the flavored water but showed no particular response to the light or buzzer (Garcia & Koelling, 1966). Notice that these associations are useful and adaptive: Nausea is more likely to be produced by something that is eaten or drunk than by a noise or some other external stimulus. Accordingly, nausea is more likely to become a conditioned response to an internal stimulus, such as a saccharine flavor, than to an external stimulus, such as a light or buzzer. In contrast, sudden pain is more likely to have been caused by an external stimulus, so it makes evolutionary sense that organisms should be "tuned" to associate pain with external stimuli like sights or sounds.

Notice, too, that strong conditioned taste aversion can develop despite the fact that poisons or other nausea-producing substances do not usually produce their effects until minutes or hours after being ingested. These intervals are far longer than what is optimal for producing conditioning in most other situations, but people who experience food poisoning may never again eat the type of food that made them ill. This makes sense in evolutionary terms, because organisms that are biologically prepared to link taste signals with illness, even if it occurs after a considerable delay, are more likely to survive than organisms not so prepared.

Evidence from several sources suggests other ways in which animals and people are innately prepared to learn associations between certain stimuli and certain responses. For example, people are much more likely to develop a conditioned fear of harmless dogs, snakes, and rats than of equally harmless doorknobs or stereos (Kleinknecht, 1991). And experiments with animals suggest that they are prone to learn the type of associations that are most common in, or most relevant to, their environments (Staddon & Ettinger, 1989). For example, birds of prey, so strongly dependent upon their vision in searching for food, may develop taste aversions on the basis of visual stimuli. Coyotes and rats, more dependent on their sense of smell, tend to develop aversions related to odor.

Some Applications of Classical Conditioning

"In Review: Basic Phenomena in Classical Conditioning" summarizes the principles of classical conditioning. These principles have proven useful in overcoming fears, controlling predators, and diagnosing Alzheimer's disease, to name just a few examples.

Phobias Classical conditioning can play a role in the development not only of mild fears (such as a child's fear of doctors in white coats) but also of phobias (Bouton, Mineka, & Barlow, 2001). *Phobias* are extreme fears of objects or situations that either are not objectively dangerous—public speaking, for example—or are less dangerous than the phobic person's reaction suggests. In some instances, phobias can seriously disrupt a person's life. A child who is frightened by a large dog may learn a dog phobia that is so intense and generalized that it creates avoidance

in review Basic Phenomena in Classical Conditioning

Process	Description	Example
Acquisition	A neutral stimulus and an unconditioned stimulus (UCS) are paired. The neutral stimulus becomes a conditioned stimulus (CS), eliciting a conditioned response (CR).	A child learns to fear (conditioned response) the doctor's office (conditioned stimulus) by associating it with the reflexive emotional reaction (unconditioned response) to a painful injection (unconditioned stimulus).
Stimulus generalization	A conditioned response is elicited not only by the conditioned stimulus but also by stimuli similar to the conditioned stimulus.	A child fears most doctors' offices and places that smell like them.
Stimulus discrimination	Generalization is limited so that some stimuli similar to the conditioned stimulus do not elicit the conditioned response.	A child learns that his mother's doctor's office is not associated with the unconditioned stimulus.
Extinction	The conditioned stimulus is presented alone, without the unconditioned stimulus. Eventually the conditioned stimulus no longer elicits the conditioned response.	A child visits the doctor's office several times for a checkup but does not receive an injection. Fear may eventually cease.

OBJ 6.9: Describe the relationship between classical conditioning and phobias, predator control, and diagnosis of Alzheimer's disease.

Test Items 6.43–6.44

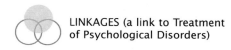

LINKAGES (a link to Treatment of Psychological Disorders)

of all dogs. Dangerous situations, too, can produce classical conditioning of very long lasting fears. Decades after their war experiences, some military veterans still respond to simulated battle sounds with large changes in heart rate, blood pressure, and other signs of emotional arousal (Edwards & Acker, 1972). These symptoms, combined with others such as distressing dreams about the troubling events, characterize posttraumatic stress disorder (PTSD, described in the chapter on health, stress, and coping).

Classical conditioning procedures can be employed to treat phobias, and even PTSD. Joseph Wolpe (1958; Wolpe & Plaud, 1997) pioneered the development of this methodology. Using techniques first developed with laboratory animals, Wolpe showed that irrational fears could be relieved through *systematic desensitization,* which involves two conditioning components: (1) extinction of classically conditioned fear responses through harmless exposure to the feared stimulus and (2) classical conditioning of a new response, such as relaxation, to the feared stimulus. Desensitization is discussed in more detail in the chapter on the treatment of psychological disorders.

Predator Control   The power of classically conditioned taste aversion has been put to work to help ranchers who are plagued by wolves and coyotes that kill and eat their sheep. To alleviate this problem without killing the predators, some ranchers have set out lithium-laced mutton for marauding wolves and coyotes to eat. The dizziness and nausea caused by the lithium becomes associated with the smell and taste of mutton, thus making sheep an undesirable meal for these predators and protecting the ranchers' livelihood (Garcia, Rusiniak, & Brett, 1977; Gustavson et al., 1974).

Diagnosis of Alzheimer's Disease   A puff of air directed at your eye is an unconditioned stimulus that causes the reflexive unconditioned response we call an *eye blink* (Hilgard & Marquis, 1936). If each air puff is preceded by a flash of light, the light will become a conditioned stimulus that can then cause an eye blink on its own. Recent research with animals has demonstrated that the hippocampus, a brain structure that is damaged in the early stages of Alzheimer's disease, is involved in the development of this type of conditioned response (Green &

Using Classical Conditioning to Save People and Tigers A program supported by the government of India has greatly reduced human deaths from tiger attacks, as well as the need to kill marauding tigers. The program involves placing human-shaped dummies— connected by hidden wires to a shock generator—in areas where tigers have killed people. When the animals approach, they receive a shock (unconditioned stimulus), which they learn to associate with the human form (conditioned stimulus), thus creating an avoidance of people (conditioned response).

Woodruff-Pak, 2000). That research is now being applied in the identification of people who are at high risk for this devastating brain disorder. One study found that elderly people whose eye blink conditioning was impaired were the ones most likely to develop Alzheimer's disease in the next two or three years (Downey-Lamb & Woodruff-Pak, 1999). Knowing who is at risk for Alzheimer's disease is important because it allows doctors to offer these people medication that can delay the emergence of the disease.

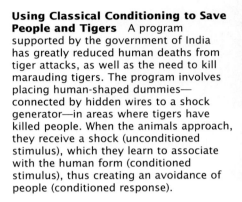

Instrumental and Operant Conditioning: Learning the Consequences of Behavior

Much of what people learn cannot be described in terms of classical conditioning. In classical conditioning, neutral and unconditioned stimuli are predictably paired, and the result is an association between the two. The association is shown by the conditioned response that occurs when the conditioned stimulus appears. Notice that both stimuli occur *before* or *along with* the conditioned response. But people also learn associations between specific actions or responses and the stimuli that *follow* them—in other words, between behavior and its consequences (Colwill, 1994). A child learns to say "Please" to get a piece of candy; a headache sufferer learns to take a pill to escape pain; a dog learns to "shake hands" to get a treat. This form of learning is called *operant conditioning*, and it constitutes the second major type of associative learning.

From the Puzzle Box to the Skinner Box

Much of the groundwork for research on the consequences of behavior was done by Edward L. Thorndike, an American psychologist. While Pavlov was exploring classical conditioning in animals, Thorndike was studying animals' intelligence and ability to solve problems. He would place an animal, usually a hungry cat, in a *puzzle box*, where it had to learn some response—say, stepping on a pedal—in order to unlock the door and get to some food (see Figure 6.5). The animal would solve the

figure 6.5

Thorndike's Puzzle Box

This drawing illustrates the kind of puzzle box used in Thorndike's research. His cats learned to open the door and reach food by stepping on the pedal, but the learning occurred gradually. Some cats actually took longer to get out of the box on one trial than on a previous trial.

ClassPrep PPT 15: *Figure 6.5:* Thorndike's Puzzle Box

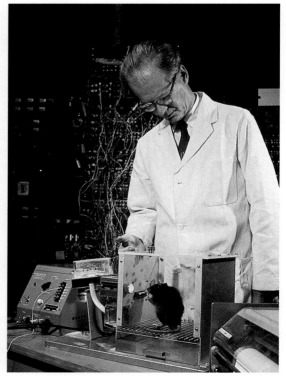

OBJ 6.10: Define the law of effect.

Test Items 6.45–6.48

ClassPrep PPT 16: Thorndike's Law of Effect

OBJ 6.11: Define instrumental, or operant, conditioning, and explain how it differs from classical conditioning.

Test Items 6.49–6.51

puzzle, but very slowly. It did not appear to understand, or suddenly gain *insight* into, the problem (Thorndike, 1898).

So what were Thorndike's cats learning? Thorndike argued that any response (such as pressing the pedal) that produces a satisfying effect (such as access to food) gradually becomes stronger, whereas any response (such as pacing or meowing) that does not produce a satisfying effect gradually becomes weaker. The cats' learning, said Thorndike, is governed by the **law of effect.** According to this law, if a response made in the presence of a particular stimulus is followed by satisfaction (such as a reward), that response is more likely to be made the next time the stimulus is encountered. Conversely, responses that produce discomfort are less likely to be performed again. Thorndike described this kind of learning as **instrumental conditioning,** because responses are strengthened when they are instrumental in producing rewards (Thorndike, 1905).

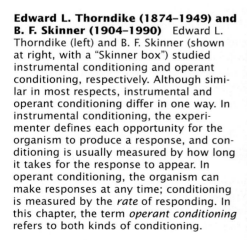

Edward L. Thorndike (1874–1949) and B. F. Skinner (1904–1990)   Edward L. Thorndike (left) and B. F. Skinner (shown at right, with a "Skinner box") studied instrumental conditioning and operant conditioning, respectively. Although similar in most respects, instrumental and operant conditioning differ in one way. In instrumental conditioning, the experimenter defines each opportunity for the organism to produce a response, and conditioning is usually measured by how long it takes for the response to appear. In operant conditioning, the organism can make responses at any time; conditioning is measured by the *rate* of responding. In this chapter, the term *operant conditioning* refers to both kinds of conditioning.

Edward Thorndike photo: Psychology Archives—The University of Akron

About forty years after Thorndike published his work, B. F. Skinner extended and formalized many of Thorndike's ideas. Skinner (1938) emphasized that during instrumental conditioning, an organism learns a response by *operating on* the environment, so he called the process of learning these responses **operant conditioning.** His primary aim was to analyze *how* behavior is changed by its consequences. To study operant conditioning, Skinner devised a chamber that became known as the *Skinner box.* The Skinner box differed from Thorndike's puzzle box in one way: The puzzle box measured learning in terms of whether an animal successfully completed a trial (i.e., got out of the box), and how long it took. The Skinner box measures learning in terms of how often an animal responds during a specified period of time (Barker, 1997).

Basic Components of Operant Conditioning

OBJ 6.12: Define the components of operant conditioning: operants and reinforcers.

Test Items 6.52–6.55

The tools Skinner devised allowed him and other researchers to precisely arrange relationships between a response and its consequences and then to analyze how those consequences affected behavior over time. They found that the basic phenomena seen in classical conditioning—such as stimulus generalization, stimulus discrimination, extinction, and spontaneous recovery—also occur in operant conditioning. However, operant conditioning involves additional concepts and processes as well. Let's consider these now.

ClassPrep PPT 17: Basic Components of Operant Conditioning

IRM Activity 6.8: Using Learning Principles to Parent

OBJ 6.13: Define positive reinforcers and negative reinforcers and give examples of each.

Test Items 6.56–6.63

Essay Q 6.2

Personal Learning Activity 6.3

Operants and Reinforcers

Skinner introduced the term *operant* or *operant response* to distinguish the responses in operant conditioning from those in classical conditioning. Recall that in classical conditioning, the conditioned response does not affect whether or when the stimulus occurs. Dogs salivated when a buzzer sounded, but the salivation had no effect on the buzzer or on whether food was presented. In contrast, an **operant** is a response that has some effect on the world; it is a response that *operates on* the environment. For example, when a child says, "Momma, I'm hungry," and is then fed, the child has made an operant response that influences when food will appear.

A **reinforcer** increases the probability that an operant behavior will occur again. There are two main types of reinforcers: positive and negative. **Positive reinforcers** strengthen a response if they are experienced after that response occurs. They are roughly equivalent to rewards. The food given to a hungry pigeon after it pecks at a switch is a positive reinforcer; its presentation increases the pigeon's switch pecking. For people, positive reinforcers can include food, smiles, money, and other desirable outcomes. Presentation of a positive reinforcer after a response is called *positive reinforcement.* **Negative reinforcers** are the *removal* of unpleasant stimuli such as pain, noise, threats, or a disapproving frown. Like positive reinforcers, negative reinforcers also strengthen responses. For example, if taking aspirin removes your headache pain, you are more likely to take aspirin the next time you have a headache. When a response is strengthened by the *removal* of an unpleasant stimulus, the process is called *negative reinforcement.* So whether reinforcement takes the form of presenting something pleasant or removing something unpleasant, it always *increases* the strength of the behavior that precedes it (see Figure 6.6).

Escape and Avoidance Conditioning

The effects of negative reinforcement can be seen in escape conditioning and avoidance conditioning. **Escape conditioning** occurs as a person or animal learns to make a response in order to stop an aversive stimulus. As shown in Figure 6.7, dogs will learn to jump over the barrier in a shuttle box to escape shock. And parents may learn to give in to a child's demands because doing so stops the child's whining. Now let's consider avoidance conditioning. Look again at Figure 6.7, and imagine that a buzzer sounds a few seconds before one side of the shuttle box is electrified. The animal will soon learn to jump over the barrier when the buzzer sounds, thus avoiding the shock. (In a

law of effect   A law stating that if a response made in the presence of a particular stimulus is followed by a reward, that response is more likely the next time the stimulus is encountered.

instrumental conditioning   A process through which responses are learned that produce some rewarding effect.

operant conditioning   A process through which an organism learns to respond to the environment in a way that produces positive consequences.

operant   A response that has some effect on the world.

reinforcer   A stimulus event that increases the probability that the response that immediately preceded it will occur again.

positive reinforcers   Stimuli that strengthen a response if they follow that response.

negative reinforcers   The removal of unpleasant stimuli, such as pain.

escape conditioning   A type of learning in which an organism learns to make a particular response in order to terminate an aversive stimulus.

figure 6.6

Positive and Negative Reinforcement

TRY THIS Behavior is strengthened through *positive reinforcement* when something pleasant or desirable follows the behavior. Behavior is strengthened through *negative reinforcement* when the behavior results in the removal of something unpleasant. To see how these operant learning principles apply in your own life, list two situations in which your behavior was affected by positive reinforcement and two in which it was affected by negative reinforcement.

ClassPrep PPT 18, OHT: *Figure 6.6:* Positive and Negative Reinforcement

IRM Activity 6.10: Negative Reinforcement Versus Punishment

OBJ 6.14: Define escape conditioning and avoidance conditioning. Give an example of each that demonstrates their similarities and differences.

Test Items 6.64–6.69

ClassPrep PPT 19: *Figure 6.7:* A Shuttle Box

IRM Discussion 2.4: On the Use of Animals in Scientific Research

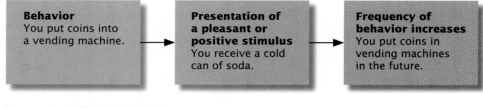

POSITIVE REINFORCEMENT

| **Behavior** You put coins into a vending machine. | → | **Presentation of a pleasant or positive stimulus** You receive a cold can of soda. | → | **Frequency of behavior increases** You put coins in vending machines in the future. |

NEGATIVE REINFORCEMENT

| **Behavior** In the middle of a boring date, you say you have a headache. | → | **Removal of an unpleasant stimulus** The date ends early. | → | **Frequency of behavior increases** You use the same tactic on future boring dates. |

similar way, some children learn that they can avoid getting in trouble for misbehavior by apologizing as soon as they see their parent's frown.) When an animal or person responds to a signal in a way that avoids an impending aversive stimulus, **avoidance conditioning** has occurred. Remember that in escape conditioning the learned response *stops* an aversive stimulus, whereas in avoidance conditioning the learned response *prevents* the aversive stimulus from occurring in the first place.

Notice that avoidance conditioning involves both classical and operant conditioning. In the shuttle box, for example, the buzzer signals the onset of an *unconditioned stimulus* (shock). Through classical conditioning, this signal becomes a *conditioned stimulus* that triggers fear, a *conditioned response*. Like the shock itself, fear is unpleasant. Once the animal learns to jump over the barrier to avoid shock, this operant response is reinforced by its consequences—the reduction of fear. In short, avoidance conditioning takes place in two steps. The first step involves classical conditioning (a signal is repeatedly paired with shock); the second step involves operant conditioning (learning to make a response that reduces fear).

Along with positive reinforcement, avoidance conditioning is one of the most important influences on everyday behavior. Most people go to work even when they would rather stay in bed, and they stop at red lights even when they are in a hurry. Each of these behaviors reflects avoidance conditioning, because each behavior allows people to avoid a negative consequence, such as lost pay or a traffic ticket.

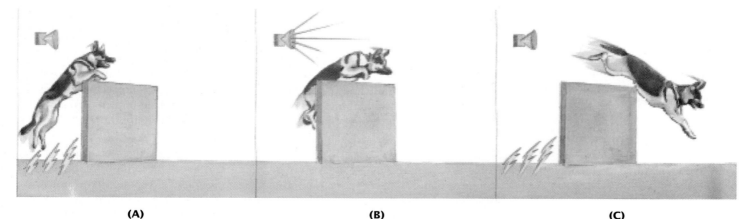

(A)   (B)   (C)

figure 6.7

A Shuttle Box

A shuttle box has two compartments, usually separated by a barrier. Its floor is an electric grid, so that shock can be delivered to either compartment. In escape conditioning (A), the animal feels a shock but can get away from it by jumping over the barrier when the shock occurs. In avoidance conditioning (B), a buzzer signals that the shock is coming, and the animal can avoid the shock if it jumps as soon as the buzzer sounds (C).

Avoidance is a difficult habit to break, partly because avoidance responses continue to be reinforced by fear reduction even if the aversive stimulus never appears (Solomon, Kamin, & Wynne, 1953). In fact, avoidance responses prevent the opportunity to learn that avoidance is no longer necessary. If you fear escalators and therefore avoid them, you will never discover that they hold no real danger. Avoidance conditioning can also prevent people from learning new, more desirable behaviors. For example, fear of doing something embarrassing may cause people with limited social skills to shy away from social situations, thus depriving themselves of the chance to become more skilled in those situations.

Discriminative Stimuli and Stimulus Control

One of the most important benefits of operant conditioning is that it enables organisms to adapt quickly to changes in their environment—an ability that has survival value in the real world. For example, even pigeons easily learn when they should respond and when they should not. If they are reinforced with food for pecking at a switch when a red light is on but are not reinforced for pecking when a green light is on, they will eventually peck only when they see a red light. Their behavior demonstrates the effect of **discriminative stimuli,** which are stimuli that signal whether reinforcement is available if a certain response is made. When an organism learns to make a particular response in the presence of one stimulus but not another, *stimulus discrimination* has occurred (see Figure 6.8). Another way to say this is that the response is now under *stimulus control.* In general, stimulus discrimination allows people or animals to learn what is appropriate (reinforced) and inappropriate (not reinforced) in particular situations. For both animals and humans, discrimination develops fastest when the discriminative stimulus signals that a behavior is appropriate, and it develops slowest when the stimulus signals that a behavior is inappropriate (Newman, Wolff, & Hearst, 1980).

Stimulus generalization also occurs in operant conditioning; that is, an animal or a person often performs a response in the presence of a stimulus that is similar, but not identical, to the one that previously signaled the availability of reinforcement. As in classical conditioning, the more similar the new stimulus is to the old, the more likely it is that the response will be performed. Suppose you ate a wonderful meal at a restaurant built to look like a big boat. In the future, you might be attracted to another restaurant that looks something like the one where you had that great meal.

OBJ 6.15: Define discriminative stimulus and stimulus control. Give an example of stimulus control. Explain how stimulus discrimination and stimulus generalization can work together.

Test Items 6.70–6.76

ClassPrep PPT 20: Stimulus Discrimination and Generalization

ClassPrep PPT 21: *Figure 6.8:* Stimulus Discrimination

figure 6.8

Stimulus Discrimination

In this experiment the rat could jump from a stand through any of three doors, but it was reinforced only if it jumped through the door that differed from the other two. The rat learned to do this quite well: On this trial, it discriminated vertical from horizontal stripes.

avoidance conditioning A type of learning in which an organism responds to a signal in a way that avoids exposure to an aversive stimulus.

discriminative stimuli Stimuli that signal whether reinforcement is available if a certain response is made.

Although the artist may not have intended it, this cartoon nicely illustrates one way in which discriminative stimuli can affect behavior.

"Oh, not bad. The light comes on, I press the bar, they write me a check. How about you?"

As in classical conditioning, stimulus discrimination and stimulus generalization often complement each other in operant conditioning. In one study, for example, pigeons received food for pecking at a switch, but only when they saw certain works of art. When other paintings were shown, pecking was not reinforced (Watanabe, Sakamoto, & Wakita, 1995). As a result, these birds learned to *discriminate* the works of the impressionist painter Claude Monet from those of the cubist painter Pablo Picasso. Later, when the birds were shown new paintings by other impressionist and cubist artists, they were able to *generalize* from the original artists to other artists who painted in the same style. In other words, they had learned what paintings fall into the "impressionist" and "cubist" categories. Humans learn to place people and things into even more finely detailed categories, such as "honest," "dangerous," or "tax deductible." We discriminate one stimulus from another and then, through generalization, respond similarly to all stimuli we perceive to be in a particular category. This ability to respond in a similar way to all members of a category can save us considerable time and effort, but it can also lead to the development of unwarranted prejudice against certain groups of people (see the chapter on social cognition).

Forming and Strengthening Operant Behavior

Daily life is full of examples of operant conditioning. People go to movies, parties, classes, and jobs primarily because doing so brings reinforcement. What is the effect of the type or timing of the reinforcers? How can new responses be established through operant conditioning?

Shaping   Imagine that you want to train your dog, Henry, to sit and to "shake hands." The basic method using positive reinforcement is obvious: Every time Henry sits and shakes hands, you give him a treat. But the problem is also obvious: Smart as Henry is, he may never spontaneously make the desired response, so you will never be able to give the reinforcer. Instead of your teaching and Henry's learning, the two of you will just stare at each other (and he'll probably wag his tail).

---

shaping The process of reinforcing responses that come successively closer to the desired response.

primary reinforcers Reinforcers that meet an organism's basic needs, such as food and water.

secondary reinforcer A reward that people or animals learn to like.

Getting the Hang of It Learning to eat with a spoon is, as you can see, a hit-or-miss process at first. However, this child will learn to hit the target more and more often as the food reward gradually shapes a more efficient, and far less messy, pattern of behavior.

OBJ 6.17: Discuss the differences between primary and secondary reinforcers.

Test Items 6.84–6.88

Critical Thinking Exercise

Personal Learning Activity 6.2

IRM Activity 6.8: Using Learning Principles to Parent

ClassPrep PPT 23: Delay and Size of Reinforcement

The way around this problem is to *shape* Henry's behavior. **Shaping** is accomplished by reinforcing *successive approximations*—that is, responses that come successively closer to the desired response. For example, you might first give Henry a treat whenever he sits down. Then you might reinforce him only when he sits and partially lifts a paw. Next, you might reinforce more complete paw lifting. Eventually, you would require that Henry perform the entire sit-lift-shake sequence before giving the treat. Shaping is an extremely powerful, widely used tool. Animal trainers have used it to teach chimpanzees to roller-skate, dolphins to jump through hoops, and pigeons to play Ping-Pong (Coren, 1999).

Secondary Reinforcement   Often, operant conditioning begins with the use of **primary reinforcers,** events or stimuli—such as food or water—that are inherently rewarding. But Henry's training will be slowed if he must stop and eat every time he makes a correct response. Furthermore, once he is full, food will no longer act as an effective reinforcer. To avoid these problems, animal trainers and others in the teaching business rely on the principle of secondary reinforcement.

A **secondary reinforcer** is a previously neutral stimulus that, if paired with a stimulus that is already reinforcing, will itself take on reinforcing properties. In other words, secondary reinforcers are rewards that people or animals learn to like. For example, if you say, "Good boy!" a moment before you give Henry each food reward, these words will become associated with the food and can then be used alone to reinforce Henry's behavior (as long as the words are again paired with food now and then). Does this remind you of classical conditioning? It should, because the primary reinforcer (food) is an unconditioned stimulus; if the sound of "Good boy!" predictably precedes, and thus signals, food, it becomes a conditioned stimulus. For this reason, secondary reinforcers are sometimes called *conditioned reinforcers.*

Secondary reinforcement greatly expands the power of operant conditioning (Schwartz & Reisberg, 1991). Money is the most obvious secondary reinforcer; some people will do anything for it (even though it tastes terrible!). Its reinforcing power lies in its association with the many rewards it can buy. Smiles and other forms of social approval (like the words "Good job!") are also important secondary reinforcers for human beings. However, what becomes a secondary reinforcer can vary a great deal from person to person and culture to culture. For example, tickets to a rock concert are an effective secondary reinforcer for some people, but not everyone. A ceremony honoring outstanding job performance might be highly reinforcing to most employees in individualist cultures, but it might be embarrassing for some employees from cultures in which group cooperation is valued more than personal distinction (Fiske et al., 1998). Still, when chosen carefully, secondary reinforcers can build or maintain behavior even when primary reinforcement is absent for long periods.

Secondary Reinforcers A touch or a smile, words of praise or thanks, and a loving or approving look are just a few of the social stimuli that can serve as secondary reinforcers for humans. Parents have used these reinforcers for generations to shape the behavior of children in accordance with their cultural values.

Delay and Size of Reinforcement   Much of human behavior is learned and maintained because it is regularly reinforced. But many people overeat, smoke, drink too much, or procrastinate, even though they know these behaviors are bad for them and even though they want to eliminate them. They just cannot seem to change; they seem to lack "self-control." If behavior is controlled by its consequences, why do people perform acts that are ultimately self-defeating?

Part of the answer lies in the *timing* of reinforcers. In general, the effect of a reinforcer is stronger when it comes soon after a response occurs (Kalish, 1981). The good feelings (positive reinforcers) that follow, say, drinking too much are immediate; hangovers and other negative consequences are usually delayed, which weakens their impact. Under some conditions, delaying a positive reinforcer for even a few seconds can decrease the effectiveness of positive reinforcement. (An advantage of praise or other secondary reinforcers is that they can easily be delivered immediately after a desired response occurs.)

TRY THIS **Reinforcement Schedules on the Job** Make a list of all the jobs you have ever held, along with the reinforcement schedule on which you received your pay for each. Now consider which of the four types of schedules (FR, FI, VR, or VI) was most common, and which was most satisfying to you.

The *size* of a reinforcer is also important. In general, operant conditioning generates more vigorous behavior when the reinforcer is large than when it is small. For example, a strong electrical shock will elicit a faster avoidance or escape response than a weak one.

Schedules of Reinforcement

We flip a light switch, and the light comes on. We put money in a vending machine, and we receive the item we want. When a reinforcer is delivered every time a particular response occurs, the arrangement is called a **continuous reinforcement schedule**. Quite often, however, reinforcement is administered only some of the time; the result is a **partial reinforcement schedule**, or *intermittent reinforcement schedule*.

Most partial reinforcement schedules can be classified according to (1) whether the delivery of reinforcers depends on the number of responses made or on the time that has elapsed since the last reinforcer and (2) whether the number of responses or the time lapse required for delivery of reinforcers is fixed or variable. Accordingly, there are four basic types of intermittent reinforcement schedules:

1. *Fixed-ratio (FR) schedules* provide a reinforcer following a fixed number of responses. So rats might receive food after every tenth time they press the lever in a Skinner box (FR 10) or after every twentieth time (FR 20); factory workers might be paid for every five computers they assemble (FR 5) or for every fiftieth (FR 50).

2. *Variable-ratio (VR) schedules* also provide a reinforcer after a given number of responses, but that number can vary. So on a VR 30 schedule, a rat might sometimes be reinforced after ten lever presses, sometimes after fifty, and sometimes after five, but the *average* number of responses required to get a reinforcer would be thirty. Gambling offers a variable-ratio schedule. A slot machine, for example, pays off only after a frustratingly unpredictable number of lever pulls, averaging perhaps one in twenty.

3. *Fixed-interval (FI) schedules* provide a reinforcer for the first response that occurs after some fixed time has passed since the last reward, regardless of how many responses have been made during that interval. For example, on an FI 60 schedule, the first response after sixty seconds have passed will be rewarded. Some radio stations use fixed-interval schedules to discourage "professional contestants" by stating that listeners cannot win a prize more than once every thirty days.

4. *Variable-interval (VI) schedules* reinforce the first response after some period of time, but the amount of time varies. On a VI 60 schedule, for example, the first response to occur after an *average* of 60 seconds is reinforced, but the actual time between reinforcements might vary from, say, 1 second to 120 seconds. Teachers use VI schedules when they give "points"—at unpredictably varying intervals—to children who are in their seats. A VI schedule has also been successfully used to encourage seat belt use: During a 10-week test in Illinois, police stopped drivers at random times and awarded prizes to those who were buckled up (Mortimer et al., 1988).

Different schedules of reinforcement produce different patterns of responding, as Figure 6.9 shows (Skinner, 1961a). The figure illustrates two important points. First, both fixed-ratio and variable-ratio schedules produce high rates of behavior, because in both cases the frequency of the reward depends directly on the rate of responding. Industrial/organizational psychologists have applied this principle to help companies increase worker productivity and lower absenteeism. Workers who are paid on the basis of the number of items they produce or the number of days they show up for work usually produce more items and miss fewer workdays (Muchinsky, 1993; Yukl, Latham, & Purcell, 1976). Similarly, gamblers reinforced

figure 6.9

Schedules of Reinforcement

These curves illustrate the patterns of behavior typically seen under different reinforcement schedules. The steeper the curve, the faster the response rate; the thin diagonal lines crossing the curves show when reinforcement was given. In general, the rate of responding is higher under ratio schedules than under interval schedules.

Source: Adapted from Skinner (1961).

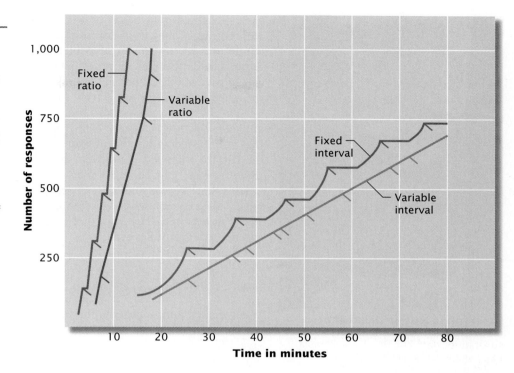

continuous reinforcement schedule A pattern in which a reinforcer is delivered every time a particular response occurs.

partial reinforcement schedule A pattern in which a reinforcer is administered only some of the time after a particular response occurs.

fixed-ratio (FR) schedule A partial reinforcement schedule that provides reinforcement following a fixed number of responses.

variable-ratio (VR) schedule A partial reinforcement schedule that provides reinforcement after a varying number of responses.

fixed-interval (FI) schedule A partial reinforcement schedule that provides reinforcement for the first response that occurs after some fixed time has passed since the last reward.

variable-interval (VI) schedule A partial reinforcement schedule that provides reinforcement for the first response after some varying period of time.

extinction The gradual disappearance of operant behavior due to elimination of rewards for that behavior.

partial reinforcement extinction effect A phenomenon in which behaviors learned under a partial reinforcement schedule are more difficult to extinguish than behaviors learned on a continuous reinforcement schedule.

on a variable-ratio schedule for pulling a slot machine handle, rolling dice, or playing other games of chance tend to maintain a high rate of responding—some so-called gambling addicts appear unable to stop.

The second important aspect of Figure 6.9 relates to the "scallops" shown in the fixed-interval schedule. Under this schedule, it does not matter how many responses are made during the time between rewards. As a result, the rate of responding typically drops dramatically immediately after a reinforcer occurs and then increases as the time for another reward approaches. When teachers schedule all their quizzes in advance, for example, some students study just before each quiz and then virtually stop studying in that course until just before the next quiz. Behavior rewarded on variable-interval schedules looks quite different. The unpredictable timing of rewards typically generates slow, steady responding. So if you know that your teacher might give a pop quiz at any class session, you might be more inclined to study more steadily from day to day (Ruscio, 2001).

Schedules and Extinction   Just as breaking the predictive link between a conditioned and an unconditioned stimulus weakens a classically conditioned response, ending the relationship between an operant response and its reinforcers weakens that response. In other words, failure to reinforce a response *extinguishes* that response; the response occurs less often and eventually may disappear. If lever pressing no longer brings food, a rat stops pressing; if repeated e-mail messages to a friend are not answered, you eventually stop sending them. As in classical conditioning, **extinction** in operant conditioning does not totally erase learned relationships. If a signaling stimulus reappears at some time after an operant response has been extinguished, that response may recur (spontaneously recover), and if it is again reinforced, it will be quickly relearned.

In general, behaviors learned under a partial reinforcement schedule are far more difficult to extinguish than those learned on a continuous reinforcement schedule. This phenomenon—called the **partial reinforcement extinction effect**—is easy to understand if you imagine yourself in a gambling casino, standing near a broken slot machine and a broken candy machine. If you deposit money in the

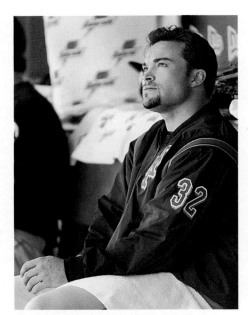

Superstition and Partial Reinforcement Partial reinforcement often creates superstitious athletic rituals—such as a fixed sequence of actions prior to hitting a golf ball or shooting a free throw in basketball. If the ritual has preceded success often enough, failure to execute the action may upset the player and disrupt performance. One professional baseball player, Wade Boggs, ate chicken before every game and warmed up by catching exactly one hundred ground balls; pitcher Mike Hamilton, shown here, always sits in a certain spot on the dugout steps between innings.

OBJ 6.19: Explain why activity preference and physiological factors influence the efficiency of reinforcement.

Test Items 6.105–6.108

ClassPrep PPT 28: Why Do Reinforcers Work?

candy machine, that behavior will probably be extinguished quickly (i.e., you will stop putting money in). Because the machine is supposed to deliver its goodies on a continuous reinforcement schedule, it is easy to tell that it is not going to provide a reinforcer. But because slot machines are known to offer rewards on an intermittent and unpredictable schedule, you might put in coin after coin, on the assumption that the machine is simply not paying off at the moment.

Partial reinforcement also helps explain why superstitious behavior is so resistant to extinction (Chance, 1988). Suppose you take a shower just before hearing that you passed an important exam. The shower did nothing to cause this outcome; the reward followed it through sheer luck. Still, for some people, this *accidental reinforcement* can function like a partial reinforcement schedule, strengthening actions that precede, and thus appear to cause, reward (Chance, 1988). So someone who wins a lottery while wearing a particular shirt may begin wearing the "lucky shirt" more often. The laws of chance dictate that if you wear a lucky shirt often enough, a rewarding event will follow now and then, on a very sparse partial schedule (Vyse, 1997).

Why Reinforcers Work

What makes reinforcers reinforcing? For primary reinforcers, at least, the reason could be that they satisfy hunger, thirst, and other physiological needs basic to survival. This explanation is incomplete, however, because substances like saccharin, which have no nutritional value, can have as much reinforcing power as sugar, which is nutritious. Further, addictive drugs are powerful reinforcers even though they pose a long-term threat to the health of people who use them. So psychologists have sought other explanations for the mechanisms of reinforcement.

Some psychologists have argued that reinforcement is based not on a stimulus itself but on the opportunity to engage in an activity that involves the stimulus. According to David Premack (1965), for example, at any moment each person maintains a list of behavioral preferences, ranked from most desirable to least desirable, like a kind of psychological "Top Ten." The higher on the list an activity is, the greater is its power as a reinforcer. This means that a preferred activity can serve as a reinforcer for any other activity that is less preferred at the moment. For example, when parents allow their teenage daughter to use the car in return for mowing the lawn, they are using something high on her preference list (driving) to reinforce an activity that is lower on the list (lawn mowing). This idea is known as the *Premack principle.*

Taking the Premack principle a step further, some psychologists have suggested that virtually any activity can become a reinforcer if a person or animal has not been allowed to perform that activity for a while (Timberlake, 1980; Timberlake & Farmer-Dougan, 1991). To understand how this *disequilibrium hypothesis* works, suppose that you would rather study than work out at the gym. Now suppose that the gym has been closed for several weeks, and you have been unable to have a workout. According to the disequilibrium hypothesis, because your opportunity to exercise has been held below its normal level, its value as a reinforcer has been raised. In fact, it might have become so preferred that it could be used to reinforce studying! In short, under certain circumstances, even activities that are normally not strongly preferred can become reinforcers for normally more preferred activities. The disequilibrium hypothesis helps explain why money is such a powerful secondary reinforcer: It can be exchanged for whatever a person finds reinforcing at the moment. In fact, some researchers believe that the disequilibrium hypothesis may provide a better overall explanation of why reinforcers work than the Premack principle does (Hergenhahn & Olson, 1997).

Psychologists taking a biological approach suggest that the stimuli and activities we know as reinforcers may work by exerting particular effects within the brain. This possibility was suggested when James Olds and Peter Milner (1954) discovered

figure 6.10

Two Kinds of Punishment

In one form of punishment, a behavior is followed by an aversive or unpleasant stimulus. In a second form of punishment, sometimes called *penalty,* a pleasant stimulus is removed following a behavior. In either case, punishment decreases the chances that the behavior will occur in the future. When a toddler reaches toward an electric outlet and her father says "NO!" and gently taps her hand, is that punishment or negative reinforcement? (If you said *punishment,* you are right, because it will *reduce* the likelihood of touching outlets in the future.)

ClassPrep PPT 30: *Figure 6.10:* Two Kinds of Punishment

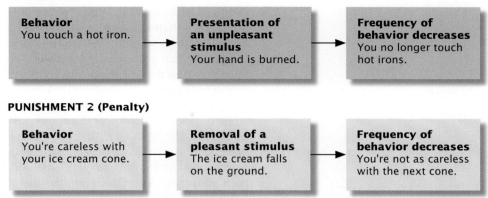

PUNISHMENT 1

| **Behavior** You touch a hot iron. | → | **Presentation of an unpleasant stimulus** Your hand is burned. | → | **Frequency of behavior decreases** You no longer touch hot irons. |

PUNISHMENT 2 (Penalty)

| **Behavior** You're careless with your ice cream cone. | → | **Removal of a pleasant stimulus** The ice cream falls on the ground. | → | **Frequency of behavior decreases** You're not as careless with the next cone. |

ClassPrep PPT 29: Punishment

OBJ 6.20: Define punishment and describe its role in operant conditioning. Discuss the disadvantages of and guidelines for using punishment.

Test Items 6.109–6.117

Essay Q 6.2

Personal Learning Activity 6.2

IRM Thinking Critically 6.1: Does Spanking Children Teach Them Aggression?

IRM Activity 6.10: Negative Reinforcement Versus Punishment

ClassPrep PPT 31: Drawbacks of Punishment

that mild electrical stimulation of certain areas of the hypothalamus can be such a powerful reinforcer that a hungry rat will ignore food in a Skinner box, preferring to spend hours pressing a lever that stimulates these "pleasure centers" in its brain (Olds, 1973). It is not yet clear whether physiological mechanisms underlie the power of all reinforcers, but evidence available so far suggests that these mechanisms are important components of the process (Waelti, Dickinson, & Schultz, 2001). For example, as mentioned in the chapter on biological aspects of psychology, the activation of dopamine systems is associated with the pleasure of many stimuli, including food; music; sex; the uncertainty involved in gambling; and some addictive drugs, such as cocaine (Berns et al., 2001; Blood & Zatorre, 2001; Breiter et al., 2001; Cardinal et al., 2001; Ciccocioppo, Sanna, & Weiss, 2001).

Punishment

So far, we have discussed positive and negative reinforcement, both of which *increase* the frequency of a response, either by presenting something pleasurable or by removing something unpleasant. In contrast, **punishment** *reduces* the frequency of an operant behavior by presenting an unpleasant stimulus or removing a pleasant one. Shouting "No!" and swatting your dog when he begins chewing on the rug illustrates punishment that presents an unpleasant stimulus following a response. Taking away a child's TV privileges because of rude behavior is a kind of punishment—sometimes called *penalty*—that removes a positive stimulus (see Figure 6.10).

Punishment is often confused with negative reinforcement, but they are actually quite different. Reinforcement of any sort always *strengthens* behavior; punishment *weakens* it. If shock is *turned off* when a rat presses a lever, that is negative reinforcement; it increases the probability that the rat will press the lever when shock occurs again. But if shock is *turned on* when the rat presses the lever, that is punishment; the rat will be less likely to press the lever again.

Although punishment can change behavior, it has several potential drawbacks. First, it does not "erase" an undesirable habit; it merely suppresses it. This suppression usually occurs in response to stimuli (such as a parent or teacher) that were present at the time of punishment, so people may repeat previously punished acts when they think they can avoid detection. This problem is summed up in the adage "When the cat's away, the mice will play." Second, punishment sometimes produces unwanted side effects. For example, if you punish a child for swearing, the child may associate the punisher with the punishment and end up being afraid of you. Third, punishment is often ineffective, especially with animals or young children, unless it is given immediately after the response and each time the response is made. If a child gets into a cookie jar and enjoys a few cookies before being discovered and

punishment Presentation of an aversive stimulus or the removal of a pleasant stimulus.

punished, the effect of the punishment will be greatly reduced. Similarly, if a child confesses to wrongdoing and is then punished, the punishment may discourage honesty rather than eliminate undesirable behavior. Fourth, physical punishment can become aggression and even abuse if administered in anger. Because children tend to imitate what they see, children who are frequently punished may be more likely to behave aggressively themselves (Gilbert, 1997). Finally, although punishment signals that inappropriate behavior occurred, it does not specify what should be done instead. An F on a term paper says the assignment was poorly done, but the grade alone tells the student nothing about how to improve.

In the 1970s and 1980s, concerns over these drawbacks led many parents and professionals to discourage spanking and other forms of punishment as a means of controlling children's behavior (Rosellini, 1998). The debate about punishment has been reopened recently by studies suggesting that spanking can be an effective behavior control technique with children three to thirteen years of age. These studies found that occasional spanking is not detrimental to children's development, if used in combination with other disciplinary practices such as requiring that the children pay some penalty for their misdeeds, having them provide some sort of restitution to the victims of their actions, and making them aware of what they did wrong (Gunnoe & Mariner, 1997; Larzelere, 1996).

When used *properly*, then, punishment can work, and in some instances it may be the only alternative. For example, some children suffer developmental disabilities in which they strike or mutilate themselves or display other potentially life threatening behaviors. As shown in Figure 6.11, punishing these behaviors has sometimes proven to be the only effective treatment (e.g., Flavell et al., 1982). Whatever the case, punishment is most effective when it is administered in accordance with several guidelines. First, the person giving punishment should specify *why* it is being given and that its purpose is to change the person's behavior, not to harm or demean the person. This step helps prevent a general fear of the punisher. Second, without being abusive, punishment should be immediate and noticeable enough to eliminate the undesirable behavior. A halfhearted "Quit it" may actually reinforce a child's misbehavior, because almost any attention is reinforcing to some children. Moreover, if children become habituated to very mild punishment, the parent may end up using substantially more severe punishment to stop inappropriate behavior than would have been necessary if a stern, but moderate, punishment had been used in the first place. (You may have witnessed this *escalation effect* in grocery stores or restaurants, where parents are often not initially firm enough in dealing with their children's misbehavior.) Finally, the use of punishment alone is usually not enough

figure 6.11

Life-Saving Punishment

This child suffered from chronic ruminative disorder, a condition in which he vomited everything he ate. At left, the boy was approximately one year old and had been vomiting for four months. At right is the same child thirteen days after punishment with electric shock had eliminated the vomiting behavior; his weight had increased 26 percent. He was physically and psychologically healthy when tested six months, one year, and two years later (Lang & Melamed, 1969).

Source: Lang & Melamed (1969).

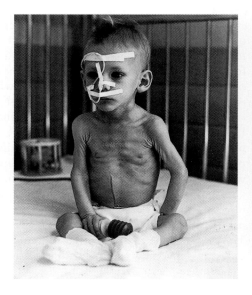 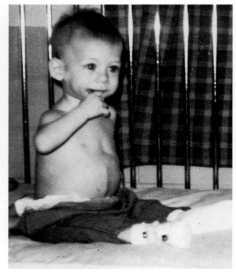

to change behavior in the long run. It is important also to identify what the person should do instead of the punished act, and then reinforce the appropriate behavior when it occurs. As the frequency of appropriate behavior increases through reinforcement, the frequency of undesirable responses (and the need for further punishment) should decline.

When these guidelines are not followed, the potentially beneficial effects of punishment may disappear or be only temporary (Hyman, 1995). As illustrated in many countries' justice systems, punishment for criminal acts is typically administered long after the acts have occurred, and initial punishments are often relatively mild—as when offenders are repeatedly given probation. Even being sent to jail or prison rarely leads to rehabilitation, because this punishment is usually not supplemented by efforts to teach and reinforce noncriminal lifestyles (Brennan & Mednick, 1994; Cassel & Bernstein, 2001). It is no wonder, then, that of the more than 2 million criminals in prison in the United States alone, about two-thirds are likely to be rearrested for serious crimes within three years of completing their sentences, and about 40 percent of them will return to prison (Cassel & Bernstein, 2001; U.S. Department of Justice, 1997).

Some Applications of Operant Conditioning

ClassPrep PPT 33: Some Applications of Operant Conditioning

The principles of operant conditioning were originally developed with animals in the laboratory, but they are valuable for understanding human behavior in an endless variety of everyday situations. ("In Review: Reinforcement and Punishment" summarizes some key principles of operant conditioning.) The unscientific but effective use of rewards and punishments by parents, teachers, and peers is vital to helping children learn what is and is not appropriate behavior at the dinner table, in the classroom, or at a birthday party. People learn how to be "civilized" in their own culture partly through positive ("Good!") and negative ("Stop that!") responses from others. As described in the chapter on human development, differing patterns

in review Reinforcement and Punishment

Concept	Description	Example or Comment
Positive reinforcement	Increasing the frequency of a behavior by following it with the presentation of a positive reinforcer—a pleasant, positive stimulus or experience	You say "Good job!" after someone works hard to perform a task.
Negative reinforcement	Increasing the frequency of a behavior by following it with the removal of an unpleasant stimulus or experience	You learn to use the "mute" button on the TV remote control to remove the sound of an obnoxious commercial.
Escape conditioning	Learning to make a response that removes an unpleasant stimulus	A little boy learns that crying will cut short the time that he must stay in his room.
Avoidance conditioning	Learning to make a response that avoids an unpleasant stimulus	You slow your car to the speed limit when you spot a police car, thus avoiding being stopped and reducing the fear of a fine; very resistant to extinction.
Punishment	Decreasing the frequency of a behavior by either presenting an unpleasant stimulus (punishment 1) or removing a pleasant one (punishment 2, or penalty)	You swat the dog after it steals food from the table, or you take a favorite toy away from a child who misbehaves. A number of cautions should be kept in mind before using punishment.

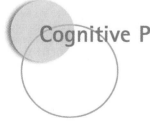

Learning Cultural Values   As described in the chapter on social influence, the prevalence of aggressive behavior varies considerably from culture to culture, in part because some cultures reward it more than others do. In some Inuit cultures, for example, aggressive behavior is actively discouraged and extremely rare (Banta, 1997). In many other cultures, it is all too common.

OBJ 6.21: Discuss how operant conditioning can be used to treat problematic behavior.

Test Items 6.118–6.119

of rewards and punishments for boys and girls also underlie the development of behaviors that fit culturally approved *gender roles.*

The scientific study of operant conditioning has led to numerous treatment programs for altering problematic behavior. Behavioral programs that combine the use of rewards for appropriate actions and extinction, or carefully administered punishment, for inappropriate behaviors have helped countless mental patients, mentally retarded individuals, autistic children, and hard-to-manage youngsters to develop the behavior patterns they need to live happier and more productive lives (Ayllon, 1999; Morisse et al., 1996). These same methods have been used successfully to help keep former drug addicts drug-free and to help patients with alcohol-related memory problems to recognize and remember new faces and names—including those of their own grandchildren (Hochhalter et al., 2001; Silverman et al., 2001). Many self-help books also incorporate principles of positive reinforcement, recommending self-reward following each small victory in efforts to lose weight, stop smoking, avoid procrastination, or reach other goals (e.g., Rachlin, 2000).

When people cannot do anything about the consequences of a behavior, discriminative stimuli may hold the key to changing the behavior. For example, people trying to quit smoking often find it easier to avoid smoking if they stay away from bars and other places that contain discriminative stimuli for smoking. Stimulus control can also help alleviate insomnia. Insomniacs are much more likely than other people to use their beds for nonsleeping activities, such as watching television, writing letters, reading magazines, worrying, and so on. Soon the bedroom becomes a discriminative stimulus for so many activities that relaxation and sleep become less and less likely. But if insomniacs begin to use their beds only for sleeping, there is a good chance that they will sleep better (Jacobs, 1999; Lichstein & Morin, 2000).

Cognitive Processes in Learning

ClassPrep PPT 34: Cognitive Processes in Learning

During the first half of the twentieth century, psychologists in North America tended to look at classical and operant conditioning through the lens of behaviorism, the theoretical approach that was dominant in psychology at the time. As described in the chapter on introducing psychology, behaviorism stresses the importance of empirical observation of lawful relationships in animal and human behavior. Behaviorists tried to identify the stimuli, responses, and consequences that build and alter overt behavior. In other words, they saw learning as resulting from the automatic, unthinking formation or modification of associations between observable events. Behaviorists paid almost no attention to the role of conscious mental activity that might accompany the learning process.

This strictly behavioral view of classical and operant conditioning is challenged by the cognitive approach, which has become increasingly influential in recent decades. Cognitive psychologists see a common thread in these apparently different forms of learning. Both classical and operant conditioning, they argue, help animals and people to detect causality—to understand what causes what (Schwartz & Robbins, 1995). By extension, both types of conditioning may result not only from automatic associations but also from more complex mental processes that organisms use to understand their environments and to interact with them adaptively (Dickinson, 2001).

Certainly there is evidence that cognitive processes—how people represent, store, and use information—play an important role in learning. This evidence includes research on learned helplessness, latent learning, cognitive maps, insight, and observational learning.

Learned Helplessness

OBJ 6.22: Define learned helplessness and give an example of it. Describe the experiments used to study learned helplessness and the results.

Test Items 6.120–6.124

IRM Activity 6.11: Learned Helplessness

Babies learn that crying brings parental attention, children learn which button turns on the TV, and adults learn what behaviors bring success in the workplace. On the basis of this learning, people come to expect that certain actions on their part cause certain consequences. If this learning is disrupted, problems may result. One such problem is **learned helplessness,** a tendency to give up any effort to control the environment (Seligman, 1975).

Learned helplessness was first demonstrated in animals. As described earlier, dogs placed in a shuttle box (see Figure 6.7) will normally learn to jump over a partition to escape a shock. However, if the dogs are first placed in a restraining harness and receive shocks that they cannot escape, they later do not even try to escape when a shock is turned on in the shuttle box (Overmier & Seligman, 1967). It is as if the animals had learned that "shock happens, and there is nothing I can do to control it."

FOCUS ON RESEARCH METHODS

A Two-Factor Experiment on Human Helplessness

The results of animal studies on learned helplessness led psychologists to wonder whether learned helplessness might play a role in human psychological problems, but they had to deal with more basic questions first. One of the most important of these questions is whether lack of control over the environment can lead to helplessness in humans.

ClassPrep PPT 45: Focus on Research Methods: A Two-Factor Experiment on Human Helplessness

● What was the researcher's question?

Donald Hiroto (1974) conducted an experiment to test the hypothesis that people would develop learned helplessness after either experiencing lack of control or simply being told that their control was limited.

● How did the researcher answer the question?

The first independent variable Hiroto manipulated in his experiment was whether or not volunteer participants could control a series of thirty randomly timed bursts of loud, obnoxious noise. Like dogs receiving inescapable shock, one group of participants had no way to stop the noise. A second group did have control; they could press a button to turn off the noise. A third group heard no noise at all.

learned helplessness A failure to try to exert control over the environment when an organism has, or believes that it has, no such control.

After this preliminary phase, all participants were exposed to eighteen more bursts of obnoxious noise, each preceded by a red warning light. During this second phase, *all* participants could stop the noise by moving a lever to the left or right, and if they acted quickly enough, they could even prevent it from starting. However, the participants did not know which lever direction would be correct on any given trial.

Before these new trials began, the experimenter manipulated a second independent variable: the participants' *expectation* about control. Half the participants were told that avoiding or escaping the noise depended on their *skill* at moving the lever. The other participants were told that no matter how hard they tried, success at avoiding or escaping noise would be a matter of *chance*. This was a *two-factor experiment,* because the dependent variable—the participants' efforts to control noise—could be affected by either or both of two independent variables: prior experience with noise (control, lack of control, or no noise) and expectation (skill or chance) about the ability to influence the noise.

● **What did the researcher find?**

On the average, participants who had previously experienced lack of control now failed to control noise on almost four times as many trials (50 percent versus 13 percent) as did participants who had earlier been in control. Further, regardless of whether participants had experienced control before, those who expected control to depend on their skill exerted control on significantly more trials than did those who expected chance to govern the outcome.

● **What do the results mean?**

These results supported Hiroto's hypothesis that people, like animals, tend to make less effort to control their environment when prior experience leads them to expect their efforts to be in vain. Unlike animals, however, people can develop expectations of helplessness either through personally experiencing lack of control or through being *told* that they are powerless. Hiroto's (1974) results appear to reflect a general phenomenon: When people's prior experience leads them to *believe* that nothing they do can change their lives or control their destiny, they generally stop trying to improve their lot (Dweck, Chiu, & Hong, 1995; Peterson, Maier, & Seligman, 1993). Instead, they tend to passively endure aversive situations and, at the cognitive level, to attribute negative events to their own permanent and general shortcomings rather than to changeable external circumstances (Abramson, Metalsky, & Alloy, 1989; Seligman, Klein, & Miller, 1976).

● **What do we still need to know?**

Although it seems clear that helplessness can be learned, not all of its consequences are known or understood. For example, Martin Seligman (1975) originally proposed that learned helplessness was a major cause of depression and other mental disorders in humans, but subsequent research (Abramson, Metalsky, & Alloy, 1989; Metalsky et al., 1993) indicates that the causal picture is more complicated. One study suggests that learned-helplessness experiences give rise to a more general *pessimistic explanatory style* that can produce depression and other mental disorders (Peterson & Seligman, 1984). People with this style tend to see the good things that happen to them as temporary and due to external factors such as luck, and the bad things as permanent and due to internal factors such as lack of ability. A pessimistic explanatory style, in fact, has been associated with negative outcomes, such as poor grades, poor sales performance, and health problems (Peterson & Barrett, 1987; Seligman & Schulman, 1986; Taylor, 1998). However, the mechanism responsible for this connection remains unknown (Wiebe & Smith, 1997); understanding how pessimistic (or optimistic) explanatory styles can lead to negative (or positive) consequences remains an important focus of research (Salovey, Rothman, & Rodin, 1998).

figure 6.12

Latent Learning

Notice that when the rats in Group C did not receive food reinforcement, they continued to make many errors in locating the goal box of a maze. The day after first finding food there, however, they took almost no wrong turns! The reinforcement, argued Tolman, affected only the rats' performance; they must have learned the maze earlier, without reinforcement.

ClassPrep PPT 45, OHT: *Figure 6.12:* Latent Learning: Tolman & Honzik (1930)

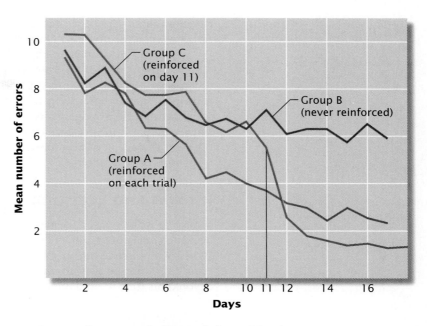

ClassPrep PPT 36: Latent Learning

Latent Learning and Cognitive Maps

The study of cognitive processes in learning goes back at least to the 1920s and Edward Tolman's research on maze learning in rats. The rats' task was to find the goal box of the maze, where food awaited them. The rats typically took many wrong turns, but over the course of many trials they made fewer and fewer mistakes. The behavioral interpretation was that the rats learned a long chain of turning responses that were ultimately reinforced by the food. Tolman disagreed and offered evidence for a cognitive interpretation.

In one of Tolman's studies, three groups of rats were placed in the same maze once a day for several consecutive days (Tolman & Honzik, 1930). For Group A, food was placed in the goal box on each trial. As shown in Figure 6.12, these rats gradually improved their performance so that by the end of the experiment, they made only one or two mistakes as they ran through the maze. Group B also ran the maze once a day, but there was never any food in their goal box. These animals continued to make many errors throughout the experiment. Neither of these results is surprising, and each is consistent with a behavioral view of learning.

The third group of rats, Group C, was the critical one. For the first ten days, they received no reinforcement for running the maze and continued to make many mistakes. But on the eleventh day, food was placed in their goal box for the first time. Then a very surprising thing happened: On the day after receiving reinforcement, these rats made almost no mistakes. In fact, their performance was as good as that of the rats who had been reinforced every day. In other words, for Group C the single reinforcement trial on day 11 produced a dramatic change in performance the next day.

Tolman argued that these results supported two conclusions. First, the reinforcement on day 11 could not have significantly affected the rats' *learning* of the maze itself; it simply changed their subsequent *performance*. They must have learned the maze earlier. Therefore, the rats demonstrated **latent learning**—learning that is not evident when it first occurs. Second, because the rats' performance changed immediately after the first reinforcement trial, the results obtained could occur only if the rats had earlier developed a **cognitive map**—that is, a mental representation of how the maze was arranged.

OBJ 6.23: Define and give an example of latent learning and a cognitive map.

Test Items 6.125–6.128

latent learning Learning that is not demonstrated at the time it occurs.

cognitive map A mental representation, or picture, of the environment.

Tolman concluded that cognitive maps develop naturally through experience with the world, even if there is no overt response or reinforcement. Research on learning in the natural environment has supported these views. For example, we develop mental maps of shopping malls and city streets, even when we receive no direct reward for doing so (Tversky & Kahneman, 1991).

Much as the Gestalt psychologists argued that the whole of a perception is different from the sum of its parts (see the chapter on perception), cognitive views hold that learning is more than just the effects of associations, reinforcements, and punishments. Just as perception may depend on the meaning attached to sensations, some forms of learning involve higher mental processes and depend on how the learner attaches meaning to events. To take just one example, being praised by a boss we respect may be more reinforcing than getting the same good evaluation from someone we hate.

Insight and Learning

Wolfgang Köhler was a Gestalt psychologist whose work on the cognitive aspects of learning came about almost by accident. He was visiting the island of Tenerife when World War I broke out in 1914. As a German in an area controlled by Germany's enemy, Britain, he was confined to the island for the duration of the war, and he devoted his time to studying problem solving by chimpanzees housed there (Köhler, 1924).

For example, Köhler would put a chimpanzee in a cage and place a piece of fruit so that it was visible, but out of the animal's reach. He sometimes hung the fruit from a string too high to reach or laid it on the ground too far outside the cage to be retrieved. Many of the chimps overcame these obstacles easily. If the fruit was out of reach on the ground outside the cage, some chimps looked around the cage and,

ClassPrep PPT 37: *Figure 6.13:* Insight

figure 6.13

Insight

Here are three impressive examples of problem solving by chimpanzees. At left, the animal fixed a fifteen-foot pole in the ground, climbed to the top, and dropped down after grabbing fruit that had previously been out of its reach. In the center photo, the chimp stacked two boxes from different areas of the compound, climbed to the top, and used a pole to knock down the fruit. The chimp at right stacked three boxes and climbed them to reach the fruit.

Source: Köhler (1976).

finding a long stick, used it to rake in the fruit. Surprised that the chimpanzees could solve these problems, Köhler tried more difficult tasks. Again, the chimps proved very adept, as Figure 6.13 illustrates.

In contrast to Thorndike, who thought that animals learn gradually through the consequences of their actions, Köhler argued that animals' problem solving does not have to depend on automatic associations developing slowly through trial and error. He supported his claim with three observations. First, once a chimpanzee solved a particular problem, it would immediately do the same thing in a similar situation. In other words, it acted as if it understood the problem. Second, Köhler's chimpanzees rarely tried a solution that did not work. Third, they often reached a solution suddenly. When confronted with a piece of fruit hanging from a string, for example, a chimp might jump for it several times. Then it would stop jumping, look up, and pace back and forth. Finally it would run over to a wooden crate, place it directly under the fruit, and climb on top of it to reach the fruit. Once, when there were no other objects available, a chimp went over to Köhler, dragged him by the arm until he stood beneath the fruit, and then started climbing up his back!

Köhler believed that the only explanation for these results was that the chimpanzees had sudden **insight,** an understanding of the problem as a whole, not just growing associations among its specific elements. However, demonstrating that a particular performance is the product of sudden insight requires experiments more sophisticated than those conducted by Köhler. Some cases of "insight" might actually be the result of a process known as *learning to learn,* in which previous experiences in problem solving are applied to new ones in a way that makes their solution seem to be instantaneous (Harlow, 1949). In other cases, according to some cognitive psychologists, insight may actually result from a "mental trial-and-error" process in which people (and some animals) envision a course of action, mentally simulate its results, compare it with the imagined outcome of other alternatives, and settle on the course of action most likely to aid complex problem solving and decision making (Klein, 1993).

Observational Learning: Learning by Imitation

Research on the role of cognitive processes in learning has been further stimulated by the finding that learning can occur not only by doing but also by observing what others do. Learning by watching others—called **observational learning,** or *social*

OBJ 6.24: Define insight. Discuss the differences in what is learned in classical conditioning, instrumental conditioning, and insight.

Test Items 6.129–6.136

ClassPrep PPT 38: Observational Learning

Sattler/Shabatay reader, 2/e: Goodwillie, "Voices From Our Future: Our Children Tell Us About Violence in America"

TRY THIS · **Learning by Imitation**   Much of our behavior is learned by imitating others, especially those who serve as role models. To appreciate the impact of social learning in your life, list five examples of how your own actions, speech, mannerisms, or appearance have come to match those of a parent, a sibling, a friend, a teacher, or even a celebrity.

insight   A sudden understanding about what is required to solve a problem.

observational learning   Learning how to perform new behaviors by watching others.

IN THE BLEACHERS   By Steve Moore

In spite of the power of observational learning, some people just have to learn things the hard way.

OBJ 6.25: Define observational learning and vicarious conditioning. Discuss their similarities and differences.

Test Items 6.137–6.144

Personal Learning Activity 6.4

learning—is efficient and adaptive. It occurs in both animals and humans. For example, young chimpanzees learn how to use a stone to crack open nuts by watching their mothers perform this action (Inoue-Nakamura & Matsuzawa, 1997). And we don't have to find out for ourselves that a door is locked or an iron is hot if we have just seen someone else try the door or suffer a burn.

Children are particularly influenced by the adults and peers who act as models for appropriate behavior in various situations. In one classic experiment, Albert Bandura showed nursery school children a film featuring an adult and a large, inflatable, bottom-heavy "Bobo" doll (Bandura, 1965). The adult in the film punched the Bobo doll in the nose, kicked it, threw objects at it, and hit its head with a hammer while saying things like "Sockeroo!" There were different endings to the film. Some children saw an ending in which the aggressive adult was called a "champion" by a second adult and rewarded with candy and soft drinks. Some saw the aggressor scolded and called a "bad person." Some saw a neutral ending in which there was neither reward nor punishment. After the film, each child was allowed to play alone with a Bobo doll. How the children played in this and similar studies led to some important conclusions about learning and about the role of cognitive factors in it.

Bandura found that children who saw the adult rewarded for aggression showed the most aggressive acts in play; they had received **vicarious conditioning,** a kind of observational learning in which one is influenced by seeing or hearing about the consequences of others' behavior. Those who had seen the adult punished for aggressive acts initially showed less aggression, but they still learned something. When later offered rewards for all the aggressive acts they could perform, these children displayed just as many as the children who had watched the rewarded adult. Observational learning can occur even when there are no vicarious consequences; many children in the neutral condition also imitated the model's aggression (see Figure 6.14).

figure 6.14

Observational Learning

Albert Bandura found that after observing an aggressive model, many children imitate the model's acts precisely, especially if the model's aggression was rewarded.

Source: Bandura, Ross, & Ross (1963).

ClassPrep PPT 39: *Figure 6.14:* Observational Learning

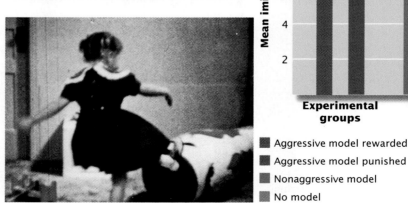

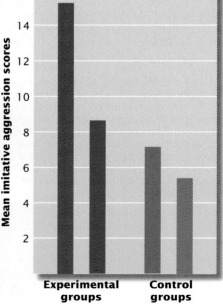

- Aggressive model rewarded
- Aggressive model punished
- Nonaggressive model
- No model

vicarious conditioning Learning conditioned responses by watching what happens to others.

Observational learning seems to be a powerful source of the *socialization* process through which children learn about which behaviors are—and are not—appropriate in their culture (Bandura, 1999). Experiments show, for example, that children are more willing to help and share after seeing a demonstration of helping by a friendly, powerful model—even after some months have elapsed (Schroeder et al., 1995). Still other studies suggest that anxiety disorders such as phobias may be learned through observation of fearful models (Cook & Mineka, 1987; Kleinknecht, 1991).

THINKING CRITICALLY

Does Watching Violence on Television Make People More Violent?

OBJ 6.26: Describe the research on the effects of television violence. State what conclusions are most reasonable, based on the evidence available.

Test Items 6.145–6.148

IRM Research Focus 6.12: I Don't Want My Music Television

ClassPrep PPT 44: Thinking Critically: Does Watching Violence on Television Make People More Violent?

If observational learning is important, then surely television—and televised violence—must teach children a great deal. For one thing, it is estimated that the average child in the United States spends more time watching television than attending school (Hepburn, 1995; Nielsen Media, 1990). Much of what children see is violent; prime-time programs in the United States present an average of 5 violent acts per hour; some Saturday morning cartoons include 20 to 25 per hour (American Psychological Association, 1993; Seppa, 1997). As a result, the average child will have witnessed at least 8,000 murders and more than 100,000 other acts of televised violence *before graduating from elementary school,* and twice that many by age 18 (Feshbach et al., 1993; Kunkel et al., 1996).

Psychologists have speculated that watching so much violence might be emotionally arousing, making viewers more likely to react violently to frustration (Huston & Wright, 1989). In fact, there is evidence that exposure to media violence can trigger or amplify viewers' aggressive thoughts and feelings, thus increasing the likelihood that they will act aggressively (Anderson & Dill, 2000; Bushman, 1998). Televised violence might also provide models that viewers imitate, particularly if the violence is carried out by attractive, powerful models—the "good guys," for example (Bandura, 1983). Finally, prolonged viewing of violent TV programs might "desensitize" viewers, making them less distressed when they see others suffer and less disturbed about inflicting pain on others (Aronson, 1999; Donnerstein et al., 1995). Concern over the influence of violence on television has recently led to the development of a violence-blocking V-Chip for new television sets in the United States.

● What am I being asked to believe or accept?

Many have argued that through one or more of the mechanisms just listed, watching violence on television causes violent behavior in viewers (Eron et al., 1996; Huesmann, 1998). A 1993 report by the National Academy of Science concluded that "overall, the vast majority of studies, whatever their methodology, showed that exposure to television violence resulted in increased aggressive behavior, both contemporaneously and over time" (Reiss & Roth, 1993, p. 371). An American Psychological Association Commission on Violence and Youth reached the same conclusion (American Psychological Association, 1993).

● What evidence is available to support the assertion?

Three types of evidence support the claim that watching violent television programs increases violent behavior. Some evidence comes from anecdotes and case studies. Children have poked one another in the eye after watching the Three Stooges appear to do so on television, and adults have claimed that watching TV shows prompted them to commit murders or other violent acts matching those seen on the shows.

Second, many longitudinal studies have found a correlation between watching violent television programs and later acts of aggression and violence. One such study tracked people from the time they were six or seven (in 1977) until they reached their early twenties (in 1992). Those who watched more violent television as children were significantly more aggressive as adults (Huesmann et al., 1997) and more likely to engage in criminal activity (Huesmann, 1995). They were also more likely to use physical punishment on their own children, who themselves tended to be much more aggressive than average. These latter results have been found not only in the United States, but in Israel, Australia, Poland, the Netherlands, and even Finland, where the number of violent TV shows is very small (Centerwall, 1990; Huesmann & Eron, 1986).

Finally, the results of numerous laboratory experiments also support the view that TV violence increases aggression among viewers (American Psychological Association, 1993; Paik & Comstock, 1994; Reiss & Roth, 1993). In one study, groups of boys watched violent or nonviolent programs in a controlled setting and then played floor hockey (Josephson, 1987). Boys who had watched the violent shows were more likely than those who had watched nonviolent programs to behave aggressively on the hockey floor. This effect was greatest for those boys who had the most aggressive tendencies to begin with. More extensive experiments in which children are exposed for long periods to carefully controlled types of television programs also suggest that exposure to large amounts of violent activity on television results in aggressive behavior (Eron et al., 1996).

● Are there alternative ways of interpreting the evidence?

Anecdotal reports and case studies are certainly open to different interpretations. When people face imprisonment or execution for their violent acts, how much credibility can we give to their claims that their actions were triggered by television programs? And how many other people might say that the same programs made them *less* likely to be violent? Anecdotes alone do not provide a good basis for drawing solid scientific conclusions.

What about the correlational evidence from longitudinal studies? As discussed in the chapter on research in psychology, a *correlation* between two variables does not necessarily mean that one is *causing* an effect on the other; both might be affected by a third factor. Why, for example, are certain people watching so much television violence in the first place? This question suggests a possible third factor that might account for the observed relationship between watching TV violence and acting aggressively: People who tend to be aggressive may prefer to watch more violent TV programs *and* behave aggressively toward others. In other words, personality may account for the observed correlations (e.g., Aluja-Fabregat & Torrubia-Beltri, 1998).

The results of controlled experiments on the effects of televised violence have been criticized as well (Geen, 1998). The major objection is that both the independent and dependent variables in these experiments are artificial, so they may not apply beyond the laboratory (Anderson, Lindsay, & Bushman, 1999). For example, the kinds of violent shows viewed by the participants during some of these experiments, as well as the ways in which their aggression has been measured, may not reflect what goes on in the real-world situations we most want to know about.

● What additional evidence would help to evaluate the alternatives?

Given the difficulty of interpreting correlational evidence, it would be useful to have evidence from controlled experiments in which equivalent groups of people were exposed for years to differing "doses" of the violence actually portrayed on TV, and the effects on their subsequent behavior were observed in real-world situations. Such experiments could also explore the circumstances under which different people (e.g., children versus adults) were affected by various forms of violence. However, studies like these create an ethical dilemma. If watching violent television programs *does* cause violent behavior, are psychologists justified in creating conditions that might lead some people to be more violent? If such violence occurred, would the researchers be partly responsible to the victims and to society? Difficulty in answering questions like these is one reason why there are so many short-term experiments and correlational studies in this area and why there is still some uncertainty about the effects of television violence.

● **What conclusions are most reasonable?**

The preponderance of evidence collected so far, including statistical analyses of correlational findings (e.g., Huesmann et al., 1997), makes it reasonable to conclude that watching TV violence may be one cause of violent behavior (Bushman & Anderson, 2001; Robinson et al., 2001; Smith & Donnerstein, 1998). Playing violent video games may be another (Anderson & Bushman, 2001). However, a causal relationship between watching TV violence and acting violently is not inevitable, and there are many circumstances in which the effect does not occur (Charleton, Gunter, & Coles, 1998; Freedman, 1992). Parents, peers, and other environmental influences, along with personality factors, may dampen or amplify the effect of watching televised violence. The viewers most likely to be affected by TV violence may be those who are most aggressive or violence-prone in the first place, a trait that could well have been acquired by observing the behavior of parents or peers (Huesmann et al., 1997). Still, the fact that violence on television *can* have a causal impact on violent behavior is reason for serious concern and continues to influence public debate about what should and should not be aired on television (Glod, 1998).

Neural Networks and Learning

Taking a cognitive approach to learning does not mean that associations are unimportant in the learning process. Associations between conditioned stimuli and reflexes or between responses and their consequences play an important role even in the mental processes that allow us to understand which events predict which other events. As a result of experience, some things remind us of other things, which remind us of still others, and so on.

How are associations actually stored in the brain? No one yet knows for sure, but the neural network models discussed in the chapter on perception provide a good way of thinking about this process. Networks of neural connections are believed to play a critical role not only in the rapid and accurate recognition of objects (Hintzman, 1991), but also in the learning process itself (Hergenhahn & Olson, 1997). These associative networks can be very complex. Consider the word *dog.* As shown in Figure 6.15, each person's experience builds many associations to this word, and the strength of each association will reflect the frequency with

figure 6.15

An Associative Network

Here is an example of a network of associations to the word *dog.* Network theorists suggest that the connections shown here represent patterns of neural connections in the brain.

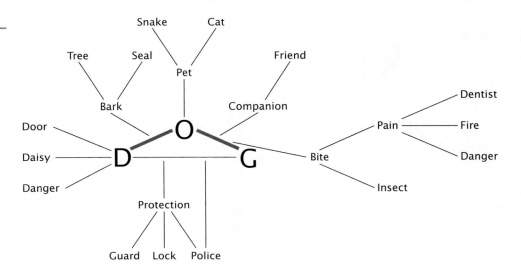

which *dog* has been mentally linked to the other objects, events, and ideas in that person's life.

Using what they know about the laws of learning and about the way neurons communicate and alter their synaptic connections, psychologists have been trying to develop models of how these associations are established (Messinger et al., 2001). We discuss some of these efforts in the chapter on perception in terms of *neural networks* and *parallel distributed processing* models of perception. A crucial aspect of such models is the idea of *distributed memory* or *distributed knowledge.* These models suggest, for example, that the knowledge of "dog" does not lie in a single location, or node, within your brain. Instead, knowledge is distributed throughout the network of associations that connect the letters *D, O,* and *G,* along with other "dog-like" experiences. In addition, as shown in Figure 6.15, each of the interconnected nodes that make up your knowledge of "dog" is connected to many other nodes as well. So the letter *D* will be connected to "Daisy," "Danger," and a host of other concepts. Networks of connections also appear to be the key to explaining how people come to understand the words and sentences they read (Wolman, van den Broek, & Lorch, 1997).

Neural network models of learning focus on how these connections are developed through experience (Hanson & Burr, 1990). For example, suppose you are learning a new word in a foreign language. Each time you read the word and associate it with its English equivalent, you strengthen the neural connections between the sight of the letters forming that word and all of the nodes activated when its English equivalent is brought to mind. Neural network, or *connectionist,* models of learning predict how much the strength of each linkage grows (in terms of the likelihood of neural communication between the two connected nodes) each time the two words are experienced together.

The details of various theories about how these connections grow are very complex (see Hanson & Burr, 1990; Schwartz & Reisberg, 1991), but a theme common to many is that the weaker the connection between two items, the greater the increase in connection strength when they are experienced together. So in a simple classical conditioning experiment, the connections between the nodes characterizing the conditioned stimulus and those characterizing the unconditioned stimulus will show the greatest increase in strength during the first few learning trials. Notice that this prediction nicely matches the typical learning curve shown in Figure 6.3 (Rescorla & Wagner, 1972).

Neural network models have yet to fully explain the learning of complex tasks, nor can they easily account for how people adapt when the "rules of the game" are suddenly changed and old habits must be unlearned and replaced (Hintzman, 1991). Nevertheless, a better understanding of what we mean by *associations* may very well lie in future research on neural network models (Anthony & Bartlett, 1999; Goldblum, 2001).

Using Research on Learning to Help People Learn

ClassPrep PPT 40: Using Research on Learning to Help People Learn

IRM Activity 1.7: Sociocultural Diversity

Teaching and training—explicit efforts to assist learners in mastering a specific skill or body of material—are major aspects of socialization in virtually every culture. So the study of how people learn has important implications for improved teaching in our schools (Lambert, 1999; Woolfolk-Hoy, 1999) and for helping people develop skills ranging from typing to tennis.

Classrooms Across Cultures

Many people are concerned that schools in the United States are not doing a very good job (Associated Press, 1997; Carnegie Task Force, 1996; Penner et al., 1994).

Reciprocal Teaching Ann Brown and her colleagues (1992) demonstrated the success of reciprocal teaching, in which children take turns teaching one another. This technique is similar to the cooperative arrangements seen in Japanese education.

IRM Thinking Critically 10.1: Do people's definitions of intelligence vary according to culture?

OBJ 6.28: Describe differences in classrooms across cultures. Define active learning and give an example.

Test Items 6.153–6.160

IRM Activity 6.13: Token Economies

IRM Handout 7.13: Study Dos and Don'ts

IRM Discussion 10.9: Teacher Expectancy

Personal Learning Activity 6.5

IRM Activity 7.4: Depth of Processing

The average performance of U.S. students on tests of reading, math, and other basic academic skills has tended to fall short of that of youngsters in other countries, especially some Asian countries (International Association for the Evaluation of Education Achievement, 1999; National Center for Education Statistics, 2000). In one comparison study, Harold Stevenson (1992) followed a sample of pupils in Taiwan, Japan, and the United States from first grade, in 1980, to eleventh grade, in 1991. In first grade, the Asian students scored no higher than their U.S. peers on tests of mathematical aptitude and skills, nor did they enjoy math more. However, by fifth grade the U.S. students had fallen far behind. Corresponding differences were seen in reading skills.

Some possible causes of these differences were found in the classroom itself. In a typical U.S. classroom session, teachers talked to students as a group; then students worked at their desks independently. Reinforcement or other feedback about performance on their work was usually delayed until the next day or, often, not provided at all. In contrast, the typical Japanese classroom placed greater emphasis on cooperative work among students (Kristof, 1997). Teachers provided more immediate feedback on a one-to-one basis. And there was an emphasis on creating teams of students with varying abilities, an arrangement in which faster learners help teach slower ones. However, before concluding that the differences in performance are the result of social factors alone, we must consider another important distinction: The Japanese children practiced more. They spent more days in school during the year and on average spent more hours doing homework. It is interesting to note that they were also given longer recesses than U.S. students and had more opportunities to get away from the classroom during a typical school day.

Although the significance of these cultural differences in learning and teaching is not yet clear, the educational community in the United States is paying attention to them. Psychologists and educators are also considering how other principles of learning can be applied to improve education (Bransford, Brown, & Cocking, 1999; Woolfolk-Hoy, 1999). Anecdotal and experimental evidence suggests that some of the most successful educational techniques are those that apply basic principles of operant conditioning, offering frequent testing, positive reinforcement for correct performance, and immediate corrective feedback following mistakes (Kass, 1999; Oppel, 2000; Walberg, 1987). Research in cognitive psychology (e.g., Bjork, 1979, 1999) also suggests that students are more likely to retain what they learn if they engage in numerous study sessions rather than in a single "cramming" session on the night before a quiz or exam. To encourage this more beneficial "distributed practice" pattern, researchers say, teachers should give enough exams and quizzes (some unannounced, perhaps) that students will be reading and studying more or less continuously. And because learning is aided by repeated opportunities to use new information, these exams and quizzes should cover material from throughout the term, not just from recent classes. Such recommendations are not necessarily popular with students, but there is good evidence that they promote long-term retention of course material (e.g., Bjork, 1999).

Active Learning

The importance of cognitive processes in learning is apparent in instructional methods that emphasize *active learning* (Bonwell & Eison, 1991). These methods take many forms, such as small-group problem-solving tasks, discussion of "one-minute essays" written in class, use of "thumbs up" or "thumbs down" to indicate agreement or disagreement with the instructor's lecture, and multiple-choice questions that give students feedback about their understanding of the previous fifteen minutes of lecture (Heward, 1997). There is little doubt that for many students, the inclusion of active learning experiences makes classes more interesting and enjoyable (Moran, 2000; Murray, 2000). Active learning methods also provide

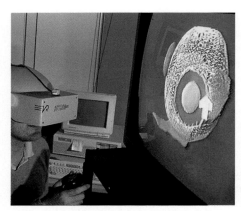

Virtual Surgery   Using a virtual reality system called "Surgery in 3-D," this medical student can actively learn and practice eye surgery skills before working with real patients.

immediate reinforcement and help students to go beyond memorizing isolated facts by encouraging them to think more deeply about new information, consider how it relates to what they already know, and apply it in new situations.

The elaborate mental processing associated with active learning makes new information not only more personally meaningful but also easier to remember. Active learning strategies have been found to be superior to passive teaching methods in a number of experiments with children and adults (Meyers & Jones, 1993). In one study, a fifth-grade science teacher spent some class periods calling on only those students whose hands were raised; the rest listened passively. On other days, all students were required to answer every question by holding up a card on which they had written their response. Scores on next-day quizzes and biweekly tests showed that students remembered more of the material covered on the active learning days than on the "passive" days (Gardner, Heward, & Grossi, 1994). Studies with students in high school, as well as with community college and university students, have found that active learning approaches result in better test performance and greater class participation compared with standard instructional techniques (e.g., Kellum, Carr, & Dozier, 2001). For example, students who passively listened to a physics lecture received significantly lower scores on a test of lecture content than did those who participated in a virtual reality lab that allowed them to "interact" actively with the physical forces covered in the lecture (Brelsford, 1993). Results like these have fueled the development of other science education programs that place students in virtual laboratory environments where they can actively manipulate materials and test hypotheses (e.g., Horwitz & Christie, 2000). Despite the enthusiasm generated by active learning methods, rigorous experimental research is still needed to compare their short- and long-term effects with those of more traditional methods in teaching various kinds of course content.

Skill Learning

The complex action sequences, or *skills,* that people learn to perform in everyday life—tying a shoe, opening a door, operating a computer, shooting a basketball, driving a car—develop through direct and vicarious learning processes involving imitation, instructions, reinforcement, and of course, lots of practice. Some skills, like those of a basketball player or violinist, demand exceptional perceptual-motor coordination. Others, like those involved in scientific thinking, have a large cogni-

Active Learning   Field trips provide students with first-hand opportunities to see and interact with the things they study in the classroom. Such experiences are just one example of the active learning exercises that can help students become more deeply involved in the learning process.

Try It This Way Good coaches provide enough guidance and performance feedback to help budding athletes develop their skills to the fullest, but not so much that the guidance interferes with the learning process. Striking this delicate balance is one of the greatest challenges faced by coaches, and by teachers in general.

OBJ 6.29: Describe the roles of practice and feedback in skill learning.

Test Items 6.161–6.165

tive component, requiring rapid understanding. In either case, the learning of skills usually involves practice and feedback.

Practice—the repeated performance of a skill—is the most critical component of skill learning (Howe, Davidson, & Sloboda, 1998). For perceptual-motor skills, both physical and mental practice are beneficial (Druckman & Bjork, 1994). To be most effective, practice should continue past the point of correct performance until the skill can be performed automatically, with little or no need for attention. As mentioned earlier, in learning many cognitive skills, what counts most seems to be practice in retrieving relevant information from memory. Trying to recall and write down facts that you have read, for example, is a more effective learning tool than simply reading the facts a second time.

Feedback about the correctness of responses is also necessary. As with any learning process, the feedback should come soon enough to be effective, but not so quickly that it interferes with the learner's efforts to learn independently. Large amounts of guidance may produce very good performance during practice, but too much guidance may impair later performance (Wickens, 1992). Coaching students about correct responses in math, for example, may impair their ability later to retrieve the correct response from memory on their own. And in coaching athletes, if feedback is given too soon after an action occurs or while it is still taking place, it may divert the learner's attention from understanding how that action was achieved and what it felt like to perform it (Schmidt & Bjork, 1992). Independent practice at retrieving previously learned responses or information requires more effort, but it is critical for skill development (Ericsson & Charness, 1994). There is little or no evidence to support "sleep learning" or other schemes designed to make learning effortless (Druckman & Bjork, 1994; Phelps & Exum, 1992). In short, "no pain, no gain."

Personal Learning Activity 6.4

ClassPrep: Linkages to Learning

LINKAGES

As noted in the chapter on introducing psychology, all of psychology's many subfields are related to one another. Our discussion of neural networks as possible models of learning illustrates just one way in which the topic of this chapter, learning, is linked to the subfield of perception, which is covered in the chapter on that topic. The Linkages diagram shows ties to two other subfields as well, and there are many more ties throughout the book. Looking for linkages among subfields will help you see how they all fit together and better appreciate the big picture that is psychology.

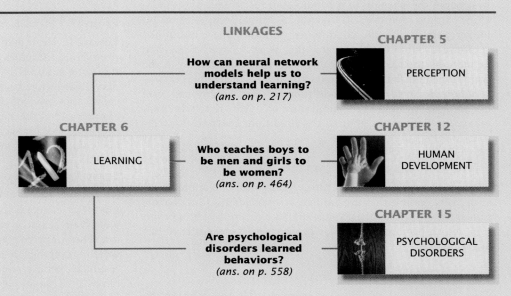

LINKAGES

How can neural network models help us to understand learning? (ans. on p. 217)

CHAPTER 5
PERCEPTION

CHAPTER 6
LEARNING

Who teaches boys to be men and girls to be women? (ans. on p. 464)

CHAPTER 12
HUMAN DEVELOPMENT

Are psychological disorders learned behaviors? (ans. on p. 558)

CHAPTER 15
PSYCHOLOGICAL DISORDERS

SUMMARY

Individuals adapt to changes in the environment through the process of *learning,* which is the modification through experience of pre-existing behavior and understanding.

Learning About Stimuli

One kind of learning is *habituation,* which is reduced responsiveness to a repeated stimulus. According to Richard Solomon's opponent-process theory, habituation results as two processes balance each other. The first process is a relatively automatic response to some stimulus. The second, or opponent, process follows and counteracts the first. This theory may help explain drug tolerance and some overdose cases.

Classical Conditioning: Learning Signals and Associations

Pavlov's Discovery

One form of associative learning is *classical conditioning.* It occurs when a *conditioned stimulus,* or *CS* (such as a tone), is repeatedly paired with an *unconditioned stimulus,* or *UCS* (such as meat powder on a dog's tongue), which naturally brings about an *unconditioned response,* or *UCR* (such as salivation). Eventually the conditioned stimulus will elicit a response, known as the *conditioned response,* or *CR,* even when the unconditioned stimulus is not presented.

Conditioned Responses Over Time: Extinction and Spontaneous Recovery

In general, the strength of a conditioned response grows as CS-UCS pairings continue. If the unconditioned stimulus is no longer paired with the conditioned stimulus, the conditioned response eventually disappears; this is *extinction.* Following extinction, the conditioned response often reappears if the conditioned stimulus is presented after some time; this is *spontaneous recovery.* In addition, if the conditioned and unconditioned stimuli are paired once or twice after extinction, *reconditioning* occurs; that is, the conditioned response reverts to its original strength.

Stimulus Generalization and Discrimination

Because of *stimulus generalization,* conditioned responses are elicited by stimuli that are similar, but not identical, to conditioned stimuli. Generalization is limited by *stimulus discrimination,* which prompts conditioned responses to some stimuli but not to others.

The Signaling of Significant Events

Classical conditioning involves learning that the conditioned stimulus is an event that predicts the occurrence of another event, the unconditioned stimulus. The conditioned response is not just an automatic reflex but also a means through which animals and people develop mental models of the relationships between events. Classical conditioning works best when the conditioned stimulus precedes the unconditioned stimulus, an arrangement known as forward conditioning. Conditioned responses develop best when the conditioned stimulus precedes the unconditioned stimulus by intervals ranging from less than a second to a minute or more, depending on the stimuli involved. Conditioning is also more likely when the conditioned stimulus reliably signals the unconditioned stimulus. In general, the strength of a conditioned response and the speed of conditioning increase as the intensity of the unconditioned stimulus increases. Stronger conditioned stimuli also speed conditioning. The particular conditioned stimulus likely to be linked to a subsequent unconditioned stimulus depends in part on which stimulus was being attended to when the unconditioned stimulus occurred. *Second-order conditioning* occurs when a conditioned stimulus becomes powerful enough to make conditioned stimuli out of stimuli associated with it. Some stimuli are easier to associate than others; organisms seem to be biologically prepared to learn certain associations, as exemplified by taste aversions.

Some Applications of Classical Conditioning

Classical conditioning plays a role in the development and treatment of phobias, in the humane control of predators in the wild, and in procedures for identifying people at risk for Alzheimer's disease.

Instrumental and Operant Conditioning: Learning the Consequences of Behavior

Learning occurs not only through associating stimuli but also through associating behavior with its consequences.

From the Puzzle Box to the Skinner Box

Edward L. Thorndike's *law of effect* holds that any response that produces satisfaction becomes more likely to occur again when the same stimulus is encountered, and any response that produces discomfort becomes less likely to occur again. Thorndike called this type of learning *instrumental conditioning.* B. F. Skinner called the same basic process *operant conditioning.* In operant conditioning the organism is free to respond at any time, and conditioning is measured by the rate of responding.

Basic Components of Operant Conditioning

An *operant* is a response that has some effect on the world. A *reinforcer* increases the probability that the operant preceding it will occur again; in other words, reinforcers strengthen behavior. There are two types of reinforcers: *positive reinforcers,* which strengthen a response if they are presented after that response occurs, and *negative reinforcers,* which are the removal of an unpleasant stimulus following some response. Both kinds of reinforcers strengthen the behaviors that precede them. *Escape conditioning* results when behavior terminates an aversive event. *Avoidance conditioning* results when behavior prevents or avoids an aversive stimulus; it reflects both classical and operant conditioning. Behaviors learned through avoidance conditioning are highly resistant to extinction. *Discriminative stimuli* indicate whether reinforcement is available for a particular behavior.

Forming and Strengthening Operant Behavior

Complex responses can be learned through *shaping,* which involves reinforcing successive approximations of the desired response. *Primary reinforcers* are inherently rewarding; *secondary reinforcers* are rewards that people or animals learn to like because of their association with primary reinforcers. In general, operant conditioning proceeds more quickly when the delay in receiving reinforcement is short rather than long, and when the reinforcer is large rather than small. Reinforcement may be delivered on a *continuous reinforcement schedule* or on one of four basic types of *partial reinforcement schedules* (also called intermittent reinforcement schedules): *fixed-ratio (FR) schedules, variable-ratio (VR) schedules, fixed-interval (FI) schedules,* and *variable-interval (VI) schedules.* Ratio schedules lead to a rapid rate of responding. Behavior learned through partial reinforcement, particularly through variable schedules, is very resistant to extinction; this phenomenon is called the *partial reinforcement extinction effect.* Partial reinforcement is involved in superstitious behavior, which results when a response is coincidentally followed by a reinforcer.

Why Reinforcers Work

Research suggests that reinforcers are rewarding because they provide an organism with the opportunity to engage in desirable activities, which may change from one situation to the next. Another possibility is that activity in the brain's pleasure centers plays a role in reinforcement.

Punishment

Punishment decreases the frequency of a behavior by following it with either an unpleasant stimulus or the removal of a pleasant stimulus. Punishment modifies behavior but has several drawbacks. It only suppresses behavior; fear of punishment may generalize to the person doing the punishing; it is ineffective when delayed; it can be physically harmful and may teach aggressiveness; and it teaches only what not to do, not what should be done to obtain reinforcement.

Some Applications of Operant Conditioning

The principles of operant conditioning have been used in many spheres of life, including the teaching of everyday social skills, the treatment of sleep disorders, the development of self-control, and the improvement of classroom education.

Cognitive Processes in Learning

Cognitive processes—how people represent, store, and use information—play an important role in learning.

Learned Helplessness

Learned helplessness appears to result when people believe that their behavior has no effect on the world.

Latent Learning and Cognitive Maps

Both animals and humans display *latent learning,* learning that is not obvious at the time it occurs. They also form *cognitive maps* of their environments, even in the absence of any reinforcement for doing so.

Insight and Learning

Experiments on *insight* also support the idea that cognitive processes and learned strategies play an important role in learning, perhaps even by animals.

Observational Learning: Learning by Imitation

The process of learning by watching others is called *observational learning,* or social learning. Some observational learning occurs through *vicarious conditioning,* in which an individual is influenced by seeing or hearing about the consequences of others' behavior. Observational learning is more likely to occur when the person observed is rewarded for the observed behavior. Observational learning is a powerful source of socialization.

Using Research on Learning to Help People Learn

Research on how people learn has implications for improved teaching and for the development of a wide range of skills.

Classrooms Across Cultures

The degree to which immediate reinforcement and extended practice are used in teaching varies considerably from culture to culture, but research suggests that the application of these and other basic learning principles is important to promoting effective teaching and learning.

Active Learning

The importance of cognitive processes in learning is seen in active learning methods designed to encourage people to think deeply about and apply new information instead of just memorizing isolated facts.

Skill Learning

Observational learning, practice, and corrective feedback play important roles in the learning of skills.

7

Memory

everal years ago an air-traffic controller at Los Angeles International Airport cleared a US Airways flight to land on runway 24L. A couple of minutes later, the US Airways pilot radioed the control tower that he was on approach for runway 24L, but the controller did not reply because she was preoccupied by a confusing exchange with another pilot. After finishing that conversation, the controller told a Sky West commuter pilot to taxi onto runway 24L for takeoff, completely forgetting about the US Airways plane that was about to land on the same runway. The US Airways jet hit the commuter plane, killing thirty-four people. The controller's forgetting was so complete that she assumed the fireball from the crash was an exploding bomb. How could her memory have failed her at such a crucial time?

Memory is full of paradoxes. It is common, for example, for people to remember the name of their first-grade teacher but not the name of someone they met just a minute before. Like perception, memory is selective. So although we retain a great deal of information, we also lose a great deal (Bjork & Vanhuele, 1992). Consider Rajan Mahadevan, who once set a world's record by reciting from memory the first 31,811 places of pi (the ratio of the circumference of a circle to its diameter). On repeated visits to the psychology building at the University of Minnesota, Mahadevan had trouble recalling the location of the nearest restroom (Biederman et al., 1992)! Similarly, Tatiana Cooley, the U.S. National Memory Champion for three years in a row, says that she is so absent-minded that she relies on Post-it Notes to remember everyday errands (Schacter, 2001). Cases like these show that memory is made up of many component abilities, some of which may operate much more effectively, or less efficiently, than others.

Memory plays a critical role in your life. Without memory, you would not know how to shut off your alarm clock, take a shower, get dressed, or recognize objects. You would be unable to communicate with other people, because you would not remember what words mean, or even what you had just said. You would be unaware of your own likes and dislikes, and you would have no idea of who you are (Craik et al., 1999). In this chapter we describe what is known about both memory and forgetting. First, we discuss what memory is—the different kinds of memory and the different ways we remember things. Then we examine how new memories are acquired and later recalled, and why they are sometimes forgotten. We continue with a discussion of the biological bases of memory, and we conclude with some practical advice for improving memory and studying skills.

Videodisc Segment: Flashbulb Memory

ClassPrep PPT 1: Ch. 7: Memory

IRM Activity 7.6: An All-Purpose Memory Demonstration

The Nature of Memory

Mathematician John Griffith estimated that in an average lifetime, each of us will have stored roughly five hundred times as much information as can be found in all the volumes of the *Encyclopaedia Britannica* (Hunt, 1982). The impressive capacity of human memory depends on the operation of a complex mental system (Schacter, 1999).

Basic Memory Processes

We know a psychologist who sometimes drives to work and sometimes walks. On one occasion, he drove, forgot that he had driven, and walked home. When his car was not in the driveway the next morning, he reported the car stolen. The police soon called to say that "some college kids" had probably stolen the car, because it was found on campus (next to the psychology building!). What went wrong? There are several possibilities, because memory depends on three basic processes: encoding, storage, and retrieval (see Figure 7.1).

First, information must be put into memory, a step that requires **encoding.** Just as incoming sensory information must be coded so that it can be communicated to the brain, information to be remembered must be put in a form that the memory

encoding   The process of putting information into a form that the memory system can accept and use.

figure 7.1

Basic Memory Processes
Remembering something requires, first, that the item be encoded—put in a form that can be placed in memory. It then must be stored and, finally, retrieved, or recovered. If any of these processes fails, forgetting will occur.

ClassPrep PPT 2: *Figure 7.1:* Basic Memory Process

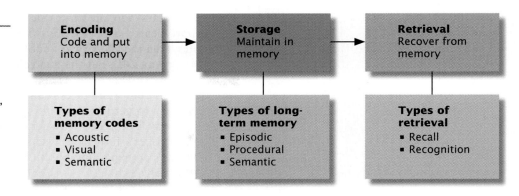

Videodisc Segment: Encoding Information into Memory

OBJ 7.1: Define and give an example of encoding, acoustic encoding, visual encoding, semantic encoding, storage, and retrieval. Discuss the importance of encoding, storage, and retrieval in memory processes.

Test Items 7.1–7.8

Essay Q 7.2

IRM Activty 7.3: Recognition Versus Recall

IRM Activity 7.5: Meaningfulness in Long-Term Memory

ClassPrep PPT 3: Types of Memory

acoustic encoding The mental representation of information as a sequence of sounds.

visual encoding The mental representation of information as images.

semantic encoding The mental representation of an experience by its general meaning.

storage The process of maintaining information in memory over time.

retrieval The process of recalling information stored in memory.

episodic memory Memory of an event that happened while one was present.

semantic memory A type of memory containing generalized knowledge of the world.

procedural memory A type of memory containing information about how to do things.

explicit memory The process in which people intentionally try to remember something.

implicit memory The unintentional influence of prior experiences.

system can accept and use. Sensory information is put into various *memory codes,* which are mental representations of physical stimuli. Suppose you see a billboard that reads "Huey's Going-Out-of-Business Sale," and you want to remember it so you can take advantage of the sale later. If you encode the sound of the words as if they had been spoken, you are using **acoustic encoding,** and the information is represented in your memory as a sequence of sounds. If you encode the image of the letters as they were arranged on the sign, you are using **visual encoding,** and the information is represented in your memory as a picture. Finally, if you encode the fact that you saw an ad for Huey's, you are using **semantic encoding,** and the information is represented in your memory by its general meaning. The type of encoding used can influence what is remembered. For example, semantic encoding might allow you to remember that a car was parked in your neighbors' driveway just before their house was robbed. If there was little or no other encoding, however, you might not be able to remember the make, model, or color of the car.

The second basic memory process is **storage,** which refers to the maintenance of information in memory over time—often over a very long time. When you find you can still use a pogo stick you haven't seen since you were a child or recall a vacation from many years ago, you are depending on the storage capacity of your memory.

The third process, **retrieval,** occurs when you locate information stored in memory and bring it into consciousness. Retrieving stored information such as your address or telephone number is usually so fast and effortless that it seems automatic. Only when you try to retrieve other kinds of information—such as the answer to a quiz question that you know but cannot quite recall—do you become aware of the searching process. Retrieval processes include both recall and recognition. To *recall* information, you have to retrieve it from memory without much help; this is what is required when you answer an essay test question or play *Jeopardy!* In *recognition,* retrieval is aided by clues, such as the response alternatives given on multiple-choice tests and the questions on *Who Wants to Be a Millionaire.* Accordingly, recognition tends to be easier than recall.

Types of Memory

When was the last time you charged something on your credit card? What part of speech is used to modify a noun? How do you keep your balance when you are skiing? To answer these questions, you must use your memory. However, each answer may require a different type of memory (Baddeley, 1998). To answer the first question, you must remember a particular event in your life; to answer the second one, you must recall a piece of general knowledge that is unlikely to be tied to a specific event. And the answer to the final question is difficult to put into words but appears in the form of remembered actions when you get up on skis. How many types of memory are there? No one is sure, but most research suggests that there are at least three basic types. Each type is named for the kind of information it handles: episodic, semantic, and procedural (Best, 1999).

How Does She Do That? As she practices, this young violinist is developing procedural memories of how to play her instrument that will be difficult to put into words. To appreciate the special nature of procedural memory, try writing a step-by-step description of *exactly* how you tie a shoe.

OBJ 7.2: Define and give an example of episodic, semantic, and procedural memories.

Test Items 7.9–7.15

Essay Q. 7.1

Personal Learning Activity 7.1

ClassPrep PPT 4: Explicit and Implicit Memory

OBJ 7.3: Define and give an example of explicit and implicit memories. Discuss the series of experiments on explicit and implicit memory.

Test Items 7.16–7.21

Making Implicit Memories By the time they reach adulthood, these boys may have no explicit memories of the interactions they had in early childhood with friends from differing ethnic groups, but research suggests that their implicit memories of such experiences could have an unconscious effect on their attitudes toward, and judgments about, members of those groups.

Memory of a specific event that happened while you were present—that is, during an "episode" in your life—is called **episodic memory** (Tulving, 1983, in press). Remembering what you had for dinner yesterday, what you did last summer, or where you were last Friday night all require episodic memory. Generalized knowledge of the world that does not involve memory of a specific event is called **semantic memory.** For instance, you can answer a question like "Are wrenches pets or tools?" without remembering any specific event in which you learned that wrenches are tools. As a general rule, people convey episodic memories by saying, "I remember when . . . ," whereas they convey semantic memories by saying, "I know that . . ." (Tulving, 1995). Finally, memory of how to do things, such as riding a bike or tying a shoelace, is called **procedural memory.** Often, procedural memory consists of a complicated sequence of movements that cannot be described adequately in words. For example, a gymnast might find it impossible to describe the exact motions in a particular routine.

Many activities require all three types of memory. Consider the game of tennis. Knowing the official rules or how many sets are needed to win a match involves semantic memory. Remembering which side served last requires episodic memory. Knowing how to lob or volley involves procedural memory.

Explicit and Implicit Memory

Memory can also be categorized in terms of its effects on thoughts and behaviors. For example, you make use of **explicit memory** when you intentionally try to remember something and are consciously aware of doing so (Masson & MacLeod, 1992). Suppose someone asks you about your last vacation. As you think about where you went, you are using explicit memory to recall this episode from your past. Similarly, when responding to an exam question, you use explicit memory to retrieve the information needed to give a correct answer. In contrast, **implicit memory** is the unintentional influence of prior experiences (McDermott, 2000; Nelson, 1999; Schacter, Chiu, & Ochsner, 1993). For example, if you were to read this chapter a second time, implicit memories of its content would help you to read it more quickly than you did the first time. For the same reason, you can solve a puzzle faster if you have solved it in the past. This facilitation of performance (often

called *priming*) is automatic, and it occurs without conscious effort. Perhaps you've found yourself disliking someone you just met, but you didn't know why. One explanation is that implicit memory may have been at work. Specifically, you may have reacted in this way because the person bore a resemblance to someone from your past who treated you badly. In such instances, people are usually unable to recall the person from the past and are unaware of any connection between the two individuals (Lewicki, 1985). Episodic, semantic, and procedural memories can be explicit or implicit, but procedural memory usually operates implicitly. This is why, for example, you can skillfully ride a bike even though you cannot explicitly remember all the procedures necessary to do so.

It is not surprising that experience affects how people behave. What is surprising is that they are often unaware that their actions have been influenced by previous events. Because some influential events cannot be recalled even when people try to do so, implicit memory has been said to involve "retention without remembering" (Roediger, 1990).

FOCUS ON RESEARCH METHODS

Measuring Explicit Versus Implicit Memory

In Canada, Endel Tulving and his colleagues undertook a series of experiments to map the differences between explicit and implicit memory (Tulving, Schacter, & Stark, 1982).

ClassPrep PPTs 4 & 46: Focus on Research Methods: Measuring Explicit Versus Implicit Memory

● What was the researcher's question?

Tulving knew he could measure explicit memory by giving a recognition test in which participants simply said which words on a list they remembered seeing on a previous list. The question was, How would it be possible to measure implicit memory?

● How did the researcher answer the question?

First, Tulving asked the participants in his experiment to study a long list of words—the "study list." An hour later, they took a recognition test involving explicit memory—saying which words on a new list had been on the original study list. Then, to test their implicit memory, Tulving asked them to perform a "fragment completion" task (Warrington & Weiskrantz, 1970). In this task, participants were shown a "test list" of word fragments, such as *d_li__u_*, and asked to complete the word (in this case, *delirium*). On the basis of priming studies such as those described in the chapter on consciousness, Tulving assumed that memory from a previous exposure to the correct word would improve the participants' ability to complete the fragment, even if they were unable to consciously recall having seen the word before. A week later, all participants took a second test of their explicit memory (recognition) and implicit memory (fragment completion) of the study list. Some of the words on this second test list had been on the original study list, but none had been used in the first set of memory tests. The independent variable in this experiment, then, was the amount of time that had elapsed since the participants read the study list (one hour versus one week), and the dependent variable was performance on each of the two types of memory tests, explicit and implicit.

● What did the researcher find?

As shown in Figure 7.2, explicit memory for the study list decreased dramatically over time, but implicit memory (or priming) was virtually unchanged. Results from several other experiments also show that the passage of time affects explicit memory more than implicit memory (Komatsu & Naito, 1992; Mitchell, 1991). For example, it appears that the aging process has fewer negative effects on implicit memory than on explicit memory (Light, 1991).

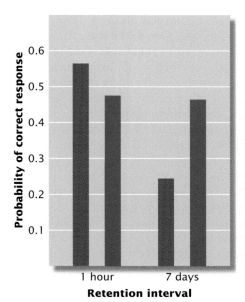

Recognition (explicit)

Fragment completion (implicit)

figure 7.2

Measures of Explicit and Implicit Memory

This experiment showed that the passage of time greatly affected people's recognition (explicit memory) of a word list but left fragment completion (implicit memory) essentially intact. Results such as these suggest that explicit and implicit memory may be different memory systems.

Source: Tulving, Schacter, & Stark (1982).

levels-of-processing model A view stating that how well something is remembered depends on the degree to which incoming information is mentally processed.

maintenance rehearsal Repeating information over and over to keep it active in short-term memory.

● **What do the results mean?**

The work of Tulving and others supports the idea of a dissociation, or independence, between explicit and implicit memory, suggesting that the two may operate on different principles (Gabrieli et al., 1995). In fact, some researchers believe that explicit and implicit memory may involve the activity of distinct neural systems in the brain (Squire, 1987; Tulving & Schacter, 1990). Others argue that the two types of memory are best described as requiring different cognitive processes (Nelson, McKinney, & Bennett, 1999; Roediger, Guynn, & Jones, 1995; Roediger & McDermott, 1995).

● **What do we still need to know?**

Psychologists are studying the role of implicit memory (and dissociations between explicit and implicit memory) in such important psychological phenomena as amnesia (Schacter, Church, & Treadwell, 1994; Tulving, 1993), depression (Elliott & Greene, 1992), problem solving (Jacoby, Marriott, & Collins, 1990), prejudice and stereotyping (Fiske, 1998), the development of self-concept in childhood (Nelson, 1993), and even the power of ads to associate brand names with good feelings (Duke & Carlson, 1994). The results of these studies should shed new light on implicit memory and how it operates in the real world.

For example, some social psychologists are trying to determine whether consciously held attitudes are independent of *implicit social cognitions*—past experiences that unconsciously influence a person's judgments about a group of people (Greenwald & Banaji, 1995). A case in point would be a person whose explicit thoughts about members of some ethnic group are positive but whose implicit thoughts are negative. Early work on implicit memory for stereotypes seemed to indicate that explicit and implicit stereotypes are independent (Devine, 1989), but more recent research suggests that they are related to some extent (Lepore & Brown, 1997). Further research is needed to determine what mechanisms are responsible for implicit versus explicit memory and how these two kinds of memory are related to one another (Lustig & Hasher, 2001; Nelson et al., 1998). That research will be facilitated by functional neuroimaging techniques. As described later, these techniques allow scientists to "watch" the brain's activity during various memory tasks, and to determine which areas are associated with the explicit and implicit cognitive processes involved in these tasks (Roediger, Buckner, & McDermott, 1999).

Models of Memory

We remember some information far better than other information. For example, suppose your friends throw a surprise party for you. When you enter the room, you might barely notice, and later fail to recall, the flash from a camera. And you might forget in a few seconds the name of a person you met at the party. But if you live to be a hundred, you will never forget where the party took place or how surprised and pleased you were. Why do some stimuli leave no more than a fleeting impression and others remain in memory forever? Each of four models of memory provides a somewhat different explanation. Let's see how the levels-of-processing, transfer-appropriate processing, parallel distributed processing, and information-processing models look at memory.

Levels of Processing   The **levels-of-processing model** suggests that the most important determinant of memory is how extensively information is encoded or processed when it is first received (Craik & Lockhart, 1972; Craik & Tulving, 1975). Consider situations in which people try to memorize something by mentally rehearsing it. There appear to be two basic types of mental rehearsal: maintenance and elaborative. **Maintenance rehearsal** involves simply repeating an item over and

IRM Activity 7.4: Depth of Processing

IRM Activity 7.5: Meaningfulness in Long-Term Memory

ClassPrep PPT 6: Transfer-Appropriate Processing Model of Memory

OBJ 7.5: Define transfer-appropriate processing. Describe the role of encoding and retrieval processes in this memory model.

Test Items 7.31–7.33

ClassPrep PPT 7: Other Models of Memory

OBJ 7.6: Define the parallel distributed processing (PDP) model of memory. Describe the role of association networks in drawing inferences and making generalizations.

Test Items 7.34–7.36

elaborative rehearsal   A memorization method that involves thinking about how new information relates to information already stored in long-term memory.

transfer-appropriate processing model   A model of memory that suggests that a critical determinant of memory is how well the retrieval process matches the original encoding process.

parallel distributed processing (PDP) models   Memory models in which new experiences change one's overall knowledge base.

information-processing model   A model of memory in which information is seen as passing through sensory memory, short-term memory, and long-term memory.

over. This method can be effective for remembering information for a short time. If you look up a phone number, pick up the phone, and then make the call, maintenance rehearsal works just fine. But what if you need to remember something for hours or months or years? In these cases, you are better off using **elaborative rehearsal**, which involves thinking about how new material relates to information already stored in memory. For, instead of trying to remember a new person's name by simply repeating it to yourself, try thinking about how the name is related to something you already know. If you are introduced to a man named Jim Crews, for example, you might think, "He is as tall as my Uncle Jim, who always wears a crew cut."

Study after study has shown that memory is enhanced when people use elaborative rather than maintenance rehearsal (Jahnke & Nowaczyk, 1998). According to the levels-of-processing model, this enhancement occurs because of the degree or "depth" to which incoming information is mentally processed during elaborative rehearsal (Lockhart & Craik, 1990). The more you think about new information, organize it, and relate it to existing knowledge, the "deeper" the processing, and the better your memory of it becomes. Teachers use this idea when they ask their students not only to define a new word but also to use it in a sentence. Figuring out how to use the new word takes deeper processing than merely defining it. (The next time you come across an unfamiliar word in this book, don't just read its definition. Try to use the word in a sentence by coming up with an example of the concept that relates to your knowledge and experience.)

Transfer-Appropriate Processing

The level of processing is not the only factor affecting what we remember (Baddeley, 1992). Another critical factor, suggested by the **transfer-appropriate processing model**, is how well the processes involved during retrieval match the way in which the information was initially encoded. Consider an experiment in which people were shown sentences with a word missing and were then asked one of two types of questions about the missing word (Morris, Bransford, & Franks, 1977). Some questions were designed so that participants would encode the target word using its meaning (semantic encoding). For example, one sentence read, "A _____ is a building," and participants were asked whether the target word *house* should go in the blank space. Other questions were designed to create a rhyming code. For example, participants were shown the sentence "_____ rhymes with legal" and asked whether the target word *eagle* rhymed with *legal*.

Later, the participants were given two kinds of memory tasks. On one task, they were asked to select from a list the target words they had been shown earlier. As Figure 7.3 shows, the participants did much better at recognizing the words for which they had used a semantic code rather than a rhyming code. On the other task, they were asked to pick out words that *rhymed* with the ones they had seen (e.g., *grouse*, which rhymes with *house*). Here, they did much better at identifying words that *rhymed* with those for which they had used a rhyming code rather than a semantic code. Results like these illustrate the concept of *transfer-appropriate processing*, which suggests that memory is better when the processes people use during retrieval match the processes they used during encoding

Parallel Distributed Processing

A third approach to memory is based on **parallel distributed processing (PDP) models** of memory (Rumelhart & McClelland, 1986). These models suggest that new experiences don't just provide new facts that are later retrieved individually; those facts are also integrated with existing knowledge or memories, changing our overall knowledge base and altering in a more general way our understanding of the world and how it operates. For example, when you first arrived at college, you learned specific facts, such as where classes are held, what time the library closes, and where to get the best pizza. Over

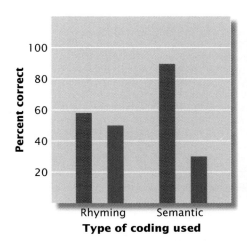

■ Recognition test

■ Identification test

figure 7.3

The Match Between Encoding and Retrieval

People who were asked to recognize words seen earlier did better if they had encoded the words on the basis of their meaning (semantic coding) rather than on the basis of what they rhymed with. But if asked to identify words that *rhymed* with those seen before, they did better on those that had been encoded using a rhyming code. These results support the transfer-appropriate processing model of memory.

OBJ 7.7: Define the information-processing model of memory. Name the three stages of processing.

Test Items 7.37–7.39

ClassPrep PPT 8: *Figure 7.4:* The Three Stages of Memory

time, these and many other facts of college life form a network of information that creates a more general understanding of how the whole college system works. Developing this network makes you more knowledgeable, but also more sophisticated. It allows you to, say, allocate your study time so as to do well in your most important courses, and to plan a schedule that avoids conflicts between classes, work, and recreational activities. In other words, your knowledge of college life changes day by day in a way that is much more general than any single new fact you learned.

PDP models of memory reflect this notion of knowledge networks. PDP memory theorists begin by considering how *neural networks*—described in the chapters on perception and learning—might provide a functional memory system (Anderson, 1990b). They suggest that each unit of knowledge is ultimately connected to every other unit, and that the connections between units become stronger as they are experienced together more frequently. From this perspective, then, "knowledge" is distributed across a dense network of associations. When this network is activated, *parallel processing* occurs; that is, different portions of the network operate simultaneously, allowing people to quickly and efficiently draw inferences and make generalizations. Just seeing the word *sofa*, for example, allows us immediately to gain access to knowledge about what a sofa looks like, what it is used for, where it tends to be located, who might buy one, and the like. PDP models of memory explain this process very effectively.

Information Processing   Historically, the most influential and comprehensive theories of memory have been based on a general **information-processing model** (Roediger, 1990). The information-processing model originally suggested that in order for information to become firmly embedded in memory, it must pass through three stages of mental processing: sensory memory, short-term memory, and long-term memory (Atkinson & Shiffrin, 1968; see Figure 7.4).

In *sensory memory*, information from the senses—sights or sounds, for example—is held in sensory registers for a very brief period of time, often for less than one second. Information in the sensory registers may be attended to, analyzed, and encoded as a meaningful pattern; this is the process of perception, as discussed in the chapter on that topic. If the information in sensory memory is perceived, it can enter *short-term memory*. If nothing further is done, the information will disappear in less than twenty seconds. But if the information in short-term memory is further processed, it may be encoded into *long-term memory*, where it may remain indefinitely.

Contemporary versions of the information-processing model emphasize the constant interactions among sensory, short-term, and long-term memory (Massaro & Cowan, 1993; Wagner, 1999). For example, sensory memory can be thought of as that part of your knowledge base (or long-term memory) that is momentarily activated by information sent to the brain via the sensory nerves. And short-term memory can be thought of as that part of your knowledge base that is the focus of attention at any given moment. Like perception, memory is an active process, and what is already in long-term memory influences how new information is encoded (Cowan, 1988). To understand this interaction better, try the exercise in Figure 7.5.

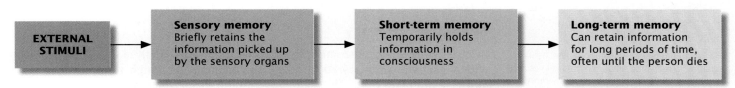

EXTERNAL STIMULI

Sensory memory Briefly retains the information picked up by the sensory organs

Short-term memory Temporarily holds information in consciousness

Long-term memory Can retain information for long periods of time, often until the person dies

figure 7.4

The Three Stages of Memory

This traditional information-processing model describes three stages in the memory system.

figure 7.5

The Role of Memory in Comprehension

TRY THIS Read the passage shown here; then turn away and try to recall as much of it as possible. Then read the footnote on page 234, and reread the passage. The second reading probably made a lot more sense and was much easier to remember, because knowing the title of the passage allowed you to retrieve from long-term memory your knowledge about the topic.

Source: Bransford & Johnson (1972).

The procedure is actually quite simple. First, you arrange items into different groups. Of course, one pile may be sufficient, depending on how much there is to do. If you have to go somewhere else due to lack of facilities that is the next step; otherwise, you are pretty well set. It is important not to overdo things. That is, it is better to do too few things at once than too many. In the short run, this may not seem important, but complications can easily arise. A mistake can be expensive as well. At first, the whole procedure will seem complicated. Soon, however, it will become just another facet of life. It is difficult to foresee any end to the necessity for this task in the immediate future, but then, one never can tell. After the procedure is completed, one arranges the materials into different groups again. Then they can be put into their appropriate places. Eventually they will be used once more, and the whole cycle will then have to be repeated. However, that is part of life.

in review — Models of Memory

Model	Assumptions
Levels of processing	The more deeply material is provessed, the better the memory of it.
Transfer-appropriate processing	Retrieval is improved when we try to recall material in a way that matches how the material was encoded.
Parallel distributed processing (PDP)	New experiences add to and alter our overall knowledge base; they are not separate, unconnected facts. PDP networks allow us to draw inferences and make generalizations about the world.
Information processing	Information is processed in three stages: sensory, short-term, and long-term memory.

For a summary of the four models we have discussed, see "In Review: Models of Memory." Each of these models provides an explanation of why we remember some things and forget others, but which one offers the best explanation? The answer is that more than one model may be required to understand memory. Just as it is helpful for physicists to characterize light in terms of both waves and particles, psychologists find it useful to think of memory as both a serial or sequential process, as suggested by the information-processing model, and as a parallel process, as suggested by parallel distributed processing models.

ClassPrep PPT 9: Sensory Memory

Storing New Memories

Videodisc Still: Encoding Information into Memory

The information-processing model suggests that sensory, short-term, and long-term memory each provide a different type of storage system.

Sensory Memory

OBJ 7.8: Define sensory memory and sensory registers. Discuss the amount of information and the length of time it stays in sensory memory.

Test Items 7.40–7.44

In order to recognize incoming stimuli, the brain must analyze and compare them with what is already stored in long-term memory. Although this process is very quick, it still takes time. The major function of **sensory memory** is to hold information long enough for it to be processed further. This maintenance is the job of the **sensory registers**, whose storage capability retains an almost complete representation of a sensory stimulus (Best, 1999). There is a separate register for each of the

 Sensory Memory at Work In a darkened room, ask a friend to hold a small flashlight, and move it very slowly in a circle. You will see a moving point of light. If it appears to have a "tail," like a comet, that is your sensory memory of the light before the memory fades. Now ask your friend to speed up the movement. You should now see a complete circle of light, because as the light moves, its impression on your sensory memory does not have time to fade before the circle is completed. A similar process allows us to see "sparkler circles" and still images that "move" when we watch a film or video (see our discussion of stroboscopic motion in the chapter on sensation).

Test Items 7.45–7.46

Test Items 7.47–7.51

TRY THIS

ClassPrep PPT 10: Short-Term and Working Memory

Personal Learning Activity 7.3

---

sensory memory A type of memory that holds large amounts of incoming information very briefly, but long enough to connect one impression to the next.

sensory registers Memory systems that hold incoming information long enough for it to be processed further.

selective attention The focusing of mental resources on only part of the stimulus field.

short-term memory (STM) The maintenance component of working memory, which holds unrehearsed information for a limited time.

working memory The part of the memory system that allows us to mentally work with, or manipulate, information being held in short-term memory.

---

five senses, and every register is capable of storing a relatively large amount of stimulus information.

Memories held in the sensory registers are fleeting, but they last long enough for stimulus identification to begin (Eysenck & Keane, 1995). As you read a sentence, for example, you identify and interpret the first few words. At the same time, subsequent words are being scanned, and these are maintained in your visual sensory register until you can process them as well.

Sensory memory helps bring coherence and continuity to your world. To appreciate this fact, turn your head slowly from left to right. Your eyes may seem to be moving smoothly, like a movie camera scanning a scene, but this is not what is happening. Your eyes fixate at one point for about one-fourth of a second and then rapidly jump to a new position. The sensation of smoothness occurs because the scene is held in the visual sensory register until your eyes fixate again. Similarly, when you listen to someone speak, the auditory sensory register allows you to experience a smooth flow of information. Information persists for varying amounts of time in the five sensory registers. For example, information in the auditory sensory register lasts longer than information in the visual sensory register.

The fact that sensory memories quickly fade if they are not processed further is an adaptive characteristic of the memory system (Martindale, 1991). One simply cannot deal with all of the sights, sounds, odors, tastes, and tactile sensations that impinge on the sense organs at any given moment. As mentioned in the chapter on perception, **selective attention** focuses mental resources on only part of the stimulus field, thus controlling what information is processed further. It is through the process of perception that the elusive impressions of sensory memory are captured and transferred to short-term memory.

Short-Term Memory and Working Memory

The sensory registers allow your memory system to develop a representation of a stimulus, but they do not allow the more thorough representation and analysis needed if the information is going to be used in some way. These functions are accomplished by short-term memory and working memory.

Short-term memory (STM) is the part of our memory system that stores limited amounts of information for a limited amount of time. When you check *TV Guide* for the channel number of a show and then switch to that channel, you are using short-term memory. **Working memory** is the part of the memory system that allows us to mentally work with, or manipulate, the information being held in short-term memory. So short-term memory is actually a component of working memory. Together, they enable us to do many kinds of mental work (Baddeley, 1992; Engle & Oransky, 1999). Suppose you are buying something for 83 cents, and you go through your change and pick out two quarters, two dimes, two nickels, and three pennies. To do this, you use both short-term and working memory to remember the price, retrieve the rules of addition from long-term memory, *and* keep a running count of how much change you have so far. Now try to recall how many windows there are on the front of the house or apartment where you grew up. In attempting to answer this question, you probably formed a mental image of the building, which required one kind of working-memory process, and then, while maintaining that image in short-term memory, you "worked" on it by counting the windows. In short, working memory has at least two components: *maintenance* (holding information in short-term memory) and *manipulation* (working on that information).

Encoding in Short-Term Memory
The encoding of information in short-term memory is much more elaborative and varied than that in the sensory registers (Brandimonte, Hitch, & Bishop, 1992). *Acoustic encoding* (by sound) seems to dominate. Evidence in support of this assertion comes from analyzing the mistakes people make when encoding information in short-term memory. These

figure 7.6

Capacity of Short-Term Memory

TRY THIS — Here is a test of your immediate memory span. Ask someone to read to you the numbers in the top row at the rate of about one per second; then try to repeat them back in the same order. Then try the next row, and the one after that, until you make a mistake. Your immediate memory span is the maximum number of items you can repeat back perfectly. Similar tests can be performed using the rows of letters and words.

ClassPrep PPT 11: Test Your Short-Term Memory

ClassPrep PPT 12: Figure 7.6: Capacity of Short-Term Memory

```
9  2  5                        G  M  N
8  6  4  2                     S  L  R  R
3  7  6  5  4                  V  O  E  P  G
6  2  7  4  1  8               X  W  D  X  Q  O
0  4  0  1  4  7  3            E  P  H  H  J  A  E
1  9  2  2  3  5  3  0         Z  D  O  F  W  D  S  V
4  8  6  8  5  4  3  3  2      D  T  Y  N  R  H  E  H  Q
2  5  3  1  9  7  1  7  6  8   K  H  W  D  A  G  R  O  F  Z
8  5  1  2  9  6  1  9  4  5  0  U  D  F  F  W  H  D  Q  D  G  E
9  1  8  5  4  6  9  4  2  9  3  7  Q  M  R  H  X  Z  D  P  R  R  E  H
```

```
CAT  BOAT  RUG
RUN  BEACH  PLANT  LIGHT
SUIT  WATCH  CUT  STAIRS  CAR
JUNK  LONE  GAME  CALL  WOOD  HEART
FRAME  PATCH  CROSS  DRUG  DESK  HORSE  LAW
CLOTHES  CHOOSE  GIFT  DRIVE  BOOK  TREE  HAIR  THIS
DRESS  CLERK  FILM  BASE  SPEND  SERVE  BOOK  LOW  TIME
STONE  ALL  NAIL  DOOR  HOPE  EARL  FEEL  BUY  COPE  GRAPE
AGE  SOFT  FALL  STORE  PUT  TRUE  SMALL  FREE  CHECK  MAIL  LEAF
LOG  DAY  TIME  CHESS  LAKE  CUT  BIRD  SHEET  YOUR  SEE  STREET  WHEEL
```

OBJ 7.11: Describe short-term memory encoding.

Test Items 7.52–7.56

IRM Activity 7.8: Short-Term Memory

OBJ 7.12: Define immediate memory span and chunks. Discuss the role of long-term memory in the chunking process.

Test Items 7.57–7.64

immediate memory span The maximum number of items a person can recall perfectly after one presentation of the items.

chunks Stimuli that are perceived as one unit or as a meaningful grouping of information.

mistakes tend to be acoustically related, which means that they involve the substitution of similar sounds. For example, Robert Conrad (1964) showed people strings of letters and asked them to repeat the letters immediately. Their mistakes tended to involve replacing the correct letter (say, *C*) with another that *sounded* like it (such as *D*, *P*, or *T*). These mistakes occurred even though the letters were presented visually, without any sound.

Evidence for acoustic coding in short-term memory also comes from studies showing that items are more difficult to remember if their spoken sounds are similar. For example, native English speakers do less well when asked to remember a string of letters like *ECVTGB* (which all have similar sounds) than when asked to remember one like *KRLDQS* (which have distinct sounds). Encoding in short-term memory is not *always* acoustic, however. Visual codes are also used (Zhang & Simon, 1985), but information coded visually tends to fade much more quickly from short-term memory than information that is encoded acoustically (Cornoldi, DeBeni, & Baldi, 1989). There is also evidence for kinesthetic encoding, which involves physical movements (Best, 1999). In one study, deaf people were shown a list of words and then asked to immediately write them down from memory (Shand, 1982). When these people made errors, they wrote words that are expressed through similar *hand movements* in American Sign Language, rather than words that *sounded* similar to the correct words. Apparently, these individuals had encoded the words on the basis of the movements they would use when signing them.

Storage Capacity of Short-Term Memory　　You can easily determine the capacity of short-term memory by conducting the simple experiment shown in Figure 7.6 (Howard, 1983). Your **immediate memory span** is the maximum number of items you are able to recall perfectly after one presentation. If your memory span is like most people's, you can repeat about six or seven items from the test in this figure. The interesting thing is that you should come up with about

---

The title of the passage in Figure 7.5 is "Washing Clothes."

ClassPrep PPT 13: The Power of Chunking

TRY THIS

Videodisc Segment & Still: Chunking

IRM Activity 7.5: Meaningfulness in Long-Term Memory

IRM Activity 7.6: An All-Purpose Memory Demonstration

IRM Activity 7.7: Chunking Pi

the same number whether you estimate your immediate memory span with digits, letters, words, or virtually any type of unit (Pollack, 1953). George Miller (1956) noticed that studies of a wide variety of tasks showed the same limit on the ability to process information. This "magic number," which is seven plus or minus two, appears to be the capacity of short-term memory. In addition, the "magic number" refers not only to discrete elements, such as words or digits, but also to meaningful *groupings* of information, called **chunks.**

To appreciate the difference between discrete elements and chunks, read the following letters to a friend, pausing at each dash: *FB-IAO-LM-TVI-BMB-MW.* The chances are very good that your friend will not be able to repeat this string of letters perfectly. Why? There are fifteen letters, which exceeds most people's immediate memory span. Now, give your friend the test again, but group the letters like this: *FBI-AOL-MTV-IBM-BMW.* Your friend will probably repeat that string easily because, even though the same fifteen letters are involved, they will be processed as only five meaningful chunks of information (Bower, 1975).

The Power of Chunking   Chunks of information can become very complex. If someone read to you, "The boy in the red shirt kicked his mother in the shin," you could probably repeat the sentence very easily. Yet it contains twelve words and forty-three letters. How can you repeat the sentence so effortlessly? The answer is that people can build bigger and bigger chunks of information (Ericsson & Staszewski, 1989). In this case, you might represent "the boy in the red shirt" as one chunk of information rather than as six words or nineteen letters. Similarly, "kicked his mother" and "in the shin" represent separate chunks of information.

Learning to use bigger and bigger chunks of information can enhance short-term memory. Children's memories improve in part because they gradually become able to hold as many as seven chunks in memory, but also because they become better able to group information into chunks (Servan-Schreiber & Anderson, 1990). Adults, too, can greatly increase the capacity of their short-term memory by more appropriate chunking (Waldrop, 1987); one college student increased his immediate memory span from seven digits to eighty digits (Neisser, 2000). In short, although the capacity of short-term memory is more or less constant—five to nine chunks of meaningful information—the size of those chunks can vary tremendously.

Chunking in Action   People who provide instantaneous translation of speeches—such as this one by Kofi Annan, the Nobel Prize–winning secretary general of the United Nations—must store long, often complicated segments of speech in short-term memory while searching long-term memory for the equivalent second-language expressions. The task is made easier by chunking the speaker's words into phrases and sentences.

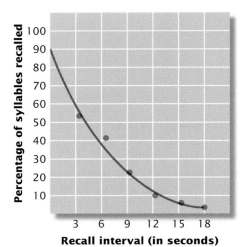

figure 7.7

Forgetting in Short-Term Memory

This graph shows the percentage of nonsense syllables recalled after various intervals during which rehearsal was prevented. Notice that virtually complete forgetting occurred after a delay of eighteen seconds.

Source: Data from Peterson & Peterson (1959).

OBJ 7.13: Define the Brown-Peterson procedure. Describe the importance of rehearsal in maintaining information in short-term memory.

Test Items 7.65–7.67

ClassPrep PPT 15: Long-Term Memory (LTM)

OBJ 7.14: Define long-term memory (LTM) and discuss the importance of semantic encoding in long-term memory. Describe the storage capacity of LTM.

Test Items 7.68–7.70

IRM Activity 7.9: Constructive Memory: The Rumor Chain

Brown-Peterson procedure A method for determining how long unrehearsed information remains in short-term memory.

long-term memory (LTM) A relatively long-lasting stage of memory whose capacity to store new information is believed to be unlimited.

Duration of Short-Term Memory   Imagine how hard it would be to, say, mentally calculate the tip you should leave in a restaurant if your short-term memory was cluttered with every other bill you had ever paid, every phone number you had ever called, and every conversation you had ever heard. This problem doesn't come up because—unless you continue repeating information to yourself (maintenance rehearsal) or use elaborative rehearsal to transfer it to long-term memory—information in short-term memory is usually forgotten quickly. You may have experienced this adaptive, though sometimes inconvenient, phenomenon if you have ever been interrupted while repeating to yourself a new phone number you were about to call, and then couldn't remember the number.

How long does unrehearsed information remain in short-term memory? To answer this question, John Brown (1958) and Lloyd and Margaret Peterson (1959) devised the **Brown-Peterson procedure**, which is a method for preventing rehearsal. A person is presented with a group of three letters, such as *GRB*, and then counts backward by threes from some number until a signal is given. Counting prevents the person from rehearsing the letters. At the signal, the person stops counting and tries to recall the letters. By varying the number of seconds that the person counts backward, the experimenter can determine how much forgetting takes place over a certain amount of time. As you can see in Figure 7.7, information in short-term memory is forgotten gradually but rapidly: After eighteen seconds, participants can remember almost nothing. Evidence from these and other experiments suggests that unrehearsed information can be maintained in short-term memory for no more than about eighteen seconds. However, if the information is rehearsed or processed further, it may be encoded into long-term memory.

Long-Term Memory

When people talk about memory, they are in fact usually talking about **long-term memory (LTM)**, which is the part of the memory system whose encoding and storage capabilities can produce memories that last a lifetime.

Videodisc Segment & Still: Encoding Into Long-Term Memory

Encoding in Long-Term Memory   Some information is encoded into long-term memory without any conscious attempt to memorize it (Ellis, 1991). However, putting information into long-term memory is often the result of a relatively deep level of conscious processing, which usually involves some degree of *semantic encoding*. In other words, encoding in long-term memory often ignores details and instead encodes the general, underlying meaning of the information.

Jacqueline Sachs (1967) demonstrated the dominance of semantic encoding in long-term memory in a classic study. She first asked people to listen to tape-recorded passages. She then showed them sentences and asked them to say which contained the exact wording heard in the taped passage. People did very well when they were tested *immediately* (using mainly short-term memory). However, after only twenty-seven seconds, at which point the information had to be retrieved from long-term memory, they could not determine which of two sentences they had heard if both sentences expressed the same meaning. For example, they could not determine whether they had heard "He sent a letter about it to Galileo, the great Italian scientist" or "A letter about it was sent to Galileo, the great Italian scientist." In short, they remembered the general meaning of what they had heard, but not the exact wording.

Perhaps you are thinking, "So what?" After all, the two sentences mean the same thing. However, psychologists have found that when people encode the general meaning of information, they may make mistakes about the specifics of what they have heard. For example, after hearing "The karate champion hit the cinderblock," people often remember having heard "The karate champion broke the cinderblock" (Brewer, 1977). When recalling exact words is important—such as in the courtroom, during business negotiations, and in discussions between parents

(A)   (B)   (C)   (D)   (E)

figure 7.8

figure 7.8

Encoding into Long-Term Memory

 Which is the correct image of a U.S. penny? (See page 238 for the answer.) Although most people often cannot explicitly remember the specific details of information stored in long-term memory, priming studies suggest that they do retain some implicit memory of them (e.g., Srinivas, 1993).

Source: Nickerson & Adams (1979).

ClassPrep PPT 16: *Figure 7.8:* Which Is the Correct Image of a U.S. Penny?

ClassPrep PPT 17: Storage Capacity of Long-Term Memory

Personal Learning Activity 7.3

and children about previous agreements—people are often wrong about what someone actually said. As discussed later in this chapter, these errors occur partly because people encode into long-term memory not only the general meaning of information but also what they think and assume about that information (Hannigan & Reinitz, 2001). Those expectations and assumptions—that karate champions always break what they hit, for example—may color what is recalled.

Counterfeiters depend on the fact that people encode only the general meaning of visual, as well as auditory, stimuli. For example, look at Figure 7.8, and find the correct drawing of the U.S. penny (Nickerson & Adams, 1979). Most people from the United States are unsuccessful at this task, just as people from Great Britain do poorly at recognizing their country's coins (Jones, 1990). Research showing that people fail to remember specific details about visual information has prompted the U.S. Treasury to begin using more distinctive drawings on the paper currencies it distributes.

Although long-term memory normally involves semantic encoding, people can also use visual encoding to process images into long-term memory. In one study, people viewed 2,500 pictures. It took 16 hours just to present the stimuli, but the participants later correctly recognized more than 90 percent of the pictures tested (Standing, Conezio, & Haber, 1970). *Dual coding theory* suggests that the reason pictures tend to be remembered better than words is that pictures are represented in two codes—visual and semantic—rather than in only one (Paivio, 1986). This assertion is supported by neuroimaging studies showing that when people are asked to memorize pictures, they tend to create a semantic label for the picture (e.g., *frog*), as well as look at the drawing's visual features (Kelley et al., 1998).

Storage Capacity of Long-Term Memory   Whereas the capacity of short-term memory is limited, the capacity of long-term memory is extremely large; in fact, most theorists believe it to be unlimited (Matlin, 1998). The unlimited capacity of long-term memory is impossible to prove, but there are no cases of people being unable to learn something new because they had too much information stored in long-term memory. We do know for sure that people store vast quantities of information in long-term memory, and that they often remember it remarkably well for long periods of time. For example, people are amazingly accurate at recognizing the faces of their high school classmates after not having seen them for over twenty-five years (Bruck, Cavanagh, & Ceci, 1991), and they do surprisingly well on tests of a foreign language or high school algebra fifty years after having formally studied these subjects (Bahrick & Hall, 1991; Bahrick et al., 1994).

However, long-term memories are also subject to distortion. In one study, college students were asked to recall their high school grades. Even though the students were motivated to be accurate, they correctly remembered 89 percent of their A grades but only 29 percent of their D grades. And perhaps it should not be surprising that when they made errors, these usually involved recalling grades as being higher than they actually were (Bahrick, Hall, & Berger, 1996). In another study, students were asked to describe where they were and what they were doing at the moment they heard about the verdict in the O. J. Simpson murder trial (Schmolck, Buffalo, & Squire, 2000). The students reported their recollections three times, first just three days after the verdict, and then again after

A Photographic Memory   Franco Magnani had been away from his hometown in Italy for more than thirty years, but he could still paint it from memory (see comparison photo; Sacks, 1992). People like Magnani display *eidetic imagery*, commonly called *photographic memory*; they have automatic, detailed, and vivid images of virtually everything they have ever seen. About 5 percent of all school-age children have eidetic imagery, but almost no adults have it (Haber, 1979).

ClassPrep PPTs 18 & 19: A Recall Experiment

OBJ 7.15: Describe the controversy over the differences between short-term and long-term memory. Define primacy and recency effects.

Test Items 7.71–7.77

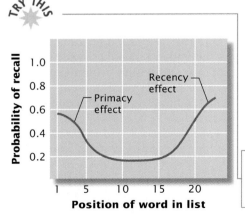

figure 7.9

A Serial-Position Curve
The probability of recalling an item is plotted here as a function of its serial position in a list of items. Generally, the first several items and the last several items are the most likely to be recalled.

fifteen and thirty-two months. At the final reporting, almost all the students claimed they could still remember accurately where they were and what they were doing, but more than 70 percent of their memories were distorted, inaccurate, or both. For example, three days after the verdict, one student said he heard about it while in a campus lounge with many other students around him. Thirty-two months later, the same student recalled hearing the news in the living room of his home with his father and sister. Most of the students whose memories had been substantially distorted over time were unaware that this distortion had occurred; they were very confident that their reports were accurate. Later, we will see that such overconfidence can also appear in courtroom testimony by eyewitnesses to crime.

ClassPrep PPT 20, OHT: Figure 7.9: A Serial-Position Curve

Distinguishing Between Short-Term and Long-Term Memory

Some psychologists claim that there is no need to distinguish between short-term and long-term memory: What people call short-term (and working) memory is simply that part of memory that they happen to be thinking about at any particular time, whereas long-term memory is the part of memory that they are not thinking about at any given moment. ("In Review: Storing New Memories" summarizes the characteristics of these systems.) However, other psychologists argue that short-term and long-term memory are qualitatively different—that they obey different laws (Cowan, 1988). Evidence that information is transferred from short-term memory to a distinct storage system comes from experiments on recall.

Experiments on Recall   To conduct your own recall experiment, look at the following list of words for thirty seconds, then look away and write down as many of the words as you can, in any order: desk, chalk, pencil, chair, paperclip, book, eraser, folder, briefcase, essays. Which words you remember depends in part on their *serial position*—that is, where the words are in the list, as Figure 7.9 shows. This figure is a *serial-position curve*, which shows the chances of recalling words appearing in each position in a list. For the first two or three words in a list, recall tends to be very good—a characteristic that is called the **primacy effect**. The

Drawing (A) shows the correct penny image in Figure 7.8.

in review	Storing New Memories		
Storage System	**Function**	**Capacity**	**Duration**
Sensory memory	Briefly holds representations of stimuli from each sense for further processing	Large: absorbs all sensory input from a particular stimulus	Less than 1 second
Short-term and working memory	Holds information in awareness and manipulates it to accomplish mental work	Five to nine distinct items or chunks of information	About 18 seconds
Long-term memory	Stores new information indefinitely	Unlimited	Unlimited

IRM Activity 7.6: An All-Purpose Memory Demonstration

probability of recall decreases for words in the middle of the list and then rises dramatically for the last few words. The ease of recalling words near the end of a list is called the **recency effect.** It has been suggested that the primacy effect reflects rehearsal that puts early words into *long-term memory*, and that the recency effect occurs because the last few words are still in *short-term memory* when we try to recall the list (Glanzer & Cunitz, 1966; Koppenaal & Glanzer, 1990).

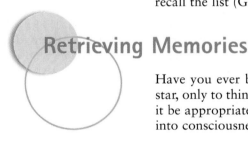

Retrieving Memories

Have you ever been unable to recall the name of an old television show or movie star, only to think of it the next day? Remembering something requires not only that it be appropriately encoded and stored but also that you have the ability to bring it into consciousness—in other words, to *retrieve* it.

OBJ 7.16: Define retrieval cue and explain why its use can increase memory efficiency. Define the encoding specificity principle.

Test Items 7.78–7.79

IRM Activity 7.3: Recognition Versus Recall

ClassPrep PPT 21: Retrieval Cues and Encoding Specificity

Retrieval Cues and Encoding Specificity

Stimuli that help people retrieve information from long-term memory are called **retrieval cues.** They allow people to recall things that were once forgotten and help them to recognize information stored in memory. In general, recognition tasks are easier than recall tasks, because they contain more retrieval cues. As noted earlier, it is usually easier to recognize the correct alternative on a multiple-choice exam than to recall material for an essay test.

The effectiveness of cues in aiding retrieval depends on the degree to which they tap into information that was encoded at the time of learning (Tulving, 1983). This rule, known as the **encoding specificity principle**, is consistent with the transfer-appropriate processing model of memory. Because long-term memories are often encoded semantically, cues related to the *meaning* of the stored information tend to work best. For example, imagine you have learned a long list of sentences, one of which is either (1) "The man lifted the piano" or (2) "The man tuned the piano." Having the cue "something heavy" during a recall test would probably help you remember the first sentence, because you probably encoded something about the weight of a piano, but "something heavy" would probably not help you recall the second sentence. Similarly, the cue "makes nice sounds" would be likely to help you recall the second sentence, but not the first (Barclay et al., 1974).

primacy effect A characteristic of memory in which recall of the first two or three items in a list is particularly good.

recency effect A characteristic of memory in which recall is particularly good for the last few items in a list.

retrieval cues Stimuli that allow people to recall or recognize information stored in memory.

encoding specificity principle A principle stating that the ability of a cue to aid retrieval depends on the degree to which it taps into information that was encoded at the time of the original learning.

Context and State Dependence

Have you ever taken a test in a classroom other than the one in which you learned the material for that test? If so, your performance may have been affected (Smith,

Context-Dependent Memories Some parents find that being in their child's schoolroom for a teacher conference provides context cues that bring back memories of their own grade school days.

context-dependent memory Memory that can be helped or hindered by similarities or differences between the context in which it is learned and the context in which it is recalled.

state-dependent memory Memory that is aided or impeded by a person's internal state.

spreading activation A principle that explains how information is retrieved in semantic network theories of memory.

Glenberg, & Bjork, 1978). In general, people remember more when their efforts at recall take place in the same environment in which they learned, because they tend to encode features of the environment where the learning occurred (Richardson-Klavehn & Bjork, 1988). These features may later act as retrieval cues. In one experiment, people studied a series of photos while in the presence of a particular odor. Later, they reviewed a larger set of photos and tried to identify the ones they had seen earlier. Half of these people were tested in the presence of the original odor and half in the presence of a different odor. Those who smelled the same odor during learning and testing did significantly better on the recognition task than those who were tested in the presence of a different odor. The matching odor served as a powerful retrieval cue (Cann & Ross, 1989).

When memory can be helped or hindered by similarities in environmental context, it is called **context-dependent memory**. This context-dependency effect is not always strong (Saufley, Otaka, & Bavaresco, 1985; Smith, Vela, & Williamson, 1988), but some students do find it helpful to study for a test in the classroom where the test will be given.

Like the external environment, the internal psychological environment can be encoded when people learn, and thus it can act as a retrieval cue When a person's internal state can aid or impede retrieval, the person has what is called **state-dependent memory**. For example, if people learn new material while under the influence of marijuana, they tend to recall it better if they are also tested under the influence of marijuana (Eich et al., 1975). Similar effects have been found with alcohol (Overton, 1984) and other drugs (Eich, 1989), although memory is best overall when people are not under the influence of any drug! Mood states, too, can affect memory (Eich & Macaulay, 2000). People tend to remember more positive incidents from their past when they are in a positive mood at the time of recall and more negative events when they are in a negative mood (Ehrlichman & Halpern, 1988; Lewinsohn & Rosenbaum, 1987). These *mood congruency effects* are strongest when people try to recall personally meaningful episodes, because such events were most likely to be colored by their mood (Eich & Metcalfe, 1989).

Retrieval from Semantic Memory

All of the retrieval situations we have discussed so far are relevant to episodic memory. ("In Review: Factors Affecting Retrieval from Long-Term Memory" summarizes this material.) But how do we retrieve information from semantic memory, where our general knowledge about the world is stored? Researchers studying this process typically ask participants general-knowledge questions, such as (1) Are fish

in review	Factors Affecting Retrieval from Long-Term Memory	
Process	**Effect on Memory**	
Encoding specificity	Retrieval cues are effective only to the extent that they tap into information that was originally encoded.	
Context dependence	Retrieval is most successful when it occurs in the same environment in which the information was originally learned.	
State dependence	Retrieval is most successful when people are in the same psychological state as when they originally learned the information.	

minerals? (2) Is a beagle a dog? (3) Do birds fly? and (4) Does a car have legs? As you might imagine, most people almost always respond correctly to such questions. By measuring the amount of time people take to answer the questions, however, psychologists gain important clues about how semantic memory is organized and how we retrieve information from it.

OBJ 7.18: Describe the semantic network theory of memory. Explain the process of spreading activation in memory.

Test Items 7.92–7.93

Semantic Networks   One of the most influential theories of semantic memory suggests that concepts are represented in a dense network of associations (Collins & Loftus, 1975). Figure 7.10 presents a fragment of what a *semantic memory network* might look like. In general, semantic network theories suggest that information is retrieved from memory through **spreading activation** (Medin, Ross, & Markman, 2001). So whenever you think about some concept, that concept becomes activated in the network, and this activation—in the form of neural energy—begins to spread along all the paths related to it. For example, if a person is asked to say whether "A robin is a bird" is true or false, the concepts of both "robin" and "bird" will become activated, and the spreading activation from each will intersect in the middle of the path between them.

Some associations within the network are stronger than others. Differing strengths are depicted by the varying thicknesses of the lines in Figure 7.10; spreading activation travels faster along thick paths than along thin ones. For example, most people probably have a stronger association between "bat" and "can fly" or "has wings" than between "bat" and "is a mammal." Accordingly, most people respond more quickly to "Can a bat fly?" than to "Is a bat a mammal?"

Because of the tight organization of semantic networks and the speed at which activation spreads through them, we can gain access to an enormous body of knowledge about the world quickly and effortlessly. We can retrieve not only the facts we have learned directly but also the knowledge that allows us to infer or compute other facts about the world (Matlin, 1998). For example, imagine answering the following two questions: (1) Is a robin a bird? and (2) Is a robin a living thing? You can probably answer the first question "directly," because you probably learned this

ClassPrep PPT 23, OHT: *Figure 7.10:* Semantic Networks

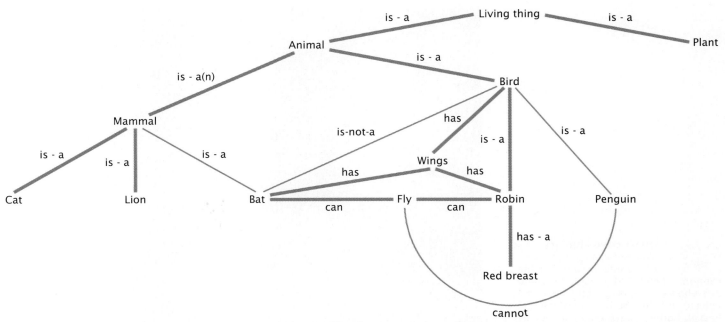

figure 7.10

Semantic Networks

This drawing represents just a small part of a network of semantic associations. Semantic network theories of memory suggest that networks like these allow us to retrieve specific pieces of previously learned information and to make new inferences about concepts.

fact at some point in your life. However, you may never have consciously thought about the second question, so answering it requires you to make an inference. Figure 7.10 illustrates the path to that inference. Because you know that a robin is a bird, a bird is an animal, and animals are living things, you can infer that a robin must be a living thing. As you might expect, however, it takes slightly longer to answer the second question than the first.

ClassPrep PPT 24: Retrieving Incomplete Knowledge

Retrieving Incomplete Knowledge   Figure 7.10 also shows that concepts—such as "bird"—are represented in semantic memory as collections of features or attributes. When you can retrieve some features of a concept from your semantic network, but not enough of them to identify what the concept is, you are said to have retrieved *incomplete knowledge.* For example, you might know that there is an animal that has wings, can fly, but is not a bird, and yet be unable to retrieve its name (Connor, Balota, & Neely, 1992).

OBJ 7.19: Define the tip-of-the-tongue and the feeling-of-knowing phenomena. Explain how these are related to the semantic network theory of memory.

Test Items 7.94–7.97

You have probably experienced a particular example of incomplete knowledge called the *tip-of-the-tongue phenomenon.* In a typical experiment on this phenomenon, people listen to dictionary definitions of words and are then asked to name each defined word (Brown & McNeill, 1966). If they cannot recall a particular word, they are asked whether they can recall any feature of it, such as its first letter or how many syllables it has. People are surprisingly good at this task, indicating that they are able to retrieve at least some knowledge of the word (Brennen et al., 1990). Most people experience the tip-of-the-tongue phenomenon about once a week (Brown, 1991).

Another example of retrieving incomplete knowledge is the *feeling-of-knowing experience,* which is often studied by asking people trivia questions (Reder & Ritter, 1992). When they cannot answer a question, they are asked to estimate the probability that they could recognize the correct answer if they were given several options. Again, people are remarkably good at this task; even though they cannot recall the answer, they can retrieve enough knowledge to determine whether the answer is actually stored in their memory (Costermans, Lories, & Ansay, 1992).

TRY THIS   **Constructive Memory** Ask a friend to examine this photo for a minute or so (cover the caption). Then take the book away and ask whether each of the following items appeared in the photo: chair, wastebasket, bottle, typewriter, coffeepot, and book. If your friend reports having seen a wastebasket or book, you will have demonstrated constructive memory.

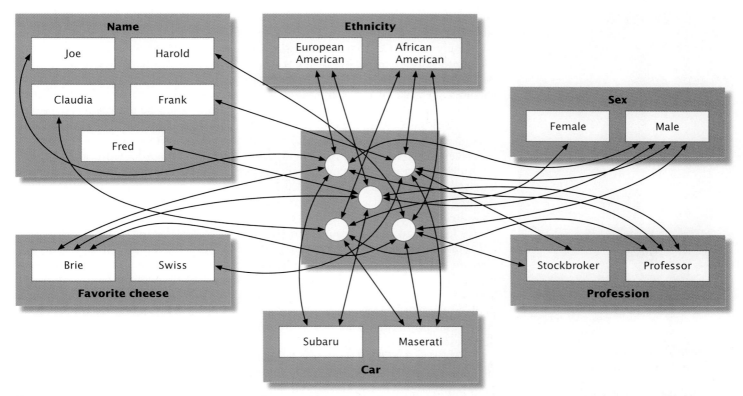

figure 7.11

A PDP Network Model

ClassPrep PPT 26: *Figure 7.11:* A PDP Network Model

This simple parallel distributed processing network model represents what someone knows about the characteristics of five people and how these characteristics are related to one another. Note that each arrow between a rectangle and a circle connects a characteristic with a person. More complex versions of such networks are capable of accounting not only for what people know but also for the inferences and generalizations they tend to make.

Source: From *Cognitive Psychology,* 1st Edition, by C. Martindale, © 1991. Reprinted with permission of Wadsworth Publishing, a division of International Thomson Publishing. Fax 800-730-2215.

ClassPrep PPT 25: Constructive Memory

OBJ 7.20: Define constructive memory. Describe how PDP memory models explain the integration of semantic and episodic memories in memory construction.

Test Items 7.98–7.101

IRM Activity 7.9: Constructive Memory: The Rumor Chain

Personal Learning Activity 7.1

IRM Activity 7.10: Remembering an Absent Memory

Personal Learning Activity 7.4

IRM Activity 2.12: A Staged Incident

Constructing Memories

The generalized knowledge about the world that each person has stored constantly affects memory (Schacter, Norman, & Koutstaal, 1998). We use our existing knowledge to organize new information as we receive it and to fill in gaps in the information we encode and retrieve (Sherman & Bessennoff, 1999). In this way, memories are constructed.

To study this process, which is sometimes called *constructive memory*, William Brewer and James Treyens (1981) asked undergraduates to wait for several minutes in the office of a graduate student. When later asked to recall everything that was in the office, most of the students mistakenly "remembered" that books were present, even though there were none. Apparently, the general knowledge that graduate students read many books influenced the participants' memory of what was in the room.

Relating Semantic and Episodic Memory: PDP Models
Parallel distributed processing models offer one way of explaining how semantic and episodic information become integrated in constructive memories. As mentioned earlier, PDP models suggest that newly learned facts alter our general knowledge of what the world is like. Figure 7.11 shows a simple PDP network model of just a tiny part of someone's knowledge of the world (Martindale, 1991). At its center lie the intersections of several learned associations between specific facts about five people, each of whom is represented by a circle. This network "knows" that Joe is a

ClassPrep PPT 27: Parallel Distributed Processing Models

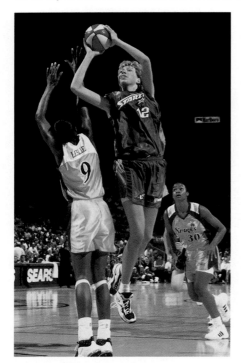

PDP Models and Constructive Memory   If you were to hear that "our basketball team won last night," your schema about basketball might prompt you to encode, and later retrieve, the fact that the players were men. Such spontaneous, though often incorrect, generalizations associated with PDP models of memory help account for constructive memory.

OBJ 7.21: Explain how PDP models produce spontaneous generalization and why they help explain the operation of schemas.

Test Items 7.102–7.106

figure 7.12

The Effect of Schemas on Recall

ClassPrep PPT 28: *Figure 7.12:* The Effect of Schemas on Recall

IRM Activity 5.11: Figure-Ground and Expectancy

IRM Activity 5.13: Top-Down Processing

IRM Activity 8.6: Cognition: Schemas

IRM Activity 8.7: Cognition: Scripts

IRM Activity 8.10: Mental Sets

male European American professor who likes Brie cheese and drives a Subaru. It also "knows" that Claudia is a female African American professor who drives a Maserati. Notice that the network has never learned what type of cheese she prefers.

Suppose Figure 7.11 represents your memory, and you now think about Claudia. Because of the connections in the network, the facts that she is a female African American professor and drives a Maserati would be activated; you would automatically remember these facts about Claudia. However, "likes Brie cheese" would also be activated, because it is linked to other professors in the network. If the level of activation for Brie cheese were low, then the proposition that Claudia likes Brie cheese might be considered a hypothesis or an educated guess. But suppose every other professor you know likes Brie. In that case, the connection between professors and "likes Brie cheese" would be strong, and the conclusion that Claudia likes Brie cheese would be held so confidently that it would take overwhelming evidence for you to change your mind (Rumelhart & McClelland, 1986).

PDP networks also produce spontaneous generalizations. If a friend told you she just bought a new car, you would know without asking that—like all other cars you have seen—it has four wheels. However, spontaneous generalizations can create significant errors if the network is based on limited or biased experience with a class of objects. For example, if the network in Figure 7.11 were asked what European American males are like, it would think that all of them drive Japanese cars.

This aspect of PDP networks—generalizing from scanty information—is actually an accurate reflection of human thought and memory. Virtually everyone makes spontaneous generalizations about males, females, European Americans, African Americans, and many other categories (Martindale, 1991).

Schemas   Parallel distributed processing models also help us understand constructive memory by explaining the operation of the schemas that guide it. **Schemas** are mental representations of categories of objects, events, and people. For example, for people who have a schema for *baseball game*, simply hearing these words is likely to activate whole clusters of information in long-term memory, including the rules of the game, images of players, bats, balls, a green field, summer days, and perhaps hot dogs and stadiums. The generalized knowledge contained in schemas

	Group 1		**Group 2**	
Figure shown to participants	Label given	Figure drawn by participants	Label given	Figure drawn by participants
○—○	Eyeglasses	○○	Dumbbell	○—○
⋈	Hourglass	⋈	Table	⋈
⇃	Seven	7	Four	4
⊐—	Gun	⟋⟋	Broom	⨜

In one early experiment, participants were shown figures like these, along with labels designed to activate certain schemas (Carmichael, Hogan, & Walter, 1932). For example, when showing the top figure, the experimenter said either "This resembles eyeglasses" or "This resembles a dumbbell." When the participants were asked to reproduce the figures from memory, their drawings tended to resemble the items mentioned by the experimenter. In other words, their memory had been altered by the labels.

schemas   Mental representations of categories of objects, events, and people.

provides a basis for making inferences about incoming information during the encoding stage. So if you hear that a baseball player was injured, your schema about baseball might prompt you to encode the incident as game related, even though the cause was not mentioned. As a result, you are likely to recall the injury as having occurred during a game (see Figure 7.12 for another example).

Memory, Perception, and Eyewitness Testimony

 LINKAGES (a link to Perception)

There are few situations in which accurate retrieval of memories is more important—and constructive memory is more dangerous—than when an eyewitness testifies in court about a crime. Eyewitnesses provide the most compelling evidence in many trials, but they can sometimes be mistaken (Kassin et al., 2001; Loftus & Ketcham, 1991). In 1984, for example, a North Carolina college student, Jennifer Thompson, confidently identified Ronald Cotton as the man who had raped her at knifepoint. Mainly on the basis of Thompson's testimony, Cotton was convicted of rape and sentenced to life in prison. He was released eleven years later, when DNA evidence revealed that he was innocent (and it identified another man as the rapist). The eyewitness-victim's certainty had convinced a jury, but her memory had been faulty (O'Neill, 2000). Let's consider the accuracy of eyewitness memory and how it can be distorted (Loftus, 1993).

Like the rest of us, eyewitnesses can remember only what they perceive, and they can perceive only what they attend to (Backman & Nilsson, 1991). As described in the perception chapter, perception is influenced by a combination of the stimulus features we find "out there" in the world and what we already know, expect, or want—that is, by both bottom-up and top-down processing.

Witnesses are asked to report exactly what they saw or heard; but no matter how hard they try to be accurate, there are limits to how faithful their reports can be (Kassin, Rigby, & Castillo, 1991). As mentioned earlier, semantic encoding into long-term memory may result in the loss of certain details. Further, new information, including questions posed by police or lawyers, can alter a witness's memory (Loftus, 1979). For example, when witnesses were asked, "How fast was the blue car going when it *smashed into* the truck?" they were likely to recall a higher speed than when they were asked, "How fast was the blue car going when it *hit* the truck?" (Loftus & Palmer, 1974; see Figure 7.13). There is also evidence that an object mentioned after the fact is often mistakenly remembered as having been

figure 7.13

The Impact of Leading Questions on Eyewitness Memory

After seeing a filmed traffic accident, people were asked, "About how fast were the cars going when they (smashed, hit, or contacted) each other?" As shown here, the witnesses' responses were influenced by the verb used in the question; *smashed* was associated with the highest average speed estimates. A week later, people who heard the question that used *smashed* remembered the accident as being more violent than did people in the other two groups (Loftus & Palmer, 1974).

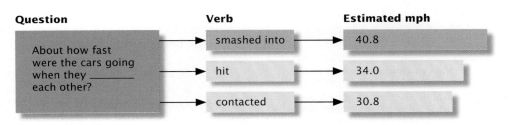

Question	Verb	Estimated mph
About how fast were the cars going when they _____ each other?	smashed into	40.8
	hit	34.0
	contacted	30.8

Original information | External information | The "memory"

About how fast were the cars going when they SMASHED INTO each other?

HERMAN

8-10   © Jim Unger/dist. by United Media, 2001

**"Can you identify the man who
punched you in the knee?"**

This is exactly the sort of biased lineup
that the new Justice Department *Guide for
Law Enforcement* (1999) is designed to
avoid. Based on research on memory and
perception, this guide recommends that
no suspect should stand out from all
the others in a lineup, that witnesses
should not assume the real criminal is in
the lineup, and that they should not be
encouraged to base identification on their
"best guess."

there in the first place (Dodson & Reisberg, 1991). So if a lawyer says that a screw-
driver was lying on the ground (when it was not), witnesses often recall with great
certainty having seen it (Ryan & Geiselman, 1991). Some theorists have speculated
that mentioning a new object makes the original memory more difficult to retrieve
(Tversky & Tuchin, 1989). However, there is now considerable evidence that when
new objects are mentioned, they are integrated into the old memory representation and subsequently are not distinguished from what was originally seen
(Loftus, 1992).

For jurors, the believability of a witness often depends as much (or even more)
on *how* the witness presents evidence as on the content or relevance of that evidence (Leippe, Manion, & Romanczyk, 1992). Many jurors are impressed, for example, by witnesses who give lots of details about what they saw or heard. Extremely
detailed testimony from prosecution witnesses is especially likely to lead to guilty
verdicts, even when the details reported are irrelevant (Bell & Loftus, 1989). When
a witness gives very detailed testimony, such as the exact time of the crime or the
color of the criminal's shoes, jurors apparently infer that the witness paid especially close attention or has a particularly accurate memory. At first glance, these
inferences might seem reasonable. However, as discussed in the chapter on perception, the ability to divide attention is limited. As a result, witnesses might focus
attention on the crime and the criminal, or on the surrounding details, but probably not on both—particularly if they were emotionally aroused and the crime happened quickly. So witnesses who accurately remember unimportant details of a
crime scene may not accurately recall the criminal's facial features or other identifying characteristics (Backman & Nilsson, 1991).

Juries also tend to believe witnesses who are confident (Leippe, Manion, &
Romanczyk, 1992), but witnesses' confidence about their testimony is frequently
much higher than its accuracy (Shaw, 1996). Repeated exposure to misinformation and the repeated recall of misinformation can increase a witness's
confidence in objectively incorrect testimony (Lamb, 1998; Mitchell & Zaragoza,
1996; Roediger, Jacoby, & McDermott, 1996). In other words, as in the Jennifer
Thompson case, even witnesses who are confident about their testimony are not
always correct.

The weaknesses inherent in eyewitness memory can be amplified by the use
of police lineups and certain other criminal identification procedures. In one study,
for example, participants watched a videotaped crime and then tried to identify
the criminal from a set of photographs (Wells & Bradfield, 1999). None of the photos showed the person who had committed the crime, but some participants nevertheless identified one of them as the criminal they saw on tape. When these
mistaken participants were led to believe that they had correctly identified the
criminal, they became even more confident in the accuracy of their false identification. These incorrect, but confident, witnesses became more likely than other
participants to claim that it had been easy for them to identify the criminal from
the photos because they had had a good view of him and had paid careful attention to him.

As of 2000, at least 96 people, including Ronald Cotton, have been released
from U.S. prisons after DNA tests or other evidence revealed that they had been
falsely convicted—mostly on the basis of faulty eyewitness testimony (Death
Penalty Information Center, 2001; Scheck, Neufeld, & Dwyer, 2000; Wells et al.,
2000). DNA evidence freed Charles Fain, who had been convicted of murder and
spent almost eighteen years on death row in Idaho (Bonner, 2001). Frank Lee
Smith, too, would have been set free after the sole eyewitness at his murder trial
retracted her testimony, but he had already died of cancer while awaiting execution in a Florida prison. Research on memory and perception helps explain how
these miscarriages of justice can occur, and it is also guiding efforts to prevent
such errors in the future. The U.S. Department of Justice has recently acknowl-
edged the potential for errors in eyewitness evidence, as well as the dangers of
asking witnesses to identify suspects from lineups and photo arrays. The result is
Eyewitness Evidence: A Guide for Law Enforcement (U.S. Department of Justice,

1999), the first-ever guide for police and prosecutors involved in obtaining eye-witness evidence. The guide warns these officials that asking leading questions about what witnesses saw can distort their memory, that witnesses should examine mug shots of possible suspects one at a time, and that false identifications are less likely if witnesses viewing suspects in a lineup are told that the real perpetrator might not be included (Foxhall, 2000; Wells et al., 2000).

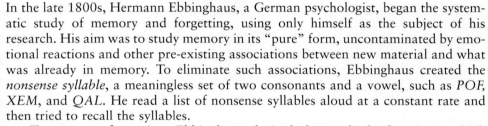

Forgetting

The frustrations of forgetting—where you left your keys, the answer to a test question, an anniversary—are apparent to most people nearly every day (Neisser, 2000). In this section we look more closely at the nature of forgetting and at some of the mechanisms that are responsible for it.

How Do We Forget?

In the late 1800s, Hermann Ebbinghaus, a German psychologist, began the systematic study of memory and forgetting, using only himself as the subject of his research. His aim was to study memory in its "pure" form, uncontaminated by emotional reactions and other pre-existing associations between new material and what was already in memory. To eliminate such associations, Ebbinghaus created the *nonsense syllable*, a meaningless set of two consonants and a vowel, such as *POF, XEM*, and *QAL*. He read a list of nonsense syllables aloud at a constant rate and then tried to recall the syllables.

To measure forgetting, Ebbinghaus devised the **method of savings**, which involves computing the difference between the number of repetitions needed to learn a list of items and the number of repetitions needed to relearn it after some time has elapsed. This difference is called the *savings*. If it took Ebbinghaus ten trials to learn a list and ten more trials to relearn it, there would be no savings, and forgetting would have been complete. If it took him ten trials to learn the list and only five trials to relearn it, there would be a savings of 50 percent.

As you can see in Figure 7.14, Ebbinghaus found a decline in savings (and an increase in forgetting) as time passes. However, the most dramatic drop in what people retain in long-term memory occurs during the first nine hours, especially in the first hour. After this initial decline, the rate of forgetting slows down considerably. In Ebbinghaus's study, some savings existed even thirty-one days after the original learning.

Ebbinghaus's research had some important limitations, but it produced two lasting discoveries. One is the shape of the forgetting curve, depicted in Figure 7.14. Psychologists have subsequently substituted words, sentences, and even stories for nonsense syllables. In virtually all cases the forgetting curve shows the same strong initial drop in memory, followed by a much more moderate decrease over time (Slamecka & McElree, 1983). Of course, people remember sensible stories better than nonsense syllables, but the *shape* of the curve is the same no matter what type of material is involved (Davis & Moore, 1935). Even the forgetting of events from daily life tends to follow Ebbinghaus's forgetting curve (Thomson, 1982).

The second of Ebbinghaus's important discoveries is just how long-lasting savings in long-term memory can be. Psychologists now know from the method of savings that information about everything from algebra to bike riding is often retained for decades (Matlin, 1998). You may forget something you have learned if you do not use the information, but it is easy to relearn the material if the need arises, indicating that the forgetting was not complete (Hall & Bahrick, 1998).

Durable Memories This man probably had not used a pogo stick since he was ten. His memory of how to do it is not entirely gone, however, so he showed some "savings": It took him less time to relearn the skill now than it took to learn it initially.

OBJ 7.23: Define Ebbinghaus's method of savings. Explain his discoveries and why they are important to memory research.

Test Items 7.111–7.115

method of savings Measuring forgetting by computing the difference between the number of repetitions needed to learn and, after a delay, relearn the same material.

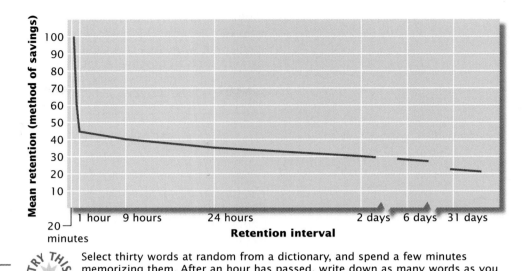

figure 7.14

Ebbinghaus's Curve of Forgetting

ClassPrep PPT 29, OHT: *Figure 7.14:* Ebbinghaus's Curve of Forgetting

ClassPrep PPT 30: Why Do We Forget?

OBJ 7.24: Compare and contrast the decay and interference theories regarding forgetting information stored in long-term memory. Define retroactive interference and proactive interference.

Test Items 7.116–7.131

IRM Activity 7.11: Interference Experiment

TRY THIS   Select thirty words at random from a dictionary, and spend a few minutes memorizing them. After an hour has passed, write down as many words as you can remember, but don't look at the original list again. Do the same self-test eight hours later, a day later, and two days later. Now look at the original list, and see how well you did on each recall test. Ebbinghaus found that most forgetting occurs during the first nine hours after learning, and especially during the first hour. If this was not the case for you, why do you think your results were different?

Why Do We Forget? The Roles of Decay and Interference

Nothing we have said so far explains *why* forgetting occurs. In principle, either of two processes can be responsible (Best, 1999). One process is **decay**, the gradual disappearance of the mental representation of a stimulus. Decay occurs in memory much as the inscription engraved on a ring or bracelet wears away and becomes less distinct over time. Forgetting might also occur because of **interference**, a process through which either the storage or retrieval of information is impaired by the presence of other information. Interference might occur either because one piece of information actually *displaces* other information, pushing it out of memory, or because one piece of information makes storing or recalling other information more difficult.

In the case of short-term memory, we noted that if an item is not rehearsed or elaborated, memory of it decreases consistently over the course of about eighteen seconds. So decay appears to play a prominent role in forgetting information in short-term memory. But interference through displacement also produces forgetting from short-term memory. Like a desktop, short-term memory can hold only so much. When additional items are added, the old ones tend to "fall off" and are no longer available (Haberlandt, 1999). Displacement is one reason why the phone number you just looked up is likely to drop out of short-term memory if you read another number before making your call. Rehearsal prevents displacement by continually re-entering the same information into short-term memory.

The causes of forgetting from long-term memory are more complicated. In long-term memory there can be **retroactive interference**, in which learning of new information interferes with recall of older information, or **proactive interference**, in which old information interferes with learning or remembering new information. For example, retroactive interference would help explain why studying French vocabulary this term might make it more difficult to remember the Spanish words you learned last term. And because of proactive interference, the French words you are learning now might make it harder to learn German next term. Figure 7.15 outlines the types of experiments used to study the influence of each form of interference in long-term memory.

decay   The gradual disappearance of the mental representation of a stimulus.

interference   The process through which either the storage or the retrieval of information is impaired by the presence of other information.

retroactive interference   A cause of forgetting in which new information placed in memory interferes with the ability to recall information already in memory.

proactive interference   A cause of forgetting in which information already in long-term memory interferes with the ability to remember new information.

PROACTIVE INTERFERENCE

Group	Time 1	Time 2	Time 3	Result
Experimental	Learn list A	Learn list B	Recall list B	The experimental group will suffer from proactive interference, and the control group will be able to recall more material from list B.
Control		Learn list B	Recall list B	

RETROACTIVE INTERFERENCE

Group	Time 1	Time 2	Time 3	Result
Experimental	Learn list A	Learn list B	Recall list A	The experimental group will suffer from retroactive interference, and the control group will be able to recall more material from list A.
Control	Learn list A		Recall list A	

figure 7.15

Procedures for Studying Interference

ClassPrep PPT 31: *Figure 7.15:* Procedures for Studying Interference

To recall the two types of interference, remember that the prefixes—*pro* and *retro*—indicate directions in time. In *pro*active interference, previously learned material interferes with *future* learning; *retro*active interference occurs when new information interferes with the recall of *past* learning.

Suppose a person learns something and then, when tested on it after various intervals, remembers less and less as the delay becomes longer. Is this forgetting due to decay or to interference? It is not easy to tell, because longer delays produce both more decay and more retroactive interference as the person is exposed to further information while waiting. To separate the effects of decay from those of interference, Karl Dallenbach sought to create situations in which time passed but there was no accompanying interference. Evidence of forgetting in such a situation would suggest that decay, not interference, was operating.

ClassPrep PPT 32: *Figure 7.16:* Interference and Forgetting

In one of Dallenbach's studies, college students learned a list of nonsense syllables and then either continued with their waking routine or were sheltered from interference by going to sleep (Jenkins & Dallenbach, 1924). Although the delay (and thus the potential for decay) was held constant for both groups, the greater interference associated with being awake produced much more forgetting (see Figure 7.16).

Results like these suggest that although decay sometimes occurs, interference is the major cause of forgetting from long-term memory. But does interference actually push the forgotten information out of memory, or does it just impair the retrieval process? To find out, Endel Tulving and Joseph Psotka (1971) presented people with different numbers of word lists. Each list contained words from one of six categories, such as types of buildings *(hut, cottage, tent, hotel)* or earth formations *(cliff, river, hill, volcano)*. Some people learned a list and then recalled as many of the words as possible. Other groups learned the first list and then learned different numbers of other lists before trying to recall the first one.

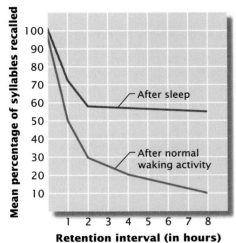

figure 7.16

Interference and Forgetting

In this study, college students' forgetting was more rapid if they engaged in normal activity after learning than if they spent the time asleep. These results suggest that interference is more important than decay in forgetting information in long-term memory.

Source: Minimi & Dallenbach (1946).

The results were dramatic. As the number of intervening lists increased, the number of words that people could recall from the original list declined. This finding reflected strong retroactive interference. Then the researchers gave a second test, in which they provided people with a *retrieval cue* by telling them the category of the words (such as types of buildings) to be recalled. Now the number of intervening lists had almost no effect on the number of words recalled from the original list, as Figure 7.17 shows. These results indicate that the words were still in long-term memory; they had not been pushed out, but the participants had been unable to recall them without appropriate retrieval cues. In other words, the original forgetting

figure 7.17

Retrieval Failures and Forgetting

In Tulving and Psotka's experiment, people's ability to recall a list of items was strongly affected by the number of other lists they learned before being tested on the first one. When item-category (retrieval) cues were provided on a second test, however, retroactive interference from the intervening lists almost disappeared.

Source: Tulving & Psotka (1971).

ClassPrep PPT 33: *Figure 7.17:* Retrieval Failure and Forgetting

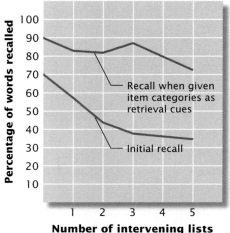

was due to a failure in retrieval. So putting more and more information in long-term memory may be like putting more and more CDs into a storage case. None of the CDs disappears, but it becomes increasingly difficult to find the specific one you are looking for.

Some theorists have concluded that all forgetting from long-term memory is due to some form of retrieval failure (Ratcliff & McKoon, 1989). Does this mean that everything in long-term memory remains there until death, even if you cannot always, or ever, recall it? No one knows for sure, but as described in the next section, this question lies at the heart of some highly controversial court cases.

*Freburg **Perspectives:*** Neimark, "The Diva of Disclosure"

*Freburg **Stand!:*** Horn, "Memories Lost and Found," Loftus, "Creating False Memories," and Horn, "Recalling the Past, Embracing the Future"

Can Traumatic Memories Be Repressed, Then Recovered?

In 1989, Eileen Franklin-Lipsker told police in California that when she looked into her young daughter's eyes one day, she suddenly remembered seeing her father kill her childhood friend more than twenty years earlier. Her father, George Franklin, Sr., was sent to prison for murder on the basis of her testimony about that memory (Loftus & Ketcham, 1994). This case sparked a debate that has continued to grow in intensity and involves not only psychologists but the North American legal system as well. The controversy concerns the validity of claims of recovered memory. Some psychologists accept the idea that it is possible for people to *repress*, or push into unconsciousness, memories of traumatic incidents and then recover these memories many years later. Other psychologists are skeptical about recovered memory claims.

● **What am I being asked to believe or accept?**

The prosecution in the Franklin case successfully argued that Eileen had repressed, and then recovered, her memory of a murder. Similar arguments in a number of other cases tried in the early 1990s resulted in the imprisonment of other parents whose now-adult children claimed to have recovered childhood memories of being physically or sexually abused by them. The juries in these trials accepted the assertion that all memory of shocking events can be repressed, or pushed into an inaccessible corner of the mind where for decades, subconscious processes keep it out of awareness, yet potentially subject to accurate recollection (Hyman, 2000). Jurors are not the only believers in this phenomenon. A few years ago a large American news organization reported that the United States had illegally used nerve gas during the war in Vietnam. The story was based, in part, on a Vietnam

LINKAGES (a link to Consciousness)

OBJ 7.25: Discuss the controversy surrounding repressed memories. Describe motivated forgetting, false memories, and flashbulb memories.

Test Items 7.132–7.135

ClassPrep PPT 45: Thinking Critically: Can Traumatic Memories Be Repressed, Then Recovered?

veteran's account of recovered memories of having been subjected to a nerve gas attack.

● What evidence is available to support the assertion?

Proponents of the recovered memory argument point to several lines of evidence to support their claims. First, there is evidence that a substantial amount of mental activity occurs outside conscious awareness (Kihlstrom, 1999; see the chapter on consciousness). Second, research on implicit memory shows that information of which we are unaware can influence our behavior (Schacter, Chiu, & Ochsner, 1993). Third, research on *motivated forgetting* suggests that people are able to willfully suppress information so that it is no longer accessible on a later memory test (Anderson & Green, 2001). Even suppressing one's emotional reactions to events can interfere with memories of those events (Richards & Gross, 2000). And people appear more likely to forget unpleasant rather than pleasant events (Erdelyi, 1985). In one study, a psychologist kept a detailed record of his daily life over a six-year period. When he later tried to recall those experiences, he remembered more than half of the positive ones, but only one-third of the negative ones. In another study, 38 percent of women who, as children, had been brought to a hospital because of sexual abuse did not report the incident as adults (Williams, 1994). Fourth, retrieval cues can help people recall memories that had previously been inaccessible to conscious awareness (Andrews et al., 2000; Landsdale & Laming, 1995). For example, these cues have helped soldiers remember for the first time the circumstances under which they had been wounded many years before (Karon & Widener, 1997). Finally, there is the confidence with which people report recovered memories; they say they are just too vivid to be anything but real.

● Are there alternative ways of interpreting the evidence?

Those who are skeptical about recovered memories do not deny the operation of subconscious memory and retrieval processes (Kihlstrom, 1999). They also recognize that unfortunately, child abuse and other traumas are all too common. But to these psychologists, the available evidence is not strong enough to support the conclusion that traumatic memories can be repressed and then accurately recalled (Pope, 1998; Pope & Hudson, 1995). Any given "recovered" memory, they say, might actually be a distorted, or constructed, memory (Clancy et al., 2000; Hyman, 2000; Loftus, 1998). As already mentioned, our recall of past events is affected by what happened at the time, what we knew beforehand, and everything we have experienced since. The people described earlier who "remembered" nonexistent books in a graduate student's office constructed that memory based on what prior knowledge led them to *assume* was there. Similarly, the "recovered memory" of the Vietnam veteran mentioned earlier appears to have no basis in fact; the news story about the alleged nerve gas attack was later retracted.

Research shows that *false memories*—distortions of actual events and the recall of events that didn't actually happen—can be at least as vivid as accurate ones, and people can be just as confident in them (Brainerd & Reyna, 1998; Brainerd, Reyna, & Brandse, 1995; Roediger & McDermott, 1995, 2000). Most of us have experienced everyday versions of false memories; it is common for people to "remember" turning off the coffeepot or mailing the rent check, only to discover later that they did not. Researchers have demonstrated that false memories can occur in relation to more emotional events, too. In one case study, a teenager named Chris was given descriptions of four incidents from his childhood and asked to write about each of them every day for five days (Loftus, 1997a). One of those incidents—being lost in a shopping mall at age five—never really happened. Yet Chris not only eventually "remembered" this event but added many details about the mall and the stranger whose hand he was supposedly found holding. He also rated this (false) memory as being more vivid than two of the other three (real) incidents. Similar results occurred in about half of seventy-seven child participants in a more recent set of case studies (Porter, Yuille, & Lehman, 1999). The same pattern of results has appeared in formal experiments on the planting of emotion-laden false memories (Hyman & Pentland, 1996). Researchers have been able to

Exploring Memory Processes
Research by Elizabeth Loftus (shown here with a student) and other cognitive psychologists has demonstrated mechanisms through which false memories can be created. The researchers have shown, for example, that false memories appear even in research participants who are told about them and asked to avoid them (McDermott & Roediger, 1998). Their work has helped to focus scientific scrutiny on reports of recovered memories, especially those arising from contact with therapists who assume that most people have repressed memories of abuse.

create vivid and striking, but *completely false*, memories of events that people thought they experienced when they were one day old (DuBreuil, Garry, & Loftus, 1998). In other experiments, children who were repeatedly asked about a nonexistent trauma (getting a hand caught in a mousetrap) eventually developed a vivid and unshakable false memory of experiencing it (Ceci et al., 1994).

In other words, people sometimes have a difficult time distinguishing between what has happened to them and what they have only imagined, or have come to believe, has happened (Garry & Polaschek, 2000; Johnson & Raye, 1998; Zaragosa et al., 2001). Some studies indicate that people who score high on tests of introversion, fantasy-proneness, and dissociation—the latter of which includes a tendency toward lapses of memory and attention—are more likely than others to develop false memories and may also be more likely to report the recovery of repressed memories (McNally et al., 2000b; Porter et al., 2000). Also, two studies have found that women who have suffered physical or sexual abuse are more likely to falsely remember words on a laboratory recall test (Bremner, Shobe, & Kihlstrom, 2000; Zoellner et al., 2000). This tendency appears strongest among abused women who show signs of posttraumatic stress disorder (Bremner, Shobe, & Kihlstrom, 2000). Another study found that susceptibility to false memory in a word recall task was greater in women who reported recovered memories of sexual abuse than in nonabused women or in those who had always remembered the abuse they suffered (Clancy et al., 2000).

Why would anyone "remember" a traumatic event that did not actually occur? Elizabeth Loftus (1997b) suggests that for one thing, popular books such as *The Courage to Heal* (Bass & Davis, 1994) and *Secret Survivors* (Blume, 1998) may lead people to believe that anyone who experiences guilt, depression, low self-esteem, overemotionality, or any of a long list of other problems is harboring repressed memories of abuse. This message, says Loftus, tends to be reinforced and extended by therapists who specialize in using guided imagination, hypnosis, and other methods to "help" clients recover repressed memories (Polusny & Follette, 1996; Poole et al., 1995). These therapists may influence people to construct false memories by encouraging them to imagine experiencing events that might never have actually occurred, or that occurred only in a dream (Mazzoni & Loftus, 1996; Olio, 1994). As one client described her therapy, "I was rapidly losing the ability to differentiate between my imagination and my real memory" (Loftus & Ketcham, 1994, p. 25). To such therapists, a client's failure to recover memories of abuse, or refusal to accept their existence, is evidence of "denial" of the truth (Loftus, 1997a).

The possibility that recovered memories might actually be false memories has led to dismissed charges or not-guilty verdicts for defendants in some repressed memory cases. In others, previously convicted defendants have been set free. (George Franklin's conviction was overturned, but only after he served five years in prison.) Concern over the potential damage resulting from false memories led to the establishment of the False Memory Syndrome Foundation, a support group for families affected by abuse accusations stemming from allegedly repressed memories. More than a hundred of these families (including Franklin's family) have filed lawsuits against hospitals and therapists (False Memory Syndrome Foundation, 1997). In 1994, California winery executive Gary Ramona received $500,000 in damages from two therapists who had "helped" his daughter recall alleged sexual abuse at his hands. More recent suits led to a $2 million judgment against a Minnesota therapist whose client realized that her "recovered" memories of childhood abuse were false; a similar case in Wisconsin brought a $5 million judgment against two therapists. And an Illinois case resulted in a $10.6 million settlement and the suspension of the license of the psychiatrist who had "found" his patient's "lost" memories (Loftus, 1998).

● **What additional evidence would help to evaluate the alternatives?**

Evaluating reports of recovered memories would be aided by more information about whether it is possible for people to repress traumatic events. If it is possible, we also need to know how common it is and how accurate recovered memories might be. So far, we know that some people apparently do forget intense emotional experiences, but that most people's memories of them are vivid and long lasting (Pope et al., 1998; Strongman & Kemp, 1991). Some are called *flashbulb memories* because they preserve particular experiences in great detail (Brown & Kulik, 1977). In fact, many people who live through trauma are *unable* to forget it. In the sexual abuse study mentioned earlier, for example (Williams, 1994a), 62 percent of the abuse victims did recall their trauma (some of the others may have recalled it, but chose not to report it). More studies like that one—studies that track the fate of memories in known abuse cases—not only would help estimate the prevalence of this kind of forgetting but also might offer clues as to the kinds of people and events most likely to be associated with it.

It would also be valuable to know more about the processes through which repression might occur and how they are related to empirically established theories and models of human memory. Is there a mechanism that specifically pushes traumatic memories out of awareness, then keeps them at a subconscious level for long periods and allows them to be accurately recalled? So far, cognitive psychologists have not found evidence for such a mechanism (Loftus, 1997a; McNally, Clancy, & Schacter, 2001; McNally et al., 2000a; Pope et al., 1998).

● What conclusions are most reasonable?

An objective reading of the available research evidence supports the view that recovery of memories of trauma is at least possible, but that the implantation of false memories is also possible—and has been demonstrated experimentally. Accordingly, it may be difficult to decide whether any particular case is an instance of recovered memory or false memory, especially in the absence of objective corroborating evidence.

The intense conflict between the False Memory Syndrome Foundation and those psychologists who accept as genuine most of the memories recovered in therapy reflects a fundamental disagreement about recovered memories: Client reports constitute "proof" for therapists who deal daily with victims of sexual abuse and other traumas, and who rely more on personal experiences than on scientific research findings. Those reports are viewed with far more skepticism by psychologists who engage in, or rely on, empirical research on the processes of memory and forgetting (Pope, 1998).

So whether or not one believes a claim of recovered memory may be determined by the relative weight one assigns to personal experiences and intuition versus empirical evidence. Still, the apparent ease with which false memories can be created should lead judges, juries, and the general public to exercise great caution before accepting as valid unverified memories of traumatic events. At the same time, we should not automatically and uncritically reject the claims of people who appear to have recovered memories. Perhaps the wisest course is to use all the scientific and circumstantial evidence available to carefully and critically examine such claims, while keeping in mind that constructive memory processes *might* have influenced them. This careful, scientific approach is vital if we are to protect the rights and welfare of those who report recovered memories, as well as of those who face accusations arising from them.

Biological Bases of Memory

Many psychologists study memory by exploring the physical, electrical, and chemical changes that take place in the brain when people encode, store, and retrieve information (Cabeza & Nyberg, 2000; Smith, 2000). The story of the scientific search for the biological bases of memory begins with the work of Karl Lashley and Donald Hebb, who spent many years studying how memory is related to brain structures and processes. Lashley (1950) taught rats new behaviors and then observed how damage to various parts of the rats' brains changed their ability to perform the tasks they had learned. Lashley hoped that his work would identify the brain area that contained the "engram"—the physical manifestation of memory in the brain. However, after many experiments, he concluded that memories are not localized in one specific region, but instead are distributed throughout large areas of brain tissue (Lashley, 1950).

Hebb, who was a student of Lashley's, proposed another biological theory of memory. Hebb believed that a given memory is represented by a group of interconnected neurons in the brain. This set of neurons, which he called a *cell assembly*, form a network in the cortex. The connections among these neurons were strengthened, he said, when the neurons were simultaneously stimulated through sensory experiences (Hebb, 1949). Though not correct in all its details, Hebb's theory stimulated research and contributed to an understanding of the physical basis of memory. His theory is also consistent, in many respects, with contemporary parallel distributed processing models of memory (Hergenhahn & Olson, 1997).

Let's consider more recent research on the biochemical mechanisms and brain structures that are most directly involved in memory processes.

The Biochemistry of Memory

As described in the chapter on biological aspects of psychology, communication among brain cells takes place at the synapses between axons and dendrites, and it depends on chemicals, called *neurotransmitters*, released at the synapses. The formation and storage of new memories are associated with at least two kinds of changes in synapses.

The first kind of change occurs when stimulation from the environment promotes the formation of *new* synapses, thus increasing the complexity of the communication networks through which neurons receive information (Black & Greenough, 1991; Rosenzweig & Bennett, 1996). Scientists have now actually seen this process occur. As shown in Figure 7.18, repeatedly sending signals across a particular synapse increases the number of special little branches, called *spines*, that appear on the receiving cell's dendrites (Toni et al., 1999).

The second kind of change occurs as new experiences alter the functioning of *existing* synapses. Researchers have discovered that when two neurons fire at the same time and together stimulate a third neuron, that third neuron will later be more responsive than before to stimulation by either neuron alone (Sejnowski, Chattarji, & Stanton, 1990). This process of "sensitizing" synapses is called *long-term potentiation* (Rioult-Pedotti, Friedman, & Donoghue, 2000). Changing patterns of electrical stimulation can also weaken synaptic connections (Malenka,

figure 7.18

Building Memories

These models of synapses are based on electron microscope images of neurons in the brain. Notice that before the synapse has been "sensitized," just one spine (shown in white) appears on this part of the dendrite. Afterward, there are two spines. The creation and changing of many individual synapses in the brain appear to underlie the formation and storage of new memories.

Source: Toni et al. (1999).

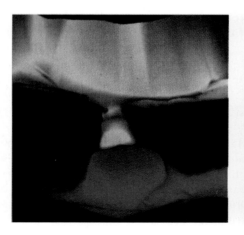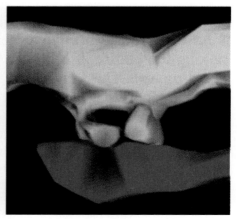

Some Brain Structures Involved in Memory

Combined neural activity in many parts of the brain allows us to encode, store, and retrieve memories. The complexity of the biological bases of these processes is underscored by research showing that different aspects of a memory—such as the sights and sounds associated with some event—are stored in different parts of the cerebral cortex (Gallagher & Chiba, 1996).

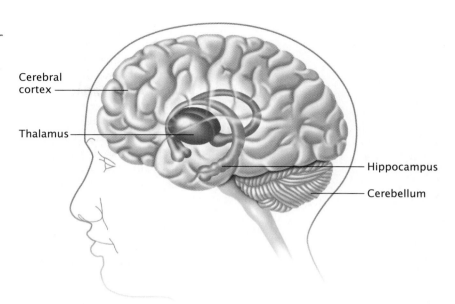

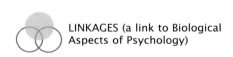 LINKAGES (a link to Biological Aspects of Psychology)

1995). Such changes in sensitivity could account for the development of conditioned responses and other types of learning.

In the hippocampus (see Figure 7.19), these changes appear to occur at synapses that use the neurotransmitter glutamate (Malenka & Nicoll, 1999). Other neurotransmitters, such as acetylcholine, also play important roles in memory formation (e.g., Furey, Pietrini, & Haxby, 2000). The memory problems seen in people with Alzheimer's disease are related to a deficiency in neurons that use acetylcholine and send fibers to the hippocampus and the cortex (Muir, 1997). Drugs that interfere with the action of acetylcholine impair memory, and drugs that increase the amount of acetylcholine in synapses improve memory in aging animals and humans (Pettit, Shao, & Yakel, 2001; Sirvio, 1999).

In short, research has shown that the formation of memories is associated with changes in many individual synapses that, together, strengthen and improve the communication in networks of neurons (Malleret et al., 2001; Rosenzweig & Bennett, 1996). These findings provide some support for the ideas formulated by Hebb many years ago.

Brain Structures and Memory

Are the biochemical processes involved in memory concentrated in certain regions, or are they distributed throughout the brain? The latest research suggests that memory involves both specialized regions for various types of memory formation and widespread areas for storage. Several of the brain regions shown in Figure 7.19, including the hippocampus and nearby parts of the cortex and the thalamus, are vital to the formation of new memories (Brewer et al., 1998; Squire & Zola, 1996; Wagner et al., 1998). Evidence for the memory-related functions of these regions comes from two main sources. First, there are case studies of patients with brain injuries that allow neuropsychologists to determine how damage to specific brain areas is related to specific kinds of memory problems. Second, studies using PET scans, functional MRI, and other neuroimaging methods (described in the chapter on biological aspects of psychology) have allowed neuroscientists to observe where brain activity is concentrated as normal people perform various memory tasks.

The Impact of Brain Damage   Both kinds of research have confirmed that the hippocampus, which is part of the limbic system, is among the brain regions involved in the formation of new memories. Damage to the hippocampus often

OBJ 7.27: Define anterograde and retrograde amnesia and discuss their relevance to the STM/LTM difference controversy.

Test Items 7.144–7.154

ClassPrep PPT 37: Impact of Brain Damage on Memory

results in **anterograde amnesia**, a loss of memory for any event occurring *after* the injury. The case of H.M. provides a striking example of anterograde amnesia (Milner, 1966). When H.M. was twenty-seven years old, part of his hippocampus was removed to end his severe epileptic seizures. Afterward, both his long-term and short-term memory appeared normal, but he had a severe problem. Two years after the operation, he still believed that he was twenty-seven. When his family moved into a new house, H.M. could not remember the new address or even how to get there. When told that his uncle had died, he grieved in a normal way. But soon afterward, he began to ask why his uncle had not visited him. He had to be repeatedly reminded of the death, and each time, he became just as upset as when he was first told. The surgery had apparently destroyed the mechanism that transfers information from short-term to long-term memory.

Although such patients cannot form episodic memories following hippocampal damage, they may still be able to form implicit memories. For example, H.M. was presented with a complicated puzzle on which mistakes are common and performance gradually improves with practice. Over several days his performance steadily improved, just as it does with normal people, and eventually it became virtually perfect. But each time he tried the puzzle, he insisted that he had never seen it before (Cohen & Corkin, 1981; see Figure 9.4). A musician with a similar kind of brain damage was able to use his implicit memory to continue leading choral groups (Vattano, 2000). Other researchers, too, have found intact implicit memory in patients who have anterograde amnesia for new episodic material (Squire & McKee, 1992; Tulving, Hayman, & Macdonald, 1991). These patients are also able to keep information temporarily in working memory, which depends on the activity of dopamine neurons in the prefrontal cortex (Williams & Goldman-Rakic, 1995). So the hippocampus is crucial in the formation of new episodic memories, but implicit memory, procedural memory, and working memory appear to be governed by other regions of the brain (Squire, 1992).

Retrograde amnesia, which involves a loss of memory for events *prior* to a brain injury, is also consistent with the idea that memory processes are widely distributed. Often, a person with this condition is unable to remember anything that took place in the months, or even years, before the injury (Kapur, 1999). In 1994, head injuries from a car crash left thirty-six-year-old Perlene Griffith-Barwell with retrograde amnesia so severe that she forgot virtually everything she had learned about everything and everybody over the previous twenty years. She thought she was still sixteen and did not recognize her husband, Malcolm, or her four children. She said, "The children were sweet, but they didn't seem like mine," and she "didn't feel anything" for Malcolm. Her memories of the last twenty years have never fully returned. She is divorced, but she still lives with her children and holds a job in a bank (Weinstein, 1999). Unlike Perlene, most victims of retrograde amnesia gradually recover their memories. The most distant events are recalled first, and the person gradually regains memory for events leading up to the injury. Recovery is seldom complete, however, and the person may never remember the last few seconds before the injury. One man received a severe blow to the head after being thrown from his motorcycle. After regaining consciousness, he claimed that he was eleven years old. Over the next three months, he gradually recovered his memory right up until the time he was riding his motorcycle the day of the accident. But he was never able to remember what happened just before the accident (Baddeley, 1982). Those final events must have been encoded into short-term memory, but apparently they were never transferred into long-term memory.

An additional clue to the role of specific brain areas in memory comes from research on people with *Korsakoff's syndrome*, a disorder that usually occurs in chronic alcoholics. These people's brains become unable to use glucose as fuel, resulting in severe and widespread brain damage. Damage to the mediodorsal nucleus of the thalamus is particularly implicated in the memory problems typical

anterograde amnesia A loss of memory for any event that occurs after a brain injury.

retrograde amnesia A loss of memory for events prior to a brain injury.

A Case of Retrograde Amnesia Trevor Rees-Jones, a bodyguard for Diana, Princess of Wales, is the sole survivor of the 1997 car crash that killed Diana, her companion Dodi al-Fayed, and her driver. Investigators had hoped that Rees-Jones could shed light on what caused the accident, but the head injury he received left him with retrograde amnesia. It was months before he could begin to recall anything about the events leading up to the accident, and he still cannot remember the accident itself. This type of amnesia is relatively common following concussions, so if you ride a motorcycle, wear that helmet!

of these patients, which can include both anterograde and retrograde amnesia (Squire, Amara, & Press, 1992). Moreover, like patients with hippocampal damage, Korsakoff's patients show impairments in the ability to form new episodic memories but retain some implicit memory abilities. Research has demonstrated that damage to the prefrontal cortex (also common in Korsakoff's patients) is related to disruptions in remembering the order in which events occur (Squire, 1992). Other studies have found that regions within the prefrontal cortex are involved in working memory in both animals and humans (D'Esposito et al., 1995; Goldman-Rakic, 1994, 1995; Smith, 2000).

Multiple Storage Areas   It seems clear that neither the hippocampus nor the thalamus provides permanent long-term memory storage (Rosenbaum et al., 2000). However, both structures send nerve fibers to the cerebral cortex, suggesting that memory is impaired following hippocampal and thalamic damage at least in part because injury to these areas disrupts pathways leading to the cortex. Memories are probably stored in and around the cortex—but not all in one place (Gabrieli, 1998; Miceli et al., 2001).

As described in the chapters on biological aspects of psychology and on sensation, messages from different senses are represented in different regions of the cortex, so information about specific aspects of an experience is probably stored in or near these regions. This arrangement would explain why damage to the auditory cortex disrupts memory for sounds (Colombo et al., 1990). A memory, however, involves more than one sensory system. Even in the simple case of a rat remembering a maze, the experience of the maze includes vision, smell, movement, and emotions, each of which may be stored in different regions of the brain (Gallagher & Chiba, 1996). So memories are both localized and distributed; certain brain areas store specific aspects of each remembered event, but many brain regions are involved in experiencing a whole event (Brewer et al., 1998). The cerebellum, for instance (see Figure 7.19), is involved in the storage of procedural memories, such as dance steps and other movements.

The memory deficits observed in cases of damage to various brain areas are consistent with the view that short-term and long-term memory are distinct systems, and that the deficits themselves result from an inability to transfer information from one system to the other. However, the precise physiological processes involved in this transfer are not yet clear. According to one line of thought, a physiological trace that codes the experience must be gradually transformed and stabilized, or consolidated, if the memory is to endure (Shimizu, Tang, & Tsien, 2000; Verfaellie & Cermak, 1991). Recent research with animals also suggests that when emotional (fear-related) memories are recalled, they are subject to a biological re-storage process during which they are open to alteration (Nader, Schafe, & Le Doux, 2000). Future research on this phenomenon may eventually shed additional light on the processes of constructive memory and the bases for false memories.

It seems likely that memory consolidation depends primarily on the movement of electrochemical impulses within clusters of neurons in the brain (Berman, 1991; Taubenfeld et al., 2001). Events that suppress neural activity in the brain (e.g., physical blows to the head, anesthetics, and carbon monoxide and other types of poisoning) can disrupt the transfer of information from short-term to long-term memory—as can strong but random sets of electrical impulses, such as those that occur in the electroshock treatments sometimes used to treat psychological disorders. The information being transferred from short-term to long-term memory seems to be particularly vulnerable to destruction during the first minute or so (Donegan & Thompson, 1991).

What happens in the brain as we retrieve memories? Functional neuroimaging studies consistently show that the hippocampus, as well as regions of the parietal cortex and prefrontal cortex, are active during memory retrieval (Buckner &

Wheeler, 2001; Cabeza & Nyberg, 2000; Cabeza et al., 2001; Eldridge et al., 2000; McDermott & Buckner, in press; Rugg & Wilding, 2000). There is also evidence to suggest that retrieving memories of certain experiences, such as a conversation or a tennis game, reactivates the sensory and motor regions of the brain that had been involved during the event itself (Nyberg et al., 2001). Cognitive neuroscientists are currently trying to learn more about the retrieval process, including whether different patterns of brain activity are associated with the retrieval of accurate versus inaccurate memories (Gonsalves & Paller, 2000). This research will have obvious applications in areas such as lie detection and the evaluation of recovered memory claims.

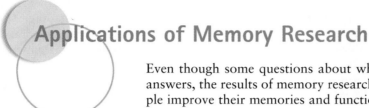

Applications of Memory Research

Even though some questions about what memory is and how it works resist final answers, the results of memory research offer many valuable guidelines to help people improve their memories and function more effectively (Neisser, 2000).

ClassPrep PPT 38: Applications of Memory Research

ClassPrep PPT 39: Mnemonics

OBJ 7.28: Define mnemonics and explain why they improve memory. Give an example of the method of loci.

Test Items 7.155–7.158

IRM Activity 7.7: Chunking Pi

IRM Discussion 7.12: Mnemonics

Improving Your Memory

The most valuable memory enhancement strategies are based on the elaboration of incoming information, and especially on linking new information to what you already know.

Sattler/Shabatay reader, 2/e: Luria, "The Mind of a Mnemonist"

Mnemonics   Psychologists have found that people with normal memory skills, and even those with brain damage, can improve their memory through the use of *mnemonics* (pronounced "nee-MON-ix"). Named for Mnemosyne, the Greek goddess of memory, **mnemonics** are strategies for placing information into an organized context in order to remember it. For example, to remember the names of the Great Lakes, you might use the acronym HOMES (for Huron, Ontario, Michigan, Erie, and Superior). Verbal organization is the basis for many mnemonics. You can link items by weaving them into a story, a sentence, or a rhyme. To help customers remember where they have parked their cars, some large garages have replaced section designations such as "A1" or "G8" with labels that use colors, animal names, or months. Customers can then tie the location of their cars to information already in long-term memory—for example, "I parked in the month of my mother's birthday."

One simple but powerful mnemonic is called the *method of loci* (pronounced "LOW-sigh"), or the method of places. To use this method, first think about a set of familiar locations—in your home, for example. You might imagine walking through the front door, around all four corners of the living room, and through each of the other rooms. Next, imagine that each item to be remembered is in one of these locations. Whenever you want to remember a list, use the same locations, in the same order. Creating vivid, unusual images of how these items appear in each location seems to be particularly effective (Kline & Groninger, 1991). For example, tomatoes smashed against the front door or bananas hanging from the bedroom ceiling might be helpful in recalling these items on a grocery list.

IRM Research Focus 2.5: Listening to Music While Studying

ClassPrep PPT 40: Guidelines for More Effective Studying

IRM Activity 7.4: Depth of Processing

Guidelines for More Effective Studying
The success of mnemonic strategies demonstrates again the importance of relating new information to knowledge already stored in memory. All mnemonic systems require that you have a well-learned body of knowledge (such as locations) that can be used to provide a context for organizing incoming information (Hilton, 1986). When you want to remember more complex material, such as a textbook chapter, the same principles apply (Palmisano & Herrmann, 1991). You can improve your memory for text material by

mnemonics Strategies for placing information in an organized context in order to remember it.

first creating an outline or some other overall context for learning, rather than by just reading and rereading (Glover et al., 1990). Repetition may *seem* effective, because it keeps material in short-term memory; but for retaining information over long periods, repetition alone tends to be ineffective, no matter how much time you spend on it (Bjork, 1999; Bjorklund & Green, 1992). In short, "work smarter, not harder."

In addition, spend your time wisely. *Distributed practice* is much more effective than *massed practice* for learning new information. If you are going to spend ten hours studying for a test, you will be much better off studying for ten one-hour blocks (separated by periods of sleep and other activity) than "cramming" for one ten-hour block. By scheduling more study sessions, you will stay fresh and tend to think about the material from a new perspective at each session. This method will help you elaborate on the material (elaborative rehearsal) and remember it.

Reading a Textbook

More specific advice for remembering textbook material comes from a study that examined how successful and unsuccessful college students approach their reading (Whimbey, 1976). Unsuccessful students tend to read the material straight through; they do not slow down when they reach a difficult section; and they keep going even when they do not understand what they are reading. In contrast, successful college students monitor their understanding, reread difficult sections, and periodically stop to review what they have learned. In other words, effective learners engage in a deep level of processing. They are active learners, thinking of each new fact in relation to other material, and they develop a context in which many new facts can be organized effectively.

Research on memory suggests two specific guidelines for reading a textbook. First, make sure that you understand what you are reading before moving on (Herrmann & Searleman, 1992). Second, use the *PQ4R method* (Thomas & Robinson, 1972), which is one of the most successful strategies for remembering textbook material (Anderson, 1990b; Chastain & Thurber, 1989). *PQ4R* stands for six activities to engage in when you read a chapter: *preview, question, read, reflect, recite,* and *review.* These activities are designed to increase the depth to which you process the information you read and should be done as follows:

1. *Preview.* First, take a few minutes to skim the chapter. Look at the section headings and any boldfaced or italicized terms. Get a general idea of what material will be discussed, the way it is organized, and how its topics relate to one another and to what you already know. Some students find it useful to survey the entire chapter once and then survey each major section in a little more detail before reading it.

2. *Question.* Before reading each section, ask yourself what content will be covered and what information you should be getting from it.

3. *Read.* Now read the text, but *think about* the material as you read. Are you understanding the material? Are the questions you raised earlier being answered?

4. *Reflect.* As you read, think of your own examples—and create visual images—of the concepts and phenomena you encounter. Ask yourself what the material means, and consider how each section relates to other sections in the chapter and to other chapters in the book (this book's Linkages features are designed to promote this kind of reflection).

5. *Recite.* At the end of each section, recite the major points. Resist the temptation to be passive and say, "Oh, I'll remember that." Be active. Put the ideas into your own words by reciting them aloud.

6. *Review.* Finally, at the end of the chapter, review all the material. You should see connections not only within each section but also among sections. The

Understand and Remember Research on memory suggests that students who simply read their textbooks will not remember as much as those who, like this woman, read for understanding using the PQ4R method. Further, memory for the material is likely to be better if you read and study it over a number of weeks rather than in one marathon session on the night before a test.

objective is to see how the material is organized. Once you grasp the organization, the individual facts will be far easier to remember.

By following these procedures you will learn and remember the material better, and you will also save yourself considerable time.

ClassPrep PPT 42: Lecture Notes

Lecture Notes   Effective note-taking during lectures is vital, but it is an acquired skill. Research on memory suggests some simple strategies for taking and using notes effectively.

Realize first that in note-taking, more is not necessarily better. Taking detailed notes of everything you hear requires that you pay close attention to unimportant, as well as important, content, leaving little time for thinking about the material. Note-takers who concentrate on expressing the major ideas in relatively few words remember more than those who try to catch every detail (Pauk & Fiore, 2000). The best way to take notes is to think about what is being said, draw connections with other material in the lecture, and then summarize the major points clearly and concisely (Kiewra, 1989).

Once you have a set of lecture notes, review them as soon as possible after the lecture so that you can fill in missing details. (Remember that most forgetting from long-term memory occurs within the first few hours after learning.) When the time comes for serious study, use your notes as if they were a chapter in a textbook. Write a detailed outline. Think about how various points are related. Once you have organized the material, the details will make more sense and will be much easier to remember. ("In Review: Improving Your Memory" summarizes tips for studying.)

Design for Memory

The scientific study of memory has influenced the design of the electronic and mechanical devices that play an increasingly important role in our lives. Those who design computers, VCRs, DVD players, digital cameras, and even stoves are faced with a choice: Either place the operating instructions on the devices themselves, or assume that users will remember how to operate them. Understanding the limits of both working memory and long-term memory has helped designers distinguish between information that is likely to be stored in (and easily retrieved from) the user's memory, and information that should be presented in the form of labels,

in review	Improving Your Memory	
Goal	**Helpful Techniques**
Remembering lists of items	Use mnemonics. Look for meaningful acronyms. Try the method of loci.
Remembering textbook material	Follow the PQ4R system. Allocate your time to allow for distributed practice. Read actively, not passively.
Taking lecture notes	Take notes, but record only the main points. Think about the overall organization of the material. Review your notes as soon after the lecture as possible in order to fill in missing points.
Studying for exams	Write a detailed outline of your lecture notes rather than passively reading them.

instructions, or other cues that reduce memory demands (Norman, 1988). Placing unfamiliar or hard-to-recall information in plain view makes it easier to use the device as intended, and with less chance of errors (Segal & Suri, 1999).

Psychologists have influenced advertisers and designers to create many other "user-friendly" systems (Wickens, Gordon, & Liu, 1998). As a result, toll-free numbers are designed to take advantage of chunking, which, as mentioned earlier, provides an efficient way to maintain information in working memory. Which do you think would be easier to remember: 1-800-438-4357 or 1-800-GET-HELP? Obviously, the more meaningful "get help" number is more memorable (there are web sites that can help you translate any phone number into words or a phrase). In the automotive arena, designers ensure that turn signals emit an audible cue when activated, a feature that reduces your memory load while driving and leaves you with enough working memory capacity to keep in mind that there is a car in your "blind spot."

As ever more complex devices appear in the marketplace, it will be increasingly important that instructions about how to operate them are presented clearly and memorably. With guidance from research on memory it should be possible for almost anyone to operate these devices efficiently. Yes, even the programming of a VCR will no longer be a mystery!

ClassPrep: Linkages to Memory

LINKAGES

As noted in the chapter on introducing psychology, all of psychology's subfields are related to one another. Our discussion of the accuracy of eyewitnesses' memories illustrates just one way in which the topic of this chapter, memory, is linked to the subfield of perception (see the chapter on perception). The Linkages diagram shows ties to two other subfields as well, and there are many more ties throughout the book. Looking for linkages among subfields will help you see how they all fit together and help you better appreciate the big picture that is psychology.

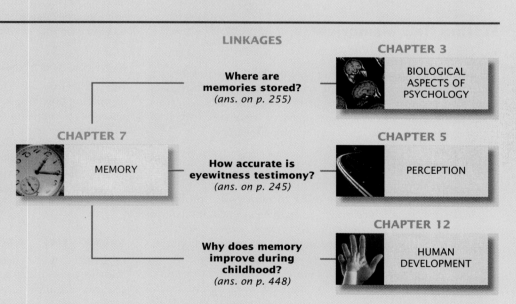

SUMMARY

The Nature of Memory

Human memory depends on a complex mental system.

Basic Memory Processes

There are three basic memory processes. *Encoding* transforms information into some type of mental representation. Encoding can be *acoustic* (by sound), *visual* (by appearance), or *semantic* (by meaning). *Storage* maintains information in the memory system over time. *Retrieval* is the process of gaining access to previously stored information.

Types of Memory

Most psychologists agree that there are at least three types of memory. *Episodic memory* contains information about specific events in a person's life. *Semantic memory* contains generalized knowledge about the world. *Procedural memory* contains information about how to do various things.

Explicit and Implicit Memory

Some research on memory concerns *explicit memory,* the processes through which people intentionally try to remember something. Psychologists also examine *implicit memory,* which refers to the unintentional influence of prior experiences.

Models of Memory

Four theoretical models of memory have guided most research. According to the *levels-of-processing model,* the most important determinant of memory is how extensively information is encoded or processed when it is first received. In general, *elaborative rehearsal* is more effective than *maintenance rehearsal* in learning new information, because it represents a deeper level of processing. According to the *transfer-appropriate processing model,* the critical determinant of memory is not how deeply information is encoded but whether processes used during retrieval match those used during encoding. *Parallel distributed processing (PDP) models* of memory suggest that new experiences not only provide specific information but also become part of, and alter, a whole network of associations. And the *information-processing model* suggests that in order for information to become firmly embedded in memory, it must pass through three stages of processing: sensory memory, short-term memory, and long-term memory.

Storing New Memories

Sensory Memory

Sensory memory maintains incoming information in the *sensory registers* for a very brief time. *Selective attention,* which focuses mental resources on only part of the stimulus field, controls what information in the sensory registers is actually perceived and transferred to short-term and working memory.

Short-Term Memory and Working Memory

Working memory is a system that allows us to store, organize, and manipulate information in order to think, solve problems, and make decisions. The storage, or maintenance, component of working memory is referred to as *short-term memory.* Remembering a phone number long enough to call it involves simple maintenance of the information in short-term memory.

Various memory codes can be used in short-term memory, but acoustic codes seem to dominate in most verbal tasks. Studies of the *immediate memory span* indicate that the storage capacity of short-term memory is approximately seven *chunks,* or meaningful groupings of information. Studies using the *Brown-Peterson procedure* show that information in short-term memory is usually forgotten within about eighteen seconds if it is not rehearsed.

Long-Term Memory

Long-term memory normally involves semantic encoding, which means that people tend to encode the general meaning of information, not specific details, in long-term memory. The capacity of long-term memory to store new information is extremely large, and perhaps even unlimited.

Distinguishing Between Short-Term and Long-Term Memory

According to some psychologists, there is no need to distinguish between short-term and long-term memory. Still, some evidence suggests that these systems are distinct. For example, the *primacy* and *recency effects* that occur when people try to recall a list of words may indicate the presence of two different systems.

Retrieving Memories

Retrieval Cues and Encoding Specificity

Retrieval cues help people remember things that they would otherwise not be able to recall. The effectiveness of retrieval cues follows the *encoding specificity principle:* Cues help retrieval only if they match some feature of the information that was originally encoded.

Context and State Dependence

All else being equal, memory may be better when one attempts to retrieve information in the same environment in which it was learned; this is called *context-dependent memory.* When a person's internal state can aid or impede retrieval, the person is said to have *state-dependent memory.*

Retrieval from Semantic Memory

Researchers usually study retrieval from semantic memory by examining how long it takes people to answer world knowledge questions. It appears that ideas are represented as associations in a dense semantic memory network, and that the retrieval of information occurs by a process of *spreading activation.* Each concept in the network is represented as a collection of features or attributes. The tip-of-the-tongue phenomenon and the feeling-of-knowing experience represent the retrieval of incomplete knowledge.

Constructing Memories

In the process of constructive memory, people use their existing knowledge to fill in gaps in the information they encode and retrieve. Parallel distributed processing models provide one explanation of how people make spontaneous generalizations about the world. They also explain the *schemas* that shape the memories people construct.

Forgetting

How Do We Forget?

In his research on long-term memory and forgetting, Hermann Ebbinghaus introduced the *method of savings.* He found that most forgetting from long-term memory occurs during the first several hours after learning and that savings can be extremely long lasting.

Why Do We Forget?: The Roles of Decay and Interference

Decay and *interference* are two mechanisms of forgetting. Although there is evidence of both decay and interference in short-term memory, it appears that most forgetting from long-term memory is due to either *retroactive interference* or *proactive interference.*

Biological Bases of Memory

The Biochemistry of Memory

Research has shown that memory can result as new synapses are formed in the brain and as communication at existing synapses is improved. Several neurotransmitters appear to be involved in the strengthening that occurs at synapses.

Brain Structures and Memory

Neuroimaging studies of normal people, as well as research with patients whose brain damage has resulted in *anterograde amnesia, retrograde amnesia,* Korsakoff's syndrome, and other memory problems, provide valuable information about the brain structures involved in memory. The hippocampus and thalamus are known to play a role in the formation of memories. These structures send nerve fibers to the cerebral cortex, which is where memories are probably stored and which is activated during memory retrieval. Memories appear to be both localized and distributed throughout the brain.

Applications of Memory Research

Improving Your Memory

Among the many applications of memory research are *mnemonics,* devices that are used to remember things better. One of the simplest but most powerful mnemonics is the method of loci. It is useful because it provides a context for organizing material more effectively. Guidelines for effective studying have also been derived from memory research. For example, the key to remembering textbook material is to read actively rather than passively. One of the most effective ways to do this is to follow the PQ4R method: preview, question, read, reflect, recite, and review. To take good lecture notes and to study them effectively, organize the points into a meaningful framework, and think about how each main point relates to the others.

Design for Memory

Research on the limits of memory has helped product designers to create electronic and mechanical systems and devices that are "user-friendly."

8

Cognition and Language

D r. Joyce Wallace, a New York City internist, was trying to figure out what was the matter with a forty-three-year-old patient, "Laura McBride." Laura reported pains in her stomach and abdomen, aching muscles, irritability, dizzy spells, and fatigue (Rouéché, 1986). The doctor's first hypothesis was that the patient had iron-deficiency anemia, a condition in which there is too little oxygen-carrying hemoglobin in the blood. There was some evidence to support that hypothesis. Laura's spleen was somewhat enlarged, and blood tests showed low hemoglobin and high production of red blood cells, suggesting that Laura's body was attempting to compensate for the loss of hemoglobin. However, other tests revealed normal iron levels. Perhaps she was losing blood through internal bleeding, but an additional test ruled that out. Had Laura been vomiting blood? She said no. Blood in the urine? No. Abnormally heavy menstrual flow? No. During the next week, as Dr. Wallace puzzled over the problem, Laura reported more intense pain, cramps, shortness of breath, and severe loss of energy. Her blood was becoming less and less capable of sustaining her, but if it was not being lost, what was happening to it? When the doctor looked at a smear of Laura's blood under the microscope, she saw that some kind of poison was destroying the red blood cells. What could it be? Laura spent most of her time at home, but her teenage daughters, who lived with her, were healthy. Dr. Wallace asked herself, "What does Laura do that the girls don't?" She repairs and restores paintings. Paint. Lead! She might be suffering from lead poisoning! When a blood test showed a lead level seven times higher than normal, Dr. Wallace knew she had solved this medical mystery at last.

To do so, Dr. Wallace relied on her ability to think, solve problems, and make judgments and decisions. She used these higher mental processes to weigh the pros and cons of various hypotheses and to reach decisions about what tests to order and how to interpret them. She also consulted with the patient and other physicians, using that remarkable human ability known as *language*.

As described in the chapter on biological aspects of psychology, these vital skills depend on the proper functioning of the brain; anything that disrupts that functioning can drastically impair cognitive abilities. For example, "Elliot," an intelligent and successful young businessman, had a cancerous tumor removed from the frontal area of his brain. After the surgery, neurologist Antonio Damasio found that Elliot's language, memory, and perceptual processes remained intact, but his ability to make complex business decisions and rational plans was virtually gone. In fact, a series of reckless, impulsive business schemes had already forced him into bankruptcy (Damasio, 1994).

These cases highlight the fact that our success as individuals depends largely on our cognitive and language skills. When those skills are impaired, by biological or other factors, we become vulnerable to all sorts of failures and errors. What pitfalls threaten the effectiveness of human cognition? What factors influence our success? How are our thoughts transformed into language? Many of the answers to these questions come from **cognitive psychology**, the study of the mental processes by which the information humans receive from their environment is modified, made meaningful, stored, retrieved, used, and communicated to others (Neisser, 1967).

In this chapter we examine two major aspects of human cognition: thought and language. First we consider what thought is and what functions it serves. Then we examine the basic ingredients of thought and the cognitive processes people use as they interact with their environment. These cognitive processes include reasoning, problem solving, and decision making. Next, we discuss language and how it is acquired and used. We discuss thought and language in the same chapter because thinking and communicating often involve the same cognitive processes. Learning about thought helps us to better understand language, and learning about language helps us to better understand thought.

cognitive psychology   The study of the mental processes by which information from the environment is modified, made meaningful, stored, retrieved, used, and communicated to others.

Basic Functions of Thought

Let's begin our exploration of human cognition by considering the five core functions of thought, which are to *describe*, *elaborate*, *decide*, *plan*, and *guide action*. These functions can be seen as forming a *circle of thought* (see Figure 8.1).

OBJ 8.2: Describe the core functions that form a circle of thought.

Test Items 8.3–8.4

IRM Activity 7.5: Meaningfulness in Long-Term Memory

OBJ 8.3: Define information-processing system and thinking. Discuss the relationship between information-processing systems and decision making in humans.

Test Items 8.5–8.8

IRM In Your Own Words 8.2: An Auto Accident

The Circle of Thought

Consider how the circle of thought operated in Dr. Wallace. It began when she received the information about Laura's symptoms that allowed her to *describe* the problem. Next, she *elaborated* on this information by using her knowledge and experience to consider what disorders might cause such symptoms. Then she made a *decision* to investigate a possible cause, such as anemia. To implement this decision, she made a *plan*—to order a blood test—and then *acted* on that plan. But the circle of thought did not stop there. Information from the blood test provided new descriptive information, which Dr. Wallace *elaborated* further to reach another decision, create a new plan, and guide her next action.

Because the circle of thought spins constantly and rapidly and cannot be observed directly, it is difficult to study scientifically. One way to do so is to approach mental processes as a kind of information-processing system. An **information-processing system** receives information, represents the information with symbols, and then manipulates those representations. According to this information-processing model, then, **thinking** is defined as the manipulation of mental representations. Figure 8.2 shows how an information-processing model might view the sequence of events that form each cycle in the circle of thought. Notice that according to this model, information from the world is transformed somewhat as it passes through each stage of processing (Wickens, Gordon, & Liu, 1998).

figure 8.1

The Circle of Thought

ClassPrep PPT 3: *Figure 8.1:* The Circle of Thought

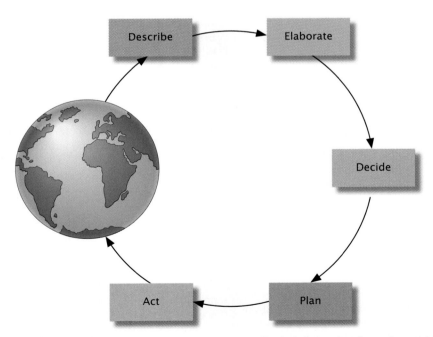

The circle of thought begins as our sensory systems take in information from the world. Our perceptual system describes and elaborates this information, which is represented in the brain in ways that allow us to make decisions, formulate plans, and guide our actions. As those actions change our world, we receive new information—and the circle of thought begins again.

information-processing system Mechanisms for receiving information, representing it with symbols, and manipulating it.

thinking The manipulation of mental representations.

reaction time The time between the presentation of a stimulus and an overt response to it.

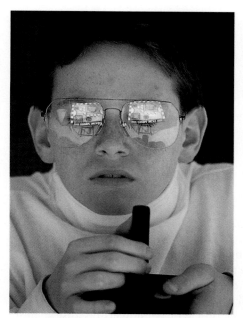

"Automatic" Thinking The sensory, perceptual, decision-making, and response-planning components that make up the circle of thought often occur so rapidly that we may be unaware of anything other than incoming information and our quick response to it. This is especially likely in skilled computer-game players, because as described in the chapter on perception, well-practiced tasks can be performed automatically.

OBJ 8.4: Define mental chronometry and reaction time. Describe the factors that influence reaction time.

Test Items 8.9–8.17

IRM Activity 8.3: Reaction Time and Cognitive Complexity

Videodisc Segment: Kahneman on Thinking and Perception

In the first stage, information about the world reaches the brain by way of the sensory receptors described in the chapter on sensation. This stage does not require attention. In the second stage, the information must be perceived and recognized, using the attentional and perceptual processes described in the chapter on perception. It is also during this stage that the information is consciously elaborated, using short-term and working memory processes that allow us to think about it in relation to knowledge stored in long-term memory. Once the information has been elaborated in this way, we must decide what to do with it. This third stage—decision making—also demands attention. The decision may be simply to store the information in memory. If, however, a decision is made to take some action, a response must be planned in the third stage and then carried out through a coordinated pattern of responses—the action itself—in the fourth and fifth stages. As suggested in Figure 8.1, this action usually affects the environment, providing new information that, in turn, is "fed back" to the system for processing in the ongoing circle of thought.

Measuring Information Processing

The brain damage suffered by Dr. Damasio's patient Elliot appeared to have mainly affected the decision-making and response selection stages of information processing. Analyzing the effects of brain damage is just one of several methods that scientists use to study the details of how the entire information-processing sequence normally works and what can interfere with it.

Mental Chronometry   Drivers and video-game players know that there is always a slight delay between seeing a red light or a space alien and hitting the brakes or firing the laser gun. The delay occurs because each of the processes described in Figure 8.2 takes some time. Psychologists began the laboratory investigation of thinking by exploring *mental chronometry,* the timing of mental events (Posner, 1978). Specifically, they examined **reaction time,** the time elapsing between the presentation of a stimulus and the appearance of an overt response to it. Reaction time, they reasoned, would give us an idea of how long it takes for all the processes shown in Figure 8.2 to occur. In a typical reaction-time experiment, a person is asked to say a word or to push a button as rapidly as possible after a stimulus appears. Even in such simple situations, several factors influence reaction times (Wickens, Gordon, & Liu, 1998).

IRM Activity 3.5: Mental Chronometry and Speed of Neural Transmission

ClassPrep: Measuring Information Processing

ClassPrep PPT 4, OHT: *Figure 8.2:* An Information-Processing Model

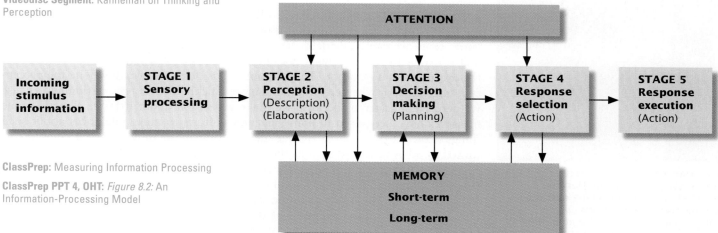

figure 8.2

An Information-Processing Model

According to the information-processing model, each stage in the circle of thought takes a certain amount of time. Some stages depend heavily on both short-term and long-term memory and require some attention—that limited supply of mental energy required for information processing to be carried out efficiently.

figure 8.3

Stimulus-Response Compatibility

Imagine standing in front of an unfamiliar stove when a pot starts to boil over. Your reaction time in turning down the heat will depend in part on the stove's design. The response you make will be quicker on the stove in Part A, because each knob is next to the burner it controls; there is compatibility between the source of the stimulus and the location of the response. The stove in Part B shows less compatibility; here, which knob you should turn is not as obvious, so your reaction time will be slower.

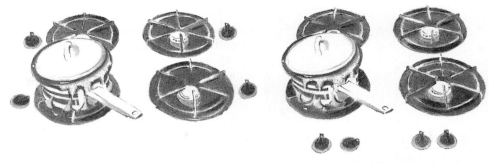

A compatible relationship   **An incompatible relationship**

(A)   **(B)**

One important factor in reaction time is the *complexity* of the decision. The larger the number of possible actions that might be carried out in response to a set of stimuli, the longer the reaction time. The tennis player who knows that her opponent usually serves to a particular spot on the court will have a simple decision to make when the serve is completed and will react rapidly. But if she faces an opponent whose serve is less predictable, her reaction will be slower, because a more complex decision about which way to move is now required.

Reaction time is also influenced by *stimulus-response compatibility*. If the relationship between a set of stimuli and possible responses is a natural or compatible one, reaction time will be fast. If not, reaction time will be slower. Figure 8.3 illustrates compatible and incompatible relationships. Incompatible stimulus-response relationships are major culprits in causing errors in the use of all kinds of equipment (Proctor & Van Zandt, 1994; Segal & Suri, 1999).

Expectancy, too, affects reaction time. People respond faster to stimuli that they expect to occur and more slowly to stimuli that surprise them. So your reaction time will be shorter when braking for a traffic light that you knew might turn red than when dodging a ball thrown at you unexpectedly.

Finally, in any reaction-time task there is a *speed-accuracy tradeoff*. If you try to respond quickly, errors increase; if you try for an error-free performance, reaction time increases (Wickens & Carswell, 1997). Sprinters who try too hard to anticipate the starting gun may have especially quick starts but may also have especially frequent false starts that disqualify them.

Evoked Brain Potentials

Research on reaction time has helped establish the time required for information processing to occur; it has also revealed how the entire sequence can be made faster or slower. But reaction times alone cannot provide a detailed picture of what goes on between the presentation of a stimulus and the execution of a response. They do not tell us, for example, how long the perception stage lasts, or whether we respond more quickly to an expected stimulus because we perceive it faster or because we make a decision about it faster. Reaction-time measures have been used in many ingenious efforts to make inferences about such things (Coles, 1989); but to analyze mental events more directly, psychologists have turned to other methods, such as the analysis of evoked brain potentials.

The **evoked brain potential** is a small, temporary change in voltage on an *electroencephalogram (EEG)* that occurs in response to specific events (Rugg & Coles, 1995). Figure 8.4 shows an example. Each peak reflects the firing of large groups of neurons, within different regions of the brain, at different times during the information-processing sequence. The pattern of the peaks provides information that is more precise than overall reaction time. For example, a large positive peak, called the P300, occurs 300 to 500 milliseconds after a stimulus is presented. The exact timing of the P300 depends in part on factors that affect the speed of perceptual processes, such as the difficulty of detecting a stimulus. But the timing of the P300

On Your Mark . . . The runner who reacts quickest when the starting gun is fired will have an advantage over other competitors, but too much eagerness can cause an athlete to literally jump the gun and lose the race before it starts. At the same time, too much concern over avoiding a false start can slow reaction time and cost precious time in getting off the mark. This is the speed-accuracy tradeoff in action.

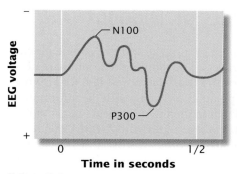

figure 8.4

Evoked Potentials

Here is the average EEG, or brain wave tracing, produced from several trials on which a participant's name was presented. Evoked potentials are averaged in this way so as to eliminate random variations in the tracings. The result is the appearance of a *negative* peak (N100) followed by a large *positive* peak (P300). Traditionally, positive peaks are shown as decreases on such tracings, whereas negative ones are shown as increases.

ClassPrep PPT 8: *Figure 8.4:* Evoked Potentials

OBJ 8.6: Describe neuroimaging techniques and how they are useful in studying information-processing.

Test Items 8.22–8.23

is not affected by factors—such as changes in stimulus-response compatibility—that merely alter the speed with which a response is selected and executed (Rugg & Coles, 1995; Siddle et al., 1991). Thus, the length of time before a P300 occurs may reflect the duration of the first two stages of information processing shown in Figure 8.2.

Neuroimaging   Using positron emission tomography (PET), functional magnetic resonance imaging (fMRI), and other neuroimaging techniques described in the chapter on biological aspects of psychology, cognitive psychologists and other cognitive neuroscientists are finding ways to watch what happens in the brain during information processing (e.g., Miller & Cohen, 2001; Posner & DiGirolamo, 2001). In one study, for example, participants performed a task that required complex problem-solving skills. As shown by the red-shaded areas in Figure 8.5, the frontal lobe of the brain was especially active when this task was still relatively new and difficult. As the participants learned the skills, however, this frontal lobe involvement decreased. When the task was well learned, the hippocampus became especially active (see the green-shaded areas in the bottom panel of Figure 8.5). Activation in the hippocampus suggests that the participants were no longer struggling with a problem-solving task but instead were performing it from memory.

A number of other studies of brain activity during the performance of cognitive tasks have also found that the frontal lobes are especially important for problem solving and other cognitive tasks that place heavy demands on attention and working memory (Duncan & Owen, 2000; Wallis, Anderson, & Miller, 2001; this chapter's Focus on Research Methods shows another example). It is no wonder, then, that the damage Elliot suffered in the frontal area of his brain disrupted his decision-making abilities.

IRM Discussion 8.5: Applications of Evoked Potential Research

figure 8.5

Watching People Think

Cognitive psychologists can now actually watch information processing as it takes place in the brain. These fMRI pictures show activity in two "slices" of the brain of a research participant who was practicing a complex problem-solving task. The areas shown in red were activated early in the learning process; as skill developed, the areas shown in green became activated.

Source: Anderson (2000).

ClassPrep PPT 9: *Figure 8.5:* Watching People Think Using fMRI Scans

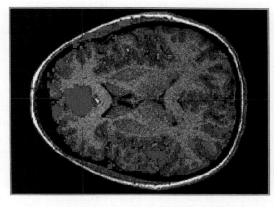

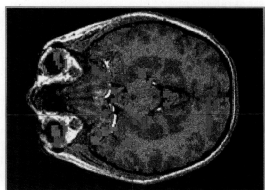

evoked brain potential A small, temporary change in EEG voltage that is evoked by some stimulus.

Mental Representations: The Ingredients of Thought

Just as measuring, stirring, and baking are only part of the story of cookie making, so timing, describing, and visualizing the processes of thinking tell only part of the story behind the circle of thought. To understand thinking more fully, we also need to know what it is that these processes manipulate. Consistent with the information-processing model, most psychologists usually describe the ingredients of thought as *information*. But this is like saying that you make cookies with "stuff." What specific forms does information take in our minds? In other words, how do we mentally represent information? Researchers in cognitive psychology have found that information can be mentally represented in many ways, including as *concepts, propositions, schemas, scripts, mental models, images,* and *cognitive maps*. Let's consider each of these ingredients of thought and how people manipulate them as they think.

ClassPrep PPT 10: How Can Information Be Mentally Represented?

OBJ 8.7: Define concept. Describe the difference between formal and natural concepts and give an example of each. Explain the role of prototypes in natural concepts.

Test Items 8.24–8.31

Concepts   *Videodisc Segment & Still:* A Concept Hierarchy

The most fundamental building blocks of thought are **concepts,** which are categories of objects, events, or ideas with common properties (Jahnke & Nowaczyk, 1998; Katz & Fodor, 1963). To "have a concept" is to recognize the properties, or *features,* that tend to be shared by the members of the category. For example, the concept "bird" includes such properties as having feathers, laying eggs, and being able to fly. The concept "scissors" includes such properties as having two blades, a connecting hinge, and a pair of hand holes. Concepts allow you to relate each object, event, or idea you encounter to a category you already know. Concepts also make it possible to think logically. If you have the concepts "whale" and "bird," you can decide whether a whale is bigger than a bird without having either creature in the room with you.

Some concepts—called **formal concepts**—can be clearly defined by a set of rules or properties such that each member of the concept has all of the defining properties, and no nonmember does. For example, the concept "square" can be defined as "a shape with four equal sides and four right-angle corners." Any object that does not have all of these features simply is not a square, and any object with all these features is a square. To study concept learning in the laboratory, psychologists often use formal concepts, because the members of the concept can be neatly defined (Trabasso & Bower, 1968).

In contrast, try to define the concept "home" or "game." These are examples of **natural concepts,** concepts that have no fixed set of defining features but instead share a set of typical, or characteristic, features. Members of a natural concept need not have all of these characteristic features. One characteristic feature of the natural concept "bird," for example, is the ability to fly; but an ostrich is a bird even though it cannot fly, because it possesses enough other characteristic features of "bird" (feathers, wings, and the like). Having just one bird property is not enough; a snake lays eggs and a bat flies, but neither is a bird. It is usually a combination of properties that defines a concept. Outside the laboratory, most of the concepts people use in thinking are natural rather than formal concepts. Natural concepts include relatively concrete object categories, such as "bird" or "house"; abstract idea categories, such as "honesty" or "justice"; and temporary goal-related categories that help people make plans, such as "things I need to pack in my suitcase" (Barsalou, 1991, 1993).

The boundaries of a natural concept are fuzzy, and some members of it are better examples of the concept than others because they share more of its characteristic features (Rosch, 1975). A robin, a chicken, an ostrich, and a penguin are all birds. But a robin is a better example than the other three, because a robin can fly and is closer to the size and proportion of what most people, through experience,

TRY THIS

Personal Learning Activity 8.1

concepts   Categories of objects, events, or ideas that have common properties.

formal concepts   Concepts that can be clearly defined by a set of rules or properties.

natural concepts   Concepts that have no fixed set of defining features but instead share a set of characteristic features.

prototype   A member of a natural concept that possesses all or most of its characteristic features.

propositions   Mental representations of the relationship between concepts.

schemas   Generalizations about categories of objects, places, events, and people.

A Natural Concept A space shuttle and a hot-air balloon are two examples of the natural concept "aircraft," but most people think of the space shuttle, with its wings, as the better example. A prototype of the concept is probably an airplane.

think of as a typical bird. A member of a natural concept that possesses all or most of its characteristic features is called a **prototype,** or is said to be *prototypical* (Smith, 1998). A robin, then, is a prototypical bird. The more prototypical a member of a concept is, the more quickly people can decide if it is an example of the concept. Thus, it takes less time to answer the question "Is a robin a bird?" than "Is a penguin is a bird?"

Propositions

OBJ 8.8: Define propositions, schemas, scripts, and mental models and describe their role in the thinking process.

Test Items 8.32–8.39

ClassPrep PPT 10: How Can Information Be Mentally Represented? (cont.)

We often combine concepts in units known as **propositions.** A proposition is a mental representation that expresses a relationship between concepts. Propositions can be true or false. Suppose you hear someone say that your friend Heather broke up with her boyfriend, Jason. Your mental representation of this event will include a proposition that links your concepts of "Heather" and "Jason" in a particular way. This proposition could be diagrammed (using unscientific terms) as follows: Heather—dumped → Jason.

The diagram looks like a sentence, but it is not. Propositions can be expressed as sentences, but they are actually general ideas that can be conveyed in any number of specific ways. In this case, "Jason was dumped by Heather" and "Heather is not dating Jason anymore" would all express the same proposition. If you later discover that it was Jason who caused the breakup, your proposition about the event would become the following: Heather ← dumped—Jason. Propositions are part of the network of associations that many psychologists see as the basis for our knowledge of the world (see Figures 7.10 and 7.11 in the chapter on memory). So hearing the name Heather, for example, will activate lots of associated information about her, including the proposition about her relationship to Jason.

IRM In Your Own Words 8.2: An Auto Accident

Schemas, Scripts, and Mental Models

IRM Activity 8.6: Cognition: Schemas

Sets of propositions are often so closely associated that they form more complex mental representations called **schemas.** As described in the chapters on perception, memory, and human development, schemas are generalizations that we develop about categories of objects, places, events, and people. Our schemas help us to understand the world. If you borrow a friend's car, your "car" schema will give you

You Can't Judge a Book by Its Cover
Does this person look like a millionaire to you? Our schemas tell us what to expect about objects, events, and people, but those expectations can sometimes be wrong. This fact was dramatically illustrated in October 1999 when Gordon Elwood died. The Medford, Oregon, man, who dressed in rags and collected cans, left over $9 million to charity (McMahon, 2000).

IRM Activity 8.7: Cognition: Scripts

IRM Activity 1.7: Sociocultural Diversity

IRM Activity 2.12: A Staged Incident

IRM Activity 5.13: Top-Down Processing

IRM Activity 5.14: Biases in Perception

ClassPrep PPT 11: How Can Information Be Mentally Represented? (cont.)

a good idea of where to put the ignition key, where the accelerator and brake are, and how to raise and lower the windows. Schemas also generate expectations about objects, places, events, and people—telling us that stereo systems have speakers, that picnics occur in the summer, that rock concerts are loud, and so on.

Scripts   Schemas about familiar activities, such as going to a restaurant, are known as **scripts** (Anderson, 2000). Your "restaurant" script represents the sequence of events you can expect when you go out to eat (see Figure 8.6). That script tells you what to do when you are in a restaurant and helps you to understand stories involving restaurants (Whitney, 2001). Scripts also shape your interpretation of events. For example, on your first day of college, you no doubt assumed that the person standing at the front of the class was a teacher, not a mugger.

If our scripts are violated, however, it is easy to misinterpret events. In 1993, a heart attack victim in London lay for nine hours in the hallway of an apartment building after an ambulance crew smelled alcohol on his breath and assumed he was "sleeping it off." The crew's script for what happens in the poorer sections of big cities told them that someone slumped in a hallway is drunk, not sick. Because script-violating events are unexpected, our reactions to them tend to be slower and less effective than are our reactions to expected events. Your "grocery shopping" script, for example, probably includes pushing a cart, putting items in it, going to the checkout stand, and paying for your purchases. But suppose you are at the back of the store when a robber near the entrance fires a gun and shouts at the manager to open the safe. People sometimes ignore these script-violating events, interpreting gunshots as a car backfiring and shouted orders as "someone fooling around." Others simply "freeze," unsure of what to do.

Mental Models   Sets of propositions can be organized not only as schemas and scripts but also as **mental models** (Johnson-Laird, 1983). For example, suppose someone tells you, "My living room has blue walls, a white ceiling, and an oval window across from the door." You will mentally represent this information as propositions about how the concepts "wall," "blue," "ceiling," "white," "door," "oval," and "window" are related. However, you will also combine these propositions to create in your mind a three-dimensional model of the room. As more infor-

scripts Mental representations of familiar sequences of activity.
mental model A cluster of propositions representing our understanding of objects and processes that guides our interaction with those things.
images Mental representations of visual information.
cognitive map A mental representation of familiar parts of the environment.

figure 8.6

Eating at a Restaurant

Schemas about what happens in restaurants and how to behave in them take the form of a *script*, represented here in four "scenes." Scripts guide our actions in all sorts of familiar situations and also help us to understand descriptions of events occurring in those situations (e.g., "Our service was really slow").

Source: Whitney (2001).

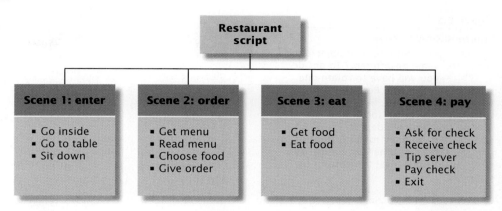

Restaurant script

Scene 1: enter
- Go inside
- Go to table
- Sit down

Scene 2: order
- Get menu
- Read menu
- Choose food
- Give order

Scene 3: eat
- Get food
- Eat food

Scene 4: pay
- Ask for check
- Receive check
- Tip server
- Pay check
- Exit

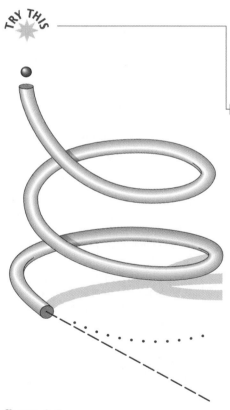

TRY THIS

figure 8.7

Applying a Mental Model

TRY THIS Try to imagine the path that the marble will follow when it leaves the curved tube. In one study, most people drew the incorrect (curved) path indicated by the dotted line rather than the correct (straight) path indicated by the dashed line (McClosky, 1983). Their error was based on a faulty mental model of the behavior of physical objects.

mation about the world becomes available, either from existing memories or from new information we receive, our mental models become more complete.

Accurate mental models are excellent guides for thinking about, and interacting with, many of the things we encounter (Galotti, 1999). If a mental model is incorrect, however, we are likely to make mistakes (see Figure 8.7). For example, people who hold an incorrect mental model of how physical illness is cured might stop taking an antibiotic when their symptoms begin to disappear, well before the bacteria causing those symptoms have been eliminated (Medin, Ross, & Markman, 2001). Others overdose on medication because according to their faulty mental model, "if taking three pills a day is good, taking six would be even better."

Images and Cognitive Maps

Think about how your best friend would look in a clown suit. The "mental picture" you just got illustrates that often, thinking involves the manipulation of **images**—which are mental representations of visual information. Cognitive psychologists refer to mental images as *analogical representations,* because we manipulate these images in a way that is similar, or *analogous* to, manipulating the objects themselves (Reed, 2000). This similarity was demonstrated in a classic study by Roger Shepard and Jacqueline Metzler (1971). They measured how long it took people to decide whether pairs of objects like those in Figure 8.8 were the same or different. They found that decision time depended on how far one object had to be "mentally rotated" to compare it with the other. The more rotation required, the longer the decision took. In other words, rotating the mental image of an object was like rotating the real object. More recent studies using neuroimaging have confirmed that manipulating mental images activates some of the same visual and spatial areas of the brain that are active during comparable tasks with real objects (Farah, 2000).

Our ability to think using images extends beyond the manipulation of stimuli like those in Figure 8.8. We also create mental images from written or spoken descriptions, as you probably did a minute ago when you read about that blue-walled room. The same thing happens when someone gives you directions to that new pizza place in town. In this case, you scan your **cognitive map**—a mental representation of familiar parts of your world—to find the location. In doing so, you use a mental process similar to the visual process of scanning a paper map (Anderson, 2000; Taylor & Tversky, 1992). Manipulating images on another cognitive map would help you if a power failure left your home pitch dark. Even though you couldn't see a thing, you could still find a flashlight or candle, because your cognitive map would show the floor plan, furniture placement, door locations, and other physical features of your home. You would not have this mental map in an unfamiliar house; there, you would have to walk slowly, arms outstretched, to avoid wrong turns and painful collisions. In the chapter on learning we describe how experience shapes cognitive maps that help animals navigate mazes and people navigate shopping malls.

figure 8.8

Manipulating Images

TRY THIS Are these pairs of objects the same or different? To decide, you will have to rotate one member of each pair. Because manipulating mental images, like manipulating actual objects, takes some time, the speed of your decision will depend on how far you have to mentally rotate one object to line it up with the other for comparison. (The top pair matches; the bottom pair does not.)

Source: Shepard & Metzler (1971).

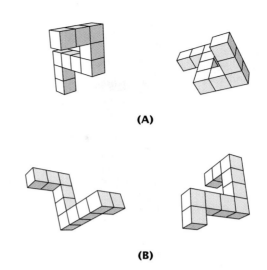

(A)

(B)

Thinking Strategies

reasoning The process by which people generate and evaluate arguments and reach conclusions about them.

formal reasoning The process of following a set of rigorous procedures for reaching valid conclusions.

algorithms Systematic procedures that cannot fail to produce a correct solution to a problem, if a solution exists.

rules of logic Sets of statements that provide a formula for drawing valid conclusions.

We have seen that our thinking capacity is based largely on our ability to manipulate mental representations—the ingredients of thought—much as a baker manipulates the ingredients of cookies (see "In Review: Ingredients of Thought" for a summary of these representations). But whereas the baker's food-processing system combines and transforms flour, sugar, milk, eggs, and chocolate into a delicious treat, our information-processing system combines, transforms, and elaborates mental representations in ways that allow us to engage in reasoning, problem solving, and decision making. Let's begin our discussion of these thinking strategies by considering **reasoning,** the process through which we generate and evaluate arguments, as well as reach conclusions about them.

Formal Reasoning

Astronomers tell us that the temperature at the core of the sun is about 27 million degrees Fahrenheit. They can't put a temperature probe inside the sun, so how can they be so confident about this assertion? Their estimate is based on *inferences* from other things that they know about the sun and about physical objects in general. Telescopic observations of the sun's volume and mass allowed astronomers to calculate its density, using the formula Density = Mass ÷ Volume. These observations also enabled them to measure the energy coming from one small region of the sun and—using what geometry told them about the surface area of spheres—to estimate the energy output from the sun as a whole. Further calculations told them how hot a body would have to be to generate that much energy.

In short, the astronomers' highly educated guess about the sun's core temperature was based on **formal reasoning** (also called *logical reasoning*), the process of following a set of rigorous procedures to reach valid, or correct, conclusions. Some of these procedures included the application of specific mathematical formulas to existing data in order to generate new data. Such formulas are examples of **algorithms,** systematic methods that always produce a correct solution to a problem, if a solution exists (Jahnke & Nowaczyk, 1998). The astronomers also followed the **rules of logic,** sets of statements that provide a formula for drawing valid conclusions about the world. For example, each step in the astronomers' thinking took the form of "if-then" statements: If we know how much energy comes from one part of the sun's surface, and if we know how big the whole surface is, then we can calculate the total energy output. You use the same formal reasoning processes when you conclude, for example, that if your friend José is two years older than you are, then

in review	Ingredients of Thought	
Ingredient	**Description**	**Examples**
Concepts	Categories of objects, events, or ideas, with common properties; basic building blocks of thought	"Square" (a formal concept); "game" (a natural concept).
Propositions	Mental representations that express relationships between concepts; can be true or false	Assertions such as "The cow jumped over the the moon."
Schemas	Sets of propositions that create generalizations and expectations about categories of objects, places, events, and people	A schema might suggest that all grandmothers are elderly, gray haired, and bake a lot of cookies.
Scripts	Schemas about familiar activities and situations; guide behavior in those situations	You pay before eating in fast-food restaurants and after eating in fancier restaurants.
Mental models	Sets of propositions about how things relate to each other in the real world; can be correct or incorrect	Assuming that airflow around an open car will send thrown objects upward, a driver tosses a lighted cigarette butt overhead, causing it to land in the back seat.
Images	Mental representations of visual information	Hearing a description of your blind date creates a mental picture of him or her.
Cognitive maps	Mental representations of familiar parts of the world	You can get to class by an alternate route even if your usual route is blocked by construction.

his twin brother, Juan, will be two years older, too. This kind of reasoning is called *deductive* because it takes a general rule (e.g., twins are the same age) and applies it to deduce conclusions about specific cases (e.g., José and Juan).

The rules of logic, which are traceable to the Greek philosopher Aristotle, have evolved into a system for drawing correct conclusions from a set of statements known as *premises*. Consider, for example, what conclusion can be drawn from the following premises:

> *Premise 1: People who study hard do well in this course.*

> *Premise 2: You have studied hard.*

According to the rules of logic, it would be valid to conclude that you will do well in this course. Logical arguments containing two or more premises and a conclusion are known as **syllogisms** (pronounced "SILL-o-jisms"). Notice that the conclusion in a syllogism goes beyond what the premises actually say. The conclusion is an inference based on the premises and on the rules of logic. In this case, the logical rule was that if something is true of all members of a category, and A is in that category, then that something will also be true of A.

Most of us try to use formal reasoning to reach valid conclusions and avoid false ones (Rips, 1994), but we have to watch out for two pitfalls: incorrect premises and violations of the rules of logic. Consider this example:

> *Premise 1: All psychologists are brilliant.*

> *Premise 2: The authors of this book are psychologists.*

> *Conclusion: The authors of this book are brilliant.*

syllogisms Arguments made up of two or more propositions, called *premises*, and a conclusion based on those premises.

ClassPrep PPT 18: Errors in Logical Reasoning

ClassPrep PPT 19: Why Do We Make These Errors?

ClassPrep PPT 20: Informal Reasoning

OBJ 8.11: Define informal reasoning and heuristics. Describe and give an example of the anchoring, representativeness, and availability heuristics.

Test Items 8.55–8.66

IRM Activity 7.8: Short-Term Memory

confirmation bias   The tendency to pay more attention to evidence in support of one's beliefs than to evidence that refutes them.
informal reasoning   The process of evaluating a conclusion, theory, or course of action on the basis of the believability of evidence.
heuristics   Time-saving mental short-cuts used in reasoning.
anchoring heuristic   A mental shortcut that involves basing judgments on existing information.

Do you agree? The conclusion follows logically from the premises, but because the first premise is false, we cannot determine whether or not the conclusion is true. Now consider this syllogism:

> *Premise 1: All gun owners are people.*
>
> *Premise 2: All criminals are people.*
>
> *Conclusion: All gun owners are criminals.*

Here, the premises are correct, but the logic is faulty. If *all As are B* and *all Cs are B*, it does not follow that *all As are C*. In other words, even conclusions based on correct premises can be false if they do not follow the rules of logic.

Psychologists have discovered that both kinds of pitfalls lead people to make errors in formal reasoning, which is one reason why misleading advertisements or speeches can still attract sales and votes (Cialdini, 2001). At least two related factors can also promote errors in logical reasoning (Ashcraft, 2002):

1. *Bias about conclusions.* Consider this syllogism: *The United States is a free country. In a free country all people have equal opportunity. Therefore, in the United States all people have equal opportunity.* People who agree with this conclusion often do so not because they have carefully considered the premises but because they hold a prior belief about it. This example illustrates **confirmation bias,** the tendency to seek evidence and reach conclusions that confirm existing beliefs. Confirmation bias can affect thinking in many situations. When people first fall in love, they often focus only on their loved one's best qualities and ignore evidence of less desirable ones. In the courtroom, jurors may pay little attention to evidence of a defendant's guilt if that defendant is, say, a beloved celebrity or a harmless-looking senior citizen. In such cases, prosecutors' logical arguments based on true premises may not lead to conviction, because the logical conclusion ("guilty") does not match jurors' beliefs about celebrities, the elderly, or some other favored group. Similarly, if jurors believe the defendant represents a category of people who tend to commit crimes, they may not be swayed much by evidence suggesting innocence. In other words, the conclusions that people reach are often based on both logical and wishful thinking (Evans et al., 1999).

2. *Limits on working memory. Some As are B. All Bs are C. Therefore, some As are C.* Do you agree? This syllogism is correct, but evaluating it requires you to hold a lot of material in short-term memory while mentally manipulating it. This task is particularly difficult if elements in a syllogism involve negatives, as in *No dogs are nonanimals.* If the amount of material to be mentally manipulated exceeds the capacity of short-term memory (see the chapter on memory), logical errors can easily result.

Informal Reasoning

The use of algorithms and logic to discover new facts and draw inferences is only one kind of reasoning. A second kind, **informal reasoning,** comes into play in situations where we are trying to assess the *believability* of a conclusion based on the evidence available to support it. Informal reasoning is also known as *inductive reasoning,* because its goal is to induce a general conclusion to appear on the basis of specific facts or examples. Psychologists use this kind of reasoning when they design experiments and other research methods whose results will provide evidence for (or against) a theory; jurors use informal reasoning when weighing evidence for the guilt or innocence of a defendant.

Formal reasoning is guided by algorithms and the rules of logic, but there are no foolproof methods for informal reasoning. Consider, for example, how many white swans you would have to see before concluding that all swans were white.

Pitfalls in Logical Reasoning *Elderly people cannot be astronauts. This is an elderly man. Therefore, he cannot be an astronaut.* The logic of this syllogism is correct, but because the first premise is wrong, so is the conclusion. John Glenn, the astronaut who in 1962 became the first American to orbit the earth, returned to space in 1998 at the age of seventy-seven as a full-fledged member of the crew of the space shuttle *Discovery.*

Fifty? A hundred? A million? A strictly formal, algorithmic approach would require that you observe every swan in existence to be sure they are all white, but such a task would be impossible. A more practical approach is to base your conclusion on the number of observations that you *believe* is "enough." In other words, you would take a mental "shortcut" to reach a conclusion that is probably, but not necessarily, correct (there are, in fact, black swans). Such mental shortcuts are called **heuristics** (pronounced "hyoor-IST-ix").

Suppose you are about to leave home but cannot find your watch. Applying an algorithm would mean searching in every possible location, room by room, until you find the watch. But you can reach the same outcome more quickly by using a heuristic—that is, by searching only where your experience suggests you might have left the watch. In short, heuristics are often valuable in guiding judgments about which events are probable or which hypotheses are likely to be true. They are easy to use and frequently work well (Gigerenzer et al., 2000).

However, heuristics can also bias cognitive processes and result in errors. For example, if a heuristic leads you to vote for all the candidates in a particular political party instead of researching the views of each candidate, you might help elect someone with whom you strongly disagree on some issues. The degree to which heuristics are responsible for important errors in judgment and decision making is a matter of continuing research and debate by cognitive psychologists (Medin & Bazerman, 1999; Mellers, Schwartz, & Cooke, 1998). Amos Tversky and Daniel Kahneman (1974, 1993) have described three potentially problematic heuristics that people seem to use intuitively in making judgments. We discuss these heuristics in the following sections.

ClassPrep PPT 21: Potentially Problematic Heuristics

The Anchoring Heuristic

People use the **anchoring heuristic** when they estimate the probability of an event not by starting from scratch but by adjusting an earlier estimate (Rottenstreich & Tversky, 1997). This strategy sounds reasonable,

Formal reasoning follows the rules of logic, but there are no foolproof rules for informal reasoning, as this fool demonstrates.

DILBERT reprinted by permission of United Feature Syndicates, Inc.

but the starting value biases the final estimate. Once people have fixed a starting point, their adjustments of the initial judgment tend to be too small. It is as if they drop a "mental anchor" at one hypothesis or estimate and then are reluctant to move very far from that original judgment. For example, if you thought that the probability of being mugged in Los Angeles is 90 percent and then heard evidence that the figure was closer to 1 percent, you might reduce your estimate, but only to 80 percent, so your judgment would still be way off. The anchoring heuristic presents a challenge for defense attorneys in U.S. courtrooms because once jurors have been affected by the prosecution's evidence (which is presented first), it may be difficult to alter their belief in a defendant's guilt or in the amount of money the defendant should have to pay (Greene & Loftus, 1998; Hogarth & Einhorn, 1992). Similarly, our first impressions of people are not easily shifted by later evidence.

IRM Activity 8.8: The Representativeness Heuristic

The Representativeness Heuristic   Using the **representativeness heuristic,** people decide whether an example belongs in a certain class on the basis of how similar it is to other items in that class. For example, suppose you encounter a man who is tidy, small in stature, wears glasses, speaks quietly, and is somewhat shy. If asked whether this person is more likely to be a librarian or a farmer, what would you say? Tversky and Kahneman (1974) found that most of their research participants chose *librarian*. The chances are that this answer would be wrong, though. Why? Because of differences in the *base rates,* or commonness, of the two occupations. True, the description is more similar to the prototypical librarian than to the prototypical farmer, but because there are many more farmers in the world than librarians, there are probably more farmers than librarians who match this description. Therefore, a man matching this description is more likely to be a farmer than a librarian. In fact, almost any set of physical features is more likely to belong to a farmer than to a librarian.

Another study found that jurors' decisions to convict or acquit a defendant may depend partly on the degree to which the defendant's actions were representative of a crime category. For example, someone who abducts a child and asks for ransom (actions that clearly fit the crime category of "kidnapping") is more likely to be convicted than someone who abducts an adult and demands no ransom—even though both crimes constitute kidnapping, and the evidence is equally strong in each case (Smith, 1991).

The Availability Heuristic   Even when people use probability information to help them judge group membership or to assess a hypothesis, a third heuristic can bias their thinking. The **availability heuristic** involves judging the probability that an event may occur or that a hypothesis may be true by how easily the hypothesis or examples of the event can be brought to mind (Reed, 2000). People tend to choose the hypothesis or alternative that is most mentally "available" to them, much as you might choose which T-shirt to wear on the basis of which one is on top in the drawer.

Like other heuristics, this shortcut tends to work well. After all, what people remember most easily are frequent events or likely hypotheses. However, the availability heuristic can lead to biased judgments, especially when mental availability does not reflect actual frequency. For example, television news reports showing the grisly aftermath of urban shootings and train wrecks may make these relatively rare events so memorable that some people avoid certain cities or avoid train travel because they overestimate the frequency of crime or the probability of a crash (Carmody, 1998; Slovic, 1984).

representativeness heuristic A mental shortcut that involves judging whether something belongs in a given class on the basis of its similarity to other members of that class.

availability heuristic A mental shortcut through which judgments are based on information that is most easily brought to mind.

The heuristics we have discussed represent only three of the many mental shortcuts that people use, and they describe only some of the biases and limitations that affect human reasoning (Hogarth & Einhorn, 1992). Some other biases and limitations are described in the following sections as we consider two important goals of thinking: problem solving and decision making.

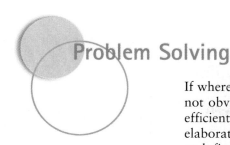

Problem Solving

If where you are is not where you want to be, and when the path to getting there is not obvious, you have a *problem*. As suggested by the circle of thought, the most efficient approach to problem solving would be first to diagnose the problem in the elaboration stage, then to formulate a plan for solving it, then to execute the plan, and finally to evaluate the results to determine whether the problem remains (Bransford & Stein, 1993). But people's problem-solving efforts are not always so systematic, which is one reason why medical tests are sometimes given unnecessarily, diseases are sometimes misdiagnosed, and auto parts are sometimes replaced when there is nothing wrong with them.

Strategies for Problem Solving

When you are trying to get from a starting point to some goal, the best path may not necessarily be a straight line. In fact, obstacles may dictate going in the opposite direction. So it is with problem solving. Sometimes, the best strategy is not to take mental steps aimed straight at your goal. For example, when a problem is especially difficult, it can sometimes be helpful to allow it to "incubate" by setting it aside for a while. A solution that once seemed out of reach may suddenly appear after you think about other things for a time. The benefits of incubation probably arise from forgetting incorrect ideas that may have been blocking the path to a correct solution (Anderson, 2000). Psychologists have identified several other useful problem-solving strategies.

Means-End Analysis   One of the most generally applicable of these strategies is called *means-end analysis*. It involves continuously asking where you are in relation to your final goal, and then deciding on the means by which you can get one step closer to the end that you desire (Newell & Simon, 1972). In other words, rather than trying to solve the problem all at once, you identify a subgoal that will take you toward a solution (this process is also referred to as *decomposition*). After reaching that subgoal, you identify another one that will get you even closer to the solution, and you continue this step-by-step process until the problem is solved. Some students apply this approach to the problem of writing a major term paper. The task might seem overwhelming at first, but their first subgoal is simply to write an outline of what they think the paper should cover. When the outline is complete, they decide whether a paper based on it will satisfy the assignment. If so, the next subgoal might be to search the library and the Internet for information about each section. If they decide that this information is adequate, the next subgoal would be to write a rough draft of the introduction, and so on.

Working Backward   A second problem-solving strategy is to *work backward*. Many problems are like a tree. The trunk is the information you are given;

ClassPrep PPT 22: Strategies for Problem Solving

OBJ 8.12: Describe the problem-solving strategies: means-end analysis, working backward, and analogies.

Test Items 8.67–8.74

Personal Learning Activity 8.2

Simply knowing about problem-solving strategies, such as means-end analysis, is not enough. As described in the chapter on motivation and emotion, people must perceive the effort involved to be worth the rewards it is likely to bring.

Calvin and Hobbes   by Bill Watterson

Working Backward to Forge Ahead
Whether you are organizing a family vacation or, as Ellen MacArthur did recently, sailing alone in an around-the-world race, working backward from the final goal through all the steps necessary to reach that goal is a helpful approach to solving complex problems.

IRM Activity 8.9: Brain Teasers

the solution is a twig on one of the limbs. If you work forward by taking the "givens" of the problem and trying to find the solution, it will be easy to branch off in the wrong direction. A more efficient approach may be to start at the twig end and work backward toward your goal (Galotti, 1999). Consider, for example, the problem of planning a climb to the summit of Mount Everest. The best strategy is to figure out, first, what equipment and supplies are needed at the highest camp on the night before the summit attempt, then how many people are needed to stock that camp the day before, then how many people are needed to supply those who must stock the camp, and so on until a plan for the entire expedition is established. It is easy to overlook the working-backward strategy, however, because it runs counter to the way we have learned to think. It is hard to imagine that the first step in solving a problem could be to assume that you have already solved it. Unfortunately, six climbers died on Mount Everest in 1996 in part because of failure to apply this strategy (Krakauer, 1997).

Using Analogies   A third problem-solving strategy is trying to find *analogies*, or similarities between today's problem and others you have encountered before. A supervisor may find, for example, that a seemingly hopeless problem between co-workers may be resolved by the same compromise that worked during a recent family squabble. To take advantage of analogies, we must first recognize the similarities between current and previous problems and then recall the solution that worked before. Although it may be surprising, most people are not very good at drawing analogies from one problem to another (Anderson, 2000). They tend to concentrate on the surface features that make problems appear different.

FOCUS ON RESEARCH METHODS

Locating Analogical Thinking

ClassPrep PPT 51: Focus on Research Methods: Locating Analogical Thinking

The value of using analogies in problem solving was beautifully illustrated after the Hubble Space Telescope was placed in orbit around the Earth in 1990. It was designed to take detailed photographs of distant galaxies, but because its main mirror was not focusing light properly, the pictures were blurry. Then NASA engineer James Crocker happened to notice the way a hotel room showerhead pivoted, and it gave him the idea for a system of movable mirrors to correct for the

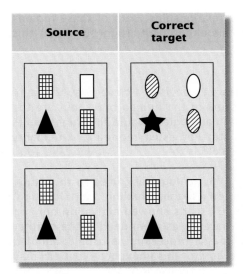

figure 8.9

Comparing Stimulus Patterns

The top row shows examples of the stimulus patterns that were compared in an analogy task. Participants had to say whether the pattern on the right is similar, or *analogous,* to the one on the left. (In this case it is, because even though the specific shapes used in one pattern differ from those in the other pattern, their shading and physical arrangement are similar.) The bottom row shows examples of the patterns that were compared in a "same-different" task. Here, participants were asked only to decide whether the two patterns are exactly the same (Wharton et al., 2000).

ClassPrep PPT 52: Focus on Research Methods: *Figure 8.9:* Comparing Stimulus Patterns

flaw in the Hubble's mirror. When shuttle astronauts installed these mirrors in 1993, the problem was solved (Stein, 1993).

● **What was the researchers' question?**

Charles Wharton and his colleagues wanted to know what goes on in the brain when people do this kind of *analogical mapping*—recognizing similarities between things that appear to be different and even unrelated (Wharton et al., 2000).

● **How did the researchers answer the question?**

The researchers knew that PET scan technology could show brain activity while participants performed an analogy task, but how could the researchers separate the activity associated with analogical mapping from everything else going on in the brain at the same time? Their answer was to use a *subtraction technique.* They asked people to perform two tasks—one after the other—that involved making comparisons between patterns of rectangles, ovals, triangles, and other shapes. Both tasks placed similar demands on the brain, but only one of them required the participants to *make analogies* between the patterns (see Figure 8.9). The researchers then compared the resulting PET scans, looking for areas of the brain that were active in the analogy task but not in the other one. What their computers did, in essence, was to take all brain activity that occurred during the analogy task and "subtract" from it all the activity that occurred during the other task. The activity remaining was presumed to reflect analogical mapping.

● **What did the researchers find?**

As you can see in Figure 8.10, the brain areas uniquely activated during the analogy task were in the left hemisphere, particularly in the frontal and parietal areas. Other neuroimaging studies have shown activation of similar areas during abstract problem solving and reasoning (e.g., Osherson et al., 1998).

● **What do the results mean?**

These results show that it is possible to locate specific brain activities associated with a specific kind of cognitive activity. They also fit well into what we already know about where certain brain functions are localized. As mentioned earlier, the frontal areas of the brain are involved in complex processing tasks, including those requiring coordination of information in working memory with information coming from the senses. There is also evidence that parietal areas are involved in our

figure 8.10

Brain Activity During Analogical Mapping

Comparing PET scans of brain activity during an analogy task and a task not requiring analogical thinking revealed that making analogies appears to involve areas of the left frontal and parietal lobes, as seen here from below and highlighted in red.

Source: Wharton et al. (2000).

ClassPrep PPT 53: Focus on Research Methods: *Figure 8.10:* Brain Activity During Analogical Mapping

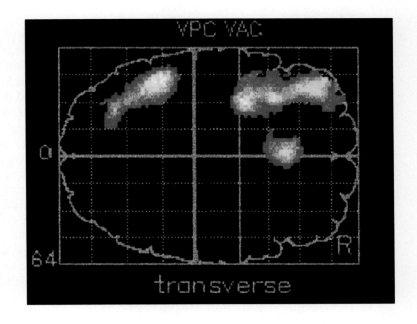

ability to perceive spatial arrangements and relationships. Both of these regions were activated during the analogy task in this experiment, suggesting that this task required both kinds of abilities.

● What do we still need to know?

There is no doubt that Wharton and his colleagues devised a clever way to examine the analogical mapping process as it occurs in the human brain, but are the brain areas identified the only ones involved in analogies? Would the same results appear if the analogy task had been verbal instead of visual, requiring participants to make analogies such as "Dark is to light as cold is to _____"? It will take additional research to answer this question.

Consider also the fact that even though the analogy task used in this study involved processing visual-spatial information (shape, shading, and location) rather than verbal information (words), the PET scans showed activation only on the left side of the brain. This is surprising, because as mentioned in the chapter on biological aspects of psychology, visual-spatial processing is usually handled mainly in the brain's right hemisphere. One reason for this unexpected pattern may be that, as noted in that same chapter, the right hemisphere actually does have some verbal processing abilities. However, the results also warn us to be careful about misinterpreting PET scan activity. Increased activity in a particular brain region doesn't always mean that the region is performing the processing we are trying to locate. The activity observed might also result if the area were being suppressed so as not to interfere with processing going on elsewhere. The study of brain activity during higher-level thinking is still quite new, so it will take some time, and a lot more research, to learn how to correctly interpret the data coming from neuroimaging techniques.

Obstacles to Problem Solving

Failing to use analogies is just one example of the obstacles that face problem solvers every day. Difficulties frequently occur at the start, during the diagnosis stage, when a person forms and then tests hypotheses about a problem.

As a case in point, consider this true story: In September 1998, John Gatiss was in the kitchen of his rented house in Cheltenham, England, when he heard a faint meowing sound. He could not find the source of the sound, but he assumed that a kitten had become trapped in the walls or under the flooring, so he called for the fire brigade to rescue the animal. The sound seemed to be coming from the electric oven, so the rescuers dismantled it, disconnecting the power cord in the process. The sound stopped, but everyone assumed that wherever the kitten was, it had become too frightened to meow. The search was reluctantly abandoned, and the oven was reconnected. Four days later, though, the meowing began anew. This time, Gatiss and his landlord called the Royal Society for the Prevention of Cruelty to Animals (RSPCA), whose inspectors heard the kitten in distress and asked the fire brigade to return. They spent the next three days searching for the cat. First, they dismantled parts of the kitchen walls and ripped up the floorboards. Next, they called in plumbing and drainage specialists, who used cables tipped with fiber-optic cameras to search remote cavities where a kitten might hide. Rescuers then brought in a disaster search team, which tried to find the kitten using acoustic and ultrasonic equipment designed to locate victims trapped in the debris of earthquakes and explosions. Not a sound could be heard. Increasingly concerned about how much longer the kitten could survive, the fire brigade tried to coax it from hiding with the finest-quality fish, but to no avail. Suddenly, there was a burst of "purring," which to everyone's surprise (and the landlord's dismay), the ultrasonic equipment traced to the clock in the electric oven! Later, the landlord commented that everyone had assumed that Gatiss's hypothesis was correct—that the meowing sound came from a cat trapped

IRM Activity 8.9: Brain Teasers

figure 8.11

The Luchins Jar Problem

TRY THIS   The problem is to obtain the quantities of liquid shown in the first column by using jars with the capacities shown in the next three columns. Each line represents a different problem. See if you can solve the first six problems without looking at the answer in the text; then try the last one. In dealing with such problems, people often fall prey to mental sets that prevent them from using the most efficient solution.

ClassPrep PPT 24: *Figure 8.11:* The Luchins Jar Problem

IRM Activity 8.10: Mental Sets

ClassPrep PPT 23: Obstacles to Problem Solving

OBJ 8.13: Explain why multiple hypotheses, mental sets, functional fixedness, confirmation bias, and lack of attention to negative evidence can hinder problem solving. Give an example of each.

Test Items 8.75–8.84

ClassPrep: *Figure 8.12:* The Nine-Dot Problem

Personal Learning Activity 8.3

Critical Thinking Exercise

Videodisc Segment & Still: An Example of Functional Fixedness

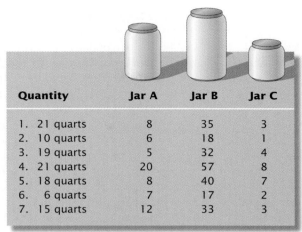

Quantity	Jar A	Jar B	Jar C
1. 21 quarts	8	35	3
2. 10 quarts	6	18	1
3. 19 quarts	5	32	4
4. 21 quarts	20	57	8
5. 18 quarts	8	40	7
6. 6 quarts	7	17	2
7. 15 quarts	12	33	3

Problem: Measure out the quantities listed in the first column using jars with the stated capacities (in quarts).

somewhere in the kitchen. "I just let them carry on. If there is an animal in there, you have to do what it takes. The funniest thing was that it seemed to reply when we called out to it" (*London Daily Telegraph,* September 19, 1998).

How could fifteen fire-rescue workers, three RSPCA inspectors, four drainage workers, and two acoustics experts waste eight days and cause nearly $2,000 in damage to a house in pursuit of a nonexistent kitten? The answer lies in the fact that they, like the rest of us, are prone to four main obstacles to efficient problem solving, described in the following sections.

Multiple Hypotheses

Often, people begin to solve a problem with only a vague notion of which hypotheses to test. Suppose you heard a strange sound in your kitchen. It could be caused by several things, but which hypotheses should you test, and in what order?

People have a difficult time considering more than two or three hypotheses at a time (Mehle, 1982). The limited capacity of short-term memory may be part of the reason. As discussed in the chapter on memory, we can hold only about seven chunks of information in short-term memory; because a single hypothesis, let alone two or three, might include many more than seven chunks, it might be difficult or impossible to keep them all in mind at once. As a result, the correct hypothesis is often neglected. Which hypothesis a person considers may depend on the availability heuristic. In other words, the particular hypothesis considered may be the one that most easily comes to mind, not the one most likely to be correct (Tversky & Kahneman, 1974). Thus, Gatiss diagnosed the sound he heard as a kitten, not a clock, because such sounds usually come from kittens, not clocks.

Mental Sets

Sometimes people are so blinded by one hypothesis or strategy that they continue to apply it even when better alternatives should be obvious (a clear case of the anchoring heuristic at work). Once Gatiss reported hearing a "trapped kitten," his description created an assumption that everyone else accepted and no one challenged.

A laboratory example of this phenomenon devised by Abraham Luchins (1942) is shown in Figure 8.11. The object of each problem in the figure is to use three jars with specified capacities to obtain a certain amount of liquid. For example, in the first problem you are to obtain 21 quarts by using 3 jars that have capacities of 8, 35, and 3 quarts, respectively. The solution is to fill Jar B to its capacity, 35 quarts, and then use its contents to fill Jar A to its capacity of 8 quarts, leaving 27 quarts in Jar B. Then pour liquid from Jar B to fill Jar C to its capacity twice, leaving

figure 8.12

The Nine-Dot Problem

TRY THIS   The problem is to draw no more than four straight lines that run through all nine dots on the page without lifting your pencil from the paper. Figure 8.14 shows two ways of going beyond mental constraints to solve this problem.

21 quarts in Jar B [27 − (2 × 3) = 21]. In other words, the general solution is
$B - A - 2C$. Now solve the remaining problems before reading further.

If you solved all the problems in Figure 8.11, you found that a similar solution
worked each time. By the time you reached Problem 7, you had probably developed
a **mental set,** a tendency for old patterns of problem solving to persist (Sweller &
Gee, 1978). That mental set may have caused you to use the same solution formula
($B - A - 2C$) for Problem 7 even though a simpler one ($A + C$) would have worked
just as well. Figures 8.12 and 8.14 show that a mental set can also restrict your perception of the problem itself.

Another restriction on problem solving may come from experience with objects.
Once people are accustomed to using an object for one purpose, they may be
blinded to its other possible functions. Long experience may produce **functional
fixedness,** a tendency to use familiar objects in familiar rather than creative ways.
Figure 8.13 illustrates an example. An incubation strategy often helps to break mental sets.

Confirmation Bias   Anyone who has had a series of medical tests knows
that diagnosis is not a one-shot decision. Instead, physicians choose their first
hypothesis on the basis of observed symptoms and then order tests or evaluate additional symptoms to confirm or refute that hypothesis (Trillin, 2001). This process
can be distorted by the *confirmation bias* mentioned earlier: Humans have a strong
bias to confirm rather than to refute the hypothesis they have chosen, even in the
face of strong evidence against it (Aronson, Wilson, & Akert, 1999; Groopman,
2000). Confirmation bias can be seen as a form of the anchoring heuristic, in that
it involves "anchoring" to an initial hypothesis and being unwilling to abandon it.
The would-be rescuers of the "trapped kitten" were so intent on their efforts to pinpoint its location that they never stopped to question its existence.

Ignoring Negative Evidence   On September 26, 1983, Soviet Lt. Col.
Stanislav Petrov was in command of a facility that analyzed information from his
country's early-warning satellites. Suddenly, alarms went off as computers detected
evidence of five U.S. missiles being launched toward the Soviet Union. There was
great tension between the two countries at the time, so based on the availability
heuristic, Petrov hypothesized that a nuclear attack was under way. He was about

figure 8. 13

An Example of Functional Fixedness

Before reading further, consider
how you would fasten together
two strings that are hanging
from the ceiling but are out of reach of
each other. Several tools are available, yet
most people do not think of attaching,
say, the pliers to one string and swinging
it like a pendulum until it can be reached
while holding the other string. This solution is not obvious because we tend to
fixate on the function of pliers as a tool
rather than as a weight. People are more
likely to solve this problem if the tools are
scattered around the room. When the
pliers are in a toolbox, their function as a
tool is emphasized, and functional fixedness becomes nearly impossible to break.

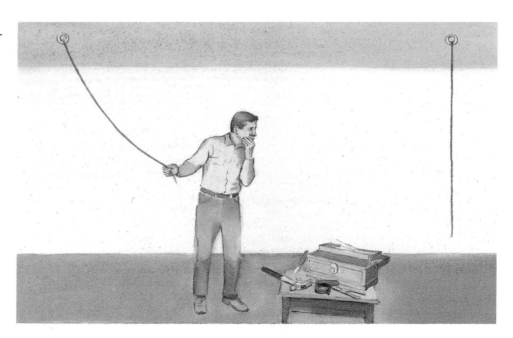

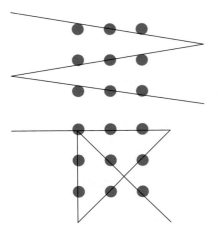

figure 8.14

Two Creative Solutions to the Nine-Dot Problem

Many people find puzzles like this difficult because their mental sets create artificial constraints on the range of solutions. In this case, the mental sets involve the tendency to draw within the frame of the dots and the tendency to draw through the middle of each dot. As shown here, however, there are other possibilities.

ClassPrep PPT 25, OHT: *Figure 8.14:* Two Creative Solutions to the Nine-Dot Problem

OBJ 8.14: Explain why an "expert" is better at solving problems. Explain why experts use chunking more efficiently than novices do. Discuss the dangers of being an expert when solving problems.

Test Items 8.85–8.90

ClassPrep PPT 29: How Do Experts Avoid Obstacles to Problem Solving?

mental set The tendency for old patterns of problem solving to persist, even when they might not always be the most efficient alternative.

functional fixedness A tendency to think about familiar objects in familiar ways that may prevent using them in other ways.

to alert his superiors to launch a counterattack on the United States when it occurred to him that if this were a real nuclear attack, there should be evidence of many more than five missiles. Fortunately for everyone, he realized that the "attack" was a false alarm (Hoffman, 1999). As this near-disaster shows, the absence of symptoms or events can sometimes provide important evidence for or against a hypothesis. Compared with evidence that is present, however, symptoms or events that do not occur are less likely to be noticed (Hunt & Rouse, 1981).

People have a difficult time using the absence of evidence to help eliminate hypotheses from consideration (Ashcraft, 1989). In the "trapped kitten" case, when the "meowing" stopped for several days after the stove was reconnected, rescuers assumed that the animal was frightened into silence. They ignored the possibility that their hypothesis was incorrect in the first place.

Building Problem-Solving Skills

Some psychologists suggest that it should be possible to train people to avoid the biases that impair problem solving, and their efforts to do so have produced some modest benefits. In one study, cautioning people against their tendency to anchor on a hypothesis reduced the magnitude of confirmation bias and increased participants' openness to alternative evidence (Lopes, 1982).

How do experts avoid obstacles to problem solving? What do they bring to a situation that a beginner does not? Knowledge based on experience is particularly important (Mayer, 1992). Experts frequently proceed by looking for analogies between current and past problems. Compared with beginners, they are better able to relate new information and new experiences to past experiences and existing knowledge (Anderson, 1995b; Bedard & Chi, 1992). Accordingly, experts can use existing knowledge to organize new information into chunks, a process described in the chapter on memory. By chunking many elements of a problem into a smaller number of units, experts apparently can visualize problems more clearly and efficiently than beginners (Reingold et al., 2001).

Experts can use their experience as a guide because they tend to perceive the similarity between new and old problems more deeply than beginners (Hardimann, Dufresne, & Mestre, 1989). Specifically, experts see the similarity of underlying principles, whereas beginners perceive similarity only in surface features. As a result, experts can more quickly and easily apply these principles to solve the new problem. In one study, expert physicists and beginning physics students sorted physics problems into groups (Chi, Feltovitch, & Glaser, 1981). The beginners grouped together problems that looked similar (such as those involving blocks lying on an inclined plane), whereas the experts grouped together problems that could be solved by the same principle (such as Newton's second law of motion).

Experience also gives experts a broader perspective on the problem domain, allowing them to perceive the whole problem "tree" so that they can work forward without error, thus avoiding the slower "working backward" strategy more suited to the beginner. Finally, successful problem solvers can explain each step in the solution, and they can remain aware of precisely what is and is not understood along the way (Medin, Ross, & Markman, 2001).

Although experts are often better problem solvers than beginners, expertise also carries a danger: Using past experience can lead to the traps of functional fixedness and mental sets. Top-down, knowledge-driven processes can bias you toward seeing what you expect or want to see and prevent you from seeing a problem in new ways. As in the case of the "trapped kitten," confirmation bias sometimes prevents experts from appreciating that a proposed solution is incorrect (Fischoff & Slovic, 1980). Several studies have shown that although experts may be more confident in their solutions (Payne, Bettman, & Johnson, 1992), they are not always more accurate than others in such areas as medical diagnosis, accounting, and pilot judgment (Wickens et al., 1992).

Experts typically have a large store of knowledge about their area of expertise, but even confidently stated opinions based on this knowledge can turn out to be wrong. In 1768, one expert critic called William Shakespeare's now-revered play *Hamlet* "the work of a drunken savage" (Henderson & Bernard, 1998). Here are some equally incorrect expert pronouncements from *The Experts Speak* (Cerf & Navasky, 1998).

LSV: Artificial Intelligence

Freburg *Perspectives:* MacFarquhar, "Point and Click Software for Shrinks"

table 8.1
Some Expert Opinions

On the possibility of painless surgery through anesthesia:
"'Knife' and 'pain' are two words in surgery that must forever be associated. . . . To this compulsory combination we shall have to adjust ourselves." (Dr. Alfred Velpeau, professor of surgery, Paris Faculty of Medicine, 1839)

On the hazards of cigarette smoking:
"If excessive smoking actually plays a role in the production of lung cancer, it seems to be a minor one." (Dr. W. C. Heuper, National Cancer Institute, 1954)

On the stock market (one week before the disastrous 1929 crash that wiped out over $50 billion in investments):
"Stocks have reached what looks like a permanently high plateau." (Irving Fisher, professor of economics, Yale University, 1929)

On the prospects of war with Japan (three years before the December 1941 Japanese attack on Pearl Harbor):
"A Japanese attack on Pearl Harbor is a strategic impossibility." (Maj. George F. Eliot, military science writer, 1938)

On the value of personal computers:
"There is no reason for any individual to have a computer in their home." (Ken Olson, president, Digital Equipment Corporation, 1977)

On the concept of the airplane:
"Heavier-than-air flying machines are impossible." (Lord Kelvin, mathematician, physicist, and president of the British Royal Society, 1895)

In short, there is a fine line between using past experience and being trapped by it. Experience alone does not ensure excellence at problem solving, and practice may not make perfect (see Table 8.1). (For a summary of our discussion of human problem solving, see "In Review: Solving Problems.")

Problem Solving by Computer

Medical and scientific researchers have created artificial limbs, retinas, cochleae, and even hearts to help disabled people move, see, hear, and live more normally. They are developing artificial brains, too, in the form of computer systems that not only see, hear, and manipulate objects but also reason and solve problems. These systems are the product of research in **artificial intelligence** (**AI**), a field that seeks to develop computers that imitate the processes of human perception and thought. For problems such as those involved in making certain kinds of medical diagnoses, locating minerals, forecasting solar flares, or evaluating loan applications, computerized *expert systems* can already perform just as well as humans, and sometimes better (e.g., Gawande, 1998a; Khan et al., 2001).

Symbolic Reasoning and Computer Logic   Early efforts at developing artificial intelligence focused on computers' enormous capabilities for formal reasoning and symbol manipulation and on their abilities to follow general problem-solving strategies, such as working backward (Newell & Simon, 1972). Valuable as it is, this logic-based approach to AI has important limitations. For one thing, expert systems are successful only in narrowly defined fields, and even within a specific domain, computers show limited ability. There are no ways of putting into computer code all aspects of the reasoning of human experts. Sometimes, the experts can only say, "I know it when I see it, but I can't put it into words." Second, the vital ability to draw analogies and make other connections among remote knowledge

OBJ 8.15: Define artificial intelligence, symbolic reasoning, and neural networks. Describe how expert systems can be used.

Test Items 8.91–8.93

ClassPrep PPT 30: Artificial Intelligence (AI)

artificial intelligence (AI) The field that studies how to program computers to imitate the products of human perception, understanding, and thought.

in review Solving Problems

Steps	Pitfalls	Remedies
Define the problem	Inexperience: the tendency to see each problem as unique.	Gain experience and practice in seeing the similarity between present problems and previous problems.
Form hypotheses about solutions	Availability heuristic: the tendency to recall the hypothesis or solution that is most available to memory.	Force yourself to entertain different hypotheses.
	Anchoring heuristic or mental set: the tendency to anchor on the first solution or hypothesis and not adjust your beliefs in light of new evidence or failures of the current approach.	Break the mental set, stop, and try a fresh approach.
Test hypotheses	The tendency to ignore negative evidence.	In evaluating a hypothesis, consider the things you should be seeing (but are not) if the hypothesis is true.
	Confirmation bias: the tendency to seek only evidence that confirms your hypothesis.	Look for disconfirming evidence that, if found, would show your hypothesis to be false.

domains is still beyond the grasp of current expert systems, partly because the builders of the systems seldom know ahead of time which other areas of knowledge might lead to insight. They can't always tell computers where to look for new ideas or how to use them. Finally, logic-based AI systems depend on "if-then" rules, and it is often difficult to tell a computer how to recognize the "if" condition in the real world (Dreyfus & Dreyfus, 1988). Consider just one example: *If it's a clock, then set it.* Humans can recognize all kinds of clocks because they have the natural concept of "clock," but computers perform this task very poorly. As discussed earlier, forming natural concepts requires putting into the same category many examples that may have very different physical features—from a bedside digital alarm clock to Big Ben.

Neural Network Models   Recognizing the problems posed by the need to teach computers to form natural concepts, many researchers in AI have shifted to the *connectionist,* or *neural network,* approach discussed in earlier chapters

Artificial Intelligence Chess master Garry Kasparov had his hands full when he was challenged by "Deep Blue," a chess-playing computer that was programmed so well that it has won games against the world's best competitors, including Kasparov. Still, even the most sophisticated computers cannot perceive and think about the world in general anywhere near as well as humans can. Some observers believe that this situation will eventually change as progress in computer technology—and a deepening understanding of human cognitive processes—leads to dramatic breakthroughs in artificial intelligence.

(Anderson, 1995b). This approach—which simulates the information processing taking place at many different, but interconnected, locations in the brain—is very effective for modeling many aspects of perceptual recognition. It has contributed to the development of computers that are able to recognize voices, understand speech, read print, guide missiles, and perform many other complex tasks. One program, called PAPNET, actually outperforms human technicians at detecting abnormal cells in smears collected during cervical examinations (Kok & Boon, 1996).

The capacities of current computer models of neural networks still fall well short of those of the human perceptual system, however. For example, computers are slow to learn how to classify visual patterns, and they do not show sudden insight when a key common feature is identified. Even though neural networks are far from perfect "thinking machines," however, they are sure to play an important role in psychologists' efforts to build ever more intelligent systems and to better understand the principles of human problem solving.

Computer-Assisted Problem Solving   One approach to minimizing the limitations of both computers and humans is to have them work together in ways that create a better outcome than either could achieve alone. In medical diagnosis, for example, the human's role is to establish the presence and nature of a patient's symptoms. The computer then combines this information in a completely unbiased way to identify the most likely diagnosis (Swets, Dawes, & Monahan, 2000). Similarly, laboratory technologists who examine blood samples for the causes of disease are assisted by computer programs that serve to reduce errors and memory lapses by (1) keeping track of the findings from previous tests, (2) listing possible tests that remain to be tried, and (3) indicating either that certain tests have been left undone or that a new sequence of tests should be done (Guerlain, 1993, 1995). This kind of teamwork can also help in the assessment of psychological problems (Nietzel et al., 2003).

Decision Making      LSV: "Decision Making"

Dr. Wallace's patient, Laura McBride, faced a simple decision: risk death by doing nothing or protect herself from lead poisoning. Most decisions are not so easy. Patients must decide whether to undergo a dangerous operation; a college graduate must choose a career; a corporate executive must decide whether to shut down a factory. Unlike the high-speed decisions discussed earlier, these decisions require considerable time, planning, and mental effort.

Even carefully considered decisions sometimes lead to undesirable outcomes, however, because the world is uncertain. Decisions made when the outcome is uncertain are called *risky decisions* or *decisions under uncertainty*. Psychologists have discovered many reasons why human decisions may lead to unsatisfactory outcomes, and we describe some of them here.

Evaluating Options

Suppose that you must choose between (1) a fascinating academic major that is unlikely to lead to a good job and (2) a boring major that virtually guarantees a high-paying job. The fact that each option has positive and negative features, or *attributes,* greatly complicates decision making. Deciding which car to buy, which college to attend, or even how to spend the evening are all examples of *multiattribute decision making* (Edwards, 1987). Often these decisions are further complicated by difficulties in comparing the attributes and in estimating the probabilities of various outcomes.

Personal Learning Activity 8.4

IRM Activity 8.12: Problem Solving Using Multiattribute Utility Theory

Comparing Attributes

Multi-attribute decisions can be difficult in part because the limited storage capacity of short-term memory does not permit us to keep in mind all of the attributes of all of our options long enough to compare them (Bettman, Johnson, & Payne, 1990). Instead, people tend to focus on the one attribute that is most important to them (Kardes, 1999; Tversky, 1972). If, for instance, finishing a degree quickly is most important to you, then you might choose courses based mainly on graduation requirements, without giving much consideration to professors' reputations. (Listing the pros and cons of each option offers a helpful way of keeping them all in mind as you think about decisions.)

Furthermore, the attributes of the options involved in most important decisions cannot be measured in dollars or other objective terms. We are often forced to compare "apples and oranges." Psychologists use the term **utility** to describe the subjective value that each attribute holds for each of us. In deciding on a major, for example, you have to think about the positive and negative utilities of each attribute—such as the job prospects and interest level—of each major. Then you must somehow weigh and combine these utilities. Will the positive utility of enjoying your courses be higher than the negative utility of risking unemployment?

Estimating Probabilities

Uncertainty adds other difficulties to the decision-making process: To make a good decision, you should take into account not only the attributes of each option but also the probabilities and risks of their possible outcomes. For example, the economy could change by the time you graduate, closing many of today's job opportunities in one of the majors you are considering and perhaps opening opportunities in another.

In studying risky decision making, psychologists begin by assuming that the best decision is the one that maximizes **expected value,** or the total amount of benefit you could expect if the decision were repeated on several occasions. Suppose someone asks you to buy a charity raffle ticket. You know that it costs $2 to enter and that the probability of winning the $100 prize is one in ten (.10). Assuming you are more interested in the prize money than in donating to the charity, should you enter the contest? The expected value of entering is determined by multiplying the probability of gain (.10) by the size of the gain ($100); this is the average benefit you would receive if you entered the raffle many times. Next, from this product you subtract the probability of loss, which is 1.0 (the entry fee is a certain loss), multiplied by the amount of the loss ($2). That is, $(.10 \times \$100) - (1.0 \times \$2) = \$8$. Because this $8 expected value is greater than the expected value of not entering (which is zero), you should enter. However, if the odds of winning the raffle were one in a hundred (.01), then the expected value of entering would be $(.01 \times \$100) - (1.0 \times \$2) = -\$1$. In this case, the expected value is negative, so you should not enter the raffle.

ClassPrep PPT 32: Biases and Flaws in Decision Making

OBJ 8.17: Describe the sources of bias and flaws in decision making in regard to perceptions of utilities, losses, and probabilities. Be sure to include loss aversion and gambler's fallacy.

Test Items 8.98–8.104

Essay Q 8.2

Biases and Flaws in Decision Making

Most people think of themselves as logical and rational, but in making decisions about everything from giving up smoking to investing in the stock market, they do not always act in ways that maximize expected value (Arkes & Ayton, 1999; Gilovich, 1997; Shiller, 2001). Why not?

Gains, Losses, and Probabilities

For one thing, positive utilities are not mirror images of negative utilities. People usually feel worse about losing a certain amount than they feel good about gaining the same amount, a phenomenon known as *loss aversion* (Dawes, 1998; Mellers, Schwartz, & Cooke, 1998; Tversky & Kahneman, 1991). They may be willing to exert more effort to try collecting a $100 debt, for example, than to try winning a $100 prize.

It also appears that the utility of a specific gain depends not on how large the gain actually is but on what the starting point was. Suppose you can do something

utility A subjective measure of value.

expected value The total benefit to be expected if a decision were to be repeated several times.

to receive a coupon for a free dinner worth $10. Does this gain have the same utility as having an extra $10 added to your paycheck? The amount of gain is the same, but people tend to behave as if the difference in utility between $0 and $10 is much greater than the difference between, say, $300 and $310. So the person who refuses to do an after-work errand across town for an extra $10 on payday might gladly make the same trip to pick up a $10 coupon. This tendency conforms to Weber's law of psychophysics, discussed in the chapter on perception. The subjective value of a gain depends on how much you already have (Dawes, 1998); the more you have, the less it means.

Biases in our perception of probabilities are also a source of less-than-optimal decisions. One of these biases comes into play when decisions involve extremely likely or extremely unlikely events. In making such decisions, we tend to overestimate the probability of very unlikely events and to underestimate the probability of very likely ones (Kahneman & Tversky, 1984). This bias helps explain why people gamble and enter lotteries, even though the odds are against them and the decision to do so has a negative expected value. According to the formula for expected value, buying a $1 lottery ticket when the probability of winning $4 million is 1 in 10 million yields an expected value of −60 cents. But because people overestimate the probability of winning, they believe there is a positive expected value. The tendency to overestimate the likelihood of unlikely events is amplified by the availability heuristic: Vivid memories of rare gambling successes and the publicity given to lottery winners help people recall gains rather than losses when deciding about future gambles (Wagenaar, 1989).

Another bias relating to probability is called the *gambler's fallacy:* People believe that events in a random process will correct themselves. This belief is false. If you flip a coin and it comes up heads ten times in a row, the chance that it will come up heads on the eleventh try is still 50 percent. Some gamblers, however, will continue feeding a slot machine that hasn't paid off much for hours, assuming it is "due." This assumption may be partly responsible for the resistance to extinction of intermittently reinforced behaviors, as described in the chapter on learning.

Yet another factor underlying flaws in human decision making is the tendency for people to be unrealistically confident in the accuracy of their predictions. Baruch Fischoff and Donald MacGregor (1982) used an ingenious approach to study this bias. They asked people whether they believed that a certain event would occur— for example, that a certain sports team would win—and how confident they were about this prediction. After the events took place, the accuracy of the forecasts was compared with the confidence these people had in those forecasts. Sure enough, people's confidence in their predictions was consistently greater than their accuracy.

This kind of overconfidence appears in many cultures, but it is more common in some than others. For example, Chinese students are more likely to show this bias than students in North America (Wright & Phillips, 1980; Yates et al., 1989). One possible explanation is that students in China are discouraged from challenging what they are told by teachers, so they may be less likely than North Americans to question what they tell themselves and thus more likely to be overconfident (Yates, Lee, & Shinotsuka, 1992).

The moral of the story is to be wary when people in any culture express confidence that a forecast or decision is correct. They will be wrong more often than they think.

A Highly Unlikely Outcome By focusing public attention on the very few people who win big prizes, lottery agencies take advantage of the human tendency to overestimate the probability of rare events. Lottery ads never show the millions of people whose tickets turn out to be worthless.

How Biased Are We?   Almost everyone makes decisions they later regret, but psychologists are divided on the extent to which cognitive biases are to blame (Cohen, 1993; Payne, Bettman, & Johnson, 1992). Some decisions are not intended to maximize expected value but rather to satisfy other criteria, such as minimizing expected loss, producing a quick and easy resolution, or preserving a moral principle (Arkes & Ayton, 1999; Zsambok & Klein, 1997). For example, decisions may depend not just on how likely we are to gain or lose a certain amount of something but also on what that something is. So a decision that could cost or save a human life might be made differently than one that could cost or gain a few dollars, even though the probabilities of each outcome were exactly the same in both cases.

Even the "goodness" or "badness" of decisions can be difficult to measure. Many of them depend on personal values (utilities), which can vary from person to person and from culture to culture. People in individualist cultures, for example, may tend to assign high utilities to attributes that promote personal goals, whereas people in collectivist cultures might place greater value on attributes that bring group harmony and the approval of family and friends (Markus, Kitayama, & Heiman, 1996).

IRM Thinking Critically 8.1: Can Culture Influence Cognitive Processing?

ClassPrep PPT 34: Naturalistic Decision Making

OBJ 8.18: Describe naturalistic decision-making. Define situation awareness.

Test Items 8.105–8.107

Naturalistic Decision Making

Sattler/Shabatay reader, 2/e: Ganas, "Using Teamwork and Goal Setting in the Classroom"

Circumstances in the real world often make it difficult or impossible to go through all the steps needed to complete a successful multi-attribute decision process (Zsambok & Klein, 1997). An alternative approach, called *naturalistic decision making,* is used when experts—working in organizational teams and facing limitations on time and resources—must find solutions to complex problems (Klein, 1997).

Naturalistic decision making involves the use of prior experiences to develop mental representations of how organizational systems really work. Suppose that a production team needs some computer graphics to complete a brochure for a sales meeting to be held in three days. The company's stated policy is that all computer graphics work will be completed in two days, but company veterans know that it always takes at least a week to get the work done. On the basis of prior organizational experience, the production team will probably decide to use an outside service to do the graphics task.

Although naturalistic decision making models vary somewhat, most of them predict that experts make decisions based on mental representations that they have developed as a consequence of prior experiences with similar problems. Based on the perceived parallels between current and past experiences, these experts develop what is known as *situation awareness*—the ability to appreciate all elements of a problem, as well as all elements of the environment within which it appears, and to make decisions that take them all into account. Situation awareness is vital to effective decision making and problem solving in the real world.

ClassPrep PPT 47: Linkages: Group Processes in Problem Solving and Decision Making

LINKAGES (a link to Social Influence)

OBJ 8.19: Describe the impact of groups on decision making. Outline the typical discussion patterns in groups trying to make a decision. Define group polarization, and list the factors that improve or impair group decision making.

Test Items 8.108–8.112

Group Processes in Problem Solving and Decision Making

As with the production team we just described, problem solving and decision making are often done in groups. The processes that influence an individual's problem solving and decision making continue to operate when the individual is in a group, but group interactions also shape the outcome.

When groups are trying to choose from among several options, for example, the discussions typically follow a consistent pattern (Hastie, Penrod, & Pennington, 1983). First, various options are proposed and debated until the group sees that no one has strong objections to one option. That option becomes the *minimally acceptable solution.* From then on, the group criticizes any other proposal and argues more and more strongly for the minimally acceptable solution, which is likely to become the group's decision. This sequence is an example of the anchoring heuristic operating in a group, and it suggests that the order in which options are considered can determine decisions (Wittenbaum & Stasser, 1996).

Groups Working at a Distance
Research on group problem solving and decision making is beginning to focus on "electronic groups," whose members use e-mail and teleconferencing to work together from a distance. Some evidence suggests that compared with meeting in person, communication via e-mail tends to be slower, more explicit, and blunt (sometimes qualifying as "flaming"), and it may result in especially extreme decisions (Kiesler & Sproull, 1992).

Group discussions often result in decisions that are more extreme than the group members would make individually. This tendency toward extreme decisions by groups is called *group polarization* (Kaplan, 1987). Two mechanisms appear to underlie group polarization. First, most arguments presented during the discussion favor the majority view, most criticisms are directed at the minority view, and (influenced by confirmation bias) group members tend to seek additional information that supports the majority position (Schulz-Hardt et al., 2000). So it seems rational to those favoring the majority view to adopt an even stronger version of it (Stasser, 1991). Second, once some group members begin to agree that a particular decision is desirable, other members may try to associate themselves with that decision, perhaps by advocating an even more extreme version (Kaplan & Miller, 1987).

Are people better at problem solving and decision making when they work in groups than when on their own? This is one of the questions about human thought studied by social psychologists. In a typical experiment, a group of people is asked to solve a problem like the one in Figure 8.12 or to make a decision about the guilt or innocence of a fictional defendant. Each person is asked to reach an individual answer and then to join with the others in the group to try to reach a consensus. These studies have found that when problems have solutions that can be demonstrated easily to all members, groups will usually outperform individuals at solving them (Laughlin, 1999). When problems have less obvious solutions, though, groups may be somewhat better at solving them than their average member, but usually no better than their most talented member (Hackman, 1998). And because of a phenomenon called *social loafing* (discussed in the chapter on social influence), people working in a group are often less productive than people working alone (Williams & Sommer, 1997).

Other research (e.g., Stasser, Stewart, & Wittenbaum, 1995) suggests that a critical element in successful group problem solving is the sharing of individual members' unique information and expertise. For example, when asked to diagnose an illness, groups of physicians were much more accurate when they pooled the information possessed by each doctor (Larson et al., 1998). However, *brainstorming,* a popular strategy that supposedly encourages group members to generate innovative solutions to a problem, may actually produce fewer ideas than are generated by individuals working alone (Levine & Moreland, 1998)—possibly because the comments of other group members interfere with the creative process in individuals. Group members who are confident or have high status are most likely to influence a group's deliberations (Levine & Moreland, 1998), but whether these people will help or hurt the group's output depends on whether they have good ideas (Hinsz, 1990). Unfortunately, there is little evidence that members with the best ideas or greatest competence (as opposed to the highest status) always contribute more to group deliberations (Littlepage et al., 1995).

As they work to solve a problem, the members of a group manipulate their own concepts, propositions, images, and other mental representations. How does each member share these private events so as to help the group perform its task? The answer lies in the use of language.

Language

Language is the primary means through which we communicate our thoughts to others. We use language not only to share the thoughts we have at the moment but also to pass on cultural information and traditions from one generation to the next. In this section, we describe the elements that make up a language, the ways that people use language to communicate, the means by which language is learned, and how language influences our thinking.

ClassPrep PPT 35: Basic Elements of Language

OBJ 8.20: List the components of language. Define language symbols and grammar.

Test Items 8.113–8.114

ClassPrep PPT 36: From Sounds to Sentences

OBJ 8.21: Define phoneme, morpheme, and words. Give an example of the phonemes and morphemes in a word.

Test Items 8.115–8.122

IRM Research Focus 8.13: Male and Female Brains and Language

OBJ 8.22: Define syntax and semantics. Explain how syntax and semantics help us comprehend language.

Test Items 8.123–8.127

language Symbols and a set of rules for combining them that provide a vehicle for communication.

grammar A set of rules for combining the words used in a given language.

phoneme The smallest unit of sound that affects the meaning of speech.

morpheme The smallest unit of language that has meaning.

words Units of language composed of one or more morphemes.

syntax The set of rules that govern the formation of phrases and sentences in a language.

semantics Rules governing the meaning of words and sentences.

The Elements of Language

A **language** has two basic elements: (1) symbols, such as words, and (2) a set of rules, called **grammar,** for combining those symbols. These two components allow human language to be at once rule bound and creative. With their knowledge of approximately 50,000 to 100,000 words (Miller, 1991), humans can create and understand an infinite number of sentences. All of the sentences ever spoken are created from just a few dozen categories of sounds. The power of language comes from the way these rather unimpressive raw materials are organized according to rules. This organization occurs at several levels.

From Sounds to Sentences
Organization occurs first at the level of sounds. A **phoneme** is the smallest unit of sound that affects the meaning of speech. Changing a phoneme changes the meaning of a spoken word, much as changing a letter in a printed word changes its meaning. *Tea* has a meaning different from *sea,* and *sight* is different from *sigh.*

The number of phonemes in the world's languages varies from a low of thirteen (Hawaiian) to a high of over sixty (Hindi). Most languages have between thirty and fifty phonemes; English uses about forty. With forty basic sounds and an alphabet of only twenty-six letters, you can see that the same letters must sometimes signal different sounds. For example, the letter *a* stands for different phonemes in the words *cat* and *cake.*

Although changing a phoneme affects the meaning of speech, phonemes themselves are not meaningful. We combine them to form a higher level of organization: morphemes. A **morpheme** is the smallest unit of language that has meaning. For example, because they have meaning, *dog* and *run* are morphemes; but so are prefixes like *un-* and suffixes like *-ed,* because they, too, have meaning, even though they cannot stand alone.

Words are made up of one or more morphemes. Words, in turn, are combined to form phrases and sentences according to a set of grammatical rules called **syntax** (Fromkin & Rodman, 1992). According to English syntax, a subject and a verb must be combined in a sentence, adjectives typically appear before the nouns that they modify, and so on. Compare the following sentences:

Fatal accidents deter careful drivers.

Snows sudden floods melting cause.

The first sentence makes sense, but the second sentence violates English syntax. If the words were reordered, however, they would produce the perfectly acceptable sentence "Melting snows cause sudden floods."

Even if you use English phonemes combined in proper ways to form morphemes strung together according to the laws of English syntax, you may not end up with an acceptable English sentence. Consider the sentence "Rapid bouquets deter sudden neighbors." It somehow sounds right, but it is nonsense. Why? It has syntax, but it ignores the set of rules, called **semantics,** that govern the meaning of words and sentences. For example, because of its meaning, the noun *bouquets* cannot be modified by the word *rapid.*

Surface Structure and Deep Structure
So far, we have discussed elements of language that are apparent in the sentences people produce. These elements were the focus of study by linguists for many decades. Then, in 1965, Noam Chomsky started a revolution in the study of language. He argued that if linguists studied only the language that people produce, they would never uncover the principles that account for all aspects of language. They could not explain, for example, how the sentence "This is my old friend" has more than one meaning. Nor could they account for the close relationship between the meanings of such sentences as "Don't give up just because things look bad" and "It ain't over 'til it's over."

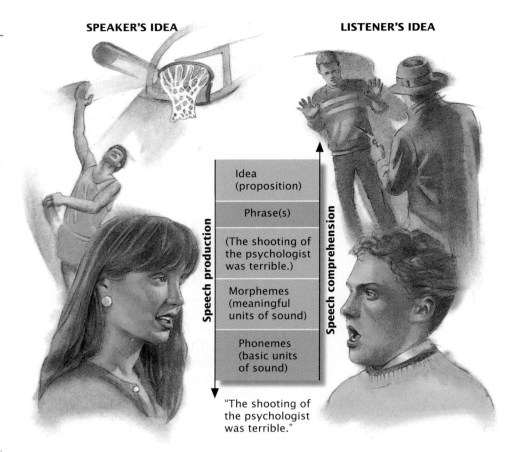

To take these aspects of language into account, Chomsky proposed a more abstract level of analysis. Behind the word strings that people produce, called **surface structures,** there is, he said, a **deep structure,** an abstract representation of the relationships expressed in a sentence. For example, as Figure 8.15 illustrates, the surface structure "The shooting of the psychologist was terrible" can represent either of two deep structures: (1) that the psychologist had terrible aim or (2) that it was terrible that someone shot the psychologist. Chomsky's original analysis of deep and surface structures was important because it encouraged psychologists to analyze not just verbal behavior and grammatical rules but also mental representations.

Understanding Speech

When someone speaks to you in your own language, your sensory, perceptual, and other cognitive systems reconstruct the sounds of speech in a way that allows you to detect, recognize, and understand what the person is saying. The process may seem effortless, but it involves amazingly complex feats of information processing. Scientists trying to develop speech-recognition software systems have discovered just how complex the process is. After decades of effort, the accuracy and efficiency of these systems are still not much better than those of the average five-year-old child. What makes understanding speech so complicated?

One factor is that the physical features of a particular speech sound are not always the same. This phenomenon is illustrated in Figure 8.16, which shows how the sounds of particular letters differ depending on the sounds that follow them. A second factor complicating our understanding of speech is that each of us creates

surface structures   The order in which words are arranged in sentences.

deep structure   An abstract representation of the underlying meanings of a given sentence.

Making sure that the surface structures we create accurately convey the deep structures we intend is one of the greatest challenges people face when communicating through language.

slightly different speech sounds, even when saying the same words. Third, as people speak, their words are not usually separated by silence. So if the speech spectrograms in Figure 8.16 showed whole sentences, you would not be able to tell where one word ended and the next began.

OBJ 8.24: Discuss the role of top-down processing, context, scripts, conventions, and nonverbal cues in the comprehension of language.

Test Items 8.136–8.139

Perceiving Words and Sentences   Despite these challenges, humans can instantly recognize and understand the words and sentences produced by almost anyone speaking a familiar language. In contrast, even the best voice-recognition software must learn to recognize words spoken by a new voice, and even then may make many mistakes. (A man we know recently requested the toll-free number for the Maglite Corporation, and the voice-recognition software in a directory assistance computer gave him the number for Metlife insurance.)

Scientists have yet to discover all the details about how people overcome the challenges of understanding speech, but some general answers are emerging. Just as we recognize objects by analyzing their visual features (see the chapter on perception), it appears that humans identify and recognize the specific—and changing—features of the sounds created when someone speaks. And as in visual perception, this *bottom-up processing* of stimulus features combines with *top-down processing* guided by knowledge-based factors, such as context and expectation, to aid understanding (Samuel, 2001). For example, knowing the general topic of conversation helps you to recognize individual words that might otherwise be hard to understand (Cole & Jakimik, 1978).

Finally, we are often guided to an understanding of speech by nonverbal cues. The frown, the enthusiastic nod, or the bored yawn that accompanies speech each carries information that helps you understand what the person is saying. So if someone says "Wow, are you smart!" but really means "I think you're a jerk," you will detect the true meaning based on the context, facial expression, and tone of voice. No wonder it is usually easier to understand someone in a face-to-face conversation than on the telephone or via e-mail (Massaro & Stork, 1998).

figure 8.16

Speech Spectrograms

These speech spectrograms show what the sound frequencies of speech look like as people say various words. Notice how the shape of the whole speech signal differs from one word to another, even when the initial consonant (*b* or *d*) is the same.

Source: Jusczyk et al. (1981).

ClassPrep PPT 38: *Figure 8.16:* Speech Spectrograms

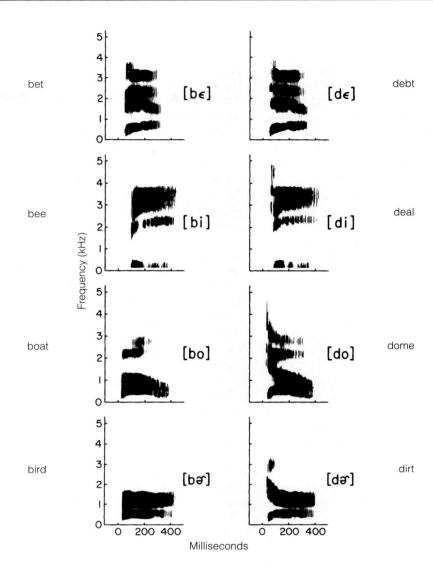

The Development of Language

LINKAGES (a link to Human Development)

Children the world over develop language with impressive speed; the average six-year-old already has a vocabulary of about 13,000 words (Pinker, 1994). But acquiring a language involves more than just learning vocabulary. We also have to learn how words are combined and how to produce and understand sentences. Psychologists who study the development of language have found that the process begins in the earliest days of a child's life and follows some predictable steps (Saffran, Senghas, & Trueswell, 2001).

The First Year   Within the first few months of life, babies can tell the difference between the sounds of their native language and those of other languages (Gerken, 1994), and by ten months of age they pay closer attention to speech in

babblings The first sounds infants make that resemble speech.

Understanding Spoken Language
Top-down perceptual processes, described in the chapter on perception, help explain why speech in a language you do not understand sounds like a continuous stream being spoken faster than speech in your own language. You do not know where each unfamiliar word starts and stops, so without perceived gaps, the speech sounds run together at what seems to be a faster-than-normal rate. To people unfamiliar with your language, your speech, too, sounds extremely fast!

their native language (Werker et al., 1996). In the first year, then, infants become more and more attuned to the sounds that will be important in acquiring their native language.

The first year is also the time when babies begin to produce **babblings,** which are patterns of meaningless sounds that first resemble speech. Infants of all nationalities begin with the same set of babbling sounds. At about nine months, however, babies who hear only English start to lose their German gutturals and French nasals. At this time, babbling becomes more complex and begins to sound like "sentences" in the babies' native language. Starting around this time, too, babies who hear English begin to shorten some of their vocalizations to "da," "duh," and "ma." These sounds seem very much like language, and babies use them in specific contexts and with obvious purpose (Blake & de Boysson-Bardies, 1992). Accompanied by appropriate gestures, they may be used to express joy ("oohwow") or anger ("uh-uh-uh"), to get something that is out of reach ("engh-engh"), or to point out something interesting ("dah!").

By ten to twelve months of age, babies can understand several words—certainly more words than they can say (Fenson et al., 1994). Proper names and object labels

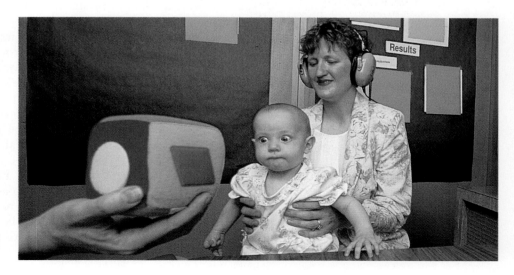

Getting Ready to Talk
Long before they utter their first words, babies are getting ready to talk. Experiments in Patricia Kuhl's laboratory show that even six-month-olds tend to look longer at faces whose lip movements match the sounds of spoken words. This tendency reflects babies' abilities to focus on, recognize, and discriminate among the sounds of speech, especially in their native language. These abilities are crucial to the development of language.

IRM Activity 3.12: Question Formation

are among the earliest words they understand. Often the first word they understand is a pet's name.

Proper names and object words—such *as mama, daddy, cookie, doggy,* and *car*—are also among the first words children are likely to say when, at around twelve months of age, they begin to talk (some do this a little earlier and some a little later). Nouns for simple object categories *(dog, flower)* are acquired before more general nouns *(animal, plant)* or more specific names *(collie, rose)* (Rosch et al., 1976).

Of course, these early words do not sound exactly like adult language. English-speaking babies usually reduce them to a shorter, easier form, like "duh" for *duck* or "mih" for *milk*. Children make themselves understood, however, by using gestures, intonations, facial expressions, and endless repetitions. If they have a word for an object, they may "overextend" it to cover more ground. So they might use *dog* for cats, bears, and horses; they might use *fly* for all insects and perhaps for other small things like raisins and M&Ms (Clark, 1983, 1993). Children make these "errors" because their vocabularies are limited, not because they fail to notice the difference between dogs and cats or because they want to eat a fly (Fremgen & Fay, 1980; Rescorla, 1981).

Until they can say the conventional words for objects, children overextend the words they have, use all-purpose sounds (like "dat" or "dis"), and coin new words (like *pepping* for "shaking the pepper shaker") (Becker, 1994). Being around people who don't understand these overextensions encourages children to learn and use more precise words (Markman, 1994). During this period, children build up their vocabularies one word at a time. They also use their limited vocabulary one word at a time; they cannot yet put words together into sentences.

The Second Year

ClassPrep PPT 41: Stages of Language Development (cont.)

The **one-word stage** of speech lasts for about six months. Then, sometime around eighteen months of age, children's vocabularies expand dramatically (Gleitman & Landau, 1994). They may learn several new words each day, and by the age of two, most youngsters can use fifty to well over one hundred words. They also start using two-word combinations to form efficient little sentences. These two-word sentences are called *telegraphic* because they are brief and to the point, leaving out anything that is not absolutely essential. So if she wants her mother to give her a book, a twenty-month-old might first say, "Give book," then "Mommy give," and if that does not work, "Mommy book." The child also uses rising tones to indicate a question ("Go out?") and puts stress on certain words to indicate location ("Play *park*") or new information ("*Big* car").

Three-word sentences come next in the development of language. They are still telegraphic, but more nearly complete: "Mommy give book." The child can now speak in sentences that have the usual subject-verb-object form of adult sentences. Other words and word endings begin appearing, too, such as the suffix *-ing*, the prepositions *in* and *on*, the plural *-s*, and irregular past tenses ("It broke," "I ate") (Brown, 1973; Dale, 1976). Children learn to use the suffix *-ed* for the past tense ("I walked"), but then they often overapply this rule to irregular verbs that they previously used correctly, saying, for example, "It breaked," "It broked," or "I eated" (Marcus, 1996).

Children also expand their sentences with adjectives, although at first they make some mistakes. For example, they are likely to use both *less* and *more* to mean "more" or both *tall* and *short* to mean "tall" (Smith & Sera, 1992).

The Third Year and Beyond

ClassPrep PPT 42: Stages of Language Development (cont.)

By age three or so, children begin to use auxiliary verbs ("Adam is going") and to ask questions using *wh-* words, such as *what, where, who,* and *why*. They begin to put together clauses to form complex sentences ("Here's the ball I was looking for"). By age five, children have acquired most of the grammatical rules of their native language.

one-word stage A stage of language development during which children tend to use one word at a time.

ClassPrep PPT 43: How Is Language Acquired?

OBJ 8.26: Discuss the roles of conditioning, imitation, nature and nurture in language development.

Test Items 8.147–8.152

Essay Q 8.3

IRM Activity 6.9: A Demonstration of Shaping

IRM Research Focus 8.13: Male and Female Brains and Language

How Is Language Acquired?

Despite all that has been discovered about the steps children follow in acquiring language, mystery and debate still surround the question of just how they do it. Obviously, children pick up the specific content of language from the speech they hear around them; English children learn English, and French children learn French. As parents and children share meals, playtime, and conversations, children learn that words refer to objects and actions and what the labels for them are. But how do children learn syntax, the rules of grammar?

Conditioning, Imitation, and Rules   Our discussion of conditioning in the chapter on learning would suggest that children learn syntax because their parents reinforce them for using it. This sounds reasonable, but observational studies show that positive reinforcement does not tell the whole story. Parents are usually more concerned about what is said than about its grammatical form (Hirsch-Pasek, Treiman, & Schneiderman, 1984). So when the little boy with chocolate crumbs on his face says, "I not eat cookie," his mother is more likely to say, "Yes, you did" than to ask the child to say, "I did not eat the cookie" and then reinforce him for grammatical correctness.

Learning through modeling, or imitation, appears to be more influential. Children learn grammar most rapidly when adults demonstrate the correct syntax in the course of a conversation, as in the following example:

CHILD: Mommy fix.

MOTHER: Okay, Mommy will fix the truck.

CHILD: It breaked.

MOTHER: Yes, it broke.

CHILD: Truck broke.

MOTHER: Let's see if we can fix it.

But if children learn syntax by imitation, why would they overgeneralize rules, such as the rule for making the past tense? Why, for example, do children who at one time said "I went" later say "I goed"? Adults never use this form of speech. Its sudden appearance indicates that the child either has mastered the rule of adding -ed or has generalized from similar-sounding words (such as *mowed* or *rowed*). In short, neither conditioning nor imitation seems entirely adequate to explain how children learn language. Children must still analyze for themselves the underlying patterns in the language examples they hear around them (Bloom, 1995).

Innate Sources of Language Acquisition   The ease with which children everywhere discover these underlying patterns and learn language has led some to argue that language acquisition is at least partly innate. For example, Chomsky believes that we have a built-in *universal grammar,* a mechanism that allows us to identify the basic dimensions of language (Baker, 2002; Chomsky, 1986; Nowak, Komarova, & Niyogi, 2001). One of these dimensions is how important word order is in the syntax of a particular language. For example, in English, word order tells us who is doing what to whom (the sentences "Heather dumped Jason" and "Jason dumped Heather" contain the same words, but they have different meanings). In languages such as Russian, however, word order is less important than modifiers attached to the word, also called *inflections.* According to Chomsky, a child's universal grammar might initially be "set" to assume that word order is important to syntax, but it would change if the child hears language in which word order is not crucial. In Chomsky's system, then, we don't entirely learn language—we develop it as genetic predispositions interact with experience (Senghas & Coppola, 2001).

Other theorists disagree with Chomsky, arguing that the development of language reflects the development of more general cognitive skills rather than innate, language-specific mechanisms (e.g., Bates, 1993). Still, there is other evidence to support the existence of biological factors in language acquisition. For example, the unique speech-generating properties of the human mouth and throat, the language-related brain regions such as Broca's area and Wernicke's area (see Figure 3.16), and recent genetic research all suggest that humans are innately "prewired," or biologically programmed, for language (Buxhoeveden et al., 2001; Lai et al., 2001). In addition, there appears to be a *critical period* in childhood during which we can learn language more easily than at any other time (Ridley, 2000). The existence of this critical period is supported by the difficulties adults have in learning a second language (e.g., Lenneberg, 1967), and also by cases in which unfortunate children spent their early years in isolation from human contact and the sound of adult language. Even after years of therapy and language training, these individuals are not able to combine ideas into sentences (Rymer, 1993b). These cases suggest that in order to acquire the complex features of our language, we must be exposed to speech before a certain age.

Bilingualism   Does trying to learn two languages at once, even before the critical period is over, impair the learning of either? Research suggests just the opposite. Although their early language utterances may be confused or delayed, children who are raised in a bilingual environment before the end of the critical period seem to show enhanced performance in each language (deHouwer, 1995). There is also some evidence that *balanced bilinguals*—people who developed roughly equal mastery of two languages as children—are superior to others in cognitive flexibility, concept formation, and creativity. It is as if each language offers a slightly different perspective on thinking, and this dual perspective makes the brain more flexible (Hong et al., 2000).

The apparent benefits of bilingualism have important implications for U.S. school systems, where children from non-English-speaking homes often receive instruction in their native language while taking classes in English. Although lack of control over school environments makes it difficult to perform true experiments on the effects of this practice, available evidence suggests that these bilingual programs

ClassPrep PPT 44: Bilingualism

OBJ 8.27: Describe the impact of a bilingual environment on the development of language abilities.

Test Items 8.153–8.156

Sattler/Shabatay reader, 2/e: Rodriguez, "A Memoir of a Bilingual Childhood"

Learning a Second Language The notion of a critical period for language acquisition is supported by the fact that after the age of thirteen or fourteen, people learn a second language more slowly (Johnson & Newport, 1989) and virtually never learn to speak it without an accent (Lenneberg, 1967).

facilitate educational achievement (Cavaliere, 1996). The evidence also suggests that rapid immersion in an English-only program may do considerable educational harm to children who enter school with no English-language background (Crawford, 1989).

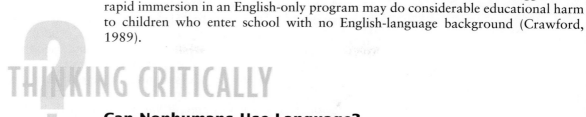

THINKING CRITICALLY

Can Nonhumans Use Language?

OBJ 8.28: Discuss the controversy surrounding the question, "Can nonhumans use language?" and describe what conclusions are reasonable given the evidence so far.

Test Items 8.157–8.161

ClassPrep PPT 50: Thinking Critically: Can Nonhumans Use Language?

Some psychologists say that it is the ability of humans to acquire and use language that sets them apart from all other creatures. Yet those creatures, too, use symbols to communicate. Bees perform a dance that tells other bees where they found sources of nectar; the grunts and gestures of chimpanzees signify varying desires and emotions. These forms of communication do not necessarily have the grammatical characteristics of language, however (Rendall, Cheney, & Seyfarth, 2000). Are any animals other than humans capable of learning language?

● What am I being asked to believe or accept?

Over the last forty years, several researchers have asserted that nonhumans can master language. Chimpanzees and gorillas have been the most popular targets of study, because at maturity they are estimated to have the intelligence of two- or three-year-old children, who are usually well on their way to learning language. Dolphins, too, have been studied because they have a complex communication system and exceptionally large brains relative to their body size (Janik, 2000; Reiss & Marino, 2001). It would seem that if these animals were unable to learn language, their general intelligence could not be blamed. Instead, failure would be attributed to the absence of a genetic makeup that permits language learning.

● What evidence is available to support the assertion?

The question of whether nonhuman mammals can learn to use language is not a simple one, for at least two reasons. First, language is more than just communication, but defining just when animals are exhibiting that "something more" is a source of debate. What seems to set human language apart from the gestures, grunts, chirps, whistles, or cries of other animals is grammar—a formal set of rules for combining words. Also, because of their anatomical structures, nonhuman mammals will never be able to "speak" in the same way that humans do (Lieberman, 1991). To test these animals' ability to learn language, investigators therefore must devise novel ways for them to communicate.

David and Ann Premack taught their chimp, Sarah, to communicate by placing differently shaped chips, each symbolizing a word, on a magnetic board (Premack, 1971). Lana, a chimpanzee studied by Duane Rumbaugh (1977), learned to communicate by pressing keys on a specially designed computer. American Sign Language (ASL), the hand-gesture language used by people who are deaf, has been used by Beatrice and Allen Gardner with the chimp Washoe, and by Herbert Terrace with Nim Chimsky, a chimp named after Noam Chomsky. And Kanzi, a bonobo (commonly known as a pygmy chimpanzee) studied by Sue Savage-Rumbaugh (1990; Savage-Rumbaugh et al., 1993), learned to recognize spoken words and to communicate by both gesturing and pressing word-symbol keys on a computer that would "speak" them. Kanzi was a special case: He learned to communicate by listening and watching as his mother, Matata, was being taught and then used what he had learned to interact with her trainers.

Studies of these animals suggested that they could spontaneously use combinations of words to refer to things that were not present. Washoe, Lana, Sarah, Nim, and Kanzi all mastered between 130 and 500 words. Their vocabulary included names for concrete objects, such as *apple* or *me*; verbs, such as *tickle* and *eat*; adjectives, such as *happy* and *big*; and adverbs, such as *again*. The animals combined the words in sentences, expressing wishes such as "You tickle me" or "If

Sarah good, then apple." Sometimes the sentences referred to things in the past. When an investigator called attention to a wound that Kanzi had received, the animal produced the sentence "Matata hurt," referring to a disciplinary bite his mother had recently given him (Savage-Rumbaugh, 1990). Finally, all these animals seemed to enjoy their communication tools and used them spontaneously to interact with their caretakers and with other animals.

Most of the investigators mentioned here have argued that their animals mastered a crude grammar (Premack & Premack, 1983; Savage-Rumbaugh, Shankar, & Taylor, 1999). For example, if Washoe wanted to be tickled, she would gesture, "You tickle Washoe." But if she wanted to do the tickling, she would gesture, "Washoe tickle you." The correct placement of object and subject in these sentences suggested that Washoe was following a set of rules for word combination—in other words, a grammar (Gardner & Gardner, 1978). Louis Herman and his colleagues documented similar grammatical sensitivity in dolphins, who rarely confused subject-verb order in following instructions given by human hand signals (Herman, Richards, & Wolz, 1984). Furthermore, Savage-Rumbaugh observed several hundred instances in which Kanzi understood sentences he had never heard before. Once, for example, while his back was turned to the speaker, Kanzi heard the sentence "Jeanie hid the pine needles in her shirt." He turned around, approached Jeanie, and searched her shirt to find the pine needles. His actions would seem to indicate that he understood this new sentence the first time he heard it.

● Are there alternative ways of interpreting the evidence?

Many of the early conclusions about primate language learning were challenged by Herbert Terrace and his colleagues in their investigation of Nim (Terrace et al., 1979). Terrace noticed many subtle characteristics of Nim's communications that seemed quite different from a child's use of language, and he argued that animals in other studies demonstrated these same characteristics.

First, he said, their sentences were always very short. Nim could combine two or three gestures but never used strings that conveyed more sophisticated messages. The ape was never able to say anything equivalent to a three-year-old child's "I want to go to Wendy's for a hamburger, OK?" Second, Terrace questioned whether the animals' use of language demonstrated the spontaneity, creativity, and expanding complexity characteristic of children's language. Many of the animals' sentences were requests for food, tickling, baths, pets, and other pleasurable objects and experiences. Is such behavior different from the kind of behavior shown by the family dog who learns to sit up and beg for table scraps? Other researchers also pointed out that chimps are not naturally predisposed to associate seen objects with heard words, as human infants are (Savage-Rumbaugh et al., 1983). Finally, Terrace questioned whether experimenter bias influenced the reports of the chimps' communications. Consciously or not, experimenters who want to conclude that chimps learn language might tend to ignore strings that violate grammatical order or to reinterpret ambiguous strings so that they make grammatical sense. If Nim sees someone holding a banana and signs, "Nim banana," the experimenter might assume the word order is correct and means "Nim wants the banana" rather than, for example, "That banana belongs to Nim," in which case the word order would be wrong.

● What additional evidence would help to evaluate the alternatives?

Studies of animals' ability to learn language are expensive and take many years. Accordingly, the amount of evidence in the area is small—just a handful of studies, each based on a few animals. Obviously, more data are needed from more studies that use a common methodology.

It is important, as well, to study the extent to which limits on the length of primates' spontaneous sentences result from limits on short-term and working memory (Savage-Rumbaugh & Brakke, 1996). If memory is in fact the main limiting factor, then the failure to produce progressively longer sentences does not necessarily reflect an inability to master language.

Animal Language? Here, a gorilla named Koko makes the American Sign Language (ASL) sign for "smoke" as her trainer, Penny Patterson, holds a cat named Smoky. Koko recently responded to questions sent to her on the Internet. Because Koko can't read or type, her trainer relayed the questions in ASL and typed the gorilla's signed responses. This procedure left some questioners wondering whether they were talking to Koko or her trainer.

Research on how primates might spontaneously acquire language by listening and imitating, as Kanzi did, as well as naturalistic observations of communications among primates in their natural habitat, would also help scientists better understand primates' capacity to communicate (Savage-Rumbaugh, Shankar, & Taylor, 1999; Sevcik & Savage-Rumbaugh, 1994).

● **What conclusions are most reasonable?**

Psychologists are still not in full agreement about whether our sophisticated mammalian cousins can learn language. Two things are clear, however. First, whatever the chimp, gorilla, and dolphin have learned is a much more primitive and limited form of communication than that learned by children. Second, their level of communication does not do justice to their overall intelligence; these animals are smarter than their "language" production suggests. In short, the evidence to date favors the view that humans have language abilities that are unique (Buxhoeveden et al., 2001), but that under the right circumstances, and with the right tools, other animals can master many language-like skills.

ClassPrep PPT 45: Culture, Language, and Thought

OBJ 8.29: Discuss the relationship among language, culture, and perception.

Test Items 8.162–8.165

Culture, Language, and Thought

When ideas from one language are translated into another, the intended meaning can easily be distorted, as shown in Table 8.2. But differences in language and culture may have more serious and important implications as well. The language that people speak forms part of their knowledge of the world, and that knowledge, as noted in the chapter on perception, guides perceptions. This relationship raises the question of whether differences among languages create differences in the ways that people perceive and think about the world.

Benjamin Whorf (1956) claimed that language actually determines how we can think, a process he called *linguistic determinism*. He noted, for example, that Inuit Eskimos have several different words for "snow" and proposed that this feature of their language should lead to a greater perceptual ability to discriminate among varieties of snow. When these discrimination abilities of Inuits and other people are

Sometimes a lack of familiarity with the formal and informal aspects of other languages get American advertisers in trouble. Here are three examples.

table 8.2
Lost in Translation

When the Clairol Company introduced its "Mist Stick" curling iron in Germany, it was unaware that *mist* is a German slang word meaning "manure." Not many people wanted to buy a manure stick.

In Chinese, the Kentucky Fried Chicken slogan "Finger lickin' good" came out as "Eat your fingers off."

In Chinese, the slogan for Pepsi, "Come alive with the Pepsi Generation," became "Pepsi brings your ancestors back from the grave."

compared, there are indeed significant differences. But are these differences in perception the *result* of differences in language?

One of the most interesting tests of Whorf's ideas was conducted by Eleanor Rosch (1975). She compared the perception of colors by North Americans with that by members of the Dani tribe of New Guinea. In the language of the Dani, there are only two color names—one for dark, "cold" colors and one for lighter, "warm" ones. In contrast, English speakers have names for a vast number of different hues. Of these, it is possible to identify eleven focal colors; these are prototypes, the particular wavelengths of light that are the best examples of the eleven major categories (red, yellow, green, blue, black, gray, white, purple, orange, pink, and brown). Fire-engine red is the focal color for red. Rosch reasoned that if Whorf's views were correct, then English speakers, who have verbal labels for focal colors, should recognize them better than nonfocal colors, but that for the Dani, the focal-nonfocal distinction should make no difference. In fact, however, Rosch found that both the Dani and the English-speaking North Americans perceived focal colors more efficiently than nonfocal ones (Heider, 1972).

Although our language may not determine what we think about, it does appear to influence how we think. For example, Alfred Bloom (1981) reported that Chinese-speaking residents of Hong Kong had a hard time thinking about questions such as "How would you react if the government were to pass a law requiring people to make weekly reports of their activities?" Responding to such questions requires dealing with *counterfactual arguments*—which are propositions that could be true but are not. The problem, he said, is that the Chinese language does not have an easy way to express such arguments. Bloom's results do not mean that the Chinese are incapable of counterfactual thinking (Au, 1992; Chan, 2000; Liu, 1985); rather, they remind us that thinking habits are shaped by our culture, including the language in which we do our thinking (Nisbett et al., 2002).

Another example of the influence of language on thinking comes from a study showing that compared with children who speak Japanese or Korean, English- and French-speaking children have more trouble understanding the mathematical concept of "place value"—such as that the number *eleven* means "one 10 and one 1" (Miura et al., 1993). As described in the chapter on human development, one important reason for this difference is that some languages make place values more obvious than others. The Korean word for *eleven*, which is *shib-il*, means "ten-one." English speakers have to remember what *eleven* refers to every time they hear it.

Even within a culture, language can affect reasoning, problem solving, and decision making. For example, consider whether you would choose A or B in each of the following situations:

The government is preparing for the outbreak of an unusual disease, which you know will kill 600 people if nothing is done. Two programs are proposed. If program A is adopted, 200 people will be saved. If program B is adopted, there is a one-third chance that all 600 people will be saved and a two-thirds chance that no people will be saved.

IRM Thinking Critically 8.1: Can Culture Influence Cognitive Processing?

A ship hits a mine in the middle of the ocean, and 600 passengers on board will die if action is not taken immediately. There are two options. If option A is adopted, 400 passengers will die. If option B is adopted, there is a one-third chance that no passengers will die and a two-thirds chance that no passengers will be saved.

The logic of each situation is the same (program A and option A will both save 200 lives), so people who choose program A in one case should choose option A in the other. But this is not what happens. In one study, 72 percent of participants chose program A in the disease situation, but 78 percent chose option B in the shipwreck situation (Kahneman & Tversky, 1984). Their choices were not logically consistent, because people's thinking tends to be influenced by the words used to describe situations. Here, program A was framed in terms of lives saved; option B was framed in terms of lives lost. Advertisers are well aware of how this *framing effect* alters decisions; as a result, your grocer stocks ground beef labeled as "75 percent lean," not "25 percent fat."

ClassPrep PPT 46: Linkages to Cognition and Language

LINKAGES

As noted in the chapter on introducing psychology, all of psychology's subfields are related to one another. Our discussion of group processes in problem solving illustrates just one way in which the topic of this chapter, cognition and language, is linked to the subfield of social psychology (especially to the chapter on social influence). The Linkages diagram shows ties to two other subfields as well, and there are many more ties throughout the book. Looking for linkages among subfields will help you see how they all fit together and help you better appreciate the big picture that is psychology.

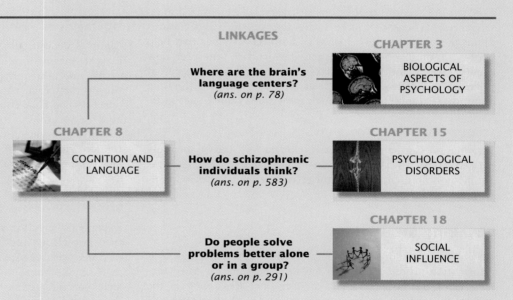

LINKAGES

CHAPTER 8
COGNITION AND LANGUAGE

Where are the brain's language centers?
(ans. on p. 78)

CHAPTER 3
BIOLOGICAL ASPECTS OF PSYCHOLOGY

How do schizophrenic individuals think?
(ans. on p. 583)

CHAPTER 15
PSYCHOLOGICAL DISORDERS

Do people solve problems better alone or in a group?
(ans. on p. 291)

CHAPTER 18
SOCIAL INFLUENCE

SUMMARY

Cognitive psychology is the study of the mental processes by which the information humans receive from their environment is modified, made meaningful, stored, retrieved, used, and communicated to others.

Basic Functions of Thought

The five core functions of thought are to describe, elaborate, decide, plan, and guide action.

The Circle of Thought

Many psychologists think of the components of the circle of thought as constituting an *information-processing system* that

receives, represents, transforms, and acts on incoming stimuli. *Thinking*, then, is defined as the manipulation of mental representations by this system.

Measuring Information Processing

The time elapsing between the presentation of a stimulus and an overt response to it is the *reaction time*. Among the factors affecting reaction times are the complexity of the choice of a response, stimulus-response compatibility, expectancy, and the tradeoff between speed and accuracy. Using methods such as the EEG and neuroimaging techniques, psychologists can also measure mental events as reflected in *evoked brain potentials* and other brain activity.

Mental Representations: The Ingredients of Thought

Mental representations take the form of concepts, propositions, schemas, scripts, mental models, images, and cognitive maps.

Concepts

Concepts are categories of objects, events, or ideas with common properties. They may be formal or natural. *Formal concepts* are precisely defined by the presence or absence of certain features. *Natural concepts* are fuzzy; no fixed set of defining properties determines membership in a natural concept. A member of a natural concept that displays all or most of its characteristic features is called a *prototype*.

Propositions

Propositions are assertions that state how concepts are related. Propositions can be true or false.

Schemas, Scripts, and Mental Models

Schemas are sets of propositions that serve as generalized mental representations of concepts and also generate expectations about them. *Scripts* are schemas of familiar activities that help people to think about those activities and to interpret new events. *Mental models* are clusters of propositions that represent physical objects and processes, as well as guide our thinking about those things; mental models may or may not be accurate.

Images and Cognitive Maps

Information can be represented as *images* and can be mentally rotated, inspected, and otherwise manipulated. *Cognitive maps* are mental representations of the spatial arrangements in familiar parts of the world.

Thinking Strategies

By combining and transforming mental representations, our information-processing system makes it possible for us to reason, solve problems, and make decisions. *Reasoning* is the process through which people generate and evaluate arguments, as well as reach conclusions about them.

Formal Reasoning

Formal reasoning seeks valid conclusions through the application of rigorous procedures. These procedures include formulas, or *algorithms*, which are guaranteed to produce correct solutions if they exist, and the *rules of logic*, which are useful in evaluating sets of premises and conclusions called *syllogisms*. To reach a sound conclusion, we must consider both the truth or falsity of the premises and the logic of the argument itself. People are prone to logical errors; their belief in a conclusion is often affected by the extent to which the conclusion is consistent with their attitudes, as well as by other factors, including *confirmation bias* and limits on working memory.

Informal Reasoning

People use *informal reasoning* to assess the believability of a conclusion based on the evidence for it. Errors in informal reasoning often stem from the misuse of *heuristics,* or mental shortcuts. Three important heuristics are the *anchoring heuristic* (estimating the probability of an event by adjusting a starting value), the *representativeness heuristic* (categorizing an event by how representative it is of a category of events), and the *availability heuristic* (estimating probability by how available an event is in memory).

Problem Solving

Steps in problem solving include diagnosing the problem and then planning, executing, and evaluating a solution.

Strategies for Problem Solving

Especially when solutions are not obvious, problem solving can be aided by the use of strategies such as incubation, means-end analysis, working backward, and using analogies.

Obstacles to Problem Solving

Many of the difficulties that people experience in solving problems arise when they are dealing with hypotheses. People do not easily entertain multiple hypotheses. Because of *mental sets,* people may stick to a particular hypothesis even when it is unsuccessful and, through *functional fixedness,* may tend to miss opportunities to use familiar objects in unusual ways. Confirmation bias may lead people to be reluctant to revise or change hypotheses, especially cherished ones, on the basis of new evidence, and they may fail to use the absence of symptoms as evidence in solving problems.

Building Problem-Solving Skills

Experts are superior to beginners in problem solving because of their knowledge and experience. They can draw on knowledge of similar problems, visualize related components of a problem as a single chunk, and perceive relations among problems in terms of underlying principles rather than surface features. Extensive knowledge is the main component of expertise, yet expertise itself can prevent the expert from seeing problems in new ways.

Problem Solving by Computer

Some specific problems can be solved by computer programs known as expert systems. These systems are one application of *artificial intelligence (AI).* One approach to AI focuses on programming computers to imitate the logical manipulation of symbols that occurs in human thought; another approach (involving connectionist, or neural network, models) attempts to imitate the connections among neurons in the human brain. Current problem-solving computer systems deal most successfully with specific domains. Often, the best outcomes occur when humans and computers work together.

Decision Making

Evaluating Options

Decisions are sometimes difficult because there are too many alternatives and too many attributes of each alternative to consider at one time. Furthermore, decisions often involve comparisons of *utility,* not objective value. Decision making is also complicated by the fact that the world is unpredictable, which makes decisions risky. In risky decision making, the best decision is one that maximizes *expected value.*

Biases and Flaws in Decision Making

People often fail to maximize expected value in their decisions for two reasons: First, losses are perceived differently from gains of equal size; second, people tend to overestimate the probability of unlikely events, underestimate the probability of likely events, and feel overconfident in the accuracy of their forecasts. The gambler's fallacy leads people to believe that outcomes in a random process are affected by previous outcomes. People sometimes make decisions aimed at goals other than maximizing expected value; these goals may be determined by personal and cultural factors.

Naturalistic Decision Making

Many real-world circumstances require naturalistic decision making, in which prior experiences are used to develop mental representations of how organizational systems really work.

Language

The Elements of Language

Language consists of symbols such as words and rules for their combination—a *grammar.* Spoken *words* are made up of *phonemes,* which are combined to make *morphemes.* Combinations of words must have both *syntax* (grammar) and *semantics* (meaning). Behind the word strings, or *surface structures,* is an underlying representation, or *deep structure,* that expresses the relationship among the ideas in a sentence. Ambiguous sentences occur when one surface structure reflects two or more deep structures.

Understanding Speech

When people listen to speech, their perceptual system allows them to perceive gaps between words, even when those gaps are not physically present. To understand language generally, and conversations in particular, people use their knowledge of the context and of the world. In addition, understanding is guided by nonverbal cues.

The Development of Language

Children develop grammar according to an orderly pattern. *Babblings* and the *one-word stage* of speech come first, then telegraphic two-word sentences. Next come three-word sentences and certain grammatical forms that appear in a somewhat predictable order. Once children learn certain regular verb forms and plural endings, they may overgeneralize rules. Children acquire most of the syntax of their native language by the time they are five years old.

How Is Language Acquired?

Conditioning and imitation both play a role in a child's acquisition of language, but neither can provide a complete explanation of how children acquire syntax. Humans may be biologically programmed to learn language. In any event, it appears that language must be learned during a certain critical period if normal language is to occur. The critical-period notion is supported by research on second-language acquisition.

Culture, Language, and Thought

Research across cultures, and within North American culture, suggests that although language does not determine what we can think, it does influence how we think, solve problems, and make decisions.

Consciousness

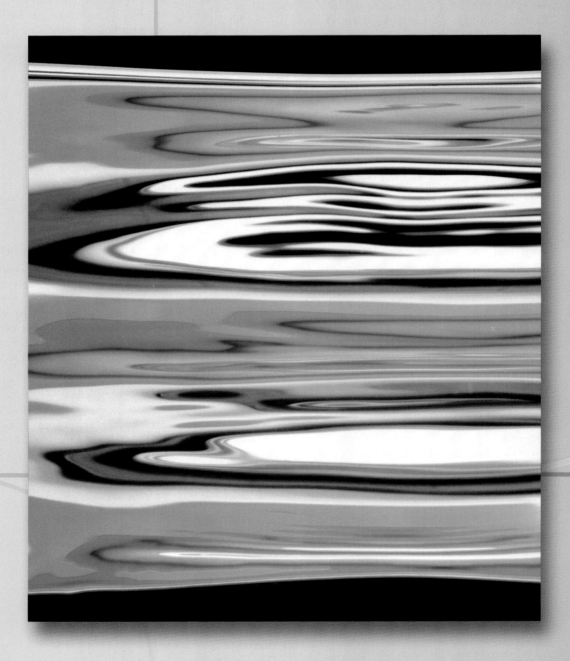

T here is an old *Sesame Street* episode in which Ernie is trying to find out whether Bert is asleep or awake. In other words, Ernie is trying to determine Bert's state of consciousness. Ernie observes that Bert's eyes are closed, and he comments that Bert usually closes his eyes when he is asleep. Ernie also notes that when Bert is asleep, he does not respond to pokes, so naturally, he delivers a few pokes. At first, Bert does not respond; but after being poked a few times, he awakes, very annoyed, and yells at Ernie for waking him. Ernie then informs Bert that he just wanted to let him know it was time for his nap.

In a way, doctors face a similar situation in dealing with the more than 30 million people each year who receive general anesthesia during surgery. These patients certainly appear to go to sleep, but it may surprise you to learn that there is no reliable way of knowing whether they are actually unconscious. It turns out that about 1 percent of them retain some degree of consciousness during the surgical procedure (Ranta, Jussila, & Hynynen, 1990; Sandin et al., 2000). In rare cases, patients have conscious awareness of surgical pain and remember the trauma. Although their surgical incisions heal, these people may be psychologically scarred by the experience and may even show symptoms of posttraumatic stress disorder (Schwender et al., 1995).

The fact that people can be conscious while "asleep" under the influence of powerful anesthetic drugs obviously makes defining consciousness quite difficult. After decades of discussion and research by philosophers, psychologists, and even physicists, some believe that consciousness is still not yet understood well enough to be precisely defined (Crick & Koch, 1998; King & Pribram, 1995). Given the ethical and legal concerns raised by the need to ensure that patients are not subjected to pain during surgery, doctors tend to define *consciousness* as awareness that is demonstrated by either explicit or implicit recall (Schwender et al., 1995). In psychology, the definition is somewhat broader: **Consciousness** is generally defined as your awareness of the outside world and of your thoughts, feelings, perceptions, and other mental processes (Metzinger, 2000). This definition suggests that consciousness is a property of many mental processes rather than a unique mental process unto itself. For example, memories can be conscious, but consciousness is not just memory. Perceptions can be conscious, but consciousness is not just perception. This definition also allows for the possibility that humans are not the only creatures that experience consciousness. It would appear that some animals whose brains are similar to our own have self-awareness, even though they do not have the language abilities to tell us about it. One way to assess this awareness is to determine if a creature recognizes itself in a mirror. Children can do so at about two years of age. Monkeys never display this ability, but chimpanzees do, and it has recently been discovered that dolphins do, too (Reiss & Marino, 2001). Although consciousness may not be a uniquely human capacity, it is central to our experience of life.

In this chapter we begin by analyzing the nature of consciousness and the ways in which it affects mental activity and behavior. Then we examine what happens when consciousness is altered by sleep, hypnosis, and meditation. Finally, we explore the changes in consciousness that occur when people use certain drugs.

ClassPrep PPT 1: Consciousness

OBJ 9.1: Define consciousness. Describe the work of cognitive scientists and cognitive neuroscientists.

Test Items 9.1–9.2

A "Self-aware" Dolphin? Scientists have provided evidence that animals other than humans have aspects of self-awareness such as mirror-recognition. For example, this dolphin is said to recognize itself because it showed self-directed behaviors at a mirror and used the mirror to view specific parts of its body that had been marked (Reiss & Marino, 2001).

ClassPrep PPT 2: What Is Consciousness?

Analyzing Consciousness

Psychologists have been fascinated by the study of consciousness for more than a century, but only in the last thirty years or so has consciousness emerged as an active and vital research area in psychology. This is because, as described in the chapter on introducing psychology, behaviorism dominated psychological research in the United States from the 1920s through the 1960s. Accordingly, little research was conducted on mental processes, including the structure and functions of consciousness. But since the late 1960s, as CT scans, PET scans, MRI, and other new techniques described in the biological psychology chapter allowed ever more precise

consciousness Awareness of external stimuli and one's own mental activity.

OBJ 9.2: Describe the three main questions that dominate the psychological study of consciousness today. Include dualism and materialism, the theater view vs. the parallel distributed processing models of consciousness, and the link between mental activity and conscious awareness.

Test Items 9.3–9.6

ClassPrep PPT 3: Central Questions

analysis of brain activity, the study of consciousness has returned to the mainstream of research in psychology. Scientists who study consciousness sometimes describe their work as *cognitive science* or *cognitive neuroscience,* because their research is so closely tied to the subfields of biological psychology, sensation, perception, memory, and human cognition. In fact, many cognitive psychologists can be said to study consciousness through their work on memory, reasoning, problem solving, and decision making.

Other psychologists study consciousness more directly by addressing three central questions about it. First, like the philosophers who preceded them, psychologists have grappled with the *mind-body problem:* What is the relationship between the conscious mind and the physical brain? One approach, known as *dualism,* sees the mind and brain as different entities. This idea was championed in the seventeenth century by French philosopher René Descartes. Descartes claimed that a person's soul, or consciousness, is separate from the brain but can "view" and interact with brain events through the pineal gland, a brain structure about the size of a grape. Once a popular point of view, dualism has virtually disappeared from psychology.

Another perspective, known as *materialism,* suggests that mind is brain. Materialists argue that complex interactions among the brain's nerve cells create consciousness, much as hardware and software interact to create the image that appears on a computer screen. A good deal of support for the materialist view comes from case studies in which disruptions of consciousness occur following brain damage.

A second question focuses on whether or not consciousness is a unitary entity: Does consciousness occur as a single "point" in mental processing or as several parallel mental operations that occur independently? According to the *"theater"* view, consciousness is a single phenomenon, a kind of "stage" on which all the different events of awareness converge to "play" before the "audience" of your mind. Those adopting this view say it is supported by the fact that the subjective intensities of lights, sounds, weights, and other stimuli follow similar psychophysical laws (described in the chapter on perception), as if each sensory system passes its inputs to a single "monitor" that coordinates the experience of magnitude (Teghtsoonian, 1992).

In contrast, the *parallel distributed processing (PDP) models* described in the perception chapter describe the mind as processing many parallel streams of information, which interact somehow to create the unitary experience we know as consciousness (Devinsky, 1997). PDP models became influential when research on sensation, perception, memory, cognition, and language suggested that components of these processes are analyzed in separate brain regions. For example, perception of a visual scene involves activity in a number of separate brain regions that analyze "what" each object is, "where" it is, and whether the object is actually there or merely imagined (Ishai et al., 2000). Scientists still do not know whether these parallel streams of information ever unite in a common brain region.

A third question about consciousness addresses the relationship between nonconscious mental activities and conscious awareness. More than a century ago, Sigmund Freud theorized that some mental processes occur without our awareness and that these processes can affect us in many ways. Most aspects of Freud's theory are not supported by modern laboratory research, but studies have shown that many important mental activities do occur outside of awareness. Let's examine some of these activities and consider the functions they serve.

ClassPrep PPT 4: Some Functions of Consciousness

Some Functions of Consciousness

conscious level The level at which mental activities that people are normally aware of occur.

nonconscious level A level of mental activity that is inaccessible to conscious awareness.

preconscious level A level of mental activity that is not currently conscious, but of which we can easily become conscious.

Francis Crick and Christof Koch have suggested that one function of consciousness is to produce the best current interpretation of sensory information in light of past experience, and to make this interpretation available to those parts of the brain that can act on it (Crick & Koch, 1998). Having a *single* conscious representation, rather than multiple ones, allows us to be less hesitant and more decisive in taking action. The conscious brain, then, experiences a representation of the sensory world that is the result of many complex computations; it has access to the *results* of these computational processes but not to the processes themselves. The conscious representation experienced is not necessarily the quickest processing available, however. For example, tennis players may respond to a hard serve before they consciously "see" the ball. However, for complex problems, consciousness allows the most adaptive and efficient interactions among sensory input, motor responses, and a range of knowledge resources in the brain (Baars, 1998).

As described in the chapter on memory, the contents of consciousness at any given moment are limited by the capacity of short-term memory, but the overall process of consciousness allows access to a vast store of memories and other information. In one study, for example, participants paid brief conscious attention to ten thousand different pictures over several days. A week later they were able to recognize more than 90 percent of the photographs. Evidently, mere consciousness of an event helps to store a recognizable memory that can later be brought into consciousness (Kosslyn, 1994).

Almost a hundred years ago William James compared consciousness to a stream, describing it as ever changing, multilayered, and varying in both quantity and quality. Variations in quantity—in the degree to which one is aware of mental events—result in different *levels of consciousness*. Variations in quality—in the nature of the mental processing available to awareness—lead to different *states of consciousness*. Appreciating the difference between levels of consciousness and states of consciousness takes a little thought. When you are alert and aware of your mental activity and of incoming sensations, you are fully conscious, and experiencing yourself as "I." At the same time, however, other mental activity is taking place within your brain at varying "distances" from your conscious awareness. These activities are occurring at differing *levels* of consciousness. It is when your experience of yourself as "I" varies in focus and clarity—as when you sleep or are under the influence of a mind-altering drug—that there are variations in your *state* of consciousness. Let's first consider various levels of consciousness.

Levels of Consciousness   ClassPrep PPT 6: Levels of Consciousness

At any moment, the mental events that you are aware of are said to exist at the **conscious level.** For example, look at the Necker cube in Figure 9.1. If you are like most people, you can hold the cube in one configuration for only a few seconds before the other configuration "pops out" at you. The configuration that you experience at any moment is at your conscious level of awareness for that moment.

Some mental events, however, cannot be experienced consciously. For example, you are not directly aware of the fact that your brain constantly regulates your blood pressure. Such mental processing occurs at the **nonconscious level,** totally removed from conscious awareness. Other mental events are not conscious, but they can either become conscious or influence conscious experience; these mental events make up the *cognitive unconscious* (Reber, 1992), which is further divided into preconscious and unconscious (or subconscious) levels. Mental events at the **preconscious level** are outside of awareness but can easily be brought into awareness. For example, stop reading for a moment, and think about last night's dinner. As you do so, you become aware of what and where you ate, and with whom. But moments ago, you were probably not thinking about that information; it was preconscious, ready to be brought to the conscious level. Varying amounts of effort may be required to bring preconscious information into consciousness. In a trivia game you may draw on your large storehouse of preconscious memories to come up with obscure facts, sometimes easily and sometimes only with difficulty.

TRY THIS

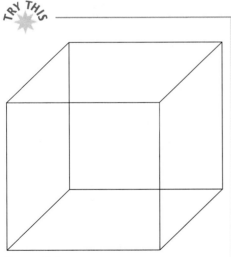

figure 9.1

The Necker Cube

TRY THIS Each of the two squares in the Necker cube can be perceived as either the front or rear surface of the cube. Try to make the cube switch back and forth between these two configurations. Now try to hold only one configuration. You probably cannot maintain the whole cube in consciousness for longer than about three seconds before it "flips" from one configuration to the other.

Evidence for the operation of sub-conscious mental processing includes research showing that surgery patients may be able to hear and later comply with instructions or suggestions given while they are under anesthesia and of which they have no memory (Bennett, Giannini, & Davis, 1985). In another study, people showed physiological arousal to emotionally charged words even when they were not paying attention to them (Von Wright, Anderson, & Stenman, 1975).

Reprinted by permission of International Creative Management, Inc. Copyright © 2002 Berke Breathed.

BLOOM COUNTY   **by Berke Breathed**

LINKAGES (a link to Sensation)

OBJ 9.4: Describe priming.

Test Items 9.21–9.25

unconscious level A level of mental activity that influences consciousness, but is not conscious.

There are still other mental activities that can alter thoughts, feelings, and actions but are more difficult to bring into awareness (Ratner, 1994). As described in the chapter on personality, Freud suggested that mental events at the **unconscious level**—especially those involving unacceptable sexual and aggressive urges—are actively kept out of consciousness. Many psychologists do not accept this view but still use the term *unconscious* (or *subconscious*) to describe the level of mental activity that influences consciousness but is not conscious.

Mental Processing Without Awareness

A fascinating demonstration of mental processing without awareness was provided by an experiment with patients who were under anesthesia for surgery. While the still-unconscious patients were in a postoperative recovery room, an audiotape of fifteen word pairs was played over and over. After regaining consciousness, these patients could not say what words had been played in the recovery room—or even whether a tape had been played at all. Yet when given one word from each of the word pairs and asked to say the first word that came to mind, the patients were able to produce the other member of the word pair from the tape (Cork, Kihlstrom, & Hameroff, 1992).

Even when people are conscious and alert, information can sometimes be processed and used without their awareness (Ward, 1997). In one study of this phenomenon, participants watched a computer screen as an X flashed in one of four locations. The participants' task was to indicate where the X appeared by rapidly pushing one of four buttons. The X's location seemed to vary randomly, but the placement sequence actually followed a set of complex rules, such as "If the X moves horizontally twice in a row, then it will move vertically next." The participants' responses became progressively faster and more accurate, but their performance instantly deteriorated when the rules were dropped and the Xs began appearing in truly random locations. Without being aware of doing so, these participants had apparently learned a complex rule-bound strategy to improve their performance. However, even when offered $100 to state the rules that had guided the location sequence, they could not do so, nor were they sure that any such rules existed (Lewicki, 1992).

Visual processing without awareness may also occur in cases of blindness caused by damage that is limited to the primary visual cortex. In such cases, fibers from the eyes are still connected to other brain areas that process visual information. Some of these surviving pathways may permit visual processing, but without visual awareness—a condition known as *blindsight* (Gazzaniga, Fendrich, & Wessinger, 1994). Even though such patients say they see nothing, if forced to guess, they can still locate visual targets, identify the direction and orientation of moving images, reach for objects, name the color of lights, and even discriminate happy from fearful faces that they cannot consciously see (Morris et al., 2001).

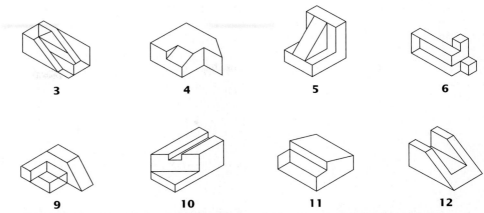

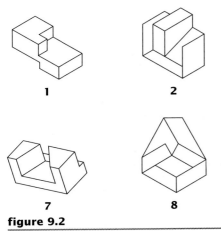

figure 9.2

Possible or Impossible?

TRY THIS Look at these figures and decide, as quickly as you can, whether each can actually exist. Priming studies show that this task would be easier for figures you have seen in the past, even if you don't recall seeing them. How did you do? (The correct answers appear on page 314.)

Source: Schacter et al. (1991).

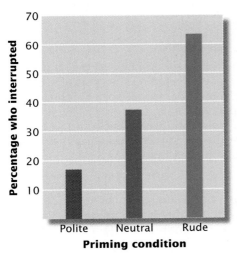

figure 9.3

Priming Behavior Without Awareness

Participants in this study were primed with rude, polite, or neutral words before being confronted with the problem of interrupting an ongoing conversation. Although they were not consciously aware of the priming process, participants previously exposed to rude words were most likely to interrupt, whereas those previously exposed to polite words were least likely to do so.

Source: Bargh, Chen, & Burrows (1996, Figure 1).

Research on *priming* also demonstrates mental processing without awareness. In a typical priming study, people tend to respond faster or more accurately to previously seen stimuli, even when they cannot consciously recall having seen those stimuli (Abrams & Greenwald, 2000; Arndt et al., 1997; Bar & Biederman, 1998; Schacter & Cooper, 1993). In one study, people were asked to look at a set of drawings like those in Figure 9.2 and decide which of the objects depicted could actually exist in three-dimensional space and which could not. The participants were better at classifying pictures that they had seen before, even when they could not remember having seen them (Cooper et al., 1992b; Schacter et al., 1991).

Other studies show how priming can alter certain behaviors even when participants are not consciously aware of being influenced. In one such study, for example (Bargh, Chen, & Burrows, 1996), participants were asked to unscramble sentences in which the words were out of order (e.g., "He it finds instantly."). In one condition of the experiment, the scrambled sentences contained words associated with the attribute of rudeness (e.g., *rude, bother,* and *annoying*); in a second condition, the scrambled words were associated with politeness (e.g., *respect, honor,* and *polite*); and in a third condition, the words were neutral (e.g., *normally, sends,* and *rapidly*). After completing the unscrambling task, the participants were asked to go to another room to get further instructions from the experimenter. But by design, the experimenter was always found talking to a research assistant. The dependent variable in this experiment was whether participants in the three conditions would interrupt the experimenter. As shown in Figure 9.3, the participants in the "rude priming" condition were most likely to interrupt, whereas those in the "polite priming" condition were least likely to do so. Those in the "neutral" condition fell in between the other two groups.

The results of priming studies challenge some of the traditional Freudian views about the unconscious. According to Freud, unconscious processes function mainly to protect us from painful or frightening thoughts, feelings, and memories by keeping them out of consciousness (Pervin, 1996). However, many psychologists studying unconscious processes now believe that, in fact, one of the primary functions of these processes is to help us more effectively carry out mundane, day-to-day mental activities.

Numerous questions about the relationship between conscious and unconscious processes remain to be answered. One of the most significant of these questions is whether conscious and unconscious thoughts occur independently of each other.

Priming studies seem to suggest that they are independent, but other research suggests that they may not be. For example, one study found a correlation between unconscious indicators of age prejudice—as seen in implicit memory for negative stereotypes about the elderly—and consciously held attitudes toward the elderly (Hense, Penner, & Nelson, 1995). Another study (Lepore & Brown, 1997) also found similarity between unconscious and conscious forms of ethnic prejudice. Overall, however, if there is a relationship between explicit and implicit cognitions, it appears to be weak and not yet clearly understood (Dovidio, Kawakami, & Beach, 2001). We consider this issue further in the chapter on social cognition.

FOCUS ON RESEARCH METHODS

ClassPrep PPT 50: Focus on Research Methods

Subliminal Messages in Rock Music

OBJ 9.5: Discuss the research on subliminal messages in rock music.

Numerous Internet web sites present claims that Satanic or drug-related messages have been embedded in the recorded music of rock bands such as Marilyn Manson, Nine Inch Nails, Judas Priest, Led Zeppelin, and the Rolling Stones. The story goes that because these alleged messages were recorded backward, they are *subliminal* (not consciously perceived), but they have supposedly influenced listeners to commit suicide or murder. For this assertion to be true, however, the content of the subliminal backward message would have to be perceived at some level of consciousness.

Test Items 9.26–9.27

● What was the researchers' question?

There is no compelling evidence that backward messages are actually present in most of the music cited. However, John R. Vokey and J. Don Read (1985) asked whether any backward messages that might exist could be perceived and understood when the music is playing forward. They also asked whether such messages have any effect on behavior.

● How did the researchers answer the question?

Vokey and Read conducted a series of multiple case studies of the impact of backward-recorded messages. They first recorded readings of portions of the Twenty-third Psalm and Lewis Carroll's poem "The Jabberwocky." This poem includes many nonsense words, but it follows grammar rules (e.g., "'Twas brillig and the slithy toves . . ."). These recordings were then played backward to groups of college students. The students were asked to judge whether what they heard would have been nonsensical or meaningful if played forward.

● What did the researchers find?

When the students heard the material played backward, they could not discriminate sense from nonsense. They could not tell the difference between declarative sentences and questions. They could not even identify the original material on which the recordings were based. In short, the participants could not make sense of the backward messages at a conscious level. Could they do so subconsciously? To find out, the researchers asked the participants to sort the backward statements they heard into one of five categories: nursery rhymes, Christian, Satanic, pornographic, or advertising. They reasoned that if some sort of meaning could be subconsciously understood, the participants would be able to sort the statements nonrandomly. As it turned out, however, the accuracy of the participants' category judgments was no better than chance.

Can even *unperceived* backward messages unconsciously shape behavior? To answer this question, Vokey and Read presented a backward version of a message whose sentences contained homophones (words that sound alike but have two spellings and two different meanings, such as *feat* and *feet*). When heard in the

Answer key for Figure 9.2: Figures 1, 4, 5, 7, 10, and 12 can exist in three-dimensional space.

315

Subliminal Messages in Rock Music?
Picketers in Florida hold up a large cross as they protest outside a Marilyn Manson concert. Some believe that Manson's music, as well as that of rock stars ranging from Michael Jackson to Madonna, contains subliminal messages advocating drug use, violence, and Satanism.

normal forward direction, such messages affect people's spelling of ambiguous words that are read aloud to them at a later time. (For example, people tend to spell out *f-e-a-t* rather than *f-e-e-t* if they previously heard the sentence "It was a great feat of strength.") This example of priming occurs even if people do not recall having heard the message. After hearing a backward version of the message, however, the participants in this study did not produce the expected spelling bias.

● **What do the results mean?**

Obviously, it wasn't possible for the participants to subconsciously understand meaning in the backward messages. Backward messages are evidently not consciously or unconsciously understood, nor do they influence behavior.

● **What do we still need to know?**

Researchers would like to understand why the incorrect idea persists that backward messages can influence behavior. Beliefs and suspicions do not simply disappear in the face of contrary scientific evidence (Vyse, 1997). Perhaps such evidence needs to be publicized more widely in order to lay the misconceptions to rest, but it seems likely that some people so deeply want to believe in the existence and power of backward messages in rock music that such beliefs will forever hold the status of folk myths in Western culture.

ClassPrep PPT 9: The Neuropsychology of Consciousness

The Neuropsychology of Consciousness

OBJ 9.6: Describe the effects of prosopagnosia and anterograde amnesia on consciousness.

Test Items 9.28–9.34

IRM Activity 9.4: Line Bisection

The nature of various levels of consciousness and the role of the brain regions that support them have been illuminated by studies of the results of brain damage. Consider the case of Karen Ann Quinlan. After drug-induced heart failure starved her brain of oxygen, Quinlan entered a coma; she was unconscious, unresponsive, and—in medical terms—brain-dead. Amid worldwide controversy, her parents obtained a court order that allowed them to shut off their daughter's life-support machines; but to everyone's surprise, she continued to live in a vegetative state for ten more years. A detailed study of her autopsied brain revealed that it had sustained damage mainly in the thalamus, an area described in the chapter on biological psychology as a "relay station" for most sensory signals entering the brain (Kinney et al., 1994). Some researchers have used this finding to argue that the thalamus may be critical for the experience of consciousness (e.g., Bogen, 1995). Given the discovery of reciprocal feedback between the thalamus and the cortex, there is reason to believe that the thalamus does, in fact, play a role in directing the spotlight of conscious attention to information in particular parts of the cortex "where the action is" (Baars, 1998).

A condition known as *prosopagnosia* provides an example of how brain damage can also cause more limited impairments in consciousness. People with prosopagnosia cannot consciously recognize faces—including their own face in the mirror—yet they can still see and recognize many other objects and can still recognize people by their voices (Young & De Haan, 1992). This deficit may reflect a more general inability to recognize curved objects (Laeng & Caviness, 2001), but in practice the problem is relatively specific for faces. One individual with prosopagnosia who became a farmer could recognize and name his sheep, but he never was able to recognize humans (McNeil & Warrington, 1993). Still, when such people see a familiar—but not consciously recognized—face, they show eye movement patterns, changes in brain activity, and autonomic nervous system responses that do not occur when viewing an unfamiliar face (Bruyer, 1991). So some vestige of face

figure 9.4

Memory Formation in Anterograde Amnesia

"H.M.," a patient with anterograde amnesia, was asked to trace the outline of an object while using only a mirror (which reverses left and right) to guide him. His performance on this difficult task improved daily, indicating that he learned and remembered how to do the task. Yet he had no conscious memory of the practice sessions that allowed his skill to develop (Milner, 1965).

Source: Data from Milner (1965).

Mirror-tracing task

(A)

Performance of H.M. on mirror-tracing task

(B)

recognition is preserved in prosopagnosia, but it remains unavailable to conscious experience.

Brain damage can also impair conscious access to other mental abilities. Consider *anterograde amnesia*, the inability to form new memories, which often accompanies damage to the hippocampus (Eichenbaum, Otto, & Cohen, 1994). Anterograde amnesics seem unable to remember any new information, even about the passage of time. One man who developed this condition in 1957 still needed to be reminded more than thirty years later that it was no longer 1957 (Smith, 1988). Yet as Figure 9.4 shows, anterograde amnesics can learn new skills, even though they cannot consciously recall the practice sessions (Milner, 1965). Their brain activity, too, shows different reactions to words they have recently studied than to other words, even though they have no memory of studying them (Düzel et al., 2001).

States of Consciousness

OBJ 9.7: Define state of consciousness and altered state of consciousness.

Mental activity is always changing. The features of consciousness at any instant—what reaches your awareness, the decisions you are making, and so on—make up your **state of consciousness** at that moment. States of consciousness can range from deep sleep to alert wakefulness; they can also be affected by drugs and other influences. Consider, for example, the varying states of consciousness that might occur aboard an airplane en route from New York to Los Angeles. In the cockpit, the pilot calmly scans instrument displays while talking to an air-traffic controller. In seat 9B, a lawyer has just finished her second cocktail while planning a courtroom strategy. Nearby, a young father gazes out a window, daydreaming, while his small daughter sleeps in his lap, dreaming dreams of her own.

Test Items 9.35–9.38

ClassPrep PPT 11: States of Consciousness

All these people are experiencing different states of consciousness. Some states are active and some are passive (Hilgard, 1980). The daydreaming father is letting his mind wander, passively noting images, memories, and other mental events that come unbidden to mind. The lawyer is actively directing her mental activity, evaluating various options and considering their likely outcomes.

Most people spend most of their time in a *waking* state of consciousness. Mental processing in this state varies with changes in attention or arousal. While reading, for example, you may temporarily ignore sounds around you. Similarly, if you are upset, or bored, or talking on a cell phone, you may miss important environmental cues, making it dangerous to drive a car.

When changes in mental processes are great enough for you or others to notice significant differences in how you function, you have entered an **altered state of consciousness.** In an altered state, mental processing shows distinct changes unique to that state. Cognitive processes or perceptions of yourself or the world may change, and normal inhibitions or self-control may weaken (Martindale, 1981).

ClassPrep PPT 12: Altered States of Consciousness

The phrase *altered states of consciousness* recognizes waking consciousness as the most common state, a baseline against which "altered" states are compared. However, this is not to say that waking consciousness is universally considered more normal, proper, or valued than other states. In fact, value judgments about different states of consciousness vary considerably across cultures (Ward, 1994).

Consider, for instance, *hallucinations*, which are perceptual experiences—such as hearing voices—that occur in the absence of sensory stimuli. In the United States, hallucinations are viewed as undesirable. Mental patients who hallucinate often feel stress and self-blame; many may choose not to report their hallucinations. Those who do so tend to be considered more disturbed and may receive more drastic treatments than patients who do not report hallucinations (Wilson et al., 1996). Among the Moche of Peru, however, hallucinations have a culturally approved place. When someone is beset by illness or misfortune, a healer conducts an elaborate ritual to find causes and treatments. During the ceremony, the healer ingests mescaline, a drug that causes hallucinations. These hallucinations are thought to give the healer

state of consciousness The characteristics of consciousness at any particular moment.

altered state of consciousness A condition in which changes in mental processes are extensive enough that a person or others notice significant differences in psychological and behavioral functioning.

Altered States and Cultural Values
Cultures define which altered states of consciousness are approved. Here we see members of a Brazilian spirit possession cult in various stages of trance, and in Peru, a Moche *curandero* (curer) attempting to heal a patient by using fumes from a potion—and a drug derived from the San Pedro cactus—to put himself in an altered state of consciousness.

spiritual insight into the patient's problems (de Rios, 1992). In the context of many other tribal cultures, too, purposeful hallucinations are revered, not demeaned (Grob & Dobkin-de-Rios, 1992).

In other words, states of consciousness differ not only in their basic characteristics but also in their value to members of particular cultures. In the sections to follow, we describe some of the most interesting altered states of consciousness, beginning with the most common one, sleep.

Sleeping and Dreaming

According to ancient myths, sleepers lose control of their minds, flirting with death as their souls wander freely. Early researchers thought sleep was a time of mental inactivity. In fact, however, sleep is an active, complex state.

OBJ 9.8: Compare and contrast slow-wave and REM sleep. List the stages of quiet sleep.

Test Items 9.39–9.44

OBJ 9.9: Explain the differences among the EEGs of each sleep stage.

Test Items 9.45–9.52

Stages of Sleep

Sleep researchers use an *electroencephalograph,* or *EEG,* to record the brain's electrical activity during sleep. EEG recordings, often called *brain waves,* vary in height (amplitude) and speed (frequency) as behavior or mental processes change. The brain waves of an awake, alert person have high frequency and low amplitude. They appear as small, closely spaced, irregular EEG spikes. A relaxed person with closed eyes shows *alpha waves,* which are more rhythmic brain waves occurring at speeds of eight to twelve cycles per second. During a normal night's sleep, brain waves show distinctive and systematic changes in amplitude and frequency as you pass through various stages of sleep (Guevara et al., 1995).

slow-wave sleep Sleep stages 1 through 4, which are accompanied by slow, deep breathing; a calm, regular heartbeat; and reduced blood pressure.
rapid eye movement (REM) sleep A stage of sleep in which brain activity and other functions resemble the waking state, but that is accompanied by rapid eye movements and virtual muscle paralysis.

Slow-Wave Sleep   Imagine that you are participating in a sleep study. You are hooked up to an EEG and various monitors, and filmed as you sleep through the night. If you were to watch that film, here's what you'd see: At first, you are relaxed, with eyes closed, but awake. At this point, your muscle tone and eye movements are normal, and your EEG shows the slow brain waves associated with relaxation. You then drift into what is called **slow-wave sleep,** which is named for the fact that your EEG shows even slower brain waves. Your breathing deepens,

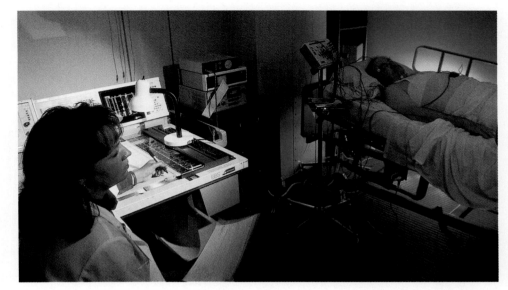

A Sleep Lab The electroencephalograph (EEG) allows scientists to record brain activity through electrodes attached to the skull. The advent of this technology opened the door to the scientific study of sleep.

LINKAGES (a link to Biological Aspects of Psychology)

OBJ 9.10: Discuss the changes that occur during REM sleep. Describe a night's sleep and the changes in sleeping patterns that occur across the lifespan.

Test Items 9.53–9.62

your heartbeat slows, and your blood pressure drops. Over the next half hour, you descend ever deeper into stages of sleep that are characterized by even slower brain waves with even higher amplitude (see Figure 9.5). When you reach stage 4, the deepest stage of slow-wave sleep, it is quite difficult to be awakened. If you were roused from this stage of deep sleep, you would be groggy and confused.

REM Sleep After thirty to forty-five minutes in stage 4, you quickly return to stage 2 and then enter a special stage in which your eyes move rapidly under your closed eyelids. This is called **rapid eye movement (REM) sleep,** or *paradoxical sleep.*

figure 9.5

EEG Recordings Typical of Various Sleep Stages

EEG recordings of brain wave activity disclose four relatively distinct stages of slow-wave sleep. Notice the regular patterns of alpha waves that occur just before a person goes to sleep, followed by the slowing of brain waves as sleep becomes deeper (stages 1 through 4). In rapid eye movement (REM) sleep, the frequency of brain waves increases dramatically and in some ways resembles patterns seen in people who are awake.

Source: Horne (1988).

ClassPrep PPT 13, OHT: *Figure 9.5:* EEG Recordings Typical of Various Sleep Stages

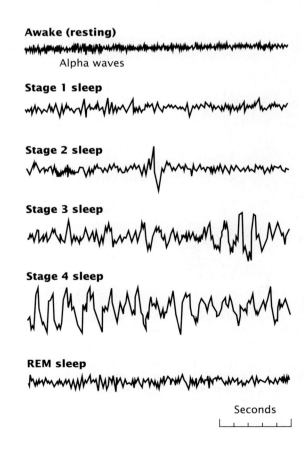

figure 9.6

A Night's Sleep

During a typical night a sleeper goes through this sequence of EEG stages. Notice that sleep is deepest during the first part of the night and more shallow later on, when REM sleep becomes more prominent.

Source: Cartwright (1978).

ClassPrep PPT 14, OHT: *Figure 9.6:* A Night's Sleep

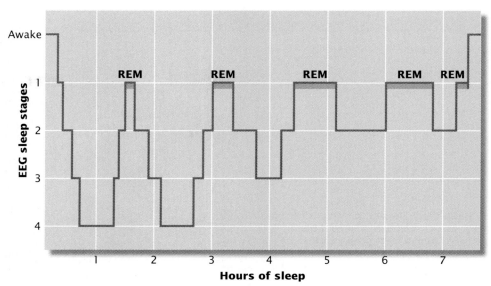

Stimulus Control Therapy   Insomnia can often be reduced through a combination of relaxation techniques and *stimulus control therapy,* in which the person goes to bed only when sleepy and gets out of bed if sleep does not come within fifteen to twenty minutes. The goal is for one's bed to become a stimulus associated with sleeping, and perhaps sex, but not with reading, eating, watching television, worrying, or anything else that is incompatible with sleep (Edinger et al., 2001).

It is called *paradoxical* because its characteristics pose a paradox, or contradiction. In REM sleep, your EEG resembles that of an awake, alert person, and your physiological arousal—heart rate, breathing, and blood pressure—is also similar to when you are awake. However, your muscles are nearly paralyzed. Sudden, twitchy spasms appear, especially in your face and hands, but your brain actively suppresses other movements (Blumberg & Lucas, 1994).

In other words, there are two different types of sleep, REM sleep and slow-wave sleep (which is sometimes called *non-REM,* or *NREM,* sleep).

Videodisc Segment & Still: A Night's Sleep

A Night's Sleep   Most people pass through the cycle of sleep stages four to six times each night. Each cycle lasts about ninety minutes, but with a somewhat changing pattern of stages and stage duration. Early in the night, most of the time is spent in the deeper stages of slow-wave sleep, with only a few minutes in REM sleep (see Figure 9.6). As sleep continues, though, it is dominated by stage 2 and REM sleep, from which sleepers finally awaken.

Sleep patterns change with age. The average infant sleeps about sixteen hours a day, and the average seventy-year-old sleeps only about six hours (Roffwarg, Muzio, & Dement, 1966). The composition of sleep changes, too (see Figure 9.7). REM sleep accounts for half of total sleep at birth but less than 25 percent in young adults. People may vary widely from these averages, however; some people feel well rested after four hours of sleep, whereas others of similar age require ten hours to feel satisfied (Clausen, Sersen, & Lidsky, 1974). There are also wide variations among cultural and socioeconomic groups in the tendency to take daytime naps. Contrary to the stereotype about the popularity of siestas in Latin and South American countries, urban Mexican college students actually nap less than many other college populations (Valencia-Flores et al., 1998).

Sleep Disorders   ClassPrep PPTs 16 & 17: Sleep Disorders

Most people experience sleep-related problems at some point in their lives. These problems range from occasional nights of tossing and turning to more serious and long-term *sleep disorders.* The most common sleeping problem is **insomnia,** in which one feels daytime fatigue due to trouble falling asleep or staying asleep. If you have difficulty getting to sleep or staying asleep that persists for longer than one month at a time, you may be suffering from insomnia. Besides being tiring, insomnia is tied to mental distress and impaired functioning. Insomnia is especially associated with depressive and anxiety disorders (U.S. Surgeon General, 1999);

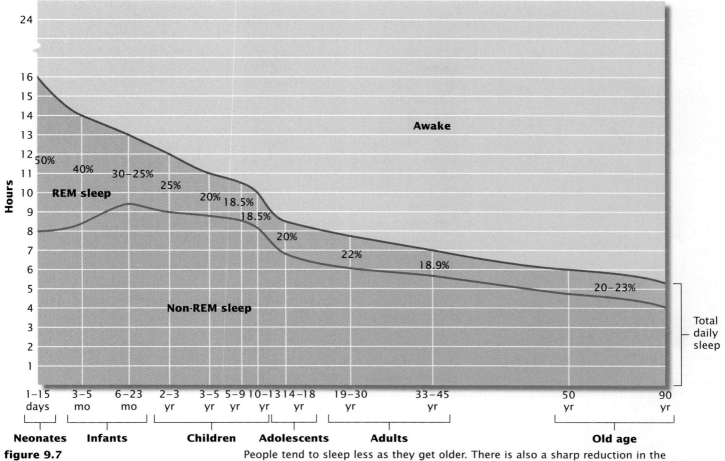

figure 9.7

Sleep and Dreaming over the Life Span

People tend to sleep less as they get older. There is also a sharp reduction in the percentage of REM sleep, from about eight hours per day in infancy to about an hour per day by age seventy. Non-REM sleep time also decreases but, compared with the drop in REM, remains relatively stable. After age twenty, however, non-REM sleep contains less and less of the deepest, or stage 4, sleep.

Note: Percentages indicate portion of total sleep time in REM sleep.

Source: Roffwarg, Muzio, & Dement (1966/1969).

overall, insomniacs are three times as likely to show a mental disorder as those with no sleep complaints. It is unclear from such correlations, however, whether insomnia causes mental disorders, mental disorders cause insomnia, or some other factor causes both.

Sleeping pills can relieve insomnia, but they are dangerous when a person also drinks alcohol and may eventually lead to *increased* sleeplessness (Ashton, 1995). In the long run, methods based on learning principles may be more helpful (Stepanski & Perlis, 2000). For example, stress management techniques such as relaxation training have been shown to help insomniacs reduce unusually strong physiological reactions to stress, thus allowing sleep (Bernstein, Borkovec, & Hazlette-Stevens, 2000).

Narcolepsy is a disturbing daytime sleep disorder that usually begins when a person is between fifteen and twenty-five years old (Choo & Guilleminault, 1998). Its victims abruptly switch from active, often emotional waking states into a few minutes of REM sleep. Because of the loss of muscle tone in REM, the narcoleptic collapses and remains briefly immobile even after awakening. The cause of narcolepsy may involve genetic factors and lack of a neurotransmitter called *hypocretin* (Krahn et al., 2001). Planned napping can be a helpful treatment, as can stimulant

insomnia A sleep disorder in which a person feels tired during the day because of trouble falling asleep or staying asleep at night.

narcolepsy A daytime sleep disorder in which a person switches abruptly from an active, often emotional waking state into several minutes of REM sleep.

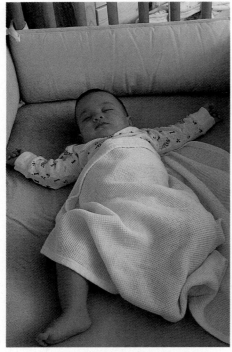

Sudden Infant Death Syndrome (SIDS)
In SIDS cases, seemingly healthy infants stop breathing while asleep in their cribs. All the causes of SIDS are not known, but the "Back to Sleep" program promoted by health authorities suggests that infants should sleep on their backs, as this baby demonstrates.

---

sleep apnea   A sleep disorder in which people briefly, but repeatedly, stop breathing during the night.

sudden infant death syndrome (SIDS) A disorder in which a sleeping baby stops breathing and suffocates.

nightmares Frightening dreams that take place during REM sleep.

night terrors Horrific dreams that cause rapid awakening from stage 3 or 4 sleep and intense fear for up to thirty minutes.

sleepwalking A phenomenon occurring in non-REM sleep in which people walk while asleep.

REM behavior disorder   A sleep disorder in which there is no loss of muscle tone during REM sleep, allowing the person to act out dreams.

---

drugs. One of these, modafinil, appears to be effective not only for narcolepsy but for counteracting the effects of sleep deprivation as well (Silber, 2001).

People suffering from **sleep apnea** briefly stop breathing hundreds of times every night, waking up each time long enough to resume breathing. In the morning, they do not recall the awakenings, yet they feel tired and tend to show reductions in attention and learning ability (Naëgelé et al., 1995). Sleep apnea has many causes, including genetic predisposition, obesity, and compression of the windpipe (Dixon, Schachter, & O'Brien, 2001; Kadotani et al., 2001). Effective treatments include weight loss and use of a nasal mask that provides a steady stream of air (Davies & Stradling, 2000; Peppard et al., 2000).

In cases of **sudden infant death syndrome (SIDS)**, sleeping infants stop breathing and die. In the United States, SIDS strikes about two of every thousand infants, usually when they are two to four months old (Hirschfeld, 1995). Some SIDS cases may stem from problems with brain systems regulating breathing, from exposure to cigarette smoke, and possibly from genetic causes (Ackerman et al., 2001; Harper et al., 1988; Klonoff-Cohen & Edelstein, 1995; Narita et al., 2001). Because SIDS is less common in cultures where infants and parents sleep in the same bed, it may also be that sleeping position is involved in sudden infant death (Gessner, Ives, & Perham-Hester, 2001). It has been estimated that about half of apparent SIDS cases might actually be accidental suffocations caused when infants sleep facedown on a soft surface (Guntheroth & Spiers, 1992). Since doctors began advising parents to be sure their babies sleep faceup, the number of infants dying from SIDS in the United States has dropped by 40 percent (Gibson et al., 2000).

Nightmares are frightening REM sleep dreams that occur in 4 to 8 percent of the general population, but in a much higher percentage of people suffering post-traumatic stress disorder following military combat or rape (Kryger et al., 2000). Imagery therapy, in which people repeatedly imagine new and less frightening outcomes to their nightmares, has been effective in reducing their frequency (Forbes et al., 2001; Krakow et al., 2001). Whereas nightmares occur during REM sleep, **night terrors** are horrific dream images that occur during stage 3 or 4 sleep. Sleepers often awake from a night terror with a bloodcurdling scream and remain intensely frightened for up to thirty minutes, yet they may not recall the episode in the morning. Night terrors are especially common in boys, but adults can suffer milder versions. The condition is sometimes treatable with drugs (Lillywhite, Wilson, & Nutt, 1994).

Like night terrors, **sleepwalking** occurs during non-REM sleep, usually in childhood (Masand, Popli, & Welburg, 1995). By morning, most sleepwalkers have forgotten their travels. Despite myths to the contrary, waking a sleepwalker is not harmful. One adult sleepwalker was cured when his wife blew a whistle whenever he began a nocturnal stroll (Meyer, 1975). Drugs help reduce sleepwalking, but most children simply outgrow the problem.

In **REM behavior disorder,** the near paralysis that normally accompanies REM sleep is absent, so sleepers move as if acting out their dreams (Watanabe & Sugita, 1998). The disorder can be dangerous to the dreamer or those nearby. In January 2001, a nine-year-old boy in New York City was seriously injured when he jumped from a third floor window while dreaming that his parents were being murdered. In another case, a man grabbed his wife's throat during the night because, he claimed, he was dreaming about breaking a deer's neck. The disorder sometimes occurs along with daytime narcolepsy (Schenck & Mahowald, 1992). Fortunately, drug treatments are usually effective.

Why Do People Sleep?

In trying to understand sleep, psychologists have studied both the functions that sleep serves and the ways in which brain mechanisms shape its characteristics.

figure 9.8

Westward/Eastward Travel and Jet Lag

Changing time zones causes more intense symptoms of jet lag after eastward travel (when time is lost) than after westward travel (when time is gained). These data show how long it took people flying between London and Detroit (a five-hour time change) to fall asleep once in bed, both on the night before the trip (B1) and on the five nights afterward. Those who flew eastward, from Detroit to London, needed more time to fall asleep than those who flew westward, from London to Detroit (Nicholson et al., 1986).

Source: Data from Nicholson et al. (1986).

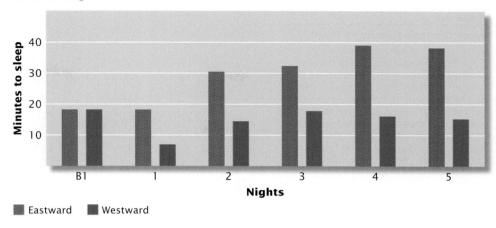

Sleep as a Circadian Rhythm

The sleep-wake cycle is one example of the rhythmic nature of life. Almost all animals (including humans) display cycles of behavior and physiology that repeat about every twenty-four hours in a pattern called a **circadian rhythm** (from the Latin *circa dies,* meaning "about a day"). Longer and shorter rhythms also occur, but they are less common. Circadian (pronounced "sir-KAY-dee-en") rhythms are linked, or *entrained,* to signals such as the light and dark of day and night, but most of them continue even without such time cues. Volunteers living for months without external cues maintain daily rhythms in sleeping and waking, hormone release, eating, urination, and other physiological functions. Under such conditions, these cycles repeat about every twenty-four hours (Czeisler et al., 1999).

Disrupting the sleep-wake cycle can create problems. For example, air travel across several time zones often causes **jet lag,** a pattern of fatigue, irritability, inattention, and sleeping problems that can last several days. The traveler's body feels ready to sleep at the wrong time for the new locale. Similar problems affect workers changing between day and night shifts. Because it tends to be easier to stay awake longer than usual than to go to sleep earlier than usual, sleep-wake rhythms readjust to altered light-dark cycles more easily when sleep is shifted to a later, rather than an earlier, time (see Figure 9.8).

Because circadian-like rhythms continue without external cues, an internal "biological clock" in the brain must keep track of time. This clock is in the *suprachiasmatic nuclei (SCN)* of the hypothalamus (see Figure 9.9). Signals from the SCN reach areas in the hindbrain that initiate sleep or wakefulness (Moore, 1997). SCN neurons show a firing rhythm of twenty-four to twenty-five hours, even when removed from the brain and put in a laboratory dish (Gillette, 1986). And when animals with SCN damage receive transplanted SCN cells, the restored circadian rhythms are similar to those of the donor animal (Menaker & Vogelbaum, 1993). SCN neurons also regulate the release of the hormone *melatonin* from the pineal gland, via an autonomic pathway. Melatonin, in turn, appears to be important in maintaining circadian rhythms; timely injections of melatonin may reduce fatigue and disorientation stemming from jet lag or other sleep-wake cycle changes by acting on melatonin receptors in the SCN (Liu et al., 1997; Sack et al., 1997). The length of circadian rhythms can vary from person to person such that some have a natural tendency to stay up later at night ("owls") or to wake up earlier in the morning ("larks"). Scientists have recently discovered that extreme variations in these rhythms are associated with mutations in the genes that code for biological clock proteins, and that certain variations can help in distinguishing Alzheimer's disease from other brain disorders (Harper et al., 2001; Toh et al., 2001).

circadian rhythm A cycle, such as waking and sleeping, that repeats about once a day.

jet lag A syndrome of fatigue, irritability, inattention, and sleeping problems caused by air travel across several time zones.

figure 9.9

Sleep, Dreaming, and the Brain

This diagram shows the location of some of the brain structures thought to be involved in sleep and dreaming, as well as in other altered states discussed later in the chapter. Scientists have discovered that cells in a region near the suprachiasmatic nuclei may act as a "master switch" for sleep by sending signals that shut down arousal systems in the hindbrain (Gallopin et al., 2000; Sherin et al., 1996).

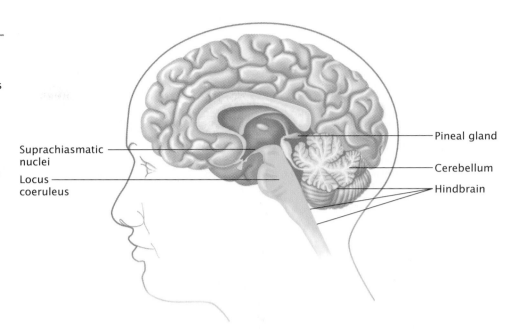

Suprachiasmatic nuclei

Locus coeruleus

Pineal gland

Cerebellum

Hindbrain

Sattler/Shabatay reader, 2/e: Dotto, "Asleep in the Fast Lane"

ClassPrep PPT 21: Functions of Sleep

OBJ 9.13: Define REM rebound. Discuss the various hypotheses on the reasons for slow-wave and REM sleep.

Test Items 9.84–9.90

The Functions of Sleep   Examining the effects of sleep deprivation may help explain why people sleep at all. People who go without sleep for as long as a week usually do not suffer serious long-term effects, but sleeplessness does lead to fatigue, irritability, and inattention (Drummond et al., 2000; Smith & Maben, 1993). The effects of short-term sleep deprivation—which is a common condition among busy adolescents and adults—can also take their toll (Stapleton, 2001). For example, most fatal auto accidents in the United States occur during the "fatigue hazard" hours of midnight to 6 A.M. (Coleman, 1992), leading some researchers to consider "sleepy driving" to be as dangerous as drunk driving. Fatigue has been implicated as the primary cause of up to 25 percent of all auto accidents (Philip et al., 2001; Summala & Mikkola, 1994) and of many injuries suffered by sleepy young children at play or in day care (Valent, Brusaferro, & Barbone, 2001). Learning, too, is more difficult after sleep deprivation, but certain parts of the

The Effects of Sleep Deprivation

Here, scientists at Loughborough University, England, test the effects of sleep deprivation on motor coordination. Driving while sleep deprived can be dangerous, but some other functions may not suffer as much. One man reportedly stayed awake for 231 hours and was still lucid and capable of serious intellectual work, including the creation of a lovely poem on his tenth day without sleep (Katz & Landis, 1935).

cerebral cortex actually increase their activity when a sleep-deprived person faces a learning task, so the person is able to compensate for a while (Drummond et al., 2000).

Some researchers believe that sleep, especially non-REM sleep, helps restore the body and the brain for future activity (Porkka-Heiskanen et al., 1997). The waking brain uses more metabolic fuel than the sleeping brain, and during wakefulness, the byproducts of metabolism accumulate. The accumulation of one such byproduct, *adenosine,* inhibits cholinergic systems in the forebrain and hindbrain, inducing sleepiness (Porkka-Heiskanen et al., 1997). During sleep, adenosine levels gradually decline.

Sleep-deprived people do not make up lost sleep hour for hour. Instead, they sleep about 50 percent more than usual, then awake feeling rested. But if people are deprived only of REM sleep, they later compensate more directly. In a classic study, participants were awakened whenever their EEG tracings showed REM sleep. When allowed to sleep uninterrupted the next night, the participants "rebounded," nearly doubling the percentage of time spent in REM sleep (Dement, 1960). Even after *total* sleep deprivation, the next night of uninterrupted sleep includes an unusually high percentage of REM sleep (Feinberg & Campbell, 1993). This apparent need for REM sleep suggests that it has special functions.

What these special functions might be is still unclear, but there are several possibilities. First, REM sleep may improve the functioning of neurons that use norepinephrine (Siegel & Rogawski, 1988). Norepinephrine is a neurotransmitter released by cells in the *locus coeruleus* (see Figure 9.9); during waking hours, it affects alertness and mood. But the brain's neurons lose sensitivity to norepinephrine if it is released continuously for too long. Because the locus coeruleus is almost completely inactive during REM sleep, researchers suggest that REM helps restore sensitivity to norepinephrine and thus its ability to keep us alert (Steriade & McCarley, 1990). Animals deprived of REM sleep show unusually high norepinephrine levels and decreased daytime alertness (Brock et al., 1994).

REM sleep may also be a time for developing, checking, and expanding the brain's nerve connections (Roffwarg, Muzio, & Dement, 1966). If so, it would explain why children and infants, whose brains are still developing, spend so much time in REM sleep (see Figure 9.7). Evidence favoring this possibility comes from recent research showing that REM sleep enhances the creation of neural connections (synaptic plasticity) in response to altered visual experience during the development of the visual cortex (Frank et al., 2001). REM sleep may also help solidify and assimilate the day's experiences in adults. In one study, people who were REM deprived showed poorer retention of a skill learned the day before than people who were either deprived of non-REM sleep or allowed to sleep normally (Karni et al., 1994). In another study, establishing memories of emotional information was particularly dependent on REM sleep (Wagner et al., 2001). Certain types of skill learning, too, may improve overnight, but only if both REM and slow-wave sleep occur (Sejnowski & Destexhe, 2000; Stickgold et al., 2000).

Dreams and Dreaming   ClassPrep PPT 22: Dreams and Dreaming

We have seen that the brain is active in all sleep stages, but **dreams** differ from other mental activity in sleep because they are usually story-like, lasting from seconds to minutes. Dreams may be organized or chaotic, realistic or fantastic, tranquil or exciting (Hobson & Stickgold, 1994). Sometimes, dreams lead to creative insights about waking problems. For example, after trying for days to write a story about good and evil in the same person, author Robert Louis Stevenson dreamed about a man who drank a potion that turned him into a monster (Hill, 1968). This dream inspired *The Strange Case of Dr. Jekyll and Mr. Hyde.* On the whole, however, there are no scientific data indicating that dreams lead to more creative insights than do waking thoughts.

ClassPrep PPT 21: Functions of Sleep

OBJ 9.14: Define dreams and lucid dreaming.

Test Items 9.91–9.93

dreams   Story-like sequences of images, sensations, and perception that occur mainly during REM sleep.

OBJ 9.15: Discuss the various theories that explain why people dream, including wish fulfillment, activation-synthesis theory, and problem-solving theory.

Test Items 9.94–9.97

Personal Learning Activities 9.3, 9.4

Essay Q 9.1

IRM Activity 9.7: Dream Analysis

IRM Activity 9.8: Intending to Dream

ClassPrep PPT 23: Why Do We Dream?

Some dreaming occurs during non-REM sleep, but most dreams—and the most bizarre and vivid dreams—occur during REM sleep (Casagrande et al., 1996; Dement & Kleitman, 1957; Stickgold, Rittenhouse, & Hobson, 1994). Even when they seem to make no sense, dreams may contain a certain amount of logic. In one study, for example, when segments from dream reports were randomly reordered, readers could correctly say which had been rearranged and which were intact (Stickgold, Rittenhouse, & Hobson, 1994). And although dreams often involve one person becoming another person or one object turning into another object, it is rare that objects become people or vice versa (Stickgold, Rittenhouse, & Hobson, 1994).

Daytime activities may influence the content of dreams, though their impact is probably minor (Foulkes, 1985). In one study, when people wore red-tinted goggles for a few minutes before going to sleep, they reported more red images in their dreams than people who had not worn the goggles (Roffwarg, Hermann, & Bowe-Anders, 1978). It is also sometimes possible to intentionally direct dream content, especially during **lucid dreaming,** in which the sleeper is aware of dreaming while a dream is happening (Stickgold et al., 2000).

Research leaves little doubt that everyone dreams during the course of every normal night's sleep. Even blind people dream, although their perceptual experiences are usually not visual. Whether you remember a dream depends on how you sleep and wake up. Recall is better if you awaken abruptly and lie quietly while writing or tape-recording your recollections.

Why do we dream? Theories abound. Some see dreaming as a fundamental process by which all mammals analyze and consolidate information that has personal significance or survival value (Porte & Hobson, 1996). This view is supported by the fact that dreaming appears to occur in most mammals, as indicated by the appearance of REM sleep. For example, after researchers disabled the neurons that cause REM sleep paralysis, sleeping cats ran around and attacked, or seemed alarmed by, unseen objects, presumably the images from dreams (Winson, 1990).

According to Freud (1900), dreams are a disguised form of *wish fulfillment,* a way to satisfy unconscious urges or resolve unconscious conflicts that are too upsetting to deal with consciously. Seeing patients' dreams as a "royal road to a knowledge of the unconscious," Freud interpreted their meaning as part of his psychoanalytic therapy (see the chapter on treatment of psychological disorders).

In contrast, the *activation-synthesis theory* sees dreams as the meaningless, random byproducts of REM sleep (Hobson, 1997). According to this theory, hindbrain arousal during REM sleep creates random messages that *activate* the brain, especially the cerebral cortex. Dreams result as the cortex *synthesizes* these random messages as best it can, using stored memories and current feelings to impose a coherent perceptual organization on confusingly random inputs. From this perspective, dreams represent the brain's attempt to make sense of meaningless stimulation during sleep, much as it does when a person, while awake, tries to find meaningful shapes in cloud formations (Bernstein & Roberts, 1995).

Even if dreams arise from random physiological activity, their content can still have psychological significance. Some psychologists believe that dreams give people a chance to review and address some of the problems they face during waking hours (Cartwright, 1993). This view is supported by evidence that people's current concerns can affect both the content of their dreams and the ways in which dreams are organized and recalled (Domhoff, 1996; Stevens, 1996). However, research using brain imaging techniques shows that while we are asleep, brain areas involved in emotion tend to be overactivated, whereas areas controlling logical thought tend to be suppressed (Braun, Balkin, & Wesensten, 1998; Hobson et al., 1998). In fact, as we reach deeper sleep stages, and then enter REM sleep, thinking subsides and hallucinations increase (Fosse, Stickgold, & Hobson, 2001). This is probably why dreams rarely provide realistic, logical solutions to our problems (Blagrove, 1996).

lucid dreaming Awareness that a dream is a dream while it is happening.

hypnosis A phenomenon brought on by special induction techniques and characterized by varying degrees of responsiveness to suggestions for changes in experience and behavior.

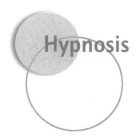

Hypnosis

Inducing Hypnosis In the late 1700s, an Austrian physician named Franz Anton Mesmer became famous for his treatment of physical disorders using *mesmerism,* a forerunner of hypnosis. His patients touched their afflicted body parts to magnetized metal rods extending from a tub of water and then, when touched by Mesmer, fell into a curative "crisis" or trance, sometimes accompanied by convulsions. We now know that hypnosis can be induced more easily, often simply by asking a person to stare at an object.

The word *hypnosis* comes from the Greek word *hypnos,* meaning "sleep," but hypnotized people are not sleeping. People who have been hypnotized say that their bodies felt "asleep," but their minds were active and alert. **Hypnosis** has traditionally been defined as an altered state of consciousness brought on by special techniques and producing responsiveness to suggestions for changes in experience and behavior (Kirsch, 1994b). Most hypnotized people do not feel forced to follow the hypnotist's instructions; they simply see no reason to refuse (Hilgard, 1965).

Experiencing Hypnosis

Usually, hypnosis begins with suggestions that the participant feels relaxed and sleepy. The hypnotist then gradually focuses the participant's attention on a restricted, often monotonous set of stimuli while suggesting that the participant should ignore everything else and imagine certain feelings.

Not everyone can be hypnotized. Special tests measure *hypnotic susceptibility,* the degree to which people respond to hypnotic suggestions (Gfeller, 1994). Such tests categorize about 10 percent of adults as difficult or impossible to hypnotize (Hilgard, 1982). Hypnotically susceptible people, in contrast, typically differ from others in several ways. They have a better ability to focus attention and ignore distraction (Crawford, Brown, & Moon, 1993), a more active imagination (Spanos, Burnley, & Cross, 1993), a tendency to fantasize (Lynn & Rhue, 1986), a capacity for processing information quickly and easily (Dixon, Brunet, & Lawrence, 1990), a tendency to be suggestible (Kirsch & Braffman, 2001), and more positive attitudes toward hypnosis (Gfeller, 1994; Spanos, Burnley, & Cross, 1993). Their *willingness* to be hypnotized is the most important factor of all; contrary to myth, people cannot be hypnotized against their will.

The results of hypnosis can be fascinating. People told that their eyes cannot open may struggle fruitlessly to open them. They may appear deaf or blind or insensitive to pain. They may forget their own names. Some appear to remember forgotten things. Others show *age regression,* apparently recalling or reenacting their childhood. Hypnotic effects can last for hours or days through *posthypnotic suggestions*—instructions about behavior that is to take place after hypnosis has ended (such as smiling whenever someone says "England"). Some participants show *posthypnotic amnesia,* an inability to recall what happened while they were hypnotized, even after being told what happened.

Ernest Hilgard (1965, 1992) described the main changes that people display during hypnosis. First, hypnotized people show *reduced planfulness.* They tend not to begin actions on their own, waiting instead for the hypnotist's instructions. One participant said, "I was trying to decide if my legs were crossed, but I couldn't tell, and didn't quite have the initiative to move to find out" (Hilgard, 1965, p. 6). Second, they tend to ignore all but the hypnotist's voice and whatever it points out; their *attention is redistributed.* Third, hypnosis enhances the *ability to fantasize,* so participants more vividly imagine a scene or relive a memory. Fourth, hypnotized people display *increased role taking;* they more easily act like a person of a different age or a member of the opposite sex, for example. Fifth, hypnotic participants show *reduced reality testing,* tending not to question if statements are true and more willingly accepting apparent distortions of reality. A hypnotized person might shiver in a warm room if a hypnotist says it is snowing.

Explaining Hypnosis Main Changes in People During Hypnosis

Hypnotized people look and act differently from nonhypnotized people (Hilgard, 1965). Do these differences actually indicate an altered state of consciousness?

ClassPrep PPT 28: *Figure 9.10:* Can Hypnosis Produce Blindness?

figure 9.10

Can Hypnosis Produce Blindness?

OBJ 9.18: Compare and contrast the state, role, and dissociation theories of hypnosis.

Test Items 9.107–9.111

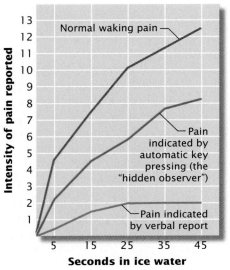

figure 9.11

Reports of Pain in Hypnosis

This graph shows average reports of pain when people's hands were immersed in painfully cold water under three different conditions. The green line represents the oral reports by nonhypnotized participants. The pink line represents the reports by hypnotized participants who were told they would feel no pain. The purple line represents the responses by hypnotized participants who were told they would feel no pain but were asked to press a key if "any part of them" felt pain. The key pressing by this "hidden observer" suggests that under hypnosis, the experience of pain was dissociated from conscious awareness (Hilgard, 1977).

state theory A theory that hypnosis is an altered state of consciousness.

role theory A theory that hypnotized people act in accordance with a social role that provides a reason to follow the hypnotist's suggestions.

dissociation theory A theory defining hypnosis as a socially agreed upon opportunity to display one's ability to let mental functions become dissociated.

The top row looks like gibberish, but you could read it as the numbers and letters in the lower row if you closed one eye and viewed it through special glasses. Yet when hypnotized subjects who had been given suggestions for blindness in one eye wore the glasses, they were unable to read the display (as they should have been able to do if one eye were blind), indicating that both eyes were in fact working normally (Pattie, 1935).

Source: Pattie (1935).

ClassPrep PPT 27: Explaining Hypnosis

ClassPrep PPT 29: Explaining Hypnosis (cont.)

Advocates of the **state theory** of hypnosis say that they do. They point to the dramatic effects that hypnosis can produce, including insensitivity to pain and the disappearance of warts (Noll, 1994). They also note that there are subtle differences in the way hypnotized and nonhypnotized people carry out suggestions. In one study, hypnotized people and those who had been asked to simulate hypnosis were told to run their hands through their hair whenever they heard the word *experiment* (Orne, Sheehan, & Evans, 1968). Simulators did so only when the hypnotist said the cue word. Hypnotized participants complied no matter who said it. Another study found that hypnotized people complied more often than simulators with a posthypnotic suggestion to mail postcards to the experimenter (Barnier & McConkey, 1998).

Proponents of the **role theory** of hypnosis argue that hypnosis is *not* a special state of consciousness, and that hypnotized people are merely complying with social demands and acting in accordance with a special social role (Kirsch, 1994a). In other words, they say, hypnosis provides a socially acceptable reason to follow someone's suggestions, much as a doctor's white coat provides a good reason for patients to remove clothing on command.

Support for role theory comes from several sources. For example, laboratory experiments show that motivated, but nonhypnotized, volunteers can duplicate many, if not all, aspects of hypnotic behavior, from arm rigidity to age regression (Dasgupta et al., 1995; Orne & Evans, 1965). Other studies using special tests have found that people rendered blind or deaf by hypnosis can still see or hear, even though their actions and beliefs suggest that they cannot (Bryant & McConkey, 1989; Pattie, 1935; see Figure 9.10).

Hilgard (1992) proposed a **dissociation theory** of hypnosis to blend role and state theories. He suggested that hypnosis is not one specific state but a general condition in which our normally centralized control of thoughts and actions is temporarily reorganized, or broken up, through a process called *dissociation*, meaning a split in consciousness (Hilgard, 1979). As a result, body movements normally under voluntary control can occur on their own, and normally involuntary processes (such as overt reactions to pain) can be controlled voluntarily. Hilgard argued that this relaxation of central control occurs as part of a *social agreement* to share control with the hypnotist. In other words, people usually decide for themselves how to act or what to attend to, perceive, or remember, but during hypnosis, the hypnotist is "allowed" to control some of these experiences and actions. So Hilgard saw hypnosis as a socially agreed upon display of dissociated mental functions. Compliance with a social role may account for part of the story, he said, but hypnosis also leads to significant changes in mental processes.

Evidence for dissociation theory comes from a study in which hypnotized participants immersed one hand in ice water after being told that they would feel no pain (Hilgard, Morgan, & MacDonald, 1975). With the other hand, participants

Surgery Under Hypnosis Bernadine Coady, of Wimblington, England, has a condition that makes it dangerous for her to have general anesthesia. So in April 1999, when a hypnotherapist failed to show up to help her through a foot operation, she used self-hypnosis as her only anesthetic. The surgery would have been extremely painful without anesthesia, but she said that she imagined the pain as "waves lashing against a sea wall . . . [and] going away, like the tide." Coady's report that the operation was painless is believable because in December 2000 she underwent the same operation on her other foot, again using only self-hypnosis for pain control (Morris, 2000).

were to press a key to indicate if "any part of them" felt pain. Participants' oral reports indicated almost no pain, but their key pressing told a different story (see Figure 9.11). Hilgard concluded that a "hidden observer" was reporting on pain that was reaching the person but had been separated, or dissociated, from conscious awareness (Hilgard, 1977). Contemporary research continues to test the validity of various explanatory theories of hypnosis, but traditional distinctions between state and role theories have become less relevant as researchers focus on larger questions, such as the impact of social and cognitive factors in hypnotic phenomena, the nature of the hypnotic experience, and the psychological and physiological basis for hypnotic susceptibility (Kirsch & Lynn, 1995).

Applications of Hypnosis

Whatever hypnosis is, it has proven useful, especially in relation to pain. Hypnosis seems to be the only anesthetic some people need to block the pain of dental work, childbirth, burns, and abdominal surgery (Van Sickel, 1992). For others, hypnosis relieves chronic pain from arthritis, nerve damage, migraine headaches, and cancer (Nolan et al., 1995). MRI studies of hypnotized pain patients show altered activity in the anterior cingulate cortex, a brain region mentioned in the chapter on sensation as being associated with the emotional component of pain (Faymonville et al., 2000). Hypnotic suggestions can also reduce nausea and vomiting due to chemotherapy (Redd, 1984) and can help reduce surgical bleeding (Gerschman, Reade, & Burrows, 1980).

Other applications of hypnosis are more controversial, especially the use of hypnosis to aid memory. For example, hypnotic age regression is sometimes attempted in an effort to help people recover lost memories. In actuality, however, the memories of past events reported by age-regressed individuals are less accurate than those of nonhypnotized individuals (Lynn, Myers, & Malinoski, 1997). Similarly, it is doubtful that hypnosis can improve the ability of witnesses to recall details of a crime (Lynn, Myers, & Malinoski, 1997). Instead, their expectations about, and confidence in, hypnosis may cause them to unintentionally distort information or reconstruct memories for the events in question (Garry & Loftus, 1994; Weekes et al., 1992). These distortions can be especially problematic because although hypnosis may not enhance people's memory for information, it may make them more confident about their reports, even if they are inaccurate.

LINKAGES (a link to Health, Stress, and Coping)

Meditation, Health, and Stress

Meditation provides a set of techniques intended to create an altered state of consciousness characterized by inner peace and tranquility (Shapiro & Walsh, 1984). Some claim that meditation increases awareness and understanding of themselves and their environment, reduces anxiety, improves health, and aids performance in everything from work to tennis (Bodian, 1999; Mahesh Yogi, 1994).

The techniques used to achieve a meditative state differ, depending on belief and philosophy (for example, Eastern meditation, Sufism, yoga, or prayer). However, in the most common meditation methods, attention is focused on just one thing—a word, sound, or object—until the meditator stops thinking about anything and experiences nothing but "pure awareness" (Benson, 1975). In this way, the individual becomes more fully aware of the present moment rather than being caught up in the past or the future.

What a meditator focuses on is far less important than doing so with a passive attitude. To organize attention, meditators might inwardly name every sound or

"Are you not thinking what I'm not thinking?"

thought that reaches consciousness, focus on the sound of their own breathing, or slowly repeat a *mantra,* which is a soothing word or phrase. During a typical meditation session, breathing, heart rate, muscle tension, blood pressure, and oxygen consumption decrease (Wallace & Benson, 1972). Most forms of meditation induce alpha-wave EEG activity, the brain wave pattern commonly found in a relaxed, eyes-closed, waking state (see Figure 9.5).

Meditators often report significant reductions in stress-related problems such as general anxiety, high blood pressure, and insomnia (Beauchamp-Turner & Levinson, 1992). More generally, meditators' scores on personality tests indicate increases in general mental health, self-esteem, and social openness (Janowiak & Hackman, 1994; Sakairi, 1992). Exactly how meditation produces its effects is unclear. Many of its effects can also be achieved by biofeedback, hypnosis, and just relaxing (Beyerstein, 1999; Holmes, 1984).

Psychoactive Drugs   ClassPrep PPT 31: Psychoactive Drugs
Test Items 9.122–9.128

OBJ 9.21: Define psychoactive drugs and psychopharmacology. Explain the function of the blood-brain barrier and discuss how agonist and antagonist drugs work.

psychoactive drugs Substances that act on the brain to create some psychological effect.

psychopharmacology The study of psychoactive drugs and their effects.

Every day, most people in the world use drugs that alter brain activity and consciousness (Levinthal, 1996). For example, 80 to 90 percent of people in North America use caffeine, the stimulant found in coffee (Gilbert, 1984). A drug is a chemical not usually needed for physiological activity and that can affect the body upon entering it. (Some people use the word *drug* to mean therapeutic medicines but refer to nonmedicinal drugs as *substances,* as in *substance abuse*). Drugs that affect the brain, changing consciousness and other psychological processes, are called **psychoactive drugs.** The study of psychoactive drugs is called **psychopharmacology.**

Psychopharmacology   Sattler/Shabatay reader, 2/e: Rodriguez, "Always Running"

Most psychoactive drugs affect the brain by altering the interactions between neurotransmitters and receptors, as described in the chapter on biological aspects of

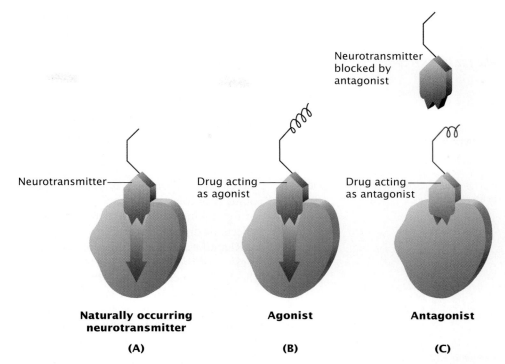

Neurotransmitter
blocked by
antagonist

Neurotransmitter——

Drug acting——
as agonist

Drug acting——
as antagonist

**Naturally occurring
neurotransmitter**

Agonist

Antagonist

(A)

(B)

(C)

Personal Learning Activity 9.5

Essay Q 9.3

ClassPrep PPT 33: *Figure 9.12:* Agonists and
Antagonists

figure 9.12

Agonists and Antagonists

In Part A, a molecule of neurotransmitter interacts with a receptor on a neuron's dendrites
by fitting into and stimulating it. Part B shows a drug molecule acting as an *agonist,*
affecting the receptor in the same way a neurotransmitter would. Part C depicts an
antagonist drug molecule blocking a natural neurotransmitter from reaching and acting
upon the receptor.

psychology. To create their effects, these drugs must cross the **blood-brain barrier,** a
feature of blood vessels in the brain that prevents some substances from entering
brain tissue. Once past this barrier, a psychoactive drug's effects depend on several
factors: With which neurotransmitter systems does the drug interact? How does the
drug affect these neurotransmitters or their receptors? What psychological functions
are performed by the brain systems that use these neurotransmitters?

Drugs can affect neurotransmitters or their receptors through several mechanisms. As Figure 9.12 shows, neurotransmitters fit into their own receptors; however, some drugs are similar enough to a particular neurotransmitter to fool its
receptors. These drugs, called **agonists,** bind to the receptor and mimic the effects of
the normal neurotransmitter. Other drugs are similar enough to a neurotransmitter
to occupy its receptors but cannot mimic its effects; they bind to a receptor and prevent the normal neurotransmitter from binding. These drugs are called **antagonists.**
Still other drugs work by increasing or decreasing the release of a specific neurotransmitter. Finally, some drugs work by speeding or slowing the *removal* of a neurotransmitter from synapses.

Predicting a drug's behavioral effects is complicated by the fact that some drugs
interact with many neurotransmitter systems. Also, the nervous system may compensate for a disturbance. For example, repeated exposure to a drug that blocks
receptors for a certain neurotransmitter often leads to a compensatory increase in
the number of receptors available to accept the neurotransmitter.

blood-brain barrier   A feature of blood
vessels in the brain that allows only certain substances to leave the blood and
interact with brain tissue.

agonists   Drugs that mimic the effects
of the neurotransmitter that normally
binds to a neural receptor.

antagonists   Drugs that bind to a
receptor and prevent the normal neurotransmitter from binding to it.

The Varying Effects of Drugs

Drugs affect biological systems in accordance with their chemical properties.
Unfortunately, their medically desirable *main effects,* such as pain relief, are often
accompanied by undesirable *side effects,* which may include the potential for abuse.

OBJ 9.22: Define substance abuse.

Test Items 9.129–9.130

OBJ 9.23: Define psychological dependence and physical dependence, or addiction. Explain the mechanisms of withdrawal syndrome and tolerance.

Test Items 9.131–9.135

IRM In Your Own Words 9.2: Drug Effects

OBJ 9.24: Explain the role of expectations in the influence of drugs on behavior.

Test Items 9.136–9.139

ClassPrep PPT 32: Factors That Influence the Effects of Psychoactive Drugs

substance abuse The self-administration of psychoactive drugs in ways that deviate from a culture's social norms.

psychological dependence A condition in which a person uses a drug despite adverse effects, needs the drug for a sense of well-being, and becomes preoccupied with obtaining it.

physical dependence Development of a physical need for a psychoactive drug.

withdrawal syndrome Symptoms associated with discontinuing the use of a drug.

tolerance A condition in which increasingly larger drug doses are needed to produce a given effect.

Substance abuse is a pattern of use that causes serious social, legal, or interpersonal problems for the user (American Psychiatric Association, 1994).

Substance abuse may lead to psychological or physical dependence. **Psychological dependence** is a condition in which a person continues drug use despite adverse effects, needs the drug for a sense of well-being, and becomes preoccupied with obtaining the drug. However, the person can still function without the drug. Psychological dependence can occur with or without **physical dependence**, or **addiction**, which is a physiological state in which drug use is needed to prevent a **withdrawal syndrome**. Withdrawal symptoms vary across drugs but often include an intense craving for the drug and effects generally opposite to those of the drug itself. Eventually, *drug tolerance* may appear. **Tolerance** is a condition in which increasingly larger drug doses are needed to produce the same effect. With the development of tolerance, many addicts need the drug just to prevent the negative effects of not taking it. However, most researchers believe that a craving for the positive effects of drugs is what keeps addicts coming back to drug use (Weiss et al., 2001). MRI studies of addicts imagining cocaine or alcohol use reveal that craving activates regions of the brain related to the rewards, positive emotions, and other pleasures they have learned to associate with using the drug (George et al., 2001; Kilts et al., 2001). Stimulating these regions in the brains of rats that had once been physically dependent on cocaine causes them to again seek out the drug (Vorel et al., 2001).

It is tempting to think of "addicts" as being unlike ourselves, but we should never underestimate the potential for "normal" people to develop drug dependence. Physical dependence can develop gradually, without a person's awareness. In fact, scientists now believe that the changes in the brain that underlie addiction may be similar to those that occur during learning (Overton et al., 1999). All addictive drugs stimulate the brain's "pleasure centers," regions that are sensitive to the neurotransmitter dopamine. Neuronal activity in these areas produces intensely pleasurable feelings; it also helps generate the pleasant feelings of a good meal, a "runner's high," or sex (Grunberg, 1994; Harris & Aston-Jones, 1995). Neuroscientists long believed that these feelings stem directly from the action of dopamine itself, but activity in dopamine systems may actually be more involved in responding to the novelty associated with pleasurable events than in actually creating the experience of pleasure (Bevins, 2001; Garris et al., 1999). In any case, by affecting dopamine regulation and related biochemical processes in "pleasure centers," addictive drugs have the capacity to create tremendously rewarding effects in most people.

Expectations and Drug Effects   Drug effects are determined by more than biochemistry. *Learned expectations* also play a role (Cumsille, Sayer, & Graham, 2000; Goldman, Del Boca, & Darkes, 1999; Stein, Goldman, & Del Boca, 2000). In one experiment, for example, college students reported being drunk after consuming drinks that tasted and smelled like alcohol—even though the drinks contained no alcohol (Darkes & Goldman, 1993). Other studies have demonstrated that people's expectancies about the effects of alcohol had a greater influence on their aggressive behavior than did alcohol itself (e.g., Lang et al., 1975). Expectations about drug effects develop, in part, as people watch other people react to drugs. Because what they see can be different from one individual and culture to the next, drug effects vary considerably throughout the world (MacAndrew & Edgerton, 1969). For example, the loss of inhibition and the violence commonly associated with alcohol use in the United States is partly attributable to custom, inasmuch as these effects are not universal. Consider the contrasting example of Bolivia's Camba culture, in which people drink, in extended bouts, a brew that is 89 percent alcohol. These people repeatedly pass out, wake up, and start drinking again—all the while maintaining tranquil social relations. Other studies have shown that learned expectancies also contribute to the effects of heroin, cocaine, and marijuana (Robbins & Everitt, 1999; Schafer & Brown, 1991; Smith et al., 1992).

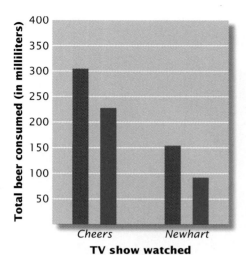

Alcohol-positive adjectives

Neutral adjectives

figure 9.13

Expectancies and Alcohol Consumption

People may drink more when their expectancies about the positive effects of alcohol have been primed. In this study, participants who (1) watched a TV show in which the characters enjoyed themselves while drinking alcohol and (2) were exposed to adjectives associated with positive expectancies about alcohol subsequently drank more (nonalcoholic) beer than participants who watched a show not related to alcohol and who were not exposed to the adjectives.

Source: Roehrich & Goldman (1995, Figure 1).

ClassPrep PPT 37: *Figure 9.13:* Expectancies and Alcohol Consumption

ClassPrep PPT 38: Depressants

OBJ 9.25: Define depressant. Describe the effects of alcohol and barbiturates on the nervous system and behavior.

Test Items 9.140–9.146

depressants Psychoactive drugs that inhibit the functioning of the central nervous system.

The learned nature of responses to alcohol is also demonstrated by cases in which people are exposed to new ideas about what those responses can be. For example, when Europeans brought alcohol to Tahiti in the 1700s, the Tahitians' initial response to drinking it was to become relaxed and befuddled, much as when consuming *kava,* their traditional nonalcoholic tranquilizing drink. But after years of watching European sailors' drunken violence, Tahitian alcohol drinkers became violent themselves. Fortunately, subsequent learning experiences once again made their response to alcohol more peaceful (MacAndrew & Edgerton, 1969).

Expectations about a drug's effects can also influence how much of it people will consume (Goldman, Darkes, & Del Boca, 1999). In one study, for example, participants thought they were taking part in a memory experiment, but in fact, their expectations about the positive effects of alcohol were being primed, without their awareness, in one or both of two ways (Roehrich & Goldman, 1995): (1) Participants viewed an episode of a television show *(Cheers)* that portrayed alcohol consumption in a positive light, and/or (2) they were subtly exposed to positive adjectives associated with alcohol consumption (e.g., *funny, happy,* and *talkative*). Later, the participants were given an opportunity to drink what they thought was alcohol (but was actually nonalcoholic beer) as part of a separate "taste-rating study." Figure 9.13 shows the results of this experiment. Although the participants saw no connection between the priming stages of the study and the subsequent taste test, those who had watched *Cheers* drank more than those who had watched a TV show not related to alcohol. Those who were exposed to the positive alcohol-consumption adjectives drank more than those who were exposed to neutral adjectives.

These examples and experiments show that the effects of psychoactive drugs are complex and variable. In the chapter on treatment of psychological disorders, we discuss some of the psychoactive drugs being used to help people who display psychopathology. Here, we consider several major categories of psychoactive drugs that are used primarily for the alterations they produce in consciousness, including depressants, stimulants, opiates, and hallucinogens.

ClassPrep PPT 34: The Varying Effects of Drugs

Depressants

Depressants are drugs that reduce activity of the central nervous system. Examples are alcohol and barbiturates, both of which increase the activity of GABA, a neurotransmitter described in the chapter on biological aspects of psychology. Because GABA reduces, or inhibits, neuron activity, enhancing GABA function reduces the excitability of many neural circuits. Because of the impact of depressants on GABA, using them creates feelings of relaxation, drowsiness, and sometimes depression (Hanson & Venturelli, 1995).

Alcohol   In the United States, over 100 million people drink *alcohol;* it is equally popular worldwide (Alvarez, Delrio, & Prada, 1995). Alcohol affects several neurotransmitters, including dopamine, endorphins, glutamate, serotonin, and most notably, GABA (Koob et al., 1998). For this reason, drugs that interact with GABA receptors can block some of alcohol's effects, as shown in Figure 9.14 (Suzdak et al., 1986). Alcohol also enhances the effect of endorphins (the body's natural painkillers, described in the chapter on sensation). This action may underlie the "high" that people feel when drinking alcohol and may explain why *naltrexone* and *naloxone,* which are endorphin antagonists, are better than placebos at reducing alcohol craving and relapse rates in recovering alcoholics (Salloum et al., 1998). Alcohol also interacts with dopamine systems, a component of the brain's reward mechanisms (Thanos et al., 2001). Prolonged alcohol use can have lasting effects on the brain's ability to regulate dopamine levels (Tiihonen et al., 1995), and dopamine agonists reduce alcohol craving and withdrawal effects (Lawford et al., 1995).

figure 9.14

GABA Receptors and Alcohol

Both of these rats received the same amount of alcohol, enough to incapacitate them with drunkenness. However, the rat on the right then received a drug that reverses alcohol's intoxicating effects by blocking the ability of alcohol to stimulate GABA receptors. Within two minutes, the rat was completely sober. Researchers found a serious problem with the drug, however: It did not reverse the effects of alcohol on the brain's breathing centers. So if people were drinking to get intoxicated, the drug would frustrate their efforts, and they might consume a lethal overdose of alcohol. Accordingly, the drug's manufacturer has discontinued its development.

IRM Discussion 9.11: A "Designer" Drug Gone Bad

ClassPrep PPTs 39 & 40: Effects of Alcohol

Alcohol affects specific brain regions. For example, it depresses activity in the locus coeruleus, an area that helps activate the cerebral cortex (Koob & Bloom, 1988). Reduced cortical activity tends to cause cognitive changes and a release of inhibitions. Some drinkers begin talking loudly, acting silly, or telling others what they think of them. Emotional reactions range from euphoria to despair. Normally shy people may become impulsive or violent. Alcohol's impairment of the hippocampus causes memory problems, making it more difficult to form memories for new information (Givens, 1995). And its suppression of the cerebellum causes poor motor coordination (Rogers et al., 1986). Alcohol's ability to depress hindbrain mechanisms that control breathing and heartbeat can make overdoses fatal.

As mentioned earlier, some effects of alcohol—such as anger and aggressiveness—depend on both biochemical factors and learned expectations (Goldman, Darkes, & Del Boca, 1999; Kushner et al., 2000). But other effects—especially disruptions in motor coordination, speech, and thought—result from biochemical factors alone. These biological effects depend on the amount of alcohol the blood carries to the brain. It takes the liver about an hour to break down one ounce of alcohol (the amount in one average drink), so alcohol has milder effects if consumed slowly. Effects increase with faster drinking, or if you drink on an empty stomach, thereby speeding absorption into the blood. Even after allowing for differences in average male and female body weight, researchers have found metabolic differences that allow male bodies to tolerate somewhat higher amounts of alcohol. As a result, equal doses of alcohol may create greater effects in women compared with men (York & Welte, 1994).

Genetics also seems to play a role in determining the biochemical effects of alcohol. Some people appear to have a genetic predisposition toward alcohol dependence (Agarwal, 1997), although the specific genes involved have not yet been identified. Others, such as the Japanese, may have inherited metabolic characteristics that increase the adverse effects of alcohol, thus possibly inhibiting the development of alcohol abuse (Iwahashi et al., 1995).

Barbiturates   Sometimes called "downers" or "sleeping pills," *barbiturates* are extremely addictive. Small doses cause relaxation, mild euphoria, loss of muscle coordination, and lowered attention. Higher doses cause deep sleep, but continued use actually distorts sleep patterns (Kales & Kales, 1973). Obviously, then, long-

Drinking and Driving Don't Mix
Although practice makes it seem easy, driving a car is a complex information-processing task. As described in the chapter on cognition and language, such tasks require constant vigilance, quick decisions, and skillful execution of responses. Alcohol can impair all these processes, as well as the ability to judge the degree of impairment—thus making drinking and driving a deadly combination that kills tens of thousands of people each year in the United States alone.

term use of barbiturates as sleeping pills is unwise. Overdoses can be fatal. Withdrawal symptoms are among the most severe for any drug and can include intense agitation, violent outbursts, convulsions, hallucinations, and even sudden death.

Stimulants ClassPrep PPT 42: Stimulants

Amphetamines, cocaine, caffeine, and nicotine are all examples of **stimulants,** drugs that increase behavioral and mental activity.

OBJ 9.26: Define stimulant. Describe the effects of amphetamines, cocaine, caffeine, nicotine, and MDMA on the nervous system and behavior.

Test Items 9.147–9.154

IRM Discussion 9.10: Cocaine Babies

Amphetamines

Also called "uppers" or "speed," *amphetamines* (Benzedrine, for example) increase the release and decrease the removal of norepinephrine and dopamine at synapses, causing increased activity at these neurotransmitters' receptors. These drugs' rewarding properties are probably due in part to their activation of dopamine systems, because taking dopamine antagonists reduces amphetamine use (Holman, 1994).

Amphetamines stimulate both the brain and the sympathetic branch of the autonomic nervous system, raising heart rate and blood pressure, constricting blood vessels, shrinking mucous membranes (thus relieving stuffy noses), and reducing appetite. Amphetamines also increase alertness and response speed, especially in tasks requiring prolonged attention (Koelega, 1993), and they may improve memory for verbal material (Soetens et al., 1995).

Amphetamine abuse usually begins as an effort to lose weight, stay awake, or experience a "high." Continued use leads to anxiety, insomnia, heart problems, brain damage, movement disorders, confusion, paranoia, nonstop talking, and psychological and physical dependence (Volkow et al., 2001). In some cases, the symptoms of amphetamine abuse are virtually identical to those of paranoid schizophrenia, a serious mental disorder associated with malfunctioning dopamine systems.

Cocaine

Like amphetamines, *cocaine* increases norepinephrine and dopamine activity, and thus it produces many amphetamine-like effects. Cocaine's particularly powerful effect on dopamine activity and its rapid onset may underlie its remarkably addictive nature (Holman, 1994; Ungless et al., 2001). Drugs with rapid onset

stimulants Psychoactive drugs that have the ability to increase behavioral and mental activity.

Deadly Drug Use In his short career as a comedian, Chris Farley starred on *Saturday Night Live* and in several movies. At the age of thirty-three, he died from an overdose of cocaine and opium.

and short duration are generally more addictive than others (Kato, Wakasa, & Yamagita, 1987), which may explain why *crack*—a purified, fast-acting, highly potent, smokable form of cocaine—is especially addictive.

Cocaine stimulates self-confidence, a sense of well-being, and optimism. But continued use brings nausea, overactivity, insomnia, paranoia, a sudden depressive "crash," hallucinations, sexual dysfunction, and seizures (Lacayo, 1995). Overdoses, especially of crack, can be deadly, and even small doses can cause a fatal heart attack or stroke (Marzuk et al., 1995). There is now little doubt that a pregnant woman who uses cocaine harms her fetus (Hurt et al., 1995; Konkol et al., 1994; Snodgrass, 1994). However, many of the severe, long-term behavioral problems seen in "cocaine babies" may have at least as much to do with poverty and neglect after birth as with the mother's cocaine use beforehand. Early intervention can reduce the effects of both cocaine and the hostile environment that confronts most cocaine babies (Wren, 1998).

Ending a cocaine addiction is difficult. One possible treatment involves *buprenorphine,* an opiate antagonist that suppresses cocaine self-administration in addicted monkeys (Mello et al., 1989). Other drugs that affect selective types of dopamine receptors have been found effective in preventing relapse when mice previously addicted to cocaine were exposed to drug-related cues, but these drugs have not yet been tested in humans (Beardsley et al., 2001). The results of other methods have been mixed; fewer than 25 percent of human cocaine addicts who have undergone even long-term pharmacological and psychological treatments are drug-free five years later (*Harvard Mental Health Letter,* 2001).

Caffeine   *Caffeine* may be the world's most popular drug. It is found in coffee, tea, chocolate, and many soft drinks. Caffeine reduces drowsiness by inhibiting receptors for the neuromodulator adenosine, which we discussed earlier in relation to sleep (Nehlig, Daval, & Debry, 1992). It improves problem solving, increases the capacity for physical work, and raises urine production (Warburton, 1995). At high doses it induces anxiety and tremors. Caffeine use can result in tolerance, as well as physical dependence (Strain et al., 1994). Withdrawal symptoms—including headaches, fatigue, anxiety, shakiness, and craving—appear on the first day of abstinence and last about a week (Silverman et al., 1992). Caffeine may make it harder for women to become pregnant and may increase the risk of miscarriage (Alderete, Eskenazi, & Sholtz, 1995; Cnattingius et al., 2000), but overall, moderate daily caffeine use appears to have few, if any, negative effects (Kleemola et al., 2000; Thompson, 1995).

Nicotine   A powerful stimulant of the autonomic nervous system, *nicotine* is the psychoactive ingredient in tobacco. Nicotine is an acetylcholine agonist, but it also increases neuronal release of glutamate, the brain's primary excitatory neurotransmitter (McGehee et al., 1995). Nicotine has many psychoactive effects, including elevated mood and improved memory and attention (Ernst et al., 2001; Pomerleau & Pomerleau, 1992). Its ability to create dependence is now well established (White, 1998). This claim is supported by evidence of a nicotine withdrawal syndrome, which includes craving, anxiety, irritability, lowered heart rate, and weight gain (Hughes, Higgins, & Bickel, 1994). Although nicotine does not create the "rush" characteristic of many drugs of abuse, withdrawal from it reduces activity in the brain's reward pathways (Epping-Jordan et al., 1998). Other research suggests that nicotine creates more psychological than physical dependence (Robinson & Pritchard, 1995), but whatever blend of physical and psychological dependence may be involved, there is no doubt that smoking is a difficult habit for most smokers to break (Shiffman et al., 1997). As discussed in the chapter on health, stress, and coping, it is also clearly recognized as a major risk factor for cancer, heart disease, and respiratory disorders (U.S. Department of Health and Human Services, 2001b).

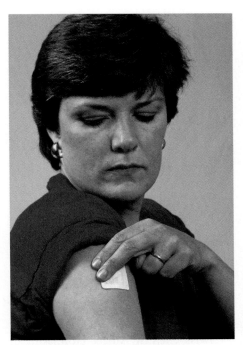

Giving Up Smoking The chemical effects of nicotine, combined with strong learned associations between smoking and relaxation, stimulation, mealtimes, alcohol, and a wide variety of pleasant social interactions, make it extremely difficult for most smokers to give up their unhealthy habit. One of the more promising treatment programs available today combines nicotine administration (through a patch like the one this woman is wearing) with antidepressant medication and behavioral training in how to cope with smoking-related situations—and with the stress of quitting.

OBJ 9.27: Define opiates. Describe the effects of opium, morphine, codeine, and heroin on the nervous system.

Test Items 9.155–9.160

opiates Psychoactive drugs, such as opium, morphine, or heroin, that produce both sleep-inducing and pain-relieving effects.

hallucinogens Psychoactive drugs that alter consciousness by producing a temporary loss of contact with reality and changes in emotion, perception, and thought.

MDMA "Ecstasy," or *MDMA* (short for 3,4-methylenedioxymethamphetamine), causes visual hallucinations, a feeling of greater closeness to others, dry mouth, hyperactivity, and jaw muscle spasms resulting in "lockjaw." Because MDMA increases the activity of dopamine-releasing neurons, it leads to some of the same effects as those produced by cocaine and amphetamines (Steele, McCann, & Ricaurte, 1994). At serotonin synapses, MDMA is a receptor agonist and also causes neurotransmitter release, thus possibly accounting for the drug's hallucinatory effects (Green, Cross, & Goodwin, 1995). On the day after using MDMA— also known as "XTC," "clarity," "essence," "E," and "Adam"—people often experience muscle aches, fatigue, depression, and poor concentration (Peroutka, Newman, & Harris, 1988). With continued use, MDMA's positive effects decrease, but its negative effects persist.

Although it does not appear to be physically addictive, MDMA is a dangerous, potentially deadly drug (National Institute on Drug Abuse, 2000b). For one thing, it permanently damages the brain, killing neurons that use serotonin (Green, Cross, & Goodwin, 1995); the damage increases with higher doses and continued use (Battaglia, Yeh, & De Souza, 1988). MDMA impairs memory, even after its use is discontinued (Reneman et al., 2001; Rodgers, 2000; Zakzanis & Young, 2001), and users may develop *panic disorder,* a problem whose symptoms include intense anxiety and a sense of impending death (see the chapter on psychological disorders).

Opiates ClassPrep PPT 43: Opiates

The **opiates** (opium, morphine, heroin, and codeine) are unique in their capacity for inducing sleep and relieving pain (Julien, 2001). *Opium,* derived from the poppy plant, relieves pain and causes feelings of well-being and dreamy relaxation. One of its most active ingredients, *morphine,* was first isolated in the early 1800s and is used worldwide for pain relief. Percodan and Demerol are two common morphine-like drugs. *Heroin* is derived from morphine but is three times more powerful, causing intensely pleasurable reactions when first taken.

Opiates have complex effects on consciousness. Drowsy, cloudy feelings occur because opiates depress activity in areas of the cerebral cortex. But they also create excitation in other parts, causing some users to experience euphoria (Bozarth & Wise, 1984). Opiates exert many of their effects through their role as agonists for endorphins. When opiates activate endorphin receptors, they are "tricking" the brain into an exaggerated activation of its painkilling and mood-altering systems (Julien, 2001).

Opiates are highly addictive, perhaps because they stimulate a particular type of glutamate receptor in the brain that can bring physical changes in a neuron's structure. It may be, then, that opiates alter neurons so that they come to require the drug to function properly. Supporting this idea are data showing that glutamate antagonists appear to prevent morphine dependence yet leave the drug's painkilling effects intact (Trujillo & Akil, 1991). Beyond the hazards of addiction itself, heroin addicts risk death through overdoses, contaminated drugs, or AIDS contracted by sharing drug-injection needles (Hser et al., 2001).

Hallucinogens ClassPrep PPT 44: Hallucinogens

Hallucinogens, also called *psychedelics,* create a loss of contact with reality and alter other aspects of emotion, perception, and thought. They can cause distortions in body image (the user may feel gigantic or tiny), loss of identity (confusion about who one actually is), dream-like fantasies, and hallucinations. Because these effects resemble many severe forms of mental disorder, hallucinogens are also called *psychotomimetics* (mimicking psychosis).

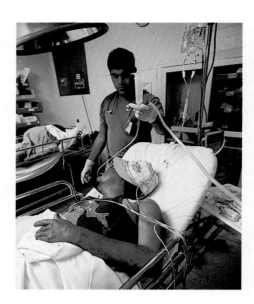

A New Drug Danger Oxycodone, a morphine-like drug prescribed by doctors under the label OxyContin, has recently become popular among recreational substance abusers. It was designed as a timed-release painkiller, but when people crush OxyContin tablets and then inject or inhale the drug, they get a much stronger and potentially lethal dose. Deaths from OxyContin abuse are already on the rise in the United States (National Drug Intelligence Center, 2001).

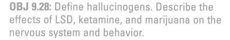

OBJ 9.28: Define hallucinogens. Describe the effects of LSD, ketamine, and marijuana on the nervous system and behavior.

Test Items 9.161–9.164

LSD   One of the most powerful psychedelics is *lysergic acid diethylamide,* or *LSD,* first synthesized from a rye fungus by Swiss chemist Albert Hofmann. In 1938, after Hofmann accidentally ingested a minuscule amount of the substance, he discovered the drug's strange effects in the world's first LSD "trip" (Julien, 1995). LSD's hallucinations can be quite bizarre. Time may seem distorted, sounds may cause visual sensations, and users may feel as if they have left their bodies.

LSD's hallucinatory effects are probably due to its ability to stimulate a specific type of receptor in the forebrain, called $5\text{-}HT_{2a}$ receptors, that normally respond to serotonin (Carlson, 1998; Leonard, 1992). Supporting this assertion is evidence that serotonin antagonists greatly reduce LSD's hallucinatory effects (Leonard, 1992).

The precise effects of LSD on a particular individual are unpredictable. Unpleasant hallucinations and delusions can occur during a person's first—or two hundredth—LSD experience. Although LSD is not addictive, tolerance to its effects does develop. Some users suffer lasting adverse effects, including severe short-term memory loss, paranoia, violent outbursts, nightmares, and panic attacks (Gold, 1994). Distortions in visual sensations can remain years after the end of heavy use (Abraham & Wolf, 1988). Sometimes flashbacks occur, in which a person suddenly returns to an LSD-like state of consciousness weeks or even years after using the drug.

Ketamine   *Ketamine* is an anesthetic widely used by veterinarians to ease pain in their animal patients, but because it also has hallucinogenic effects, it is being stolen and sold as a recreational drug known as "Special K." Its effects include dissociative feelings that create what some users describe as an "out-of-body" or "near death" experience. Unfortunately, ketamine also causes enduring memory impairment (Curran & Monaghan, 2001), which may result from damage to memory-related brain structures such as the hippocampus (Jevtovic-Todorovic et al., 2001).

Marijuana   A mixture of the crushed leaves, flowers, and stems from the hemp plant *(Cannabis sativa)* makes up *marijuana.* The active ingredient is *tetrahydrocannabinol,* or *THC.* When inhaled, THC is absorbed in minutes by many organs, including the brain, and it continues to affect consciousness for a few hours. THC tends to collect in fatty deposits of the brain and reproductive organs, where it can be detected for weeks. The specific receptors for THC include those sensitive to *anandamide* (from a Sanskrit word meaning "bliss"), a naturally occurring brain substance that research suggests may be a neurotransmitter (Fride & Mechoulam,

in review — Major Classes of Psychoactive Drugs

Drug	Trade/Street Name	Main Effects	Potential for Physical/Psychological Dependence
Depressants			
Alcohol	"booze"	Relaxation, anxiety reduction, sleep	High/high
Barbiturates	Seconal, Tuinal, Nembutal ("downers")		High/high
Stimulants			
Amphetamines	Benzedrine, Dexedrine, Methadrine ("speed," "uppers," "ice")	Alertness, euphoria	Moderate/high
Cocaine	"coke," "crack"		Moderate to high/high
Caffeine		Alertness	Moderate/moderate
Nicotine	"smokes," "coffin nails"	Alertness	High (?)/high
MDMA	ecstasy, clarity	Hallucinations	Low/(?)
Opiates			
Opium		Euphoria	High/high
Morphine	Percodan, Demerol	Euphoria, pain control	High/high
Heroin	"junk," "smack"	Euphoria, pain control	High/high
Hallucinogens			
LSD/Ketamine	"acid"/"Special K"	Altered perceptions, hallucinations	Low/low
Marijuana (cannabis)	"pot," "dope," "reefer"	Euphoria, relaxation	Low/moderate

1993). Another substance in the brain that binds to THC receptors is called *2-AG*, which may affect the neural basis of memory in the hippocampus (Stella, Schweitzer, & Piomelli, 1997).

Low doses of marijuana may initially create restlessness and hilarity, followed by a dreamy, carefree relaxation, an expanded sense of space and time, more vivid sensations, food cravings, and subtle changes in thinking (Kelly et al., 1990). For a summary of the effects of marijuana and other psychoactive drugs, see "In Review: Major Classes of Psychoactive Drugs."

Is Marijuana Dangerous?   ClassPrep PPT 49: Is Marijuana Dangerous?

OBJ 9.29: Discuss research on the level of danger associated with marijuana use.

Test Item 9.165

A large-scale study of U.S. teenagers indicated a dramatic rise in their use of marijuana from 1991 to 1996. Usage almost tripled among eighth-graders (from 4 to 11 percent) and more than doubled among tenth-graders (from 9 to 20 percent). During this same period, the number of students who believed that there is a "great risk" associated with using marijuana declined in about the same proportions (Hall, 1997). Marijuana use has continued to increase in recent years (National Institute on Drug Abuse, 2000a), and in response to these trends, U.S. government officials have condemned marijuana use as "dangerous, illegal, and wrong." Concern about the drug has also been voiced in many other countries.

At the same time, the medical community has been engaged in serious discussion about whether marijuana should be used for medicinal purposes, and in the United States and around the world many individuals and organizations continue to argue for the decriminalization of marijuana use (Hall, 1997; Iversen & Snyder, 2000; Strang, Witten, & Hall, 2000).

Those who support legalization of marijuana cite its medical benefits; some doctors claim to have successfully used marijuana in the treatment of asthma,

The Cannabis Controversy Marijuana is illegal in North America and in many other places, too, but the question of whether it should remain so is a matter of hot debate between those who see the drug as a dangerous gateway to more addictive substances and those who view it as a benign source of pleasure that may also have important medical benefits.

glaucoma, epilepsy, chronic pain, and nausea from cancer chemotherapy (Tramer et al., 2001; Voelker, 1997). But critics insist that medical legalization of marijuana is premature, because its medicinal value has not been clearly established (Bennet, 1994) and because—even though patients may prefer marijuana-based drugs—other medications may be equally effective and less dangerous (e.g., Campbell et al., 2001).

● **What am I being asked to believe or accept?**

Those who see marijuana as dangerous usually assert four beliefs: (1) that marijuana is addictive; (2) that it leads to the use of "hard drugs," such as heroin; (3) that marijuana intoxication endangers the user and other individuals; and (4) that long-term marijuana use leads to undesirable behavioral changes, disruption of brain functions, and other adverse effects on health.

● **What evidence is available to support the assertion?**

Without a doubt, some people do use marijuana to such an extent that it disrupts their lives. According to the criteria normally used to define alcohol abuse, these people are dependent on marijuana—at least psychologically (Stephens, Roffman, & Simpson, 1994). The question of physical dependence (addiction) is less clear, inasmuch as withdrawal from chronic marijuana use has long been thought not to produce any severe physical symptoms. However, some evidence of a mild withdrawal syndrome has been reported in rats, and in humans, withdrawal from marijuana may be accompanied by increases in anxiety, depression, and aggressiveness (Budney et al., 2001; Haney et al., 1999; Kouri, Pope, & Lukas, 1999; Rodriguez de Fonseca et al., 1997). Other research (e.g., Tanda, Pontieri, & Di Chiara, 1997) has found that marijuana interacts with the same dopamine and opiate receptors as does heroin, implying that marijuana could be a "gateway drug" to the use of more addictive drugs.

Regardless of whether marijuana is addicting or leads to "harder drugs," it can create a number of problems. It disrupts memory formation, making it difficult to carry out complex tasks (Lichtman, Dimen, & Martin, 1995; Pope et al., 2001). And because marijuana affects muscle coordination, driving while under its influence is quite hazardous. Compounding the danger is the fact that motor impairment continues long after the obvious effects of the drug have worn off. In one study, for example, pilots had difficulty landing a simulated aircraft even a full day after smoking one marijuana cigarette (Yesavage et al., 1985). As for marijuana's effects on intellectual and cognitive performance, long-term use can lead to lasting impairments in reasoning and memory (Solowij et al., 2002). One study found that adults who frequently used marijuana scored lower on a twelfth-grade academic achievement test than did nonusers with the same IQs (Block & Ghoneim, 1993).

● Are there alternative ways of interpreting the evidence?

Those who see marijuana as a benign or even beneficial substance criticize studies like those just mentioned as providing an inaccurate or incomplete picture of marijuana's effects (Grinspoon, 1999). They argue, for example, that the same dopamine receptors activated by marijuana and heroin are also activated by sex and chocolate—and that few people would call for the criminalization of those pleasures (Grinspoon et al., 1997). Moreover, the correlation between early marijuana use and later use of hard drugs could be due more to the people with whom users become involved than to any property of the drug per se (Fergusson & Horwood, 1997).

The question of marijuana's long-term effects on memory and reasoning is also difficult to resolve, partly because studies of academic achievement scores and marijuana use tend to be correlational in nature. As noted in the chapter on research in psychology, cause and effect cannot easily be determined in such studies. Does marijuana use lead to poor academic performance, or does poor academic performance lead to increased marijuana use? Both possibilities are credible.

● What additional evidence would help to evaluate the alternatives?

More definitive evidence on marijuana's short- and long-term effects is obviously needed, but evaluating the meaning of that evidence will be difficult. The issues involved in the marijuana debate involve questions of degree and relative risk. For example, is the risk of marijuana dependence greater than that of alcohol dependence? There are clearly differences among people in the extent to which marijuana use poses a risk for them. So far, however, we have not determined what personal characteristics account for such differences. Nor do we know why some people use marijuana only occasionally, whereas others use it so often and in such quantities that it seriously disrupts their ability to function in a normal and adaptive manner. The physical and psychological factors underlying these differences have yet to be identified.

● What conclusions are most reasonable?

Those who would decriminalize the use of marijuana argue that when marijuana was declared illegal in the United States in the 1930s, there was no evidence that it was any more harmful than alcohol or tobacco. Scientific evidence supports that claim, but more by illuminating the dangers of alcohol and tobacco than by exonerating marijuana. Although marijuana is less dangerous than, say, cocaine or heroin, it is by no means totally benign. Marijuana easily reaches a developing fetus and should not be used by pregnant women (Fried, Watkinson, & Gray, 1992); it suppresses some immune functions in humans (Cabral & Dove Pettit, 1998); and marijuana smoke is as irritating to lungs as tobacco smoke (Roth et al., 1998). Further, because possession of marijuana is still a crime almost everywhere in the United States, as well as in many other countries throughout the world, it would be foolish to flaunt existing laws without regard for the legal consequences of such actions.

However, in Canada, it is legal to grow and use marijuana for medicinal purposes, and despite federal laws to the contrary, the same is true in eight U.S. states. Although the American Medical Association has recently rejected the idea of medical uses for marijuana, scientists are intent on objectively studying its potential value in the treatment of certain diseases, as well as its dangers (or lack thereof). Their work is being encouraged by bodies such as the National Institute of Medicine (Joy, Watson, & Benson, 1999), and a British company is working on new cannabis-based medicines (Altman, 2000). The United Nations, too, has recommended that governments worldwide sponsor additional work on the medical uses of marijuana (Wren, 1999). Ultimately, the most reasonable conclusions about marijuana use must await the outcome of this research (Joy, Watson, & Benson, 1999).

LINKAGES

As noted in the chapter on introducing psychology, all of psychology's subfields are related to one another. Our discussion of meditation, health, and stress illustrates just one way in which the topic of this chapter, consciousness, is linked to the subfield of health psychology (which is a focus of the chapter on health, stress, and coping). The Linkages diagram shows ties to two other subfields as well, and there are many more ties throughout the book. Looking for linkages among subfields will help you see how they all fit together and help you better appreciate the big picture that is psychology.

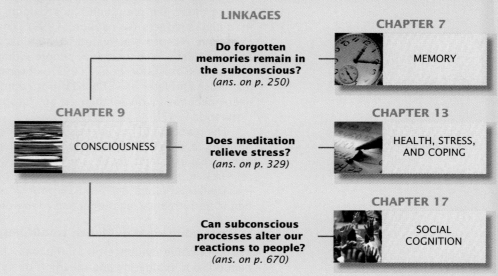

LINKAGES

Do forgotten memories remain in the subconscious?
(ans. on p. 250)

CHAPTER 7
MEMORY

CHAPTER 9
CONSCIOUSNESS

Does meditation relieve stress?
(ans. on p. 329)

CHAPTER 13
HEALTH, STRESS, AND COPING

Can subconscious processes alter our reactions to people?
(ans. on p. 670)

CHAPTER 17
SOCIAL COGNITION

SUMMARY

Consciousness can be defined as awareness of the outside world and of one's own thoughts, feelings, perceptions, and other mental processes.

Analyzing Consciousness

Current research on consciousness focuses on three main questions. First, what is the relationship between the mind and the brain? Second, does consciousness occur as a single "point" in mental processing or as several parallel mental operations that operate independently? Third, what mental processes are outside awareness, and how do they affect conscious processes?

Some Functions of Consciousness

Consciousness produces the best current interpretation of sensory information in light of past experience and makes this interpretation available to the parts of the brain that plan voluntary actions and speech.

Levels of Consciousness

Variations in how much awareness you have for a mental function are described by different levels of consciousness. The *preconscious level* includes mental activities that are outside of awareness but can easily be brought to the *conscious level*. The *unconscious level* involves thoughts, memories, and processes that are more difficult to bring to awareness. Mental processes that cannot be brought into awareness occur at the *nonconscious level*.

Mental Processing Without Awareness

Awareness is not always required for mental operations. Priming studies show that people's responses to some stimuli can be sped up, improved, or modified, even when the people are not consciously aware of the priming stimuli.

The Neuropsychology of Consciousness

Brain injuries often reveal ways in which mental processing can occur without conscious awareness. For instance, patients with anterograde amnesia continue to acquire new skills without later awareness of learning them.

States of Consciousness

A person's *state of consciousness* is constantly changing. When the changes are particularly noticeable, they are called *altered states of consciousness*. Examples include sleep, hypnosis, meditation, and some drug-induced states. Different cultures vary considerably in the value placed on different states of consciousness.

Sleeping and Dreaming

Sleep is an active and complex state.

Stages of Sleep

Different stages of sleep are defined on the basis of changes in brain activity (as recorded by an electroencephalograph, or EEG) and physiological arousal. Sleep normally begins with stage 1 sleep and progresses gradually to stage 4 sleep. Sleep stages 1 through 4 constitute *slow-wave sleep,* or non-REM sleep. Most dreaming occurs when people enter *rapid eye movement (REM) sleep.* The sleeping person cycles through these stages several times each night, gradually spending more time in stage 2 and REM sleep later in the night.

Sleep Disorders

Sleep disorders can disrupt the natural rhythm of sleep. Among the most common is *insomnia*, in which one feels tired because of trouble falling asleep or staying asleep. *Narcolepsy* produces sudden daytime sleeping episodes. In *sleep apnea*, people briefly, but repeatedly, stop breathing during sleep. *Sudden infant death syndrome (SIDS)* may be due to brain abnormalities or accidental suffocation. *Nightmares* and *night terrors* are different kinds of frightening dreams. *Sleepwalking* occurs most frequently during childhood. *REM behavior disorder* is potentially dangerous because it allows people to act out REM dreams.

Why Do People Sleep?

The cycle of waking and sleeping is a natural *circadian rhythm*, controlled by the suprachiasmatic nuclei in the brain. *Jet lag* can be one result of disrupting the normal sleep-wake cycle. The purpose of sleep is much debated. Non-REM sleep may aid bodily rest and repair. REM sleep may help maintain activity in brain areas that provide daytime alertness, or it may allow the brain to "check circuits" and solidify learning from the previous day.

Dreams and Dreaming

Dreams are story-like sequences of images, sensations, and perceptions that occur during sleep. Evidence from research on *lucid dreaming* suggests that people may sometimes be able to control their own dream content. Some claim that dreams are the meaningless byproducts of brain activity, but dreams may still have psychological significance.

Hypnosis

Hypnosis is a well-known but still poorly understood phenomenon.

Experiencing Hypnosis

Tests of hypnotic susceptibility suggest that some people cannot be hypnotized. Hypnotized people tend to focus attention on the hypnotist and passively follow instructions. They become very good at fantasizing and role taking. They may exhibit apparent age regression, experience posthypnotic amnesia, and obey posthypnotic suggestions.

Explaining Hypnosis

State theory sees hypnosis as a special state of consciousness. *Role theory* suggests that hypnosis creates a special social role that gives people permission to act in unusual ways. *Dissociation theory* combines aspects of role and state theories, suggesting that hypnotic participants enter into a social contract with the hypnotist to allow normally integrated mental processes to become dissociated and to share control over these processes.

Applications of Hypnosis

Hypnosis is useful in the control of pain and the reduction of nausea associated with cancer chemotherapy. Its use as a memory aid is open to serious question.

Psychoactive Drugs

Psychoactive drugs affect the brain, changing consciousness and other psychological processes. *Psychopharmacology* is the field that studies drug effects and their mechanisms.

Psychopharmacology

Psychoactive drugs exert their effects primarily by influencing specific neurotransmitter systems and, hence, certain brain activities. To reach brain tissue, drugs must cross the *blood-brain barrier*. Drugs that mimic the receptor effects of a neurotransmitter are called *agonists,* and drugs that block the receptor effects of a neurotransmitter are called *antagonists*. Some drugs alter the release or removal of specific neurotransmitters, thus affecting the amount of neurotransmitter available for receptor effects.

The Varying Effects of Drugs

Adverse effects such as *substance abuse* often accompany the use of psychoactive drugs. *Psychological dependence, physical dependence (addiction), tolerance,* and a *withdrawal syndrome* may result. Drugs that produce dependence share the property of directly stimulating certain areas of the brain known as pleasure centers. The consequences of using a psychoactive drug depend both on how the drug affects neurotransmitters and on the user's expectations.

Depressants

Alcohol and barbiturates are examples of *depressants*. They reduce activity in the central nervous system, often by enhancing the action of inhibitory neurotransmitters. They have considerable potential for producing both psychological and physical dependence.

Stimulants

Stimulants such as amphetamines and cocaine increase behavioral and mental activity mainly by increasing the action of dopamine and norepinephrine. These drugs can produce both psychological and physical dependence. Caffeine, one of the world's most popular stimulants, may also create dependency. Nicotine is a potent stimulant. MDMA is one of several psychoactive drugs that can permanently damage brain tissue.

Opiates

Opiates such as opium, morphine, and heroin are highly addictive drugs that induce sleep and relieve pain.

Hallucinogens

LSD, ketamine, and marijuana are examples of *hallucinogens,* or psychedelics. Hallucinogens alter consciousness by producing a temporary loss of contact with reality and changes in emotion, perception, and thought.

Cognitive Abilities

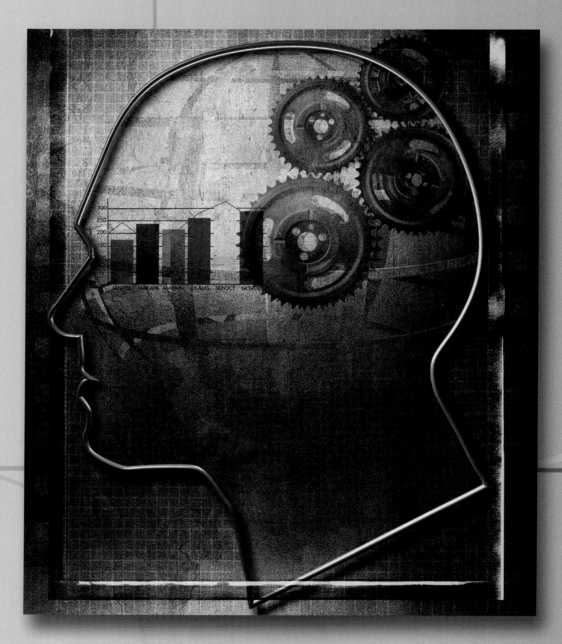

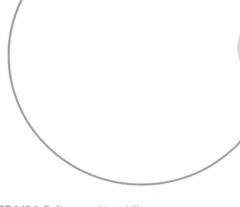

Consider the following sketches of four college seniors and their varying abilities and interests. Do any of these descriptions remind you of anyone you know? Do any of them sound like you?

Jack's big-city "street smarts" were not reflected in his high school grades. After testing revealed a learning disability, Jack worked to compensate for it, graduating with a grade-point average (GPA) of 3.78; but when he took the Scholastic Aptitude Test (SAT), his score was only 860 out of a possible 1600. He attended a local college, where he was given extra time to complete exams because of his learning disability. He held a half-time job throughout all four years, and his GPA was 2.95. When he completes his undergraduate degree, Jack will apply to master's degree programs in special education.

Deneace earned straight As in public grade school. She attended a private high school, where she placed in the top fifth of her class and played the violin. Her SAT score was 1340, but because her school did not give letter grades, she had no grade-point average to include in college applications. Instead, she submitted teachers' evaluations and a portfolio containing papers and class projects. Deneace was accepted at several prestigious small colleges, but not at major research universities. She is enrolled in a pre-med program, and with a GPA of 3.60, Deneace is hoping to be accepted by a medical school.

Ruthie has a wide range of interests and many friends, loves physical activities, and can talk to anybody about almost anything. Her high school grades, however, were only fair, averaging 2.60; but she played four sports, was captain of the state champion volleyball team, and was vice president of her senior class. She scored rather poorly on the SAT but received an athletic scholarship at a large university. She majored in sociology and minored in sport psychology. Focusing on just one sport helped her achieve a 3.25 GPA. She has applied to graduate schools but has also looked into a job as a city recreation director.

George showed an early interest in computers. In high school, he earned straight As in math, art, and shop, but his overall GPA was only 2.55, and he didn't get along with other students. Everyone was surprised when he scored 1320 on the SAT and went on to major in math and computer science at a large public university. His grades suffered initially as he began to spend time with people who shared his interests, but his GPA is now 3.33. He writes computer animation software and has applied to graduate programs in fields relating to artificial intelligence and human factors engineering.

Before reading further, rank these four people on **cognitive ability**—the capacity to reason, remember, understand, solve problems, and make decisions. Who came out on top? Now ask a friend to do the same, and see if your rankings match. They may not, because each of the four students excels in different ways.

Deneace might score highest on general intelligence tests, which emphasize remembering, reasoning, and verbal and mathematical abilities. But would these tests measure Ruthie's social skills, Jack's street smarts, or George's artistic ability? If you were hiring an employee or evaluating a student, what characteristics would you want a test to measure? Can test scores be compared without consideration of social and academic background? The answers to these questions are important. Research on cognitive abilities helps us to understand human cognition and which factors help or hinder people's ability to learn from and adapt to their environment; and as our examples illustrate, measures of cognitive abilities often determine the educational and employment opportunities people have or don't have.

cognitive ability The capacity to reason, remember, understand, solve problems, and make decisions.

As you can see from its definition, *cognitive ability* is a very broad term. In this chapter, we will focus mainly on one aspect of it, known as *intelligence*. Like many other concepts in psychology, intelligence cannot be directly observed. Therefore, we must draw inferences about it from what can be observed and measured—namely, from scores on tests designed to assess intelligence.

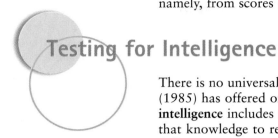

Testing for Intelligence   *Videodisc Segment & Still:* Correlations of IQ Scores

OBJ 10.2: Define intelligence. Discuss the reasons that intelligence is so difficult to define.

Test Items 10.2–10.3

Personal Learning Activity 10.1

Essay Q 10.1

OBJ 10.3: Discuss the history of intelligence test, or IQ test, construction. Explain the scoring methods used in the Binet and Stanford-Binet intelligence tests.

Test Items 10.4–10.13

OBJ 10.4: Discuss the use and abuse of intelligence testing in the United States in the early 1900s.

Test Items 10.14–10.17

ClassPrep PPTs 4 & 5: A Brief History of Intelligence Tests

There is no universally agreed upon definition of *intelligence,* but Robert Sternberg (1985) has offered one that is accepted by many psychologists. Sternberg says that **intelligence** includes three main characteristics: having knowledge, efficiently using that knowledge to reason about the world, and using that reasoning adaptively in different environments. Standard tests of intelligence measure some of these characteristics, but they don't address all of them. Accordingly, some psychologists argue that these tools are not able to capture all that should be tested if we want to get a complete picture of someone's intelligence in its broadest sense. To better understand the controversy, let's take a look at how standard intelligence tests were created, what they are designed to measure, and how well they do their job.

ClassPrep PPT 3: What Is Intelligence?

A Brief History of Intelligence Tests

The story of modern intelligence tests begins in France in 1904, when the French government appointed psychologist Alfred Binet to a commission charged with identifying, studying, and providing special educational programs for children who were not doing well in school. As part of his work, Binet developed a set of test items that provided the model for today's intelligence tests. Binet assumed that intelligence is involved in many reasoning, thinking, and problem-solving activities. Therefore, he looked for tasks that would highlight differences in children's ability to reason, judge, and solve problems (Binet & Simon, 1905). His test included tasks such as unwrapping a piece of candy, repeating numbers or sentences from memory, and identifying familiar objects (Rogers, 1995). Binet also assumed that children's abilities increase with age. He tested the items on children of various ages and then categorized items according to the age at which the typical child could respond correctly. For example, a "six-year-old item" was one that a substantial majority of six-year-olds could answer. Binet's test was thus a set of age-graded items. It measured a child's "mental level"—now called *mental age*—by determining the age level of the most advanced items a child could consistently answer correctly. Children whose mental age equaled their actual age, or *chronological age,* were considered to be of "regular" intelligence (Schultz & Schultz, 2000).

About a decade after Binet published his test, Lewis Terman at Stanford University developed an English version known as the **Stanford-Binet** (Terman, 1916). Table 10.1 gives examples of the kinds of items included on this test. Terman added items to measure the intelligence of adults and revised the scoring procedure. Mental age was divided by chronological age, and the result, multiplied by 100, was called the *intelligence quotient,* or *IQ.* So a child whose mental age and chronological age were equal would have an IQ of 100, which is considered "average" intelligence. A ten-year-old who scored at the mental age of twelve would have an IQ of $12/10 \times 100 = 120$. From this method of scoring came the term **IQ test,** a name that is widely used for any test designed to measure intelligence on an objective, standardized scale.

This scoring method allowed testers to rank people on IQ, which was seen as an important advantage by Terman and others who promoted the test in the United States. Unlike Binet—who believed that intelligence improved with practice—they saw intelligence as a fixed and inherited entity, and they believed that IQ tests could pinpoint who did and who did not have a suitable amount of intelligence. These

intelligence   Those attributes that center around reasoning skills, knowledge of one's culture, and the ability to arrive at innovative solutions to problems.

Stanford-Binet   A test for determining a person's intelligence quotient, or IQ.

IQ test   A test designed to measure intelligence on an objective, standardized scale.

Here are samples of the types of items included on Lewis Terman's original Stanford-Binet test. As in Alfred Binet's test, an age level was assigned to each item.

table 10.1
The Stanford-Binet

Age	Task
2	Place geometric shapes into corresponding openings; identify body parts; stack blocks; identify common objects.
4	Name objects from memory; complete analogies (e.g., fire is hot; ice is _____); identify objects of similar shape; answer simple questions (e.g., "Why do we have schools?").
6	Define simple words; explain differences (e.g., between a fish and a horse); identify missing parts of a picture; count out objects.
8	Answer questions about a simple story; identify absurdities (e.g., in statements like "John had to walk on crutches because he hurt his arm"); explain similarities and differences among objects; tell how to handle certain situations (e.g., finding a stray puppy).
10	Define more difficult words; give explanations (e.g., about why people should be quiet in a library); list as many words as possible; repeat 6-digit numbers.
12	Identify more difficult verbal and pictured absurdities; repeat 5-digit numbers in reverse order; define abstract words (e.g., *sorrow*); fill in a missing word in a sentence.
14	Solve reasoning problems; identify relationships among points of the compass; find similarities in apparently opposite concepts (e.g., "high" and "low"); predict the number of holes that will appear when folded paper is cut and then opened.
Adult	Supply several missing words for incomplete sentences; repeat 6-digit numbers in reverse order; create a sentence, using several unrelated words (e.g., *forest, business-like,* and *dismayed*); describe similarities between concepts (e.g., "teaching" and "business").

Source: Nietzel & Bernstein (1987).

beliefs were controversial because in some instances, they led to prejudicial attitudes and acts of discrimination as enthusiasm for testing outpaced understanding of what was being tested.

Actually, controversy over intelligence testing arose even before the Stanford-Binet was published. In 1910, the U.S. government asked Henry Goddard to help identify immigrants who might be mentally defective. Goddard (1917) created an English translation of Binet's test and then administered it to immigrants by orally translating each item into their native languages. Scores resulting from this error-prone procedure led to the conclusion that 83 percent of Jews, 80 percent of Hungarians, 87 percent of Russians, and 79 percent of Italians immigrating to America were "feeble-minded"! The fact that this was not a fair test is painfully obvious today; even Goddard came to doubt the accuracy of his conclusions and eventually retracted them (Schultz & Schultz, 2000). Some of the same testing problems remained when the United States entered World War I, in 1918. To assess the cognitive abilities of military recruits, the government asked a team of psychologists to develop the first group-administered intelligence tests. The Army Alpha test assessed abilities such as arithmetic, analogies, and general knowledge among recruits who could read English. The Army Beta test was for recruits who could not read or did not speak English; it measured ability using nonverbal tasks, such as

Coming to America   Early in the twentieth century, immigrants to the United States, including these new arrivals at Ellis Island in New York Harbor, were tested for both physical and mental frailties. Especially for those who could not read, speak, or understand English, the intelligence tests they took tended to greatly underestimate their intellectual capacity.

IRM Discussion 10.3: A Brief History of the Heredity Versus Environment Argument Regarding Intelligence

ClassPrep PPT 6: A Brief History of Intelligence Tests (cont.)

OBJ 10.5: Describe Wechsler's intelligence test. Explain why it is different from tests that were used previously. Define verbal and performance scales.

Test Items 10.18–10.22

OBJ 10.6: Describe the process of IQ test scoring used today to yield an intelligence quotient, or IQ score.

Test Items 10.23–10.27

intelligence quotient   An index of intelligence that reflects the degree to which a person's score on an intelligence test deviates from the average score of others in the same age group.

visualizing three-dimensional objects and solving mazes. Unfortunately, the verbal tests contained items that were unfamiliar to many recruits. Further, both versions were given in crowded rooms, where instructions were not always audible or, for non-English speakers, understandable. When 47 percent of the recruits scored at a mental age of thirteen years or lower (Yerkes, 1921), C. C. Brigham (1923) arrived at the incorrect conclusion that (1) from 1890 to 1915 the mental age of immigrants to America had declined and (2) the main source of this decline was the increase in immigration from southern and eastern Europe. Like Goddard, however, Brigham (1930) later retracted his statements (Gould, 1983).

In the late 1930s, David Wechsler (1939, 1949) developed new tests designed to improve on the earlier ones in three key ways. First, both verbal and nonverbal subtests were completed by all test takers. Second, knowing correct answers depended less on familiarity with a particular culture. Third, each subtest was scored separately, producing a profile that described an individual's performance in terms of several cognitive abilities.

ClassPrep PPT 7: Wechsler Adult Intelligence Scale–3rd Edition (WAIS-III)

Intelligence Tests Today

Today's editions of the Wechsler tests and the Stanford-Binet are the most widely used individually administered intelligence tests. The Wechsler Adult Intelligence Scale-Third Edition (WAIS-III) includes fourteen subtests. Seven of them measure verbal skills such as remembering a series of digits, solving arithmetic problems, defining vocabulary words, and understanding and answering general-information questions (e.g., What did Shakespeare do?). The other seven subtests have little or no verbal content; they are designed to measure performance skills such as manipulating materials and understanding the relationships between objects. These nonverbal subtests include tasks such as assembling blocks, solving mazes, arranging pictures to form a story, and completing unfinished pictures (Figure 10.1 shows examples of such performance items from a Wechsler test designed for children). Using the WAIS-III, the tester can calculate a verbal IQ, performance IQ, and a full-

figure 10.1

Performance Items Similar to Those on the Wechsler Intelligence Scale for Children (WISC-III-R)

Items like these are designed to measure aspects of intelligence that involve little or no verbal ability. The WISC-III-R contains six verbal subtests and seven performance tests.

Source: Simulated items similar to those in the Wechsler Intelligence Scales for Adults and Children. Copyright © 1949, 1955, 1974, 1981, 1991 by the Psychological Corporation. Reproduced by permission. All rights reserved.

ClassPrep PPT 8: Picture completion

ClassPrep PPT 9: Picture arrangement

ClassPrep PPT 10: Block design

ClassPrep PPT 11: Calculating IQ

Picture completion
What part is missing from this picture?

Picture arrangement
These pictures tell a story, but they are in the wrong order. Put them in the right order so that they tell a story.

Block design

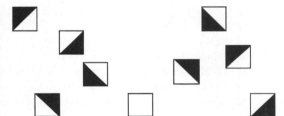

Put the blocks together to make this picture.

Taking the Wechsler Test Comparison of verbal and performance scores on the Wechsler test can be useful. For example, a high performance score and a low verbal score could mean that a child has a language deficiency. Knowing that this deficiency might account, in part, for the relatively low verbal score could help testers make more accurate inferences about the child's cognitive abilities.

Source: Simulated items similar to those in the Wechsler Intelligence Scales for Adults and Children. Copyright 1949, 1955, 1974, 1981, 1991, 1997 by The Psychological Corporation. Reproduced by permission. All rights reserved. Photo © Dan McCoy/ Rainbow.

scale IQ, as well as factor scores that reflect a person's *cognitive processing speed, working memory, perceptual organization,* and *verbal comprehension.*

Like the Wechsler scales, the latest edition of the Stanford-Binet also uses subtests. It provides scores on *verbal reasoning* (e.g., What is similar about an orange, an apple, and a grape?), *quantitative reasoning* (e.g., math problems), *abstract/ visual reasoning* (e.g., explaining why you should wear a coat in winter), and *working memory* (e.g., repeating a string of numbers in reverse order), along with an overall IQ score (Thorndike, Hagan, & Sattler, 2001).

If you take an IQ test today, your score will not be calculated by dividing your mental age by your chronological age and multiplying by 100. Instead, the points you earn for each correct answer are summed. Then the summed score is compared with the scores earned by other people. The average score obtained by people at each age level is *assigned* the IQ value of 100. Other scores are assigned IQ values that reflect how far each score deviates from that average. If you do better on the test than the average person in your age group, you will receive an IQ score above 100; how far above depends on how much better than average you do. Similarly, a person scoring below the age-group average will have an IQ below 100. This procedure may sound arbitrary, but it is based on a well-documented assumption about many characteristics: Most people's scores fall in the middle of the range of possible scores, creating a bell-shaped curve known as the *normal distribution,* shown in Figure 10.2. (The statistics appendix provides a fuller explanation of the normal distribution and how IQ tests are scored.) As a result of this scoring method, your **intelligence quotient,** or **IQ score,** reflects your *relative* standing within a population of your age.

figure 10.2

The Normal Distribution of IQ Scores in a Population

When the IQ scores in the overall population are plotted on a graph, a bell-shaped curve appears. The average IQ score of any given age group is 100. Half of the scores are higher than 100, and half are lower than 100. Approximately two-thirds of the IQ scores of any age group fall between 84 and 116; about one-sixth fall below 84, and one-sixth fall above 116.

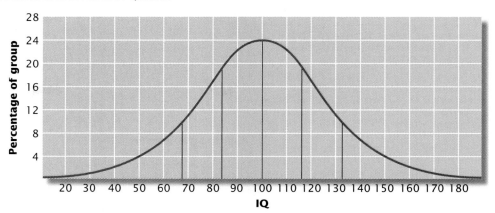

ClassPrep PPT 13: Aptitude and Achievement Tests

OBJ 10.7: Describe the differences between an aptitude test and an achievement test.

Test Items 10.28–10.31

Aptitude and Achievement Tests

Closely related to intelligence tests are aptitude and achievement tests. **Aptitude tests** are designed to measure a person's capability to learn certain things or perform certain tasks. Although such tests may contain questions about what you already know, their ultimate goal is to assess your *potential* to learn (Aiken, 1994). The *SAT* (originally called the *Scholastic Aptitude Test*), the *American College Testing Assessment (ACT),* and the verbal, quantitative, and analytic components of the *Graduate Records Examination (GRE)* are the aptitude tests most commonly used by colleges and universities in the United States to help guide decisions about which applicants to admit (e.g., Kuncel, Hezlett, & Ones, 2001). Corporations also use aptitude tests as part of the process of selecting new employees. These tests usually involve brief assessments of cognitive abilities; examples include the Otis-Lennon Mental Abilities Test and the Wonderlic Personnel Test (Aiken, 1994). Corporations may also use the General Aptitude Test Battery (GATB) to assess both general and specific skills ranging from learning ability and verbal aptitude to motor coordination and finger dexterity at computer or clerical tasks.

Schools and employers also commonly administer **achievement tests,** which measure what a person has accomplished or learned in a particular area. For example, schoolchildren are tested on what they have learned about language, mathematics, and reading (Rogers, 1995). Their performance on these tests is then compared with that of other students in the same grade to evaluate their educational progress. Similarly, college students' scores on the Graduate Record Examination's Subject Tests assess how much they have learned about the field in which they wish to pursue graduate work.

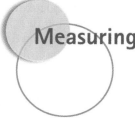

Measuring the Quality of Tests   **ClassPrep PPT 14:** Measuring the Quality of Tests

OBJ 10.8: Define test. Describe the advantages of tests over other evaluation methods.

Test Item 10.32

ClassPrep PPT 15: Advantages of Tests

A **test** is a systematic procedure for observing behavior in a standard situation and describing it with the help of a numerical scale or a system of categories (Cronbach, 1990). Any test, including an IQ test, should fairly and accurately measure a person's performance. Accordingly, schools and employers in the United States are required by law to use fair and accurate tests for placing students in particular classes and for choosing new employees.

Tests have two major advantages over interviews and other means of evaluating people. First, they are *standardized;* that is, conditions surrounding a test are as similar as possible for everyone who takes it. Standardization helps ensure, for example, that test results will not be significantly affected by who gives and scores the test. Incidental factors, such as variations in how a question is phrased, are also less likely to affect the results of standardized tests. Because the biases of those

OBJ 10.9: Define norms. Describe their usefulness.

Test Item 10.33

OBJ 10.10: Define reliability. Describe the process of assessing reliability using test-retest, alternate-forms, and split-half correlations. Give an example of each.

Test Items 10.34–10.46

OBJ 10.11: Define validity as well as content, construct, criterion, and predictive validity.

Test Items 10.47–10.60

IRM Activity 10.5: Test Validity

aptitude tests Tests designed to measure a person's capacity to learn certain things or perform certain tasks.

achievement tests Measures of what a person has accomplished or learned in a particular area.

test A systematic procedure for observing behavior in a standard situation and describing it with the help of a numerical scale or a category system.

norms Descriptions of the frequency at which particular scores occur, allowing scores to be compared statistically.

reliability The degree to which a test can be repeated with the same results.

validity The degree to which a test measures what it is supposed to measure and leads to correct inferences about people.

giving or scoring the test do not influence the results, a standardized test is said to be *objective*. Second, tests summarize the test taker's performance with a specific number, known as a *score*. Scores, in turn, allow the calculation of **norms,** which describe the frequency of particular scores. Norms tell us, for example, what percentage of high school students obtained each possible score on a college entrance exam and whether a particular person's score is above or below the average.

The two most important things to know about when determining the value of a test are its reliability and validity.

Reliability   ClassPrep PPT 16: Reliability

If you stepped on a scale, checked your weight, stepped off, stepped back on, and found that your weight had increased by twenty pounds, you would know it was time to buy a new scale. A good scale, like a good test, must have **reliability;** in other words, the results must be repeatable or stable. A test must measure the same thing in the same way every time. If you received a very high score on a reasoning test the first time you took it but a very low score when the test was repeated the next day, the test is probably unreliable. The higher the reliability of a test, the less likely it is that its scores will be affected by temperature, hunger, or other irrelevant changes in the environment or the test taker.

To estimate the reliability of a test, researchers usually get two sets of scores on the same test from the same people and then compute a *correlation coefficient* between the two (see the chapter on research in psychology and the statistics appendix). If the correlation is high and positive (usually above +.80 or so), the test is considered reliable. The two sets of scores can be obtained in several ways. In the *test-retest* method, a group of people take the same test twice. Using this method assumes, of course, that whatever is being measured will not change much between the two testings. If you practiced on your keyboard before taking a second test of typing skill, your second score would be higher than the first, but not because the test was unreliable. Using an *alternate form* of the test at the second testing can reduce this practice effect, but great care must be taken to ensure that the second test is truly equivalent to the first. Perhaps the most common approach is the *split-half* method, in which a correlation coefficient is calculated between each person's scores on two comparable halves of the test (Thorndike & Dinnel, 2001). Some researchers employ more than one of these methods to check the reliability of their tests.

Validity   ClassPrep PPT 17: Types of Validity

Imagine that your scale is reliable, giving you the same reading every time you step on it, but that it says you weigh thirty pounds. Unless you are a small child, this scale would provide a reliable but incorrect, or *invalid,* measure of your weight. Tests, like scales, can be reliable without being valid. In simplest terms, the **validity** of a test is reflected in the degree to which it measures what it is supposed to measure and leads to correct inferences about people (American Educational Research Association, American Psychological Association, and National Council on Measurement in Education, 1999; Anastasi, 1997). Assessing validity is not easy, partly because tests do not have "high" or "low" validity built into them. *The validity of a test depends on how it is used.* Suppose, for example, that you test people's intelligence by seeing how long they can hold their hands in ice water. This test's validity *as an intelligence test* would be low, because it does not measure what most of us think of as intelligence; it would not allow us to make accurate inferences about the cognitive abilities of the people tested. However, this same test might be a valid test of *pain tolerance,* because its results allow us to make accurate statements about people's sensitivity to discomfort. In other words, a test can be valid for one purpose but invalid for another.

A test's validity can be measured in several ways. For example, we can look at *content validity,* the degree to which the test's content is related to what the test is supposed to measure. If an instructor spends only five minutes out of forty lectures discussing the mating behavior of the tree frog and then devotes half of the final exam to this topic, that exam would be low on content validity. It would not allow us to make accurate inferences about students' learning in the course as a whole. Similarly, a test that measures only math skills would not have acceptable content validity as an intelligence test. A content-valid test includes items relating to the entire area of interest, not just a narrow slice (Lanyon & Goodstein, 1997).

Another way to evaluate a test's validity is to determine how well it correlates with an independent measure of whatever the test is supposed to assess. This independent measure is called a *criterion.* For example, a test of eye-hand coordination would have high *criterion validity* for hiring diamond cutters if scores on the test were highly correlated with a hands-on test of actual skill at diamond cutting. Why give a test if there is an independent criterion we can measure? The reasons often relate to convenience and cost. It would be silly to hire all job applicants and then fire those who are unskilled, if a ten-minute test could identify the best candidates. Criterion validity is called *predictive validity* when test scores are correlated with a criterion that cannot be measured until some time in the future—such as success in a pilot training program or grade-point average at graduation.

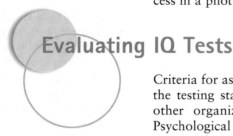

Evaluating IQ Tests   Sattler/Shabatay reader, 2/e: Assessment of Children

OBJ 10.12: Describe the results of checks on IQ test validity. Describe studies of the validity of IQ tests.

Test Items 10.61–10.66

IRM Activity 10.7: A Mock Intelligence Test

Criteria for assessing the reliability and validity of tests have been incorporated into the testing standards established by the American Psychological Association and other organizations (American Educational Research Association, American Psychological Association, and National Council on Measurement in Education, 1999). These standards are designed to maintain quality in educational and psychological testing by providing guidelines for the administration, interpretation, and application of tests in such areas as therapy, education, employment, certification or licensure, and program evaluation (Turner et al., 2001). Despite the best efforts of testers and test developers, however, scores on IQ tests must still be interpreted with caution, mainly because no one test can accurately measure all aspects of what various people think of as intelligence. So what does an IQ score say about you? Can it predict your performance in school or on the job? Is it a fair summary of your cognitive abilities? To scientifically answer questions like these, we must take into account not only the reliability and validity of the tests from which IQ scores come but also a number of sociocultural factors that might influence those scores.

ClassPrep PPT 18: Test Reliability and Validity

The Reliability and Validity of IQ Tests

The reliability and validity of IQ tests are generally evaluated on the basis of the stability, or consistency, of IQ scores (reliability) and the accuracy of these scores in measuring cognitive abilities associated with intelligence (validity).

How Reliable Are IQ Tests?
IQ scores obtained before the age of seven typically do not correlate very well with scores on IQ tests given later, for two key reasons: (1) Test items used with very young children are different from those used with older children, and (2) cognitive abilities change rapidly in the early years (see the chapter on human development). During the school years, however, IQ scores tend to remain stable (Mayer & Sutton, 1996). For teenagers and adults, the reliability of IQ tests is high, generally above +.90.

Of course, a person's score may vary from one time to another if testing conditions, degree of motivation or anxiety, physical status, or other factors change. For

If only measuring intelligence were this easy!

this reason, testers today do not make decisions about a person's abilities on the basis of a single score. Overall, though, modern IQ tests usually provide exceptionally consistent results—especially compared with most other kinds of mental tests.

How Valid Are IQ Tests?

If everyone agreed on exactly what intelligence is (having a good memory, for example), we could evaluate the validity of IQ tests simply by correlating people's IQ scores with their performance on particular tasks (in this case, memory tasks). IQ tests whose scores correlated most highly with scores on memory tests would be the most valid measures of intelligence. But because psychologists do not fully agree on a single definition of intelligence, they don't have a single standard against which to compare IQ tests. Therefore, they cannot say whether IQ tests are valid measures of intelligence. They can only assess the validity of IQ tests for *specific purposes*.

IQ tests appear to be most valid for assessing aspects of intelligence that are related to schoolwork, such as abstract reasoning and verbal comprehension. Their validity—as measured by correlating IQ scores with high school grades—is reasonably good, about +.50 (Brody & Ehrlichman, 1998).

In addition, there is evidence that employees who score high on tests of verbal and mathematical reasoning tend to perform better on the job (and are paid more) than those who earned lower scores (Borman, Hanson, & Hedge, 1997; Johnson & Neal, 1998). Later, we describe a study that kept track of people for sixty years and found that children with high IQ scores tended to be well above average in terms of academic and financial success in adulthood (Oden, 1968; Terman & Oden, 1947). IQ scores also appear to be highly correlated with performance on "real-life" tasks such as reading medicine labels and using the telephone book (Gottfredson, 1997).

So, by the standard measures for judging psychological tests, IQ tests have good reliability and reasonably good validity for predicting certain abilities, such as success in school. As noted earlier, however, an IQ score is not an infallible measure of how "smart" a person is. Because IQ tests do not measure the full array of cognitive abilities, a particular test score tells only part of the story, and even that part may be distorted. Many factors other than cognitive ability—including response to the tester—can influence test performance. Children might not do as well if they

IQ and Job Performance IQ scores are reasonably good at predicting the ability to learn job-relevant information and to deal with unpredictable, changing aspects of the work environment (Hunter, 1986)—characteristics that are needed for success in complex jobs such as the ones these Navy navigator trainees will undertake.

are suspicious of strangers, for example (Jones & Appelbaum, 1989). Test scores can also be affected by anxiety, motor disabilities, and language differences and other cultural barriers (Fagan, 2000; Steele, 1997). For example, older adults who worry about making mistakes in unfamiliar situations may fail to even try to answer some questions, thus artificially lowering their IQ scores (Zelinski, Schaie, & Gribben, 1977).

How Fair Are IQ Tests?   Our review of the history of intelligence testing in the United States suggests that early IQ tests were biased against people who were unfamiliar with English or with the vocabulary and experiences associated mainly with middle-class culture at the time. For example, consider the question "Which is most similar to a xylophone? (violin, tuba, drum, marimba, piano)." No matter how intelligent children are, if they have never had a chance to see an orchestra or to learn about these instruments, they may miss the question. Test designers today try to avoid obviously biased questions (American Educational Research Association, American Psychological Association, and National Council on Measurement in Education, 1999; Serpell, 2000). Furthermore, because IQ tests now include more than one scale, areas that are most influenced by culture, such as vocabulary, can be assessed separately from areas that are less vulnerable to cultural bias.

The solutions to many of the technical problems in IQ tests, however, have not resolved the controversy over the fairness of intelligence *testing*. The debate continues partly because results of IQ tests can have important consequences (Messick, 1982, 1989). Recall that intelligence tests were initially developed to identify and assist children with special educational needs. Yet today, such children may find themselves in special classes that not only isolate them from other students but also carry negative social labels. Obviously, the social consequences of testing can be evaluated separately from the quality of the tests themselves (Maguire, Hattie, & Haig, 1994); but those consequences cannot be ignored, especially if they tend to affect some groups more than others.

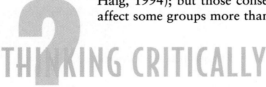

THINKING CRITICALLY

Are IQ Tests Unfairly Biased Against Certain Groups?

Despite attempts to eliminate cultural bias from IQ tests, there are differences in the average scores of various ethnic and cultural groups in the United States (e.g., Fagan, 2000; Herrnstein & Murray, 1994; Lynn, 1996; Taylor & Richards, 1991). Asian Americans typically score highest, followed, in order, by European Americans, Hispanic Americans, and African Americans. Similar patterns appear on a number of other tests of cognitive ability (e.g., Bobko, Roth, & Potosky, 1999; Sackett et al., 2001).

● **What am I being asked to believe or accept?**

Some critics of IQ tests argue that a disproportionately large number of people in some ethnic minority groups score low on IQ tests for reasons that are unrelated to cognitive ability, job potential, or other criteria that the tests are supposed to predict (Helms, 1992; Kwate, 2001; Neisser et al., 1996). They say that using IQ tests—and related cognitive aptitude tests—to make decisions about people may unfairly deprive members of some ethnic minority groups of equal employment or educational opportunities.

● **What evidence is available to support the assertion?**

Research reveals several possible sources of bias in tests of cognitive abilities. First, as noted earlier, noncognitive factors such as motivation, trust, and anxiety influence performance on IQ tests and may put certain groups at a disadvantage. Children from some minority groups may be less motivated to perform well on

IRM In Your Own Words 10.2: What Is
Intelligence? What Is Culture-Fair?

Essay Q 10.2

standardized tests and less likely to trust the adult tester (Bradley-Johnson, Graham, & Johnson, 1986; Jones & Appelbaum, 1989; Steele, 1997). Consequently, differences in test scores may reflect motivational differences among various groups.

Second, many test items are still drawn from the vocabulary and experiences of the dominant middle-class culture in the United States. As a result, these tests often measure *achievement* in acquiring knowledge valued by that culture. Not all cultures value the same things, however (Serpell, 1994). A study of Cree Indians in northern Canada revealed that words and phrases associated with *competence* included *good sense of direction;* at the incompetent end of the scale was the phrase *lives like a white person* (Berry & Bennett, 1992). A European American might not perform well on a Cree intelligence test based on these criteria. In fact, as illustrated in Table 10.2, poor performance on a culture-specific test is probably due more to unfamiliarity with culture-based concepts than to lack of cognitive ability. "Culture-fair" tests—such as the Universal Nonverbal Intelligence Test—that reduce, if not eliminate, dependence on language skills and other knowledge of a specific culture do indeed produce smaller differences between majority and minority groups than more traditional measures (Bracken & McCallum, 1998).

Third, some tests may reward those who interpret questions as expected by the test designer. Conventional IQ tests have clearly defined "right" and "wrong" answers. Yet a person may interpret test questions in a manner that is "intelligent" or "correct," but that produces a "wrong" answer. For example, when one child was asked, "In what way are an apple and a banana alike?" he replied, "Both give me diarrhea." The fact that you don't give the answer that the test designer was looking for does not mean that you *can't*. When rice farmers from Liberia were asked to sort objects, they tended to put a knife in the same group as vegetables. This was the clever way to do it, they said, because the knife is used to cut vegetables. When asked to sort the objects as a "stupid" person would, they grouped the cutting tools together, the vegetables together, and so on, much as most North Americans would (Segall et al., 1990).

● **Are there alternative ways of interpreting the evidence?**

The evidence might be interpreted as showing that although IQ tests do not provide an unbiased measure of cognitive abilities in general, they do provide a fair test of whether a person is likely to succeed in school or in certain jobs. In short, they may be biased—but not in a way that discriminates *unfairly* among groups. Perhaps familiarity with the culture reflected in IQ tests is just as important for success at school or work in that culture as it is for success on the tests themselves. After all, the ranking among groups on measures of academic achievement is similar to the ranking for average IQ scores (Sue & Okazaki, 1990). According to this view, it doesn't matter very much if tests that are supposed to measure intellectual aptitude actually measure culture-related achievement, as long as they are useful

ClassPrep PPT 45: *Table 10.2:* An Intelligence
Test?

TRY THIS How did you do on this "intelligence test"? If, like most people, you are unfamiliar with the material being tested by these rather obscure questions, your score was probably low. Would it be fair to say, then, that you are not very intelligent?

table 10.2
An Intelligence Test?

Take a minute to answer each of these questions, and check your answers against the key below.

1. What fictional detective was created by Leslie Charteris?

2. What planet travels around the sun every 248 years?

3. What vegetable yields the most pounds of produce per acre?

4. What was the infamous pseudonym of broadcaster Iva Toguri d'Aquino?

5. What kind of animal is Dr. Dolittle's pushmi-pullyu?

Answers: (1) Simon Templar (2) Pluto (3) Cabbage (4) Tokyo Rose (5) A two-headed llama.

in predicting whatever criterion is of interest. In fact, "culture-fair" tests do not predict academic achievement as well as conventional IQ tests do (Aiken, 1994; Humphreys, 1988).

● **What additional evidence would help to evaluate the alternatives?**

Evaluation of whether tests fairly or unfairly differentiate among people depends on whether the sources of test-score differences are relevant to predicting performance in the environment for which the test is intended. To take an extreme example, perhaps average differences in IQ scores between ethnic groups result entirely from certain test items that have nothing to do with how well the test as a whole predicts academic success. It is important to conduct research on this possibility.

Alternative tests must also be explored, particularly those that include assessment of problem-solving skills and other abilities not measured by most IQ tests (e.g., Sternberg & Kaufman, 1998). If new tests prove to be less biased than traditional tests but have equal or better predictive validity, many of the issues discussed in this section will have been resolved.

● **What conclusions are most reasonable?**

The effort to reduce unfair cultural biases in tests is well founded, but "culture-fair" tests will be of little benefit if they fail to predict success as well as conventional tests do. Whether one considers this circumstance good or bad, fair or unfair, it is important for people to have information and skills that are valued by the culture in which they live and work. As long as this is the case, tests designed to predict success in such areas are reasonable insofar as they measure a person's skills and access to the information valued by that culture.

Stopping at that conclusion, however, would mean freezing the status quo, whereby members of certain groups are denied many educational and economic benefits. As discussed later, if more attention were focused on combating poverty, poor schools, inadequate nutrition, lack of health care, and other conditions that result in lower average IQ scores and reduced economic opportunities for certain groups of people, many of the reasons for concern about test bias might be eliminated. In the meantime, researchers are working to develop ways to reduce unnecessary culture-specific content on IQ and other cognitive ability tests, to motivate test takers to do their best on these tests, and to base ability-related decisions on a combination of cognitive ability tests and other relevant measures. The goal of this work is to maximize the predictive validity of the testing process while also maximizing the ethnic diversity of the people selected through that process for important educational and occupational opportunities (Sackett et al., 2001).

IQ Scores as a Measure of Innate Ability

Years of research have led psychologists to conclude that both hereditary and environmental factors interact to influence cognitive abilities. For example, by asking many questions, bright children help generate an enriching environment for themselves; thus, innate abilities allow people to take better advantage of their environment (Scarr & Carter-Saltzman, 1982). In addition, if their own biologically influenced intelligence allows bright parents to give their children an environment that helps the development of intelligence, their children are favored by both heredity and environment.

Psychologists have explored the influence of genetics on individual differences in IQ by comparing the correlation between the IQ scores of people who have differing degrees of similarity in their genetic makeup and environment. For example, they have examined the IQ scores of identical twins—pairs with exactly the same genetic makeup—who were separated when very young and reared in different environments. They have also examined the scores of identical twins raised together.

ClassPrep PPT 20: IQ Scores as a Measure of Innate Ability

OBJ 10.14: Discuss the possible interpretations of evidence from correlational twin studies on the role of heredity and the environment in the development of intelligence.

Test Items 10.74–10.82

(You may want to review the Linkages section of the chapter on research in psychology, as well as the behavioral genetics appendix, for more on the research designs typically used to analyze hereditary and environmental influences.)

These studies find, first, that hereditary factors are strongly related to IQ scores. When identical twins who were separated at birth and adopted by different families are tested many years later, the correlation between their scores is usually high and positive, at least +.60 (Bouchard et al., 1990; McGue et al., 1993; Pederson et al., 1992). If one twin receives a high IQ score, the other probably will, too; if one is low, the other is likely to be low as well. However, studies of IQ correlations also highlight the importance of the environment (Scarr, 1998). Consider any two people—twins, siblings, or unrelated children—brought together in a foster home. No matter what the degree of genetic similarity in these pairs, the correlation between their IQ scores is higher if they share the same home than if they are raised in different environments, as Figure 10.3 shows (Scarr & Carter-Saltzman, 1982).

The role of environmental influences is also seen in the results of studies that compare children's IQ scores before and after environmental changes such as adoption. Generally, when children from relatively impoverished backgrounds were adopted into homes offering a more enriching intellectual environment—including interesting materials and experiences, as well as a supportive, responsive adult—they showed modest increases in IQ scores (Weinberg, Scarr, & Waldman, 1992).

A study of French children who were adopted soon after birth demonstrates the importance of both genetic and environmental influences. These children were tested after years of living in their adopted homes. Children whose biological parents were from upper socioeconomic groups (where higher IQ scores are more common) had higher IQ scores than children whose biological parents came from lower socioeconomic groups, regardless of the socioeconomic status of the adoptive homes (Capron & Duyme, 1989). These findings were supported by data from the Colorado Adoption Project (Cardon & Fulker, 1993; Cardon et al., 1992), and they suggest that a genetic component of children's cognitive abilities continues to exert an influence even in their adoptive environment. At the same time, when children from low socioeconomic backgrounds were adopted by parents who provided academically enriched environments, their IQ scores rose by twelve to fifteen points (Capron & Duyme, 1989). Other studies have also found that the IQ scores of adopted children were an average of fourteen points higher than those of siblings who remained with their biological parents in poorer, less enriching environments (Schiff et al., 1978).

figure 10.3

Correlations of IQ Scores

The correlation in IQ scores between pairs increases with increasing similarity in heredity or environment.

Source: Reprinted with permission from "Familial Studies of Intelligence: A Review," T. Bouchard et al., *Science,* Vol. 212, #4498, pp. 1055–9, 29 May 1981. Copyright © 1981 American Association for the Advancement of Science.

ClassPrep PPT 21: *Figure 10.3:* Correlations of IQ Scores

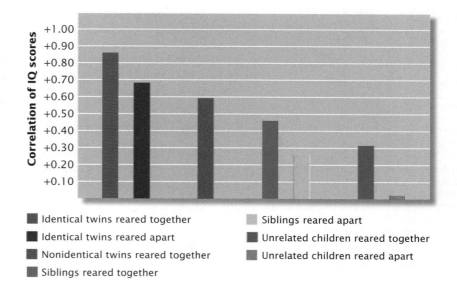

■ Identical twins reared together
■ Identical twins reared apart
■ Nonidentical twins reared together
■ Siblings reared together

■ Siblings reared apart
■ Unrelated children reared together
■ Unrelated children reared apart

figure 10.4

IQ Test Scores, Then and Now

Comparisons of performance on the Stanford-Binet IQ test reveal that today's children are answering more questions correctly than did children in the 1930s. In fact, the average child today would receive an IQ score of 120 on the 1932 test, a very high score! No one is sure why this increase in performance has occurred, but some psychologists suspect that better nutrition and improvements in education programs are partly responsible.

Source: Neisser (1998).

ClassPrep PPT 22: *Figure 10.4:* IQ Test Scores, Then and Now

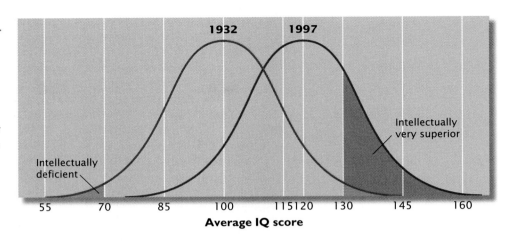

OBJ 10.15: Explain why a group intelligence score tells you nothing about the individuals in the group. Discuss the variables that affect group intelligence scores.

Test Items 10.83–10.88

Personal Learning Activity 10.4

Research on genetic and environmental influences can help us understand the differences we see *among* people in terms of cognitive abilities and other characteristics, but it cannot tell us how strong each influence is in any *particular* person.

Other factors that may have negative effects on cognitive abilities include poor nutrition, exposure to lead or alcohol, low birth weight, and complications during birth (Matte et al., 2001; Strathearn et al., 2001). In contrast, exposure to early interventions that improve school readiness and academic ability tend to improve children's scores on tests of intelligence (Neisser et al., 1996; Ripple et al., 1999). These intervention programs, some of which are described later, may be responsible for the steady increase in average IQ scores throughout the world over the past six decades (Flynn, 1999; Neisser, 1998). Note that this increase cannot be due to the influence of new and "better" genes, because genetic changes or mutations do not occur this rapidly in humans (see Figure 10.4).

Some researchers have concluded that the influence of heredity and environment on differences in cognitive abilities appears to be about equal; others see a somewhat larger role for heredity (Herrnstein & Murray, 1994; Loehlin, 1989; Petrill et al., 1998; Plomin, 1994b). One research team has even suggested that specific genes are associated with extremely high IQs (Chorney et al., 1998). Still, it must be emphasized that such estimates of the relative contributions of heredity and environment apply only to groups, not to individuals. It would be inaccurate to say that 50 percent of *your* IQ score is inherited and 50 percent learned. It is far more accurate to say that about half of the *variability* in the IQ scores of a group of people can be attributed to hereditary influences, and about half can be attributed to environmental influences.

Intelligence provides yet another example of nature and nurture working together to shape behavior and mental processes. It also illustrates how the relative contributions of genetic and environmental influences can change over time. Environmental influences, for example, seem to be greater at younger ages (Plomin, 1994b) and tend to diminish over the years. So IQ differences in a group of children will probably be affected more by parental help with preschool reading than by, say, the courses they take in junior high school ten years later.

Group Differences in IQ Scores

Much of the controversy over the roles played by genes and the environment in intelligence has been sparked by efforts to explain differences in the average IQ scores earned by particular groups of people. As noted earlier, for example, the average scores of Asian Americans are typically the highest among various ethnic groups in the U.S. (e.g., Taylor & Richards, 1991). Further, the average IQ scores of people from high-income areas in the United States and elsewhere are consistently higher than those of people from low-income communities with the same ethnic makeup (Fergusson, Lloyd, & Horwood, 1991; Jordan, Huttenlocher, & Levine, 1992; McLoyd, 1998; Murthy & Panda, 1987; Rowe, Jacobson, & Van den Oord, 1999).

To correctly interpret these differences and analyze their sources, we must remember two things. First, group scores are just that; they do not describe individuals. Although the mean IQ score of Asian Americans is higher than the mean score of European Americans, there will still be large numbers of European Americans who score well above the Asian American mean and large numbers of Asian Americans who score below the European American mean (see Figure 10.5).

Second, increases in IQ scores over the past sixty years (Flynn, 1999; Neisser, 1998) and other similar findings suggest that inherited characteristics are not necessarily fixed. A favorable environment may improve a child's performance somewhat, even if the inherited influences on that child's IQ are negative (Humphreys, 1984).

Socioeconomic Differences

Why should there be a relationship between IQ scores and socioeconomic status? Four factors seem to be involved. First, parents' jobs and status depend on characteristics related to their own intelligence, and this intelligence is partly determined by a genetic component that, in turn, contributes to their children's IQ scores. Second, parents' income affects their children's environment in ways that can increase or decrease IQ scores (Bacharach & Baumeister, 1998; MacKenzie, 1984; Suzuki & Valencia, 1997). Third, motivational differences may play a role. Parents in upper- and middle-income families tend to provide more financial and psychological support for their children's motivation to succeed and excel in academic endeavors (Atkinson & Raynor, 1974; Nelson-LeGall & Resnick, 1998). As a result, children from middle- and upper-class families may exert more effort in testing situations and therefore obtain higher scores (Bradley-Johnson, Graham, & Johnson, 1986; Zigler & Seitz, 1982). Some suggest that this effect is strongest in smaller families, where each individual child, or an only child, can receive more parental support for academic achievement (Downey, 2001), while others see siblings themselves as a potential source of additional motivation (Zajonc, 2001a). Fourth, because colleges, universities, and businesses usually select people who score high on various cognitive ability tests, those with higher IQs—who tend to do better on such tests—may have greater opportunities to earn more money (Sackett et al., 2001).

Ethnic Differences

Some have argued that the average differences in IQ scores among various ethnic groups in the United States are due mostly to heredity. Note, however, that the existence of hereditary differences *within* groups does not indicate whether differences *among* groups result from similar genetic causes (Lewontin, 1976). As shown in Figure 10.5, variation within ethnic groups is much greater than variation among the mean scores of those groups (Zuckerman, 1990).

figure 10.5

A Representation of Ethnic Group Differences in IQ Scores

The average IQ score of Asian Americans is about four to six points higher than the average score of European Americans, who average twelve to fifteen points higher than African Americans and Hispanic Americans. Notice, however, that the variation *within* these groups is much greater than the differences among their average scores.

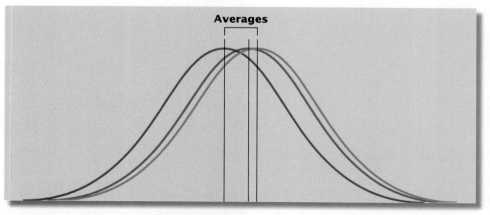

Averages

— African Americans and Hispanic Americans
— European Americans
— Asian Americans

ClassPrep PPT 25: Ethnic Differences

We must also take into account the significantly different environments in which the average child in various ethnic groups grows up. To take only the most blatant evidence, the latest U.S. Census Bureau figures show 22.1 percent of African American families and 21.2 percent of Hispanic American families living below the poverty level, compared with 9.4 percent of European American families (U.S. Census Bureau, 2001). Among children under age sixteen, the figures show about 15 percent of European Americans, 36 percent of African Americans, and about 36 percent of Hispanic Americans living below the poverty line. Compared with European Americans, African Americans are more likely to have parents with poor educational backgrounds, as well as inferior nutrition, health care, and schools (Wilson, 1997). All of these conditions are likely to pull down scores on IQ tests (Brooks-Gunn, Klebanov, & Duncan, 1996).

Evidence for the influence of environmental factors on the average black-white difference in IQ scores is supported by data from adoption studies. One such study involved African American children from disadvantaged homes who were adopted by middle- to upper-class European American families in the first years of their lives (Scarr & Weinberg, 1976). When measured a few years later, the mean IQ score of these children was 110. A comparison of this mean score with that of nonadopted children from similar backgrounds suggests that the new environment raised the children's IQ scores at least ten points. A ten-year follow-up study of these youngsters showed that their average IQ scores were still higher than the average scores of African American children raised in disadvantaged homes (Weinberg, Scarr, & Waldman, 1992).

As discussed in the chapter on human development, cultural factors may also contribute to differences among the mean scores of various ethnic groups. For example, those means may partly reflect differences in motivation based on how much value is placed on academic achievement. In one study of 15,000 African American, Asian American, Hispanic American, and European American high school students, parental and peer influences related to achievement tended to vary by ethnic group (Steinberg, Dornbusch, & Brown, 1992). The Asian American students received strong support for academic pursuits from both their parents and

Helping with Homework There are differences in the average IQ scores of European Americans and African Americans, but people who attribute these differences primarily to hereditary factors are ignoring a number of environmental, social, and other nongenetic factors that are important in creating, and that are now narrowing, this IQ gap.

their peers. European American students whose parents expected high academic achievement tended to associate with peers who also encouraged achievement, and they tended to do better academically than African American and Hispanic American students. The parents of the African American students in the study supported academic achievement, but because these students' peers did not, the students may have been less motivated, and their performance may have suffered. The performance of the Hispanic American students may have suffered because, in this study at least, they were more likely than the others to have authoritarian parents, whose emphasis on obedience (see the chapter on human development) may have created conflicts with the schools' emphasis on independent learning.

In short, it appears that some important nongenetic factors decrease the mean scores of African American and Hispanic American children. The currently narrowing gap between African American and European American children on tests of intelligence and mathematical aptitude may be related to changing environmental conditions for many African American children (College Board, 1994; Vincent, 1991). Whatever heredity might contribute to children's performance, it may be possible for them to improve greatly, given the right conditions.

Conditions That Can Raise IQ Scores

A number of environmental conditions can help or deter cognitive development (see the chapter on human development). For example, lack of caring attention or of normal intellectual stimulation can inhibit a child's mental growth. Low test scores have been linked with poverty, chaos, and noise in the home; poor schools; and inadequate nutrition and health care (Alaimo, Olson, & Frongillo, 2001; Kwate, 2001; Serpell, 2000; Weinberg, 1989). Can the effects of bad environments be reversed? Not always, but efforts to intervene in the lives of children and enrich their environments have had some success. Conditions for improving children's performance include rewards for progress, encouragement of effort, and creation of expectations for success.

In the United States, the best-known attempt to enrich children's environments is Project Head Start, a set of programs established by the federal government in the 1960s to help preschoolers from lower-income backgrounds. In some of these programs, teachers visit the home and work with the child and parents on cognitive skills. In others, the children attend classes in nursery schools. Some programs emphasize health and nutrition and, in recent years, family mental health and social skills as well (Murray, 1995). Head Start has brought measurable benefits to children's health, as well as improvements in their academic and intellectual skills (Barnett, 1998; Lee, Brooks-Gunn, & Schnur, 1988; Ramey, 1999). Closely related to Project Head Start are intervention programs for infants at risk because of low birth weight, low socioeconomic status, or low parental IQ scores. Such programs appear to enhance IQ scores by as much as nine points by the age of three; the effects appear especially strong for the infants of mothers with a high school education or less (Brooks-Gunn et al., 1992; Ramey et al., 2000; Wasik et al., 1990).

Do the gains achieved by preschool enrichment programs last? Although program developers sometimes claim long-term benefits (Schweinhart & Weikart, 1991), such claims are disputed (Spitz, 1991). Various findings from more than a thousand such programs are often contradictory, but the effect on IQ scores typically diminishes after a year or two (Woodhead, 1988). A study evaluating two of the better preschool programs concluded that their effects are at best only temporary (Locurto, 1991a). The fading of effects is probably due to reduced motivation, not loss of cognitive ability (Zigler & Seitz, 1982). Children may lose motivation when they leave a special preschool program and enter the substandard schools that often serve poor children.

Fading effects were also seen in programs such as the Abecedarian Project (Ramey, 1992). Children at risk for mental retardation were identified while they

OBJ 10.16: Describe the conditions that can raise IQ scores. Explain why a teacher's expectancies can affect students' classroom performance and improvement.

Test Items 10.89–10.93

Personal Learning Activity 10.5

IRM Discussion 10.9: Teacher Expectancy

ClassPrep PPT 26: Conditions That Can Raise IQ Scores

Project Head Start This teacher is working in Project Head Start, a U.S. government program designed to enrich the academic environments of preschoolers from lower-income backgrounds and improve their chances of succeeding in grade school.

were still in the womb. They then received five years of intense interventions to improve their chances of success once they entered school. When they started school, children in this enrichment program had IQ scores that were seven points higher than the scores of at-risk children who were not in the program. At age twelve, they still scored higher on IQ tests, but the size of the difference at that time was just five points. This difference was still evident nearly a decade later, when the participants were assessed recently at the age of twenty-one (Campbell et al., 2001).

Martin Woodhead (1988) concluded that the primary benefits of early-enrichment programs probably lie in their effect on children's attitudes toward school. One consistent, though very small, effect is that children who have taken part in enrichment programs are less likely to be held back in school or to need special-education programs (Locurto, 1991b; Palmer & Anderson, 1979). Especially in borderline cases, favorable attitudes toward school may help reduce the chances that children will be held back a grade or placed in special-education classes. Children who avoid these experiences may retain positive attitudes about school and enter a cycle in which gains due to early enrichment are maintained and amplified on a long-term basis (Myerson et al., 1998; Zigler & Styfco, 1994).

IQ Scores in the Classroom

IQ scores do not act as a crystal ball that can infallibly predict a person's destiny, nor are they a measure of some fixed quantity of cognitive ability. However, they can subtly affect how people are treated and how they behave. Decades ago, Robert Rosenthal and Lenore Jacobson (1968) argued that labels placed on students create teacher *expectancies* that can become self-fulfilling prophecies. This assertion was based on what happened after they gave grade school teachers the names of students who were about to enter a "blooming" period of rapid academic growth. These students had supposedly scored high on a special test, but the researchers had actually selected the "bloomers" at random. During the next year, however, the IQ scores of two-thirds of the bloomers dramatically increased, whereas only one-quarter of the other children showed the same increase. Apparently, the teachers' expectancies about certain children influenced those children in ways that showed up on IQ tests.

Some attempts to replicate Rosenthal and Jacobson's findings have failed (Elashoff, 1979); others have found that the effect of teacher expectancies, though statistically significant, is relatively small (Jussim, 1989; Snow, 1995). Still, there is little doubt that IQ-based teacher expectancies can have an effect on students (Rosenthal, 1994b). To find out how, Alan Chaiken and his colleagues (1974) videotaped teacher-child interactions in a classroom in which teachers had been informed (falsely) that certain pupils were particularly bright. They found that the teachers tended to favor the supposedly brighter students—smiling at them more often than at other students, making more eye contact, and reacting more positively to their comments. Children receiving extra social reinforcement not only get more intense teaching but are also more likely to enjoy school, to have their mistakes corrected, and to continue trying to improve. Later research found that teachers provide a wider range of classroom activities for students for whom they have higher expectations, suggesting another way in which expectancies might influence IQ scores (Blatchford et al., 1989).

These results suggest that the "rich get richer": Those perceived to be blessed with better cognitive abilities are given better opportunities to improve those abilities. There may also be a "poor get poorer" effect. Some studies have found that teachers tend to be less patient, less encouraging, and less likely to try teaching as much material to students whom they do not consider bright (Cooper, 1979; Trujillo, 1986). Further, differential expectations among teachers—and even parents—about the academic potential of boys and girls may contribute to gender differences in performance in certain areas, such as science (e.g., Crowley et al., 2001).

IQ tests have been criticized for being biased and for labeling people on the basis of scores or profiles. ("In Review: Influences on IQ Scores" lists the factors that can shape IQ scores.) "Summarizing" a person through an IQ score does indeed run the risk of oversimplifying reality and making errors, but intelligence tests can also *prevent* errors by reducing the number of important educational and employment decisions that are made on the basis of inaccurate stereotypes, false preconceptions, and faulty generalizations. For example, boredom or lack of motivation at school might make a child appear mentally slow, or even retarded. But a test of cognitive abilities conducted under the right conditions is likely to reveal the child's potential. The test can prevent the mistake of moving a child of average intelligence to a class for the mentally handicapped. And as Alfred Binet had hoped, intelligence tests have been enormously helpful in identifying children who need special educational attention. So despite their limitations and potential for bias, IQ tests can minimize the likelihood of assigning children to remedial work they do not need or to advanced work they cannot yet handle.

in review — Influences on IQ Scores

Source of Effect	Description	Examples of Evidence for Effect
Genetics	Genes appear to play a significant role in differences among people on IQ test performance.	The IQ scores of siblings who share no common environment are positively correlated. There is a greater correlation between scores of identical twins than between those of nonidentical twins.
Environment	Environmental conditions interact with genetic inheritance. Nutrition, medical care, sensory and intellectual stimulation, interpersonal relations, and influences on motivation are all significant features of the environment.	IQ scores have risen among children who are adopted into homes that offer a stimulating, enriching environment. Correlations between IQs of identical twins reared together are higher than for those reared apart.

LINKAGES (a link to Motivation and Emotion)

OBJ 10.17: Describe how emotional arousal affects the measurement of mental abilities. Define test anxiety and stereotype threat.

Test Items 10.94–10.96

IRM Activity 10.4: Performance Effects

ClassPrep PPT 43: *Figure 10.6:* The Stereotype Threat Effect

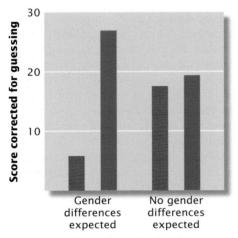

figure 10.6

The Stereotype Threat Effect

In this experiment, male and female college students took a difficult math test. Beforehand, some of the students were told that men usually outscore women on such tests. Women who heard this gender-stereotype information scored lower than women who did not hear it; they also scored lower than the men, even though their mathematical ability was equal to that of the men. Men's scores were not significantly affected by gender-stereotype information.

Emotionality and the Measurement of Cognitive Abilities

As mentioned earlier, factors other than cognitive ability can potentially influence scores on cognitive ability tests. One of the most important of these factors is emotional arousal. In the chapter on motivation and emotion, we note that people tend to perform best when their arousal level is moderate, whereas too much arousal, or even too little, tends to result in decreased performance. People whose overarousal impairs their ability to do well in testing situations are said to suffer from *test anxiety.*

These people fear that they will do poorly on the test and that others will think they are "stupid." In a testing situation, they may experience physical symptoms such as heart palpitations and sweating, as well as negative thoughts such as "I am going to blow this exam" or "They are going to think I am a real idiot." In the most severe cases of test anxiety, individuals may be so distressed that they are unable to successfully complete the test.

Test anxiety may affect up to 40 percent of elementary school students and about the same percentage of college students. It afflicts boys and girls equally (Turner et al., 1993). High test anxiety is correlated with lower IQ scores, and even among people with high IQ scores, those who experience severe test anxiety do poorly on achievement tests such as the SAT. Test-anxious grade school students are likely to receive low grades and to perform poorly on evaluated tasks and on those that require new learning (Campbell, 1986). Some children with test anxiety refuse to attend school or they "play sick" on test days, thus becoming caught up in a vicious circle that further harms their performance on standardized achievement tests.

Anxiety, frustration, and other emotions may also be at work in a testing phenomenon identified by Claude Steele and his colleagues. In one study, when test instructions were written in such a way as to cause bright African American students to become more sensitive to negative stereotypes about the intelligence of their ethnic group, these students performed less well on a standardized test than equally bright African American students whose sensitivity to the stereotypes had not been increased (Steele & Aronson, 1995). In another study, math-proficient women were randomly divided into two groups. The first group was given information that elicited concern over the stereotype that women are less good at math than men; specifically, they were told that men usually do better on the difficult math test they were about to take. The second group was not given such information. As shown in Figure 10.6, the women in the second group performed much better on the test than did those in the first. In fact, their performance was equal to that of men who took the same test (Spencer, Steele, & Quinn, 1997). Steele refers to this phenomenon as *stereotype threat* (Steele & Aronson, 2000): Concern over negative stereotypes about the cognitive abilities of the group to which they belong can impair the performance of some women—and some members of ethnic minorities—such that the test scores they earn underestimate their cognitive abilities (Blascovich et al., 2001; Inzlicht & Ben-Zeev, 2000).

The good news for people who suffer from test anxiety is that the counseling centers at most colleges and universities have effective programs for dealing with it. Test anxiety can be remedied through some of the same procedures used to treat other anxiety disorders (see the chapter on treatment of psychological disorders). There is also reason to be cautiously optimistic about reducing the impact of the stereotype threat phenomenon on the academic performance of African Americans and other minority groups. A program at the University of Michigan that directly addresses this phenomenon has produced substantial improvements in the grades of first-year minority students (Steele, 1997).

These and other research findings indicate that the relationship between anxiety and test performance is a complex one, but one generalization seems to hold true: People who are severely test anxious do not perform to the best of their ability on IQ tests.

Understanding Intelligence

We have said that standard IQ tests such as the Stanford-Binet and the Wechsler do not measure all aspects of intelligence. This is true because psychologists have taken several approaches to studying intelligence, some of which include a wider array of cognitive abilities than those focused on by Binet, Terman, and Wechsler. Let's consider these approaches and a few of the nontraditional intelligence tests that have emerged from some of them.

The Psychometric Approach

Standard IQ tests are associated with the **psychometric approach,** which is a way of studying intelligence that emphasizes the *products* of intelligence, including IQ scores. Researchers taking this approach ask whether intelligence is one general trait or a bundle of more specific abilities. The answer matters, because if intelligence is a single "thing," an employer might assume that someone with a low IQ could not do any tasks well. But if intelligence is composed of many independent abilities, a poor showing in one area—say, spatial abilities—would not rule out good performance in others, such as understanding information or solving word problems.

Early in the twentieth century, statistician Charles Spearman made a suggestion that began the modern debate about the nature of intelligence. Spearman noticed that scores on almost all tests of cognitive abilities were positively correlated (Spearman, 1904, 1927). That is, people who did well on one test also tended to do well on all of the others. Spearman concluded that these correlations were created by general cognitive ability, which he called *g,* for *general intelligence,* and a group of special intelligences, which he collectively referred to as *s.* The *s*-factors, he said, are the specific information and skills needed for particular tasks.

Spearman argued that people's scores on a particular test depend on both *g* and *s.* Further examination of test scores, however, revealed correlations that could not be explained by either *g* or *s* and were called *group factors.* Although Spearman modified his theory to accommodate these factors, he continued to assert that *g* represented a measure of mental force, or intellectual power.

In 1938, L. L. Thurstone published a paper criticizing Spearman's mathematical methods. Using the statistical technique of factor analysis, he analyzed the correlations among IQ tests to identify the underlying factors, or abilities, being measured by those tests. Thurstone's analyses did not reveal a single, dominating *g*-factor; instead, he found seven relatively independent *primary mental abilities:* numerical ability, reasoning, verbal fluency, spatial visualization, perceptual ability, memory, and verbal comprehension. Thurstone did not deny that *g* exists, but he argued that it was not as important as primary mental abilities in describing a particular person. Similarly, Spearman did not deny the existence of special abilities, but he maintained that *g* tells us most of what we need to know about a person's cognitive ability.

Raymond B. Cattell (1963) agreed with Spearman, but his own factor analyses suggested that there are two kinds of *g,* which he labeled *fluid* and *crystallized.* **Fluid intelligence,** he said, is the basic power of reasoning and problem solving. **Crystallized intelligence,** in contrast, involves specific knowledge gained as a result of applying fluid intelligence. It produces, for example, a good vocabulary and familiarity with the multiplication tables.

OBJ 10.18: Describe the psychometric approach to studying intelligence. Define *"g," "s,"* group factors, primary mental abilities, fluid intelligence, and crystallized intelligence. Give an example of each.

Test Items 10.97–10.110

ClassPrep PPTs 28 & 29: The Psychometric Approach to Understanding Intelligence

psychometric approach A way of studying intelligence that emphasizes analysis of the products of intelligence, especially scores on intelligence tests.

g A general intelligence factor that Charles Spearman postulated as accounting for positive correlations between people's scores on all sorts of mental ability tests.

s A group of special abilities that Charles Spearman saw as accompanying general intelligence *(g).*

fluid intelligence The basic power of reasoning and problem solving.

crystallized intelligence The specific knowledge gained as a result of applying fluid intelligence.

Who is right? After decades of research and debate, most psychologists today agree that there is a positive correlation among various tests of cognitive ability, a correlation that is due to a factor known as *g*. However, the brain probably does not contain some unified "thing" corresponding to what people call intelligence. Instead, it is suggested, cognitive abilities may be organized in "layers," beginning with skills that are narrow and specific and progressing through those that are broader and more general; *g* is the most general of all (Carroll, 1993).

The Information-Processing Approach

OBJ 10.19: Describe the information-processing approach to studying intelligence. Describe the role of attention in intelligence behavior.

Test Items 10.111–10.116

ClassPrep PPT 30: Information-Processing Approach to Understanding Intelligence

The **information-processing approach** analyzes the *processes* involved in intelligent behavior, rather than test scores and other *products* of intelligence (Das, 2002; Hunt, 1983; Naglieri et al., 1991; Vernon, 1987). Researchers taking this approach ask, What mental operations are necessary to perform intellectual tasks? What aspects depend on past learning, and what aspects depend on attention, working memory, and processing speed? In other words, the information-processing approach relates the basic mental processes discussed in the chapters on perception, learning, memory, and cognition to the concept of intelligence. Are there individual differences in these processes that correlate with measures of intelligence? More specifically, are measures of intelligence related to differences in the attention available for basic mental processes or in the speed of these processes?

The notion that intelligence may be related to attention builds on the results of research by Earl Hunt and others (Ackerman, 1994; Eysenck, 1987; Hunt, 1980). As discussed in the chapter on perception, attention represents a pool of resources or mental energy. When people perform difficult tasks or perform more than one task at a time, they must call on greater amounts of these resources. Does intelligent behavior depend on the amount of attention that can be mobilized? Early research by Hunt (1980) suggests that it does—that people with greater intellectual ability have more attentional resources available. There is also evidence of a positive correlation between IQ scores and performance on tasks requiring attention, such as mentally tallying the frequency of words in the "animal" category while reading a list of varied terms aloud (Stankov, 1989).

Another possible link between differences in information processing and differences in intelligence relates to processing speed. Perhaps intelligent people have "faster brains" than other people—perhaps they carry out basic mental processes more quickly. When a task is complex, having a "fast brain" might decrease the chance that information will disappear from memory before it can be used (Jensen, 1993; Larson & Saccuzzo, 1989). A fast brain might also allow people to do a better job of mastering material in everyday life and therefore to build up a good knowledge base (Miller & Vernon, 1992). Hans Eysenck (1986) even proposed that intelligence can be defined as the error-free transmission of information through the brain. Following his lead, some researchers have attempted to measure various aspects of intelligence by looking at electrical activity in particular parts of the brain (Deary & Caryl, 1993; Eysenck, 1994).

These hypotheses sound reasonable, but research suggests that only about 25 percent of the variation seen in people's performance on general cognitive abilities tests can be accounted for by differences in speed of access to long-term memory, the capacity of short-term and working memory, or other information-processing abilities (Baker, Vernon, & Ho, 1991; Miller & Vernon, 1992).

OBJ 10.20: Describe the triarchic theory of intelligence. Define analytic intelligence, creative intelligence, and practical intelligence.

Test Items 10.117–10.123

ClassPrep PPT 31, OHT: Sternberg's Triarchic Theory of Intelligence

The Triarchic Theory of Intelligence

According to Robert Sternberg (1988b, 1999), a complete theory of intelligence must deal with three different types of intelligence: analytic, creative, and practical intelligence. *Analytic intelligence,* the kind that is measured by traditional IQ tests, would help you solve a physics problem; *creative intelligence* is what you would use

information-processing approach An approach to the study of intelligence that focuses on mental operations, such as attention and memory, that underlie intelligent behavior.

Brainpower and Intelligence The information-processing approach to intelligence suggests that people with the most rapid information processors (the "fastest brains") should do best on cognitive ability tests, including IQ tests and college entrance exams. Research suggests, however, that there is more to intelligent behavior than sheer processing speed.

IRM Activity 10.10: Applying the Theories of Intelligence

triarchic theory of intelligence Robert Sternberg's theory that describes intelligence as having analytic, creative, and practical dimensions.

to compose music; and you would draw on *practical intelligence* to figure out what to do if you were stranded on a lonely road during a blizzard. Sternberg's **triarchic theory of intelligence** deals with all three types of intelligence.

Sternberg acknowledges the importance of analytic intelligence for success at school and in other areas, but he argues that universities and employers should not select people solely on the basis of tests of this kind of intelligence (Sternberg, 1996; Sternberg & Williams, 1997). Why? Because the tasks posed by tests of analytic intelligence are often of little interest to the people taking them and typically have little relationship to their daily experience; each task is usually clearly defined and comes with all the information needed to find the one right answer (Neisser, 1996). In contrast, the practical problems people face every day are generally of personal interest and are related to their actual experiences; they are ill-defined and do not contain all the information necessary to solve them; they typically have more than one correct solution; and there may be several methods by which one can arrive at a solution (Sternberg et al., 1995).

It is no wonder, then, that children who do poorly in school can nevertheless show high degrees of practical intelligence. Some Brazilian street children, for example, are capable of doing the math required for their street business, despite having failed mathematics in school (Carraher, Carraher, & Schliemann, 1985). And a study of avid race-track bettors revealed that even bettors whose IQ scores were as low as 82 were highly accurate at predicting race odds at post time by combining many different kinds of complex information about horses, jockeys, and track conditions (Ceci & Liker, 1986). In other words, their practical intelligence was unrelated to measures of their IQ.

Sternberg's theory is important because it extends the concept of intelligence into areas that most psychologists traditionally did not examine and emphasizes what intelligence means in everyday life. The theory is so broad, however, that many parts of it are difficult to test. Determining exactly how to measure practical "street smarts," for example, is a challenge that is now being addressed (Sternberg et al., 1995, 2001). Sternberg and his colleagues have developed new intelligence tests designed to assess analytic, practical, and creative intelligence, and there is some evidence that scores on these tests can predict success at some jobs at least as well as standard IQ tests (Leonhardt, 2000; Sternberg & Kaufman, 1998; Sternberg et al., 1995). Figure 10.7 provides examples of several items from Sternberg's test that are designed to measure practical and creative aspects of intelligence.

figure 10.7

Testing for Practical and Creative Intelligence

 Robert Sternberg argues that traditional IQ tests measure mainly analytic intelligence. Here are sample items from tests he developed that test practical and creative intelligence as well. The answers are given at the bottom of the figure. How did you do?

Source: Sternberg (1996).

PRACTICAL

1. Think of a problem that you are currently experiencing in real life. Briefly describe the problem, including how long it has been present and who else is involved (if anyone). Then describe three different practical things you could do to try to solve the problem. *(Students are given up to 15 minutes and up to 2 pages.)*

2. Choose the answer that provides the **best** solution, given the specific situation and desired outcome.

   John's family moved to Iowa from Arizona during his junior year in high school. He enrolled as a new student in the local high school two months ago but still has not made friends and feels bored and lonely. One of his favorite activities is writing stories. What is likely to be the most effective solution to this problem?

   A. Volunteer to work on the school newspaper staff.

   B. Spend more time at home writing columns for the school newsletter.

   C. Try to convince his parents to move back to Arizona.

   D. Invite a friend from Arizona to visit during Christmas break.

3. Each question asks you to use information about everyday things. Read each question carefully and choose the best answer.

   Mike wants to buy two seats together and is told there are pairs of seats available only in Rows 8, 12, 49, and 95–100. Which of the following is not one of his choices for the total price of the two tickets?

   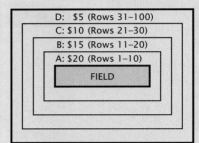

   A. $10.   **B.** $20.   **C.** $30.   **D.** $40.

CREATIVE

1. Suppose you are the student representative to a committee that has the power and the money to reform your school system. Describe your ideal school system, including buildings, teachers, curriculum, and any other aspects you feel are important. *(Students are given up to 15 minutes and up to 2 pages.)*

2. Each question has a "Pretend" statement. You must suppose that this statement is true. Decide which word goes with the third underlined word in the same way that the first two underlined words go together.

   Colors are audible.

   flavor is to *tongue* as *shade* is to

   A. ear.   **B.** light.   **C.** sound.   **D.** hue.

3. First, read how the operation is defined. Then, decide what is the correct answer to the question.

   There is a new mathematical operation called **flix**. *It is defined as follows:*

   $$A \text{ flix } B = A + B, \text{ if } A > B$$
   $$\text{but} \quad A \text{ flix } B = A \times B, \text{ if } A < B$$
   $$\text{and} \quad A \text{ flix } B = A / B, \text{ if } A = B$$

   How much is 4 flix 7?

   A. 28.   **B.** 11.   **C.** 3.   **D.** –11.

ANSWERS. Practical: (2) A, (3) B. Creative: (2) A, (3) A.

multiple intelligences Eight semi-independent kinds of intelligence postulated by Howard Gardner.

Multiple Intelligences

A Musical Prodigy? According to Gardner's theory of multiple intelligences, skilled artists, athletes, and musicians—such as the young pianist shown here—display forms of intelligence not assessed by standard intelligence tests.

Some people whose IQ scores are only average, or even below-average, may have exceptional ability in specific areas (Miller, 1999). One child whose IQ score was 50 could correctly state the day of the week for any date between 1880 and 1950 (Scheerer, Rothmann, & Goldstein, 1945). He could also play melodies on the piano by ear and sing Italian operatic pieces he had heard. In addition, he could spell—forward or backward—any word spoken to him and could memorize long speeches, although he had no understanding of what he was doing.

Cases of remarkable ability in specific areas constitute part of the evidence cited by Howard Gardner in support of his theory of **multiple intelligences** (Gardner, 1993). To study intelligence, Gardner focused on how people learn and use symbol systems such as language, mathematics, and music. He asked, Do these systems all require the same abilities and processes, the same "intelligence"? According to Gardner, the answer is no. All people, he says, possess a number of intellectual potentials, or intelligences, each of which involves a somewhat different set of skills. Biology provides raw capacities; cultures provide symbolic systems—such as language—to mobilize those raw capacities. Although the intelligences normally interact, they can function with some independence, and individuals may develop certain intelligences further than others. ("In Review: Analyzing Cognitive Abilities" summarizes Gardner's theory, along with the other views of intelligence we have discussed.)

The specific intelligences that Gardner (1998) proposes are (1) *linguistic* intelligence (reflected in good vocabulary and reading comprehension), (2) *logical-mathematical* intelligence (as indicated by skill at arithmetic and certain kinds of reasoning), (3) *spatial* intelligence (seen in understanding relationships between objects), (4) *musical* intelligence (as in abilities involving rhythm, tempo, and sound identification), (5) *body-kinesthetic* intelligence (reflected in skill at dancing,

in review	Analyzing Cognitive Abilities	
Approach	**Method**	**Key Findings or Propositions**
Psychometric	Define the structure of intelligence by examining factor analyses of the correlations between scores on tests of mental abilities.	Performance on many tests of mental abilities is highly correlated, but this correlation, represented by *g*, reflects a bundle of abilities, not just one trait.
Information processing	Understand intelligence by examining the mental operations involved in intelligent behavior.	The speed of basic processes and the amount of attentional resources available make significant contributions to performance on IQ tests.
Sternberg's triarchic theory	Understand intelligence by examining the information processing involved in thinking, changes with experience, and effects in different environments.	There are three distinct kinds of intelligence: analytic, creative, and practical. IQ tests measure only analytic intelligence, but creative intelligence (which involves dealing with new problems) and practical intelligence (which involves adapting to one's environment) may also be important to success in school and at work.
Gardner's theory of multiple intelligences	Understand intelligence by examining test scores, information processing, biological and developmental research, the skills valued by different cultures, and exceptional people.	Biology provides the capacity for eight distinct "intelligences": linguistic, logical-mathematical, spatial, musical, body-kinesthetic, intrapersonal, interpersonal, and naturalistic.

OBJ 10.21: Explain Gardner's theory of multiple intelligences. List the eight types of intelligences he proposed.

Test Items 10.124–10.132

Personal Learning Activity 10.3

ClassPrep PPTs 32 & 33: Gardner's Multiple Intelligences

athletics, and eye-hand coordination), (6) *intrapersonal* intelligence (displayed by self-understanding), (7) *interpersonal intelligence* (seen in the ability to understand and interact with others), and (8) *naturalistic* intelligence (the ability to see patterns in nature). Other researchers have suggested that people also possess *emotional* intelligence, which involves the capacity to perceive emotions and to link them to one's thinking (Meyer & Salovey, 1997). Gardner says that traditional IQ tests sample only the first three of these intelligences, mainly because these are the forms of intelligence most valued in school. To measure intelligences not tapped by standard IQ tests, Gardner suggests collecting samples of children's writing, assessing their ability to appreciate or produce music, and obtaining teacher reports of their strengths and weaknesses in athletic and social skills.

Gardner's view of intelligence is appealing, partly because it allows virtually everyone to be highly intelligent in at least one way. However, critics argue that including athletic or musical skill dilutes the validity and usefulness of the intelligence concept, especially as it is applied in school and in many kinds of jobs. Nevertheless, Gardner and his colleagues are working on new ways to assess potentially important multiple intelligences that are ignored by traditional IQ tests (Kornhaber, Krechevsky, & Gardner, 1990). The value of these methods will be decided by further research.

ClassPrep PPT 46: Focus on Research Methods

FOCUS ON RESEARCH METHODS

Tracking Cognitive Abilities over the Life Span

As described in the chapter on human development, significant changes in cognitive abilities occur from infancy through adolescence, but development does not stop there. One major study has focused specifically on the changes in cognitive abilities that occur during adulthood.

OBJ 10.22: Explain the differences between cross-sectional and longitudinal studies as tools for examining age-related changes in intelligence. Describe the cross-sequential with resampling design and the confounds for which it corrects.

Test Items 10.133–10.137

LINKAGES (a link to Research in Psychology)

OBJ 10.23: Describe the types of changes in intelligence that occur with aging.

Test Items 10.138–10.141

Freburg *Perspectives:* Greider, "Making Our Minds Last a Lifetime"

● What was the researchers' question?

The researchers began by asking what appears to be a relatively simple question: How do adults' cognitive abilities change over time?

● How did the researchers answer the question?

Answering this question is extremely difficult because findings about age-related changes in cognitive abilities depend to some extent on the methods that are used to observe those changes. None of the methods includes true experiments, because psychologists cannot randomly assign people to be a certain age and then give them mental tests. So changes in cognitive abilities must be explored through a number of other research designs.

One of these, the *cross-sectional study,* compares data collected simultaneously from people of different ages. However, cross-sectional studies contain a major confounding variable: Because people are born at different times, they may have had very different educational, cultural, nutritional, and medical experiences. This confounding variable is referred to as a *cohort effect.* Suppose two cohorts, or age groups, are given a test of their ability to imagine the rotation of an object in space. The cohort born around 1940 might not do as well as the one born around 1980, but the difference may not be due so much to declining spatial ability in the older people as to the younger group's greater experience with video games and other spatial tasks. In short, it may be differences in experience, and not just age, that account for differences in ability among older and younger people in a cross-sectional study.

Changes associated with age can also be examined through *longitudinal studies,* in which a group of people are repeatedly tested as they grow older. But

longitudinal designs have their own inherent problems. For one thing, fewer and fewer members of an age cohort can be tested over time as death, physical disability, relocation, and lack of interest reduce the sample size. Researchers call this problem the *mortality effect*. Further, the remaining members are likely to be the healthiest in the group and may also have retained better mental powers than the dropouts (Botwinick, 1977). As a result, longitudinal studies may underestimate the degree to which abilities decline with age. Another confounding factor can come from the *history effect*. Here, some event—such as a reduction in health care benefits for senior citizens—might have an effect on cognitive ability scores that is mistakenly attributed to age. Finally, longitudinal studies may be confounded by *testing effects,* meaning that participants may improve over time because of what they learn during repeated testing procedures. People who become "test wise" in this way might even remember answers from one testing session to the next.

As part of the Seattle Longitudinal Study of cognitive aging, K. Warner Schaie (1993) developed a design that measures the impact of the confounding variables we have discussed and thus allows corrections to be made for them. In 1956, Schaie identified a random sample of five thousand members of a health maintenance organization and invited some of them to volunteer for his study. These volunteers, who ranged in age from twenty to eighty, were given a battery of intelligence tests designed to measure Thurstone's primary mental abilities (PMA). The cross-sectional comparisons allowed by this first step were, of course, confounded by cohort effects. To control for those effects, the researchers retested the same participants seven years later, in 1963. Thus, the study combined cross-sectional with longitudinal methods in what is called a *cross-sequential with resampling design.* This design allowed the researchers to compare the size of the *difference* in PMA scores between, say, the twenty-year-olds and twenty-seven-year-olds tested in 1956 with the size of the *change* in PMA scores for these same people as they aged from twenty to twenty-seven and from twenty-seven to thirty-four. Schaie reasoned that if the size of the longitudinal change was about the same as the size of the cross-sectional difference, the cross-sectional difference could probably be attributed to aging, not to the era in which the participants were born.

What about the effect of confounding variables on the longitudinal changes themselves? To measure the impact of testing effects, the researchers randomly drew a new set of participants from their original pool of five thousand. These people were of the same age range as the first sample, but they had not yet been tested. If people from the first sample did better on their second PMA testing than the people of the same age who now took the PMA for the first time, a testing effect would be suggested. (In this case, the size of the difference would indicate the size of the testing effect.) To control for history effects, the researchers examined the scores of people who were the same age in different years. For example, they compared people who were thirty in 1956 with those who were thirty in 1963, people who were forty in 1956 with those who were forty in 1963, and so on. If PMA scores were the same for people of the same age no matter what year they were tested, it is unlikely that events that happened in any particular year would have influenced test results. The researchers tested participants six times between 1956 and 1991; on each occasion they retested some previous participants and tested others for the first time.

● What did the researchers find?

The results of the Seattle Longitudinal Study and other, more limited longitudinal studies suggest a reasonably consistent conclusion: Unless people are impaired by Alzheimer's disease or other brain disorders, their cognitive abilities usually remain about the same from early adulthood until about sixty to seventy years of age. Some components of intelligence, but not others, then begin to fail.

Crystallized intelligence, which depends on retrieving information and facts about the world from long-term memory, may continue to grow well into old age. *Fluid intelligence,* which involves rapid and flexible manipulations of ideas and

The Voice of Experience Even in old age, most people's crystallized intelligence remains intact. Their extensive storehouse of knowledge, experience, and wisdom makes older people a valuable resource for the young.

symbols, remains stable during adulthood and then declines in later life (Horn, 1982; Schaie, 1996). Among people over sixty-five or seventy, problems in several areas of information processing may impair problem-solving ability (Sullivan & Stankov, 1990). This decline shows up in the following areas:

1. ***Working memory.*** The ability to hold and organize material in working memory declines beyond age fifty or sixty, particularly when attention must be redirected (Parkin & Walter, 1991).

2. ***Processing speed.*** There is a general slowing of all mental processes (Salthouse, 1996, 2000). Research has not yet isolated whether this slowing is due to reduced storage capacity, impaired processing efficiency, problems in coordinating simultaneous activities, or some combination of these factors (Babcock & Salthouse, 1990; Salthouse, 1990). For many tasks, this slowing does not create obstacles. But if a problem requires manipulating material in working memory, quick processing of information is critical (Rabbitt, 1977). To multiply two 2-digit numbers mentally, for example, you must combine the subsums before you forget them.

3. ***Organization.*** Older people seem to be less likely to solve problems by adopting specific strategies, or mental shortcuts (Charness, 1987; Young, 1971). For example, to locate a wiring problem, you might perform a test that narrows down the regions where the problem might be. The tests carried out by older people tend to be more random and haphazard (Young, 1971). This result may occur partly because many older people are out of practice at solving such problems.

4. ***Flexibility.*** Older people tend to be less flexible in problem solving than their younger counterparts. They are less likely to consider alternative solutions (Salthouse & Prill, 1987), and they require more information before making a tentative decision (Rabbitt, 1977). Laboratory studies suggest that older people are also more likely than younger ones to choose conservative, risk-free options (Botwinick, 1966).

5. ***Control of attention.*** The ability to direct or control attention declines with age (Kramer et al., 1999). When required to switch their attention from one task to another, older participants typically perform less well than younger ones.

● **What do the results mean?**

This study indicates that different kinds of cognitive abilities change in different ways throughout our lifetime. In general, there is a gradual, continual accumulation of knowledge about the world, some systematic changes in the limits of cognitive processes, and qualitative changes in the way those processes are carried out. This finding suggests that a general decline in cognitive abilities during adulthood is neither inevitable nor universal.

● **What do we still need to know?**

An important question that the Schaie (1993) study leaves unanswered is why age-related changes in cognitive abilities occur. Some researchers suggest that these changes are largely due to a decline in the speed with which older people process information (Salthouse, 2000). If this interpretation is correct, it would explain why some older people are less successful than younger ones at tasks that require rapidly integrating several pieces of information in working memory prior to making a choice or a decision. Finally, it is vital that we learn why some people do *not* show declines in cognitive abilities—even when they reach their eighties. By understanding the biological and psychological factors responsible for these exceptions to the general rule, we might be able to reverse or delay some of the intellectual consequences of growing old.

Diversity in Cognitive Abilities

Although psychologists still don't agree on the details of what intelligence is, the study of IQ tests and intelligent behavior has yielded many insights into human cognitive abilities. It also has highlighted the diversity of those abilities. In this section we briefly examine some of that diversity.

OBJ 10.24: Discuss the relationship between creativity and intelligence. Define divergent and convergent thinking.

Test Items 10.142–10.151

Essay Q 10.3

Creativity   ClassPrep PPT 34: Creativity

If you watch *The Simpsons* on television, you have probably noticed that Bart writes a different "punishment" sentence on the blackboard at the beginning of every episode. To maintain this tradition, the show's writers have had to create a unique—and funny—gag sentence for each of the more than two hundred shows that have aired since 1989. In every area of human endeavor, there are people who demonstrate **creativity,** the ability to produce new, high-quality ideas or products (Simonton, 1999; Sternberg, 2001). Whether a corporate executive or a homemaker, a scientist or an artist, everyone is more or less creative (Klahr & Simon, 1999). Yet like *intelligence, creativity* is difficult to define (Amabile, Goldfarb, & Brackfield, 1990). Does creativity include innovation based on previous ideas, or must it be utterly new? And must it be new to the world, as in Pablo Picasso's paintings, or only new to the creator, as when a child "makes up" the word *waterbird* without having heard it before? As with intelligence, psychologists have defined *creativity* not as a "thing" that people have or don't have but rather as a process or cognitive activity that can be inferred from performance on creativity tests, as well as from the books and artwork and other products resulting from the creative process (Sternberg & Dess, 2001)

To measure creativity, some psychologists have generated tests of **divergent thinking,** the ability to think along many paths to generate many solutions to a problem (Guilford & Hoepfner, 1971). The Consequences Test is an example. It contains items such as "Imagine all of the things that might possibly happen if all national and local laws were suddenly abolished" (Guilford, 1959). Divergent-thinking tests are scored by counting the number of reasonable responses that a person can list for each item, and how many of those responses differ from other people's responses.

Of course, the ability to come up with different answers or different ways of looking at a situation does not guarantee that anything creative will be produced. Creative behavior requires divergent thinking that is *appropriate* for a given situation or problem. To be productive rather than just weird, a creative person must be firmly anchored to reality, understand society's needs, and learn from the experience and knowledge of others (Sternberg & Lubert, 1992). Teresa Amabile has identified three kinds of cognitive and personality characteristics necessary for creativity (Amabile, 1996; Amabile, Hennessey, & Grossman, 1986):

1. *Expertise* in the field of endeavor, which is directly tied to what a person has learned. For example, a painter or composer must know the paints, techniques, or instruments available.

2. A set of *creative skills,* including willingness to work hard, persistence at problem solving, capacity for divergent thinking, ability to break out of old problem-solving habits, and willingness to take risks. Amabile believes that training can influence many of these skills (some of which are closely linked to the strategies for problem solving discussed in the chapter on cognition and language).

3. The *motivation* to pursue creative production for internal reasons, such as satisfaction, rather than for external reasons, such as prize money. In fact,

Freburg *Perspectives:* Csikszentmihalyi, "The Creative Personality," and Critin, "That Fine Madness"

---

creativity   The capacity to produce new, high-quality ideas or products.

divergent thinking   The ability to think along many alternative paths to generate many different solutions to a problem.

Amabile and her colleagues found that external rewards can deter creativity (e.g., Amabile, Hennessey, & Grossman, 1986). In one study, they asked groups of children or adults to create artistic products such as collages or stories. Some were simply asked to work on the project. Others were told that their project would be judged for its creativity and excellence and that rewards would be given or winners announced. Experts, who had no idea which products were created by which group, judged those from the "reward" group to be significantly less creative. Similar effects have been found in many other studies (Deci, Koestner, & Ryan, 1999, 2001).

Is creativity inherited? To some extent, perhaps it is; but there is evidence that a person's environment—including the social, economic, and political forces in it—can influence creative behavior at least as much as it influences intelligence (Amabile, 2001; Nakamura & Csikszentmihalyi, 2001). For example, the correlation between the creativity scores of identical twins reared apart is lower than that between their IQ scores (Nichols, 1978). Do you have to be smart to be creative? Creativity does appear to require a certain degree of intelligence (Simonton, 1984; Sternberg, 2001), but it may not necessarily appear as an extremely high IQ score (Simonton, 1984). Correlations between scores on IQ tests and on tests of creativity are only modest, between +.10 and +.30 (Barron & Harrington, 1981; Rushton, 1990; Simonton, 1999). This result is not surprising, because creativity as psychologists measure it requires broad, divergent thinking, whereas traditional IQ tests assess **convergent thinking**—the ability to apply logic and knowledge in order to *narrow down* the number of possible solutions to a problem. The pace of research on creativity, and its relationship to intelligence, has picked up lately (Sternberg & Dess, 2001). One result of that research has been to define the combination of intelligence and creativity in the same person as *wisdom* (Sternberg, 2001; Sternberg & O'Hara, 1999).

Unusual Cognitive Ability   ClassPrep PPT 37: Unusual Cognitive Ability

Our understanding of cognitive abilities has been advanced by research on people whose cognitive abilities are unusual—people who are gifted, mentally retarded, or have learning disabilities (Robinson, Zigler, & Gallagher, 2000).

Giftedness
People with especially high IQ scores are often referred to as *gifted,* but this does not mean that they share exactly the same pattern of exceptional cognitive abilities. In one study, Robert Sternberg (2000) found that gifted people can display at least seven different combinations of the analytic, creative, and practical skills measured by his Triarchic Abilities Test.

Do all people with unusually high IQs become famous and successful in their chosen fields? One of the best-known studies of the intellectually gifted was conducted by Louis Terman and his colleagues (Oden, 1968; Sears, 1977; Terman & Oden, 1947, 1959). This study began in 1921 with the identification of more than 1,500 children whose IQ scores were very high—most higher than 135 by age 10. Periodic interviews and tests over the next 60 years revealed that few, if any, became truly creative geniuses—such as world-famous inventors, authors, artists, or composers—but only 11 failed to graduate from high school, and more than two-thirds graduated from college. Ninety-seven earned Ph.D.s; 92, law degrees; and 57, medical degrees. In 1955 their median family income was well above the national average (Terman & Oden, 1959). In general, they were physically and mentally healthier than the nongifted people and appear to have led happier, or at least more fortunate, lives (see the Focus on Research Methods section of the chapter on health, stress, and coping).

In short, although high IQ scores tend to predict longer, more successful lives (Whalley & Deary, 2001), an extremely high IQ does not guarantee special

OBJ 10.25: Describe the correlation between giftedness and success in our society. Define mental retardation, familial retardation, and metacognition.

Test Items 10.152–10.161

IRM Discussion 10.11: A Brief Note on Retardation and Giftedness

IRM Discussion 10.13: Savants

convergent thinking The ability to apply logic and knowledge to narrow down the number of possible solutions to a problem or perform some other complex cognitive task.

distinction. Some research suggests that gifted children are not fundamentally different from other children; they just have "more" of the same basic cognitive abilities seen in all children (Dark & Benbow, 1993). Other work suggests that there may be other differences as well, such as an unusually intense motivation to master certain tasks or areas of intellectual endeavor (Lubinski et al., 2001; Winner, 2000).

Sattler/Shabatay reader, 2/e: Hayakawa, "Our Son Mark," & Vigil, "I Don't Get Lost Very Often"

Mental Retardation   People whose score on an IQ test is less than about 70 *and* who fail to display the skill at daily living, communication, and other tasks expected of those their age have traditionally been described as *mentally retarded* (American Psychiatric Association, 1994). They now are often referred to as *developmentally disabled* or *mentally challenged*. People within this very broad category differ greatly in their cognitive abilities, as well as in their ability to function independently in daily life. Table 10.3 shows a classification that divides the range of low IQ scores into categories that reflect these differences.

Some cases of mental retardation have a clearly identifiable origin. The best-known example is *Down syndrome,* which occurs when an abnormality during conception results in an extra twenty-first chromosome (Hattori et al., 2000). Children with Down syndrome typically have IQ scores in the range of 40 to 55, though some may score higher than that. There are also several inherited causes of mental retardation. The most common of these is *Fragile X* syndrome, caused by a defect on chromosome 23 (known as the *X chromosome*). More rarely, retardation is caused by inheriting *Williams syndrome* (a defect on chromosome 7) or by inheriting a gene for *phenylketonuria,* or *PKU* (which causes the body to create toxins out of milk and other foods). Retardation can also result from environmental causes, such as exposure to German measles (rubella) or alcohol or other toxins before birth; oxygen deprivation during birth; and head injuries, brain tumors, and infectious diseases (such as meningitis or encephalitis) in childhood (U.S. Surgeon General, 1999).

These categories are approximate. Especially at the upper end of the scale, many retarded persons can be taught to handle tasks well beyond what their IQ scores might suggest. Furthermore, IQ is not the only diagnostic criterion for retardation. Many people with IQs lower than 70 can function adequately in their communities and so would not be classified as mentally retarded.

table 10.3
Categories of Mental Retardation

Level of Retardation	IQ Scores	Characteristics
Mild	50–70	A majority of all the mentally retarded. Usually show no physical symptoms of abnormality. Individuals with higher IQs can marry, maintain a family, and work in unskilled jobs. Abstract reasoning is difficult for those with the lower IQs of this category. Capable of some academic learning to a sixth-grade level.
Moderate	35–49	Often lack physical coordination. Can be trained to take care of themselves and to acquire some reading and writing skills. Abilities of a 4- to 7-year-old. Capable of living outside an institution with their families.
Severe	20–34	Only a few can benefit from any schooling. Can communicate vocally after extensive training. Most require constant supervision.
Profound	Below 20	Mental age less than 3. Very limited communication. Require constant supervision. Can learn to walk, utter a few simple phrases, and feed themselves.

The Eagle Has Landed In February 2000, Richard Keebler, twenty-seven, became an Eagle Scout, the highest rank in the Boy Scouts of America. His achievement is notable not only because only 4 percent of all Scouts reach this pinnacle but also because Keebler has Down syndrome. As we come to better understand the potential, and not just the limitations, of mentally retarded people, their opportunities and their role in society will continue to expand.

 LINKAGES (a link to Memory)

metacognition The knowledge of what strategies to apply, when to apply them, and how to deploy them in new situations.

Familial retardation refers to the 30 to 40 percent of (usually mild) cases in which there is no obvious genetic or environmental cause (American Psychiatric Association, 1994). In these cases, retardation appears to result from a complex, and as yet unknown, interaction between heredity and environment that researchers are continuing to explore (Croen, Grether, & Selvin, 2001).

In what ways are the cognitive skills of mentally retarded people deficient? Actually, they are just as good as others at recognizing simple stimuli, and their rate of forgetting information from short-term memory is no more rapid (Belmont & Butterfield, 1971). But mildly retarded people do differ from other people in three important ways (Campione, Brown, & Ferrara, 1982):

1. They perform certain mental operations more slowly, such as retrieving information from long-term memory. When asked to repeat something they have learned, they are not as quick as a person of normal intelligence.

2. They simply know fewer facts about the world. It is likely that this deficiency is a consequence of the third problem.

3. They are not very good at using particular mental strategies that may be important in learning and problem solving. For example, they do not spontaneously rehearse material that must be held in short-term memory.

What are the reasons for these deficiencies? In some ways, the differences between normal and retarded children resemble the differences between older and younger children discussed in the chapter on human development. Both younger children and retarded children show deficiencies in *metamemory*—the knowledge of how their memory works. More generally, retarded children are deficient in **metacognition:** the knowledge of what strategies to apply, when to apply them, and how to deploy them in new situations so that new specific knowledge can be gained and different problems mastered (Ferretti & Butterfield, 1989).

It is their deficiencies in metacognition that most limit the intellectual performance of mildly retarded people. For example, if retarded children are simply taught a strategy, they are not likely to use it again on their own or to transfer the strategy to a different task. It is important, therefore, to teach retarded children to evaluate the appropriateness of strategies (Wong, 1986) and to monitor the success of their strategies. Finally, like other children, retarded children must be shown that effort, combined with effective strategies, pays off (Borkowski, Weyhing, & Turner, 1986).

Despite such difficulties, the intellectual abilities of mentally retarded people can be improved to some extent. One program emphasizing positive parent-child communications began when the children were as young as thirty months old. It ultimately helped children with Down syndrome to master reading skills at a second-grade level, providing the foundation for further achievement (Rynders & Horrobin, 1980; Turkington, 1987). However, designing effective programs for retarded children is complicated because the way people learn depends not just on cognitive skills but also on social and emotional factors, including *where* they learn. Currently, there is debate about *mainstreaming,* the policy of teaching children with disabilities, including those who are retarded, in regular classrooms with children who do not have disabilities. Is mainstreaming good for retarded children? A number of studies of the cognitive and social skills of students who have been mainstreamed and those who were separated show few significant differences overall, although it appears that students at higher ability levels may gain more from being mainstreamed than their less mentally able peers (Cole et al., 1991).

Learning Disabilities   People who show a significant discrepancy between their measured intelligence and their academic performance may have a *learning disability* (National Information Center for Children and Youth with Disabilities, 2000). Learning disabilities are often seen in people with average or above-average IQs. For example, the problems with reading, writing, and math that Leonardo da Vinci and Thomas Edison had as children may have been due to such a disability; the problems certainly did not reflect a lack of cognitive ability!

There are several kinds of learning disabilities (Myers & Hammill, 1990; Wadsworth et al., 2000). People with *dyslexia* find it difficult to understand the meaning of what they read; they may also have difficulty in sounding out and identifying written words. *Dysphasia* is difficulty with understanding spoken words or with recalling the words one needs for effective speech. *Dysgraphia*—problems with writing—appears as an inability to form letters or as the omission or reordering of words and parts of words in one's writing. The least common learning disability, *dyscalculia,* is a difficulty with arithmetic that reflects not poor mathematical ability but rather an impairment in the understanding of quantity and/or in the comprehension of basic arithmetic principles and operations, such as addition and subtraction.

The National Joint Committee on Learning Disabilities (1994) suggests that these disorders are caused by dysfunctions in the brain; however, although brain imaging studies are helping to locate areas of dysfunction (e.g., Pugh et al., 2000; Richards et al., 2000), specific neurological causes have not yet been found. Accordingly, most researchers describe learning disabilities in terms of dysfunctional information processing (Kujala et al., 2001; Shaw et al., 1995). Diagnosis of a learning disability includes several steps. First, it is important to look for significant weaknesses in a person's listening, speaking, reading, writing, reasoning, or arithmetic skills (Brinckerhoff, Shaw, & McGuire, 1993). The person's actual ability is compared with that predicted by the person's IQ score. Tests for brain damage are also given. To help rule out alternative explanations of poor academic performance, the person's hearing, vision, and other sensory systems are tested, and factors such as poverty, family conflicts, and inadequate instruction are reviewed. Finally, alternative diagnoses such as attention deficit disorder (see the chapter on psychological disorders) must be eliminated.

An Inventive Genius When, as in the case of inventor Thomas Edison, students' academic performance falls short of what intelligence tests say they are capable of, a learning disability may be present. However, poor study skills, lack of motivation, and even the need for eyeglasses are among the many factors other than learning disabilities that can create a discrepancy between IQ scores and academic achievement. Accordingly, accurately diagnosing learning disabilities is not an easy task.

ClassPrep PPTs 41 & 42, OHT: Linkages

LINKAGES

As noted in the chapter that introduced psychology, all of psychology's subfields are related to one another. Our discussion of test anxiety illustrates just one way in which the topic of this chapter, cognitive abilities, is linked to the subfield of motivation and emotion (which is the focus of the chapter by that name). The Linkages diagram shows ties to two other subfields as well, and there are many more ties throughout the book. Looking for linkages among subfields will help you see how they all fit together and help you better appreciate the big picture that is psychology.

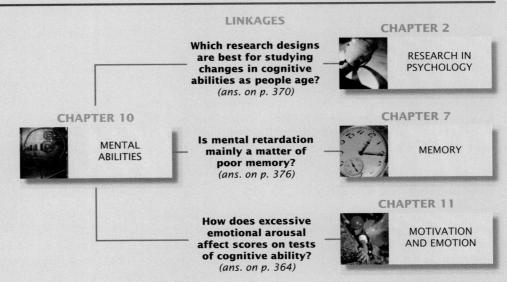

LINKAGES

Which research designs are best for studying changes in cognitive abilities as people age?
(ans. on p. 370)

CHAPTER 2
RESEARCH IN PSYCHOLOGY

CHAPTER 10
MENTAL ABILITIES

Is mental retardation mainly a matter of poor memory?
(ans. on p. 376)

CHAPTER 7
MEMORY

How does excessive emotional arousal affect scores on tests of cognitive ability?
(ans. on p. 364)

CHAPTER 11
MOTIVATION AND EMOTION

SUMMARY

Cognitive ability refers to the capacity to perform the higher mental processes of reasoning, remembering, understanding, problem solving, and decision making.

Testing for Intelligence

Psychologists have not reached a consensus on how best to define *intelligence*. A working definition describes intelligence in terms of reasoning, problem solving, and dealing with the environment.

A Brief History of Intelligence Tests

Alfred Binet's pioneering test of intelligence included questions that required reasoning and problem solving of varying levels of difficulty, graded by age. Lewis Terman developed a revision of Binet's test that became known as the *Stanford-Binet*; it included items designed to assess the intelligence of adults as well as children and became the model for *IQ tests*. Early IQ tests in the United States required not just cognitive ability but also knowledge of U.S. culture. David Wechsler's tests remedied some of the deficiencies of the earlier IQ tests. Made up of sub-tests, some of which have little verbal content, these tests allowed testers to generate scores for different aspects of cognitive ability.

Intelligence Tests Today

The Stanford-Binet and Wechsler tests are the most popular individually administered intelligence tests. Both include sub-tests and provide scores for parts of the test as well as an over-all score. For example, the Wechsler tests yield verbal, performance, and full-scale IQ as well as scores reflecting cognitive processing speed, working memory, perceptual organization, and verbal comprehension. Currently, a person's *intelligence quotient,* or *IQ score,* reflects how far that person's performance on the test deviates from the average performance by people in the same age group. An average performance is assigned an IQ score of 100.

Aptitude and Achievement Tests

Aptitude tests are intended to measure a person's potential to learn new skills; *achievement tests* are intended to measure what a person has already learned. Both kinds of tests are used by schools for the placement or admission of students and by com-panies for the selection of new employees.

Measuring the Quality of Tests

Tests have two key advantages over other techniques of evalua-tion. They are standardized, so that the performances of differ-ent people can be compared, and they produce scores that can be compared with *norms*.

Reliability

A good test must be *reliable*, which means that the results for each person are consistent, or stable. Reliability can be meas-ured by the test-retest, alternate-form, and split-half methods.

Validity

A test is said to be *valid* if it measures what it is supposed to measure and leads to correct inferences about people. A test's *validity* for a particular purpose can be evaluated in several ways, including the measurement of content validity or criterion validity; the latter entails measuring the correlation between the test score and some criterion. If the criterion is not measured until after the test is given, criterion validity is considered to be predictive validity.

Evaluating IQ Tests

The Reliability and Validity of IQ Tests

IQ tests are reasonably reliable, and they do a good job of pre-dicting academic success. However, IQ tests assess only some of the abilities that might be considered aspects of intelligence, and they may favor people most familiar with middle-class culture. Nonetheless, this familiarity is important for academic and occupational success.

IQ Scores as a Measure of Innate Ability

Both heredity and the environment influence IQ scores, and their effects interact. The influence of heredity is shown by the high correlation between IQ scores of identical twins raised in separate households and by the similarity in the IQ scores of children adopted at birth and their biological parents. The influ-ence of the environment is revealed by the higher correlation of IQ scores among siblings who share the same environment than among siblings who do not, as well as by the effects of environ-mental changes such as adoption.

Group Differences in IQ Scores

Average IQ scores differ across socioeconomic and ethnic groups. These differences appear to be due to numerous factors, including differences in motivation, family support, educational opportunity, and other environmental conditions.

Conditions That Can Raise IQ Scores

An enriched environment sometimes raises IQ scores. Initial gains in cognitive performance that result from interventions like Project Head Start may decline over time, but the programs may improve children's attitudes toward school.

IQ Scores in the Classroom

Like any label, an IQ score can generate expectations that affect both how other people respond to a person and how that person behaves. Children labeled with low IQ scores may be offered fewer or lower-quality educational opportunities. However, IQ scores help educators to identify a student's strengths and weaknesses and to offer the curriculum that will best serve that student.

Understanding Intelligence

The Psychometric Approach

The *psychometric approach* attempts to analyze the structure of intelligence by examining correlations between tests of cognitive ability. Because scores on almost all tests of cognitive ability are positively correlated, Charles Spearman concluded that such tests measure a general factor of mental ability, called *g*, as well as more specific factors, called *s*. As a result of factor analysis, other researchers have concluded that intelligence is not a single general ability but a collection of abilities and subskills needed to succeed on any test of intelligence. Raymond B. Cattell distinguished between *fluid intelligence*, the basic power of reasoning and problem solving, and *crystallized intelligence*, the specific knowledge gained as a result of applying fluid intelligence.

The Information-Processing Approach

The *information-processing approach* to intelligence focuses on the process of intelligent behavior. Varying degrees of correlation have been found between IQ scores and measures of the flexibility and capacity of attention, and between IQ scores and measures of the speed of information processing.

The Triarchic Theory of Intelligence

According to Robert Sternberg's *triarchic theory of intelligence*, there are three different types of intelligence: analytic, creative, and practical. IQ tests typically focus on analytic intelligence, but recent research has suggested ways to assess practical and creative intelligence.

Multiple Intelligences

Howard Gardner's approach to intelligence suggests that biology equips us with the capacities for *multiple intelligences* that can function with some independence—specifically, linguistic, logical-mathematical, spatial, musical, body-kinesthetic, intra-personal, interpersonal, and naturalistic intelligences.

Diversity in Cognitive Abilities

Creativity

Tests of *divergent thinking* are used to measure differences in *creativity*. In contrast, IQ tests typically require *convergent thinking*. Although creativity and IQ scores are not highly cor-related, creative behavior requires a certain amount of intelligence, along with expertise in a creative field, skills at problem solving and divergent thinking, and motivation to pursue a creative endeavor for its own sake.

Unusual Cognitive Ability

Knowledge about cognitive abilities has been expanded by research on giftedness, mental retardation, and learning disabilities. People with very high IQ scores tend to be successful in life, but they are not necessarily geniuses. People are considered mentally retarded if their IQ score is below about 70 and if their communication and daily living skills are less than expected of people their age. Some cases of retardation have a known cause; in familial retardation the mix of genetic and environmental causes is unknown. Compared with people of normal intelligence, retarded people process information more slowly, know fewer facts, and are deficient at *metacognition*—that is, at knowing and using mental strategies. Mentally retarded people can be taught strategies, but they must also be taught how and when to use those strategies. People who show a significant discrepancy between their measured intelligence and their academic performance may have a learning disability. Learning disabilities can take several forms and must be carefully diagnosed.

11

Motivation and Emotion

I n January 1994, despite temperatures reaching 30 degrees below zero, Brian Carr caught 155 fish, beating out 36 competitors to win the annual ice-fishing contest at upstate New York's Lake Como Fish and Game Club. He also netted the grand prize of $8 (Shepherd, 1994). Why would these people endure such harsh conditions in pursuit of such a paltry reward? Why, for that matter, do any of us do what we do? Why do we help others or ignore them, overeat or diet, haunt art museums or sleazy bars, attend college or drop out of high school?

These are questions about **motivation,** the factors that influence the initiation, direction, intensity, and persistence of behavior (Reeve, 1996). Psychologists who study motivation ask questions such as these: What prompts a person to start looking for food, to register for dance lessons, or to act in any other particular way? What determines whether a person chooses to go mountain climbing or to stay home and read? What makes some people go all out to reach a goal while others exert only halfhearted efforts and quit at the first obstacle?

Part of the motivation for behavior is to feel certain emotions, such as the joy of scaling a lofty peak or of becoming a parent. Motivation also affects emotion, as when hunger makes you more likely to become angry if people annoy you. In short, motivation and emotion are closely intertwined.

The first part of this chapter concerns motivation. We begin with some general theories of motivation and then discuss three specific motives—hunger, sexual desire, and the need for achievement. Next, we examine the nature of human emotion, as well as some major theories of how and why certain emotions are experienced. The chapter concludes with a discussion of how humans communicate their emotions to one another.

OBJ 11.1: Define motivation. Discuss the types of behaviors that motivation may help to explain.

Test Items 11.1–11.2

IRM Activity 11.4: Why Are You in School?

ClassPrep PPT 1: Motivation and Emotion

Freburg *Perspectives:* Frick, "Hire a Coach to Shape Up Your Life"

Concepts and Theories of Motivation   **ClassPrep PPT 2:** What Is Motivation?

The concept of motivation helps psychologists accomplish what Albert Einstein once called the whole purpose of science: to discover unity in diversity. Suppose that a man works two jobs, refuses party invitations, wears old clothes, drives a beat-up car, eats food others leave behind at lunch, never gives to charity, and keeps his furnace set at sixty degrees all winter. In trying to explain why he does what he does, you could propose a separate reason for each behavior: Perhaps he likes to work hard, hates parties, despises shopping for clothes and cars, enjoys other people's leftovers, has no concern for the poor, and loves cold air. Or you could suggest a **motive,** a reason or purpose that provides a single explanation for this man's diverse and apparently unrelated behaviors. That unifying motive might be the man's desire to save as much money as possible.

This example illustrates the fact that motivation cannot be observed directly; its presence is inferred from what we *can* observe. Psychologists think of motivation, whether it be hunger or thirst or love or greed, as an *intervening variable*—something that is used to explain the relationships between environmental stimuli and behavioral responses. The three different responses shown in Figure 11.1, for example, can be understood as guided by a single unifying motive: thirst. In order for an intervening variable to be considered a motive, it must be able to change behavior in some way. For example, suppose we arrange for some party guests to eat only salted peanuts and other guests to eat only unsalted peanuts. We will probably find that the people who ate salted peanuts drink more liquids, and perhaps take longer sips, than do those who ate the unsalted nuts. We can then explain differences in the initiation and intensity of drinking behavior in terms of differences in thirst.

Figure 11.1 shows that motivation can help explain why different stimuli can lead to the same response, and why the same stimulus can evoke different responses. Motivation also helps explain why behavior varies over time. For example, many people cannot bring themselves to lose weight, quit smoking, or exercise until they

OBJ 11.2: Define motive and intervening variables, and explain the latter's role in understanding motivation.

Test Items 11.3–11.4

motivation The influences that account for the initiation, direction, intensity, and persistence of behavior.

motive A reason or purpose for behavior.

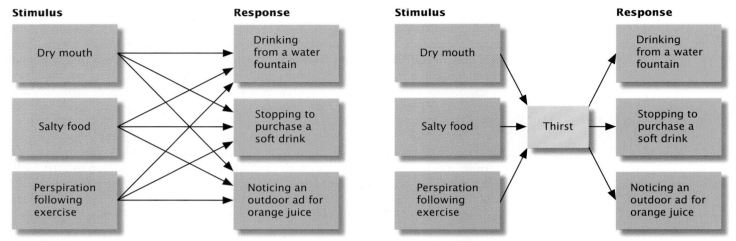

figure 11.1

Motives as Intervening Variables

Motives can act as explanatory links between apparently unrelated stimuli and responses. In this example, seeing thirst as the common motive provides an explanation for why each stimulus triggers the responses shown.

ClassPrep PPT 3, OHT: *Figure 11.1:* Motives as Intervening Variables

OBJ 11.3: Describe the sources of motivation.

Test Items 11.5–11.7

Essay Q 11.1

experience a heart attack or symptoms of other serious health problems. At that point, these people may suddenly start eating a low-fat diet, give up tobacco, and exercise regularly. In other words, because of changes in motivation, particular stimuli—such as ice cream, cigarettes, and health clubs—elicit different responses at different times.

Sources of Motivation   ClassPrep PPT 4: Sources of Motivation

The number of possible motives for human behavior seems endless. People are motivated to satisfy their needs for food and water, of course, but they have many other needs as well. Some people seek the pleasures of creativity, whereas many others are motivated by money or praise or power. And as social creatures, people are also influenced by motives to form emotional attachments to others, to become parents, and to join groups.

These and many other sources of human motivation fall into four general, somewhat overlapping categories. First, human behavior is motivated by basic *biological factors,* particularly the need for food, water, sex, and temperature regulation (Tinbergen, 1989). *Emotional factors* are a second source of motivation (Izard, 1993). Panic, fear, anger, love, and hatred can influence behavior ranging from selfless giving to brutal murder. Third, *cognitive factors* can motivate human behavior (Weiner, 1993). People behave in certain ways—becoming arrogant or timid, for example—partly because of these cognitive factors, which include their perceptions of the world, their beliefs about what they can or cannot do, and their expectations about how others will respond to them. Fourth, motivation may stem from *social factors,* that is, from reactions to parents, teachers, siblings, friends, television, and other sociocultural forces. The combined influence of these social factors in motivation has a profound effect on almost all human behavior (Baumeister & Leary, 1995). For example, have you ever bought a jacket or tried a particular hairstyle not because you liked it but because it was in fashion?

Psychologists have used various combinations of these factors to develop four prominent theories of human motivation. None of these theories can completely explain all aspects of how and why we behave as we do, but each of them—instinct theory, drive reduction theory, arousal theory, and incentive theory—helps tell part of the story.

Motivation and Emotion The link between motivation and emotion is obvious in many everyday situations. For example, her motivation to win the U.S. National Spelling Bee creates strong emotions in this contestant as she struggles with a tough word. And emotions can create motivation, as when anger leads a parent to become aggressive toward a child or when love leads that parent to provide for the child.

Fixed Action Patterns   The male three-spined stickleback fish attacks aggressively when it sees the red underbelly of another male. This automatic response is called a *fixed action pattern,* because it can be triggered by almost any red stimulus. These fish have been known to fly into an aggressive frenzy in response to a wooden fish model sporting a red spot, or even in response to a red truck driving past a window near their tank!

instinct theory   A view that explains human behavior as motivated by automatic, involuntary, and unlearned responses.
instincts   Innate, automatic dispositions toward responding in a particular way when confronted with a specific stimulus.

Instinct Theory and Its Descendants

Early in the twentieth century, many psychologists favored **instinct theory** as an explanation for the motivation of humans and animals alike. **Instincts** are automatic, involuntary behavior patterns consistently triggered, or "released," by particular stimuli (Tinbergen, 1989). Such behaviors are often called *fixed-action patterns* because they are unlearned, genetically coded responses to specific "releaser" stimuli. For example, these stimuli cause birds to build nests or engage in complex mating dances, and the birds do so perfectly the first time they try.

In 1908, William McDougall listed eighteen human instincts, including self-assertion, reproduction, pugnacity, and gregariousness. Within a few years, McDougall and others had named more than ten thousand more, prompting one critic to suggest that his colleagues had "an instinct to produce instincts" (Bernard, 1924). The problem was that instincts had become labels that simply describe what people do. Saying that someone gambles because of a gambling instinct, golfs because of a golfing instinct, and works because of a work instinct explains nothing about why these behaviors do or do not occur, how they developed, or the like.

Despite the shortcomings of early instinct theories, psychologists have continued to explore the possibility that at least some aspects of human motivation are innate. Their interest has been stimulated partly by research showing that a number of human behaviors are present at birth. Among these are sucking and other reflexes, as well as certain facial expressions, such as smiling. There is also the fact that people do not have to learn to be hungry or thirsty or to want to stay warm, and—as discussed in the chapters on learning and psychological disorders—that they appear to be biologically prepared to fear snakes and other potentially dangerous stimuli. Psychologists who take the evolutionary approach suggest that all such behaviors have evolved because they were adaptive for promoting individual survival; the individuals who possessed these behavioral predispositions were more likely than others to father or give birth to offspring. We are the descendants of these ancestral human survivors, so to the extent that our ancestors' behavioral predispositions were transmitted genetically, we should show similar predispositions. Even many aspects of human social behavior, such as helping and aggression, are seen by evolutionary psychologists as motivated by inborn factors—especially by the desire to maximize our genetic contribution to the next generation (Buss, 1999). We may not be aware of this specific desire, they say, but we nevertheless behave in ways that promote it (Geary, 2000). So you are more likely to hear someone say "I can't wait to have children" than to say "I want to contribute genes to the next generation."

The evolutionary approach suggests, for example, that the choice of a marriage partner has a biological basis; heterosexual love and marriage are seen as the result of inborn desires to create and nurture offspring so that parents' genes will survive in their children. According to this view, the mating strategies of males and females differ in ways that reflect traditional differences in how much males and females invest in their offspring (Bjorklund & Shackelford, 1999; Trivers, 1972). Because women can produce relatively few children in their lifetime, they are more psychologically invested than men are in the survival and development of those children (Townsend, Kline, & Wasserman, 1995). This greater investment motivates women to choose mates more cautiously, seeking males who are not only genetically fit but also able to provide the protection and resources necessary to ensure children's survival. The search for genetic fitness, say evolutionary psychologists, helps account for the fact that women tend to prefer men who display athleticism and facial symmetry (Barber, 1995; Gangestad & Thornhill, 1997). But good looks and well-built bodies may not be enough; women are also drawn to men who have demonstrated an ability to acquire resources, as signified by maturity, ambition, and earning power. It takes some time to assess these resource-related characteristics (He drives a nice car, but can he afford it?), which is why, according to the evolutionary view, women are more likely than men to prefer a period of courtship prior to mating. Men tend to want to begin a sexual relationship sooner than women (Buss & Schmitt, 1993) because, compared with their female partners, they have little to lose from doing so. On the contrary, their eagerness to engage in sex early in a relationship is seen as reflecting their evolutionary ancestors' tendency toward casual sex as a means of maximizing their genetic contribution to the next generation. In fact, evolutionary psychologists see the desire to produce as many children as possible as motivating males' preference to mate with women whose reproductive capacity and genetic fitness are signified by youth, attractiveness, and good health (Symons, 1995).

These controversial speculations have received some support. For instance, according to a survey of more than ten thousand men and women in thirty-three countries on six continents and five isolated islands, males generally preferred youth and good health in prospective female mates, and females generally preferred males who were mature and wealthy (Kenrick, 1994). One example of this sex difference is illustrated in Figure 11.2, which shows the age preferences of men and women who advertised for dates in the personal sections of newspapers in the United States. In general, men were interested in women younger than themselves, but women were interested in older men (Kenrick et al., 1995).

Critics argue that such preferences could stem from cultural traditions, not genetic programming. Among the Zulu of South Africa, where women are expected to build houses, carry water, and perform other physically demanding tasks, men tend to value maturity and ambition in a mate more than women do (Buss, 1989).

figure 11.2

Age Preferences Reflected in Personal Advertisements

An analysis of 486 personal section ads placed in newspapers around the United States showed a sex difference in age preferences. As men got older, their preferences for younger women increased, whereas women, regardless of age, preferred men who were about their own age or older.

Source: Kenrick et al. (1995, Figure 1).

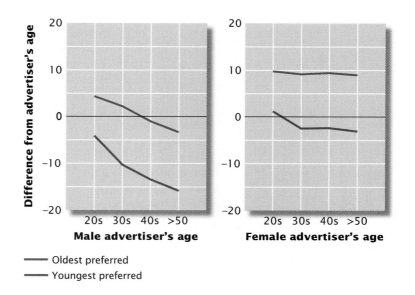

Evolution at Work? Film stars Michael Douglas and Catherine Zeta-Jones married when he was 57 and she was 32, exemplifying the worldwide tendency for older men to prefer younger women, and vice versa. This tendency has been interpreted as evidence supporting an evolutionary explanation of mate selection, but skeptics see social and economic forces at work in establishing these preference patterns.

OBJ 11.5: Define homeostasis, need, drive, and drive reduction theory. Define primary and secondary drive and discuss their role in motivation. Explain what behaviors drive theory can and cannot account for.

Test Items 11.13–11.19

---

homeostasis The tendency for organisms to keep their physiological systems at a stable, steady level by constantly adjusting themselves in response to change.

drive reduction theory A theory of motivation stating that much motivation arises from constant imbalances in homeostasis.

need A biological requirement for well-being that is created by an imbalance in homeostasis.

drive A psychological state of arousal created by an imbalance in homeostasis that prompts an organism to take action to restore the balance and reduce the drive.

primary drives Drives that arise from basic biological needs.

secondary drives Stimuli that acquire the motivational properties of primary drives through classical conditioning or other learning mechanisms.

The fact that women have been systematically denied economic and political power in many cultures may also account for their tendency to rely on the security and economic power provided by men (Silverstein, 1996).

Drive Reduction Theory

Like instinct theory, drive reduction theory emphasizes biological factors, but it is based on the concept of homeostasis. **Homeostasis** is the tendency for organisms to keep physiological systems at a steady level, or *equilibrium*, by constantly making adjustments in response to change. We describe a version of this concept in the chapter on biological aspects of psychology, in relation to feedback loops that keep hormones at desirable levels.

According to **drive reduction theory,** an imbalance in homeostasis creates a **need**—a biological requirement for well-being. The brain responds to such needs, in the service of homeostasis, by creating a psychological state called a **drive**—a feeling of arousal that prompts an organism to take action, restore the balance, and as a result, reduce the drive (Hull, 1943). For example, if you have had no water for some time, the chemical balance of your body fluids is disturbed, creating a biological need for water. One consequence of this need is a drive—thirst—that motivates you to find and drink water. After you drink, the need for water is met, so the drive to drink is reduced. In other words, drives push people to satisfy needs, thus reducing the drives as well as the arousal they create (see Figure 11.3).

Drive reduction theory recognizes the influence of learning on motivation by distinguishing between primary and secondary drives. **Primary drives** stem from biological needs, such as the need for food or water. (In the chapter on learning, we note that food, water, and other things that satisfy primary drives are called *primary reinforcers*.) People do not have to learn either these basic biological needs or the primary drives to satisfy them (Hull, 1951). However, we do learn other drives, called *secondary drives*. Once acquired, **secondary drives** motivate us to act *as if* we have an unmet basic need. For example, as people learn to associate money with the satisfaction of primary drives for food, shelter, and so on, having money may become a secondary drive. Having too little money then motivates many behaviors—from hard work to thievery—to obtain more funds.

figure 11.3

Drive Reduction Theory and Homeostasis

Homeostatic mechanisms, such as the regulation of body temperature or food and water intake, are often compared to thermostats. If the temperature in a house drops below the thermostat setting, the furnace comes on and brings the temperature up to that preset level, achieving homeostasis. When the temperature reaches the preset point, the furnace shuts off.

```
Unbalanced          →    Need              →    Drive
equilibrium              (biological            (psychological
                         disturbance)           state that provides
                                                motivation to
                                                satisfy need)

Equilibrium         ←    Behavior that     ←
restored                 satisfies need and
                         reduces drive
```

OBJ 11.6: Define arousal. Describe arousal theories of motivation. Discuss the role of an optimal level of arousal in motivation and the impact of more or less than an optimal level of arousal on performance.

Test Items 11.20–11.24

Optimal Arousal and Personality
People whose optimal arousal is high are likely to smoke, drink alcohol, engage in frequent sexual activity, listen to loud music, eat spicy foods, and do things that are novel and risky (Farley, 1986; Zuckerman, 1979). Those with lower optimal arousal tend to behave in ways that bring less intense stimulation and to take fewer risks. Most of the differences in optimal arousal have a strong biological basis and, as discussed in the chapter on personality, may help shape broader differences, such as introversion-extraversion.

By recognizing secondary as well as primary drives, drive reduction theory can account for a wider range of behaviors than instinct theory. But humans and animals often go to great lengths to do things that do not appear to reduce any drive. Consider curiosity. Animals explore and manipulate their surroundings, even though such activities do not lead to drive reduction. They will also exert considerable effort simply to enter a new environment, especially if it is complex and full of novel objects (Bolles, 1975; Loewenstein, 1994). People are no less curious. Most of us cannot resist checking out anything new or unusual. We go to the new mall, read the newspaper, surf the Web, and travel the world just to see what there is to see.

Arousal Theory   ClassPrep PPT 10: Arousal Theory

People also go out of their way to ride roller coasters, skydive, drive racecars, and do countless other things that, like curiosity-motivated behaviors, do not reduce any known drive (Zuckerman, 1996). In fact, these behaviors *increase* people's levels of activation, or arousal. The realization that people sometimes try to decrease arousal and sometimes try to increase it has led theorists to argue that motivation is tied to the regulation of arousal.

Most of these theorists think of **arousal** as a general level of activation reflected in the state of several physiological systems (Plutchik & Conte, 1997). Your level of arousal can be measured by your brain's electrical activity, by heart action, or by muscle tension (Deschaumes et al., 1991). Normally, arousal is lowest during deep sleep and highest during panic or great excitement. Many factors increase arousal, including hunger, thirst, intense stimuli, unexpected events, and stimulants (such as amphetamines). It is interesting to note that people who tend to actively seek novelty in life also tend to be at increased risk for abusing stimulants. This phenomenon may be related to individual differences in the brain's dopamine system, which is activated by novelty and by most drugs of abuse (Bardo, Donohew, & Harrington, 1996; Berns et al., 2001). Through especially creative applications of brain imaging techniques, researchers have found that the dopamine system is activated even when a person gambles or plays a video game (Breiter et al., 2001; Koepp et al., 1998).

People perform best, and may feel best, when arousal is moderate (Teigen, 1994). Figure 11.4 illustrates the general relationship between arousal and performance. Overarousal can be harmful to performance; it can also disrupt activities ranging from intellectual tasks to athletic competition (Penner & Craiger, 1992; Smith et al., 2000; Wright et al., 1995).

Arousal theories of motivation suggest that people are motivated to behave in ways that keep them at their own *optimal* level of arousal (Hebb, 1955). This optimal level is higher for some people than for others (Zuckerman, 1984). Generally, however, people try to increase arousal when it is too low and decrease it when it is

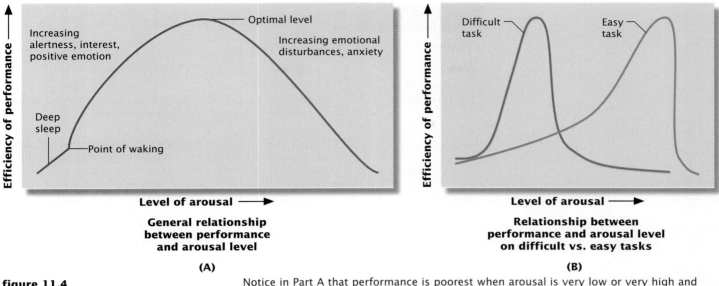

(A)

General relationship between performance and arousal level

(B)

Relationship between performance and arousal level on difficult vs. easy tasks

figure 11.4

The Arousal-Performance Relationship

ClassPrep PPT 11: *Figure 11.4:* The Arousal-Performance Relationship

Notice in Part A that performance is poorest when arousal is very low or very high and best when arousal is at some intermediate level. When you are either nearly asleep or overly excited, for example, it may be difficult to think clearly or to be physically coordinated. In general, optimal performance comes at a lower level of arousal on difficult or complex tasks and at a higher level of arousal on easy tasks, as shown in Part B. So even a relatively small amount of overarousal can cause students to perform far below their potential on difficult tests (Sarason, 1984). Because animal research early in this century by Robert Yerkes and his colleagues provided supportive evidence, this arousal-performance relationship is sometimes referred to as the *Yerkes-Dodson law,* even though Yerkes never actually discussed performance as a function of arousal (Teigen, 1994).

too high. They seek excitement when bored and relaxation when overaroused. After classes and studying, for example, you may want to see an exciting movie. But if your day was spent playing baseball, fiercely debating a political issue, and helping a friend move, an evening of quiet relaxation may seem ideal.

OBJ 11.7: Define incentive theory. Describe incentive theory's attempt to explain behavior and distinguish "wanting" from "liking."

Test Items 11.25–11.29

ClassPrep PPT 13: Incentive-Related Systems

Incentive Theory   ClassPrep PPT 12: Incentive Theory

Instinct, drive reduction, and arousal theories of motivation all focus on internal processes that prompt people to behave in certain ways. By contrast, **incentive theory** emphasizes the role of environmental stimuli that can motivate behavior by pulling us toward them or pushing us away from them. According to this view, people act to obtain positive incentives and avoid negative incentives. Differences in behavior from one person to another, or in the same person from one situation to another, can be traced to the incentives available and the value a person places on them at the time. So if you expect a behavior (such as buying a lottery ticket) to lead to a valued outcome (winning money), you will want to engage in that behavior. The value of an incentive is influenced by biological as well as cognitive factors. For example, food is a more motivating incentive when you are hungry than when you are full (Balleine & Dickinson, 1994).

Today, incentive theorists distinguish between two incentive-related systems: wanting and liking. *Wanting* is the process of being attracted to stimuli, whereas *liking* is the immediate evaluation of how pleasurable a stimulus is (Berridge, 1999). Studies with animals have shown that these two systems involve separate parts of the brain, that the wanting system guides behavior to a greater extent than does the liking system, and that the operation of the wanting system varies according to whether an individual has been deprived or not (Nader, Bechara, & Van der Kooy,

arousal A general level of activation that is reflected in several physiological systems.

arousal theories Theories of motivation stating that people are motivated to behave in ways that maintain what is, for them, an optimal level of arousal.

incentive theory A theory of motivation stating that behavior is directed toward attaining desirable stimuli and avoiding unwanted stimuli.

in review	Theories of Motivation	
Theory	**Main Points**	
Instinct	Innate biological instincts guide behavior.	
Drive reduction	Behavior is guided by biological needs and learned ways of reducing drives arising from those needs.	
Arousal	People seek to maintain an optimal level of physiological arousal, which differs from person to person. Maximum performance occurs at optimal arousal levels.	
Incentive	Behavior is guided by the lure of positive incentives and the avoidance of negative incentives. Cognitive factors influence expectations of the value of various rewards and the likelihood of attaining them.	

1997). For example, different brain regions would affect the motivation to consume a piece of apple pie, depending on whether it is served as an appetizer or as a dessert.

The theoretical approaches we have outlined (see "In Review: Theories of Motivation") complement one another. Each emphasizes different sources of motivation, and each has helped to guide research into motivated behaviors such as eating, sex, and achievement-related activities, which we consider in the sections that follow.

Hunger and Eating   ClassPrep PPT 14: Hunger and Eating

Hunger is deceptively simple; you get hungry when you do not eat. Much as a car needs gas, you need fuel from food. Is there a bodily mechanism that, like a car's gas gauge, signals the need for fuel? What causes hunger? What determines which foods you eat, and how do you know when to stop? The answers to these questions involve not only interactions between the brain and the rest of the body but also learning, social, and environmental factors (Hill & Peters, 1998).

OBJ 11.8: Define hunger and satiety. List the nutrients and hormones that the brain monitors in the bloodstream as it regulates hunger and eating. Explain the role of the ventromedial nucleus, lateral hypothalamus, and paraventricular nucleus in hunger and eating. Define set point.

Test Items 11.30–11.39

Biological Signals for Hunger and Satiety

A variety of mechanisms underlie **hunger,** the general state of wanting to eat, and **satiety** (pronounced "se-TY-a-tee"), the general state of no longer wanting to eat. In order to maintain body weight, we must have ways to regulate food intake over the short term (a question of how often we eat and when we stop eating a given meal) and to regulate the body's stored energy reserves (fat) over the long term.

ClassPrep PPT 15: Biological Signals for Hunger and Satiety

Signals from the Stomach   The stomach would seem to be a logical source of signals for hunger and satiety. After all, people say they feel "hunger pangs" from an "empty" stomach, and they complain of a "full stomach" after overeating. True, the stomach does contract during hunger pangs, and increased pressure within the stomach can reduce appetite (Cannon & Washburn, 1912; Houpt, 1994). But people who have lost their stomachs due to illness still get hungry when they do not eat and still eat normal amounts of food (Janowitz, 1967). So stomach cues can affect eating, but they do not play a major role in the normal control of eating. These cues appear to operate mainly when you are very hungry or very full.

hunger   The general state of wanting to eat.

satiety   The condition of no longer wanting to eat.

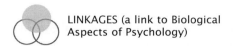

LINKAGES (a link to Biological Aspects of Psychology)

Signals from the Blood

The most important signals about the body's fuel level and nutrient needs are sent to the brain from the blood. The brain's ability to "read" blood-borne signals about the body's nutritional needs was shown years ago when researchers deprived rats of food for a long period and then injected them with blood from rats that had just eaten. When offered food, the injected rats ate little or nothing (Davis et al., 1969); something in the injected blood of the well-fed animals apparently signaled the hungry rats' brains that there was no need to eat. What sent that satiety signal? Subsequent research has shown that the brain constantly monitors both the level of food *nutrients* absorbed into the bloodstream from the stomach and the level of *hormones* released into the blood in response to those nutrients and from stored fat.

Some blood-borne signals affect short-term intake—telling us when to start and stop eating a meal—whereas others reflect and regulate the body's long-term supply of fat. The short-term signals are called *satiety factors.* One such signal comes from *cholecystokinin (CCK)* (pronounced "cole-ee-sis-toe-KY-nin"), which regulates meal size (Woods et al., 1998). During a meal, cholecystokinin is released as a hormone in the gut and as a neurotransmitter in the brain (Crawley & Corwin, 1994). The activation of CCK in the brain causes animals to stop eating (Parrott, 1994), and even a well-fed animal will start to eat if receptors in the brain for CCK are blocked (Brenner & Ritter, 1995). Moderate doses of CCK given to humans cause them to eat less of a given meal, whereas high doses can cause nausea—thus possibly explaining why people sometimes feel sick after overeating. However, research with animals suggests that simply increasing production of CCK would probably not result in weight loss, because the animals made up for smaller meals by eating more often. This phenomenon reflects the fact that the brain monitors the long-term storage of fat, as well as the short-term status of nutrients.

The nutrients that the brain monitors include *glucose,* the main form of sugar used by body cells. Decades ago, researchers noted that when the level of blood glucose drops, eating increases sharply (e.g., Mogenson, 1976). More recent work has shown that glucose acts indirectly by affecting certain chemical messengers. For example, when glucose levels rise, the pancreas releases *insulin,* a hormone that most body cells need in order to use the glucose they receive. Insulin may enhance the brain's satiety response to CCK. In one study, animals receiving CCK preceded by insulin infusions into the brain ate less food and gained less weight than animals getting either CCK or insulin alone (Riedy et al., 1995). Insulin itself may also provide a satiety signal by acting directly on brain cells (Brüning et al., 2000; Schwartz et al., 2000).

The long-term regulation of fat stores involves a hormone called *leptin* (from the Greek word *leptos,* meaning "thin"). The process works like this: Cells that store fat have genes that produce leptin in response to increases in fat supplies. The leptin is released into the bloodstream, and when it reaches special receptors for it in the hypothalamus, it provides information to the brain about the increasing fat supplies (Farooqi et al., 2001; Huang & Li, 2000; Tartaglia et al., 1996). When leptin levels are high, hunger decreases, helping to reduce food intake. When leptin levels are low, hunger increases, as illustrated in animals that are obese because of defects in leptin-producing genes (Zhang et al., 1994). Researchers have found that injections of leptin cause these animals to lose weight and body fat rapidly, with no effect on muscle or other body tissue (Forbes et al., 2001). Leptin injections can produce the same effects in normal animals, too (e.g., Campfield et al., 1995; Fox & Olster, 2000). At first, these results raised hope that leptin might be a "magic bullet" for treating obesity, or severe overweight, in humans, but this is not the case. It can help those rare individuals who are obese because their cells make no leptin (Farooqi et al., 1999), but leptin injections are far less effective for people whose obesity results from a high-fat diet (Gura, 1999; Heymsfield et al., 1999). In these far more common cases of obesity, the brain appears to become less sensitive to leptin's signals (Ahima & Flier, 2000; Lin et al., 2000).

Hunger and the Brain

Many parts of the brain contribute to the control of hunger and eating, but research has focused on several regions of the hypothalamus that may play primary roles in detecting and reacting to the blood's signals about the need to eat (see Figure 11.5). Some regions of the hypothalamus detect leptin and insulin; these regions generate signals that either increase hunger and reduce energy expenditure, or else reduce hunger and increase energy expenditure. At least twenty neurotransmitters and *neuromodulators*—substances that modify the action of neurotransmitters—convey these signals to networks in other parts of the hypothalamus and in the rest of the brain (Woods et al., 1998, 2000).

Activity in a part of the network that passes through the *ventromedial nucleus* of the hypothalamus tells an animal that there is no need to eat. So if a rat's ventromedial nucleus is electrically or chemically stimulated, the animal will stop eating (Kent et al., 1994). However, if the ventromedial nucleus is destroyed, the animal will eat continuously, increasing its weight up to threefold.

In contrast, the *lateral hypothalamus* contains networks that stimulate eating. When the lateral hypothalamus is electrically or chemically stimulated, rats eat huge quantities, even if they have just had a large meal (Stanley et al., 1993). When the lateral hypothalamus is destroyed, however, rats stop eating almost entirely.

One theory suggests that, much as a thermostat maintains a constant temperature in a house, these two hypothalamic regions interact to create a *set point* based on food intake or related metabolic signals that keeps body weight within a narrow range (Cabanac & Morrissette, 1992). According to this *range theory*, normal animals (and people) eat until their set point is reached, then stop eating until desirable intake falls below the set point. Destroying or stimulating the lateral or ventromedial hypothalamus may alter the set point.

However, research on other regions of the hypothalamus suggests that the brain's control of eating involves more than just the interaction of "stop-eating" and

figure 11.5

The Hypothalamus and Hunger

Regions of the hypothalamus generate signals that either increase hunger and reduce energy expenditure, called *anabolic effects,* or reduce hunger and increase energy expenditure, called *catabolic effects.*

Source: Adapted from Schwartz et al. (2000).

ClassPrep PPT 16: *Figure 11.5:* The Hypothalamus and Hunger

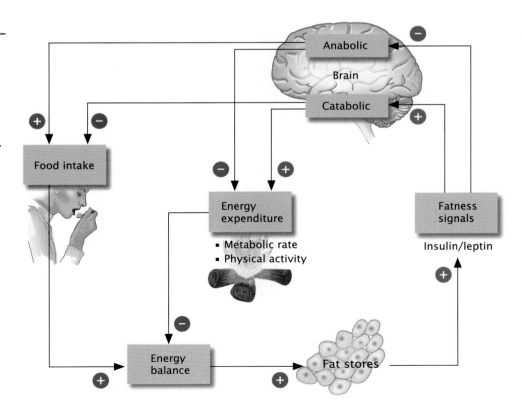

One Fat Mouse After surgical destruction of its ventromedial nucleus, this mouse ate enough to triple its body weight. Such animals become picky eaters, choosing only foods that taste good and ignoring all others.

OBJ 11.9: Specify the role of flavor and learning in the regulation of eating. Define appetite. Describe the mechanisms controlling specific hungers. Give examples of the effects of a food culture.

Test Items 11.40–11.43

IRM Discussion 11.8: The Curiosity of Chili Pepper: Anatomy of a Motivation

Personal Learning Activity 11.2

Personal Learning Activity 11.3

ClassPrep PPT 17: Flavor, Cultural Learning, and Food Selection

"start-eating" areas (Winn, 1995). For example, hunger—and hunger for particular types of food—is also related to the effects of certain neurotransmitters on certain neurons (Lee, Schiffman, & Pappas, 1994; Woods et al., 1998). One of these neurotransmitters, called *neuropeptide Y*, stimulates carbohydrate eating (Jhanwar et al., 1993), whereas another, *serotonin*, suppresses it (Blundell & Halford, 1998). Similarly, *galanin* motivates the eating of high-fat food (Krykouli et al., 1990), and *enterostatin* reduces it (Lin et al., 1998). *Endocannabinoids* stimulate eating in general. They affect the same hypothalamic receptors as does the active ingredient in marijuana, which may account for "the munchies," a sudden hunger that marijuana often creates (Di Marzo et al., 2001).

In short, several brain regions and many brain chemicals help to regulate hunger and eating. And although eating is controlled by processes that suggest the existence of a set point, that set point appears variable enough to be overridden by other factors.

Flavor, Cultural Learning, and Food Selection

One factor that can override a set point is the *flavor* of food. In one experiment, some animals were offered just a single type of food while others were offered foods of several different flavors. The group getting the varied menu ate nearly four times more than the one-food group. As each new food appeared, the animals began to eat voraciously, regardless of how much they had already eaten (Peck, 1978). Humans behave similarly. All things being equal, people eat more food during a multicourse meal than when only one food is served (Raynor & Epstein, 2001). Apparently, the flavor of any particular food becomes less enjoyable as more of it is eaten (Swithers & Hall, 1994). In one study, for example, people rated how much they liked four kinds of food; then they ate one of the foods and rated all four again. The food they had just eaten now got a lower rating, whereas liking increased for all the rest (Johnson & Vickers, 1993).

Another factor that can override blood-borne signals about satiety is *appetite*, the motivation to seek food's pleasures. For example, the appearance and aroma of certain foods come to elicit conditioned physiological responses—such as secretion of saliva, gastric juices, and insulin—in anticipation of eating those foods. (The process is based on the principles of classical conditioning described in the chapter on learning.) These responses then increase appetite. So merely seeing a pizza on television may prompt you to order one—even if you hadn't been feeling hungry—and if you see a delicious-looking cookie, you do not have to be hungry to start eating it. In fact, brain-damaged patients who cannot remember anything for more than a minute will eat a full meal ten to thirty minutes after finishing one just like it, and may even start a third meal ten to thirty minutes later, simply because the food looks good (Rozin et al., 1998). In other words, people eat not only to satisfy nutritional needs but also to experience enjoyment.

A different mechanism appears to be responsible for *specific hungers*, or desires for particular foods at particular times. These hungers appear to reflect the biological need for the nutrients contained in certain foods. In one study, rats were allowed to eat from a bowl of carbohydrate-rich but protein-free food and also from a bowl of protein-rich but carbohydrate-free food. These animals learned to eat from both bowls in amounts that gave them a proper balance of carbohydrates and protein (Miller & Teates, 1985). In another study, rats were given three bowls of tasty, protein-free food and one bowl of food that tasted bad but was rich in protein. Again, the rats learned to eat enough of the bad-tasting food to get a proper supply of dietary protein (Galef & Wright, 1995).

These results are remarkable in part because food nutrients such as carbohydrates, fats, and proteins have no taste or odor. How, then, can they guide food choices that maintain nutritional balance? As with appetite, learning principles are probably involved. It may be that *volatile odorants* (odor molecules) in foods come

Bon Appétit! The definition of *delicacy* differs from culture to culture. At this elegant restaurant in Mexico, diners pay to feast on baby alligators, insects, and other dishes that some people from other cultures would not eat even if the restaurant paid *them*. To appreciate your own food culture, make a list of foods that are traditionally valued by your family or cultural group but that people from other groups do not, or might even be unwilling, to eat.

OBJ 11.10: Define obesity, anorexia nervosa, and bulimia nervosa. Describe behavior associated with each of these eating disorders.

Test Items 11.44–11.51

IRM Discussion 11.3: Anorexia Nervosa

ClassPrep PPT 18: Obesity

obesity A condition in which a person is severely overweight, as measured by a body-mass index greater than 30.

to be associated with the nutritional value of their fat and protein content. Evidence for this kind of learning comes from experiments in which rats received infusions of liquid directly into their stomachs. Some of these infusions consisted of plain water; others included nutritious cornstarch. Each kind of infusion was paired with a different taste—either sour or bitter—in the animals' normal supply of drinking water. After all the infusions were completed, both sour water and bitter water were made available. When the animals became hungry, they showed a strong preference for the water whose taste had been associated with the cornstarch infusions (Drucker, Ackroff, & Sclafani, 1994). Related research shows that children come to prefer flavors that have been associated with high-fat ingredients (Johnson, McPhee, & Birch, 1991).

The role of learning in food selection is also seen in the social rules and cultural traditions that influence eating. Munching popcorn at movies and hot dogs at baseball games are common examples from North American culture of how certain social situations can stimulate appetite for particular food items. Similarly, how much you eat may depend on what others do. Courtesy or custom might prompt you to select foods you might otherwise have avoided. Generally, the mere presence of others, even strangers, tends to increase consumption: Most people consume 60 to 75 percent more food when they are with others than when eating alone (Clendenen, Herman, & Polivy, 1995; Redd & de Castro, 1992).

Eating and food selection are central to the way people function within their cultures. Celebrations, holidays, vacations, and even daily family interactions often revolve around food and what some call a *food culture* (Rozin, 1996). As any world traveler knows, there are wide cultural and subcultural variations in food selection. For example, chewing coca leaves is popular in the Bolivian highlands but illegal in the United States (Burchard, 1992). In China, people in urban areas eat a high-cholesterol diet rich in animal meat, whereas those in rural areas eat so little meat as to be cholesterol deficient (Tian et al., 1995). And the insects known as *palm weevils,* a popular food for people in Papua New Guinea (Paoletti, 1995), are regarded by many Westerners as disgusting (Springer & Belk, 1994). Even within the same general culture, different groups may have sharply contrasting food traditions. Squirrel brains won't be found on most dinner tables in the United States, but some people in the rural South consider them to be a tasty treat. In short, eating serves functions beyond nutrition—functions that help to remind us of who we are and with whom we identify.

Eating Disorders

Problems in the processes regulating hunger and eating may cause an *eating disorder.* The most common and dangerous examples are obesity, anorexia nervosa, and bulimia nervosa.

Obesity   The World Health Organization defines **obesity** as a condition in which a person's body-mass index, or BMI, is greater than 30. People whose BMI is 25 to 29.9 are considered to be overweight. (BMI is determined by dividing a person's weight in kilograms by the square of the person's height in meters. So someone who is 5 feet 2 inches tall and weighs 164 pounds would be classified as obese, as would someone 5 feet 10 inches tall who weighs 207 pounds. BMI calculators appear on web sites such as www.consumer.gov/weightloss/bmi.htm.) Using these BMI criteria, 36 percent of adults in the United States are overweight, and another 27 percent are obese (USDHHS, 2000a). Worse yet, obesity appears to be on the rise, not only in the United States but also in regions as diverse as Europe, Asia, South America, and Africa (Kopelman, 2000; Lewis et al., 2000; Mokdad et al., 2000, 2001; Rudolph et al., 2001; Taubes, 1998). It is associated with health problems such as diabetes, high blood pressure, pancreatic cancer, and increased risk of

ClassPrep PPT 19: The Health Risks of Obesity

ClassPrep PPTs 20 & 21: Causes of Obesity

ClassPrep PPT 22: Fighting Obesity

heart attack (Field et al., 2001; Michaud et al., 2001; Sturm & Wells, 2001). With nearly 300,000 deaths in the United States alone attributed to obesity each year, it has been described as at least as dangerous as smoking and alcohol abuse (Allison et al., 1999; Sturm & Wells, 2001).

The precise reasons for this obesity epidemic are unknown (Hill & Peters, 1998), but possible causes include increased portion sizes at fast-food outlets, greater prevalence of high-fat foods, and decreases in physical activity associated with both work and recreation. These are important factors, because the body maintains a given weight through a combination of food intake and energy output (Keesey & Powley, 1986). Obese people get more energy from food than their body *metabolizes*, or "burns up"; the excess energy, measured in *calories*, is stored as fat. Metabolism declines during sleep and rises with physical activity. Because women tend to have a lower metabolic rate than men, even when equally active, they tend to gain weight more easily than do men with similar diets (Ferraro et al., 1992). Most obese people have normal resting metabolic rates, but they tend to eat above-average amounts of high-calorie, tasty foods and below-average amounts of less tasty foods (Kauffman, Herman, & Polivy, 1995; Peck, 1978). Further, some obese people are less active than lean people, a pattern that often begins in childhood (Strauss & Pollack, 2001). Spending long hours watching television or playing computer games is a major cause of the inactivity seen in overweight children (USDHHS, 1996; Vioque, Torres, & Quiles, 2000). In short, inadequate physical activity, combined with overeating—especially of the high-fat foods so prevalent in most Western cultures—has a lot to do with obesity.

But not everyone who is inactive and eats a high-fat diet becomes obese, and some obese people are as active as lean people, so other factors must also be involved (Blundell & Cooling, 2000). Some people probably have a genetic predisposition toward obesity (Arner, 2000; Rosmond, Bouchard, & Björntorp, 2001). For example, although most obese people have the genes to make leptin, they may not be sensitive to its weight-suppressing effects—perhaps because of a genetic defect in leptin receptors in the hypothalamus. Recent brain-imaging studies also suggest that obese people's brains may be slower to "read" satiety signals coming from their blood, thus causing them to continue eating when leaner people would have stopped (Liu et al., 2000). These factors, along with the presence of one or more recently discovered viruses in the body (Dhurandhar et al., 2000), may help explain obese people's tendency to eat more, to accumulate fat, and to feel more hunger than lean people.

Psychological explanations for obesity focus on factors such as learning from examples set by parents who overeat (Hood et al., 2000) and maladaptive reactions to stress. Many people do tend to eat more when under stress, a reaction that may be especially extreme among those who become obese (Friedman & Brownell, 1995). However, obese people are no more likely than other people to display mental disorders (Stunkard & Wadden, 1992).

Losing weight, and keeping it off for at least five years, is extremely difficult for many people, especially those who are obese (Lewis et al., 2000; McGuire et al., 1999). Part of the problem may be due to metabolic changes that accompany weight loss. When food intake is reduced, the process of homeostasis leads to a drop in metabolic rate, thus saving energy and curbing weight loss (Leibel, Rosenbaum, & Hirsch, 1995). This response makes evolutionary sense; conservation of energy during famine, for example, is adaptive for survival. But when obese people try to lose weight, their metabolic rate drops below normal. As a result, they can gain weight even while eating amounts that would maintain constant weight in other people.

These facts suggest that attempts to lose a great deal of weight quickly will be met with compensatory changes in one's set point (Brownell & Rodin, 1994). Animal studies show that losing and then regaining large amounts of weight, a process called *cycling*, actually leads to a gradual rise in average weight

Thin Is In In Western cultures today, thinness is a much-sought-after ideal, especially among young women who are dissatisfied with their appearance. That ideal is seen in fashion models, as well as in Miss America pageant winners, whose body-mass index has decreased from the "normal" range of 20 to 25 in the 1920s to an "undernourished" 18.5 in recent years (Rubinstein & Caballero, 2000). In the United States, 35 percent of normal-weight girls—and 12 percent of under-weight girls!—begin dieting when they are as young as nine or ten. Many of these children try to lose weight in response to criticism by their mothers (Schreiber et al., 1996); for some, the result is anorexia.

anorexia nervosa An eating disorder characterized by self-starvation and dramatic weight loss.

bulimia nervosa An eating disorder that involves eating massive amounts of food and then eliminating the food by self-induced vomiting or the use of strong laxatives.

(Archambault et al., 1989). Moreover, people whose body weight "cycles" tend to experience more depression and stress-related symptoms than do people whose weight does not fluctuate (Foreyt et al., 1995).

Several anti-obesity drugs have been developed recently, including one that prevents fat in foods from being digested (e.g., Finer et al., 2000; Hauptman et al., 2000). Another drug has been found to interfere with an enzyme that forms fat. This "fatty acid synthase inhibitor" not only caused rapid weight loss in mice but also reduced their hunger (Loftus et al., 2000). The drug has not yet been tested for safety and effectiveness in humans, but researchers hope that it may someday be possible to give obese people medications that alter brain mechanisms involved in overeating and fat storage (Abu-Elheiga et al., 2001; Arterburn & Noël, 2001; Halford & Blundell, 2000).

Even the best drug treatments are unlikely to solve the problem of obesity on their own, however. To achieve the kind of gradual weight loss that is most likely to last, obese people are advised to increase exercise, because it burns calories without slowing metabolism (Tremblay & Bueman, 1995). In fact, a regular regimen of aerobic exercise and weight training *raises* the metabolic rate (Binzen, Swan, & Manore, 2001; McCarty, 1995). The most effective weight-loss programs include components designed to reduce food intake, change eating habits and attitudes toward food, and increase energy expenditure through exercise (Bray & Tartaglia, 2000; National Task Force on the Prevention and Treatment of Obesity, 2000; Wadden et al., 2001).

Anorexia Nervosa

At the opposite extreme from obesity is **anorexia nervosa**, an eating disorder characterized by some combination of self-starvation, self-induced vomiting, and laxative use that results in weight loss to below 85 percent of normal (Kaye et al., 2000; U.S. Surgeon General, 1999). About 95 percent of people who suffer from anorexia are young females. Anorexic individuals often feel hungry, and many are obsessed with food and its preparation, yet they refuse to eat. Anorexic self-starvation causes serious, often irreversible physical damage, including reduction in bone density that enhances the risk of fractures (Grinspoon et al., 2000). Between 4 and 30 percent of anorexics die of starvation, biochemical imbalances, or suicide; their risk of death is twelve times higher than that of other young women (Herzog et al., 2000; Sullivan, 1995). Anorexia tends to appear in adolescence, when concern over appearance becomes intense. The incidence of anorexia appears to be on the increase; it now affects about 1 percent of young women in the United States and is a growing problem in many other industrialized nations as well (Feingold & Mazzella, 1998; Thompson, 1996a).

The causes of anorexia are not yet clear. Anorexic individuals do have abnormally low levels of certain neurotransmitters; but because these levels return to normal when weight is restored, the deficit may be a response to starvation, not its cause (Kaye et al., 1988). Genetic factors may be involved in anorexia, but their strength is not yet determined (Bulik et al., 2000; Vink et al., 2001). Psychological factors that may contribute to the problem include a self-punishing, perfectionistic personality and a culturally reinforced obsession with thinness and attractiveness (Thompson & Stice, 2001; Tiller et al., 1995). People with anorexia appear to develop a fear of being fat, which they take to dangerous extremes (de Castro & Goldstein, 1995). Many anorexics continue to view themselves as fat or misshapen even as they are wasting away.

Drugs, hospitalization, and psychotherapy are all used to treat anorexia. In most cases, some combination of treatment and the passage of time brings recovery and maintenance of normal weight (Herzog et al., 1999).

Bulimia Nervosa

Like anorexia, bulimia nervosa involves intense fear of being fat, but the person may be thin, normal in weight, or even overweight (U.S. Surgeon General, 1999). **Bulimia nervosa** involves eating huge amounts of food

in review	Major Factors Controlling Hunger and Eating	
	Stimulate Eating	**Inhibit Eating**
Biological factors	Levels of glucose and insulin in the blood provide signals that stimulate eating; neurotransmitters that affect neurons in different regions of the hypothalamus also stimulate food intake and influence hungers for specific kinds of foods, such as fats and carbohydrates. Stomach contractions are associated with subjective feelings of hunger, but they do not play a substantial role in the stimulation of eating.	Hormones released into the bloodstream produce signals that inhibit eating; hormones such as leptin, CCK, and insulin act as neurotransmitters or neuromodulators and affect neurons in the hypothalamus and inhibit eating. The ventromedial nucleus of the hypothalamus may be a "satiety center" that monitors these hormones.
Nonbiological factors	Sights and smells of particular foods elicit eating because of prior associations; family customs and social occasions often include norms for eating in particular ways; stress is often associated with eating more.	Values in contemporary U.S. society encourage thinness, and thus can inhibit eating.

(say, several boxes of cookies, a half-gallon of ice cream, and a bucket of fried chicken) and then getting rid of the food through self-induced vomiting or strong laxatives. These "binge-purge" episodes may occur as often as twice a day (Weltzin et al., 1995).

ClassPrep PPT 26: Bulimia versus Anorexia

Like people with anorexia, bulimic individuals are usually female, and like anorexia, bulimia usually begins with a desire to be slender. However, bulimia and anorexia are separate disorders (Pryor, 1995). For one thing, most bulimics see their eating habits as problematic, whereas most anorexics do not. In addition, bulimia nervosa is usually not life threatening (Thompson, 1996b). There are consequences, however, including dehydration, nutritional problems, and intestinal damage. Many bulimics develop dental problems from the acids associated with vomiting. Frequent vomiting and the insertion of objects to trigger it can also cause damage to the throat. More generally, a preoccupation with eating and avoiding weight gain prevents many bulimics from working productively (Herzog, 1982).

Sattler/Shabatay reader, 2/e: Pope & Hudson, "New Hope for Binge Eaters"

Estimates of the frequency of bulimia range from 1 to 3 percent of adolescent and college-age women (Thompson, 1996a; U.S. Surgeon General, 1999). It appears to be caused by a combination of factors, including perfectionism, low self-esteem, stress, culturally encouraged preoccupation with being thin, depression and other emotional problems, and as-yet-undetermined biological problems that might include defective satiety mechanisms (Crowther et al., 2001; Steiger et al., 2001; Stice, 2001; Wade, Martin, & Tiggemann, 1998). Treatment for bulimia typically includes individual or group therapy and, sometimes, antidepressant drugs; these treatments help the vast majority of bulimic people to eat more normally (Herzog et al., 1999; Wilson et al., 1999).

(For a summary of the processes involved in hunger and eating, see "In Review: Major Factors Controlling Hunger and Eating.")

Sexual Behavior   **ClassPrep PPT 27:** Sexual Behavior

Unlike food, sex is not necessary for individual survival. A strong desire for reproduction does help ensure the survival of a species, however (Keeling & Roger, 1995). The various factors shaping sexual motivation and behavior differ in strength across species, but they often include a combination of the individual's physiology, learned behavior, and physical and social environment. For example, one species of desert bird requires adequate sex hormones, a suitable mate, and a particular environment before it begins sexual behavior. As long as the dry season lasts, it shows no interest in sex, but within ten minutes of the first rainfall the birds vigorously copulate.

Rainfall is obviously much less influential as a sexual trigger for humans. People show a staggering diversity of *sexual scripts,* or patterns of behavior that lead to sex. One survey of college-age men and women identified 122 specific acts and 34 different tactics used for promoting sexual encounters (Greer & Buss, 1994). What happens next? The matter is exceedingly difficult to address scientifically, because most people are reluctant to respond to specific questions about their sexual practices, let alone to allow researchers to observe their sexual behavior (Bancroft, 1997). Yet having valid information about the nature of human sexual behavior is a vital first step for psychologists and other scientists who study such topics as individual differences in sexuality, sources of sexual orientation, types of sexual dysfunctions, and the pathways through which AIDS and other sexually transmitted diseases (STDs) reach new victims. This information also has important implications for helping people understand themselves, alleviating sexual problems, and curbing the spread of STDs.

FOCUS ON RESEARCH METHODS

A Survey of Human Sexual Behavior

ClassPrep PPT 65: Survey of Human Sexual Behavior

The first extensive studies of sexual behavior in the United States were done by Alfred Kinsey during the late 1940s and early 1950s (Kinsey, Pomeroy, & Martin, 1948; Kinsey et al., 1953), followed in the 1960s by the work of William Masters and Virginia Johnson. The Kinsey studies surveyed people about their sex lives; Masters and Johnson actually measured sexual arousal and behavior in volunteers who received natural or artificial stimulation in a laboratory. These studies broke new ground in the exploration of human sexuality, but the people who volunteered for them probably did not constitute a representative sample of humankind. Accordingly, the results—and any conclusions drawn from them—may

Do They Look Ready? Research on sexual behavior provides psychologists, public health officials, and others who are concerned about poverty and child abuse with important information that helps them to more precisely tailor advertising campaigns and other efforts to prevent these problems.

not apply to people in general. The results of more recent surveys, such as reader polls in *Cosmopolitan* and other magazines, are also flawed by the use of unrepresentative samples (Davis & Smith, 1990).

● What was the researchers' question?

Is there a way to gather data on sexual behavior that is more representative and thus more revealing about people in general? A team of researchers at the University of Chicago believe there is, so they undertook the National Health and Social Life Survey, the first extensive survey of sexual behavior in the United States since the Kinsey studies (Laumann et al., 1994).

● How did the researchers answer the question?

This survey included important design features that had been neglected in most other surveys of sexual behavior. First, the study did not depend on self-selected volunteers. The researchers sought out a particular sample of 3,432 people, ranging in age from eighteen to fifty-nine. Second, careful construction of the sample made it reflective of the sociocultural diversity of the U.S. population in terms of gender, ethnicity, socioeconomic status, geographical location, and the like. Third, unlike previous mail-in surveys, the Chicago study was based on face-to-face interviews. This approach made it easier to ensure that the participants understood each question and could explain their responses. To encourage honesty, the researchers allowed participants to answer some questions anonymously, by placing written responses in a sealed envelope.

● What did the researchers find?

For one thing, the researchers found that people in the United States have sex less often and with fewer people than many had assumed. For most, sex occurs about once a week, and only with a partner with whom they share a stable relationship. About a third of the participants reported having sex only a few times, or not at all, in the past year. And in contrast to certain celebrities' splashy tales of dozens, even hundreds, of sexual partners per year, the average male survey participant had only six sexual partners in his entire life. The average female respondent reported a lifetime total of two. Further, the survey data suggested that people in committed, one-partner relationships had the most frequent and the most satisfying sex. And although a wide variety of specific sexual practices were reported, the overwhelming majority of heterosexual couples said they tend to engage mainly in penis-vagina intercourse.

● What do the results mean?

The Chicago survey challenges some of the cultural and media images of sexuality in the United States. In particular, it suggests that people in the United States may be more sexually conservative than one might think on the basis of magazine reader polls and the testimony of guests on daytime talk shows.

● What do we still need to know?

Many questions remain. The Chicago survey did not ask about some of the more controversial aspects of human sexuality, such as the effects of pornography, the nature and incidence of pedophilia (sexual attraction to children), and the role in sexual activity of sexual fetishes such as shoes or other clothing. Had the researchers asked about such topics, their results might have painted a less conservative picture. Further, because the Chicago survey focused on people in the United States, it told us little or nothing about the sexual practices, traditions, and values of people in the rest of the world.

The Chicago team has continued to conduct interviews, and the results are beginning to fill in the picture about sexual behavior in the United States and around the world. They have found, for example, that nearly one quarter of U.S. women prefer to achieve sexual satisfaction without partners of either sex. And although people in the United States tend to engage in a wider variety of sexual behaviors than those in Britain, there is less tolerance in the United States of disapproved sexual practices (Laumann & Michael, 2000; Michael et al., 1998).

Even the best survey methods—like the best of all other research methods—usually yield results that raise as many questions as they answer. When do people become interested in sex, and why? How do they choose to express these desires, and why? What determines their sexual likes and dislikes? How do learning and sociocultural factors modify the biological forces that seem to provide the raw material of human sexual motivation? These are some of the questions about human sexual behavior that a survey cannot easily or accurately explore.

The Biology of Sex

Some aspects of the sexual behavior observed by Masters and Johnson in their laboratory may not have reflected exactly what goes on when people have sex in more familiar surroundings. Still, those observations led to important findings about the **sexual response cycle**, the pattern of physiological arousal during and after sexual activity (see Figure 11.6).

People's motivation to engage in sexual activity has biological roots in **sex hormones**. The female sex hormones are **estrogens** and **progestins**; the main ones are *estradiol* and *progesterone*. The male hormones are **androgens**; the principal example is *testosterone*. Each sex hormone flows in the blood of both sexes, but males have relatively more androgens, and women have relatively more estrogens and progestins. Sex hormones have both organizational and activational effects. The *organizational* effects are permanent changes in the brain that alter the way a person thereafter responds to hormones. The *activational* effects are temporary behavioral changes that last only during the time a hormone level remains elevated, such as during puberty or in the ovulation phase of the monthly menstrual cycle.

The organizational effects of hormones occur around the time of birth, when certain brain areas are sculpted into a "male-like" or "female-like" pattern. These areas are thus described as *sexually dimorphic*. In rodents, for example, a sexually dimorphic area of the hypothalamus appears to underlie specific sexual behaviors. When these areas are destroyed in male gerbils, the animals can no longer copulate; yet damage to other nearby brain regions does not affect sexual behavior (Yahr & Jacobsen, 1994). Sexually dimorphic areas also exist in the human hypothalamus and elsewhere in the brain (Breedlove, 1994; Kimura, 1999). For example, a hypothalamic area called *BSTc* is generally smaller in women than in men. Its possible role in some aspects of human sexuality was suggested by a study of transsexual men—genetic males who feel like women and who may request sex-change surgery in order to "be" female. The BSTc in these men was smaller than in other men; in fact, it was about the size usually seen in women (Zhou et al., 1995).

Rising levels of sex hormones during puberty have activational effects, resulting in increased sexual desire and interest in sexual behavior. Generally, estrogens and androgens stimulate females' sexual interest (Burleson, Gregory, & Trevarthen, 1995; Sherwin & Gelfand, 1987). Androgens raise males' sexual interest (Davidson, Camargo, & Smith, 1979). The activational effects of hormones are also seen in reduced sexual motivation and behavior among people whose hormone-secreting ovaries or testes have been removed for medical reasons. Injections of hormones help restore these people's sexual interest and activity.

Generally, hormones affect sexual *desire*, not the physical *ability* to have sex (Wallen & Lovejoy, 1993). This fact may explain why castration does not prevent sex crimes in male offenders. Men with low testosterone levels due to medical problems or castration show less sexual desire, but they still experience physiological responses to erotic stimuli (Kwan et al., 1983). So a sex offender treated with androgen antagonists or castration would be less likely to seek out sex, but he would still respond as before to his favorite sexual stimuli (Wallen & Lovejoy, 1993).

OBJ 11.11: Describe the survey of human sexual behavior and discuss its findings. Describe the sexual response cycle. Name the male and female sex hormones. Explain their organizational and activational effects.

Test Items 11.52–11.56

sexual response cycle   The pattern of physiological arousal during and after sexual activity.

sex hormones   Chemicals in the blood of males and females that have both organizational and activational effects on sexual behavior.

estrogens   Feminine hormones that circulate in the bloodstream of both men and women; relatively more estrogens circulate in women.

progestins   Feminine hormones that circulate in the bloodstream of both men and women; relatively more progestins circulate in women.

androgens   Masculine hormones that circulate in the bloodstream and regulate sexual motivation in both sexes; relatively more androgens circulate in men than in women.

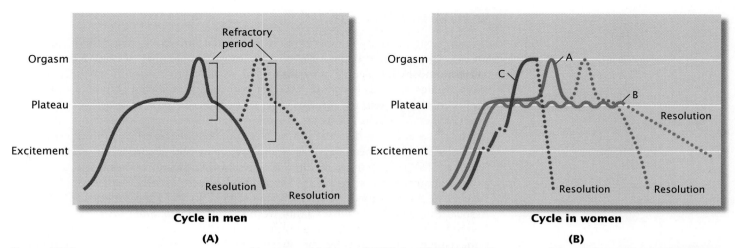

figure 11.6

The Sexual Response Cycle

Masters and Johnson (1966) found that men show one primary pattern of sexual response, depicted in Part A, and that women display at least three different patterns from time to time—labeled A, B, and C in Part B. For both men and women, the *excitement* phase begins with sexual stimulation from the environment or one's own thoughts. Continued stimulation leads to intensified excitement in the *plateau* phase and, if stimulation continues, to the intensely pleasurable release of tension in the *orgasmic* phase. During the *resolution* phase, both men and women experience a state of relaxation. Following resolution, men enter a *refractory* phase, during which they are unresponsive to sexual stimulation; women are capable of immediately repeating the cycle.

Source: Adapted from Masters & Johnson (1966).

Social and Cultural Factors in Sexuality

In humans, sexuality is profoundly shaped by a lifetime of learning and thinking that modifies the biological "raw materials" provided by hormones. For example, children learn some of their sexual attitudes and behaviors as part of the development of *gender roles,* which we discuss in the chapter on human development. The specific attitudes and behaviors learned depend partly on the nature of gender roles in their culture (Baumeister, 2000; Hyde & Durik, 2000). One survey of the sexual experiences of more than 1,500 college students in the United States, Japan, and Russia found numerous cross-cultural differences in the ways that men and women behave in sexual situations (Sprecher et al., 1994). For example, the results indicated that more women than men in the United States had consented to sex when they did not really want it; in both Russia and Japan, men and women were about equally likely to have had this experience.

Sexual behavior is also shaped by a variety of other sociocultural forces. In the United States, for example, concern over transmission of the AIDS virus during sex has prompted mass-media campaigns and school-based educational programs to encourage sexual abstinence prior to marriage or "safe sex" using condoms (e.g., Smith & DiClemente, 2000; some examples of such programs are described in the chapter on health, stress, and coping). These efforts seem to be shaping young people's sexual attitudes and practices. At the beginning of one sex education program, only 36 percent of 1,800 students in grades 7 through 10 thought premarital sex was a bad idea, and only 35 percent saw many benefits in premarital abstinence from sex. By the end of the semester-long program, these figures had risen to 66 percent and 58 percent, respectively (Eisenman, 1994). Another survey of 1,100 adolescents and young adults in the United States found that prior to 1985, first-time intercourse seldom included use of a condom. With growing AIDS awareness since 1985, however, condom use has become far more common in first-time intercourse and in later sexual activity (Everett et al., 2000; Leigh, Schafer, & Temple, 1995).

Sexual Orientation

Human sexual activity is most often **heterosexual,** involving members of the opposite sex. When sexual behavior is directed toward a member of one's own sex, it is called **homosexual.** People who engage in sexual activities with partners of both sexes are described as **bisexual.** Whether you engage in sexual activities with members of your own sex, the opposite sex, or both is one part of your *sexual orientation* (Ellis & Mitchell, 2000).

In many cultures, heterosexuality has long been regarded as a moral norm, and homosexuality has been seen as a disease, a mental disorder, or even a crime (Hooker, 1993). Attempts to alter the sexual orientation of homosexuals—using psychotherapy, brain surgery, or electric shock—were usually ineffective (American Psychiatric Association, 1999; Haldeman, 1994). In 1973 the American Psychiatric Association dropped homosexuality from the *Diagnostic and Statistical Manual of Mental Disorders,* thus ending its official status as a form of psychopathology. The same change was made by the World Health Organization in its *International Classification of Diseases* in 1993, by Japan's psychiatric organization in 1995, and by the Chinese Psychiatric Association in 2001.

Nevertheless, some people still disapprove of homosexuality. Because homosexuals and bisexuals are often the victims of discrimination and even hate crimes, many are reluctant to let their sexual orientation be known (Bernat et al., 2001). It is difficult, therefore, to obtain an accurate picture of the mix of heterosexual, homosexual, and bisexual orientations in a population. In the Chicago sex survey mentioned earlier, 1.4 percent of women and 2.8 percent of men identified themselves as exclusively homosexual (Laumann et al., 1994), figures much lower than the 10 percent found in Kinsey's studies. However, that survey did not allow respondents to give anonymous answers to questions about sexual orientation. It has been suggested that if anonymous responses to those questions had been permitted, the prevalence figures for homosexual and bisexual orientations would have been higher (Bullough, 1995). In fact, studies that have allowed anonymous responding estimate the percentage of homosexual people in the United States, Canada, and Western Europe at between 5 and 15 percent (Bagley & Tremblay, 1998; Diamond, 1993; Rogers & Turner, 1991; Sell, Wells, & Wypij, 1995).

THINKING CRITICALLY

Does Biology Determine Sexual Orientation?

The question of where sexual orientation comes from is a topic of intense debate in scientific circles, on talk shows, in everyday conversations, and even in the halls of the U.S. Congress.

● **What am I being asked to believe or accept?**

One point of view suggests that genes dictate sexual orientation. According to this view, we do not learn a sexual orientation but rather are born with it.

● **What evidence is available to support the assertion?**

In 1995, a report by a respected research group suggested that one kind of sexual orientation—namely, homosexuality in males—was associated with a particular gene on the X chromosome (Hu et al., 1995). This finding was not supported by later studies (Rice et al., 1999), but a growing body of evidence from research in behavioral genetics (see the chapter on research in psychology) suggests that genes might influence sexual orientation (Kendler et al., 2000; Pillard & Bailey, 1998). One study examined pairs of monozygotic male twins (whose genes are

ClassPrep PPT 64: Does Biology Determine Sexual Orientation?

ClassPrep PPT 31: Sexual Orientation

Freburg *Stand!:* Nimmons, "Sex and the Brain," and Billings and Bedwith, "Born Gay?"

heterosexual A description of sexual motivation that is focused on members of the opposite sex.
homosexual A description of sexual motivation that is focused on members of one's own sex.
bisexual A description of people who engage in sexual activities with partners of both sexes.

identical), nonidentical twin pairs (whose genes are no more alike than those of any brothers), and pairs of adopted brothers (who are genetically unrelated). To participate in this study, at least one brother in each pair had to be homosexual. As it turned out, the other brother was also homosexual or bisexual in 52 percent of the identical-twin pairs, but in only 22 percent of the nonidentical twin pairs and in just 11 percent of the pairs of adopted brothers (Bailey & Pillard, 1991). Similar findings have been reported for male identical twins raised apart; in such cases, a shared sexual orientation cannot be attributed to the effects of a shared environment (Whitam, Diamond, & Martin, 1993). The few available studies of female sexual orientation have yielded similar results (Bailey & Benishay, 1993; Bailey, Dunne, & Martin, 2000).

ClassPrep PPT 29, OHT: Role of Sex Hormones

Evidence for the role of other biological factors in sexual orientation comes from research on the impact of sex hormones. In adults, differences in the level of these hormones are not generally associated with differences in sexual orientation. However, hormonal differences during prenatal development might be involved in the shaping of sexual orientation (Williams et al., 2000). Support for this view is provided by research on a congenital disorder that causes the adrenal glands to secrete extremely high levels of androgens prior to birth (Carlson, 1998). Women who suffered from this disorder, and who thus had been exposed to high levels of androgens during their fetal development, were much more likely to become lesbians than their sisters who had not been exposed (Meyer et al., 1995). In animals, such hormonal influences alter the structure of the hypothalamus, a brain region known to underlie some aspects of sexual functioning (Swaab & Hofman, 1995). In humans, hormones may likewise be responsible for anatomical differences in the hypothalamus that are seen not only in males versus females but in homosexual versus heterosexual men as well (LeVay, 1991; Swaab & Hofman, 1990). The anterior commissure, an area near the hypothalamus, also appears to differ in people with differing sexual orientations (Allen & Gorski, 1992; Gladue, 1994).

Further support for the influence of hormones on sexual orientation comes from a study of *otoacoustic emissions,* which are faint sounds that come from the human ear (McFadden & Pasanen, 1998). These sounds, known to be affected by hormones during prenatal development, are louder in heterosexual women than in men. In lesbians, however, the sounds are more similar to men's than to heterosexual women's, suggesting a biological process of sexual differentiation. This study did *not* find a difference between homosexual and heterosexual men, which is contrary to what would be expected if sexual orientation were invariably associated with otoacoustic emissions.

Finally, a biological basis for sexual orientation is suggested by the fact that environmental factors have a relatively weak impact on it. For example, several studies have shown that the sexual orientation of children's caregivers has little or no effect on those children's own sexual orientation.

● Are there alternative ways of interpreting the evidence?

Correlations between genetics and sexual orientation, like all correlational data, are open to alternative interpretations. As discussed in the chapter on research in psychology, a correlation describes the strength and direction of a relationship between variables, but it does not guarantee that one variable is actually influencing the other. Consider again the data showing that brothers who shared the most genes were also most likely to share a homosexual orientation. It is possible that what the brothers shared was not a gene for homosexuality but rather a set of genes that influenced their activity level, emotionality, aggressiveness, or the like. One example is "gender nonconformity" in childhood, the tendency for some boys to display "feminine" behaviors and for some girls to behave in "masculine" ways (Bailey, Dunne, & Martin, 2000). It could be such general aspects of temperament or personality—and other people's reactions to them—that influence the likelihood of a particular sexual orientation (Bem, 1996). In other words, sexual orientation could arise as a reaction to the way people respond to a genetically

A Committed Relationship Hetero-sexual and homosexual relationships can be brief and stormy, or stable and long lasting. These gay men are committed to each other for the long haul, as evidenced by their decision to adopt two children together. The strong role of biological factors in sexual orientation is seen in research showing that these children's orientation will not be influenced much, if at all, by that of their adopted parents (e.g., Bailey et al., 1995; Stacey & Biblarz, 2001; Tasker & Golombok, 1995).

ClassPrep PPT 30: Social & Cultural Factors in Sexuality

determined, but nonsexual, aspect of personality. Prenatal hormone levels, too, could influence sexual orientation by shaping aggressiveness or other nonsexual aspects of behavior.

It is also important to look at behavioral genetics evidence for what it can tell us about the role of *environmental factors* in sexual orientation. When we read that both members of identical twin pairs have a homosexual or bisexual orientation 52 percent of the time, it is easy to ignore the fact that the orientation of the twin pair members was *different* in nearly half the cases. Viewed in this way, the results suggest that genes do not tell the entire story of sexual orientation.

So even if sexual orientation has a biological base, it is probably not determined by genetic and hormonal forces alone. As described in the chapter on biological aspects of psychology, the bodies we inherit are quite responsive to environmental input; the behaviors we engage in and the environmental experiences we have often result in physical changes in the brain and elsewhere (Wang et al., 1995). For example, changes occur in the brain's synapses as we form new memories. So differences in the brains of people with differing sexual orientations could be the effect, not the cause, of their behavior or experiences.

● What additional evidence would help to evaluate the alternatives?

Much more evidence is needed regarding the extent to which genetic characteristics directly determine sexual orientation, as well as the extent to which genes and hormones shape physical and psychological characteristics that lead to the social construction of various sexual orientations. For example, the few available reports of sexual dimorphism in human brains have yet to be replicated. In studying this issue, researchers need to learn more not only about the genetic characteristics of people with different sexual orientations but also about their mental and behavioral styles. Are there personality characteristics associated with different sexual orientations? If so, do those characteristics have a strong genetic component? To what extent are heterosexuals, bisexuals, and homosexuals similar—and to what extent are they different—in terms of cognitive styles, biases, coping skills, developmental histories, and the like? And are there any differences in how sexual orientation is shaped in males versus females (Bailey, Dunne, & Martin, 2000)?

The more we learn about sexual orientation generally, the easier it will be to interpret data relating to its origins; but even defining sexual orientation is not simple. Alfred Kinsey and his colleagues (1948) viewed sexual orientation as occurring along a continuum rather than falling into a few discrete categories. Should a man who identifies himself as gay be considered bisexual because he occasionally has heterosexual daydreams? What sexual orientation label would be appropriate for a forty-year-old woman who experienced a few lesbian encounters in her teens but has engaged in exclusively heterosexual sex since then? Progress in understanding the origins of sexual orientation would be enhanced by a generally accepted system for describing and defining what is meant by *sexual orientation* (Stein, 1999).

● **What conclusions are most reasonable?**

Given the antagonism and physical danger often faced by people with nonheterosexual orientations (Cramer, 1999), it seems unlikely that a homosexual or bisexual identity is entirely a matter of choice. On the contrary, much of the evidence reviewed suggests that our sexual orientation chooses us, rather than the other way around. In light of this evidence, a reasonable hypothesis is that genetic factors, probably operating through prenatal hormones, create differences in the brains of people with different sexual orientations. Even if this hypothesis is correct, however, the manner in which a person expresses a genetically influenced sexual orientation will be profoundly shaped by what that person learns through social and cultural experiences (Bancroft, 1994). In short, sexual orientation most likely results from the complex interplay of both genetic and nongenetic mechanisms—both nature and nurture. Those who characterize sexual orientation as being either all "in the genes" or entirely a matter of choice are probably wrong.

Sexual Dysfunctions   ClassPrep PPT 32: Sexual Dysfunctions

The same biological, social, and psychological factors that shape human sexual behavior can also result in **sexual dysfunctions**, problems in a person's desire for or ability to have satisfying sexual activity. Fortunately, most of these problems—which affect 30 to 40 percent of U.S. adults (Laumann, Paik, & Rosen, 1999)—respond to psychotherapy, drugs, or both (de Silva, 1994). For men, a common problem is *erectile disorder* (once called *impotence*), a persistent inability to have or maintain an erection adequate for sex. Physical causes—such as fatigue, diabetes, hypertension, aging, and alcohol or other drugs—account for some cases, but psychological causes such as anxiety are also common (Everaerd & Laan, 1994). Viagra, a drug that increases blood flow in the penis, is effectively treating many cases of erectile disorder (Lue, 2000), and other drugs are in development. *Premature ejaculation*, another common dysfunction, involves a recurring tendency to ejaculate during sex sooner than the man or his partner desires. Most men experience episodes of at least one of these problems at some point in their lives, but such episodes are considered dysfunctions only if they become a distressing obstacle to sexual functioning (American Psychiatric Association, 1994).

For women, the most common sexual dysfunction is *arousal disorder* (once called *frigidity*), which is characterized by a recurring inability to become physiologically aroused during sexual activity (Phillips, 2000; Wilson et al., 1996). Arousal disorder can stem from inadequate genital stimulation, insufficient vaginal lubrication, or inadequate blood flow to the clitoris (Mansfield, Voda, & Koch, 1995; Wilson et al., 1996). However, it is also often tied to psychological factors such as guilt or self-consciousness, which can affect men as well as women (Davidson & Moore, 1994; Laan et al., 1993).

sexual dysfunctions Problems with sex that involve sexual motivation, arousal, or orgasmic response.

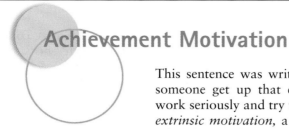

Achievement Motivation   ClassPrep PPT 33: Extrinsic vs. Intrinsic Motivation

OBJ 11.13: Define need achievement. Describe the characteristics of achievement motivation and the factors that can affect its development.

Test Items 11.63–11.70

Personal Learning Activity 11.1

IRM Activity 11.5: Achievement Motivation Through Children's Literature

IRM Activity 11.6: An In-Class Basketball Game to Show Achievement Motivation

Essay Q 11.2

This sentence was written at 6 A.M. on a beautiful Sunday in June. Why would someone get up that early to work on a weekend? Why do people take their work seriously and try to do the best that they can? People work hard partly due to *extrinsic motivation,* a desire for external rewards such as money. But work and other human behaviors also reflect *intrinsic motivation,* a desire to attain internal satisfaction.

The next time you visit someone's home or office, look at the mementos displayed there. You may see framed diplomas and awards, trophies and ribbons, pictures of memorable personal events, and photos of children and grandchildren. These badges of achievement affirm that a person has accomplished tasks that merit approval or establish worth. Much of our behavior is motivated by a desire for approval, admiration, and achievement—in short, for *esteem*—from others and from ourselves. In this section, we examine two of the most common avenues to esteem: achievement in general and a job in particular.

Need for Achievement   ClassPrep PPT 34: Need for Achievement

Many athletes who already hold world records still train intensely; many people who have built multimillion-dollar businesses still work fourteen-hour days. What motivates these people?

One possible answer is a motive called **need achievement** (Murray, 1938). People with a high need for achievement seek to master tasks—be they sports, business ventures, intellectual puzzles, or artistic creations—and feel intense satisfaction from doing so. They exert strenuous efforts in striving for excellence, enjoy themselves in the process, and take great pride in achieving at a high level (McClelland, 1985).

ClassPrep PPT 35: Individual Differences in Need for Achievement

Individual Differences   How do people with strong achievement motivation differ from others? To find out, researchers gave children a test to measure their need for achievement (Figure 11.7 shows a test for adults) and then asked them to play a ring-toss game. Children scoring low on the need-achievement test usually stood so close to, or so far away from, the ring-toss target that they either could not fail or could not succeed. In contrast, children scoring high on the need-achievement test stood at a moderate distance from the target, making the game challenging but not impossible (McClelland, 1958). These and other experiments suggest that people with high achievement needs tend to set challenging—but realistic—goals. They actively seek success, take risks when necessary, and are intensely satisfied with success. But if they feel they have tried their best, people with high achievement motivation are not too upset by failure. Those with low achievement motivation also like to succeed, but instead of joy, success tends to bring them relief at having avoided failure (Winter, 1996).

Differences in achievement motivation also appear in people's goals in achievement-related situations (Molden & Dweck, 2000). Some people tend to adopt *learning goals.* When they play golf, take piano lessons, work at puzzles and problems, go to school, and get involved in other achievement-oriented activities, they do so mainly to develop competence in those activities. Realizing that they may not yet possess the skills necessary to achieve at a high level, they tend to learn by watching others and to struggle with problems on their own rather than asking for help (Mayer & Sutton, 1996). When they do seek help, people with learning goals are likely to ask for explanations, hints, and other forms of task-related information, not for quick, easy answers that remove the challenge from the situation. In contrast, people who adopt *performance goals* are usually more concerned with demonstrating the competence they believe they already possess. They tend to seek information about how well they have performed compared with others rather than

figure 11.7

Assessment of Need Achievement
This picture is from the Thematic Apperception Test, or TAT (Morgan & Murray, 1935). The strength of people's achievement motivation is inferred from the stories they tell about TAT pictures. A response such as "The young woman is hoping that she will be able to make her grandmother proud of her" would be seen as reflecting high achievement motivation.

Source: Murray (1971).

Helping Them Do Their Best
Learning-oriented goals are especially appropriate in classrooms, where students typically have little knowledge of the subject matter. This is why most teachers tolerate errors and reward gradual improvement. They do not usually encourage performance goals, which emphasize doing better than others and demonstrating immediate competence (Reeve, 1996). Still, to help students do their best in the long run, teachers sometimes promote performance goals, too. The proper combination of both kinds of goals may be more motivating than either kind alone (Barron & Harackiewicz, 2001).

ClassPrep PPT 36: Goal Differences in Achievement-Related Situations

IRM Handout 11.7: Characteristics of the Self-Actualizer

ClassPrep PPT 37: Influences on Development of Achievement Motivation

need achievement A motive influenced by the degree to which a person establishes specific goals, cares about meeting those goals, and experiences feelings of satisfaction by doing so.

about how to improve their performance (Butler, 1999). When they seek help, it is usually to ask for "the right answer" rather than for tips on how to find the answer themselves. Because their primary goal is to demonstrate their competence, people with performance goals tend to avoid new challenges if they are not confident that they will be successful, and they tend to quit in response to failure (Weiner, 1980).

Development of Achievement Motivation   Achievement motivation tends to be learned in early childhood, especially from parents. For example, in one study young boys were given a very hard task at which they were sure to fail. Fathers whose sons scored low on achievement motivation tests often became annoyed as they watched their boys, discouraged them from continuing, and interfered or even completed the task themselves (Rosen & D'Andrade, 1959). A different pattern of behavior emerged among parents of children who scored high on tests of achievement motivation. Those parents tended to (1) encourage the child to try difficult tasks, especially new ones; (2) give praise and other rewards for success; (3) encourage the child to find ways to succeed rather than merely complaining about failure; and (4) prompt the child to go on to the next, more difficult challenge (McClelland, 1985).

More general cultural influences also affect the development of achievement motivation. For example, subtle messages about a culture's view of how achievement occurs often appear in the books children read and the stories they hear. Does the story's main character work hard and overcome obstacles (creating expectations of a payoff for persistence) or loaf and then win the lottery (suggesting that rewards come randomly, regardless of effort)? If the main character succeeds, is this outcome the result of personal initiative (typical of an individualist culture) or of ties to a cooperative and supportive group (typical of a collectivist culture)? These themes appear to act as blueprints for reaching culturally approved goals. It should not be surprising, then, that ideas about how people achieve differ from culture to culture. In one study, for example, individuals from Saudi Arabia and from the United States were asked to comment on short stories describing people succeeding at various tasks. Saudis tended to see the people in the stories as having succeeded because of the help they got from others, whereas Americans tended to attribute success to the internal characteristics of each story's main character (Zahrani & Kaplowitz, 1993). Achievement motivation is also influenced by how much a particular culture *values* achievement. For example, in cultures where demanding standards lead students to fear rejection for failure to attain high grades, the motivation to excel is likely to be especially strong (Eaton & Dembo, 1997; Hess, Chih-Mei, & McDevitt, 1987).

It is possible to increase achievement motivation among people whose cultural training did not foster it in childhood (Mayer & Sutton, 1996). In one study, high school and college students with low achievement motivation were helped to develop fantasies about their own success. They imagined setting goals that were difficult, but not impossible. Then they imagined themselves concentrating on breaking a complex problem into small, manageable steps. They fantasized about working hard, failing but not being discouraged, continuing to work, and finally feeling elated at success. Afterward, the students' grades and academic success improved, suggesting an increase in their achievement motivation (McClelland, 1985). In short, achievement motivation is strongly influenced by social and cultural learning experiences, as well as by the beliefs about oneself that these experiences help to create. People who come to believe in their ability to achieve are more likely to do so than those who expect to fail (Butler, 1998; Dweck, 1998; Wigfield & Eccles, 2000).

ClassPrep PPT 38: Goal Setting and Achievement Motivation

Goal Setting and Achievement Motivation

Why are you reading this chapter instead of watching television or hanging out with your friends? Your motivation to study is probably based on your goal of doing well in a psychology course, which relates to broader goals, such as attaining a degree, having a career, and the like. Psychologists have found that we set goals when we recognize a discrepancy between our current situation and how we want that situation to be (Oettingen, Pak, & Schnetter, 2001). Establishing a goal motivates us to engage in behaviors designed to reduce the discrepancy we have identified. The kinds of goals we set can influence the amount of effort, persistence, attention, and planning we devote to a task.

In general, the more difficult a goal, the harder people will try to reach it. This rule assumes, of course, that the goal is seen as attainable. Goals that are impossibly difficult may not motivate maximum effort. It also assumes that the person accepts the goal. If a difficult goal is set by someone else—as when a parent assigns a teenager to keep a large lawn and garden trimmed and weeded—people may not accept it as their own and may not work very hard to attain it. Setting goals that are

Children raised in environments that support the development of strong achievement motivation tend not to give up on difficult tasks—even if all the king's horses and all the king's men do!

"Maybe they didn't try hard enough."

Motivated by a Goal People are more motivated to persist in efforts to improve their appearance and avoid health risks when they are pursuing a clear, specific goal such as "lose twenty pounds," "do aerobics three times a week," or "quit smoking" rather than pursuing a vague goal such as "get in shape."

clear and specific tends to increase people's motivation to persist at a task. For example, you are more likely to keep reading this chapter if your goal is to "read the motivation and emotion chapter today" than if it is to "do some studying." Clarifying your goal makes it easier to know when you have reached it, and when it is time to stop. Without clear goals, a person can be more easily distracted by fatigue, boredom, or frustration and more likely to give up before completing a task. Goals, especially clear goals, also tend to focus people's attention on creating plans for pursuing them, on the activities they believe will lead to goal attainment, and on evaluating their progress. In short, the process of goal setting is more than just wishful thinking. It is an important first step in motivating all kinds of behavior.

Achievement and Success in the Workplace

OBJ 11.14: Describe the extrinsic and intrinsic factors that affect job satisfaction and dissatisfaction. Give an example of a job that has been designed to increase satisfaction and motivation.

Test Items 11.71–11.77

IRM In Your Own Words 11.2: Evaluate Your Job

ClassPrep PPT 39: Achievement & Success in the Workplace

In the workplace, there is usually less concern with employees' general level of achievement motivation than with their motivation to work hard during business hours. In fact, employers tend to set up jobs in accordance with their ideas about how intrinsic and extrinsic motivation combine to shape their employees' performance (Riggio, 1989). Employers who see workers as lazy, untrustworthy creatures with no ambition tend to offer highly structured, heavily supervised jobs that give employees little say in deciding what to do or how to do it. These employers assume that workers are motivated mainly by extrinsic rewards—money, in particular. So they tend to be surprised when, in spite of good pay and benefits, employees sometimes express dissatisfaction with their jobs and show little motivation to work hard (Amabile et al., 1994; Igalens & Roussel, 2000).

If good pay and benefits alone do not bring job satisfaction and the desire to excel on the job, what does? Research suggests that low worker motivation in Western cultures comes largely from the feeling of having little or no control over the work environment (Rosen, 1991). Compared with those in rigidly structured jobs, workers tend to be more satisfied and productive if they are (1) encouraged to participate in decisions about how work should be done; (2) given problems to solve, without being told how to solve them; (3) taught more than one skill; (4) given individual responsibility; and (5) given public recognition, not just money, for good performance.

Allowing people to set and achieve clear goals is one way to increase both job performance and job satisfaction (Abramis, 1994). As suggested by our earlier discussion, some goals are especially effective at maintaining work motivation (Katzell

Teamwork Pays Off A number of U.S. companies are following Japanese examples by redesigning jobs to increase workers' responsibility and flexibility. The goal is to increase productivity and job satisfaction by creating teams in which employees are responsible for solving production problems and making decisions about how best to do their jobs. Team members are publicly recognized for outstanding work, and part of their pay depends on the quality (not just the number) of their products and on the profitability of the company as a whole.

& Thompson, 1990). First, they are personally meaningful. When a memo from a remote administrator decrees that employees should increase production, they tend to feel put upon and not particularly motivated to meet the goal. Before assigning difficult goals, good managers try to ensure that employees accept those goals (Klein et al., 1999). They include employees in the goal-setting process, make sure that the employees have the skills and resources to reach the goal, and emphasize the benefits to be gained from success—perhaps including financial incentives (Jenkins et al., 1998; Locke & Latham, 1990). Second, effective goals are specific and concrete. The goal of "doing better" is usually not a strong motivator, because it provides no direction about how to proceed and also fails to specify when the goal has been met. A specific target, such as increasing sales by 10 percent, is a far more motivating goal; it can be measured objectively, allowing feedback on progress, and it tells workers whether the goal has been reached. Finally, goals are most effective if management supports the workers' own goal setting, offers special rewards for reaching goals, and gives encouragement for renewed efforts after failure (Kluger & DeNisi, 1998).

In summary, motivating jobs offer personal challenges, independence, and both intrinsic and extrinsic rewards. They provide enough satisfaction for people to feel excitement and pleasure in working hard. For employers, meanwhile, the rewards are more productivity, less absenteeism, and lower turnover (Ilgen & Pulakos, 1999).

Achievement and Subjective Well-Being

OBJ 11.15: Discuss the relation between achievement and subjective well-being.

Test Items 11.78–11.80

ClassPrep PPT 40: Achievement and Subjective Well-Being

Some people believe that the more they achieve at work and elsewhere, and the more money and other material goods they acquire as a result, the happier they will be. Will they? As part of a recent focus on *positive psychology* (Seligman & Csikszentmihalyi, 2000; Sheldon & King, 2001), researchers have become increasingly interested in studying what it actually takes to achieve happiness, or more formally, subjective well-being. **Subjective well-being** is a combination of a cognitive judgment of satisfaction with life, the frequent experiencing of positive moods and emotions, and the relatively infrequent experiencing of unpleasant moods and emotions (Diener, 2000).

subjective well-being A combination of a cognitive judgment of satisfaction with life, the frequent experiencing of positive moods and emotions, and the relatively infrequent experiencing of unpleasant moods and emotions.

Research on subjective well-being indicates that, as you might expect, people living in extreme poverty or in war-torn or politically chaotic countries are less happy than people in better circumstances. And people everywhere react to good or bad events with corresponding changes in mood. As described in the chapter on health, stress, and coping, for example, severe or long-lasting stressors—such as the death of a loved one—can lead to psychological and physical problems. But although events do have an impact, the saddening or elevating effects of major changes, such as being promoted or fired, or even being imprisoned or seriously injured, tend not to last as long as we might think they would. In other words, how happy you are may have less to do with what happens to you than you might expect (Gilbert & Wilson, 1998).

Most event-related changes in mood subside within days or weeks, and most people then return to their previous level of happiness (Suh, Diener, & Fujita, 1996). Even when events create permanent changes in circumstances, most people adapt by changing their expectancies and goals, not by radically and permanently changing their baseline level of happiness. For example, people may be thrilled after getting a big salary increase, but as they get used to having it, the thrill fades, and they may eventually feel just as underpaid as before. In fact, people's level of subjective well-being tends to be remarkably stable throughout their lives. This stable baseline may be related to temperament, or personality, and it has been likened to a set point for body weight (Lykken, 1999). Like many other aspects of temperament, our baseline level of happiness may be influenced by genetics. Twin studies have shown, for example, that individual differences in happiness are more strongly associated with inherited personality characteristics than with environmental factors such as money, popularity, or physical attractiveness (Lykken, 1999; Tellegen et al., 1988).

Beyond inherited tendencies, the things that appear to matter most in generating happiness are close social ties (especially a satisfying marriage or partnership and good friends), religious faith, and having the resources necessary to allow progress toward one's goals (Diener, 2000; Myers, 2000b). So you don't have to be a rich, physically attractive high achiever to be happy, and it turns out that most people in Western cultures are relatively happy (Diener & Diener, 1995).

These results are consistent with the views expressed over many centuries by philosophers, psychologists, and wise people in all cultures. For example, decades ago, Abraham Maslow (1970) noted that when people in Western cultures experience unhappiness and psychological problems, those problems can often be traced to a *deficiency orientation*. That is, these people tend to seek happiness by trying to acquire the goods and reach the status they *don't* have—but think they need—rather than by appreciating life itself and the value of the material and nonmaterial riches they *already* have. Others have amplified this point, suggesting that efforts to get more of the things we think will bring happiness may actually contribute to unhappiness if what we get is never "enough" (Csikszentmihalyi, 1999; Myers, 2000a; Srivastava, Locke, & Bartol, 2001).

Relations and Conflicts Among Motives

Maslow's views about deficiency motivation stemmed from his more general model, in which human behavior is seen as based on a hierarchy of needs, or motives (see Figure 11.8). Needs at the lowest level of the hierarchy, he said, must be at least partially satisfied before people can be motivated by higher-level goals. From the bottom to the top of Maslow's hierarchy, these five motives are as follows:

OBJ 11.16: Describe Maslow's hierarchy of needs. Give examples of each kind of need.

Test Items 11.81–11.86

1. *Biological,* such as the need for food, water, oxygen, activity, and sleep.

2. *Safety,* such as the need to be cared for as a child and have a secure income as an adult.

3. *Belongingness and love,* such as the need to be part of social groups and to participate in affectionate sexual and nonsexual relationships.

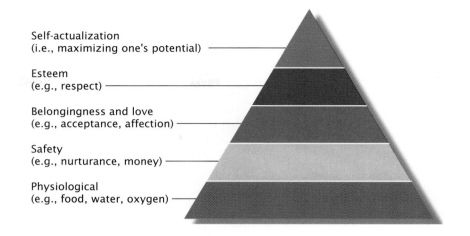

Self-actualization
(i.e., maximizing one's potential)

Esteem
(e.g., respect)

Belongingness and love
(e.g., acceptance, affection)

Safety
(e.g., nurturance, money)

Physiological
(e.g., food, water, oxygen)

4. *Esteem,* such as the need to be respected as a useful, honorable individual.

5. *Self-actualization,* which means reaching one's fullest potential. People motivated by this need explore and enhance relationships with others; follow interests for intrinsic pleasure rather than for money, status, or esteem; and are concerned with issues affecting all people, not just themselves.

Maslow's theoretical hierarchy has been very influential over the years, but critics see it as far too simplistic (Hall, Lindsay, & Campbell, 1998; Neher, 1991). It does not predict or explain, for example, the motivation of people who starve themselves to death to draw attention to political or moral causes. Further, people may not have to satisfy one kind of need before addressing others; we can seek several needs at once. And though the needs associated with basic survival and security do generally take precedence over those related to self-enhancement or personal growth (Baumeister & Leary, 1995; Oishi et al., 1999), the needs that are most important to people's satisfaction with life do not always correspond to Maslow's hierarchy. One set of studies with college students found that the needs for autonomy (independence), relatedness to others, competence, and self-esteem were more important than the need for luxury *or* self-actualization (Sheldon et al., 2001). Further, the ordering of needs within the survival/security and enhancement/growth categories differs from culture to culture, suggesting that there may not be a single, universal hierarchy of needs.

Conflicting Motives and Stress

As in the case of hunger strikes, human motives can sometimes conflict. The usual result is some degree of discomfort. For example, imagine that you are alone and bored on a Saturday night, and you think about going to the store to buy some snacks. What are your motives? Hunger might prompt you to go out, as might the prospect of increased arousal that a change of scene will provide. Even sexual motivation might be involved, as you fantasize about meeting someone exciting in the snack-food aisle. But safety-related motives may also kick in—what if you get mugged? Even an esteem motive might come into play, making you hesitate to be seen alone on a weekend night.

These are just a few motives that may shape a trivial decision. When the decision is more important, the number and strength of motivational pushes and pulls are often greater, creating far more internal conflict. Four basic types of motivational conflict have been identified (Miller, 1959):

1. *Approach-approach conflicts.* When a person must choose only one of two desirable activities—say, going to a movie or going to a play—an *approach-approach conflict* exists. As the importance of the choice increases, so does the difficulty of making it.

2. *Avoidance-avoidance conflicts.* An *avoidance-avoidance conflict* arises when a person must select one of two undesirable alternatives. Someone forced either to sell the family farm or to declare bankruptcy faces an avoidance-avoidance conflict. Such conflicts are very difficult to resolve and often create intense emotions.

3. *Approach-avoidance conflicts.* If someone you couldn't stand had tickets to your favorite group's sold-out concert and invited you to come along, what would you do? When a single event or activity has both attractive and unattractive features, an *approach-avoidance conflict* is created. Conflicts of this type are also difficult to resolve and often result in long periods of indecision.

4. *Multiple approach-avoidance conflicts.* Suppose you must choose between two jobs. One offers a high salary with a well-known company, but it requires long hours and relocation to a miserable climate. The other boasts advancement opportunities, fringe benefits, and a better climate, but it offers lower pay and an unpredictable work schedule. This is an example of a *multiple approach-avoidance conflict,* in which two or more alternatives each have both positive and negative features. Such conflicts are difficult to resolve partly because the attributes of each option are often difficult to compare. For example, how many dollars a year does it take to compensate you for living in a bad climate?

Each of these conflicts can create a significant amount of stress, a topic described at length in the chapter on health, stress, and coping. Most people in the midst of motivational conflicts are tense, irritable, and more vulnerable than usual to physical and psychological problems. These reactions are especially likely when there is no obviously "right" choice, when conflicting motives have approximately equal strength, and when the choice can have serious consequences (as in decisions to marry, to divorce, or to approve disconnection of a relative's life-support system). People may take a long time to resolve these conflicts, or they may act impulsively and thoughtlessly, if only to end the discomfort of uncertainty. And even after a conflict is resolved, stress responses may continue in the form of anxiety about the wisdom of the decision or self-blame over bad choices. These and other consequences of conflicting motives can even lead to depression or other serious disorders.

Opponent Processes, Motivation, and Emotion

OBJ 11.18: Discuss the opponent-process theory of motivation. Give an example of the kinds of behavior it explains.

Test Items 11.98–11.103

ClassPrep PPT 42: Opponent Process Theory

Resolving approach-avoidance conflicts is often complicated by the fact that some behaviors have more than one emotional effect, and those effects may be opposite to one another. People who ride roller coasters or skydive, for example, often say that the experience is scary, but also thrilling. How do they decide whether or not to repeat these behaviors? One answer lies in the changing value of incentives and the regulation of arousal described in Richard Solomon's *opponent-process theory,* which is discussed in the chapter on learning (Solomon & Corbit, 1974). Opponent-process theory is based on two assumptions. The first is that any reaction to a stimulus is followed by an opposite reaction, called the *opponent process.* For example, being startled by a sudden sound is typically followed by relaxation and relief. Second, after repeated exposure to the same stimulus, the initial reaction weakens, and the opponent process becomes quicker and stronger.

Research on opponent-process theory has revealed a predictable pattern of emotional changes that helps explain some people's motivation to repeatedly engage in arousing but fearsome activities, such as skydiving. Prior to the first several episodes, people usually experience stark terror, followed by intense relief when they reach the ground. With more experience, however, the terror becomes mild anxiety, and what had been relief grows to a euphoria that can appear *during* the activity (Solomon, 1980). As a result, says Solomon, some people's motivation to pursue such activities can become a virtual addiction.

The emotions associated with motivational conflicts and with the operation of opponent processes provide just two examples of the intimate links between motivation and emotion. Motivation can intensify emotion, as when a normally timid person's hunger results in an angry phone call about a late pizza delivery. But emotions can also create motivation. Happiness, for example, is an emotion that people want to feel, so they engage in whatever behaviors—studying, creating art, investing, beachcombing—they think will achieve it. Similarly, as an emotion that most people want to avoid, anxiety prompts many behaviors, from leaving the scene of an accident to avoiding poisonous snakes. In the next section of this chapter, we take a closer look at emotions.

The Nature of Emotion

Everyone seems to agree that joy, sorrow, anger, fear, love, and hate are emotions, but it is hard to identify exactly what it is that makes these experiences emotions rather than, say, thoughts or impulses. In fact, some cultures see emotion and thought as the same thing. The Chewong of Malaysia, for example, consider the liver the seat of both what we call thoughts and feelings (Russell, 1991).

OBJ 11.19: Describe the defining characteristics of the subjective experience of emotion.

Test Items 11.104–11.107

ClassPrep PPT 43: Emotions

Freburg *Perspectives:* Nelton, "Emotion in the Workplace"

Defining Characteristics

Most psychologists in Western cultures tend to see emotions as organized psychological and physiological reactions to changes in our relationship to the world. These reactions are partly inner, or *subjective,* experiences and partly objectively measurable patterns of behavior and physiological arousal. The subjective experience of emotion has several characteristics:

Winners and Losers Emotional experiences depend in part on our interpretation of situations and how those situations relate to our goals. A single stimulus—the announcement of the results of a cheerleading contest—triggered drastically different emotional reactions in these women, depending on whether they perceived it as making them winners or losers.

1. Emotion is usually *temporary;* it tends to have a relatively clear beginning and end, as well as a relatively short duration. Moods, by contrast, tend to last longer.

2. Emotional experience is either *positive* or *negative,* that is, pleasant or unpleasant.

3. Emotional experience is elicited partly by a *cognitive appraisal* of how a situation relates to your goals. The same event can bring about different emotions depending on your interpretation of what the event means. An exam score of 75 percent could excite you if your previous score had been 50 percent, but it might upset you if you had never before scored below 90 percent and you saw the result as a disaster.

4. Emotional experience *alters thought processes,* often by directing attention toward some things and away from others. The anguish of parents whose child is killed by a drunken driver, for example, might change their perception of the importance of drunk-driving laws.

5. Emotional experience triggers an *action tendency,* the motivation to behave in certain ways. The grieving parents' anger, for example, might motivate them to harm the driver or to work for stronger penalties for drunk driving.

6. Emotional experiences are *passions* that happen to you, usually whether you want them to or not. You can exert at least some control over emotions in the sense that they depend partly on how you interpret situations (Gross, 2001). For example, your emotional reaction might be less extreme after a house fire if you remind yourself that no one was hurt and you are insured. Still, such control is limited. You cannot *decide* to experience joy or sorrow; instead, you "fall in love" or are "overcome by grief." Emotional experiences, much like personality traits, have a different relation to the self than do conscious thoughts.

In other words, the subjective aspects of emotions are both *triggered* by the thinking self and felt as *happening* to the self. They reveal each individual as both agent and object, both I and me, both the controller of thoughts and the recipient of passions. The extent to which we are "victims" of our passions versus rational designers of our emotions is a central dilemma of human existence, as much a subject of literature as of psychology.

The *objective* aspects of emotion include learned and innate *expressive displays* and *physiological responses.* Expressive displays—a smile, a frown—communicate feelings to others. Physiological responses—changes in heart rate, for example—are the biological adjustments needed to perform the action tendencies generated by emotional experience. If you throw a temper tantrum or jump for joy, your heart must deliver additional oxygen and fuel to your muscles.

In summary, an **emotion** is a temporary experience with either positive or negative qualities. It is felt with some intensity as happening to the self, generated in part by a cognitive appraisal of situations, and accompanied by both learned and innate physical responses. Through emotion, people communicate their internal states and intentions to others, but emotion also functions to direct and energize a person's own thoughts and actions. Emotion often disrupts thought and behavior, but it also triggers and guides cognitions and organizes, motivates, and sustains behavior and social relations.

emotion   A transitory positive or negative experience that is felt as happening to the self, is generated in part by cognitive appraisal of a situation, and is accompanied by both learned and reflexive physical responses.

The Biology of Emotion

The role of biology in emotion is seen in mechanisms of the central nervous system and the autonomic nervous system. In the *central nervous system,* specific brain areas are involved in the generation of emotions as well as in our experience of those

ClassPrep PPT 48, OHT: *Figure 11.9:* Brain Regions Involved in Emotion

figure 11.9

Brain Regions Involved in Emotion

Incoming sensory information alerts the brain to an emotion-evoking situation. Most of the information goes through the thalamus; the cingulate cortex and hippocampus are involved in the interpretation of this sensory input. Output from these areas goes to the amygdala and hypothalamus, which control the autonomic nervous system via hindbrain connections. There are also connections from the thalamus directly to the amygdala. The locus coeruleus is an area of the hindbrain that causes both widespread arousal of cortical areas and changes in autonomic activity.

ClassPrep PPT 47: Three Basic Features of the Brain's Control of Emotions

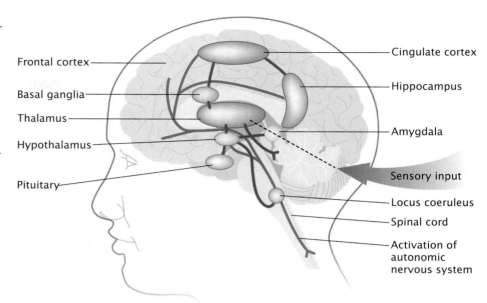

Frontal cortex — Basal ganglia — Thalamus — Hypothalamus — Pituitary — Cingulate cortex — Hippocampus — Amygdala — Sensory input — Locus coeruleus — Spinal cord — Activation of autonomic nervous system

emotions. The *autonomic nervous system (ANS)* gives rise to many of the physiological changes associated with emotional arousal.

Brain Mechanisms   Although many questions remain, researchers have described three basic features of the brain's control of emotion. First, it appears that activity in the *limbic system,* especially in the *amygdala,* is central to various aspects of emotion (LeDoux, 1996; see Figure 11.9). Disruption of the amygdala's functioning prevents animals from being able to associate fear with a negative stimulus (Davis et al., 1993). In humans, too, the amygdala plays a critical role in the ability to learn emotional associations, recognize emotional expressions, and perceive emotionally charged words (e.g., Anderson & Phelps, 2001). In one functional magnetic resonance imaging study, when researchers paired an aversively loud noise with pictures of faces, the participants' brains revealed activation of the amygdala while the noise-picture association was being learned (LaBar et al., 1998). In another study, victims of a disease that destroys only the amygdala were found to be unable to judge other people's emotional states by looking at their faces (Adolphs et al., 1994). Faces that normal people rated as expressing strong negative emotions were rated by the amygdala-damaged individuals as approachable and trustworthy (Adolphs, Tranel, & Damasio, 1998).

A second aspect of the brain's involvement in emotion is seen in its control over emotional and nonemotional facial expressions (Rinn, 1984). Take a moment to look in a mirror and put on your best fake smile. The voluntary facial movements you just made, like all voluntary movements, are controlled by the *pyramidal motor system,* a brain system that includes the motor cortex (see Figure 3.17). However, a smile that expresses genuine happiness is involuntary. That kind of smile, like the other facial movements associated with emotions, is governed by the *extrapyramidal motor system,* which depends on areas beneath the cortex. Brain damage can disrupt either system (see Figure 11.10). People with pyramidal motor system damage show normal facial expressions during genuine emotion, but they cannot fake a smile. In contrast, people with damage to the extrapyramidal system can pose facial expressions at will, but they remain straight-faced even when feeling genuine joy or profound sadness (Hopf, Muller, & Hopf, 1992).

A third aspect of the brain's role in emotion is revealed by research on the cerebral cortex and the differing contributions of its two cerebral hemispheres to the perception, experience, and expression of emotion (Davidson, 2000). For example, after suffering damage to the right, but not the left, hemisphere, people no longer

figure 11.10

Control of Voluntary and Emotional Facial Movements

This man has a tumor in his motor cortex that prevents him from voluntarily moving the muscles on the left side of his face. In the photograph at the left he is trying to smile in response to instructions from the examiner. He cannot smile on command, but he can smile with happiness, as the photograph at the right shows, because the movements associated with genuine emotion are controlled by the extrapyramidal motor system.

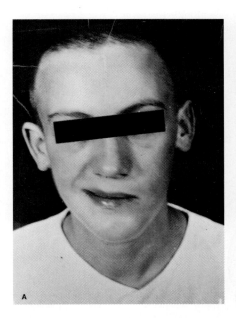
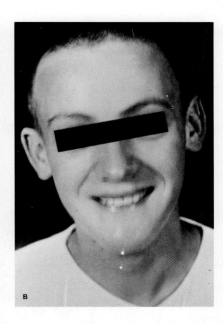

laugh at jokes—even though they can still understand the jokes' words, the logic (or illogic) underlying them, and the punch lines (Critchley, 1991). Further, when people are asked to name the emotions shown in slides of facial expressions, blood flow increases in the right hemisphere more than in the left hemisphere (Gur, Skolnic, & Gur, 1994). People are also faster and more accurate at this emotion-naming task when the facial expressions are presented to the brain's right hemisphere than when they are presented to the left (Hahdahl, Iversen, & Jonsen, 1993). Finally, compared with normal people, depressed people display greater electrical activity in the right frontal cortex (Schaffer, Davidson, & Saron, 1983) and perform more poorly on tasks that depend especially on the right hemisphere (Banich et al., 1992; Heller, Etienne, & Miller, 1995).

There is some debate about how hemispheric differences relate to emotion. Research has demonstrated that the right hemisphere is activated during many displays of emotion (Heller, 1993), including negative emotion. But some investigators argue that the experiencing of positive emotion depends on the left frontal cortex. For example, EEG recordings show that smiling during an experience of genuine positive emotion correlates with greater left frontal activity (Davidson et al., 1990). And consider the findings from a case study of a sixteen-year-old girl. When an area of her left frontal cortex was given mild electrical stimulation, she began to smile, and stimulation at a higher intensity elicited robust laughter (Fried et al., 1998). She attributed her laughing to whatever external stimulus was present ("You guys are just so funny . . . standing around"). Generally, however, most other aspects of emotion—the experiencing of negative emotion, the perception of any emotion exhibited in faces or other stimuli, and the facial expression of any emotion—depend on the right hemisphere more than on the left (Heller, Nitschke, & Miller, 1998; Kawasaki et al., 2001).

If the right hemisphere is relatively dominant in emotion, which side of the face would you expect to be somewhat more involved in expressing emotion? If you said the left side, you are correct, because movements of each side of the body are controlled by the opposite side of the brain (see the chapter on biological aspects of psychology).

Mechanisms of the Autonomic Nervous System   The autonomic nervous system is involved in many of the physiological changes that accompany emotions (Vernet, Robin, & Dittmar, 1995). If your hands get cold and clammy when you are nervous, it is because the ANS has increased perspiration and decreased the blood flow in your hands.

Parasympathetic functions   **Sympathetic functions**

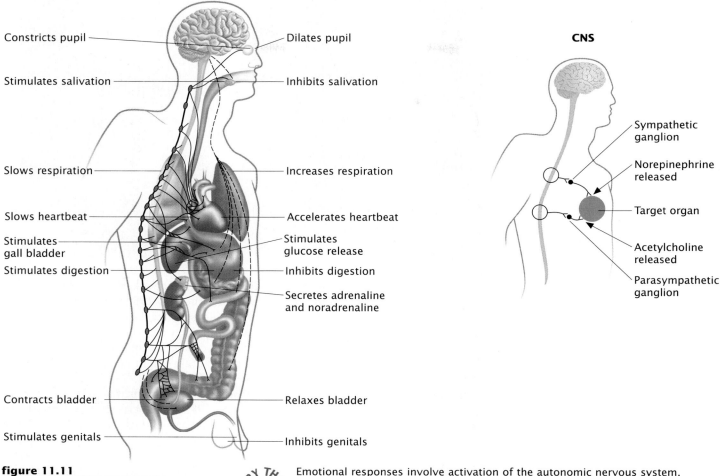

Constricts pupil — — Dilates pupil

Stimulates salivation — — Inhibits salivation

Slows respiration — — Increases respiration

Slows heartbeat — — Accelerates heartbeat

Stimulates gall bladder — — Stimulates glucose release

Stimulates digestion — — Inhibits digestion

— Secretes adrenaline and noradrenaline

Contracts bladder — — Relaxes bladder

Stimulates genitals — — Inhibits genitals

CNS

Sympathetic ganglion

Norepinephrine released

Target organ

Acetylcholine released

Parasympathetic ganglion

figure 11.11

The Autonomic Nervous System

TRY THIS   Emotional responses involve activation of the autonomic nervous system, which includes sympathetic and parasympathetic subsystems. Which of the bodily responses depicted here do you associate with emotional experiences?

ClassPrep PPT 49, OHT: *Figure 11.11:* The Autonomic Nervous System

parasympathetic system   The subsystem of the autonomic nervous system that typically influences activity related to the protection, nourishment, and growth of the body.

sympathetic system   The subsystem of the autonomic nervous system that usually prepares the organism for vigorous activity.

As described in the chapter on biological aspects of psychology, the ANS carries information between the brain and most organs of the body—the heart and blood vessels, the digestive system, and so on. Each of these organs has its own ongoing activity, but ANS input affects this activity, increasing or decreasing it. By doing so, the ANS coordinates the functioning of these organs to meet the body's general needs and to prepare it for change (Porges, Doussard, & Maita, 1995). If you are aroused to take action—to run to catch a bus, say—you need more glucose to fuel your muscles. The ANS frees needed energy by stimulating secretion of glucose-generating hormones and promoting blood flow to the muscles.

Figure 11.11 shows that the autonomic nervous system is organized into two divisions: the sympathetic nervous system and the parasympathetic nervous system. Emotions can activate either of these divisions, both of which send axon fibers to each organ in the body. Generally, the sympathetic and parasympathetic fibers have opposite effects on these so-called *target organs*. Axons from the **parasympathetic system** release *acetylcholine* onto target organs, leading to activity related to the protection, nourishment, and growth of the body. For example, parasympathetic activity increases digestion by stimulating movement of the intestinal system so that more nutrients are taken from food. Axons from the **sympathetic system** release a different neurotransmitter, *norepinephrine*, onto target organs, helping to prepare the body for vigorous activity. When one part of the sympathetic system is stimulated, other parts are activated "in sympathy" with it (Gellhorn & Loofbourrow, 1963). For example, input from sympathetic neurons to the adrenal medulla causes that gland to dump norepinephrine and epinephrine into the bloodstream, thereby activating all sympathetic target organs (see Figure 13.3). The result is the **fight-or-flight syndrome,** a pattern of increased heart rate and blood pressure, rapid or irregular breathing, dilated pupils, perspiration, dry mouth, increased blood sugar, piloerection ("goose bumps"), and other changes that help prepare the body to combat or run from a threat.

The ANS is not directly connected to brain areas involved in consciousness, so sensations about organ activity reach the brain at a nonconscious level. You may hear your stomach grumble, but you can't actually feel it secrete acids. Similarly, you can't consciously experience the brain mechanisms that alter the activity of your autonomic nervous system. This is why most people cannot exert direct, conscious control over blood pressure or other aspects of ANS activity. However, there are things you can do that have indirect effects on the ANS. For example, to arouse autonomic innervation of your sex organs, you might imagine an erotic situation. And to raise your blood pressure, you might hold your breath or strain your muscles.

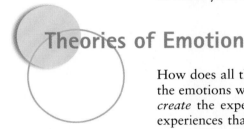

Theories of Emotion

How does all this activity in the brain and the autonomic nervous system relate to the emotions we actually experience? Are autonomic responses to events enough to *create* the experience of emotion, or are those responses the *result* of emotional experiences that begin in the brain? And how does our cognitive interpretation of events affect our emotional reactions to them? Psychologists have worked on the answers to these questions for over a century; in the process, they have developed a number of theories that explain emotion mainly in terms of biological or cognitive factors. The main biological theories are those of William James and Walter Cannon. The most prominent cognitive theories are those of Stanley Schachter and Richard Lazarus. In this section we review these theories, along with some research designed to evaluate them.

Videodisc Segment & Still: "Common Sense" Views of Emotion

James's Peripheral Theory

Suppose you are camping in the woods when a huge bear approaches your tent. Scared to death, you run for dear life. Do you run because you are afraid, or are you afraid because you run? The example and the question come from William James, who offered one of the first formal accounts of how physiological responses relate to emotional experience. James argued that you are afraid *because* you run. Your running and other physiological responses, he said, follow directly from your perception of the bear. Without some form of these responses, you would feel no fear, because, said James, recognition of physiological responses *is* fear. Because James saw activity in the peripheral nervous system, not the central nervous system, as the cause of emotional experience, his theory is known as a *peripheral theory* of emotion.

On the surface, James's theory might seem preposterous. It defies common sense, which says that it would be silly to run from something unless you already fear it. James concluded otherwise after examining his own mental processes. He decided that once you strip away all physiological responses, nothing remains of the experience of an emotion (James, 1890). Emotion, he reasoned, must therefore be the result of experiencing a particular set of physiological responses. A similar argument was offered by Carle Lange, a Danish physician, so James's view is sometimes called the *James-Lange theory* of emotion.

OBJ 11.21: Discuss James's theory of emotion. Give an example of how an emotion would occur according to this theory.

Test Items 11.122–11.126

ClassPrep PPT 50, OHT: James's Peripheral Theory of Emotion

Videodisc Segment & Still: James-Lange Theory of Emotion

fight-or-flight syndrome The physical reactions initiated by the sympathetic nervous system that prepare the body to fight or to run from a threatening situation.

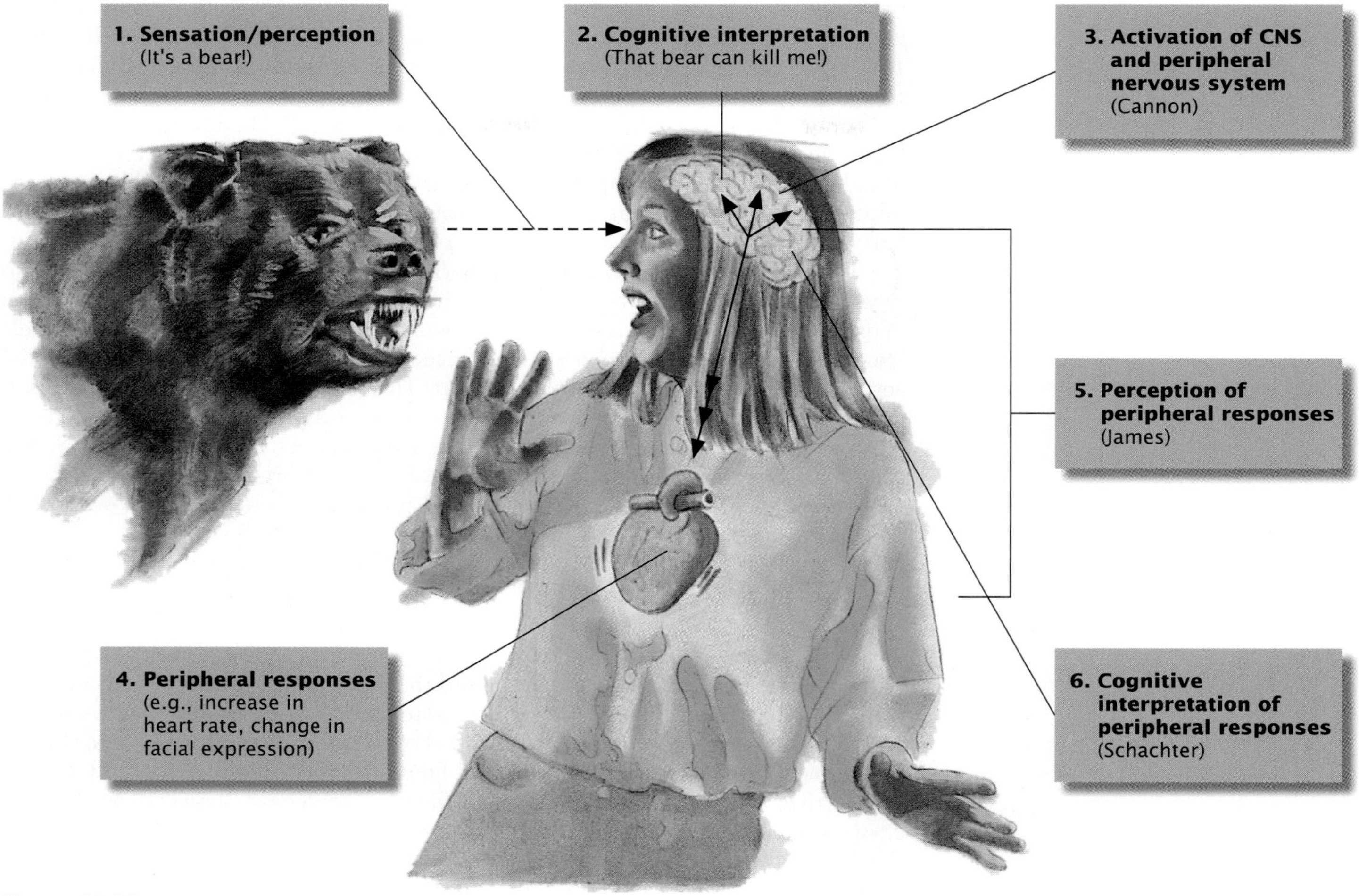

1. Sensation/perception
(It's a bear!)

2. Cognitive interpretation
(That bear can kill me!)

3. Activation of CNS and peripheral nervous system
(Cannon)

5. Perception of peripheral responses
(James)

4. Peripheral responses
(e.g., increase in heart rate, change in facial expression)

6. Cognitive interpretation of peripheral responses
(Schachter)

figure 11.12

Components of Emotion

Emotion is associated with activity in the central nervous system (the brain and spinal cord), with responses elsewhere in the body (called *peripheral* responses), and with cognitive interpretations of events. Different theories of emotion place differing emphasis on each of these components. William James emphasized the perception of peripheral responses, such as changes in heart rate. Walter Cannon asserted that emotion could occur entirely within the brain. Stanley Schachter emphasized cognitive factors, including how we interpret events and how we label our peripheral responses to them.

ClassPrep PPT 51: *Figure 11.12:* Components of Emotion

Observing Peripheral Responses   Figure 11.12 outlines the components of emotional experience, including those emphasized by James. First, a perception affects the cerebral cortex, said James; "then quick as a flash, reflex currents pass down through their pre-ordained channels, alter the condition of muscle, skin, and viscus; and these alterations, perceived, like the original object, in as many portions of the cortex, combine with it in consciousness and transform it from an object-simply-apprehended into an object-emotionally-felt" (James, 1890, p. 759). In other words, the brain interprets a situation and automatically directs a particular set of peripheral physiological changes—a palpitating heart, sinking stomach, facial grimace, perspiration, and certain patterns of blood flow. We are not conscious of the process, said James, until we become aware of these bodily changes; at that point, we experience an emotion. In other words, James's theory holds that reflexive peripheral responses precede the subjective experience of emotion, and that each particular emotion is created by a particular pattern of physiological responses. For example, fear would follow from one pattern of bodily responses, and anger would follow from a different pattern.

Notice that according to James's view, there is no emotional experience generated by activity in the brain alone—no special "emotion center" in the brain where the firing of neurons creates a direct experience of emotion. If this theory is accurate, it might account for the difficulty we sometimes have in knowing our true feelings: We must figure out what emotions we feel by perceiving subtle differences in specific physiological response patterns.

OBJ 11.22: Discuss the research that evaluates James's theory. Describe the facial feedback hypothesis. Discuss the assumptions upon which a lie detector is based.

Test Items 11.127–11.131

Evaluating James's Theory   There are more than five hundred labels for emotions in the English language (Averill, 1980). Does a distinctly different pattern of physiological activity precede each of these emotions? Research shows that certain emotional states are indeed associated with different patterns of autonomic changes (Damasio et al., 2000; Kelter & Buswell, 1996; Sinha & Parsons, 1996). For example, blood flow to the hands and feet increases in association with anger and declines in association with fear (Levenson, Ekman, & Friesen, 1990). So fear involves "cold feet"; anger does not. A pattern of activity associated with disgust includes increased muscle activity, but no change in heart rate. Even when people mentally re-live different kinds of emotional experiences, they show different patterns of autonomic activity (Ekman, Levenson, & Friesen, 1983). Such emotion-specific patterns of physiological activity have been found in widely different cultures (Levenson et al., 1992).

Furthermore, different patterns of autonomic activity are closely tied to specific emotional facial expressions, and vice versa (Ekman, 1993). In one study, when participants were told to make certain facial movements, autonomic changes occurred that resembled those normally accompanying emotion (Ekman, Levenson, & Friesen, 1983; see Figure 11.13). Almost all these participants also reported *feeling the emotion*—such as fear, anger, disgust, sadness, or happiness—associated with the expression they had created, even though they could not see their own expressions and did not realize that they had portrayed a specific emotion. Other studies, too, have shown that people feel emotions such as anger or sadness, for example, when simply making an "angry" or "sad" face. They can also ease these feelings just by relaxing their faces (Duclos & Laird, 2001). The emotional effects of this "face making" appear strongest in people who are the most sensitive to internal bodily cues. The emotions created by posed facial expressions can be significant enough to affect social judgments. Research participants who were asked to smile, for example, tended to form more positive impressions of other people than did those who received no special instructions (Ohira & Kurono, 1993).

ClassPrep PPT 52: *Figure 11.13:* Patterns of Physiological Change Associated with Different Emotions

figure 11.13

Patterns of Physiological Change Associated with Different Emotions

In this experiment, facial movements characteristic of different emotions produced different patterns of change in (A) heart rate; (B) peripheral blood flow, as measured by finger temperature; (C) skin conductance; and (D) muscle activity (Levenson, Ekman, & Friesen, 1990). For example, making an angry face caused heart rate and finger temperature to rise, whereas making a fearful face raised heart rate but lowered finger temperature.

Source: Levenson, Ekman, & Friesen (1990).

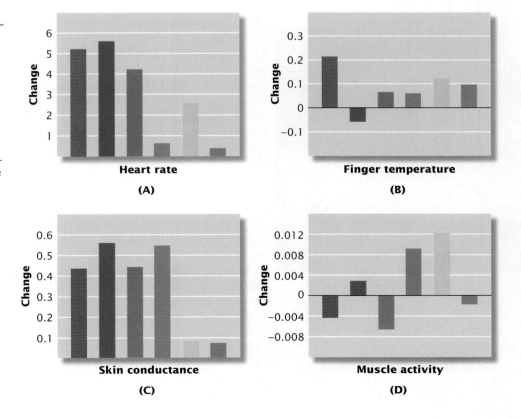

James's theory implies that the experience of emotion would be blocked if a person were unable to detect physiological changes occurring in the body's periphery. For example, spinal cord injuries that reduce feedback from peripheral responses should reduce the intensity of emotional experiences. This was the result reported in a study performed during the 1960s (Hohmann, 1966). More recently, however, studies have shown that when people with spinal injuries actively pursue their life goals, they experience a full range of emotions, including as much happiness as noninjured people (Bermond et al., 1991; Chwalisz, Diener, & Gallagher, 1988). These people report that their emotional experiences are just as intense as before their injuries, even though they notice less intense physiological changes associated with their emotions.

Such reports seem to contradict James's theory. But spinal cord injuries do not usually affect facial expressions, which James included among the bodily responses that are experienced as emotions. Some researchers have proposed a variant of James's theory, the *facial feedback hypothesis,* which maintains that involuntary facial movements provide enough peripheral information to create emotional experience (Ekman & Davidson, 1993). This hypothesis helps to explain why posed facial expressions generate the emotions normally associated with them. (The next time you want to cheer yourself up, it might help to smile—even though you don't feel like it.)

Lie Detection

James's view that different patterns of physiological activity are associated with different emotions forms the basis for the lie detection industry. If people experience anxiety or guilt when they lie, specific patterns of physiological activity accompanying these emotions should be detectable on instruments, called *polygraphs,* that record heart rate, breathing, skin conductance (which is affected by slight changes in perspiration), and other autonomic responses.

To identify the perpetrator of a crime using the *control question test,* a polygraph operator may ask questions specific to the crime, such as "Did you stab anyone on July 3, 2002?" Responses to such *relevant questions* are then compared with responses to *control questions,* such as "Have you ever tried to hurt someone?" Innocent people might have tried to hurt someone at some time and might feel guilty when asked, but they should have no reason to feel guilty about what they did on July 3, 2002. Accordingly, an innocent person should have a stronger emotional response to control questions than to relevant questions (Rosenfeld, 1995). Another approach, called the *directed lie test,* compares a person's physiological reactions when asked to lie about something and when telling what is known to be the truth. Finally, the *guilty knowledge test* seeks to determine if a person reacts in a notable way to information about a crime that only the perpetrator would know (Lykken, 1992).

Most people do have emotional responses when they lie, but statistics about the accuracy of polygraphs are difficult to obtain. Estimates vary widely, from those suggesting that polygraphs detect 90 percent of guilty, lying individuals (Honts & Quick, 1995; Kircher, Horowitz, & Raskin, 1988; Raskin, 1986) to those suggesting that polygraphs mislabel as many as 40 percent of truthful, innocent persons as guilty liars (Ben-Shakhar & Furedy, 1990; Saxe & Ben-Shakhar, 1999). Obviously, the results of a polygraph test are not determined entirely by whether a person is telling the truth. What people think about the act of lying, and about the value of the test, can also influence the accuracy of its results. For example, people who consider lying to be acceptable—and who do not believe in the power of polygraphs—are unlikely to display emotion-related physiological responses while lying during the test. However, an innocent person who believes in such tests and who thinks that "everything always goes wrong" might show a large fear response when asked about a crime, thus wrongly suggesting guilt.

Polygraphs can catch some liars, but most researchers agree that a guilty person can "fool" a polygraph lie detector, and that some innocent people can be misla-

IRM Activity 11.10: Lie Detection

ClassPrep PPT 53: Lie Detection

Videodisc Segment: Polygraph: Does It Reveal Lying?

Searching for the Truth Polygraph tests are not foolproof, though they may intimidate people who believe that they are. In a small town where the police could not afford a polygraph, one guilty suspect confessed his crime when a "lie detector" consisting of a kitchen colander was placed on his head and attached by wires to a copy machine (Shepherd, Kohut, & Sweet, 1989).

beled as guilty (Lykken, 1998). Accordingly, a large majority of psychologists in the United States have expressed serious reservations about the use of polygraph tests to detect deception (Abeles, 1985; Iacono & Lykken, 1997) and do not support their use as evidence in court.

Cannon's Central Theory

OBJ 11.23: Describe Cannon's theory of emotion. Discuss the updates to Cannon's theory.

Test Items 11.132–11.137

ClassPrep PPT 54, OHT: Cannon's Central Theory

For James, the experience of emotion depends on feedback from physiological responses occurring outside the brain, but Walter Cannon disagreed (Cannon, 1927/1987). According to Cannon, you feel fear at the sight of a wild bear even before you start to run because emotional experience starts in the central nervous system—specifically, in the thalamus, the brain structure that relays information from most sense organs to the cortex.

According to Cannon's *central theory* (also known as the *Cannon-Bard theory*, in recognition of Philip Bard's contribution), when the thalamus receives sensory information about emotional events and situations, it sends signals *simultaneously* to the autonomic nervous system and to the cerebral cortex, where the emotion becomes conscious. So when you see a bear, the brain receives sensory information about it, perceives it as a bear, and *directly* creates the experience of fear while at the same time sending messages to the heart, lungs, and muscles to do what it takes to run away. In other words, Cannon said that the experience of emotion appears directly in the brain, with or without feedback from peripheral responses (see Figure 11.12).

Videodisc Segment & Still: Cannon-Bard Theory of Emotion

Updating Cannon's Theory

Research conducted since Cannon proposed his theory indicates that the thalamus is actually not the "seat" of emotion, but through its connections to the amygdala (see Figure 11.9), the thalamus does participate in some aspects of emotional processing (Lang, 1995). For example, studies in animals and humans show that the emotion of fear is generated by connections from the thalamus to the amygdala (Anderson & Phelps, 2000; LeDoux, 1995). The implication is that strong emotions can sometimes bypass the cortex without requiring conscious thought to activate them. One study showed, for example, that people presented with stimuli such as angry faces display physiological signs of arousal even if they are not conscious of seeing those stimuli (Morris et al., 1998). The same processes might explain why people find it so difficult to overcome an intense fear, or phobia, even though they may consciously know the fear is irrational.

An updated version of Cannon's theory suggests that specific brain areas produce the feelings of pleasure or pain associated with emotion. This idea arose from studies mentioned in the chapter on learning, showing that electrical stimulation of certain brain areas is rewarding. Researchers found that rats kept returning to the place in their cage where they received this kind of stimulation. When the animals were allowed to control delivery of the stimulation by pressing a bar, they pressed it until they were physically exhausted, ignoring even food and water (Olds & Milner, 1954). Stimulation of other brain regions is so unpleasant that animals work hard to avoid it. The areas of the brain in which stimulation is experienced as especially pleasurable include the dopamine systems, which are activated by drugs such as cocaine (Bardo, 1998). When animals are given drugs that block the action of dopamine, this kind of brain stimulation is no longer experienced as pleasurable (Wise & Rompre, 1989).

Presumably, part of the direct central experience of emotions involves areas of the brain whose activity is experienced as either pleasurable or aversive. The areas of the brain activated by the kind of events that elicit emotion in humans have widespread connections throughout the brain. Therefore, the central nervous system's experience of emotion is probably widely distributed, not narrowly localized in any one "emotion center" (Derryberry & Tucker, 1992). Still, there is evidence to support the main thrust of Cannon's theory: that emotion occurs through the activation of specific parts of the central nervous system. What Cannon did not foresee is that different parts of the central nervous system may be activated for different emotions and for different aspects of the total emotional experience.

Cognitive Theories

Suppose you are about to be interviewed for your first job, or go out on a blind date, or fly in a hot-air balloon for the first time. In such situations, it is not always easy to be sure of what you are feeling. Is it fear, excitement, anticipation, worry, happiness, dread, or what? Stanley Schachter suggested that the emotions we experience every day are shaped partly by how we interpret the arousal we feel. His cognitive theory of emotion, known as the *Schachter-Singer theory* in recognition of the contributions of Jerome Singer, took shape in the early 1960s, when many psychologists were raising questions about the validity of James's theory of emotion. Schachter argued that the theory was essentially correct—but required a few modifications (Cornelius, 1996). In Schachter's view, feedback about physiological changes may not vary enough to create the many subtle shades of emotion that people can experience. He argued instead that all these emotions emerge from a combination of feedback from peripheral responses and the *cognitive interpretation* of those responses, and of what caused them (Schachter & Singer, 1962). Cognitive interpretation first comes into play, said Schachter, when you perceive the stimulus that leads to bodily responses ("It's a bear!") and again when you identify feedback from those responses as a particular emotion (see Figure 11.12). The same physiological responses might be given many different labels, depending on how you interpret those responses. So, according to Schachter, the emotion you experience when that bear approaches your campsite might be fear, excitement, astonishment, or surprise, depending on how you label your bodily reactions to seeing it.

The labeling of arousal depends, in turn, on **attribution**, the process of identifying the cause of an event. People may attribute their physiological arousal to different emotions based on the information available about the situation. If you are watching the final seconds of a close ball game, you might attribute your racing heart, rapid breathing, and perspiration to excitement; but you might attribute the same physiological reactions to anxiety if you are waiting for a big exam to begin. Schachter predicted that our emotional experiences will be less intense if we attribute arousal to a nonemotional cause. So if you notice your heart pounding before an exam but say to yourself, "Sure my heart's pounding—I just drank five cups of coffee!" then you should feel "wired" from caffeine rather than afraid or worried. This prediction has received some support (Mezzacappa, Katkin, & Palmer, 1999; Sinclair et al., 1994), but other aspects of Schachter's theory have not.

Few researchers today fully accept the Schachter-Singer theory, but it did stimulate an enormous amount of valuable research, including studies of **transferred excitation,** a phenomenon in which physiological arousal from one experience carries over to affect emotion in an independent situation (Reisenzein, 1983; Zillman, 1984). For example, people who have been aroused by physical exercise become more angry when provoked, or experience more intense sexual feelings when in the company of an attractive person, than do people who have been less physically active (Allen et al., 1989). This transfer is most likely to occur when the overt signs of physiological arousal have subsided but the sympathetic nervous system is still active. In one study, people were emotionally "primed" by reading words that were cheerful, neutral, or depressing. Next, they either engaged in physical exercise or sat quietly and then rated their mood, either immediately or after a short delay. Those who had not exercised, as well as those who rated themselves immediately after exercise, reported being in no particular mood. However, the mood of those whose reports came several minutes after exercising tended to be positive, neutral, or negative, depending on which priming words they had read earlier. Apparently, the

---

OBJ 11.24: Describe Schacter's modification of James's theory of emotion. Define attribution and give an example.

Test Items 11.138–11.143

ClassPrep PPT 55, OHT: Schachter-Singer Theory of Emotion

OBJ 11.25: Define transferred excitation and give an example of its effects.

Test Items 11.144–11.148

---

attribution   The process of explaining the causes of an event.

transferred excitation   The process of carrying over arousal from one experience to an independent situation.

people in this latter group were still somewhat aroused; but because the delay had been long enough to keep them from attributing their lingering arousal to exercise, they instead used the emotional tone of the word list as a guide to labeling their mood (Sinclair et al., 1994).

Schachter's theory also led to the development of theories emphasizing the role of other cognitive processes in emotion (Cornelius, 1996). Schachter focused on the cognitive interpretation of our *bodily responses* to events, but other theorists have argued that it is our cognitive interpretation of *events themselves* that are most important in shaping emotional experiences. For example, as we mentioned earlier, a person's emotional reaction to receiving exam results can depend partly whether the score is seen as a sign of improvement or a grade worthy of shame. According to Richard Lazarus's (1966, 1991) *cognitive appraisal* theory of emotion, these differing reactions can be best explained by how we think exam scores, job interviews, blind dates, bear sightings, and other events will affect our personal well-being. According to Lazarus, the process of cognitive appraisal, or evaluation, begins when we decide whether or not an event is relevant to our well-being; that is, do we even care about it? If we don't, as might be the case if an exam doesn't count toward our grade, we are unlikely to have an emotional experience when we get the results. If the event *is* relevant to our well-being, we will experience an emotional reaction to it. That reaction will be positive or negative, said Lazarus, depending on whether we appraise the event as advancing our personal goals or obstructing them. The *specific* emotion we experience depends on our individual goals, needs, standards, expectations, and past experiences. As a result, a particular exam score can create contentment in one person, elation in another, mild disappointment in someone else, and despair in yet another. Individual differences in goals and standards are at work, too, when a second-place finisher in a marathon race experiences bitter disappointment at having "lost," while someone at the back of the pack may be thrilled just to have completed the race alive.

"In Review: Theories of Emotion" summarizes key elements of the theories we have discussed. It appears that both peripheral autonomic responses (including facial responses) and the cognitive interpretation of those responses add to emotional experience. So does cognitive appraisal of events themselves. In addition, the brain can apparently generate emotional experience on its own, independent of

ClassPrep PPT 56: Other Cognitive Theories

OBJ 11.26: Compare and contrast James's, Schacter's modification, and Cannon's theories of emotion.

Test Items 11.149–11.151

Essay Q 11.3

in review	Theories of Emotion	
Theory	**Source of Emotions**	**Example**
James-Lange	Emotions are created by awareness of specific patterns of peripheral (autonomic) responses.	Anger is associated with increased blood flow in the hands and feet; fear is associated with decreased blood flow in these areas.
Cannon-Bard	The brain generates direct experiences of emotion.	Stimulation of certain brain areas can create pleasant or unpleasant emotions.
Cognitive (Schachter-Singer and Lazarus)	Cognitive interpretation of events, and of physiological reactions to them, shapes emotional experiences.	Autonomic arousal can be experienced as anxiety or excitement, depending on how it is labeled. A single event can lead to different emotions, depending on whether it is perceived as threatening or challenging.

physiological arousal. In short, emotion is probably both in the heart and in the head (including the face). The most basic emotions probably occur directly within the brain, whereas the many shades of discernible emotions probably arise from attributions and other cognitive interpretations of physiological responses and environmental events. No theory has completely resolved the issue of which, if any, component of emotion is primary. However, the theories we have discussed have helped psychologists better understand how these components interact to produce emotional experience. Cognitive appraisal theories, in particular, have been especially useful in studying and treating stress-related emotional problems (see the chapters on health, stress, and coping; psychological disorders; and treatment of psychological disorders).

Communicating Emotion

Imagine a woman watching television. You can see her face, but not what she sees on the screen. She might be engaged in complex thought, perhaps comparing her investments with those of the experts on *Wall Street Week*. Or she might be thinking of nothing at all as she loses herself in a rerun of *The Drew Carey Show*. In other words, your observation is not likely to tell you much about what the woman is thinking. If the television program creates an emotional experience, however, you will be able to make a reasonably accurate guess about which emotion she feels just by looking at the expression on her face. So far, we have described emotion from the inside, as people experience their own emotions. In this section, we examine the social organization of emotion—how people communicate emotions to one another.

Humans communicate emotions partly through tone of voice and body posture or movement, but mainly through facial movements and expressions. The human face can create thousands of different expressions (Zajonc, 1998), and people are good at detecting them. Observers can notice even tiny facial movements—a twitch of the mouth or eyebrow can carry a lot of information. Females consistently

TRY THIS

What Are They Feeling? People's emotions are usually "written on their faces." Jot down the emotions you think these people are feeling, and then look at the footnote on page 426 to see how well you "read" their emotions.

outperform males in identifying and interpreting the nonverbal emotion cues conveyed by facial expressions (Hall, 1984). This gender difference also appears in adolescents, children, and even infants (McClure, 2000), suggesting that it may be rooted in biology as well as in gender-specific socialization. Are emotional facial expressions innate as well, or are they learned? And how are they used in communicating emotion?

Innate Expressions of Emotion

Charles Darwin observed that some facial expressions seem to be universal (Darwin, 1872/1965). He proposed that these expressions are genetically determined, passed on biologically from one generation to the next. The facial expressions seen today, said Darwin, are those that have been most effective at telling others something about how a person is feeling. If someone is scowling with teeth clenched, for example, you will probably assume that he or she is angry, and you will be unlikely to choose that particular moment to ask for a loan.

Infants provide one source of evidence that some facial expressions are innate. Newborns do not need to be taught to grimace in pain or to smile in pleasure or to blink when startled (Balaban, 1995). Even blind infants, who cannot imitate adults' expressions, show the same emotional expressions as do sighted infants (Goodenough, 1932).

A second line of evidence for innate facial expressions comes from studies showing that for the most basic emotions, people in all cultures show similar facial responses to similar emotional stimuli (Hejmadi, Davidson, & Rozin, 2000; Zajonc, 1998). Participants in these studies look at photographs of people's faces and then try to name the emotion each person is feeling. The pattern of facial movements we call a smile, for example, is universally related to positive emotions. Sadness is almost always accompanied by slackened muscle tone and a "long" face. Likewise, in almost all cultures, people contort their faces in a similar way when shown something they find disgusting. And a furrowed brow is frequently associated with frustration (Ekman, 1994).

Anger is also linked with a facial expression recognized by almost all cultures. One study examined artwork—including ceremonial masks—of various Western and non-Western cultures (Aronoff, Barclay, & Stevenson, 1988). The angry, threatening masks of all eighteen cultures contained similar elements, such as triangular eyes and diagonal lines on the cheeks. In particular, angular and diagonal elements carry the impression of threat (see Figure 11.14). One study with high school students found that threat is conveyed most strongly by the eyebrows, followed by the mouth and eyes (Lundqvist, Esteves, & Öhman, 1999).

The Universal Smile The idea that some emotional expressions are innate is supported by the fact that the facial movement pattern we call a smile is related to happiness, pleasure, and other positive emotions in human cultures throughout the world.

ClassPrep PPT 58: *Figure 11.14:* Elements of Ceremonial Facial Masks That Convey Threat

figure 11.14

Elements of Ceremonial Facial Masks That Convey Threat

Certain geometric patterns are common to threatening masks in many cultures. When people in various cultures were asked which member of each of these pairs was more threatening, they consistently chose those, shown here on the left, containing triangular and diagonal elements. "Scary" Halloween pumpkins tend to have such elements as well.

OBJ 11.28: Describe the social and cultural factors involved in communicating emotion. Describe the role and sources of learning in human emotional expression. Define emotion culture and social referencing.

Test Items 11.159–11.165

IRM Activity 11.12: Cultural Influence on Emotional Expression

Personal Learning Activity 11.5

Social and Cultural Influences on Emotional Expression

Whereas some basic emotional expressions are innate, many others are neither innate nor universal (Ekman, 1993). Even innate expressions are flexible and modifiable, changing as necessary in the social contexts within which they occur (Fernández-Dols & Ruiz-Belda, 1995). For example, facial expressions become more intense and change more frequently while people are imagining social scenes as opposed to solitary scenes (Fridlund et al., 1990). Similarly, facial expressions in response to odors tend to be more intense when others are watching than when people are alone (Jancke & Kaufmann, 1994).

Further, although a core of emotional responses is recognized by all cultures (Hejmadi, Davidson, & Rozin, 2000), there is a certain degree of cultural variation in recognizing some emotions (Russell, 1995). In one study, for example, Japanese and North American people agreed about which facial expressions signaled happiness, surprise, and sadness, but they frequently disagreed about which faces showed anger, disgust, and fear (Matsumoto & Ekman, 1989). Members of preliterate cultures, such as the Fore of New Guinea, agree even less with people in Western cultures on the labeling of facial expressions (Russell, 1994). In addition, there are variations in how people in different cultures interpret emotions expressed by tone of voice (Mesquita & Frijda, 1992). For instance, Taiwanese participants were best at recognizing a sad tone of voice, whereas Dutch participants were best at recognizing happy tones (Van Bezooijen, Otto, & Heenan, 1983).

People learn how to express certain emotions in particular ways, as specified by cultural rules. Suppose you say, "I just bought a new car," and all your friends stick their tongues out at you. In North America, this would mean that they are envious or resentful. But in some regions of China, such a display expresses surprise.

Even smiles can vary as people learn to use them to communicate certain feelings. Paul Ekman and his colleagues categorized seventeen types of smiles, including "false smiles," which fake enjoyment, and "masking smiles," which hide unhappiness. They called the smile that occurs with real happiness the *Duchenne* (pronounced "do-SHEN") *smile,* after the French researcher who first noticed a difference between spontaneous, happy smiles and posed smiles. A genuine, Duchenne smile includes contractions of the muscles around the eyes (creating a distinctive wrinkling of the skin in these areas), as well as of the muscles that raise the lips and cheeks. Few people can successfully contract the muscles around the eyes during a posed smile, so this feature can be used to distinguish "lying smiles" from genuine ones (Frank, Ekman, & Friesen, 1993). In one study, the Duchenne smile was highly correlated with reports of positive emotions experienced while people watched a movie, as well as with a pattern of brain waves known to be associated with positive emotions. These relationships did not appear for other types of smiles (Ekman, Davidson, & Friesen, 1990).

Learning About Emotions   The effects of learning are seen in a child's growing range of emotional expressions. Although infants begin with an innate set of emotional responses, they soon learn to imitate facial expressions and use them for more and more emotions. In time, these expressions become more precise and personalized, so that a particular expression conveys a clear emotional message to anyone who knows that person well.

If facial expressions become *too* personalized, however, no one will know what the expressions mean. Operant shaping (described in the chapter on learning)

The people pictured on page 424 were waiting to hear whether Chile's former dictator Augusto Pinochet would be brought to trial in Britain for torturing their relatives in Chilean prisons. Their emotions probably included anxiety, worry, dread, uncertainty, excitement, hope, and perhaps anger. Pinochet was allowed to return to Chile, where he was found mentally unfit to stand trial.

ClassPrep PPT 59: Social and Cultural Influences on Emotional Expression

probably helps keep emotional expressions within certain limits. If you could not see other people's facial expressions or observe their responses to yours, you might show fewer, or less intense, facial signs of emotion. Indeed, as congenitally blind people grow older, their facial expressions tend to become less animated (Izard, 1977).

As children grow, they learn an *emotion culture*—rules that govern what emotions are appropriate in what circumstances and what emotional expressions are allowed. These rules can vary from culture to culture. For example, TV news cameras showed that men in the U.S. military leaving for duty in Kosovo in 1999 tended to keep their emotions in check as they said goodbye to wives, girlfriends, and parents. However, in Italy—where mother-son ties are particularly strong—many male soldiers wailed with dismay and wept openly as they left. In a laboratory study, when viewing a distressing movie with a group of peers, Japanese students exhibited much more control over their facial expressions than did North American students. When they watched the film while alone, however, the Japanese students' faces showed the same emotional expressions as those of the North American students (Ekman, Friesen, & Ellsworth, 1972).

Emotion cultures shape how people describe and categorize feelings, resulting in both similarities and differences across cultures (Russell, 1991). At least five of the seven basic emotions listed in an ancient Chinese book called the *Li Chi*—joy, anger, sadness, fear, love, disliking, and liking—are considered primary emotions by most Western theorists. Yet while English has over five hundred emotion-related words, some emotion words in other languages have no English equivalent. The Czech word *litost* apparently has no English word equivalent: "It designates a feeling as infinite as an open accordion, a feeling that is the synthesis of many others: grief, sympathy, remorse, and an indefinable longing" (quoted in Russell, 1991). The Japanese word *ijirashii* also has no English equivalent; it describes the feeling of seeing a praiseworthy person overcoming an obstacle (Russell, 1991).

Similarly, other cultures have no equivalent for some English emotion words. Many cultures do not see anger and sadness as different, for example. The Ilongot, a Philippine head-hunting group, have only one word, *liget,* for both anger and grief (Russell, 1991). Tahitians have words for forty-six different types of anger, but no word for sadness and, apparently, no concept of it. One Westerner described a Tahitian man as sad over separation from his wife and child, but the man himself felt *pe'a pe'a*—a generic word for feeling ill, troubled, or fatigued—and did not attribute it to the separation.

ClassPrep PPT 60: Learning About Emotions

Social Referencing   Facial expressions, tone of voice, body postures, and gestures not only communicate information about the emotion someone is experiencing; they can also influence others' behavior, especially the behavior of people who are not sure what to do. An inexperienced chess player, for instance, might reach out to move the queen, catch sight of a spectator's grimace, and infer that another move would be better. The process of letting another person's emotional state guide our own behavior is called **social referencing** (Campos, 1980).

The visual-cliff studies described in the chapter on perception have been used to create an uncertain situation for infants. To reach its mother, an infant in these experiments must cross the visual cliff (see Figure 5.25). If the apparent drop-off is very small or very large, there is no question about what to do; a one-year-old knows to crawl across in the first case and to stay put in the second case. However, if the apparent drop-off is shallow enough (say, two feet) to create uncertainty, the infant relies on its mother's facial expression to decide what to do. In one study, mothers were asked to make either a fearful or a happy face. When the mothers made a fearful face, no infant crossed the glass floor. But when they posed a happy face, most infants crossed (Sorce et al., 1981). Here is yet another example of the adaptive value of sending, and receiving, emotional communications.

social referencing A phenomenon in which other people's facial expressions, tone of voice, and bodily gestures serve as guidelines for how to proceed in uncertain situations.

LINKAGES   ClassPrep PPTs 61, 62, & 63: Linkages

As noted in the chapter on introducing psychology, all of psychology's subfields are related to one another. Our discussion of conflicting motives and stress illustrates just one way in which the topic of this chapter, motivation and emotion, is linked to the subfield of health psychology (which is discussed in the chapter on health, stress, and coping). The Linkages diagram shows ties to two other subfields as well, and there are many more ties throughout the book. Looking for linkages among sub-fields will help you see how they fit together and help you better appreciate the big picture that is psychology.

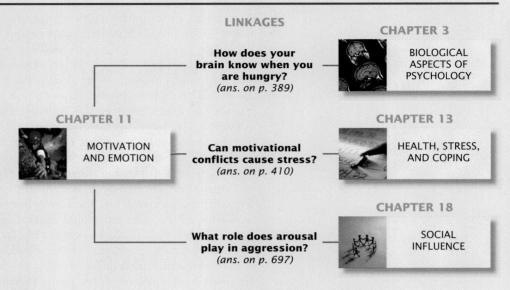

LINKAGES

CHAPTER 11
MOTIVATION AND EMOTION

How does your brain know when you are hungry?
(ans. on p. 389)

CHAPTER 3
BIOLOGICAL ASPECTS OF PSYCHOLOGY

Can motivational conflicts cause stress?
(ans. on p. 410)

CHAPTER 13
HEALTH, STRESS, AND COPING

What role does arousal play in aggression?
(ans. on p. 697)

CHAPTER 18
SOCIAL INFLUENCE

SUMMARY

Motivation refers to factors that influence the initiation, direction, intensity, and persistence of behavior. Emotion and motivation are often linked: Motivation can influence emotion, and people are often motivated to seek certain emotions.

Concepts and Theories of Motivation

Focusing on a *motive* often reveals a single theme within apparently diverse behaviors. Motivation is said to be an intervening variable, a way of linking various stimuli to the behaviors that follow them.

Sources of Motivation

The many sources of motivation fall into four categories: biological factors, emotional factors, cognitive factors, and social factors.

Instinct Theory and Its Descendants

An early argument held that motivation follows from *instincts*, which are automatic, involuntary, and unlearned behavior patterns consistently "released" by particular stimuli. Modern versions of *instinct theory* are seen in evolutionary accounts of helping, aggression, mate selection, and other aspects of social behavior.

Drive Reduction Theory

Drive reduction theory is based on *homeostasis,* a tendency to maintain equilibrium in a physical or behavioral process. When disruption of equilibrium creates a *need* of some kind, people are motivated to reduce the resulting *drive* by behaving in some way that satisfies the need and restores balance. *Primary drives* are unlearned; *secondary drives* are learned.

Arousal Theory

According to *arousal theories* of motivation, people are motivated to behave in ways that maintain a level of *arousal* that is optimal for their functioning.

Incentive Theory

Incentive theory highlights behaviors that are motivated by attaining desired stimuli (positive incentives) and avoiding undesirable ones (negative incentives).

Hunger and Eating

Hunger and eating are controlled by a complex mix of learning, culture, and biology.

Biological Signals for Hunger and Satiety

The desire to eat *(hunger)* or to stop eating *(satiety)* depends primarily on signals from blood-borne substances such as cholecystokinin (CCK), glucose, insulin, and leptin.

Hunger and the Brain

Activity in the ventromedial nucleus of the hypothalamus results in satiety, whereas activity in the lateral hypothalamus results in hunger. These brain regions might be acting together to maintain a set point of body weight, but control of eating is more complex than that. For example, a variety of neurotransmitters act in various regions of the hypothalamus to create hunger for specific types of foods.

Flavor, Cultural Learning, and Food Selection

Eating may also be influenced by the flavor of food and by appetite for the pleasure of food. Food selection is influenced by biological needs (specific hungers) for certain nutrients, as well as by food cravings, social contexts, and cultural traditions.

Eating Disorders

Obesity has been linked to overconsumption of certain kinds of foods, to low energy metabolism, and to genetic factors. People suffering from *anorexia nervosa* starve themselves to avoid becoming fat. Those who suffer from *bulimia nervosa* engage in binge eating, followed by purging through self-induced vomiting or laxatives.

Sexual Behavior

Sexual motivation and behavior result from a rich interplay of biology and culture.

The Biology of Sex

Sexual stimulation generally produces a stereotyped *sexual response cycle,* a pattern of physiological arousal during and after sexual activity. *Sex hormones,* which include male hormones *(androgens)* and female hormones *(estrogens* and *progestins),* occur in different relative amounts in both sexes. They can have organizational effects, such as physical differences in the brain, and activational effects, such as increased desire for sex.

Social and Cultural Factors in Sexuality

Gender-role learning and educational experiences are examples of cultural factors that can bring about variations in sexual attitudes and behaviors.

Sexual Orientation

Sexual orientation—*heterosexual, homosexual,* or *bisexual*— is increasingly viewed as a sociocultural variable that affects many other aspects of behavior and mental processes. Though undoubtedly shaped by a lifetime of learning, sexual orientation appears to have strong biological roots.

Sexual Dysfunctions

Common male *sexual dysfunctions* include erectile disorder and premature ejaculation. Females may experience such problems as arousal disorder.

Achievement Motivation

People gain esteem from achievement in many areas, including the workplace.

Need for Achievement

The motive to succeed is called *need achievement.* Individuals with high achievement motivation strive for excellence, persist despite failures, and set challenging but realistic goals.

Goal Setting and Achievement Motivation

Goals influence motivation, especially the amount of effort, persistence, attention, and planning we devote to a task.

Achievement and Success in the Workplace

Workers are most satisfied when they are working toward their own goals and are getting concrete feedback. Jobs that offer clear and specific goals, a variety of tasks, individual responsibility, and other intrinsic rewards are the most motivating.

Achievement and Subjective Well-Being

People tend to have a characteristic level of happiness, or *subjective well-being,* which is not necessarily related to the attainment of money, status, or other material goals.

Relations and Conflicts Among Motives

Human behavior reflects many motives, some of which may be in conflict. Abraham Maslow proposed a hierarchy of five classes of human motives, from meeting basic biological needs to attaining a state of self-actualization. Motives at the lowest levels, according to Maslow, must be at least partially satisfied before people can be motivated by higher-level goals.

Opponent Processes, Motivation, and Emotion

Motivated behavior sometimes gives rise to opponent emotional processes, such as the fear and excitement associated with a roller coaster ride. Opponent-process theory illustrates the close link between motivation and emotion.

The Nature of Emotion

Defining Characteristics

An *emotion* is a temporary experience with positive or negative qualities that is felt with some intensity as happening to the self, is generated in part by a cognitive appraisal of a situation, and is accompanied by both learned and reflexive physical responses.

The Biology of Emotion

Several brain mechanisms are involved in emotion. The amygdala, in the limbic system, is deeply involved in various aspects of emotion. The expression of emotion through involuntary facial movement is controlled by the extrapyramidal motor system. Voluntary facial movements are controlled by the pyramidal motor system. The brain's right and left hemispheres play somewhat different roles in emotional expression. In addition to specific brain mechanisms, both branches of the autonomic nervous system, the *sympathetic system* and the *parasympathetic system,* are involved in physiological changes that accompany emotional activation. The *fight-or-flight syndrome,* for example, follows from activation of the sympathetic system.

Theories of Emotion

James's Peripheral Theory

William James's theory of emotion holds that peripheral physiological responses are the primary source of emotion and that self-observation of these responses constitutes emotional experience. James's theory is supported by evidence that, at least for several basic emotions, physiological responses are distinguishable enough for emotions to be generated in this way. Distinct facial expressions are linked to particular patterns of physiological change.

Cannon's Central Theory

Walter Cannon's theory of emotion proposes that emotional experience occurs independent of peripheral physiological responses and that there is a direct experience of emotion based on activity of the central nervous system. Updated versions of this theory suggest that various parts of the central nervous system may be involved in different emotions and different aspects of emotional experience. Some pathways in the brain, such as that from the thalamus to the amygdala, allow strong emotions to occur before conscious thought can take place. And specific parts of the brain appear to be responsible for the feelings of pleasure or pain in emotion.

Cognitive Theories

Stanley Schachter's modification of James's theory proposes that physiological responses are primary sources of emotion but that the cognitive labeling of those responses—a process that depends partly on *attribution*—strongly influences the emotions we experience. Schachter's theory stimulated research on *transferred excitation.* Other cognitive theories, such as that of Richard Lazarus, emphasize that emotional experience depends heavily on how we think about the situations and events we encounter.

Communicating Emotion

Humans communicate emotions mainly through facial movement and expressions, but also through voice tones and bodily movements.

Innate Expressions of Emotion

Charles Darwin suggested that certain facial expressions of emotion are innate and universal and that these expressions evolved because they effectively communicate one creature's emotional condition to other creatures. Some facial expressions of basic emotions do appear to be innate. Even blind infants smile when happy and frown when experiencing discomfort. And certain facial movements are universally associated with certain emotions.

Social and Cultural Influences on Emotional Expression

Many emotional expressions are learned, and even innate expressions are modified by learning and social contexts. As children grow, they learn an emotion culture, the rules of emotional expression appropriate to their culture. Accordingly, the same emotion may be communicated by different facial expressions in different cultures. Especially in ambiguous situations, other people's emotional expressions may serve as a guide about what to do or what not to do, a phenomenon called *social referencing.*

Human Development

12

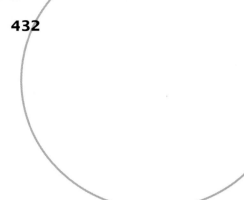

OBJ 12.1: Define developmental psychology.

Test Items 12.1–12.3

IRM Research Focus 12.3: Is Family Resemblance Real?

ClassPrep PPT 1: Human Development

ClassPrep PPT 2: Developmental Psychology

OBJ 12.2: Describe the history of the nature-nurture debate.

Test Items 12.4–12.6

Santee, California; Littleton, Colorado; Springfield, Oregon; Jonesboro, Arkansas; West Paducah, Kentucky; Edinboro, Pennsylvania; Bethel, Alaska; Pearl, Mississippi; and Taber, Alberta. These towns have shared a common tragedy—the shooting deaths of students and teachers at local schools. Overall, the number of school homicides has been dropping, but that statistic is of little solace to the friends and families of the fifty-one people who were killed and the sixty-eight others who were injured in these school shooting sprees. With each new tragedy the cry became louder: *Why do these things happen?* All the killers were boys, ranging in age from eleven to eighteen. Had they watched too many violent movies and television programs? Were their actions the fault of a "gun culture" that allows children access to firearms? Had they been victims of abuse and neglect? Were their parents too strict—or not strict enough? Did they come from "broken homes," or had they witnessed violence within their own families? Did they behave violently because they were going through a difficult "stage," because they had not been taught right from wrong, because they wanted to impress their peers, because males are more aggressive in general, or because their brains were "defective"? Were they just "bad kids"?

These are the kinds of questions developmental psychologists try to answer. They investigate when certain behaviors first appear and how they change with age. They explore how development in one area, such as moral reasoning, relates to development in other areas, such as aggressive behavior. They attempt to discover whether most people develop at the same rate and, if not, whether slow starters ever catch up to early bloomers. They ask why some children become well-adjusted, socially competent, nurturant, and empathic individuals, whereas others become murderers, and why some adolescents go on to win honors in college, whereas others drop out of high school. They seek to explain how development throughout the life span is affected by both genetics and the environment, analyzing the extent to which development is a product of what we arrive with at birth (our inherited, biological *nature*) and the extent to which it is a product of what the world provides (the *nurture* of the environment). And they pursue development into adulthood, examining the changes that occur over the years and determining how these changes are related to earlier abilities and later events. In short, **developmental psychology** is concerned with the course and causes of developmental changes over a person's lifetime.

In this chapter we examine many such changes. We begin by describing the physical and biological changes that occur from the moment of conception to the time a child is born. Then we discuss cognitive, social, and emotional development during infancy and childhood. Next, we examine the changes and challenges that confront humans during their adolescence. And we conclude by considering the significant physical, intellectual, and social changes that occur as people move through early, middle, and late adulthood.

Exploring Human Development LSV: Origins of Nature, Origins of Nurture

The question of whether development is the result of nature or nurture was the subject of philosophical debate centuries before psychologists began studying it scientifically. In essays published in the 1690s, British philosopher John Locke argued for nurture. He believed that experiences provided by the environment during childhood have a profound and permanent effect. As mentioned in the chapter that introduced psychology, Locke thought of the newborn as a blank slate, or *tabula rasa*. Adults write on that slate, he said, as they teach children about the world and how to behave in it. Some seventy years later, French philosopher Jean-Jacques Rousseau made the opposite argument. He claimed that children are capable of discovering how the world operates and how they should behave without instruction from adults, and he advocated letting children grow as their natures dictate, with little guidance or pressure from parents.

developmental psychology The psychological specialty that documents the course of social, emotional, moral, and intellectual development over the life span.

maturation Natural growth or change that unfolds in a fixed sequence relatively independent of the environment.

ClassPrep PPT 4, OHT: *Figure 12.1:* Motor Development

figure 12.1

Motor Development

When did you start walking? The left end of each bar indicates the age at which 25 percent of the infants tested were able to perform the behavior; 50 percent of the babies were performing the behavior at the age indicated by the vertical line in the bars; the right end indicates the age at which 90 percent could do so (Frankenberg & Dodds, 1967). Although different infants, especially in different cultures, achieve milestones of motor development at slightly different ages, all infants—regardless of their ethnicity, social class, or temperament—achieve them in the same order.

Sattler/Shabatay reader, 2/e: Hall, "Madeline's First Months of Life"

OBJ 12.3: Discuss the differences among Gesell's, Watson's, and Piaget's views of development. Define maturation.

Test Items 12.7–12.10

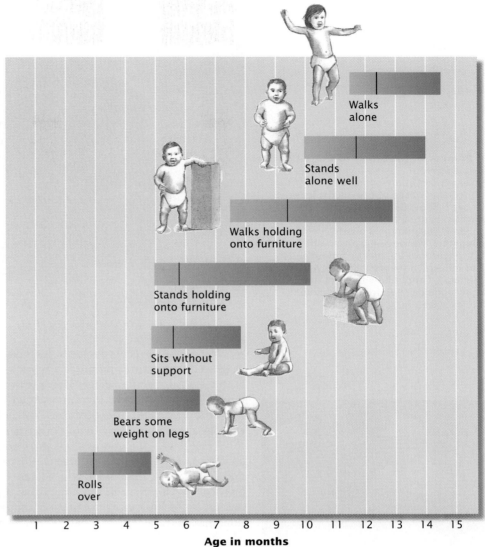

A Deadly Child Andrew Golden was barely out of diapers when he was given camouflage clothing and taught to fire a hunting rifle. In March 1998, at the age of eleven, he and his thirteen-year-old friend Mitchell Johnson used their shooting skills to kill four classmates and a teacher at their elementary school in Jonesboro, Arkansas. Many youngsters learn to hunt; what led these two to commit murder? Researchers in developmental psychology are studying the genetic and environmental factors that underlie the emergence of violent aggression and many other patterns of behavior and mental processes.

The first psychologist to systematically investigate the role of nature in behavior was Arnold Gesell. In the early 1900s, Gesell (pronounced "geh-ZELL") observed many children of all ages. He found that their motor skills, such as standing and walking, picking up a cube, and throwing a ball, developed in a fixed sequence of stages, as Figure 12.1 illustrates. The order of the stages and the age at which they develop, he suggested, are determined by nature and relatively unaffected by nurture. Only under extreme conditions, such as famine, war, or poverty, he claimed, are children thrown off their biologically programmed timetable. Gesell referred to this type of natural growth or change, which unfolds in a fixed sequence relatively independent of the environment, as **maturation.** The broader term *development* encompasses not only maturation but also the behavioral and mental processes that are due to learning.

John B. Watson, founder of the behaviorist approach to psychology, disagreed with Gesell. He claimed that the environment, not nature, molds and shapes development. Early in the twentieth century Watson began conducting experiments with children. From these experiments he inferred that children learn everything, from skills to fears.

A Pioneer in the Study of Cognitive Development   Using a variety of research procedures, including his remarkable observational skills, Jean Piaget (1896–1980) investigated the development of cognitive processes in children, including his own son and daughters. He wove his observations and inferences into the most comprehensive and influential theory that had yet been formulated about how thought and knowledge develop from infancy to adolescence.

A Tiger in Training   Human behavior develops as a function of both heredity and environment—of both nature and nurture. The joint and inseparable influence of these two factors in development is nicely illustrated in the case of professional golfer Tiger Woods, shown here as a youngster with his father, who not only provided some of Tiger's genes but also served as his golf teacher.

It was the Swiss psychologist Jean Piaget (pronounced "p-ah-ZHAY") who first suggested that nature and nurture work together, and that their influences are inseparable and interactive. Piaget had a lifelong interest in human intellectual and cognitive development. His ideas, presented in numerous books and articles published from the 1920s until his death in 1980, influenced the field of developmental psychology more than those of any other person before or since (Flavell, 1996).

Most developmental psychologists now accept the idea that nature and nurture contribute jointly to development—in two ways. First, they operate together to make all people alike as human beings. For example, we all achieve milestones of physical development in the same order and at roughly the same rate as a result of the nature of biological maturation supported by the nurture of basic care, nutrition, and exercise. Second, nature and nurture also both operate to make each person unique. The nature of inherited genes and the nurture of widely different family and cultural environments produce differences among individuals in such dimensions as athletic abilities, intelligence, and personality (Cross & Markus, 1999; Plomin & Caspi, 1999). Heredity creates *predispositions* that interact with environmental influences, including family and teachers, friends and random events, books and computers. It is this interaction that produces the developmental outcomes we see in individuals. So Michael Jordan, Eminem, and Prince William are different from one another and from other men because of both their genes and their experiences.

Just how much nature and nurture contribute varies from one characteristic to another. Nature shapes some characteristics, such as physical size and appearance, so strongly that only extreme environmental conditions can affect them. Variation in height, for example, has been estimated to be 80 to 95 percent genetic. This means that 80 to 95 percent of the differences in height that we see among people are due to their genes. Less than 20 percent of the differences are due to prenatal or postnatal diet, or to early illness or other growth-stunting environmental factors. Nature's influence on other characteristics, such as intelligence or personality, is not as strong. Complex traits like these are influenced by genes, but by many environmental factors as well (Plomin et al., 2000).

It is impossible for researchers to identify the separate influences that nature and nurture exert on such complex traits, partly because heredity and environment are *correlated*. For instance, highly intelligent biological parents give their children genes for intelligence and typically also provide a stimulating environment. Heredity and environment also influence each other. Just as the environment promotes or hampers an individual's abilities, those inherited abilities to some extent determine the individual's environment. For example, a stimulating environment full of toys, books, and lessons encourages children's mental development and increases the chances that their full inherited intelligence will emerge. At the same time, more intelligent children seek out environments that are more stimulating, ask more questions, draw more attention from adults, and ultimately, learn more from these experiences.

Beginnings

Let's now consider how nature and nurture interact to affect human development, before and after birth. Nowhere is this interaction clearer than in the womb, as a single fertilized egg becomes a functioning infant.

OBJ 12.5: Describe the process of development in each of the prenatal stages.

Test Items 12.14–12.18

Prenatal Development LSV: Prenatal Life

The process of development begins when a sperm from the father-to-be penetrates, or fertilizes, the ovum of the mother-to-be, and a brand-new cell, called a **zygote**, is formed. This new cell carries a genetic heritage from both mother and father (see the behavioral genetics appendix).

ClassPrep PPT 7, OHT: Prenatal Development: The First Weeks

Class Prep PPTs 8 & 9: Stages of Prenatal Development

Stages of Development
In the first stage of prenatal development, called the *germinal stage,* the zygote divides into many more cells, which by the end of the second week have formed an **embryo** (pronounced "EM-bree-oh"). What follows is the *embryonic stage* of development, during which the embryo quickly develops a heart, nervous system, stomach, esophagus, and ovaries or testes. By two months after conception, when the embryonic stage ends, the inch-long embryo has developed eyes, ears, a nose, a jaw, a mouth, and lips. The tiny arms have elbows, hands, and stubby fingers; the legs have knees, ankles, and toes.

During the remaining seven-month period until birth, called the *fetal stage* of prenatal development, the organs grow and start to function. By the end of the third month, the **fetus** can kick, make a fist, turn its head, open its mouth, swallow, and frown. In the sixth month, the eyelids, which have been sealed, open. The fetus now has taste buds and a well-developed grasp and, if born prematurely, can breathe regularly for as long as twenty-four hours at a time. By the end of the seventh month, the organ systems, though immature, are all functional. In the eighth and ninth months, fetuses respond to light and touch, and they can hear what is going on outside. They can also learn. For example, they will ignore a stimulus, such as a vibration or sound, after it has been repeated a number of times. In such cases, they have *habituated* to the stimulus.

ClassPrep PPT 10: Prenatal Risks

LSV: Prenatal Risks

Habituation, described in the chapter on learning, predicts cognitive abilities after birth; babies who habituate faster display higher mental abilities later on.

Nature determines the timing and stages of prenatal development, but that development is also affected by the nurture provided by the environment of the womb.

zygote A new cell, formed from a father's sperm and a mother's ovum.

embryo The developing individual from the fourteenth day after fertilization until the end of the second month after conception.

fetus The developing individual from the third month after conception until birth.

Prenatal Risks
During prenatal development, a spongy organ called the *placenta,* formed from the outside layer of the zygote, sends nutrients from the mother to the fetus and carries away wastes. It also screens out many potentially harmful substances, including most bacteria. This screening is imperfect, however: Gases and viruses, as well as nicotine, alcohol, and other drugs, can pass through.

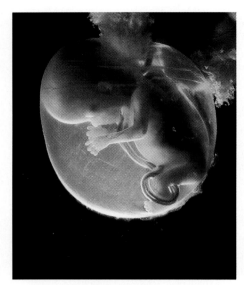

A Fetus at Twelve Weeks　At this point in prenatal development, the fetus can kick its legs, curl its toes, make a fist, turn its head, squint, open its mouth, swallow, and take a few "breaths" of amniotic fluid.

OBJ 12.6: Define teratogen. Define critical period and know the stage associated with it.

Test Items 12.19–12.25

ClassPrep PPT 11: Examples of Teratogens

teratogens　Harmful substances that can cause birth defects.

critical period　An interval during which certain kinds of growth must occur if development is to proceed normally.

fetal alcohol syndrome　A pattern of physical and mental defects found in babies born to women who abused alcohol during pregnancy.

Severe damage can occur if the baby's mother takes certain drugs, is exposed to toxic substances, or has certain illnesses while organs are forming in the embryonic stage.

Harmful external substances that invade the womb and result in birth defects are called **teratogens** (pronounced "ta-RAT-a-jens"). Teratogens are especially damaging during the embryonic stage, because it is a **critical period** in prenatal development, a time when certain kinds of growth must occur if the infant's development is to proceed normally. If the heart, eyes, ears, hands, and feet do not appear during this period, they cannot form later on; and if they form incorrectly, the defects are permanent. So even before a mother knows she is pregnant, she may accidentally damage her infant by exposing it to teratogens. A baby whose mother has rubella (German measles) during the third or fourth week after conception, for example, has a 50 percent chance of being blind, deaf, or mentally retarded, or of having a malformed heart. If the mother has rubella later in the pregnancy, after the infant's eyes, ears, brain, and heart have formed, the likelihood that the baby will have one of these defects drops substantially. Later, during the fetal stage, teratogens affect the baby's size, behavior, intelligence, and health, rather than the formation of organs and limbs.

Of special concern today are the effects of drugs on infants' development. Pregnant women who use substances such as cocaine create a substantial risk for their fetuses, which do not yet have the enzymes necessary to break down the drugs. "Cocaine babies" or "crack babies" may be born premature, underweight, tense, and fussy (Inciardi, Surratt, & Saum, 1997); they may also suffer delayed physical growth and motor development (Tarr & Pyfer, 1996). Current research suggests, however, that although cocaine babies are more likely to have behavioral and learning problems (Singer et al., 2001), their mental abilities are not substantially different from those of any baby born into an impoverished environment (Frank et al., 2001). How well they ultimately do in school depends on how supportive that environment turns out to be (Begley, 1997).

Alcohol is another dangerous teratogen. Pregnant women who drink as little as a glass or two of wine a day can harm their infants' intellectual functioning (Streissguth et al., 1999). Almost half the children born to expectant mothers who abuse alcohol will develop **fetal alcohol syndrome,** a pattern of defects that includes mental retardation and malformations of the face, such as a flattened nose and an underdeveloped upper lip (Jenkins & Culbertson, 1996). Smoking, too, can affect the developing fetus. Smokers' babies are usually born underweight and often suffer from respiratory problems (Gilliland, Li, & Peters, 2001). They may also be irritable and display problems with attention later on (Milberger et al., 1997).

Defects due to teratogens are most likely to appear when the negative effects of nature and nurture combine—when a genetically susceptible infant receives a strong dose of a damaging substance during a critical period of prenatal development. Fortunately, mental or physical problems resulting from all harmful prenatal factors affect fewer than 10 percent of the babies born in Western nations. Mechanisms built into the human organism maintain normal development under all but the most adverse conditions. The vast majority of fetuses arrive at the end of their nine-month gestation averaging a healthy seven pounds and ready to continue a normal course of development in the world.

The Newborn

Determining what newborns are able to see, hear, and do is one of the most fascinating—and frustrating—research challenges in developmental psychology. Young infants are very difficult to study. About 70 percent of the time, they are asleep; and when they are not sleeping, they may be drowsy, crying, or restlessly moving about. It is only when they are in a state of quiet alertness, which occurs infrequently and only for a few minutes at a time, that researchers can assess infants' abilities.

A Baby's-Eye View of the World The photograph on the left simulates what the mother on the right looks like to her newborn infant. Although their vision is blurry, infants particularly seem to enjoy looking at faces. As mentioned in the chapter on perception, their eyes will follow a moving face-like drawing (Johnson et al., 1991a, 1991b), and they will stare at a human face longer than at other figures (Valenza et al., 1996).

OBJ 12.7: Describe the capacities of a newborn's senses. Define reflex, and name three reflexes exhibited by newborns. Discuss how motor development is influenced by experimentation.

Test Items 12.26–12.33

Essay Q 12.1

During these brief periods, psychologists show infants objects or pictures, or present sounds to them, and watch where they look and for how long. They film the infants' eye movements and record changes in their heart rates, sucking rates, brain waves, body movements, and skin conductance (a measure of perspiration associated with emotion) to learn what infants can see and hear (Aslin, Jusczyk, & Pisoni, 1998; Kellman & Banks, 1998).

ClassPrep PPT 12: Vision Capabilities of the Newborn

Vision and Other Senses   Infants can see at birth, but their vision is blurry. Researchers estimate that newborns have 20/300 eyesight; that is, an object 20 feet away looks as clear as it would if viewed from 300 feet by an adult with normal vision. The reason infants' vision is so limited is that their eyes and brains still need time to grow and develop. Newborns' eyes are smaller than those of adults, and the cells in their foveas—the area of each retina on which images are focused—are fewer and far less sensitive. Their eye movements are slow and jerky. And pathways connecting the eyes to the brain are still inefficient, as is the processing of visual information within the brain.

Although infants cannot see small objects on the other side of the room, they are able to see large objects close up. They stare longest at objects that have large visible elements, movement, clear contours, and a lot of contrast—all qualities that exist in the human face. In fact, from the time they are born, infants will redirect their eyes to follow a moving drawing of a face, and they stare at a human face longer than at other figures (Johnson et al., 1991a, 1991b; Valenza et al., 1996). They also exhibit a degree of *size constancy*—the ability to perceive the correct physical size of an object despite changes in the size of its image on the retina (see the chapter on perception). So a baby perceives Mother's face as remaining about the same size, whether she is looking over the edge of the crib or close enough to kiss the baby's cheek. Newborns do not experience *depth perception* until some time later, however; it takes about seven months before they develop the ability to use the pictorial cues to depth described in the chapter on perception.

The course of development for hearing is similar to that of vision. Infants at birth are not deaf, but they hear poorly. At two or three days of age, they can hear soft voices and notice the difference between tones about one note apart on the musical scale; they also turn their heads toward sounds (Clifton, 1992). But their hearing is not as sharp as that of adults until well into childhood. Infants' hearing is particularly attuned to the sounds of speech. When they hear voices, babies open their eyes wider and look for the speaker. By four months of age, they can discriminate differences among almost all of the more than fifty phonetic contrasts in adult languages. Infants also prefer certain kinds of speech. They like rising tones spoken by women or children, and they like speech that is high pitched, exaggerated, and expressive. In other words, they like to hear the "baby talk" used by most adults when they talk to babies.

ClassPrep PPT 13: Other Senses of the Newborn

Newborns' sense of smell is similar to that of adults, but again, less acute. Certain smells and tastes appeal to them more than others. For instance, they like the smell of flowers and the taste of sweet drinks (Ganchrow, Steiner, & Daher,

1983). Contrary to popular myth, however, they dislike the smell of ammonia (in wet diapers). Research indicates that within a few days after birth, breastfed babies prefer the odor of their own mother to that of another mother (Porter et al., 1992). They also develop preferences for the food flavors consumed by their mothers (Mennella & Beauchamp, 1996).

Although limited, these inborn sensory abilities—smell, taste, hearing, and vision—are important for survival and development because they focus the infant's attention on the caregiver. For example, the attraction of newborns to the sweet smell and taste of mother's milk helps them locate appropriate food and identify their caregiver. Their sensitivity to speech allows them to focus on language and encourages the caregiver to talk to them. And because their vision is limited to the distance at which most interaction with a caregiver takes place and is tuned to the special qualities of faces, the caregiver's face is especially noticeable to them. Accordingly, infants are exposed to emotional expressions and come to recognize the caregiver by sight, further encouraging the caregiver to interact. As infants physically mature and learn from their environment, their sensory capacities become more complex and adult-like.

Reflexes and Motor Skills

In the first few weeks and months after birth, babies demonstrate involuntary, unlearned motor behaviors called *reflexes*. These are swift, automatic movements that occur in response to external stimuli. Figure 12.2 illustrates the *grasping reflex;* more than twenty other reflexes have been observed in newborn infants. For example, the *rooting reflex* causes the infant to turn its mouth toward a nipple (or anything else) that touches its cheek, and the *sucking reflex* causes the newborn to suck on anything that touches its lips. Many of these reflexes evolved because, like seeing and hearing, they were important for infants' survival. But infants' behavior does not remain under the control of these reflexes for long. Most reflexes disappear after the first three or four months, when infants' brain development allows them to control their muscles voluntarily. At that point, infants can develop motor skills, so they are soon able to roll over, sit up, crawl, stand, and by the end of the year, walk (see Figure 12.1).

Until a few years ago, most developmental psychologists accepted Gesell's view that barring extreme environmental conditions, these motor abilities occur spontaneously as the central nervous system and muscles mature. Recent research demonstrates, however, that maturation does not tell the whole story. Consider the fact that many babies today aren't learning to crawl on time—or at all. Why? A decade ago, in an effort to prevent sudden infant death syndrome, described in the chapter on consciousness, public health officials launched the "Back to Sleep" campaign, which urged parents to put babies to sleep on their backs rather than facedown. The campaign was successful, but researchers have discovered that many babies who were never placed on their tummies went directly from sitting to toddling, skipping the crawling stage but reaching all other motor milestones on schedule (Kolata & Markel, 2001). Observation of infants who do learn to crawl has shown that it does not happen suddenly. It takes the development of enough muscle strength to support the abdomen—and some active experimentation—to get the job done (Thelen, 1995). Six infants in one study tried various crawling techniques—moving backward, moving one limb at a time, using the arms only, and so on (Freedland & Bertenthal, 1994). It was only after a week or two of trial and error that all six arrived at the same method: moving diagonal limbs (right arm and left leg, left arm and right leg) together. This pattern turned out to be the most efficient way of getting around quickly without tipping over. Such observations suggest that as maturation increases infants' strength, they try out motor patterns and select the ones that work best (Nelson, 1999).

In short, motor development results from a combination of maturation and experience. It is not the result of an entirely automatic sequence genetically etched in the brain. Yet again, we see that nature and nurture influence each other.

IRM Activity 12.4: Development Exercise: Motor Milestones

ClassPrep PPT 14: Reflexes of the Newborn
ClassPrep PPT 15: Development of Motor Skills

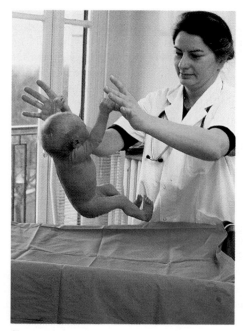

figure 12.2

Reflexes in the Newborn

When a finger is pressed into a newborn's palm, the *grasping reflex* causes the infant to hold on tightly enough to suspend its entire weight. And when a newborn is held upright over a flat surface, the *stepping reflex* leads to walking movements.

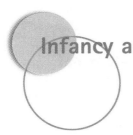

Infancy and Childhood: Cognitive Development

Over the first ten years of life, the tiny infant becomes a competent child who can read a book, write a poem, and argue for access to the family's new computer. Several changes lead to the dramatic shifts in thinking, knowing, and remembering that occur between early infancy and later childhood.

ClassPrep PPT 16: Infancy and Childhood

OBJ 12.8: Describe Piaget's theory of knowledge development. Explain why it incorporates both nature and nurture. Define schemas, assimilation, and accommodation.

Test Items 12.34–12.41

IRM Activity 12.5: Playing Piaget

Changes in the Brain ClassPrep PPT 17: Changes in the Brain

One factor that underlies the cognitive leaps of infancy and childhood is continued growth and development of the brain. When infants are born, they already have a full quota of brain cells, but the neural networks connecting the cells are immature. With time, the connections grow increasingly complex and then, with pruning, more efficient. Studies reveal how, as different regions of the brain develop more complex and efficient neural networks, new cognitive abilities appear (Nelson, 1997).

In the first few months of infancy, the area of the brain that is most mature is the cerebellum. Its early maturation allows infants to display simple associative abilities such as sucking more when they see their mother's face or hear her voice. Between six and twelve months of age, neurological development in the medial temporal lobe of the cortex makes it possible for infants to remember and imitate an action they have seen earlier, or to recognize a picture of an object they have never seen before but have held in their hands. And neurological development in the frontal cortex, which occurs later in childhood, allows the individual to develop higher cognitive functions such as reasoning. Brain structures thus provide the "hardware" for children's *cognitive development*. How does the "software" of thinking develop, and how does it modify the "wiring" of the brain's "hardware"? These questions have been pursued by many developmental psychologists, beginning with Piaget.

Sattler/Shabatay reader, 2/e: Gregory, "Shame"

The Development of Knowledge: Piaget's Theory

ClassPrep PPTs 18 & 19: Piaget's Theory of Cognitive Development

LSV: Development of Identity and Attachment, Piaget's Theory of Cognitive Development

Piaget dedicated his life to a search for the origins of intelligence in infancy and the factors that lead to changes in knowledge over the life span. He was the first to chart the fascinating journey from the simple reflexes of the newborn to the complex understandings of the adolescent. Piaget's theory was not correct in every respect—later we discuss some of its weaknesses—but the fact remains that his ideas about cognitive development still guide much research in the field (Fischer & Hencke, 1996).

Piaget proposed that cognitive development proceeds through a series of distinct *periods* or *stages* (outlined in Table 12.1). He believed that all children's thinking goes through the same stages, in the same order, without skipping—building on previous stages, then moving progressively to higher ones. According to Piaget, the thinking of infants is different from the thinking of children, and the thinking of children is different from that of adolescents. He concluded that children are not just miniature adults, and they are not dumber than adults; they just think in different ways. Entering each stage involves a *qualitative* change from the previous stage, much as a caterpillar is transformed into a butterfly. What drives children to higher stages is their constant struggle to make sense of their experiences. They are active thinkers who are always trying to construct more advanced understandings of the world.

Building Blocks of Development
To explain how infants and children move to ever-higher stages of understanding and knowledge, Piaget used the concept of **schemas**. As noted in the chapters on perception, memory, and cognition, schemas are the generalizations that form as people experience the world; they organize past experiences and provide a framework for understanding future experiences. Piaget

schemas Generalizations based on experience that form the basic units of knowledge.

According to Piaget, a predictable set of features characterizes each period of children's cognitive development. The ages associated with the stages are approximate; Piaget realized that some children move through the stages slightly faster or slower than others.

table 12.1
Piaget's Periods of Cognitive Development

Period	Activities and Achievements
Sensorimotor Birth–2 years	Infants discover aspects of the world through their sensory impressions, motor activities, and coordination of the two.
	They learn to differentiate themselves from the external world. They learn that objects exist even when they are are not visible and that objects are independent of the infant's own actions. They gain some appreciation of cause and effect.
Preoperational 2–4 years	Children cannot yet manipulate and transform information in logical ways, but they now can think in images and symbols.
4–7 years	They become able to represent something with something else, acquire language, and play games that involve pretending. Intelligence at this stage is said to be intuitive, because children cannot make general, logical statements.
Concrete operational 7–11 years	Children can understand logical principles that apply to concrete external objects.
	They can appreciate that certain properties of an object remain the same despite changes in appearance, and they can sort objects into categories. They can appreciate the perspective of another viewer. They can think about two concepts, such as longer and wider, at the same time.
Formal operational Over 11 years	Only adolescents and adults can think logically about abstractions, can speculate, and can consider what might or what ought to be.
	They can work in probabilities and possibilities. They can imagine other worlds, especially ideal ones. They can reason about purely verbal or logical statements. They can relate any element or statement to any other, manipulate variables in a scientific experiment, and deal with proportions and analogies. They reflect on their own activity of thinking.

saw schemas as organized patterns of action or thought that children construct as they adapt to the environment; they are the basic units of knowledge, the building blocks of intellectual development. Schemas, he said, can involve behaviors (e.g., tying a shoelace or sucking), mental symbols (e.g., words or images), or mental activities (e.g., doing arithmetic "in our head" or imagining actions).

At first, infants form simple schemas. For example, a sucking schema consolidates their experiences of sucking into images of what objects can be sucked on (bottles, fingers, pacifiers) and what kinds of sucking can be done (soft and slow, speedy and vigorous). Later, children form more complex schemas, such as a schema for tying a knot or making a bed. Still later, adolescents form schemas about what it is to be in love.

Two complementary processes guide the development of schemas: assimilation and accommodation. In the process of **assimilation**, infants and children take in information about new objects by using existing schemas that will fit the new objects. An infant is given a new toy. He sucks on it, assimilating it into the sucking schema he has developed with his bottle and pacifier. A toddler sees a butterfly for

assimilation   The process of trying out existing schemas on objects that fit those schemas.

figure 12.3

Accommodation

Because the bars of the playpen are in the way, this child discovers that her schema for grasping and pulling objects toward her will not work. She then adjusts, or accommodates, her schema to achieve her goal.

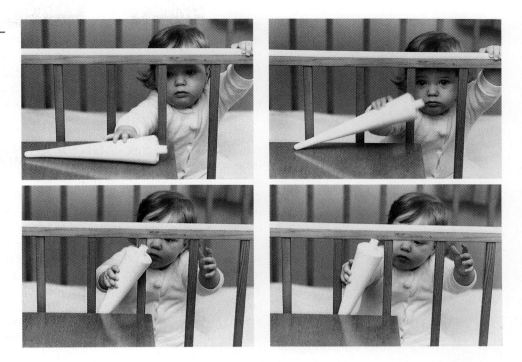

the first time. It's colorful and flies, like a bird, so she assimilates it into her "birdie" schema. An older child encounters a large dog. How she assimilates this new creature depends on her existing schema of dogs. If she has had positive experiences with a family pet, she will expect the dog to behave like her pet, and she will greet it enthusiastically. If she has been frightened by dogs in the past, she may have a negative schema and react with fear to the dog she has just met.

Sometimes, like Cinderella's sisters squeezing their oversized feet into the glass slipper, people distort information about a new object to make it fit their existing schema. When squeezing won't work, though, they are forced to change, or accommodate, their schema to the new object. In **accommodation,** a person finds that a familiar schema cannot be made to fit a new object, and changes it (see Figure 12.3). So when the infant discovers that another new toy—a squeaker—is more fun when it makes a noise, he accommodates his sucking schema and starts munching on the squeaker instead. When the toddler realizes that butterflies are not birds because they don't have beaks and feathers, she accommodates her "birdie" schema to include two kinds of "flying animals"—birds and butterflies. And if the child with the positive "doggie" schema meets a snarling stray, she discovers that her original schema does not extend to all dogs, and she refines it to distinguish between friendly dogs and those that are aggressive. Through assimilation and accommodation, said Piaget, we build our knowledge of the world, block by block.

OBJ 12.9: Describe the development of mental abilities during the sensorimotor period. Define object permanence.

Test Items 12.42–12.46

ClassPrep PPT 21: Sensorimotor Development

Sensorimotor Development　　Piaget (1952) called the first stage of cognitive development the **sensorimotor period** because, he claimed, the infant's mental activity and schemas are confined to sensory functions, like seeing and hearing, and motor skills, like grasping and sucking. According to Piaget, during this stage, infants can form schemas only of objects and actions that are present—things they can see or hear or touch. They cannot think about absent objects because they cannot act on them; thinking, for infants, is doing. They do not lie in the crib thinking about their mother or their teddy bear, because they are not yet able to form schemas that are *mental representations* of objects and actions.

The sensorimotor period ends when infants can form mental representations and thus can think about objects and actions even while the objects are not visible or the actions are not occurring. This is a remarkable milestone, according to Piaget;

accommodation　The process of modifying schemas when familiar schemas do not work.

sensorimotor period　The first of Piaget's stages of cognitive development, when the infant's mental activity is confined to sensory perception and motor skills.

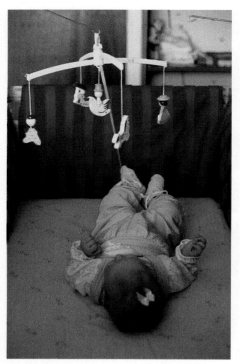

figure 12.4

Infant Memory

This three-month-old infant learned to move a mobile by kicking her left foot, which is tied to the mobile with a ribbon. Even a month later, the baby will show recognition of this particular mobile by kicking more vigorously when she sees it than when she sees another one.

OBJ 12.10: Explain how research has modified Piaget's description of infants in the sensori-motor period. Discuss the experiments on object permanence and the role of experience in developing knowledge during infancy.

Test Items 12.47–12.48

object permanence The knowledge that objects exist even when they are not in view.

it frees the child from the here-and-now of the sensory environment and allows for the development of thought. One sign that children have reached this milestone is their ability to find a hidden object. This behavior was of particular interest to Piaget because, for him, it reflected infants' knowledge that they do not have to look at, touch, or suck an object to know that it exists; it exists even when out of sight. Piaget called this knowledge **object permanence.**

Before they acquire a knowledge of object permanence, infants do not search for objects that are placed out of their sight. They act as if out of sight is literally out of mind. The first evidence of developing object permanence appears when infants are four to eight months old. At this age, for the first time, they recognize a familiar object even if part of it is hidden. They know it's their bottle even if they can see only the nipple peeking out from under the blanket. In Piaget's view, infants now have some primitive mental representation of objects. If an object is completely hidden, however, they will not search for it.

Several months later, infants will search briefly for a hidden object, but their search is random and ineffective. Not until they are eighteen to twenty-four months old, said Piaget, do infants appear able to picture and follow events in their minds. They look for the object in places other than where they saw it last, sometimes in completely new places. According to Piaget, their concept of the object as perma-nent is now fully developed; they have a mental representation of the object that is completely separate from their immediate perception of it.

New Views of Infants   In the years since Piaget's death, psychologists have found new ways to measure what is going on in infants' minds—infrared pho-tography to record infants' eye movements, time-lapse photography to detect subtle hand movements, special equipment to measure infants' sucking rates, and com-puter technology to track and analyze it all. Their research shows that infants know a lot more, and know it sooner, than Piaget ever thought they did.

Infants are not just sensing and moving in the sensorimotor period; they are already thinking as well. For example, they are able to integrate sights with sounds. In one study, infants were shown two different videotapes at the same time, while the soundtrack for one of them was played through a speaker placed between the two video screens. The infants tended to look at the video that went with the sound-track—at a toy bouncing in time with a tapping sound or at a pair of cymbals accompanied by clanging (Walker-Andrews et al., 1991). Infants can remember, too. As young as two to three months of age, they can recall a particular mobile that was hung over their crib a few days before (Rovee-Collier, 1999; see Figure 12.4).

Young babies also seem to have a sense of object permanence. Piaget had required infants to demonstrate object permanence through rather grand move-ments, such as removing a cover that had been placed over a hidden object. However, when experimenters simply turn off the lights, infants as young as five months of age have been shown to reach for now-unseen objects in the dark (Clifton et al., 1991). Researchers now recognize that finding a hidden object under a cover requires several abilities: mentally representing the hidden object, figuring out where it might be, and pulling off the cover. Piaget's tests did not allow for the possibility that infants know a hidden object still exists but do not have adequate strategies for finding it or memory skills for remembering it while they search. In research situa-tions where infants merely have to stare to indicate that they know where an object is hidden, they demonstrate this cognitive ability even before the age of one (Ahmed & Ruffman, 1998; Hespos & Baillargeon, 2001).

In short, developmental psychologists now generally agree that infants develop some mental representations earlier than Piaget had suggested. They disagree, how-ever, about whether this knowledge is "programmed" in infants (Spelke et al., 1992), quickly develops through interactions with the outside world (Baillargeon, 1995), or is constructed through the recombination of old schemas into new ones (Fischer & Bidell, 1991).

FOCUS ON RESEARCH METHODS

ClassPrep PPT 77: Focus on Research Methods

Experiments on Developing Minds

To explore how infants develop mental representations, Renee Baillargeon (pronounced "by-ar-ZHAN") investigated infants' early understanding of the principles of physics. Whether you realize it or not, you know a lot about physics. You know about gravity and balance, for example. But when did you first understand that "what goes up must come down" and that an unbalanced tray will tip over? Are these things you have always known, or did you figure them out through trial and error?

● What was the researcher's question?

Baillargeon wanted to know when and how babies first develop knowledge about balance and gravity—specifically, about the tendency of unsupported objects to fall.

● How did the researcher answer the question?

Baillargeon (1994a, 1994b) devised a creative experimental method to probe infants' knowledge. She showed infants pairs of events, one of which was physically possible and the other, physically impossible. She then determined the infants' interest in each kind of event by measuring the amount of time they spent looking at it. Their tendency to look longer at unexpected events provided an indication of which events violated what the babies knew about the world. Using this method, Baillargeon studied infants' knowledge of balance and gravity.

The independent variable in her studies was the amount of physical support applied to objects; the dependent variable was the length of time the infants looked at the objects. Specifically, the infants viewed a bright-red gloved hand pushing a box from left to right along the top of a platform. On some trials, they saw physically possible events. For example, the hand pushed the box until its edge reached the end of the platform (see event A in Figure 12.5). On other trials, they saw impossible events, as when the hand pushed the box until only the end of its bottom surface rested on the platform or the box was beyond the platform altogether (see events B and C in the figure). On still other trials, the gloved hand held onto the box while pushing it beyond the edge of the platform (as shown in event D). Trials continued until the infants had seen at least four pairs of possible and impossible events in alternating order.

● What did the researcher find?

Baillargeon found that three-month-old infants looked longest at impossible event C, in which the box was entirely off the platform, whereas they were not particularly interested in either event D (box held by the gloved hand) or event A (box still on the platform). At six and a half months, infants stared intently at both event C (box off the platform) and event B (in which only the end of the box was resting on the platform).

● What do the results mean?

According to Baillargeon (1998), these results suggest that three-month-old babies know something about physical support: They expect the box to fall if it is entirely off the platform and act surprised when it does not. But they do not yet know that a box should fall if its center of gravity is unsupported, as in event B. By the time they are six and a half months old, however, infants apparently know about centers of gravity—that most of the box must be on the platform or it will fall.

Other researchers have questioned whether infants' tendency to stare longer at a particular display necessarily indicates "surprise" (Bogartz, Shinskey, & Speaker, 1997). Perhaps they simply recognize that the image is different from what they remember it to be or find the impossible image more noticeable.

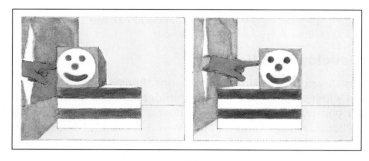

(A)

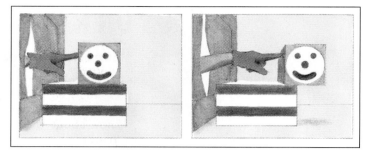

(B)

(C)

(D)

figure 12.5

**Events Demonstrating Infants'
Knowledge of Physics**

Infants look longer at things that interest them—that is, at new things rather than things they have seen before and find boring. In her research on the development of knowledge, Renee Baillargeon (1995) has found that physically impossible events B and C—made possible by an experimenter reaching through a hidden door to support a moving box—attract the most attention from infants. These results suggest that humans understand some basic laws of physics quite early in life.

Source: Baillargeon (1992).

● What do we still need to know?

The question remains as to which of these interpretations is correct. Do infants possess fundamental knowledge about the world that implies an understanding of complex physical principles, or are they just staring at something because it is novel or vivid? The answer to this question will require further research using varied visual stimuli that allows researchers to determine whether infants stare longer at physically possible events that are just as novel and vivid as physically impossible events.

Whether or not such research confirms Baillargeon's view, psychologists are still faced with the task of discovering *how* babies know about physics (Wynn & Chiang, 1998). Does their increasing understanding of physical principles result from their experience with objects, or is the knowledge innate?

In an attempt to answer this question, Baillargeon conducted another experiment in which she manipulated object-experience. She randomly assigned infants, ranging in age from three months to six and a half months, to receive either normal or extra experience with objects (the independent variable) and observed the effect on the infants' understanding of gravity (the dependent variable). After only a few demonstrations in which unsupported objects fell off platforms, infants in the extra object-experience group stared longer at a display of an unsupported object that did not fall. Other studies found similar results (Needham & Baillargeon, 1999).

It is still too early to say for sure whether Baillargeon's hypothesis about the importance of experience in developing knowledge is correct, but her results seem to support it.

OBJ 12.11: Describe the changes in cognition that occur during the preoperational period. Define conservation. Discuss the importance of symbol usage during this period. Describe the impact of visual perception on a preoperational child's thinking.

Test Items 12.50–12.54

ClassPrep PPTs 22 & 23: Preoperational Development

Videodisc Segment & Still: The Three Mountain Test

Videodisc Segment: Piagetian Volume Task

Preoperational Development

According to Piaget, the sensorimotor stage of development is followed by the **preoperational period.** During the first half of this period, children begin to understand, create, and use *symbols* (words, images, and objects) to represent things that are not present. As described in the chapter on cognition and language, they begin to use words to stand for objects: *Mommy, cup, me.* They also begin to play "pretend." They make their fingers "walk" or "shoot" and use a spoon to make a bridge. By the age of three or four, children can symbolize roles and play "house" or "doctor." They also can use drawing symbolically: Pointing to their scribble, they might say, "This is Mommy and Daddy and me going for a walk." The ability to use and understand symbols opens up vast domains for two- to four-year-olds.

During the second half of the preoperational stage, according to Piaget, four- to seven-year-olds begin to make intuitive guesses about the world as they try to figure out how things work. They claim that dreams are real: "Last night there was a circus in my room." And they believe that inanimate objects are alive and have intentions, feelings, and consciousness, a belief called *animism:* "Clouds go slowly because they have no legs" and "Empty cars feel lonely." In short, said Piaget, preoperational children cannot distinguish between the seen and the unseen, between the physical and the mental world. They are also highly *egocentric,* meaning that they appear to believe that the way things look to them is also how they look to everyone else. (This helps to explain why they may stand so as to block your view when both of you are trying to watch TV or ask "What's this?" as they look at a picture book in the back seat of the car while you're driving.)

Children's thinking is so dominated by what they can see and touch for themselves, Piaget said, that they do not realize that something is the same if its appearance changes. In one study, for example, preoperational children thought that a cat wearing a dog mask was actually a dog—because that's what it looked like (DeVries, 1969). These children do not yet have what Piaget called **conservation,** the ability to recognize that important properties of a substance or object—including its volume, weight, and species—remain constant despite changes in its shape.

In a test of conservation, Piaget first showed children equal amounts of water in two identical containers. He then poured one of them into a tall, thin glass and the other into a short, wide glass and asked whether one glass contained more water

During the second half of the pre-operational period, according to Piaget, children believe that inanimate objects are alive and have feelings, intentions, and consciousness.

©1993 Bil Keane, Inc.
Dist. by Cowles Synd., Inc.

"I think the moon likes us. It keeps on followin' us."

© Bill Keane, Inc. Reprinted with special permission of King Features Syndicate.

preoperational period According to Piaget, the second stage of cognitive development, during which children begin to use symbols to represent things that are not present.

conservation The ability to recognize that the important properties of a substance remain constant despite changes in shape, length, or position.

Testing for Conservation If you know a child who is between the ages of four and seven, get permission to test the child for what Piaget called *conservation*. Show the child two identical lumps of clay, and ask which lump is bigger. The child will probably say they are the same. Now roll one lump into a long "rope," and again ask which lump is bigger. If the child says that they are still the same, this is evidence of conservation. If the longer one is seen as bigger, conservation has not yet developed—at least not for this task. The older the child, the more likely it is that conservation will appear, but some children display conservation much earlier than Piaget thought was possible.

ClassPrep PPT 24, OHT: Conservation of Liquid

OBJ 12.12: Describe the changes in cognition that occur during Piaget's stage of concrete operation.

Test Items 12.55–12.59

OBJ 12.13: Discuss the criticisms of and alternatives to Piaget's theory of cognitive development.

Test Items 12.60–12.63

ClassPrep PPT 26: Modifying Piaget's Theory

concrete operations According to Piaget, the third stage of cognitive development, during which children's thinking is no longer dominated by visual appearances.

than the other. Children at the preoperational stage of development said that one glass (usually the taller one) contained more. They were dominated by the evidence of their eyes. If the glass looked bigger, they thought it contained more. In other words, they did not understand the logical concepts of *reversibility* (you just poured the water from one container to another, so you can pour it back, and it will still be the same amount) or *complementarity* (one glass is taller but also narrower; the other is shorter but also wider). Piaget named this stage "*pre*operational" because children at this stage do not yet understand logical mental operations such as these.

Concrete Operational Thought   Sometime around the age of six or seven, Piaget observed, children do develop the ability to conserve number and amount. When they do so, they enter what Piaget called the stage of **concrete operations**. Now, he said, they can count, measure, add, and subtract; their thinking is no longer dominated by the appearance of things. They can use simple logic and perform simple mental manipulations and mental operations on things. They can also sort objects into classes (such as tools, fruit, and vehicles) or series (such as largest to smallest).

Still, concrete operational children can perform their logical operations only on real, concrete objects—sticks and glasses, tools and fruit—not on abstract concepts like justice and freedom. They reason about what is, but not yet about what is possible. The ability to think logically about abstract ideas comes in the next stage of cognitive development, the *formal operational period*, which we discuss later in relation to adolescence.

ClassPrep PPT 25: Concrete Operational Thought

Modifying Piaget's Theory

Piaget was right in pointing out that there are significant shifts with age in children's thinking, and that thinking becomes more systematic, consistent, and integrated as children get older. His idea that children are active explorers and constructors of knowledge has been absorbed into contemporary ways of thinking about childhood. And he inspired many other psychologists to test his findings and theory with experiments of their own. The results of these experiments have suggested that Piaget's theory needs some modification.

What needs to be modified most is Piaget's notion of developmental stages. Researchers have shown that changes from one stage to the next are less consistent and global than Piaget thought. For example, three-year-olds can sometimes make the distinction between physical and mental phenomena; they know the characteristics of real dogs versus pretend dogs (Woolley, 1997). Moreover, they are not invariably egocentric; as one study demonstrated, children of this age knew that a white card, which looked pink to them because they were wearing rose-colored glasses, still looked white to someone who was not wearing the glasses (Liben, 1978). Preoperational children can even do conservation tasks if they are allowed to count the number of objects or have been trained to focus on relevant dimensions such as number, height, and width (Gelman & Baillargeon, 1983).

Taken together, these studies suggest that children's knowledge and mental strategies develop at different ages in different areas, and in "pockets" rather than at global levels of understanding (Sternberg, 1989). Knowledge in particular areas is demonstrated sooner in children who are given specific experience in those areas or who are presented with very simple questions and tasks. Children's reasoning depends not only on their general level of development but also on (1) how easy the task is, (2) how familiar they are with the objects involved, (3) how well they understand the language being used, and (4) what experiences they have had in similar situations (Siegal, 1997). Research has also shown that the level of a child's thinking varies from day to day and may even shift when the child solves the same problem twice in the same day (Siegler, 1994).

In summary, psychologists today tend to think of cognitive development in terms of rising and falling "waves," not fixed stages—in terms of changing frequencies in children's use of different ways of thinking, not sudden, permanent shifts from one way of thinking to another (Siegler, 1995). Psychologists now suggest that children systematically try out many different solutions to problems and gradually come to select the best of them.

Information Processing During Childhood

OBJ 12.14: Describe cognitive development from an information-processing approach.

Test Items 12.64–12.65

Personal Learning Activity 12.1

ClassPrep PPT 27: Information Processing During Childhood

An alternative to Piaget's theory of cognitive development is based on the *information-processing approach* discussed in the chapters on memory and on cognition and language. This approach describes cognitive activities in terms of how people take in information, use it, and remember it. Developmental psychologists taking this approach focus on gradual increases in children's mental capacities, rather than on dramatic changes in their stages of development. Their research demonstrates that as children get older, their information-processing skills gradually get better, and they can perform more complex tasks faster and easier.

First, older children have longer attention spans and are better at filtering out irrelevant information. These skills help them overcome distractions and concentrate intently on a variety of tasks, from hobbies to homework. Second, older children take in information more rapidly and can shift their attention from one task to another more quickly. (This is how they manage to do their homework while watching TV.) Third, older children can process the information they take in more rapidly and efficiently (Halford et al., 1994; Miller & Vernon, 1997). Compared with younger children, they code information into fewer dimensions and divide tasks into steps that can be processed one after another. This helps them to organize and complete their homework assignments.

Children's memory also markedly improves with age (Schneider & Bjorklund, 1998). Whereas preschoolers can keep only two or three pieces of information in their short-term memory at the same time, older children can hold four or five pieces of information. Older children can also put more information into their long-term memory storage, so they remember things longer than younger children. After about age seven, children can remember information that is more complex and abstract, such as the gist of what several people have said during a conversation. Their

in review	**Milestones of Cognitive Development in Infancy and Childhood**	

Age*	Achievement	Description
3–4 months	Maturation of senses	Immaturities that limit the newborn's vision and hearing are overcome.
	Voluntary movement	Reflexes disappear, and infants begin to gain voluntary control over their movements.
12–18 months	Mental representation	Infants can form images of objects and actions in their minds.
	Object permanence	Infants understand that objects exist even when out of sight.
18–24 months	Symbolic thought	Young children use symbols to represent things that are not present in their pretend play, drawing, and talk.
4 years	Intuitive thought	Children reason about events, real and imagined, by guessing rather than by engaging in logical analysis.
6–7 years	Concrete operations Conservation	Children can apply simple logical operations to real objects. For example, they recognize that important properties of a substance, such as number or amount, remain constant despite changes in shape or position.
7–8 years	Information processing	Children can remember more information; they begin to learn strategies for memorization.

*These ages are approximate; they indicate the order in which children first reach these milestones of cognitive development rather than the exact ages.

memories are more accurate, extensive, and well organized. And because they have accumulated more knowledge during their years of learning about the world, older children can integrate new information into a more complete network of facts. This makes it easier for them to understand and remember new information. (See "In Review: Milestones of Cognitive Development in Infancy and Childhood.")

 LINKAGES (a link to Memory)

What accounts for these increases in children's attention, information processing, and memory capacities? It should not be surprising that it's nature plus nurture. As mentioned earlier, maturation of the brain contributes to better and faster information processing as children grow older. Experience also contributes. The importance of experience has been demonstrated by researchers who have tested children's cognitive abilities using familiar versus unfamiliar materials. In one study, for example, Mayan children in Mexico lagged behind their age-mates in the United States on standard memory tests for pictures and nouns that the Mexican children had not seen before. But the children did much better when researchers gave them a more familiar task, such as recalling the objects they saw in a model of a Mayan village (Rogoff & Waddell, 1982). The children's memory for these familiar objects was better, presumably because they could process information about them more easily and quickly.

Knowing how to memorize things also improves children's memories. To a great extent, children acquire memorization strategies in school. They learn to repeat information over and over to help fix it in memory, to place information into categories, and to use memory aids like "*i* before *e* except after *c*" to help them remember. They also learn what situations call for deliberate memorization and what factors, such as the length of a list, affect memory.

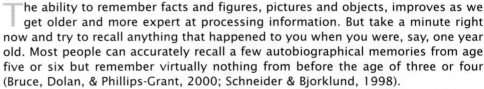

Development and Memory

LINKAGES (a link to Memory)

OBJ 12.15: Discuss the research on memory in early childhood.

Test Items 12.66–12.67

The ability to remember facts and figures, pictures and objects, improves as we get older and more expert at processing information. But take a minute right now and try to recall anything that happened to you when you were, say, one year old. Most people can accurately recall a few autobiographical memories from age five or six but remember virtually nothing from before the age of three or four (Bruce, Dolan, & Phillips-Grant, 2000; Schneider & Bjorklund, 1998).

Psychologists have not yet found a fully satisfactory explanation for this "infantile amnesia." Some have suggested that young children lack the memory encoding and storage processes described in the chapter on memory. Yet children two or three years old can clearly recall experiences that happened weeks or even months earlier (Bauer, 1996). Others suggest that infantile amnesia occurs because very young children lack a sense of self. They don't recognize themselves in a mirror, so they may not have a framework for organizing memories about what happens to them (Howe, 1995). However, this explanation cannot apply to the entire period up to three years of age, because children do recognize themselves in the mirror by the time they are two. In fact, research suggests that infants even younger than two can recognize their own faces, as well as their voices on tape (Legerstee, Anderson, & Schaffer, 1998).

Another possibility is that early memories, though "present," are implicit rather than explicit. As described in the chapter on memory, *implicit memories* form automatically and can affect our emotions and behavior even when we do not consciously recall them. Toddlers' implicit memories were demonstrated in a study in which two-and-a-half-year-olds apparently remembered a strange, pitch-dark room where they had participated in an experiment two years earlier (Perris, Myers, & Clifton, 1990). Unlike children who had never been in the room, these children were unafraid and reached for noisy objects in the dark, just as they had learned to do at the previous session. However, children's implicit memories of their early years, like their explicit memories, are quite limited. In one study, researchers showed photographs of young children to a group of ten-year-olds (Newcombe & Fox, 1994). Some of the photos were of preschool classmates whom the children had not seen since they were five years old. They explicitly recalled 21 percent of their former classmates, and their skin conductance (an index of emotion) indicated that they had implicit memories of an additional 5 percent. Yet these children had *no* memory of 74 percent of their preschool pals, as compared with adults in another study who correctly identified 90 percent of the photographs of high school classmates they had not seen in thirty years (Bahrick, Bahrick, & Wittlinger, 1975).

Other psychologists have proposed that our early memories are lost because in those years we did not yet have the language skills to talk about, and thus solidify, our memories. Nor could we be reminded of past events when others talked about them (Fivush, Haden, & Adam, 1995; Hudson & Sheffield, 1998). Still others say that early memories were stored, but because the schemas we used in early childhood to mentally represent them changed in later years, we no longer possess the retrieval cues necessary to recall them. Another possibility is that early experiences tend to be fused into *generalized event representations,* such as "going to Grandma's" or "playing at the beach," so it becomes difficult to remember any specific event. Research on hypotheses such as these may someday unravel the mystery of infantile amnesia (Eacott, 1999; Newcombe et al., 2000; Rovee-Collier, 1999).

Culture and Cognitive Development

OBJ 12.16: Describe the impact of culture on cognitive development.

Test Items 12.68–12.71

ClassPrep PPT 28: Culture and Cognitive Development

Whereas Piaget focused on the physical world of objects in explaining development, the Russian psychologist Lev Vygotsky (pronounced "vah-GOT-ski") focused on the social world of people. He viewed cognitive abilities as the product of cultural history. The child's mind, said Vygotsky, grows through interaction with other minds. Dramatic support for this idea comes from cases such as the "Wild Boy of Aveyron," a French child who, in the late 1700s, was apparently lost or abandoned by his parents at an early age and had grown up with animals. At about eleven years of age, he was captured by hunters and sent to Paris, where scientists observed him. What the scientists saw was a dirty, frightened creature who trotted like a wild animal and spent most of his time silently rocking. Although the scientists worked with the boy for more than ten years, he was never able to live unguarded among other people, and he never learned to speak.

Consistent with Vygotsky's ideas, this tragic case suggests that without society, children's minds would not develop much beyond those of animals—that children acquire their ideas through interaction with parents, teachers, and other representatives of their culture. Vygotsky's followers have studied the effects of the social world on children's cognitive development—how participation in social routines affects children's developing knowledge of the world (Gauvain, 2001). In Western societies, such routines include shopping, eating at McDonald's, going to birthday parties, and attending religious services. In other cultures they might include helping to make pottery, going hunting, and weaving baskets (Larson & Verma, 1999). Quite early, children develop mental representations, called *scripts,* for these activities (see the chapter on cognition and language). By the time they are three, children can accurately describe the scripts for their routine activities (Nelson, 1986). Scripts, in turn, affect children's knowledge and understanding of cognitive tasks. So suburban children can understand conservation problems earlier than inner-city children if the problems are presented, as Piaget's were, like miniature science experiments; but the performance of inner-city children is improved when the task is presented via a script that is more familiar to them, such as one involving what a "slick trickster" would do to fool someone (White & Glick, 1978).

From a remarkably young age, children's cognitive abilities are influenced by the language of their culture. Consider, for instance, the way people think about relations between objects in space. Children who learn a language that has no words for spatial concepts—such as *in, on, in front of, behind, to the left,* and *to the right*— will acquire cognitive categories that are different from those of people in North America. Research indicates that such individuals do, in fact, have difficulty distinguishing between the left and right sides of objects, and they tend not to invoke the symbolic associations with left and right hands that North Americans do (Bowerman, 1996; Levinson, 1996).

As a cultural tool, language can also affect academic achievement. For example, Korean and Chinese children show exceptional ability at adding and subtracting large numbers (Fuson & Kwon, 1992; Miller et al., 1995). As third-graders, they can do in their heads three-digit problems (such as 702 minus 125) that would stump most North American children. The difference seems traceable in part to the clear and explicit way that Asian languages label numbers from eleven to nineteen. In English, the meaning of the words *eleven* and *twelve,* for instance, is not as clear

Encouraging Academic Achievement
Asian American children tend to do better in school than European American children partly because Asian American children's families tend to provide especially strong support for academic achievement.

OBJ 12.17: Describe the potential impact of the environment on cognitive development.

Test Items 12.72–12.74

as the Asian *ten-one* and *ten-two.* A related cultural difference supports this mathematical expertise: Asians use the metric system of measurement and a manual computing device called the *abacus,* both of which are structured around the number ten. Korean math textbooks emphasize this tens structure by presenting the ones digits in red, the tens in blue, and the hundreds in green. Above all, in Asian cultures, educational achievement, especially in mathematics, is encouraged at home and strongly encouraged in school (Crystal et al., 1994; Naito & Miura, 2001).

In short, children's cognitive development is affected in ways large and small by the culture in which they live (Tomasello, 2000).

ClassPrep PPT 29: Variations in Cognitive Development

Variations in Cognitive Development

Even within a single culture, some children are mentally advanced, whereas others lag behind their peers. Why? As already suggested, heredity is an important factor, but experience also plays a role. To explore the significance of that role, psychologists have studied the cognitive development of children who are exposed to differing environments.

Cognitive development is profoundly delayed if children are raised in environments that deprive them of the everyday sights, sounds, and feelings provided by conversation and loving interaction with family members, by pictures and books, even by toys and television. Children subjected to this kind of severe deprivation show marked impairment in intellectual development by the time they are two or three years old, and they may never fully recover even if they are given special attention later on. These effects were seen in the "Wild Boy," and also in more recent cases of youngsters whose abusive parents deliberately isolated them from contact with the world (Rymer, 1993a, 1993b), or who grew up in the understaffed and understimulating orphanages of Russia and Romania (O'Conner et al., 2000). Cognitive development is also impaired by less extreme conditions of deprivation, including the neglect, malnourishment, noise, and chaos that occur in many poor households. One study found that children raised in poverty scored nine points lower on IQ tests by the time they were five years old than did children in families

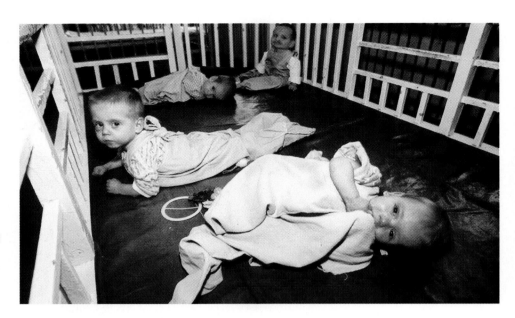

Babies at Risk   The cognitive development of infants raised in this understaffed Russian orphanage will be permanently impaired if they are not given far more stimulation in the orphanage or, better yet, adopted into a loving family at a young age.

whose incomes were twice the poverty level (Duncan, Brooks-Gunn, & Klebanov, 1994). These differences continue as poor children enter school (Stipek & Ryan, 1997). Children who remain in poverty have lower IQs and poorer school achievement, the result of a buildup of problems that often begins with prenatal complications and continues through childhood with exposure to lead, lack of cognitive stimulation, and harsh and inconsistent parenting (McLoyd, 1998).

In families above the poverty line, too, children's cognitive development is related to their surroundings, their experiences, and most notably, their parents' behavior. One longitudinal study, for instance, revealed that the parents of gifted children started stimulating their children's cognitive activity very early on (Gottfried, 1997). When they were infants, the parents read to them. When they were toddlers, the parents provided them with reference books, computerized teaching aids, and trips to museums. And when they were preschoolers and older, the parents drew out their children's natural curiosity about the world and encouraged their tendency to seek out new learning opportunities themselves. In another study, researchers examined how interactions between parents and children are related to IQ scores (Fagot & Gauvain, 1997). When the children were eighteen to thirty months old, they were asked to solve a problem—specifically, to use a hook to remove a stuffed animal from a box. The researchers recorded how the mothers interacted with their children during this task. Later, at the age of five, the children were given IQ tests. It turned out that the mothers of children with the highest IQ scores had been the ones who provided cognitive guidance by offering numerous hints and suggestions. In contrast, the mothers of children with the lowest IQ scores had forcefully told them what they needed to do to complete the task.

To improve the cognitive skills of children who do not get the optimum stimulation and guidance at home, developmental psychologists have provided extra lessons, materials, and educational contact with sensitive adults. In a variety of such programs, ranging from weekly home visits to daily preschools, children's cognitive abilities have been enhanced (Ramey & Ramey, 1998), and some effects can last into adulthood (Campbell et al., 2001). Music lessons have also been shown to promote children's cognitive development (Rauscher et al., 1997). Even electronic games, though no substitute for adult attention, can provide opportunities for school-age children to hone spatial skills that help improve their performance in math and science (Subrahmanyam & Greenfield, 1994). It appears that the earlier the stimulation begins, the better; and for some cognitive abilities, stimulation affects both the brain and behavior throughout much of the life span (Greenough, 1997).

Infancy and Childhood: Social and Emotional Development

Life for the child is more than learning about objects, doing math problems, and getting good grades. It is also about social relationships and emotional reactions. From the first months onward, infants are both attracted by and attractive to other people.

During the first hour or so after birth, mothers gaze into their infants' eyes and give them gentle touches (Klaus & Kennell, 1976). This is the first opportunity for the mother to display her *bond* to her infant—an emotional tie that begins even before the baby is born. Psychologists once believed that this immediate postbirth contact was critical—that the mother-infant bond would never be strong if the opportunity for early interaction was missed. Research has revealed, however, that such interaction in the first few hours is not a requirement for a close relationship (Myers, 1987). With or without early contact, mothers (and nowadays many fathers as well), whether biological or adoptive, gradually form close attachments to their infants by interacting with them day after day.

As the mother gazes at her baby, the baby is gazing back (Klaus & Kennell, 1976). By the time infants are two days old, they recognize—and like—their mother's face; they will suck more vigorously to see a videotaped image of her face than to see that of a stranger (Walton, Bower, & Bower, 1992). Soon, they begin to respond to the mother's facial expressions as well. By the time they are a year old, children use their mothers' emotional expressions to guide their own behavior in ambiguous situations (Saarni, Mummer, & Campos, 1998; Thompson, 1998). If the mother looks frightened when a stranger approaches, for example, the child is more likely to avoid the stranger. As mentioned in the chapter on motivation and emotion, this phenomenon is called *social referencing*.

Infants also communicate their feelings to their parents. They do so by crying and screaming, but also by more subtle behavior. When they want to interact, they look and smile; when they do not want to interact, they turn away and suck their thumbs (Tronick, 1989).

Forming a Bond   Mutual eye contact, exaggerated facial expressions, and shared "baby talk" are an important part of the early social interactions that promote an enduring bond of attachment between parent and child.

OBJ 12.18: Define temperament. Describe the three main temperament patterns discussed in your text.

Test Items 12.75–12.81

ClassPrep PPT 33: Temperament Patterns

Individual Temperament   ClassPrep PPT 32: Individual Temperament

From the moment infants are born, they differ from one another in the emotions they express most often. Some infants are happy, active, and vigorous; they splash, thrash, and wriggle. Others are usually quiet. Some infants approach new objects with enthusiasm; others turn away or fuss. Some infants whimper; others kick, scream, and wail. Characteristics like these make up the infant's disposition or **temperament**—the individual style of expressing needs and emotions. Temperament has long been known to reflect heredity's influence on the beginning of an individual's personality. But temperament may itself be affected by the prenatal environment—for example, by the mother's level of stress; her intrauterine hormones; and her health habits, such as smoking.

Early research on infant temperament indicated that most babies fall into one of three general temperament patterns (Thomas & Chess, 1977). *Easy babies* are the most common kind. They get hungry and sleepy at predictable times, react to new situations cheerfully, and seldom fuss. In contrast, *difficult babies* are irregular and irritable. And *slow-to-warm-up babies* react warily to new situations but eventually come to enjoy them.

Traces of these early temperament patterns weave their way throughout childhood (Rothbart, Ahadi, & Evans, 2000): Easy infants usually stay easy; difficult infants often remain difficult, sometimes developing attention and aggression problems in childhood (Guerin, Gottfried, & Thomas, 1997); timid, or slow-to-warm-up, toddlers tend to become shy preschoolers, restrained and inhibited eight-year-olds, and somewhat anxious teenagers (Schwartz, Kagan, & Snidman, 1995). However, these tendencies are not set in stone. In temperament, as in cognitive development, nature interacts with nurture. Many events take place between infancy and adulthood that can shift an individual's development in one direction or another. For instance, if parents are patient enough to allow their difficult baby to respond to changes in daily routines at a more relaxed pace, the child may become less difficult over time.

If the characteristics of parent and infant are in synch, chances increase that temperamental qualities will be stable. Consider, for example, the temperament patterns of Chinese American and European American children. At birth, Chinese American infants are calmer, less changeable, less perturbable, and more easily consoled when upset than is typical of European American infants. This pattern suggests that there may be an inherited predisposition toward self-control among the Chinese (Kagan et al., 1994). This tendency is then powerfully reinforced by the Chinese culture. Compared with European American parents, Chinese parents are less likely to reward and stimulate babbling and smiling, and more likely to maintain close control of their young children. The children, in turn, are more dependent on their mothers and less likely to play by themselves; by and large, they are less vocal, noisy, and active than European American children (Smith & Freedman, 1983).

These temperamental differences between children in different ethnic groups illustrate the combined contributions of nature and nurture. There are many other illustrations as well. Mayan infants, for example, are relatively inactive from birth. The Zinacantecos, a Mayan group in southern Mexico, reinforce this innate predisposition toward restrained motor activity by swaddling their infants and by nursing at the slightest sign of movement (Greenfield & Childs, 1991). This combination of genetic predisposition and cultural reinforcement is culturally adaptive: Quiet Mayan infants do not kick off their covers at night, which is important in the cold highlands where they live; inactive infants are able to spend long periods on their mother's back as she works at the loom; infants who do not begin to walk until they can understand some language do not wander into the open fire at the center of the house. This adaptive interplay of innate and cultural factors in the development of temperament operates in all cultures.

temperament An individual's basic disposition, which is evident from infancy.

attachment A deep and enduring relationship with the person with whom a baby has shared many experiences.

OBJ 12.19: Define attachment. Describe the studies of motherless monkeys. Discuss the development of attachment and describe the four types of attachment.

Test Items 12.82–12.92

Videodisc Segment & Still: Konrad Lorenz and His Imprinted Ducks, The Harlow Experiments

The Infant Grows Attached   ClassPrep PPT 34: Importance of Attachment

During the first year of life, as infants and caregivers watch and respond to one another, the infant begins to form an **attachment**—a deep, affectionate, close, and enduring relationship—to these important figures. John Bowlby, a British psychoanalyst, drew attention to the importance of attachment after he observed children who had been orphaned in World War II. These children's depression and other emotional scars led Bowlby to develop a theory about the importance of developing a strong attachment to one's primary caregivers, a tie that normally keeps infants close to their caregivers and, therefore, safe (Bowlby, 1973). Soon after Bowlby first described his theory, researchers began to investigate how such attachments are formed and what happens when they are not formed, or when they are broken by loss or separation. Some of the most dramatic of these studies were conducted by Harry Harlow.

Motherless Monkeys—and Children

Harlow (1959) explored two hypotheses about what leads infants to develop attachments to their mothers. The first hypothesis was that attachment occurs because mothers feed their babies; food, along with the experience of being fed, creates an emotional bond to the mother. Harlow's second hypothesis was that attachment is based on the warm, comforting contact the baby gets from the mother. To evaluate these hypotheses, Harlow separated newborn monkeys from their mothers and raised them in cages containing two artificial mothers. One "mother" was made of wire, but it featured a rubber nipple from which the infant could get milk (see Figure 12.6); it provided food but no physical comfort. The other artificial mother had no nipple but was made of soft, comfortable terrycloth. Harlow found that the infants preferred the terrycloth mother; they spent most of their time with it, especially when frightened. The terrycloth mother provided feelings of softness and cuddling, which were things the infants needed when they sensed danger.

Harlow also investigated what happens when attachments do not form. He isolated some newborn monkeys from all social contact. After a year of this isolation,

figure 12.6

Wire and Terrycloth "Mothers"

Here are the two types of artificial mothers used in Harlow's research. Although baby monkeys received milk from the wire mother, they spent most of their time with the terrycloth version, and they clung to it when frightened.

ClassPrep PPT 35: *Figure 12.6:* Wire and Terrycloth "Mothers"

the monkeys showed dramatic disturbances. When visited by normally active, playful monkeys, they withdrew to a corner, huddling or rocking for hours. As adults, they were unable to have normal sexual relations; but when some of the females did have babies (through artificial insemination), they tended to ignore them. When their infants became distressed, the mothers physically abused and sometimes even killed them.

Humans who spend their first few years without a consistent caregiver react in a tragically similar manner. At the Romanian and Russian orphanages mentioned earlier, where many children were neglected by institutional caregivers, visitors have discovered that the children, like Harlow's deprived monkeys, were withdrawn and engaged in constant rocking (Holden, 1996). These effects continued even after the children were adopted. In one study, researchers observed the behaviors of four-year-old children who had been in a Romanian orphanage for at least eight months before being adopted and compared them with the behaviors of children in two other groups matched for age and gender: those who had been adopted before the age of four months, and those who had remained with their biological parents (Chisholm, 1997). The late-adopted children were found to have many more serious problems. Depressed or withdrawn, they stared blankly, demanded attention, and could not control their tempers (Holden, 1996). They also interacted poorly with their adopted mothers but were indiscriminately friendly with strangers, trying to cuddle and kiss them. Neurologists suggest that the dramatic problems observed in isolated monkeys and humans are the result of developmental brain dysfunction and damage brought on by a lack of touch and body movement in infancy (Prescott, 1996).

Forming an Attachment

Fortunately, most infants do have a consistent caregiver, usually the mother, to whom they can form an attachment. By the age of six or seven months, infants show signs of preferring their mother to anyone else—watching her closely, crawling after her, clambering up into her lap, protesting when she leaves, and brightening when she returns (Ainsworth, 1973). After an attachment has been formed, separation from the mother for even thirty minutes can be a stressful experience (Larson, Gunnar, & Hertsgaard, 1991).

Later on, infants develop attachments to their fathers as well (Lamb, 1997). However, interaction with fathers is typically less frequent, and of a somewhat different nature, than with mothers (Parke, 2002). Mothers tend to feed, bathe, dress, cuddle, and talk to their infants, whereas fathers are more likely to play, jiggle, and toss them, especially sons.

ClassPrep PPT 36: Variations in Attachment

Variations in Attachment

The amount of closeness and contact infants seek with either their mother or father depends to some extent on the infant. Those who are ill, tired, or slow to warm up may require more closeness. Closeness also depends to some extent on the parent. An infant whose parent has been absent, aloof, or unresponsive is likely to need more closeness than one whose parent is accessible and responsive.

Researchers have studied the differences in infants' attachments in a special situation that simulates the natural comings and goings of parents—the so-called *Strange Situation Test* (Ainsworth et al., 1978). Mother and infant come to an unfamiliar room where they can be videotaped through a one-way window. Here the infant interacts with the mother and an unfamiliar woman in brief episodes: The infant plays with the mother and the stranger, the mother leaves the baby with the stranger for a few minutes, the mother and the stranger leave the baby alone in the room briefly, and the mother returns to the room.

Researchers have found that most infants display a *secure attachment* to the mother in the Strange Situation Test (Thompson, 1998). In the unfamiliar room, they use the mother as a home base, leaving her side to explore and play but returning to her periodically for comfort or contact. And when the mother returns after

Cultural Differences in Parent-Child Relations Variations in the intimacy of family interactions, including whether infants sleep in their parents' bed, may contribute to cross-cultural differences in attachment patterns.

ClassPrep PPT 37: Types of Insecure Attachment

the brief separation, these infants are invariably happy to see her and receptive when she initiates contact. These mother-child pairs also tend to have harmonious interactions at home. The mothers themselves are generally sensitive and responsive to their babies' needs and signals (DeWolff & van IJzendoorn, 1997).

Some infants, however, display an *insecure attachment*. Their relationship with their mother may be (1) *avoidant*—they avoid or ignore their mother when she approaches or when she returns after the brief separation; (2) *ambivalent*—they are upset when their mother leaves, but when she returns they act angry and reject her efforts at contact, and when picked up they squirm to get down; or (3) *disorganized*—their behavior is inconsistent, disturbed, and disturbing; they may begin to cry again after their mother has returned and comforted them, or they may reach out for their mother while looking away from her.

The nature of a child's attachment to parents can have long-term and far-reaching effects. For example, unless disrupted by the loss of a parent, abuse by a family member, chronic depression in the mother, or some other severe negative event (Weinfield, Sroufe, & Egeland, 2000), an infant's secure attachment continues into young adulthood—and probably throughout life (Hamilton, 2000; Waters et al., 2000). A secure attachment to the mother is also reflected in relationships with other people. Children who are securely attached receive more positive reactions from other children when they are toddlers (Fagot, 1997) and have better relations with peers in middle childhood and adolescence (Schneider, Atkinson, & Tardif, 2001). Attachment to the mother also affects the way children process emotional information. Securely attached children tend to remember positive events more accurately than negative events, whereas insecurely attached children tend to do the opposite (Belsky, Spritz, & Crnic, 1996).

Patterns of attachment vary widely in different parts of the world and are related to how parents treat their children. In northern Germany, for example, where parents promote children's independence with strict discipline, the proportion of infants who display avoidant attachments is quite high (Spangler et al., 1996). Kibbutz babies in Israel, who sleep in infant houses away from their parents, are likely to show insecure attachment, as well as other attachment difficulties, later in life (Aviezer et al., 1999). And in Japan, where mothers are completely devoted to their young children and are seldom apart from them, including at night, children develop an attachment relationship that emphasizes harmony and union (Rothbaum et al., 2000). These attachment patterns differ from the secure one that is most common in the United States: with their parents' encouragement, U.S. children balance closeness and proximity with exploration and autonomy.

Freburg *Perspectives:* Collins, "The Day Care Dilemma"

THINKING CRITICALLY

OBJ 12.20: Discuss the question of whether day care damages the formation of a healthy mother-infant attachment.

Test Items 12.93–12.95

Freburg *Stand!:* Barnett & Barnett, "Childcare Brain Drain?," Judd, "Working Mothers Need Not Feel Guilty"

Does Day Care Harm the Emotional Development of Infants?

With about 60 percent of mothers now working outside the home, concern has been expressed about how daily separations from their mothers might affect children, especially infants. Some have argued that leaving infants with a baby sitter or putting them in a day-care center damages the quality of the mother-infant relationship and increases the babies' risk for psychological problems later on (Gallagher, 1998).

● **What am I being asked to believe or accept?**

The claim to be evaluated is that daily separations brought about by the need for day care undermine the infant's ability to form a secure attachment, as well as inflict emotional harm.

● What evidence is available to support the assertion?

There is clear evidence that separation from the mother is painful for young children. Furthermore, if separation lasts a week or more, young children may become apathetic and mournful and eventually lose interest in the missing mother (Robertson & Robertson, 1971). But day care does not involve such lasting separations, and research has shown that infants in day care do form attachments to their mothers. In fact, they prefer their mothers to their daytime caregivers (Clarke-Stewart & Fein, 1983).

But are their attachments as secure as the attachments formed by infants whose mothers do not work outside the home? Researchers first examined this question by comparing infants' behavior in the Strange Situation Test. A review of the data disclosed that, on average, infants in full-time day care were somewhat more likely to be classified as insecurely attached. Specifically, 36 percent of the infants in full-time care received this classification, compared with 29 percent of the infants not in full-time day care (Clarke-Stewart, 1989). These results appear to support the suggestion that day care hinders the development of infants' attachments to their mothers.

● Are there alternative ways of interpreting the evidence?

Perhaps factors other than day care could explain this difference between infants in day care and those at home with their mothers. One such factor could be the method used to assess attachment—the Strange Situation Test. Infants in these studies were judged insecure if they did not run to their mothers after a brief separation. But maybe infants who experience daily separations from their mothers are less disturbed by the separations in the Strange Situation Test and therefore seek out less closeness with their mothers. A second factor could be differences between the infants' mothers: Working mothers may value independence in themselves and their children, whereas mothers who value closeness may choose to stay home.

● What additional evidence would help to evaluate the alternatives?

Finding a heightened rate of insecure attachment among the infants of working mothers does not, by itself, prove that day care is harmful. To judge the effects of day care, we must use other measures of emotional adjustment. If infants in day care show consistent signs of impaired emotional relations in other situations (at home, say) and with other caregivers (such as the father), this evidence would support the argument that day care harms children's emotional development. Another

The Effects of Day Care   Parents are understandably concerned that leaving their infants in a day-care center all day long might interfere with the mother-infant attachment or with other aspects of the children's development. Research shows that most infants in day care do form healthy bonds with their parents, but that if children spend many hours in day care between infancy and kindergarten, they are more likely to have behavior problems in school, such as talking back to the teacher or getting into fights with other children (NICHD Early Child Care Research Network, 2001).

useful method would be to statistically control for differences in the attitudes and behaviors of parents who do and do not use day care and then examine the differences in their children.

In fact, this research design has already been employed. In 1990 the U.S. government funded a study of infant day care in ten sites around the country. The psychological and physical development of more than 1,300 randomly selected infants was tracked from birth through age three. The results showed that when factors such as parents' education, income, and attitudes were statistically controlled for, infants in day care were no more likely to have emotional problems or to be insecurely attached to their mothers than infants not in day care. However, in cases where infants were placed in poor-quality day care, where the caregivers were insensitive and unresponsive, and where mothers were insensitive to their babies' needs at home, the infants were less likely to develop a secure attachment to their mothers (NICHD Early Child Care Research Network, 1997, 1998, 1999).

● **What conclusions are most reasonable?**

Based on available evidence, the most reasonable conclusion appears to be that day care by itself does not lead to insecure attachment or cause emotional harm to infants. But if the care is of poor quality, it can worsen a risky situation at home and increase the likelihood that infants will have problems forming a secure attachment to their mothers. The U.S. government study is still under way, and the children's progress is being followed into elementary school. Time will tell if other problems develop in the future.

Relationships with Parents and Peers

IRM Discussion 12.6: Erikson's Psychosocial Stages of Development

Erik Erikson (1968) saw the first year of life as the time when infants develop a feeling of basic trust (or mistrust) about the world. According to his theory, an infant's first year represents the first of eight stages of lifelong psychosocial development (see Table 12.2). Each stage focuses on an issue or crisis that is especially important at that time of life. Erikson believed that the ways in which people resolve these issues shape their personalities and social relationships. Positive resolution of an issue provides the foundation for characteristics such as trust, autonomy, initiative, and industry. But if the crisis is not resolved positively, according to Erikson, the person will be psychologically troubled and cope less effectively with later crises. In Erikson's theory, then, forming basic feelings of trust during infancy is the bedrock for all future emotional development.

After children have formed strong emotional attachments to their parents, their next psychological task is to begin to develop a more independent, or autonomous, relationship with them. This task is part of Erikson's second stage, when children begin to exercise their wills, develop some independence from their parents, and initiate activities on their own. According to Erikson, children who are not allowed to exercise their wills or initiate their own activities will feel uncertain about doing things for themselves and guilty about seeking independence. The extent to which parents allow or encourage their children's autonomy depends largely on their parenting style.

OBJ 12.21: Define socialization. Describe the three parental socialization styles discussed in the text. Discuss the characteristics of children who have grown up under each of these styles. Explain the impact of the parents' culture and environment on the development of their parenting styles.

Test Items 12.96–12.110

Personal Learning Activity 12.2

IRM Activity 12.8: I'm Glad I'm a Boy! I'm Glad I'm a Girl!

IRM Thinking Critically 12.1: Can Parenting Styles Explain Variations in Patterns of Adolescent Development?

Parenting Styles   Parents try to channel children's impulses into socially accepted outlets and teach them the skills and rules needed to function in their society. This process, called *socialization,* is shaped by cultural values. Parents in Hispanic cultures of Mexico, Puerto Rico, and Central America, for example, tend to be influenced by the collectivist tradition, in which family and community interests are emphasized over individual goals. Children in these cultures are expected to respect and obey their elders and to do less of the questioning, negotiating, and arguing that is encouraged—or at least allowed—in many middle-class European and European American families (Greenfield, 1995). When parents from Hispanic

In each of Erikson's stages of development, a different psychological issue presents a new crisis for the person to resolve. The person focuses attention on that issue and, by the end of the period, has worked through the crisis and resolved it either positively, in the direction of healthy development, or negatively, hindering further psychological development.

authoritarian parents Firm, punitive, and unsympathetic parents who value obedience from their child and authority for themselves.

permissive parents Parents who give their child great freedom and lax discipline.

authoritative parents Parents who reason with their child, encourage give and take, and are firm but understanding.

table 12.2
Erikson's Stages of Psychosocial Development

Age	Central Psychological Issue or Crisis
First year	**Trust versus mistrust** Infants learn to trust that their needs will be met by the world, especially by the mother—or they learn to mistrust the world.
Second year	**Autonomy versus shame and doubt** Children learn to exercise will, to make choices, and to control themselves—or they become uncertain and doubt that they can do things by themselves.
Third to fifth year	**Initiative versus guilt** Children learn to initiate activities and enjoy their accomplishments, acquiring direction and purpose. Or, if they are not allowed initiative, they feel guilty for their attempts at independence.
Sixth year through puberty	**Industry versus inferiority** Children develop a sense of industry and curiosity and are eager to learn—or they feel inferior and lose interest in the tasks before them.
Adolescence	**Identity versus role confusion** Adolescents come to see themselves as unique and integrated persons with an ideology—or they become confused about what they want out of life.
Early adulthood	**Intimacy versus isolation** Young people become able to commit themselves to another person—or they develop a sense of isolation and feel they have no one in the world but themselves.
Middle age	**Generativity versus stagnation** Adults are willing to have and care for children and to devote themselves to their work and the common good—or they become self-centered and inactive.
Old age	**Integrity versus despair** Older people enter a period of reflection, becoming assured that their lives have been meaningful and ready to face death with acceptance and dignity. Or they are in despair for their unaccomplished goals, failures, and ill-spent lives.

cultures immigrate to the United States, they may find that some of their values conflict with those of their children's European American teachers (Raeff, Greenfield, & Quiroz, 1995), and their own parenting efforts may become inconsistent (Harwood, Schulze, & Wilson, 1995).

European and European American parents tend to employ one of three distinct parenting styles, as described by Diana Baumrind (1971). **Authoritarian parents** are relatively strict, punitive, and unsympathetic. They value obedience and try to shape their children's behavior to meet a set standard and to curb the children's wills. They do not encourage independence. They are detached and seldom praise their youngsters. In contrast, **permissive parents** give their children lax discipline and a great deal of freedom. **Authoritative parents** fall between these two extremes. They reason with their children, encouraging give and take. They allow the children increasing responsibility as they get older and better at making decisions. They are firm but understanding. They set limits but also encourage independence. Their demands are reasonable, rational, and consistent.

In her research with middle-class parents, Baumrind found that these three parenting styles were related to young children's social and emotional development. The children of authoritarian parents tended to be unfriendly, distrustful, and withdrawn. Children of permissive parents tended to be immature, dependent, and unhappy; they were likely to have tantrums or to ask for help when they encountered even slight difficulties. Children raised by authoritative parents tended to be friendly, cooperative, self-reliant, and socially responsible (Baumrind, 1986).

Other researchers have found authoritative parenting styles to be associated with additional positive outcomes, including better school achievement (Steinberg et al., 1994), higher sociometric status (Hinshaw et al., 1997), and better psychological adjustment to parental divorce (Hetherington & Clingempeel, 1992). In contrast, children of authoritarian parents are more likely to cheat and to be aggressive, and less likely to be empathic or to experience guilt or accept blame after doing something wrong (Eisenberg & Fabes, 1998).

ClassPrep PPT 40: Limitations of Parenting Studies

The results of these studies of parenting styles are interesting, but they have some limitations. First, they involve *correlations,* which, as discussed in the chapter on research in psychology, do not prove causation. Finding consistent correlations between parenting styles and children's behavior does not establish that the parents' behavior is causing the differences seen in their children. In fact, parents' behavior is, itself, often shaped by their children to some extent. For example, parents may react differently to children of different ages. Children's temperament, size, and appearance may also influence the way parents treat them (Bugental & Goodnow, 1998). Second, some psychologists have suggested that it is not the parents' behavior itself that influences children but rather how the children perceive the discipline they receive—as stricter or more lenient than what an older sibling received, for example (Reiss et al., 2000).

A third limitation of these studies is that the correlations between parenting styles and children's behavior, though statistically significant, are usually not terribly strong. Expected relationships between parenting styles and children's behavior do not always appear. For example, Baumrind (1971) found a small group of "harmonious" families in which she never observed the parents disciplining the children, yet the children were thriving.

In all likelihood, it is the "fit" between parenting style and children's characteristics that affects children the most. There is no universally "best" style of parenting (Parke & Buriel, 1998, 2002). For example, authoritative parenting, so consistently linked with positive outcomes in European American families, is not related to better school performance in African American or Asian American youngsters (Steinberg, Dornbusch, & Brown, 1992; Wang & Phinney, 1998). One possible explanation is that different disciplinary styles have different meanings in different cultures. Chinese American parents use authoritarian discipline more than European American parents, but their goal is usually to "train" *(chiao shun)* and "govern" *(guan)* children so that they will know what is expected of them (Chao, 1994). By contrast, European American parents who use authoritarian discipline are more likely to do so to "break the child's will." In other words, each parenting style must be evaluated in its cultural context.

There are no hard and fast rules about how to discipline children, even when it comes to things like spanking. In her longitudinal study of children from preschool through adolescence, Baumrind found that although severe punishment was linked with negative outcomes, there were no detrimental effects of occasional mild to moderate spanking. Accordingly, Baumrind (2001) argues that parents should be free to raise their children in accordance with their own values and traditions.

Some people have suggested that parenting styles are a less significant influence on children's social development than are the influences the children encounter outside the home—especially by interacting with peers (Harris, 1995, 1998). Research

Parent-Training Programs Research in developmental psychology on the relationship between parents' socialization styles and children's behavior has helped shape parent-training programs based on both the social-cognitive and the humanistic approaches described in the chapter on personality. These programs are designed to teach parents authoritative methods that can avoid scenes like this.

OBJ 12.22: Describe the different kinds of social relationships and the development of social skills in children.

Test Items 12.111–12.114

ClassPrep PPT 41: Relationship with Peers

evidence does not justify dismissing the impact of parenting styles, but there is no denying the impact of peer influences, either (Collins et al., 2000; Leventhal & Brooks-Gunn, 2000).

Relationships with Peers   Social development over the years of childhood occurs in a social world that broadens to include brothers, sisters, playmates, and classmates. Relationships with other children start very early (Rubin, Bukowski, & Parker, 1998). By two months of age, infants engage in mutual gazing. By six months, they vocalize and smile at each other. By eight months, they prefer to look at another child rather than at an adult (Bigelow et al., 1990). So people are interested in one another, even as infants, but it's a long journey from interest to intimacy.

Observations of two-year-olds show that the most they can do with their peers is to look at them, imitate them, and exchange—or grab—toys. By age four, they begin to play "pretend" together, agreeing about roles and themes. This "sociodramatic" play is important because it provides a context for communicating meaning and offers an opportunity to form first "friendships" (Dunn & Hughes, 2001; Rubin, Bukowski, & Parker, 1998).

In the school years, peer interaction becomes more frequent, complex, and structured. Children play games with rules, join teams, tutor each other, and cooperate— or compete—in achieving goals. Friends become more important and friendships longer lasting as school-age children find that friends are a source of companionship, stimulation, support, and affection (Hartup & Stevens, 1997). In fact, companionship and fun are the most important aspects of friendship for children at this age; psychological intimacy does not enter the picture until adolescence (Parker et al., 2001).

Children's Friendships Although relationships with peers may not always be this cordial, they are often among the closest and most positive in a child's life. Friends are more interactive than non-friends. They smile and laugh together more; pay closer attention to equality in their conversation; and talk about mutual, rather than just personal, goals. Having at least one close friend in childhood predicts good psychological functioning later on.

LINKAGES (a link to Social Cognition)

Friends also help children to establish their sense of self-worth. For example, through friendships children can compare their own strengths and weaknesses with those of others in a supportive and accepting atmosphere. Unfortunately, about 10 percent of schoolchildren do not have friends. These children report extremely high levels of loneliness and rejection (Asher & Hopmeyer, 2001). They do poorly in school and usually experience psychological and behavior problems in later life (Asher & Hopmeyer, 2001; Bagwell, Newcomb, & Bukowski, 1998). It appears that having just one close, stable friend can protect schoolchildren from loneliness and other problems (Parker et al., 2001); having more than one friend does not seem to provide further benefits.

Social Skills   ClassPrep PPT 42: Social Skills

The changes in peer interactions and the formation of friendships over the years of childhood can be traced in part to children's increasing social competencies and skills. *Social skills,* like cognitive skills, must be learned (Rubin, Bukowski, & Parker, 1998).

One social skill is the ability to engage in sustained, responsive interactions with peers. Such interactions require cooperation, sharing, and taking turns—behaviors that first appear in the preschool years. Parents can aid their children's development of these skills by initiating lots of "pretend" play and other prosocial activities (Ladd & LeSieur, 1995; Parke & O'Neil, 2000) and by helping the children express their emotions constructively (Eisenberg, 1998). Older siblings, too, can help by acting out social roles during play and by talking about their feelings (Ruffman et al., 1998). Children who have been abused by their parents tend to lack these important interactional skills and are thus more likely to be victimized by their peers (Bolger & Patterson, 2001; Crick, 1997).

A second social skill learned by children is the ability to detect and interpret other people's emotional signals. In fact, effective performance in social situations depends on this ability to process information about other people (Slomkowski & Dunn, 1996). Research indicates that girls are able to read emotional signals at younger ages than boys (Dunn et al., 1991). Children who understand another person's perspective, who appreciate how that person might be feeling, and who behave accordingly tend to be the most popular members of a peer group (Izard et al., 2001; Rubin, Bukowski, & Parker, 1998). Children who do not have these skills are rejected or neglected; they may become bullies or the victims of bullies.

A related social skill is the ability to feel what another person is feeling, or something close to it, and to respond with comfort or help if the person is in distress. This skill allows children to develop both *empathy* and *sympathy*. Affectionate mothers who discuss emotions openly, and who provide clear messages about the consequences of their child's hurtful behavior, effectively encourage the child to be empathic and sympathetic (Eisenberg, 1997).

Yet another social skill that develops in childhood is the ability to control one's emotions and behavior—an ability known as **self-regulation** (Rothbart & Bates, 1998). In the first few years of life, children learn to calm or console themselves by sucking their thumbs or cuddling their favorite blanket. Later, they learn more sophisticated strategies of self-regulation, such as planning ahead to avoid a problem (e.g., getting on the first bus if the school bully usually takes the second one) and recruiting social support (e.g., casually joining a group of big kids to walk past the bully on the playground). Children who cannot regulate their emotions tend to experience anxiety and distress and have trouble recovering from stressful events. They become emotionally overaroused when they see someone in distress and are often unsympathetic and unhelpful (Eisenberg & Fabes, 1998). Further, boys who are easily aroused and have difficulty regulating this arousal become less and less popular with their peers as the months go by (Fabes et al., 1997).

Self-regulation is most effectively learned by children who experience harmonious interactions at home under the guidance of supportive and competent parents (Saarni, Mummer, & Campos, 1998). One study revealed that children skilled at regulating their emotions had parents who had soothed them in infancy by holding them, talking to them, and providing distractions. As the children grew older, the parents gradually began to introduce them to new and potentially uncomfortable events (such as their first haircut), all the while remaining close by as a safe base (Fox, 1997). Another study, specifically involving North American children, found that self-regulation and empathy are fostered by parents who talk about their own feelings and encourage their children to express emotions (Eisenberg, 1997). This phenomenon is not universal, however. For example, Japanese children are usually better emotion regulators than North American children, even though Japanese parents tend not to encourage the expression of strong emotion. (Zahn-Waxler et al., 1996).

In recent years, psychologists in the United States have been encouraging schools to teach children the social skills of self-regulation, as well as understanding, empathy, and cooperation (Goleman, 1995; Salovey & Sluyter, 1997). It is their hope that this "emotional literacy" will reduce the prevalence of childhood depression and aggression.

Gender Roles   ClassPrep PPT 43: Gender Roles

An important aspect of understanding other people and being socially skilled is knowing about social roles, including **gender roles**—the general patterns of work, appearance, and behavior associated with being a man or a woman. One survey of gender roles in twenty-five countries found that children learn these roles earliest in Muslim countries (where gender roles are perhaps most extreme), but children in all twenty-five countries eventually develop them (Williams & Best, 1990).

Gender roles persist because they are deeply rooted in both nature and nurture. Small physical and behavioral differences between the sexes are evident early on and tend to increase over the years (Eagly, 1996). For example, girls tend to speak and write earlier and to be better at grammar and spelling (Halpern, 1997), whereas boys tend to be more skilled than girls at manipulating objects, constructing three-dimensional forms, and mentally manipulating complex figures and pictures. Girls are likely to be more kind, considerate, and empathic. Their play tends to be more orderly. Boys are more physically active and aggressive; they play in larger groups and spaces, enjoying noisier, more strenuous physical games (Eisenberg & Fabes, 1998).

Sattler/Shabatay reader, 2/e: Tanner, "Put Down That Paper and Talk to Me!" and Rappaport, "Talk and Report-Talk"

  LINKAGES (a link to Learning)

OBJ 12.23: Describe the development of gender roles in and the influence of gender schemas on children.

Test Items 12.115–12.118

IRM In Your Own Words 12.2: An Exercise in Gender Stereotypes

Personal Learning Activity 12.3

self-regulation   The ability to control one's emotions and behavior.
gender roles   Patterns of work, appearance, and behavior that a society associates with being male or female.